Personality
Strategies and Issues

Personality
Strategies and Issues

Fifth Edition

Robert M. Liebert
State University of New York at Stony Brook

Michael D. Spiegler
Providence College

THE DORSEY PRESS
Chicago, Illinois 60604

© THE DORSEY PRESS, 1970, 1974, 1978, 1982, and 1987

ISBN 0-256-03397-8

Library of Congress Catalog Card No. 86–71970

Printed in the United States of America

1 2 3 4 5 6 7 8 9 0 DO 4 3 2 1 0 9 8 7

To Vin Calia

Robert M. Liebert received his B.S. degree from Tulane University in 1963 after studying psychology both at Tulane and at University College, London. He received a Ph.D. in clinical psychology from Stanford in 1966, after which he joined the faculty at Vanderbilt. He subsequently served as Senior Investigator at Fels Research Institute and as a member of the faculty at Antioch College. He is now Professor of Psychology and Psychiatry at the State University of New York at Stony Brook. He has published widely in the fields of personality, social development, and methodological issues, and is coauthor of several other books, including *Developmental Psychology* and *Science and Behavior: An Introduction to Methods of Research*. He also has strong avocational interests in poetry and philosophy.

Photo by Joy Sherman

Michael D. Spiegler received his A.B. from the University of Rochester in 1964 and his Ph.D. in clinical psychology from Vanderbilt University in 1969. He taught at Vanderbilt University and the University of Texas at Austin and was Director of the Community Training Center at the Palo Alto VA Hospital. He is currently Professor of Psychology at Providence College. His research interests include anxiety, modeling, treatment of chronic psychiatric patients, exercise addiction, and obesity. He is author of *Contemporary Behavioral Therapy* and coauthor of *The Community Training Center*. As a clinician, he has directed an obesity treatment program; he consults on behavioral interventions and maintains a private practice. Professor Spiegler is well-known for his research and training in active learning. He also can be frequently observed running, eating ice cream, and listening to early music.

PREFACE

Writing the fifth edition of *Personality: Strategies and Issues* has been exciting for us. First, personality theorists and researchers have been especially active in recent years, and the present edition has been substantially rewritten to reflect important changes in the field. Second, we have made structural changes to the text and have added new pedagogical features that make the fifth edition an even better *teaching book.*

We continue to have one fundamental goal for the book: to *present complex ideas in clear terms* that students can grasp quickly and retain beyond the final exam. We always write with the student in mind, which means eliminating jargon and translating abstruse theory into simple, concrete language that students can understand. We have also structured the book in a way that organizes complex material in a simple analytical framework. This framework uses conceptual *strategies* and fundamental *issues* to explain the basic ideas behind personality psychology.

The book examines the four conceptual strategies that have been used by psychologists in their study of personality: the *psychoanalytic, dispositional, phenomenological,* and *behavioral.* Each of the strategies is presented in an affirmative light and in the tone and format that might be selected by its adherents. Each strategy section begins with a short introductory chapter that outlines and summarizes the major assumptions of the approach. Then, after a more detailed presentation of the theories that fall within the strategy and the manner in which they have been researched and applied, the section concludes with a concise chapter on the strategy's liabilities, as seen by its critics.

All strategies for the study of personality must come to grips with the same four major issues: a clear *theoretical statement*, a set of guidelines for *personality assessment*, a systematic body of *research*, and an explicit basis for understanding and implementing *personality change.* The scientific investigation of personality is thus presented as the critical interplay of the four basic strategies—psychoanalytic, dispositional, phenomenological, and behavioral—and the four fundamental issues—theory, assessment, research, and personality change. This superordinate organizational structure is a powerful way of orienting students who are surveying the field for the first time. It clarifies and highlights differences and similarities among the various viewpoints, so that they do not seem to be an incomprehensible hodgepodge of arbitrary opinions.

As in the preceding editions of *Personality*, we have not tried to give complete coverage of every individual theory and viewpoint. Even if such a goal were attainable (which is highly doubtful), we do not believe that an encyclopedic presentation is a sound way to introduce students to the field of personality. Instead, our emphasis continues to be presenting enduring principles and contemporary issues and illustrating them with selected examples rather than exhaustive listings.

The fifth edition of *Personality* has been thoroughly updated to reflect the most current research in the field. Among the many new additions are coverage of the most contemporary psychoanalytic theories, including a new section on object relations; current findings and trends in Type A behavior patterns and inheritable personality characteristics; recent extensions and applications of the theories of Rogers and Kelly; and extensive coverage of contemporary social learning and cognitive-behavioral theory, research, and therapy.

We have reorganized the material within these sections to integrate new with existing coverage. Each chapter begins with an overview in outline form and ends with a point-by-point summary. Key terms are in boldface type. In response to reviewers' and users' suggestions, we have added a glossary at the end of the book for students' quick references.

Personality courses are among the most popular offerings in psychology, but they are often disappointing to students who want information that bears on their own lives. To serve this legitimate need, we have illustrated concepts and principles through examples that are relevant to today's college students. We have also expanded a feature of previous editions that capitalizes on and stimulates college students' intellectual inquisitiveness and skepticism. Periodically, the reader is invited to perform easily implemented *Demonstrations* that examine the validity of various propositions discussed in the text. We have used these "personalized studies" repeatedly in our teaching and have revised them on the basis of student feedback. Demonstrations appear throughout the book, and one is included in each of the strategies' introductory chapters to provide an additional avenue through which the student can experience the "way of thinking" that is characteristic of each strategy.

We believe that visual illustrations which are related in meaningful ways to the substance of a text can increase its instructional value. The fifth edition of *Personality* contains many more of such illustrations, including new photographs (some specifically shot for the book) that succinctly make or clarify ideas and consequently enhance students' understanding and retention.

We wish to thank the following reviewers, whose comments and criticisms helped our work on the fifth edition: Sanford Golin, University of Pittsburgh; Donna L. Lamping, Fordham University; Marsha M. Linehan, University of Washington; Henry Marcucella, Boston University; Donald Meichenbaum, University of Waterloo; Richard H. Passman, University of Wisconsin, Milwaukee; Robert C. Plomin, Pennsylvania State University; Robert Steele, Wesleyan University; Edward A. Thompson, Southern Connecticut State University; Alice K. Wagstaff, Ramsey Mental Health Center, St. Paul, Minnesota; and John P. Wilson, Cleveland State University.

We want to acknowledge our continuing debt to the many undergraduates in our personality courses over the past nineteen years whose comments, questions, and challenges have provided critical input that has allowed us to shape successive editions to meet their needs. We appreciate the help of Denise A. Fish and Cynthia A. Kulick in preparation of the book and the participants in Virginia Satir's family systems workshop in obtaining the one elusive photograph. Several chapters greatly benefited from extensive theoretical discussions with two very insightful and creative students, Michelle E. Parker and Mary E. Tramonti. Michael D. Spiegler is grateful for the support of Barbara K. Hanson and Kristina W. Hanson while the book was being written. Robert M. Liebert acknowledges the generous contribution of Lynn Langenbach during the final stage of the project. To all the friends, relatives, and other interested persons who persisted in asking, "Is the book finished yet?" we are pleased to finally be able to answer, "Yes." Special thanks are due to Danette M. Hann and Gregg T. Johnson for their dedicated and competent assistance in many phases of the work on the fifth edition of *Personality: Strategies and Issues.*

Robert M. Liebert
Michael D. Spiegler

CONTENTS

SECTION V

THE BEHAVIORAL STRATEGY

LIST OF FIGURES

LIST OF TABLES

Personality
Strategies and Issues

SECTION

I

INTRODUCTION

INTRODUCTION

CHAPTER 1

ISSUES IN THE STUDY OF PERSONALITY

OVERVIEW

In ancient Rome actors used no makeup. Instead they wore one of a small number of masks, or *persona*. These told the audience to expect consistent attitudes and behavior from the player who wore a given mask. Soon persona came to refer not only to the masks but also to the roles they implied and, finally, to the actors themselves (cf. Burnham, 1968).

Persona is the source of the English word *personality*. The link is more than historical. The term as we use it today also implies that we expect a consistent pattern of attitudes and behavior or at least an "orderly arrangement" in the behavior of those we know.

All people exhibit recognizable individual actions that serve to identify

In the theater of ancient Rome, actors wore a mask, called a *persona*, to indicate the personal characteristics of the roles they played. The familiar comedy and tradegy masks are examples that are still used. This fresco shows a Roman actor with three dramatic *personae. The Bettmann Archive*

them. Where do these characteristics and regularities come from? Are they ever truly unique? Or are they just particular combinations of characteristics all people possess? Are they learned, inherited, or both? Can personality be altered? If so, how? Discerning the character of human nature has been called one of the "limited number of common human problems to which all people at all times must find some solution" (Kluckhohn & Strodtbeck, 1961, p. 10). So it should come as no surprise that the questions just raised have puzzled thoughtful people for thousands of years. Originally the quest for answers to these questions was the domain of philosophy, religion, and literature; these fields continue to be interested in them. But scientific psychology, born about one hundred years ago, has also tried to understand and explain human character employing a slant of its own.

This book introduces the psychological study of personality. It deals with the issues involved in developing a scientific approach to understanding ourselves and others. Instead of an exhaustive list of approaches, we have stressed the major *strategies* psychologists have followed in conceptualizing human behavior. This will give you a general picture of the diversity of existing positions, the points the positions emphasize, the assumptions they make, and the nature of the evidence they consider. In this way, we have tried to explain the ideas underlying major theoretical positions and, at the same time, to summarize the questions they have answered and those they are still asking.

The study of personality, like all other scientific endeavors, needs a strategy. All approaches to personality that we will discuss employ one of four strategies: *psychoanalytic, dispositional, phenomenological,* or *behavioral.*

Strategy, as we use the term, encompasses four issues. The strategies differ in how they handle the four fundamental issues with which every psychological approach to personality must deal. These are developing: (1) a *theory* of personality, (2) an approach to the *assessment* (or measurement) of personality, (3) *research* procedures for testing hypotheses or implications derived from the theory, and (4) methods of *changing personality* (i.e., psychotherapeutic interventions).

There is considerable overlap in the roles of each of the four issues. Theories suggest ideas or *hypotheses* that are then tested in research. At the same time, though, the nature of the research is determined by what the particular theory leads us to expect. To do research, the personality variables of interest must be measured. This involves the development of assessment techniques which must conform to the assumptions about personality made in the theory. The success of personality-change techniques serves to partially validate the therapeutic principles derived from the theory. You can see that theory, assessment, research, and personality change are intricately linked parts of every strategy. In fact, it becomes difficult to talk about one issue without referring to one or more of the other three issues.

THE SCOPE OF THE STUDY OF PERSONALITY

Modern psychology is a very broad field, comprised of many specialized areas. Interest in interpersonal relations, attitude change, and the influence of social forces is typically the domain of *social psychology*. *Developmental psychology* emphasizes the historical antecedents of a person's behavior. It is concerned with the interplay of maturational and social influences as people advance from childhood to adulthood and old age. Someone's behavior may be markedly different from the usual norms of society. Especially when these differences are maladaptive for the person or others, the phenomena are of particular interest to *abnormal psychology*. This field includes the theoretical and experimental work of *psychopathology* and the applied work of *clinical psychology*.

Fields such as *human engineering, industrial and organizational psychology, environmental psychology, educational psychology*, and *school psychology*, concern specific human enterprises. *Experimental psychology* may involve the study of single aspects of the organism, such as physiology, sensation and perception, learning, or emotion. *Cognitive psychology* focuses on how we think and process information.

In many ways, *personality psychology* is at the crossroads of these other branches. Personality psychology is the study of all aspects of the functioning of an individual. Every person is influenced by all of the basic processes studied by experimental psychologists (e.g., perception, learning, memory) and by all of the interpersonal forces studied by social psychologists (e.g., group norms, peer pressure). At the same time, personality psychology provides the theoretical and research base for understanding psychopathology and psychotherapy.

THE CONCEPT OF PERSONALITY

Thus far we have used the term *personality* without offering a specific definition. In fact, personality psychologists use many definitions. Which definition a particular psychologist selects depends on his or her theoretical orientation. Because of the diversity of definitions, there is little point in searching for *a* definition of personality. And, as we shall see repeatedly, a complete definition of personality always implies at least a partial theory of personality as well. To fully understand what a particular psychologist means by the term *personality*, we must examine his or her theoretical approach. Thus, definitions differ from one personality psychologist to another mainly along theoretical lines. Four major areas of theoretical disagreement are introduced next.

Objective versus Subjective Aspects

Philosophers long understood that our knowledge of others is limited to what we observe of their behavior. We can never know directly what is "inside" a person; that is, we cannot observe another's subjective experiences directly. We may say that Tom is happy in order to provide a summary label for his smiles, his jokes, or his invitation to take us all out for a beer. But we are speaking of his overt behavior and not necessarily of any private, internal state that he is experiencing. Psychologists who follow a radical behavioral view hold that our sole concern should be with observable responses rather than with presumed internal states. They argue that the scientific study of personality must be concerned with an examination of objective information and observable responses. Others, though, have argued that personality psychology must acknowledge and explain private, subjective experiences as well. Tom *appears* happy; he may in fact, be miserable inside. Mary, who seems to be self-assured and "put together," may actually have numerous doubts and fears about her adequacy and competence as a person. In general, behavior may not reflect a person's "real" personality. Which view is right? That depends on how you define *personality* in the first place. It is one of the central points about which personality psychologists disagree.

The Person versus the Situation

To what extent are people consistent in the way they think, feel, and act in various situations? We often hear descriptions like "John is quiet" or "Sharon is irresponsible." People speak as if these were properties of individuals rather like the color of their eyes, which is always apparent and virtually unchangeable. But personality is plainly not as consistent as eye color. John, the "quiet boy," may be very outspoken about his hobby, stamp collecting. Sharon, the "irresponsible girl," may be very careful in keeping her club's records although she has not finished a single class assignment on time in three years. Definitions and theories of personality differ in how they deal with the inconsistencies that may be observed in a person's behavior across different situations or at different times. Some theorists have minimized the importance of such inconsistencies, whereas others have emphasized them.

The Nature of Individuality:
The Idiographic-Nomothetic Distinction

Personality psychologists generally agree that each of us is in some way unique. But there is great controversy over the implications of this for the study of personality. One view is that each of us is so distinctive that we can only be understood in terms of our own particular life and experiences. Comparison with others, according to this approach, is really not meaningful. This is called the **idiographic** [id-ee-o-GRAF-ik] approach (from the Greek *idios*, meaning personal). It has inspired extensive studies of all aspects of the lives of individuals with the aim of achieving a unique understanding of each person.

The alternative view is the **nomothetic** [no-mo-THET-ik] approach. It assumes that our uniqueness is a product of general physical, biological, and psychological laws. (*Nomos* is the Greek word for law.) According to this approach, each of us is a unique combination of "ingredients." Each ingredient, though, is produced by *general* processes. The processes can be understood by investigating specific aspects of personality in a wide variety of persons, with the aim of formulating laws of behavior that hold for people in general.

The Goals of Personality Psychology: Prediction, Control, and Understanding

In discussing personality, psychologists often use the terms *prediction*, *control*, and *understanding*. **Prediction** is the ability to accurately anticipate a person's behavior. **Control**, as the term is used in psychology, means influencing a person's behavior. Suppose a theory indicated that people with a high need to achieve tend to take moderate risks. If we know that Barbara has a high need to achieve, we would predict that she will prefer a bet with 4 to 1 odds over a bet with either 2 to 1 or 20 to 1 odds. And we could influence (control) Barbara's betting behavior by changing the odds of the available bets.

Prediction and control are straightforward ideas. The meaning of **understanding** is elusive and ambiguous. By understanding we usually mean comprehension of the process involved or an *explanation* of some sort. But how much comprehension and explanation are sufficient for a person to say "I understand" varies from individual to individual. To most drivers, it is enough to know that their car won't start because of a short in the ignition. But mechanically inclined drivers may not be satisfied until they know where the short is and what caused it. Understanding can thus mean different things to different people.

PERSONALITY THEORY

In science, theory serves four general purposes: (1) to organize and clarify observations; (2) to explain the causes of past events in such a way that future events can be predicted from the same causes; (3) to provide a sense of understanding of the subject matter; and (4) to generate new ideas and research.

Theoretical Constructs in Personality

The basic terms and building blocks of a theory are *theoretical constructs.* Energy is a theoretical construct in physics; oxidization is a theoretical construct in chemistry; and natural selection is a theoretical construct in biology. Personality theorists have used many theoretical constructs; among the more familiar are ego, anxiety, unconscious, trait, self-concept, and learning. One characteristic distinguishes all **theoretical constructs.** They have been *invented* to describe and explain observations. Thus, theoretical constructs do not actually exist; they cannot be seen or touched. They are merely useful inventions that help give order to observed phenomena.

Why are these convenient fictions necessary or even desirable? A major reason is that they economically tie together meaningful relationships among observations that would otherwise soon become a hopeless quagmire of raw facts. Figure 1–1 illustrates the advantage of using the theoretical construct *anxiety* to "pull together" various observations and outcomes. Even in the case of only three situations and three outcomes, a single concept that unites each of the three observations with the three outcomes (shown in the bottom half of Figure 1–1) is more economical, manageable, and comprehensible than describing nine separate relationships (shown in the top half of Figure 1–1).

On the Correctness of a Theory

Theories are theories. That is to say, they are *speculations* about the nature of phenomena. Facts (actual observations) are used to generate and substantiate a theory. But theories are not facts. Therefore, strictly speaking, theories cannot be "right" or "wrong." Theories, however, can be more or less "useful" depending on their intended purposes. Correctness is not one of the accepted criteria for evaluating a theory.

Criteria for Evaluating Personality Theories

Seven major criteria for evaluating a theory are: empirical validity, parsimony, extensiveness, internal consistency, testability, usefulness, and acceptability. A theory may fulfill any of the criteria to a greater or lesser degree. Even the "best" theories do not meet all seven criteria to the same degree.

FIGURE 1–1

An illustration of the advantages of using *anxiety* as a theoretical construct, operating differently in a number of circumstances (B), over a mere listing of observed, separate relationships (A)

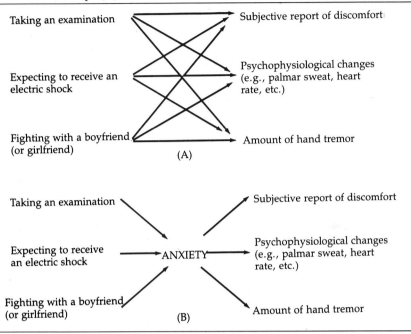

Source: Modified from "Liberalization of Basic S-R Concepts: Extensions to Conflict Behavior, Motivation, and Social Learning" by N. E. Miller, 1959 in S. Koch (Ed.), *Psychology: A study of a science* Vol. 2, New York: McGraw-Hill.

Empirical Validity

Empirical validity is the degree to which the theory is supported by evidence derived from observations. Note that a theory is not proved *or* disproved by empirical evidence. A researcher can gather evidence that supports a theory. But the absence of supporting evidence does not usually refute the theory. With each new substantiating piece of evidence, the psychologist gains more confidence in the theory. After a number of tests, however, a theory may fail to receive support. The psychologist would then have to turn to a new theory or revise the existing one. In this case, the theory would have been rendered useless for all practical purposes. Logically, though, it would not have been proved false.

Parsimony

Any phenomenon can be described and explained in different ways. Theories concerning the same phenomenon differ in the complexity and in the number of fundamental assumptions they make. When everything else is equal, theories that involve simpler explanations and fewer assumptions are better theories—they are more **parsimonious.**

Extensiveness

Extensiveness refers to the breadth of the phenomena with which the theory can deal, that is, its comprehensiveness. All other things being equal, the more phenomena a theory accounts for, the better is the theory. The more extensive a theory, the greater is the scope of the research efforts it inspires. In contrast, restricted theories tend to be *restrictive* theories. They exclude important phenomena and problems with which they are unable to deal.

Internal Consistency

A theory has **internal consistency** to the degree that its propositions and assumptions are consistent and fit together in a coherent, larger explanation. Some theories are such a loose confederation of ideas and concepts that the parts do not fit together. When this happens, the theory loses some of its explanatory power.

Testability

Testability is how well and easily a theory can be supported. Whole theories are never tested directly. Rather, specific predictions, or **hypotheses,** derived from the theory are tested through research. Testability is enhanced when a theory's concepts are clearly defined so that hypotheses derived from the theory can be stated precisely and unambiguously.

Usefulness

"Theory," wrote the Irish poet James Stephens, "is but the preparation for practice." Scientists often object to public demands for practical applications of their ideas. But theories that survive often lead to important practical applications, at least in the long run. Evaluation of the applications of personality assessment and personality change derived from various personality theories provides a measure of their usefulness.

Acceptability

To be influential, a theory must be known and taken seriously by others. This does not mean the theory must be popular or faddish. But theories proposed before or after "their time" do not fare well. A theory must have some **acceptability** among scientists if it is to be tested through research and applied in practice. Public tolerance and funding of research require believing the theory is worthwhile. The most brilliant theory cannot thrive in a social climate that does not find it acceptable and plausible.

Implicit Theories of Personality

Each of us has an implicit theory of personality. If this does not seem immediately obvious, you will almost certainly be convinced by the time you have finished this book. You are likely to find some theoretical propositions that you immediately agree with; others will immediately seem wrong. This is because you already have a set of ideas about how your own personality and the personalities of others work. You have an "implicit theory of personality." The implicit personality theories held by individuals differ from the theories in this book. The theories we will examine are formal and have been communicated to others. In contrast, our own theories of human behavior are not formalized and are often not communicated to others.

PERSONALITY ASSESSMENT

Modern psychology is said to have begun in 1879. In that year, Wilhelm Wundt established a psychological laboratory at the University of Leipzig. Only five years later, formal personality measurement was proposed by Francis Galton. Galton (1884) wrote: "The character which shapes our conduct is a definite and durable 'something,' and therefore . . . it is reasonable to attempt to measure it" (p. 179). Toward this end, Galton made a number of specific proposals about how to assess personality. The methods he proposed included ratings by teachers and peers and direct observation of the person in social situations. Modern personality psychologists use many sources of information for drawing inferences about personality and look for converging lines of evidence wherever possible.

Self-Reports: Interviews, Questionnaires, and Personality Tests

One way to find out something about a person is to ask the person directly. This can be done through an interview, by questionnaire, or using a combination of the two. Self-report data based on direct questioning gathered through interviews or from psychological tests have been used widely in studies of personality. Such procedures have the advantage of providing information quickly. They are also our only access to the person's subjective experiences (e.g., "How are you feeling today?").

Despite their appeal, direct questions alone present an incomplete picture. What people say about themselves is subject to memory lapses, misunderstanding, and a variety of distortions. This is especially true when "sensitive" content is involved. If it seems direct self-reports may be invalid or inaccurate, indirect assessment techniques are used. In most cases, these techniques are "disguised" so the person being assessed cannot easily distort the measurement. The difficulty with disguised test methods is that responses must be interpreted; psychologists may disagree on how to interpret, say, what a person reports seeing in an inkblot.

Direct Observations of Behavior

A second way to learn about people is to observe them directly in particular situations. Such situations may be simulated or natural. For example, in some well-known studies of aggression the test situation involved leading subjects to believe they were "teachers" in an experiment on punishment and learning. Subjects administered electric shocks to a learner. (In fact, the learner was a confederate of the experimenter and no shock was given.) The severity of shock subjects administered served as the measure of aggression. In contrast, a psychologist interested in aggression might simply observe children on a playground, noting and recording the nature, severity, and circumstances of various acts of aggression that occur spontaneously. Such naturalistic observation (whether by a clinician or a researcher) has more credibility than interviews or questionnaires. But naturalistic observation is often expensive or otherwise impractical; observation of even a single individual in more than a small number of situations is usually out of the question for personality assessment. Direct observations provide only part of the information needed for a complete understanding of personality.

Projective techniques are indirect methods of personality assessment in which the subject responds to an ambiguous stimulus. Here the subject is making up a story based on a Thematic Apperception Test (TAT) picture. The examiner writes down the subject's story and later scores and interprets it. *Photo by Christopher O'Keefe and Michael D. Spiegler*

Impressions of Others

Sociologist Erving Goffman (1959) suggested that personality includes both how we *express* ourselves and how others are *impressed* by us. How we are seen by others, including friends, family, supervisors, and peers, is an important part of who we are. Moreover, these people can observe us in many situations, often over a considerable period of time.

Using the impressions of others to judge someone's personality has a subtle implication, though. It blurs the line between objective judgment and mere opinion. Psychiatrist Thomas Szasz (1960), for example, believes terms such as *mental illness* and *abnormal personality* are really value judgments. They are used to talk about persons whose values, thoughts, and actions simply differ from those of most other people.

Personal Histories and Life Records

Finally, much information can be found in a person's history and life records. Educational, employment, and marital history as well as personal accomplishments can reveal much about a person. Such data have the advantage that they can be obtained or confirmed objectively, such as by consulting school records.

Bogus Personality Assessment

So far, our discussion has focused on personality assessment from the assessor's viewpoint. An equally interesting aspect is the point of view of the person being assessed.

Many popular assessment techniques are available commercially. These include everything from horoscopes to handwriting analyses. These techniques have never been shown to be scientifically valid, yet they enjoy many enthusiastic endorsements. Why is this so if the techniques are generally invalid?

Snyder (1974a, 1974b) showed that most people are quite believing when given interpretations of their personality from sources they trust. As a result, "bogus" personality descriptions that could actually apply to anyone are often accepted by otherwise thoughtful people as unique and remarkably accurate descriptions of their true selves. What this means is that there is general faith in some procedure, whether an astrological reading or a personality test administered by a Ph.D. psychologist in a prestigious clinic. This does not necessarily mean the procedure can accomplish what it purports to accomplish.

This book contains a number of Demonstrations that will allow you to test for yourself both the principles and the problems associated with the study of personality. The first of these, Demonstration 1–1, illustrates

Although there is no scientific evidence that fortune-telling can be used to assess personality, it continues to enjoy great popularity. © *Barbara Alper*

how personality assessments may seem to be "true" to the person who is offered them when, in fact, like cotton candy, they have very little real substance. Demonstration 1–1 will also allow you to try your hand at some research, the next issue we will consider in this chapter.

DEMONSTRATION 1–1

THE CREDIBILITY OF BOGUS PERSONALITY ASSESSMENTS

Most of us have read horoscopes in the newspapers and may well have commented that it is difficult to imagine anyone being "taken in" by these overly general descriptions and predictions. It is possible, however, that a more sophisticated version of the same kind of generalized descriptions can be extremely convincing and can even lead persons to believe that they have an entirely unique description of themselves. Testing this hypothesis, Ulrich, Stachnik, and Stainton (1963) asked students in educational psychology classes to take two personality tests. A week later, the students were given a written interpretation of their test scores which appeared to represent the careful efforts of the professor. As a second part of the study, other students were taught how to administer the same two personality tests to a friend. For both phases of the study, the people whose personalities were being "interpreted" were asked to rate the accuracy of the "interpretation" (on a scale ranging from excellent to very poor) and to comment on it.

Despite the individualized appearance of the personality description, *all persons were given exactly the same "interpretation"* (though the order of the statements varied), and, in fact, *no actual interpretations of the tests were made.* The description read:

> You have a strong need for other people to like you and for them to admire you. You have a tendency to be critical of yourself. You have a great deal of unused capacity which you have not turned to your advantage. While you have some personality weaknesses, you are generally able to compensate for them. Your sexual adjustment has presented some problems for you. Disciplined and controlled on the outside, you tend to be worrisome and insecure inside. At times you have serious doubts as to whether you have made the right decision or done the right thing. You prefer a certain amount of change and variety and become dissatisfied when hemmed in by restrictions and limitations. You pride yourself as being an independent thinker and do not accept others' opinions without satisfactory proof. You have found it unwise to be too frank in revealing yourself to others. At times you are extroverted, affable, [and] sociable, while at other times you are introverted, wary, and reserved. Some of your aspirations tend to be pretty unrealistic. (Ulrich et al., 1963, p. 832)

The students who had been administered the personality tests by the professor virtually all rated the "interpretations" as good or excellent. In the second phase of the study, approximately 75 percent of the subjects who had been tested by admittedly inexperienced students also rated the assessments of themselves as good or excellent. Furthermore, the subjects' comments clearly indicated an acceptance of these interpretations as accurate and individualized descriptions of their own personalities. One subject who had been given the tests and interpretation by the professor said: "On the nose! Very good. I wish you had said more, but what you did mention was all true without a doubt. I wish you could go further into this personality sometime." A subject who had been given the tests and interpretation by a student commented: "I believe this interpretation fits me individually, as there are too many facets which fit me too well to be a generalization" (Ulrich et al., 1963, p. 833).

Snyder and Larson (1972) replicated this study, extending it to show that college students accept these global evaluations as relevant, regardless of whether they are presented by a psychologist in an office or a graduate student in the laboratory. Indeed, in the Snyder and Larson study, even among students who had been led to believe that their tests had been scored by a computer (rather than evaluated by a human scorer), most rated these statements as between good and excellent. From their own and earlier experiments of this sort, Snyder and Larson (1972) concluded that the evidence provides:

> an object lesson for the users of psychological tests. People place great faith in the results of psychological tests, and their acceptance of the results as being true for them is fairly independent of test setting, administrator, and scorer. Furthermore, it must be realized that presentation of the results of psychological tests, typically presented to the individual as being for him personally, maximizes the acceptance of the psychological interpretation. Thus, the individual's acceptance of the interpretation cannot be taken as a meaningful "validation" of either the psychologist or his tests. (p. 388)

To replicate this experiment for yourself, tell a friend that you are learning how to use personality tests in class and have the person make two different drawings for you. First, ask your friend to draw a picture of her- or himself and another picture as he or she would like to look. (The Draw-a-Person Test is a projective technique that uses this procedure to assess personality; we will have more to say about projective techniques in Chapter 6.) Then, in your own handwriting, copy the interpretation used by Ulrich and his associates quoted on page 17. About a week later, offer this assessment to your friend. After he or she has had an opportunity to read it, ask your friend to rate the interpretation (excellent, good, average, poor, or very poor) and to give you some feedback as to how well you are doing as a "psychological examiner."

Finally, after obtaining feedback from your friend, it is important that you tell your friend the real nature of the Demonstration. Complete explanation of the deception, called **debriefing**, should remove the possibility that permanent misconceptions about psychological testing will result. It may also evoke further comments of interest.

THE IMPORTANCE OF RESEARCH

A strategy for studying personality includes theory, assessment, research, and personality change. The importance of theory and assessment, introduced briefly above, is obvious to most beginning students of personality; we all have implicit personality theories, and we assess other personalities (and our own) long before studying the field of psychology. Often, the importance of research seems less obvious.

Until about 100 years ago, the formal study of personality was rooted in philosophy; it proceeded almost entirely on *rational* grounds. Discussion, argument, the opinions of various authorities, and a general appeal to "reason" were the basis for settling disputes among adherents of differing viewpoints. But people often cannot agree on what is reasonable; so the rational approach to the study of personality, by itself, offers no solid way of resolving differences of opinion. What one person regards as a great insight may seem to be a preposterous fantasy to another.

An alternative to the rational approach can be traced at least to the seventeenth century and John Locke. This is the *empirical* approach. With empiricism, disputes can be settled only by admitting as "facts" what is verifiable by direct observation. Thus, empiricism brought with it a demand for objectively verifiable rather than circumstantial or subjective evidence. Rational considerations may give rise to theories, but they are not strong enough to validate theories.

Empirical research involves systematic attempts to gather evidence through observations and procedures that can be repeated and verified by others. The four strategies we will consider are all committed to supporting the validity of their theories, assessment procedures, and personality-change techniques through empirical research. It is this commitment to research that distinguishes the scientific approach to knowledge from other approaches (Neale & Liebert, 1986).

Scientific personality research is not a stereotyped or rigid enterprise, however. There are many scientifically legitimate ways of investigating personality. In Chapter 2 we will consider three basic methods: experimental, correlational, and case studies. We will also see, throughout this book, how research has helped to dispel an "obvious" but incorrect idea or establish a less-obvious principle or process that seemed implausible until the evidence came in. Scientific demonstration is never superfluous.

Personality change

The fourth issue with which personality psychologists deal is personality change. *Change* in personality actually can have two meanings: (1) naturally occurring developmental changes over time, and (2) planned changes when personality "problems" arise. Natural changes, or personality development, will be covered as we discuss theories. In this book, the term *personality change* refers only to planned personality change. For the most part, this is synonymous with *psychotherapy*.

Personality psychology, as distinguished from abnormal psychology and psychopathology, involves primarily normal personality. However, normal and abnormal personality are closely related, and personality theorists often link the two. In fact, many personality theorists began their professional careers as clinicians engaged in psychotherapy. Their theories arose from observation of their patients or clients, and dealt with the development and planned change of abnormal personality. These psychologists then used the insights they had gained from dealing with clients in psychotherapy to better understand human personality in general. Finally, personality change has a uniquely important place in the field of personality psychology because it is the single most significant practical application of personality theory.

A NOTE TO THE READER

This book is divided into five sections. Section I includes this introductory chapter and the next chapter, which deals with methods of personality research that will be illustrated throughout the book. The four succeeding sections are devoted to descriptions of the *theories, assessment techniques, research methods,* and *change procedures* characteristic of one of four strategies for the study of personality: *psychoanalytic, dispositional, phenomenological,* and *behavioral.* We are presenting the study of personality, then, in terms of a 4 × 4 matrix as illustrated in Figure 1–2.

The strategy sections begin with brief introductory chapters. In each section, the introductory chapters should be read first. You may also want

FIGURE 1–2
Personality can be studied from the perspective of four different strategies, each of which is concerned with four issues.

	ISSUES			
	Theory	Assessment	Research	Change
Psychoanalytic				
Dispositional				
Phenomenological				
Behavioral				

STRATEGIES

to reread these chapters after you finish the section to help you integrate what you've learned about the strategy.

Our aim is to convey a sense of the nature of these strategies. The format, emphasis, and writing style of Sections II through V vary somewhat so as to be consistent with the "flavor" and "customs" of each strategy. The strategies are presented in a generally positive light, emphasizing assets. In essence, each strategy is presented from the viewpoint of its proponents. We believe that this is the best way to learn about the strategy.

The last chapter in each strategy section deals with the "liabilities" of the strategy according to its critics. In these chapters, we adopt the stance of a harsh critic to highlight the weaknesses of each strategy. This complements the positive light in which the strategy was presented. The liabilities chapters are not intended as complete critiques or evenhanded evaluations of the strategies; rather, they illustrate the range of limitations and problems each strategy entails when applied to the full scope of the study of human personality. We believe that this approach gives readers an opportunity to evaluate both the merits and limitations of the strategy, thereby providing an optimal introduction to the scientific study of personality.

SUMMARY

1. All strategies for the study of personality must deal with four issues: theory, assessment, research, and personality change.

2. Personality psychology refers to the study of the total functioning of the individual person.

3. Two common themes run through most definitions of personality: organization and uniqueness.

4. Personality psychologists differ in the degree of emphasis they put on the subjective and objective aspects of human functioning. They also differ on whether prediction and control are the only goals of personality psychology, or whether understanding should be a major goal.

5. Theory serves four general purposes: (1) to organize and clarify observations; (2) to explain the causes of past events so that future events can be predicted; (3) to provide a sense of understanding; and (4) to generate new ideas and research. The basic terms used by a theory are its theoretical constructs, which help "pull together" various observations and outcomes.

6. Evaluation of theories involves seven major criteria: empirical validity, parsimony, extensiveness, internal consistency, testability, usefulness, and acceptability.

7. Most people have their own implicit theories of personality, which are typically informal and are not communicated to others.

8. There are four broad methods of personality assessment: self-reports (including interviews, questionnaires, and personality tests), direct

observations of behavior, impressions of others, and personal histories and life records. Bogus personality assessments, though highly general in their content, are often accepted as correct.

9. Empirical research is the hallmark of the scientific study of personality. Such research involves systematic attempts to gather evidence through observations and procedures that can be repeated and verified by others.

10. Personality change refers both to naturally occurring developmental changes and to those produced intentionally (through psychotherapy); we use the term in this book only in the latter sense. Many personality theorists developed their ideas mainly through observing the clients or patients they saw in psychotherapy.

INTRODUCTION

CHAPTER 2

ASKING AND ANSWERING QUESTIONS ABOUT PERSONALITY: RESEARCH

OVERVIEW

The fundamental aim of personality research is quite simple. Personality research involves asking and answering questions about why people act as they do.

AN OVERVIEW OF THE THREE BASIC APPROACHES TO PERSONALITY RESEARCH

Three major research methods have been used to gather information about personality: the *case-study, correlational,* and *experimental* methods. The three methods have one essential element in common—they all involve *observation* of behavior. The major differences are the types of observations made, the circumstances in which the observations are made, and how the data from the observations are examined. Briefly, the **case study** involves a detailed *qualitative description* of the behavior of a *single* individual. The case study yields a depth and richness of information that cannot be obtained with the correlational or the experimental method. The **correlational method** examines the *quantitative relationship* between two or more events for a group (sample) of people observed under the *same* conditions. The **experimental method** looks at the *quantitative relationship* between one or more conditions which are *systematically varied* and are expected to *cause* specific changes in people's behavior. (Note that in this book the terms *experiment* and *experimental* are reserved specifically for investigations using the experimental method.)

In many cases, a problem can be studied using any of the three basic methods. How the research questions are stated and the type of answers desired determine the method employed. Before examining each of the methods in depth, we will look at how a single, broad question—how television violence affects the aggressive behavior of children—has been investigated using each method. This comparison will point out, with a concrete example, how the same issue can be studied in different ways.

TV Violence and Aggression: Case Studies

The earliest investigations of TV violence and children's aggressive behavior were case studies of individual youngsters who had apparently become more aggressive by learning from or copying what they had seen on television. The following are two excerpts from case studies involving television violence and aggression (Schramm, Lyle, & Parker, 1961).

> In Los Angeles, a housemaid caught a seven-year-old boy in the act of sprinkling ground glass into the family's lamb stew. There was no malice behind the act. It was purely experimental, having been inspired by curiosity to learn whether it would really work as well as it did on television. (p. 161)
>
> A 13-year-old . . . boy, who said he received his inspiration from a television program, admitted to police . . . that he sent threatening notes to a . . . school teacher. His inspiration for the first letter came while he was helping the pastor of his church write some letters. When the minister left the office for an hour, the boy wrote his first poison-pen letter. "I got the idea when I saw it happen on TV," he told Juvenile Sergeant George Rathouser. "I saw it on the 'Lineup' program." (p. 164)

Such reports represent isolated incidents. But they certainly raise the possibility that television violence is related to aggressive acts. More children must be examined in a more standard manner to determine whether such a relationship exists for the general population and not just the few children in the case studies. Further, if we want to know the degree or magnitude of the relationship between television violence and aggression among children, we need quantitative data (i.e., numbers) to supplement the qualitative descriptions that case studies yield. These additional requirements are met by the correlational method.

TV Violence and Aggression: Correlational Studies

In fact, many correlational studies provide quantitative evidence of a relationship between viewing TV violence and aggression for children in general (Liebert, Sprafkin, & Davidson, 1982). For example, McIntyre and Teevan (1972) correlated viewing habits and behavior in 2,300 junior and senior high school boys and girls in Maryland. First, the youngsters were asked to list their four favorite television programs, "the ones you watch every time they are on the air." A numerical violence rating was assigned to each program. Then an average violence score was computed for every subject. Second, a measure of deviance was obtained by having each youngster complete a self-report checklist of various antisocial behaviors such as serious fights at school and involvement with police. The subjects indicated how often they engaged in each behavior using a simple numerical scale (0 = never, 1 = once, 2 = twice or more). McIntyre and Teevan thus had two numerical scores for each of the 2,300 youngsters. One was the degree of violence in subjects' preferred TV fare; the other was the extent of their deviant behavior. It was then possible to statistically examine the nature of the relationship (correlation) between these two sets of scores. This would show whether they were systematically associated and, if they were, the nature of their association. The results indicated a direct relationship between the various types of deviance and the violence ratings of the four favorite programs—the more violent the programs were, the greater the deviance.

TV Violence and Aggression: Experimental Studies

Although the correlational evidence is impressive, it does not indicate that television violence *caused* the aggressive behavior. Possibly being aggressive makes a youngster more interested in watching violent entertainment, rather than vice versa. Cause-and-effect relationships can be most clearly demonstrated by means of the experimental method. For example, in one experiment, Liebert and Baron (1972) hypothesized that children who saw a violent film would be significantly more willing to hurt other children than would children who saw a nonviolent film. Boys and girls aged five through nine were taken to a room containing a television and told that they could watch television for a few minutes, until the experimenter was ready. The sequences they saw came from actual television shows. Half of the children saw a sequence with a chase, two fistfights, two shootings, and a knifing. The other half of the children saw an equal-length exciting sports sequence.

Each child was then brought to another room and seated in front of a large box with wires leading into the next room. On the box were a green button, labeled HELP, and a red button, labeled HURT. Over the two buttons was a white light. The experimenter said the wires were connected to a game a child in another room was going to play. The game involved turning a handle; each time the child started to turn the handle, the white light would come on. The experimenter explained that, by pushing the buttons, the subject could either help the other child by making the handle easier to turn or hurt the other child by making the handle hot. The subjects were told that the longer they pushed the buttons, the more they helped or hurt, and that they had to push a button every time the light came on. (In fact, there was no other child, so the subjects' responses had no effect on anyone.) The experimenter then left the room and the light came on twenty times.

The measure of aggression was how long a child pushed the HURT button. The investigators found children who saw the aggressive program were significantly more willing to hurt another child than were those who saw the sports sequence. As shown in Figure 2–1, this finding appeared for boys and girls in both age groups. Because the only difference between the two groups of children was the TV sequence they saw—violence or sports—it is possible to conclude that the differences were due to viewing violence.

We now turn to a detailed examination of each of the three major research methods. Bear in mind that the same basic question can be approached using different methods of research, as we have just illustrated. Each strategy for the study of personality favors particular types of research. But we will see numerous examples of converging lines of evidence using varied research methods.

THE EXPERIMENTAL METHOD

In the experimental method, a factor that seems to cause the behavior studied is systematically varied while all other possible causative factors are held constant. In the simplest case, two groups of subjects are used.

FIGURE 2–1
Mean total duration of aggressive responses in Liebert and Baron's (1972) experiment

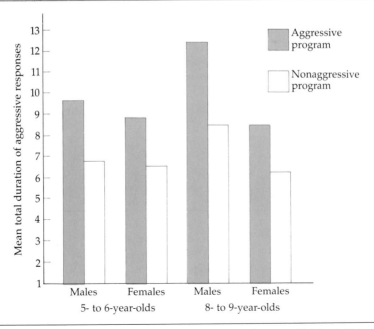

Source: From "Some Immediate Effects of Televised Violence on Children's Behavior" by R. M. Liebert and R. A. Baron, 1972, *Developmental Psychology, 6*, pp. 469–75.

Subjects in an **experimental group** are exposed to the hypothesized cause. Those in a **control group** are not exposed to it. In all other respects the groups are treated alike. If the two groups differ in the behavior being measured, the difference must be due to the hypothesized causative factor. In Liebert and Baron's (1972) experiment concerning TV violence and aggression, the experimental group saw violent TV episodes and the control group did not. The only difference between the two groups was the TV episodes they watched.

Besides treating experimental and control subjects alike, experimenters must also be sure that characteristics of the subjects do not influence the results. Suppose, for example, that Liebert and Baron's experimental group had a higher percentage of "naturally aggressive children" than did the control group. If that were the case, the greater aggression observed in experimental subjects might have been due to a difference in the characteristics of the subjects rather than to the TV sequences. To eliminate the possible effects of such extraneous factors, groups in an experiment must be equivalent in subject characteristics relevant to the experimental hypothesis. Usually, this is done by *randomly* assigning subjects to each group. This means every subject has an equal chance of being assigned to each group. Subjects are not assigned to groups in any systematic way. So, their personal characteristics, such as "natural aggressiveness," tend to equalize across groups. As a result, no group has a disproportionate number of subjects with a particular characteristic. Liebert and Baron employed random assignment of subjects. Another way to deal with this influence is to measure subject characteristics ahead of time. Subjects are then assigned to groups so that the characteristics occur equally in each group.

The experimental method controls conditions so that cause-and-effect relationships can be precisely assessed. **Control** in psychological research refers to systematically varying, randomizing, or holding constant the conditions under which observations are made. Such procedures are meant to reduce the number of alternative explanations of what influenced the behavior observed.

In an experiment, the condition that is directly varied is the **independent variable.** In our example, TV violence was the independent variable; it was varied by being either present (for experimental subjects) or absent (for control subjects). The aim of an experiment is to observe the influence of the independent variable on a specific behavior, the **dependent variable.** Total time pressing the HURT button was the dependent variable in Liebert and Baron's experiment. The term *dependent variable* comes from the fact that this variable is hypothesized to depend on or be influenced by the conditions varied by the experimenter—that is, the independent variable.

An **experimental hypothesis** states a prediction about the effect of the independent variable on the dependent variable. Liebert and Baron's experimental hypothesis was: "observing violence on TV will lead to more aggression than will observing nonviolent episodes on TV." The only difference between the experimental and control groups was the independent variable (violence or no violence). Thus, it was possible to conclude that the independent variable influenced the dependent variable (aggression), which supported the hypothesis.

Experiments can have more than two groups, and a control group is not always required. Instead of just having the independent variable present or absent, different amounts or levels may be examined. For example, a logical next step to Liebert and Baron's study might be to examine the hypothesis that the more TV violence children observed, the more aggressive they would become. To test this hypothesis, we might have several experimental groups, each watching a different amount of TV violence (e.g., 30, 60, and 120 minutes) before their aggression was measured. In this case, comparisons would be between groups exposed to different amounts of TV violence. No control group is necessary because the hypothesis only concerns varying amounts of TV violence. However, as with the simpler experiment, it would be necessary that the only difference among groups is the independent variable (amount of TV violence).

In studies that employ groups of subjects, *average* performance is examined. Liebert and Baron found that on the average, children exposed to TV violence were more aggressive than children who were exposed to nonviolent sports. However, some experimental subjects may have exhibited less aggression than some control subjects.

Evaluation of the Experimental Method

The experimental method can be used to determine definitive cause-and-effect relationships. This is its main advantage. Changes in the dependent variable can be causally linked to the independent variable when all other relevant variables (influences) are held constant. Often the experiment is conducted in a psychological laboratory where rigid control over conditions is possible. The price paid for such control is frequently some artificiality. This may limit the extent results of controlled laboratory experiments can be generalized to real-life settings. We might ask, for example, how similar is watching TV in a psychological laboratory to watching TV at home? And how similar is pushing a HURT button to physically assaulting another child on the street? If the laboratory conditions are not similar enough to the real-life circumstances, it will not be possible to generalize from what is found in the laboratory.

In laboratory experiments, we gain less information about the total problem of interest. But we gain more reliable and precise information about specific aspects of the problem. As we will see, the correlational and case-study methods involve less control over relevant variables. At the same time, they preserve more naturalness. The decision as to which method to use in studying a particular problem is complex; each method has both advantages and disadvantages.

THE CORRELATIONAL METHOD

Correlation, as the name implies, deals with the co-, or joint, relationship between variables. The method answers research questions of the form: "Do variable X and variable Y go together or vary together?" Questions of relationship are frequently asked about personality. (Is there a relationship between late toilet training and compulsiveness in adulthood? Is the frequency of dating in college related to marital success and happiness?) Using the correlational method, *observations of all subjects are made under the same conditions.* This should be contrasted with the experimental method, in which the conditions under which subjects are observed are systematically varied.

The basic data for a correlational analysis are pairs of observations collected for each member of a group of subjects. As an example, suppose a college professor were interested in whether a relationship existed between how close students sat to the front of the classroom and how much they learned in the course. The professor could list the row in which each student sat and the student's final grade in the course. The data from such a study might look like those in Table 2–1. These data could be used to correlate seating and final grade. Notice that all of the subjects (students) in this correlational study were observed under the same conditions.

Psychologists ask two specific questions about the relationship between two variables. First, if there is a correlation between the two variables, how strong is it? The *magnitude* (strength) of a correlation refers to the ability to predict one variable from the other. The stronger the correlation, the more accurate is the prediction. The second question involves the *direction* of the correlation or the way in which the variables relate to each other—either directly or inversely. A direct or **positive correlation**

TABLE 2–1
Data from a hypothetical study of the relationship between how close a student sits to the front of the classroom and final course grade

Subject	Row	Final Grade	Subject	Row	Final Grade
Andy	2	76	Linda	5	71
Ann	5	60	Mary	1	95
Bill	4	79	Pam	1	87
Bob	3	67	Pat	3	80
Eric	1	82	Polly	3	75
Howie	2	91	Robert	4	81
Jerry	2	86	Sam	2	82
Joan	5	64	Sheila	5	55
John	4	62	Shelley	3	90
Ken	4	66	Steve	1	99

between variable X and variable Y means that high scores on X tend to be associated with high scores on Y; low scores on X tend to go with low scores on Y. For example, a positive correlation is regularly found between people's height and weight; in general, taller people weigh more. Conversely, with an inverse or **negative correlation,** high scores on X are associated with low scores on Y; low scores on X go with high scores on Y. Age and quickness of reflexes are negatively correlated; as people grow older, their reflexes become slower.

The correlation between two variables can be estimated by plotting the scores on a **scatter diagram.** Figure 2–2 presents several such diagrams. The horizontal axis represents one variable, and the vertical axis represents the other. Each point indicates the scores of one subject on the two variables.

The magnitude of the correlation is estimated by how closely the points in the scatter diagram deviate from a straight line, the **line of perfect correlation**. Perfect correlations between psychological variables do not exist. If a perfect correlation did exist, all the points would fall on a straight line (Figures 2–2A and 2–2B). Knowing a person's score on one of the variables (it makes no difference which one), we could perfectly predict his or her score on the other variable (see Figure 2–3). In the case of a high (but not perfect) correlation, there is some "scatter" (deviation) around the line of perfect correlation. But the scores tend to fall within a narrow ellipse, making prediction of one variable from the other reasonably good (Figures 2–2C and 2–2D). The lower or weaker the correlation, the more scatter there is. Thus, where there is virtually no correlation (i.e., no relationship between the variables), there is much scatter of the scores (they are essentially randomly scattered); it is not possible to predict one variable from the other (Figure 2–2E).

The direction of the correlation is determined by the way the correlation line is slanted. If the points form a line from bottom left to top right, the correlation is positive or direct (Figures 2–2A and 2–2C). If the points go from bottom right to top left, the correlation is negative or inverse (Figures 2–2B and 2–2D).

The data from our hypothetical study of the correlation between where students sit in class and their grades (Table 2–1) are plotted in Figure 2–4. Most of the data points fall in a narrow ellipse, which indicates a high correlation or strong relationship. The points are oriented from lower right to upper left, indicating a negative correlation. This means a general tendency for students who sit close to the front of the room to earn higher grades.

A numerical index of the correlation between two variables is provided by a **correlation coefficient,** often abbreviated r. It is calculated by means of a mathematical formula. The direction of the correlation is indicated by the sign (plus or minus) of the coefficient; its magnitude is indicated by the absolute numeric value of the coefficient, whether positive or negative. Correlation coefficients range from $+1.00$, a perfect positive relationship, to −1.00, a perfect negative relationship. When the coefficient is equal to 1.00 (+ or −), either variable can be exactly predicted from the other. As the coefficient decreases in absolute value from 1.00, ability to predict one variable from the other decreases. In the extreme, a correlation of 0.00 indicates that the variables are totally unrelated; knowledge of one variable would not assist at all in predicting the other. Note that how closely two variables are related depends only on the absolute size of the correlation coefficient. Thus, correlation coefficients of +.60 and

FIGURE 2–2
Scatter diagrams showing various degrees of relationship between two variables

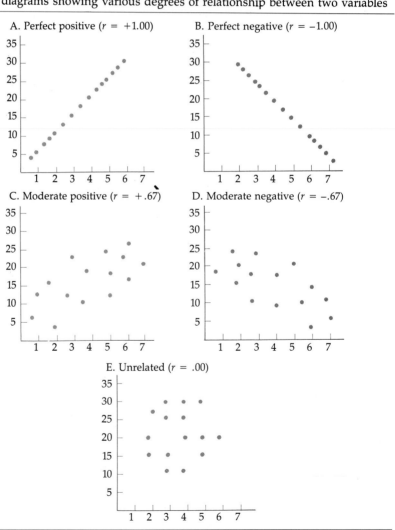

FIGURE 2–3
In a scatter plot of correlational data, the intersection on the line of perfect correlation of two lines drawn at right angles to each axis allows prediction of one variable from another. For example, a person obtaining a score of 4 on variable X would obtain a score of 22 on variable Y.

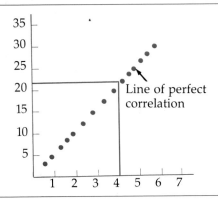

FIGURE 2–4
Scatter diagram of data (presented in Table 2–1) from a hypothetical study of the relationship between how close a student sits to the front of the classroom and final course grade ($r = -.79$)

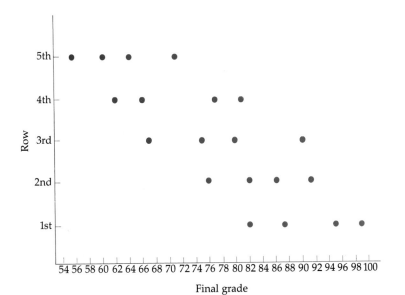

$-.60$ are equivalent in the extent to which one variable can be predicted from the other, although the direction of the correlation must be known to make the prediction. The correspondence between correlation coefficients and scatter plots can be seen in Figure 2–2, where the correlation coefficient is given in parentheses.

To conceptualize how well one variable can be predicted from the other, the correlation coefficient must be *squared*. The squared correlation coefficient (r^2) is a measure of the overlap between the two variables, or how much they "share in common." The greater the overlap, the stronger is the relationship and the more accurately one variable can be predicted from the other. A correlation coefficient of .80 indicates the two variables have an overlap of 64 percent ($.80^2 = .64 = 64\%$); a correlation coefficient of .40 indicates the two variables have an overlap of only 16 percent. A correlation coefficient of .80 *cannot* be considered twice as strong as one of .40. The relative strengths of correlation coefficients can be estimated only by comparing the squared correlation coefficients. Thus, a correlation of .80 is four times as strong as a correlation of .40 ($.80^2 = 64\%$ and $.40^2 = 16\%$), as is shown in Figure 2–5.

FIGURE 2–5
Squaring the correlation coefficient gives an estimate of the percent of overlap between the two variables. In comparing the relative strength of two correlations, the squared correlation coefficients must be compared. Thus, a correlation of .80 is not twice as strong as a correlation of .40 (left hand graph) but rather is four times as strong (right hand graph).

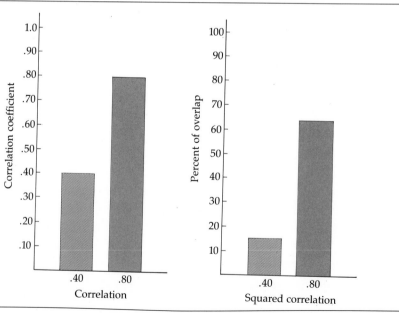

Evaluation of the Correlational Method

It is useful to contrast correlational with experimental research. The correlational method involves making observations without controlling the subjects' behavior or varying the circumstances under which the subjects are observed. Thus, the naturalness of the situation is maintained. This absence of control may bring the investigation closer to "real life" than does the experimental method.

Generally, the correlational method has three advantages over the experimental method. First, a number of variables of interest to personality researchers are difficult or impossible to vary systematically. Variables such as sex, age, birth order, and body size cannot be changed by a researcher. In a study of child-rearing, for instance, it would be virtually impossible to successfully control the lengthy and complex procedures that parents use to raise their children. And such phenomena as death, suicide, and mourning cannot ethically be controlled.

Second, it may be possible to introduce a variable only at relatively "weak" levels. Collecting data on the variable as it naturally occurs may let a researcher examine it over a broader range. An example is studying the effects of stress. It is not ethical to place individuals under more than mild stress. But in naturally stressful situations psychologists can collect data that may help us learn what factors are associated with severe and prolonged stress.

One such situation occurred during a massive power failure that encompassed much of the eastern seaboard of the United States on November 9–10, 1965. The blackout occurred in New York City at about 5:30 P.M., the height of the rush hour. Thousands of people on their way home from work had to spend the night in public facilities. In the early morning hours, psychologists collected data from people in a large bus terminal and a hotel lobby, both of which were illuminated by emergency power (Zucker, Manosevitz, & Lanyon, 1968). They asked people to complete a questionnaire calling for such information as age, education, and birth order, and their feelings about being stranded for the night. They also asked subjects to rate their preference for being alone or with other people, on a five-point scale. Anxiety was assessed through responses to the following question, also on a five-point scale: "How nervous or uneasy did you feel during this experience (i.e., the blackout) over the course of the evening?" Finally, the investigators noted, before approaching a subject, whether he or she was talking to or standing with someone else; this information became an index of actual gregariousness. Previous laboratory experiments that created mild stress in subjects indicated that firstborn persons tend to show more anxiety and a greater preference to be with other people when confronted with stress-inducing conditions than do those lower in the birth order. The data collected during the blackout generally confirmed the previous findings and extended them to a broader range of stress in a real crisis situation.

·A third advantage of correlational research over experimental research is that correlational studies are often more economical in terms of time, effort, and expense. This is because correlational data are frequently collected under conditions that already exist so that there is no need to "set up" situations.

Correlation and Causation

The major limitation of correlational research is that conclusions about *cause-and-effect* relationships usually cannot be drawn. When two variables are correlated, we do not know which is the cause of the other—the *directionality* problem. Or both variables could be caused by some other factor—the *third-variable* problem.

A correlation between two variables tells us only that they are related; it does not tell us whether one is caused by the other. For example, there is a positive correlation between grades and attending class. One possible interpretation is that better attendance increases the amount learned and thus results in higher grades. A second, equally plausible, hypothesis is that good grades lead students who obtain them to attend class more often. In many correlational studies, the problem of directionality cannot be resolved.

But the direction of a correlation can sometimes be determined. Some relationships can only be conceptualized in one direction. For example, there is a negative correlation between amount of alcohol consumed and motor coordination (such as driving or even walking). Obviously, this relationship makes sense in only one direction.

The third-variable problem concerns the possibility that neither variable produces the other. Instead, some unspecified variable is responsible for the relationship. There is, for example, a positive correlation between the number of churches in a city and the number of crimes committed in that city; the more churches a city has, the more crimes are committed in it. Does this mean that religion fosters crime? Probably not. That crime fosters religion? Unlikely. The relationship is due to a third variable—population. Growth of population leads to an increase both in churches and crime. There is also a positive correlation between the number of drownings on any given day and the consumption of ice cream on that day. Here, too, a third variable—temperature—is responsible for the relationship. When the weather is warm, more people are likely to be swimming (which is directly related to the frequency of drowning). Coincidently, more ice cream is also likely to be eaten on warm days.

We often cannot infer causation directly from correlational evidence. But this does not mean a cause-and-effect relationship does not exist. It merely means that a correlation does not let us identify the nature and the direction of causal relationships *without further information.*

There are instances in which we don't need to know whether one variable is causing the other or whether a third variable is responsible. A common example occurs in applied areas of psychology in which only prediction of a criterion is needed. For instance, a college admissions committee requires information to predict success in college. Typically there is a moderately high positive correlation between grades in high school and academic achievement in college. Using this information, the committee can do its job effectively without reference to the causes of college academic achievement.

Statistical Significance and Practical Importance

In experimental and correlational research, small groups of people, called **samples,** have been selected from much larger groups of people, called **populations.** Personality researchers study a sample—a small subset of the population of interest—because it is not feasible to deal with the entire population, which is generally quite large (e.g., children who watch TV). However, the researcher wants to be able to conclude something relevant about the population, not just the particular sample. This involves drawing *inferences* about the population from the sample.

For such inferences to be valid, findings from the sample must be **reliable,** meaning that they will occur again in another study with a different sample from the same population. Any event that occurs only once might be attributable to chance. ("Anything can happen once," as the saying goes.)

Statistical significance is the standard of reliability of quantitative research findings. It is computed by mathematical procedures called **statistical tests**. A statistical test provides the researcher with an estimate of the probability that the result is due to chance alone. A low probability means that the result was a reliable rather than an accidental or chance finding. Traditionally, in psychological research, a result is considered *statistically significant* if the odds are less than 5 in 100 that it is due to chance alone. This is written "$p < .05$" and is read "probability less than 5 percent (or 5 in 100)." Statistical significance can be computed for either an experimental or a correlational finding.

Statistical significance refers only to the reliability of the finding. It in no way implies that the finding is important, socially relevant, or practically meaningful. This is sometimes confusing because in discussing results, the word *statistically* is often omitted, as in the phrase "A significant difference was found in the study. . . ." A highly reliable (nonchance) finding may, in fact, have little or no practical import.

THE CASE-STUDY METHOD

When a detailed account of a single individual is used in psychological, sociological, or anthropological research, it is typically called a *case study* or a *case history*. Oscar Lewis' (1961) classic study of family life in a Mexico City slum, *The Children of Sanchez*, was based on extensive interviews in which the then-grown children were asked to relate their life histories. The following passage illustrates the detailed, individualistic nature of these case studies.

> Manuel, the eldest son, came closest to the pattern of traits held to be typical in a disorganized slum environment. He recalled little about his home life, though his brother and sisters remembered all too well his crude assertions of authority when father was not at home. Having an "aversion to routine," as he put it, he remembered only "the exciting things," and these occurred mainly with his gang of friends who soon became the most important part of his life. Stocky and strong, he was from the first a good fighter and earned the other boys' respect. One of his fiercest fights, started to defend his brother, led oddly to a firm friendship; he and his new companion became inseparable, exchanged many confidences, and for years supported each other during emotional hard times. Manuel did poorly in school, which after the sixth grade he gladly gave up in favor of jobs, pocket money, and girls. At 13 he was inducted into sexual intercourse, after which "the fever, this sex business," got hold of him "in such a way that all I did was to go around thinking about it. At night my dreams were full of girls and sex. I wanted every woman I saw." Presently he fell into the grip of another fever, gambling at cards. "If a day passed without a game," he said, "I was desperate." This fever soon mounted to a point where he would bet a whole week's pay, but when he won he would go out with his friends and "throw it all away." Regretfully he recalled that he "never did anything practical" with his winnings.
>
> There is a certain charm about Manuel. His narrative is full of vitality and drama, and he sometimes reveals generous impulses, especially toward male friends. On one occasion he took over a sick friend's job to hold it for him, thereby sacrificing a much better job of his own. On another occasion, set up in a small business making shoes, he paid his three helpers so well that he went bankrupt. This mishap extinguished an already feeble spark: "I lost the little confidence I had in myself and lived just from day to day, like an animal. I didn't have the will power to carry out plans." At 15 he

started a family and presently had four children. He never provided a home for his family, which finally became part of his father's household, and he increasingly neglected his wife, staying away and having a torrid affair with another woman. When his wife died he was grief-stricken. With his boyhood companion he departed for some months to work and gamble elsewhere, leaving the children to his father's support. No doubt this behavior contained some element of revenge for the humiliations and belittlements received from his father, but there was a strong undertone of shame and sadness in Manuel at having led a life "so sterile, so useless, so unhappy." (White, 1976, pp. 132–33)

The case study is mainly descriptive; its data are qualitative. It is the least systematic and least controlled research method. As we will discuss shortly, this has both advantages and disadvantages. The case study is the major research method in idiographic approaches to personality. (The experimental and correlational methods are typically used in nomothetic research.)

Many case studies deal with abnormal personality phenomena; they are used to present data concerning unusual cases. "A Case of Multiple Personality" is an account of a 25-year-old married woman, "Eve White," who displayed three very distinct personalities (Thigpen & Cleckley, 1954). Eve White had been in psychotherapy for several months because of severe headaches and blackouts. Her therapist described her as a "retiring and gently conventional figure." One day during an interview,

> As if seized by a sudden pain she put both hands to her head. After a tense moment of silence, her hands dropped. There was a quick, reckless smile and, in a bright voice that sparkled, she said, "Hi there, Doc!" The demure and constrained posture of Eve White had melted into buoyant repose. . . . This new and apparently care-free girl spoke casually of Eve White and her problems, always using *she* or *her* in every reference, always respecting the strict bounds of a separate identity. When asked her own name she immediately replied, "Oh, I'm Eve Black." (p. 137)

Following this startling discovery, Eve was observed over a period of fourteen months in a series of interviews totaling approximately one hundred hours. During this time, a third personality emerged. This case study is especially valuable because it is one of only a few detailed accounts of a rare phenomenon, a true multiple personality. Since this classic case study, a small number of additional in-depth case studies of multiple personality have been made (e.g., Keyes, 1981; Schreiber, 1974). Recently, there has been a renewed interest, partially a consequence of the case studies, among psychologists in this fascinating phenomenon (e.g., Crabtree, 1985).

Case studies are sometimes used to test hypotheses and support theories. Psychoanalysts use case studies extensively to support their personality theories. But because case studies are basically uncontrolled, using them in such ways is questionable. However, case studies can sometimes be helpful in *disconfirming* the implications of a theory. When a theory purports to be universally true, case studies can provide negative instances. A single negative instance—a relevant example that does not conform to the theory—is sufficient to disprove universality. For instance, Freud theorized that *all* male children experience an Oedipus complex (see Chapter 4). Anthropological case studies revealed cultures in which young boys do not exhibit the Oedipus complex. This cast serious doubt on Freud's original hypothesis (Malinowski, 1927). (Of course, a somewhat modified position might still be tenable, such as limiting the phenomenon to Western society.)

Evaluation of the Case-Study Method

As a method of personality research, the case study has several advantages. It is an excellent way of examining the personality of a single individual in great detail. A closely related advantage is that the case study allows an individual's idiosyncrasies [id-ee-o-SIN-kra-sees], complexities, and contradictions to be examined. No matter how general the laws of human behavior are, each person is unique. Occasionally, a psychologist interested in making statements about human behavior in general will use a number of case studies. In this situation, the idiosyncrasies that appear may be of special significance.

Data from case studies can reflect the richness and complexity of personality; they are often the source of hypotheses about human behavior. Hypotheses formulated from case-study material can then be tested using more controlled and rigorous methods.

Another advantage is that the case study typically deals with people in their natural environments as opposed to an artificial laboratory setting. In the final analysis, theories of personality are intended to explain behavior in "real-life" situations. Case studies therefore directly examine the phenomena of ultimate interest.

The case study allows circumstances to vary as they will. Thus, it offers greater potential for revealing new and surprising findings. With the other research methods, the variables measured are specified in advance, and only those measures are collected. As a result, the investigator may miss some vital observations. In contrast, the case study does not specify the observations to be made. Instead, as much of the entire situation as possible is recorded.

There are several important limitations of the case-study method. First, case-study observations are not made under controlled conditions. Thus, they cannot be directly repeated by independent investigators. As we explained previously, replication is important in science.

Second, observers in any type of research are never totally unbiased or neutral. But objectivity in case studies *may* be at additional risk because there is usually only one observer.

A third problem with case studies is that it is difficult or even impossible to make definitive statements about cause-and-effect relationships. This is true because there is no control over variables that may influence the behavior being studied.

Fourth, there is the major practical problem of being in the right place at the right time. To overcome this, the psychologist typically waits for the critical event to occur and collects the data later. These data come from detailed retrospective reports by the subject and other people who observed the subject. The problem with such retrospective data is that the observers (the subject and others) tend to forget what happened and how they felt in the original critical situation. Moreover, their "stories" also tend to change as time passes. Things are later seen in a different perspective. This is especially true when the incident studied was somewhat stressful. Memories are mixed with present thoughts and feelings. Unless the data for the case study are gathered when the crucial incident occurs, the accuracy of the case material is open to question. Lewis' (1961) case study of Manuel Sanchez is clearly subject to the problems of retrospective data collection. The case of Eve White is an example of a *non*retrospective case study; the data were systematically collected as the subject was exhibiting her multiple personalities.

A fifth limitation of a case study is that it is difficult to generalize from it to other people. This is because the data it yields are unique in that they usually come from a single individual.

Finally, the data from case studies are usually qualitative rather than quantitative. Quantification is important in scientific research because it leads to finer, more precise descriptions of behavior.

Whether the disadvantages of the case-study method outweigh its advantages depends on the purpose of the investigation. At the very least, it is reasonable to think of the case study as a preliminary research method that can generate intriguing hypotheses. The generality and validity of such hypotheses can then be tested using the correlational and experimental methods.

LOOKING AHEAD: ADVICE TO THE TRAVELER

Reading and learning about personality in terms of the four strategies described in this book is analogous to visiting four different countries. Beginning your tour of each strategy in the introductory chapter, you'll immediately notice its structure, as you would the landscape of a new country as your plane circles overhead before landing and your tour guide gives you some basic information about what to expect. As you enter the strategy, you will quickly become aware of the distinctive language. You will have to acquaint yourself with new terminology as well as with words that are familiar but are used in novel ways. Moreover, the personality psychologists in each strategy express themselves in a unique style. This style can, in subtle ways, tell you a great deal about their approach to personality.

Foreign travelers are advised to immerse themselves in the culture they are in, leaving their native customs, including their assumptions and values, behind. You will substantially increase your understanding and appreciation of each strategy if you temporarily adopt its approach and suspend your critical evaluation until you are leaving the strategy. That way, beside formulating your own ideas of the problems with the strategy, you will be able to put the frequently voiced criticisms discussed in the liability chapter in perspective.

Travel is an educational experience because it opens us to new ideas about human existence, thought, values, and behavior. You will have a similar experience in learning about personality through four very different approaches to the same phenomena. Your journey begins in the birthplace of the scientific study of personality, the psychoanalytic strategy. Bon voyage!

SUMMARY

1. All methods of personality research involve observation of behavior. The methods differ in the types of observations made, the circumstances in which they are made, and how the data are examined. Evidence bearing on a research question may be gathered using one or more methods.

2. In the experimental method, an independent variable hypothesized to be causing the behavior being studied (dependent variable) is systematically varied while all other possible causative factors are held constant. This is often done by comparing an experimental group in which the independent variable is present with a control group in which the independent variable is not present. Because the two groups are equivalent except for the presence of the independent variable, differences between the groups (on the dependent variable) can be attributed to the independent variable (a statement of cause-and-effect).

3. Experiments allow cause-and-effect relationships to be established. However, the controls they must exert to provide such information often make them narrow in scope and thus the ability to generalize from the results may be limited.

4. Correlational studies examine the degree to which variables are related or go together. A group of subjects is measured on the variables of interest, and the subjects' scores are mathematically correlated. Correlations may be direct (the variables change in the same direction) or inverse

(the variables change in opposite directions). The strength or magnitude of the correlation is determined by how accurately one variable can be predicted from the other. The higher the correlation, the more accurate the prediction.

5. Correlations can be plotted on a scatter diagram. The direction of the points indicates whether the correlation is direct or inverse; the degree of deviation of the points from the line of best fit indicates the magnitude of the correlation. Correlation coefficients are mathematically determined indexes of the direction and magnitude of a relationship. They may be positive (direct) or negative (inverse) and their values range from zero (no correlation) to 1.00 (perfect correlation).

6. Correlational research allows observations to be made in existing, natural situations because the variables are simply measured and not systematically varied. Definitive cause-and-effect relationships cannot usually be determined from correlational data alone. Either variable may cause the other, or a third variable may cause both variables.

7. Statistical significance is an estimate of the reliability of a quantitative finding (i.e., the probability that the results are not due to chance and therefore will occur again).

8. Case studies involve qualitative, detailed descriptions of single individuals. They can provide a picture of the richness and complexity of personality that neither the experimental nor the correlational method can. Case studies cannot be precisely replicated; they are subject to many biases; cause-and-effect statements cannot be made from them; they are usually retrospective; and generalizations to other people are tenuous.

SECTION

II

THE PSYCHOANALYTIC STRATEGY

THE PSYCHOANALYTIC STRATEGY

CHAPTER 3

INTRODUCTION

OVERVIEW

Before you read this chapter, you might want to write down the words or phrases you think of when you hear the word *psychoanalysis*. The odds are that you have many associations to psychoanalysis. These might include Freud, unconscious, sex, libido, Oedipus complex, repression, id, ego, superego, defense mechanism, dreams, couch. . . . Most people know more about the psychoanalytic strategy than the other three personality strategies. Psychoanalytic concepts have become part of a variety of academic disciplines other than psychology. Literary and art criticism and philosophy are among them. It has also become part of popular culture.

WHAT IS PSYCHOANALYSIS?

Psychoanalysis has three common meanings: a theory of personality, an approach to research, and procedures for changing personality. All three were originally advanced by Sigmund Freud (1856–1939). Subsequently they have been extended and modified by other psychoanalysts. Psychoanalytic personality theory emphasizes the role of (*a*) **intrapsychic events** (processes occurring in the mind), (*b*) unconscious drives, and (*c*) early childhood development. To assess and study these phenomena, psychoanalysis examines a person's thoughts, dreams, mistakes, and other behaviors to discover their underlying meaning or significance for the individual. The same analysis of the mind is used to bring about personality change. Psychoanalysis as psychotherapy is the third meaning of the term. Thus, theory, research, assessment, and personality change are highly intertwined in the psychoanalytic strategy.

The psychoanalytic strategy has been dominated by the work and writings of a single individual. All psychoanalytic thinking is (*a*) a direct outgrowth of Freud's ideas, (*b*) a variation on or expansion of them, or (*c*) very divergent from them to the point of being anti-Freudian. Accordingly, our discussion of the psychoanalytic strategy will draw heavily on Freudian conceptualizations and practices. However, we will also cover other psychoanalytic viewpoints, including the most recent trends within the strategy. Psychoanalysts fall broadly into two camps: **Freudians,** who closely subscribe to Freud's ideas and **post-Freudians** who deviate, in varying degrees, from Freud's ideas.

PSYCHOANALYTIC PERSONALITY THEORY

Freud's theory of personality is actually a number of separable but interrelated mini-theories. Freud frequently revised his thinking over the course of some forty-five years of theorizing that began in the mid-1890s. The second half of the nineteenth century was a period of great intellectual excitement. In particular, two daring ideas were set forth during this time.

The human species is in all its aspects a natural result of evolution, not different in this way from animals. Charles Darwin (1809–1882) reached this conclusion in 1871. His theory held that humans gradually evolved from other life forms through random variation and environmental selection. Darwin's theory accounted for the appearance, disappearance (extinction), and evolution of species. Darwin claimed that all life forms are motivated by two forces: the will to survive and the urge to reproduce. Darwin stopped short of providing a scientific analysis of the mind. But he set the stage for this task, and Freud accepted the challenge.

Unconscious, irrational, and primitive forces play a central role in human motivation. Philosophers Arthur Schopenhauer (1788–1860) and Friedrich Nietzsche (1844–1900) observed that human behavior is often driven by unconscious and irrational forces. Both emphasized how easily the intellect

Sigmund Freud was the founder of the psychoanalytic strategy and the first modern personality theorist. *The Bettmann Archive*

could be self-deluding. Schopenhauer considered sex to be the most important human instinct. Nietzsche suggested that we repress certain memories, turn aggression inward to become a basis for ethics and conscience, and derive our ultimate strength from the most primitive part of ourselves. By the late nineteenth century, these ideas held sway among many intellectual Europeans (Ellenberger, 1970; Kern, 1973; Sulloway, 1979). They are also clearly expressed in psychoanalytic theory.

Major Themes in Psychoanalytic Theory

Four major themes characterize psychoanalysis. It is *deterministic, dynamic, organizational,* and *developmental.*

The Deterministic Nature of Psychoanalytic Theory

Freud believes that all behavior is determined, or caused, by some force within the person. Thus, all behavior has meaning. Even the simplest examples of human behavior can be traced to complicated psychological factors of which the person may be totally unaware. Perhaps the best known occurrences are so-called *Freudian slips.* These are errors made in speech, writing, and reading. They presumably reveal something about the person's "inner" thought, or "real" intent. Obvious examples include substituting "playbody" for "playboy" and "Fraud" for "Freud."

Other examples of Freud's (1963)[1] thoroughgoing determinism relate to "accidental" forgetting or losing objects:

> If anyone forgets a proper name which is familiar to him normally or if, in spite of all his efforts, he finds it difficult to keep it in mind, it is plausible to suppose that he has something against the person who bears the name so that he prefers not to think of him. (p. 52)
>
> We lose an object if we have quarreled with the person who gave it to us and do not want to be reminded of him; or if we no longer like the object itself and want to have an excuse for getting another and better one instead. The same intention directed against an object can also play a part, of course, in cases of dropping, breaking, or destroying things. (p. 54)
>
> Here is the best example, perhaps, of such an occasion. A youngish man told me the following story: "Some years ago there were misunderstandings between me and my wife. I found her too cold, and although I willingly recognized her excellent qualities, we lived together without any tender feelings. One day, returning from a walk, she gave me a book she had bought because she thought it

---

[1]The dates used in this book refer to the actual references used (sometimes translated or reprinted editions), and thus they do not always correspond to the original publication date of the work.

would interest me. I thanked her for this mark of 'attention,' promised to read the book, and put it on one side. After that I could never find it again. Months passed by, in which I occasionally remembered the lost book and made vain attempts to find it. About six months later my dear mother, who was not living with us, fell ill. My wife left home to nurse her mother-in-law. The patient's condition became serious and gave my wife an opportunity of showing the best side of herself. One evening I returned home full of enthusiasm and gratitude for what my wife had accomplished. I walked up to my desk, and without any definite intention but with a kind of somnambulistic certainty opened one of the drawers. On the very top I found the long-lost book I had mislaid." (p. 55)

Freud analyzed and interpreted incidents like these to understand facets of an individual's personality that would not otherwise be accessible.

The Dynamic Nature of Psychoanalytic Theory

Dynamic here refers to the exchange and transformation of energy within the personality. Like most other personality theorists, Freud believes that a comprehensive understanding of personality must include the motivation for human actions. For Freud, it is a unitary energy source within the person called **psychic energy**.

The Organizational Nature of Psychoanalytic Theory

Freud organized personality in two different ways. His early theory held that personality operates at three levels of awareness: unconscious, preconscious, and conscious. Later he divided personality into three basic functions or aspects—id (primitive, pleasure-seeking impulses), ego (rational self), and superego (internalized values of society). According to Freud, natural biological instincts (id), such as the need for food, elimination, and sexual gratification, are inevitably in conflict with the restraints of reality (ego), and the rules of society (superego). This conflict determines our specific actions.

Freud emphasizes the unconscious and the id in personality development and functioning. Many post-Freudians compensate by stressing rational, conscious ego processes. Some post-Freudians also disagree with Freud about how important conflict is for understanding personality. They concentrate more on conflict-free personality functions.

The Developmental Nature of Psychoanalytic Theory

Freud's theory is developmental. He considers early childhood experiences to be the prime determinant of adult personality. In fact, Freud believes one's adult personality is fixed by about the age of five. In Freud's own words, "The little creature is often completed by the fourth or fifth year of life, and after that merely brings gradually to light what is already within him" (quoted by Roazen, 1975, p. 106). Freud theorizes that personality development follows a more or less set course from birth. He divides development into a series of discrete stages through which every one of us must pass.

All psychoanalysts view early childhood experiences as important. A number of post-Freudian theorists broadened Freud's original idea to include the entire life span. Some post-Freudians even consider later experiences equally important in determining personality.

Intention and the Search for Meaning

Psychoanalysts search for the intentions and meanings behind every bit of behavior. They are famous for offering interpretations for what, at first, seem to be chance happenings. This is consistent with their deterministic outlook. The search for underlying motives is not unique to psychoanalysis, of course. Every day we form judgments about other people and their behavior by evaluating the "worthiness" of their intentions. For example, "Why did Kathy offer to help me with my work—because she likes me or because she felt she owed me something?" Our criminal justice system places great emphasis on premeditation. For instance, a person will be sent to jail for as little as one year for killing another if intent cannot be shown. If intent to murder is clearly established, the penalty can be life imprisonment or even death.

The importance of intention is learned early in Western societies. Jean Piaget, the famous Swiss developmental psychologist, found that children as young as seven acknowledge that a small amount of intended damage is "naughtier" than a great deal of damage due to ignorance, oversight, or accident. In our culture, high status is given noble intentions, even when the outcome is undesirable. A gift is not important; it is the *thought* (the giver's intent) that counts. A parent can severely punish children "because he or she loves them."

It is important to be aware of other people's intentions in daily interactions. We are also concerned with others' understanding, or failing to understand, our intentions. Sometimes we want to make our intentions clear. If Wylie walks quickly past a close friend without saying hello, he is likely to explain his "behavior" the next time he sees his friend. He may tell his friend that he did not *mean* to be rude; he was concerned about being late for an appointment. Actually, Wylie is explaining his intention rather than his behavior.

At other times we try to conceal our intentions. A student who volunteers to do some additional research for a class in the hope of getting on the teacher's good side might tell the teacher that he or she is very interested in the topic.

We may describe our intention to another person. This doesn't mean he or she will accept the statement. If Wylie had had an argument with his close friend the night before, the friend might not be so sure Wylie was merely concerned with his pressing appointment. Similarly, the "diligent" student may have shown little interest in the course throughout the semester. The teacher might therefore be suspicious about the student's motives in volunteering to do extra work. In each case, people's reports of their intentions are being doubted. The issue is finding the "true" intent of the act, the "real" reason it was performed. We often use the word *really* to emphasize the validity of a statement of intent. "Do you *really* like the way I'm dressed?" "Phil *really* meant well." "I *really* love Julie."

The psychoanalytic strategy stresses questions of motivation and intention for understanding personality. These issues relate to other emphases of the strategy. For example, as implied by terms such as *really*, people may not always be aware of their own intentions and motivations; some of the most important aspects of an individual's personality may be *unconscious*. Therefore they are the products of motivations of which the person is entirely unaware.

Intention is always inferred from behavior. But people vary in using behavior to evaluate interpersonal interactions or in going beyond the behavior to infer intentions. Demonstration 3–1 will allow you to explore your use of behavior and intentions to evaluate personal interactions.

DEMONSTRATION 3–1

INTENTION VERSUS BEHAVIOR

In our daily lives we have many interactions with people: a roommate, salesperson, friend, teacher, bus driver. In each interaction, we have certain expectations, either explicit or implicit, about what should take place. For example, the bus driver is supposed to get us to work on time, a teacher must assign grades, and a friend should listen sympathetically to problems. Some of our expectations are doubtless satisfied (e.g., teachers almost never forget to give grades), whereas others are not (e.g., friends are not always eager to hear about our frustrations). When our expectations about how another person is supposed to act are not met, our reactions and feelings about that person are based on two sources of information: the person's *behavior* (what he or she has done or failed to do) and the person's *intent* (what he or she meant to do).

Suppose that a bus driver failed to stop at your corner. You might have been very annoyed if this resulted in your being late for a date. It would have made little difference to you in that situation that the driver had "meant" to stop. The driver's intent and behavior were at odds, and your reaction of annoyance was based on the bus driver's *behavior* of driving past your corner and not on the driver's intent.

It is important to note that, in this instance, the driver did not explicitly state an intention to stop, but the intention was a reasonable inference. Intent frequently has to be inferred. In the next example, the person's intention is explicitly stated.

Suppose you met your friend Dave at lunch, hoping to share with him the events of your frustrating morning. Dave said he wanted to listen (intent) but that he had to rush off (behavior) to study for a physics test scheduled that afternoon. You appreciated Dave's desire to listen to you and wished him well on his exam. Here again, a person's intent and behavior were inconsistent, but in this situation you evaluated the interaction in terms of Dave's *intention* to listen rather than his behavior of rushing off.

A third way of reacting to an inconsistency between intention and behavior would take both factors into account. In the preceding example, if Dave had left to play tennis, it is likely that you would have felt less good about your interaction with him than if he had "had" to leave for an exam. You would have understood that Dave had planned to play tennis but, at the same time, would have thought that he might have given your feelings and needs higher priority. By considering both behavior (Dave's playing tennis) and intention (he would have liked to listen to you), you would have viewed the situation differently than if you had taken only his intention *or* only his behavior into account.

The purpose of this Demonstration is to sensitize you to the role played by other people's intentions and behavior and the relation between the two in some of your daily interpersonal transactions. You will first compile a list of people with whom you have dealt recently and whom you either know very well or with whom you merely have a passing acquaintance. Then you will consider interactions you have had with these people in which their intentions and behavior were inconsistent.

PROCEDURE

1. First, make a list of the people with whom you have interacted over the past few weeks. Try to include as many persons as you can, but there is no need for the list to be exhaustive.

2. Next, divide the people on your list into three categories:

Close—people you know well, interact with frequently and regularly, think about, and so on (e.g., roommate, good friend, parent);

Distant—people you do not know well, interact with infrequently and irregularly, may have met only once or twice, or have only brief business-type dealings with (e.g., salesperson, teacher with whom you have minimal personal contact);

Other—people who do not fit into either the "close" or the "distant" category, those whom you would not consider intimate acquaintances but with whom you have had more than just a brief encounter (e.g., many classmates, people who live in your dorm, your mail carrier). The people in this category will *not* be used in the Demonstration.

Keep in mind that the object of this preliminary step in the Demonstration is to provide you with a list of a number of people with whom you have recently interacted and whom you would consider either "close" or "distant." Thus, if you are having difficulty coming up with six to eight people in *each* of the two categories, your criteria for either "close" or "distant" relationship may be too tough. If this seems to be the case, adjust your criteria accordingly.

3. Having compiled a sizable list of persons whom you would construe as "close" and "distant," you are ready to proceed with the major part of the Demonstration. This involves identifying as many interactions as you can with the persons on your "close" and "distant" lists *in which the persons' intentions and behavior were somehow inconsistent with each other.* Certainly all of your interpersonal interactions will not meet this requirement. Your goal should be to come up with at least four instances of intention-behavior discrepancies for each of the two categories of people (i.e., four for "close" and four for "distant"), and more, if possible.

4. For recording each of the intention-behavior discrepancies, make a large copy of the chart in Table 3–1 (omitting the examples, of course). Then, for each interaction in which intention and behavior were inconsis-

TABLE 3–1
Sample Chart for Demonstration 3–1

	I Other Person	II Nature of Interaction	III Other's Behavior	IV Other's Intent	V Your Evaluation	VI Basis for Evaluation
"Close" relationships	Dick	Met Dick after having rough morning	Went to study	Wanted to talk with me	Understood why he couldn't talk and felt okay about it	I
	Dick	Met Dick after having rough morning	Went to tennis game	Wanted to talk with me	Appreciated that he had a tennis date but was a bit angry with him	B and I
"Distant" relationships	Bus driver	On bus going to date	Drove past my stop	To stop	Annoyed at the driver for making me late for my date	B

tent, record the information outlined below. Note that the top half of the chart is designated for interactions with "close" acquaintances and the bottom half for interactions with "distant" acquaintances.

In Column I: write the *name* of the person with whom you had the interaction.

In Column II: write a brief description of the *interaction*.

In Column III: write a brief description of the other person's *behavior*.

In Column IV: write a brief description of the other person's *intention*.

In Column V: write a brief description of how you *evaluated* the incident—that is, how you felt about and reacted to the other person and to the outcome of the incident.

In Column VI: state whether the *basis for your evaluation* in Column V was primarily the other person's behavior (B), primarily the other person's intention (I), or a combination of behavior and intention (B and I).

(The examples in Table 3–1 are taken from those discussed at the beginning of the Demonstration.)

DISCUSSION

By the time you complete Demonstration 3–1, you should have a greater understanding of the difference between intention and behavior. This is an essential distinction in the psychoanalytic strategy. We usually do not differentiate intention and behavior when they are consistent with each other. However, when they are discrepant, as were the interactions you considered, then a need arises to distinguish between them. The situation may also be evaluated in terms of the person's intent, the person's behavior, or some combination of the two.

The Demonstration should give you a sense of how you tend to use intention and behavior in situations where they are inconsistent. Is there any pattern in your reliance on intention versus behavior? There are any number of variables that might affect this. One has been built into the Demonstration. Compare your Column VI entries for "close" relationships with those for "distant" relationships. You may find that you tend to use intention in situations involving one of these groups and behavior for the other group. Clearly this is an individual matter. The more interactions you considered, the greater the likelihood that consistent patterns or trends will emerge. You might wish to look at your use of intention and behavior in relation to other factors. These could include the importance of the interaction, the sex of the other person, and whether your evaluation of the other person's intention-behavior discrepancy had direct consequences for the person.

You might also want to examine instances where your own intentions and behavior were inconsistent. How did you evaluate such situations? How did others react in terms of the emphasis they placed on your intention versus your behavior?

PSYCHOANALYTIC ASSESSMENT

Psychoanalytic theory assumes that much of our motivation is unconscious. This means we are often not aware of why we act the way we do. However, it is complex and difficult to assess motives you are partially or completely unaware of. To appreciate this complexity, ask yourself some questions like: Why am I going to college? Why do I like (dislike) my roommate (friend, relative)? Why do I enjoy my favorite activity? (The answers to these questions may be readily apparent. If they are, insert the word *really* in front of the words *going* and *like*.)

Can people be ignorant of their own motives? Can they be unaware of or mistaken about their feelings? An individual may express excessive certainty about his or her own abilities. It is not uncommon to assume that such a person, like the roaring lion, is expressing not self-confidence, but self-doubt. Are there grounds for such assumptions? How often do they hold? What is the value and what are the limitations of looking at people in this light? The answers to these crucial questions about unconscious processes are the domain of the psychoanalytic strategy.

Psychoanalytic personality assessment must be *indirect* if unconscious phenomena are to be assessed. Obviously, unconscious phenomena cannot be observed directly by others. It is also not possible for people to describe motives and feelings they are unaware of.

Psychoanalytic assessment must also be indirect in another respect. According to psychoanalytic theory, personality characteristics appear as either direct or indirect expressions of underlying drives. We normally expect direct expression. For example, an individual who feels hostile may attack another person, either physically or verbally. According to psychoanalytic theory, it is equally probable that underlying motives are expressed indirectly. Hostility may be disguised, such as by ignoring others. The most indirect way to express a motive is as its opposite. Hostility may come out as friendly and loving acts. The more socially unacceptable a motive is, the more likely it is that it will be expressed indirectly. Indirect expression gives unacceptable impulses an outlet without the anxiety or guilt normally associated with socially unacceptable behavior.

PSYCHOANALYTIC RESEARCH

Freud relied entirely on the case study method. He gathered extensive information about his patients in his clinical practice. He used these observations both as the source of his personality theory and as the evidence for the theory.

Psychoanalytic case studies include more than just a detailed description of the patient/subject's behavior. The observations are *interpreted*. These interpretations become an integral part of the case study

(Steele, 1986). Any behavior occurring during the psychoanalytic session may be interpreted. This includes the patient's reports of behavior outside the session. Psychoanalysts often interpret their patients' dream reports and free associations; these are assumed to be valuable sources of unconscious material that becomes conscious in disguised fashion, such as in symbolic form. Usually the analyst waits until the same observation is made several times, so that a theme is present, before making an interpretation. An interpretation is validated partially by the degree that the patient accepts it as true, and partially by whether it leads to changes in the patient's behavior. Interpretations that are frequently made by a number of psychoanalysts and have been validated in the manner described become principles of the theory.

Freudians believe that psychoanalytic concepts can only be validated through analysis and interpretation of material obtained from case studies. Freud commented on an early attempt to validate psychoanalytic concepts through experiments.

> I have examined your experimental studies for the verification of psychoanalytic assertions with interest. I cannot put much value on these confirmations because the wealth of reliable observations on which these assertions rest make them independent of experimental verification. Still, it can do no harm. (quoted by MacKinnon & Dukes, 1962, p. 702)

Case studies, more than any other research method, allow psychologists to explore the richness and complexity of human personality. Interpretative case studies are still the main method of research in the psychoanalytic strategy. However, post-Freudians have increasingly used correlational and experimental methods to test psychoanalytic propositions (e.g., Fisher & Greenberg, 1977; Kline, 1972; Masling, 1983, 1985).

PSYCHOANALYTIC PERSONALITY CHANGE

Psychoanalytic personality theory, assessment, and research began with attempts to change abnormal personality. Even today, most psychoanalysts are psychotherapists ("personality changers") first and theorists, assessors, and researchers second.

Psychoanalytic personality change (psychotherapy) involves indirect methods, just as psychoanalytic assessment does. This is because the conflicts causing patients' problems are primarily unconscious. Thus, a major aim of psychoanalytic personality change is to make the patient aware of his or her unconscious processes and motives—that is, making conscious what is unconscious. Personality change comes about primarily through the lengthy process of patients' discovering and understanding the underlying causes of their behavior. This is often accompanied by intense emotional release. Frequently patients discover, in the course of psychoanalysis, that their motives are based on early childhood adjustment problems and conflicts. They must learn that such motives are no longer relevant to their lives and are therefore unrealistic guides for their present behavior.

SUMMARY

1. Psychoanalysis refers to a theory of personality, an approach to research, and procedures for changing personality (i.e., psychoanalytic psychotherapy). Freud is the originator of psychoanalysis, and his ideas dominate the psychoanalytic strategy.

2. Psychoanalytic theory holds that all of one's behavior is (a) determined by forces within the person and (b) has meaning for the person. No behavior is purely accidental; Freudian slips are examples of this strict determinism.

3. Psychoanalytic theory posits a dynamic system in which personality functions employ and exchange psychic energy.

4. Freud organizes personality in two ways: levels of awareness (unconscious, preconscious, and conscious) and functions of personality (id, ego, and superego).

5. Psychoanalytic theory is developmental. Early childhood experiences are critical in determining adult personality. Many psychoanalysts have identified discrete, universal stages of development.

6. A person's intentions are central to the psychoanalytic view.

7. Personality operates primarily at an unconscious level. Therefore, indirect methods of assessing personality are necessary (e.g., projective techniques and dream analysis).

8. Case studies, usually of patients in psychoanalytic psychotherapy, provide the major source of evidence for psychoanalytic personality theory.

9. Psychoanalytic personality change is a lengthy process. The patient is made aware of the underlying, often unconscious determinants of his or her behavior and personality.

ORIGINS AND DEVELOPMENT OF PERSONALITY

OVERVIEW

In this chapter we will discuss the development of personality from birth to old age. The psychoanalytic strategy, more than the other strategies, describes in great detail how personality develops, especially in early childhood. We begin with a discussion of the motivation for development.

DRIVES AND LIBIDO

Drive in psychoanalysis is an inborn, intrapsychic force. When operative, it produces a state of excitement or tension. Freud spent over forty years developing his theory. In that time, many of his conceptions were revised. This is true of his theory of drives. In Freud's early theory, there were two classes of drives. The first is *self-preservative*. These satisfy physical needs, including breathing, hunger and thirst, and excretion. When these drives are not satisfied, the organism experiences tension. For example, when we hold our breath, we feel a tightness in our chest; when we have not eaten in some time, we feel hunger pangs. Under unusual circumstances, a drive such as hunger can become abnormally strong and exert a powerful influence on behavior. In October 1972, a plane carrying a Uruguayan rugby team and their supporters crashed in the Andes. The passengers and crew were given up for lost. Miraculously, sixteen men survived for seventy-three days in subfreezing temperatures with no fuel and only enough food for twenty days. The survivors remained alive by eating parts of the bodies of those who had died. (A popular book, *Alive: The Story of the Andes Survivors* [Read, 1974] and a movie, *Survive*, are based on this incident.)

The second group of drives relate to *sexual urges*. Freud used *sexual* to refer to all pleasurable actions and thoughts, including, but not confined to, eroticism. The psychic energy of sexual drives is called **libido**. Libido is also the energy for all mental activity, including thinking, perceiving, imagining, remembering, and problem solving.

Freud initially believed all human motivation is sexual; in other words, humans behave in ways that bring them pleasure. Societies place obstacles in the way of completely or even predominantly satisfying pleasure-seeking drives. In capsule form, Freud's theory of personality deals with how we handle our sexual needs in relation to society, which usually prevents the *direct* expression of such needs. Each individual's personality is a result of her or his unique compromise between satisfying sexual drives and conforming to society's restraints.

Around 1920, shortly after World War I, Freud revised his theory of motivation. He now included the aggressive along with the sexual drive. (Freud also called the aggressive drive the *death drive, death instinct,* or *Thanatos;* this is in opposition to the life drive, or *Eros.*) The aggressive drive accounts for the destructive aspects of human behavior. It has its own kind of psychic energy. However, Freud did not give a specific name to this energy. The development and function of the aggressive drive and the sexual drive are parallel. Freud's dual theory of drives assumes that both the sexual and the aggressive drives are involved in the motivation of all behavior. (The common use of the word *fuck* to express anger in contemporary America is an example of the close interrelationship of the sexual and aggressive drives.) However, the contributions of both drives are not necessarily equal. Freud did not describe the aggressive drive as fully or clearly as the sexual drive. Despite his recognition that human motivation is more than sexual, Freud always considered the sexual drive to be paramount. Accordingly, our discussion will focus on the sexual drive.

Dynamics of the Mind

Freud's psychic energy system is a *closed* system. Additional energy cannot be added to the system; no existing energy can escape or be permanently depleted. Each person has a fixed quantity of psychic energy that is invested in or devoted to various behaviors, people, and ideas. An investment of psychic energy is known as a **cathexis; cathect,** the verb form, is the process of investing psychic energy.

Psychic energy cannot actually be attached to people or activities. But in the mind, it can be cathected to their mental representations in the form of thoughts, images, and fantasies. The strength of a cathexis, the amount of energy invested, indicates how important the focus of energy is. There is a limited amount of psychic energy. So, the greater the amount of energy given to one cathexis, the less psychic energy available for other cathexes and mental activities. A young man who is constantly thinking of a woman friend has difficulty doing other things, such as reading an assignment in his personality textbook. Cathexes are not permanent. When we turn our attention to another activity or person, the energy transfers to our new focus. You may be wondering whether some people have more psychic energy than others. Each person has a fixed amount of psychic energy, which places limits on one's actions, thoughts, and feelings. But the concept of psychic energy has never been quantified.

To explain the nature of psychic energy and how it operates, Freud used analogies. (These must not be confused with actual description.)

The pressure of psychic energy builds up as does the pressure of water in a series of pipes when no external valve is open. If there is an increase in pressure and no outlet for this pressure, the pipe will burst—and it will burst at its weakest point. Reduction of psychic tension is necessary for an individual's functioning. It also produces a highly pleasurable experience, because tension is unpleasant or painful. Tension reduction is formally called the **pleasure principle.** The individual's psychic energy may not have an opportunity to discharge in normal or socially acceptable ways. In this case, the pressure will increase and finally, using the water pipe analogy, it will burst out violently at the weakest point in the personality. Bear in mind, however, that when psychic energy "bursts out," it is not dissipated. This would not be possible in a closed energy system.

ALTERNATIVE VIEWS OF THE BASIC HUMAN MOTIVE: JUNG AND ADLER

Mention *Freud*, and many people's initial association is sex. Freud's insistence on the preeminence of the sexual drive in human motivation ultimately made his views unacceptable to many psychologists. This includes two of his ardent followers at the beginning of the century, Carl Jung (1875–1961) and Alfred Adler (1870–1937). Early in their relationship, Jung (pronounced YOONG) wrote Freud to ask:

> Is it not conceivable, in view of the limited conception of sexuality that prevails nowadays, that the sexual terminology should be reserved only for the most extreme forms of your "libido," and that a less offensive collective term should be established for *all* the libidinal manifestations? (Freud & Jung, 1974, p. 25)

Jung believes that the sexual drive is an important source of motivation. He does not believe that it was the only source.

Carl Jung

National Library of Medicine

Adler's disagreement with Freud over the importance of the sexual drive is sharper. Adler believes the fundamental human motive is *striving for superiority* as compensation for feelings of inferiority. Adler's own life was the basis of the idea. As a child, Adler was continually sick and weak. He suffered from rickets, a disease that softens the bones; this made it extremely difficult for him to engage in physical activities with his peers. In later years, Adler recalled his feelings of inferiority: "I remember sitting on a bench bandaged up on account of rickets, with my healthy elder brother sitting opposite me. He could run, jump, and move about quite effortlessly, while for me, movement of any sort was a strain and an effort" (quoted in Bottome, 1957, pp. 30–31). Adler had twice been run over in the street, and he almost died from pneumonia (Orgler, 1963). As a consequence, he decided early in life to become a physician in an effort to overcome death and his fear of death (Ansbacher & Ansbacher, 1956).

Adler did go on to become a physician. Before he turned to psychiatry, he practiced general medicine. His 1907 book titled *The Study of Organ Inferiority and Its Physical Compensation* presents an intriguing theory. It states that people develop a disease or malfunction in their weakest organ or body part. Further, Adler believes that people deal with such weakness by compensating and even *over*compensating. For example, a person born with weak legs might spend many hours developing the leg muscles (compensation). As a result, the individual might eventually become a long-distance runner (overcompensation).

When Adler began to practice psychiatry, he broadened his theory to all feelings of inferiority. These included feelings arising from psychological or interpersonal weaknesses. The individual's perceived inferiority, be it from biological, psychological, or social weaknesses, leads to striving for superiority as a form of compensation. Adler (1964) believes that the existence of these two forces—the need to overcome inferiority and the desire to do so by becoming superior—are normal in all people. They are the basic motivating tendencies in humans. In normal development,

Alfred Adler

National Library of Medicine

striving for superiority compensates for feelings of inferiority. In the resulting compensatory lifestyle that the individual adopts, feelings of inferiority, which are most prominent in childhood, may be forgotten. (There is a parallel between Adler's view that adults are unaware of their childhood feelings of inferiority and Freud's view that adults are unaware of their infantile sexuality.) When feelings of inferiority and/or strivings for superiority become exaggerated, abnormal behavior (neurosis) can occur. **Inferiority complex** was Adler's term for such an exaggerated, neurotic reaction.

Other psychoanalysts emphasize different nonsexual sources of motivation. Many consider social factors critical in the development of personality. We will explore these "social alternatives" later.

MAJOR ISSUES IN THE THEORY OF PERSONALITY DEVELOPMENT

Precisely how personality develops is critical in psychoanalytic theory. Most psychoanalysts divide personality development into a number of discrete stages that are considered to be *universal,* or relevant to all people. There is considerable controversy, however, about the number and content of the stages.

Importance of Biological versus Social Factors

One controversy involves the role of biological factors versus social factors in development. Freud believes that biological factors are paramount. His developmental stages are biologically determined. Most contemporary psychoanalysts emphasize social factors and minimize the role of biology; the developmental stages they propose are based primarily on social phenomena.

Role of Early Experiences

Another controversy concerns the extent to which early experience determines adult personality. All psychoanalysts consider early experience important. Freud believes that adult personality is relatively fixed by about age five. Many post-Freudians agree that early experiences have a definite impact on later personality. But they believe that later experiences can also have profound effects. They have pursued the fascinating questions of when and how underlying personality changes occur after childhood.

FREUD'S STAGES OF PSYCHOSEXUAL DEVELOPMENT

At particular times in the development sequence, one body area—specifically, the mouth, anus, or genital region—predominates as an *erogenous zone*, an area that is particularly sensitive to erotic stimulation. Freud's stages of development are called *psychosexual* because they are concerned with the manifestation of the sexual (pleasure) drive.

While in a given psychosexual stage, much of the individual's libido is invested in behavior involving the erogenous zone that is predominant. To progress to the next stage, the libido must be freed from the primary erogenous zone of the stage it is in and reinvested in the primary erogenous zone of the next stage. This is necessary because each individual has only a fixed amount of libido.

The ability to transfer libido from one stage to the next depends on how well the individual has resolved the developmental conflict associated with each psychosexual stage. The conflict is always between free expression of biological impulses and parental constraints. Freud uses the analogy of military troops on the march to explain this process. As the troops march, they are met by opposition (conflict). If they are highly successful in winning the battle (resolving the conflict), virtually all of the troops (libido) will move on to the next battle (stage). (Thus, there will be ample libido available to deal with the conflict of the next stage.) If they experience difficulty in winning the battle, more troops will be left behind and fewer troops will move on to fight the next battle. (In other words, less libido will be available to cope with the next conflict.)

An individual may have difficulty leaving a stage and going on to the next for two reasons: *frustration* or *overindulgence*. Either the person's needs relevant to the psychosexual stage have not been met (frustration), or the needs have been so well satisfied that the person is reluctant to leave the stage (overindulgence). Both problems result in **fixation.** This involves leaving a portion of libido permanently invested in a previous developmental stage. The more difficult it is for a person to resolve the conflict, the more libido remains fixated at the stage.

Some libido is fixated at each psychosexual stage. If the proportion of libido fixated at a stage of development is small, then only vestiges of earlier ways of obtaining satisfaction are seen in later behavior. However, a substantial proportion of libido may be fixated at an earlier stage. In this case, the individual's personality is dominated by ways of obtaining satisfaction that were used in the stage. As a result, the individual develops an adult **character type** reflecting the poorly resolved conflict. Freud (1959) believes identifiable character types result from libido being fixated at each stage of psychosexual development. Psychoanalysis states that impulses may be expressed directly or indirectly. Thus, Freud (1959) lays down

the following formula for how character develops out of the relevant instincts: "the permanent character traits are either unchanged prolonga-
tions of the original instincts, or sublimations [socially acceptable means of
direct expression] of these instincts, or reaction formations [behaving opposite to the instinct] against them" (p. 175).

Oral Stage

For the first year of life, the mouth is the prominent source of tension
reduction (e.g., eating) and pleasure (e.g., sucking). The child is in the
oral stage of development; libido is centered in the oral cavity. Weaning
is the crucial conflict of the oral stage. The more difficult it is for the
child to leave the mother's breast or the bottle and its accompanying sucking pleasure, the more libido is fixated at the oral stage. Freud focuses
primarily on the biological ramifications of the oral stage. Post-Freudians
generally expand the emphasis. As Strupp (1967) puts it: "The focal point
of the child's personality organization at this period is not necessarily
the mouth per se but *the total constellation of immaturity, dependency, the
wish to be mothered, the pleasure of being held, the enjoyment of human closeness
and warmth"* (p. 23).

Karl Abraham (1927) divides the oral stage into two phases. The
early phase is **oral eroticism.** It is characterized by the pleasure of sucking
or taking things in through the mouth (oral incorporation). The later phase
is **oral sadism.** It begins as teeth emerge and represents the development
of the aggressive drive. The child is now capable of biting and chewing
as well as of behaving aggressively and destructively.

The Oral Character

Fixation at the oral stage results in an **oral character** (Abraham, 1927). It
is difficult, however, to say exactly what such people will be like—that
is, precisely what traits they will have. The specific group of traits depends
on two factors: whether the person is fixated at the oral erotic or oral
sadistic phase, and whether the fixation is due to frustration or overindulgence. It is possible, however, to list the general components of the oral
character.

1. Preoccupation with issues of giving/taking.
2. Concern about dependence/independence and passivity/activity.
3. Special attitudes about closeness and distance to others—being
   alone versus attachment to the group.
4. Extremes of optimism/pessimism.
5. Unusual ambivalence [especially true of the oral sadistic character].
6. An openness to novel experience and ideas, which involves enhancing curiosity and interest in investigating nature.
7. A hasty, restless, impatient orientation—wanting to be "fed" with
   events and things.

8. Continued unusual use of oral channels for gratification or . . . [coping with frustration] (for example, overeating, not eating enough, smoking, excessive talking). (Fisher & Greenberg, 1977, p. 88)

How might one of these elements be manifested differently according to the specific origins of the fixation? Let us consider optimism/pessimism. People who were frustrated would be expected to be pessimistic; those who were overindulged would be expected to be optimistic. The specific form of optimism or pessimism could be broadly passive or active. This would depend on whether the individual were fixated early (erotic phase) or late (sadistic phase) in the stage. The four possible outcomes are depicted in Table 4–1.

Research on the Oral Character

Research suggests that the concept of the oral character has some validity. Many studies indicate that the traits hypothesized as comprising the oral character—particularly dependency and pessimism—often are associated.

Joseph Masling and his associates (Masling, 1985) correlated a variety of behaviors with orality, measured by subjects' responses to Rorschach

TABLE 4–1
Development of optimism/pessimism as an oral character trait

Time of Fixation	Cause of Fixation	
	Overindulgence	**Frustration**
Oral Erotic (early)	*Passive Optimism:* Believing the world will always provide for one's needs, no matter what one does	*Passive Pessimism:* Behaving as if there were nothing one can do to improve one's lot in life
	Example: Student doesn't study because he/she expects tests will be easy, teacher will understand, etc.	*Example:* Student doesn't study because he/she feels it is no use; nothing can help; will inevitably do poorly
Oral Sadistic (late)	*Active Optimism:* Aggressively taking (in) from the world to provide for one's needs	*Active Pessimism:* Behaving cynically and hostilely toward perceived harsh world; striking out at others indiscriminantly
	Example: Student studies hard; seeks extra help; does additional reading, assignments	*Example:* Student devotes time to criticizing teachers, classes, exams; bad grades attributed to system

inkblots. **Rorschach inkblots** are a projective personality assessment technique. Subjects describe what they see in ambiguous, nearly symmetrical figures. These are described in Chapter 6. Examples of responses that are taken to indicate oral-dependent behavior appear in Table 4–2.

One direct prediction from the theory is that people fixated at the oral stage would tend to drink and eat excessively. A positive relationship has been found between subjects' reporting oral imagery in Rorschach inkblots and both alcoholism and obesity (Bertrand & Masling, 1969; Masling, Rabie, & Blondheim, 1967).

Dependency is a central trait of the oral character. College students who depend on others to make decisions in ambiguous situations rather than trusting their own judgments report more oral imagery on the Rorschach than do students who hold to their own perceptions of the situation (Masling, Weiss, & Rothschild, 1968). Complying with rules is another indication of dependency on others (authorities) for approval. This tendency was demonstrated in two studies. Both found a positive correlation between orality and compliance with the research participation requirement for a psychology course (Bornstein & Masling, 1985; Masling, O'Neill, & Katkin, 1981). Students who completed the research requirement in the first half of the semester reported significantly more oral Rorschach responses than students who participated during the second half. Participation in the first half was taken as readiness to comply. People who seem focused on the mouth and themes of incorporation on various projective measures also appear to show a special motivation for closeness and support from others (Fisher & Greenberg, 1977). These and other findings tend to support the concept of the oral character. To date, however, little

TABLE 4–2
Examples of oral dependent Rorschach responses

Category	Sample Responses
Food and drink*	Milk, whiskey, boiled lobster
Food providers	Waiter, cook, bartender
Food organs	Mouth, stomach, lips, teeth
Oral instruments	Lipstick, cigarette, tuba
Nurturers	Jesus, mother, father, doctor, God
Good luck objects	Wishbone, four-leaf clover
Oral activity	Eating, talking, singing, kissing
"Baby talk" responses	Patty-cake, bunny rabbit, pussy cat
Negations of oral percepts	No mouth, not pregnant, woman without breasts

* Note: Animals are scored as an oral dependent response only if they are definitely associated with being eaten (e.g., *roast duck* would count but *duck* would not).

Source: Based on "Orality and Latency of Volunteering to Serve as Experimental Subjects: A Replication" by R. F. Bornstein and J. Masling, 1985, *Journal of Personality Assessment, 49*, p. 307.

evidence shows that the character type originates from fixation in the oral stage.

Post-Freudian Extensions of the Oral Stage

Erich Fromm (1900–1980) believes character types develop from the social interactions of children and parents. Like Abraham, Fromm (1947) distinguishes two basic oral types. He theorizes that people raised in environments that fostered an attitude of expecting to receive become **receptive characters.** (These are Abraham's oral-erotic characters). This is because the demands of the home situation were best dealt with by being receptive, friendly, and pleasing. In contrast, when home circumstances are frustrating, children develop the attitude that they must take to receive; the best source of security comes from exploiting others (Thompson, 1957). Such persons become **exploitative characters.** (These are Abraham's oral-sadistic characters.) Here the same data—two somewhat distinct types of personality—are interpreted in different ways.

Another extension of the basic Freudian notion of the oral character was made by Harry Stack Sullivan (1892–1949), who also emphasized interpersonal aspects of development. For Sullivan, the critical aspect of the first year is the social interaction between the child and the mother. This involves the child learning to evaluate and discriminate the mother's emotions. This ability to "read" the mother's feelings is a prototype for accurately perceiving and predicting other people's behavior. Masling, Johnson, and Saturansky (1974) obtained partial support for this idea. High-oral male college students—those reporting many oral images on the Rorschach—were better than low-oral males at predicting the responses of other male students on a personality test. The same result was found with a second group of college students who knew each other well and were all enrolled in a pre–Peace Corps program. In the second study, investigators correlated the measures of oral dependence and interpersonal perception with a measure of success in the Peace Corps. Obviously,

Erich Fromm

René Burri/Magnum Photos, Inc.

Harry Stack Sullivan

Courtesy of William Alanson White. Psychiatric Foundation, Inc.

accurate perception of others would be essential to working well with people in foreign cultures. Both accurate interpersonal perception and oral dependence were found to be positively related to the Peace Corps rating.

Finally, Bettelheim (1976) advanced an interesting extension of the oral stage. He conceptualizes the story of Hansel and Gretel as a tale of oral sadism. Hansel and Gretel are sent into the woods because they have been careless with milk (an oral symbol). In the woods, they greedily devour part of the gingerbread house of the witch. Like their mother, the witch is gratifying at first. But she soon reveals her intention to eat the children. The children resolve their dilemma by abandoning their strictly oral impulses in favor of using reason. They outwit and kill the witch, returning home more mature children. Bettelheim believes the story is popular precisely because it helps people deal with their oral conflicts.

Anal Stage

When a child is weaned, libido shifts from the mouth to the anus. Pleasure is obtained at first from expelling feces—the **anal sadistic phase**. Later pleasure comes from retaining them—the **anal erotic phase.** This is not to say that the child did not derive similar pleasure during the oral stage. However, during the second and third years of life, anal pleasure predominates, just as oral pleasure did in the first year of life.

Until the anal stage, few demands are made on the child. During the second year of life, however, parents in most Western cultures begin to place restrictions on their offspring's behaviors. This particularly involves bowel and bladder control. The conflict in the anal stage pits the sexual drive for pleasure, from the tension reduced by defecation, against the constraints of society that the child develop self-control with respect to excretion.

If children easily accede to their parents' toilet-training demands, they will develop the basis for successful self-control. Muscle control becomes the prototype for self-control in general, just as weaning is a prototype for dependency. However, the child may have difficulty developing control and meeting parental demands. This may lead to the development of the **anal character,** a person who is *orderly, stingy,* and *stubborn* (Freud, 1959).

The Anal Character

One way to handle difficulty in toilet training is direct opposition. This involves a "you can't make me do that" attitude. Included are attempts to "counterattack" by defecating at especially "bad" moments, such as immediately after being taken off the toilet. The child may discover that this is a successful means of social control. He or she may adopt it as a strategy for handling frustration in general and become an **anal expulsive (sadistic) character.** It is interesting that our colloquial statements of extreme anger and hostility often refer to excretion—"Piss on it" and "Oh, shit." Anal expulsives would also be expected to be stingy, hoarding, and stubborn, and to rebel or express anger by becoming wasteful, disorderly, or messy.

The other strategy is to meet parental demands by retaining feces. Gentle pressure against the intestinal walls is pleasurable. What is more, the child can indirectly strike back at his or her parents if they are concerned about their child's failure to have a bowel movement. When this tactic is successful, it may set the stage for unusually compulsive behavior patterns in later life. The person is becoming an **anal compulsive (erotic) character**. Anal compulsives are neat, careful, systematic, and orderly. They may be upset or even revolted by a mess of any kind, including, for instance, a room in disarray or poorly organized plans that lead to confusion and uncertainty.

Anal expulsiveness and anal compulsiveness are the two sides of the same fixation; both are responses to being controlled and forced. The relation of the two anal character types and Freud's three basic anal traits are given in Table 4-3.

TABLE 4-3
The anal character

Phase	Basic Trait	Examples
Anal expulsive (sadistic)	Stingy	Cheap; hoarding; withholding (e.g., love)
	Obstinate	Stubborn; defiant (including rage and revenge)
Anal compulsive (erotic)	Orderly	Body cleanliness; conscientiousness; trustworthiness; attention to details; neat; careful; systematic

Research on the Anal Character

Many correlational studies have examined whether the three basic traits Freud hypothesized as the basis of the anal character are in fact associated in people. These involved correlating responses to questionnaires about interpersonal relations, preferred activities, and general style of behavior. The evidence largely supports Freud's "anal triad." The strongest direct association is between orderly and stingy. For example, people who are overly neat also tend to be extremely cheap.

There are also some interesting experimental demonstrations. Rosenwald (1972) asked male college students to identify various geometric forms while they were immersed in a smelly, fecal-like substance and while they were immersed in water. Comparison of performance in the two conditions was taken as a measure of anal anxiety; the greater the difference in performance, the greater the anal anxiety. Men who had the most difficulty in the fecal-like material tended to be the most stubborn and also were most careful in arranging a set of magazines that had been left in disarray.

Studies of the origins of the anal character have failed to support the idea that it is related to difficulty in toilet training. Thus, empirical evidence does not support Freud's hypotheses that either the anal or oral character originates in psychosexual conflicts. This does not mean that the concept of an anal or an oral character is not valid. Freud's observations of certain basic traits associated with various adult behaviors may be accurate. His theory (inference) that the character type is related to fixation at a psychosexual stage may be inaccurate.

Phallic Stage

During the fourth and fifth years of life, the libido is centered in the genital region. Children at this age are frequently observed examining their genitals, masturbating, and asking questions about birth and sex. The conflict in the phallic stage is the last and the most crucial one with which the young child must cope. It involves the child's unconscious wish to possess the opposite-sexed parent and at the same time to eliminate the same-sexed parent. Freud called this situation the **Oedipus complex** (pronounced ED'ipus). The name is derived from the Greek myth in which the hero Oedipus kills his father and marries his mother.

The Oedipus Complex

The Oedipus complex operates somewhat differently for males and females. The little boy's first object of love is his mother. As the libido centers in the genital zone, his love for his mother becomes erotically tinged and therefore incestuous. Naturally, the boy's father stands in the way of this sexual desire for the mother. Thus, the boy sees his father as his rival, someone he would like to eliminate from the scene. These desires result in the boy's fearing that his father will retaliate. The little boy's casual observations that women lack penises suggest to him that his father's revenge will take the form of castration. This threat of castration, **castration anxiety,** forces the boy to give up his wish to possess his mother. Resolution of the Oedipus complex entails two processes: repression of his incestuous desires and defensive identification with his father. **Repression** is totally putting a thought or feeling out of consciousness. **Defensive identification** involves becoming like a threatening person ("if you can't beat him, join him"). It follows from the boy's unconscious "reasoning": "I cannot directly possess my mother, for fear of being castrated by my father. I can, however, possess her vicariously. I can get some of the joy of possessing my mother *by becoming like my father.*" The boy resolves his conflict by identifying with his father's behavior, attitudes, and values. Defensive identification allows the boy to (1) possess his mother vicariously, (2) eliminate his castration anxiety, and (3) assimilate appropriate sex-role behavior.

The female version of the Oedipus complex is sometimes called the **Electra complex.** (In Greek mythology, Electra persuaded her brother to murder their mother and their mother's lover, who together had killed their father.) The Electra complex is considerably more complicated and less clear than its male counterpart. The little girl's first object of love is also her mother. However, during the phallic stage, the little girl is likely to discover that her father and other males (such as a brother) have penises. But she and her mother (and other women) do not. She reasons that she must have had a penis at one time; she also blames her mother for her apparent castration. This, along with other inevitable disappointments in her mother, leads to some loss of love for her mother and increased love for her father. Her love for her father is erotically tinged. It is also coupled with envy because he has a penis. Freud considers **penis envy** counterpart of castration anxiety. However, castration anxiety motivates the little boy to renounce his incestuous desires; penis envy carries no threat of retaliation. Instead, the girl fears *loss of her mother's love.* This is, in fact, parallel to castration anxiety for the male in that it motivates her resolution of the Electra complex.

Freud is vague about how the Electra complex is resolved. He does state that the resolution occurs later in life and is never complete. (This implies that women always remain somewhat fixated at the phallic stage.) The mother does not hold the threat of castration over her daughter. However, she would express extreme displeasure over incestuous relations between her husband and daughter. Presumably, the impracticality of fulfillng her Oedipal wish causes the girl to repress her desires for her father and defensively identify with her mother. This protects the girl from loss of her mother's love. It also, as in the case of the boy, allows her to possess her father vicariously and develop appropriate sex-role behavior.

We have presented the general "formula" for the Oedipus complex. The exact pattern for each individual depends on the child's development in the prephallic stages. It also depends on specific family circumstances during the phallic stage. For example, if one parent is absent, the child will substitute a surrogate, such as an aunt or uncle. Freud considers resolution of the Oedipus complex the single most critical aspect of personality development. Successful resolution is necessary for a normal adult life. Unsuccessful resolution inevitably leads, Freud believes, to psychopathology.

The phallic stage is also important because during that time the child's moral principles (conscience) develop through identification with parents. (We will discuss this important aspect of personality development in Chapter 5, when we describe the formation of the superego.)

Fixation at the phallic stage results in a **phallic character type.** The **phallic character** is *reckless, resolute,* and *self-assured* (Fenichel, 1945). There is also a narcissistic element to the phallic character type. This involves excessive vanity and pride. Phallic characters have not successfully resolved their Oedipus complex. Thus, they tend to be afraid of closeness and love because they still suffer from castration anxiety. They seem courageous and show off; this behavior is overcompensation for castration anxiety.

Freud's concepts of infantile sexuality and the Oedipus complex are difficult for people to accept. This was true at the beginning of the century, when Freud introduced his revolutionary theory; it is equally true today for students being introduced to these notions. We can accept the conflicts of the oral and anal stages. We may not recall being weaned and toilet trained. But there is strong evidence in our present behavior that we were! In contrast, it is unclear that we once had incestuous desires toward our opposite-sexed parent; and the very idea is completely contrary to our morality. How would Freud answer an allegation such as "*I* never went through an Oedipus complex"? He would point out that the taboo against incest is very strong; because of the anxiety created by your incestuous desires, you have long since repressed memories of your Oedipus complex.

Evidence for the Oedipus Complex

Freud's theory of the Oedipus complex is really a collection of mini-theories. These encompass a variety of aspects of socialization (e.g., directing erotic drives, adopting sex roles). The empirical research findings concerning Oedipal identification support the following generalizations:

1. Both males and females are probably closer to mother than father in the pre-Oedipal period.

2. At some later point [beyond age nine or ten] each sex identifies more with the same-sex than with the opposite-sex parent. [Note that this is later than Freud postulates.]
3. There are defensive attitudes detectable in persons beyond the Oedipal phase, which suggest they have had to cope with erotic feelings toward the opposite-sex parent and hostility toward the same-sex parent (Fisher & Greenberg, 1977, pp. 219–20).

Empirical investigations have provided support for Oedipal phenomena. We will describe two studies of castration anxiety and penis envy, a correlational and an experimental study.

Hall and Van de Castle (1963) analyzed the dreams of 120 college students for indications of castration anxiety and penis envy. Examples taken to indicate castration anxiety included the dreamer's inability to use either his penis or a symbol of his penis (such as a pen or a gun). Acquiring a penis or a phallic symbol or changing into a man in the dream was regarded as evidence for penis envy. The results were consistent with the theoretical differences between the Oedipal situation for males and females. Men had more dreams of castration anxiety than women; women had more dreams of penis envy and the wish to be castrated. (The wish to be castrated is related to penis envy because the wish assumes one has a penis.)

In a very different type of investigation, Sarnoff and Corwin (1959) studied the relationship between castration anxiety and fear of death. Psychoanalysts consider death (as well as other less severe forms of bodily harm) a symbol of castration. Sarnoff and Corwin hypothesized that the greater the castration anxiety, the greater should be the fear of death when castration anxiety is aroused. They measured male undergraduates' fear of death before and after castration anxiety was aroused. In the first part of the experiment, subjects indicated their agreement with statements about death (e.g., "I am disturbed when I think of the shortness of life") on a brief Fear of Death scale. Castration anxiety was assessed with a projective technique. Subjects were asked to choose one of three descriptions of a cartoon presumed to depict castration. On the basis of this test, subjects were divided into high- and low-castration-anxiety groups.

In the second part of the experiment, subjects returned four weeks later. Ostensibly they were to rate the esthetic value of some pictures. Half the subjects in each of the castration anxiety groups rated pictures of nude women (high-sexual-arousal condition); half rated pictures of fully clothed fashion models (low-sexual-arousal condition). Then the subjects again completed the Fear of Death scale. As predicted, under conditions of high sexual arousal, which were presumed to arouse castration anxiety, subjects with high castration anxiety showed significantly greater increases in fear of death than did subjects with low castration anxiety. No differences were found when sexual arousal was low. Assuming that fear of death is an indication of castration anxiety, this study lends support to an important psychoanalytic concept.

Horney's Reinterpretation of the Oedipus Complex

Few psychoanalysts, or other psychologists who study child development, question Freud's *observations* that children around the age of four or five experience jealousy, rivalry, and ambivalent feelings of love and hate for their parents. Many, however, have been skeptical about the origin and content of these feelings. Specifically, they have disagreed with Freud's sexual interpretation. Analyst Karen Horney (pronounced HORN-eye) (1885–1952), for example, reinterpreted the Oedipus complex in terms of interpersonal dynamics.

> The typical conflict leading to anxiety in a child is that between dependency on the parents . . . and hostile impulses against the parents. Hostility may be aroused in a child in many ways: by the parents' lack of respect for him; by unreasonable demands and prohibitions; by injustice; by unreliability; by suppression of criticism; by the parents dominating him and ascribing these tendencies to love. . . . If a child, in addition to being dependent on his parents, is grossly or subtly intimidated by them and hence feels that any expression of hostile impulses against them endangers his security, then the existence of such hostile impulses is bound to create anxiety. . . . The resulting picture may look exactly like what Freud describes as the Oedipus complex: passionate clinging to one parent and jealousy toward the other or toward anyone interfering with the claim of exclusive possession. . . . *But the dynamic structure of these attachments is entirely different from what Freud conceives as the Oedipus complex.*

Karen Horney

National Library of Medicine

They are an early manifestation of neurotic conflicts rather than a primarily sexual phenomenon. (Horney, 1939, pp. 83–81; italics added)

Horney, unlike Freud, theorizes considerably about women. She challenges Freud's use of penis envy to explain feminine inferiority and Freud's view of motherhood as a means of compensating for that inferiority. Horney believes Freud's image of women is distorted and biased because he based it exclusively on observations of neurotic women.

Latency Period

When the Oedipus complex is resolved, at about age five, children of both sexes pass into a period known as **latency.** Latency is *not* a stage of psychosexual development; there is no further sexual development during this period. Latency lasts from the end of the phallic stage to the onset of puberty. According to Freud, latency involves massive repression of sexual as well as oral and anal impluses. During latency, the libido is rechanneled from sexual pursuits to such activities as school, friendships with children of the same age and gender, sports, and hobbies. Freud says little about this period of life; other psychoanalytic theorists place considerable emphasis on it (e.g., Erikson, 1963, 1968; Sullivan, 1953).

Genital Stage

Freud's final stage of psychosexual development begins at puberty; at this point, the young adolescent starts to mature sexually. This stage lasts through adulthood until the onset of senility, at which time the individual regresses to pregenital behavior (i.e., behavior of the oral, anal, or phallic stage). In the genital stage, libido is again focused in the genital area. But now it is directed toward heterosexual, rather than autoerotic, pleasure. The greater an individual's success in reaching the genital stage without large amounts of libido fixated in pregenital stages, the greater the person's capacity to lead a "normal" life, free of neurosis, and to enjoy genuine heterosexual relationships.

We spend the vast majority of our lives in the genital stage. Yet Freud had little to say about adulthood. This is consistent with his considering the first five years of life paramount in determining personality. Other psychoanalysts have made up for this deficit, however. For example, Freud's daughter, Anna (1895–1982), theorized about adolescence. Anna Freud was among Sigmund's most devoted colleagues. She was his constant companion in his later years. She also continued to work within her father's classic psychoanalytic framework until her death.

Anna Freud (1958) observed that adolescents are suddenly faced with

Anna Freud

National Library of Medicine

an onslaught of sexual and aggressive impulses that sharply contrast to their experiences during latency. Indeed, she wrote that "there are few situations in life which are more difficult to cope with than an adolescent son or daughter during the attempt to liberate themselves" (1958, p. 323). Anna Freud identifies strategies that adolescents use to regain some sense of control. One is *asceticism;* the adolescent tries to abandon physical pleasure, such as by strict diets or vigorous exercise. From the psychoanalytic viewpoint, this strategy is adopted by teenagers suffering from *anorexia nervosa.* This eating disorder is widespread among teenage girls who lose extreme amounts of weight because they stop eating (e.g., Bruch, 1973, 1978). Another strategy adolescents use to cope is *intellectualization;* this involves developing personal theories about the nature of love or of life.

Jung's Concept of the Midlife Crisis

Jung (1933) was well ahead of his time in targeting middle age (late 30s, early 40s) as a critical period in a person's life (cf. Levinson, Darrow, Klein, Levinson, & McKee, 1978; Sheehy, 1976, 1981; Vaillant, 1977). Jung describes this as a time when people undergo a major transition from youthful impulsiveness and extroversion to thoughtfulness and introversion, from interests and goals that have their roots in biological urges to interests and goals that are based on cultural norms. The person's values become more social, civic minded, and philosophical or religious. In short, the middle-aged individual develops into a spiritual being. These changes precipitate what Jung refers to as a **midlife crisis.** The crisis occurs even among quite successful people as they realize many of their goals have been set for them by others. "The achievements which society rewards are won at the cost of diminution of personality. Many—far too many—aspects of life which should have been experienced lie in the lumber room among dusty memories" (Jung, 1933, p. 104).

The transformation of energy during midlife should occur smoothly. If it doesn't, Jung believes, the personality might be seriously and permanently crippled. Jung was very successful in treating individuals who were having difficulties with this transition. He believes that the midlife crisis could only be resolved through *individuation*. This means finding one's own way. The process begins by "turning our energy away from the mastery of the external world, . . . and focusing on our inner selves. We feel inner urgings to listen to the unconscious, to learn about the potentials we have so far left unrealized. We begin to raise questions about the meaning of our lives" (Crain, 1980, p. 194).

ERIKSON'S EIGHT STAGES OF PSYCHOSOCIAL DEVELOPMENT

The best known alternative to Freud's psychosexual stages was advanced by Erik Erikson (1902–   ). This prominent ego analyst was a student of Anna Freud. Erikson does not discount biological and psychosexual influences on the developing individual. But he emphasizes the influence of society and culture. Thus, Erikson considers Freud's latency period to be a time of growth rather than stagnation. Erikson, like Jung, views adult development as important. He divides this development into three stages: *young adulthood, adulthood,* and *maturity.*

Erikson (1963, 1968) believes that we all deal with eight critical developmental issues in our lives. Each issue becomes the central focus of attention at a specific time of life. He outlines eight stages of psycho*social* development. Each is named for the issue that predominates and is the central conflict at that time. Every issue involves an encounter with the environment. In each, there is a conflict between an adaptive and a maladaptive way of handling the encounter (e.g., between basic trust and mistrust). Each conflict must be successfully resolved in the period in which it predominates, before a person is fully prepared to deal with the conflict that predominates next. Successful resolution is relative and involves develop-

Erik Erikson

Harvard University News Office

ing a "favorable ratio" between the adaptive and maladaptive alternative (e.g., more trust than mistrust).

In contrast to Freud's stages, Erikson's eight issues are present at birth and remain throughout the life span. For example, during the first year of life (Erikson's first stage), the child's major problems center on developing basic trust. However, the child is also struggling to develop autonomy—the central issue in Erikson's second stage—as when it wriggles to be set free if held too tightly. Similarly, adolescents are primarily concerned with identity, but they also encounter conflicts with autonomy when they struggle to be confident rather than self-conscious.

This concept of development is illustrated in Figure 4–1. The figure is a diagram of Erikson's psychosocial stages, plotted against periods of physical and/or psychosexual development. Each vertical column represents one of the eight developmental issues. The period in life when that issue becomes the central conflict is highlighted in a colored box. The

FIGURE 4–1
Erikson's diagram of the eight stages of psychosocial development

Developmental period		1	2	3	4	5	6	7	8
	VIII Maturity					Objective view of accomplishments vs. distorted view of accomplishments*			Ego integrity vs. despair
	VII Adulthood					Role diversity vs. burnout*		Generativity vs. stagnation	
	VI Young adulthood					Role acceptance vs. role rejection*	Intimacy vs. isolation		
	V Puberty and adolescence	Temporal perspective vs. time confusion	Self-certainty vs. self-consciousness	Role experimentation vs. role fixation	Apprenticeship vs. work paralysis	Identity vs. role confusion	Sexual polarization vs. bisexual confusion	Leader- and followership vs. authority confusion	Ideological commitment vs. confusion of values
	IV Latency				Industry vs. inferiority	Task identification vs. sense of futility			
	III Locomotor-genital			Initiative vs. guilt		Anticipation of roles vs. role inhibition			
	II Muscular-anal		Autonomy vs. shame, doubt			Will to be oneself vs. self-doubt			
	I Oral-sensory	Basic trust vs. mistrust				Mutual recognition vs. autistic isolation			

Psychosocial stages

* Conflict conceptualized by authors, extrapolating from Erikson's theory.

Source: Adapted from *Childhood and Society* by E. H. Erikson, 1963, New York: W. W. Norton; and *Identity, Youth, and Crisis* by E. H. Erikson, 1968, New York: W. W. Norton.

colored boxes form the diagonal of the diagram. To understand the form of one developmental issue—*identity versus role confusion*—in other periods of development, follow the fifth vertical column up from the oral-sensory period to maturity. The nature of the other seven developmental issues (that are not the central conflict during puberty and adolescence) is shown in the fifth horizontal row in the uncolored boxes.

Erikson's description of his eight stages of psychosocial development focuses on the way the person deals with the issue that is the central conflict of the stage.

Basic Trust versus Mistrust

Initially an infant must develop sufficient trust to let its mother, the provider of food and comfort, out of sight without the child experiencing anxiety or rage. Such trust involves not only confidence in the predictability of the mother's behavior but also trust in oneself. This conflict occurs during Freud's oral stage.

Autonomy versus Shame and Doubt

Next, the child must develop a sense of autonomy. This sense is originally developed through bladder and bowel control. The stage parallels Freud's anal stage. If the child fails to meet parental expectations in this regard, shame and doubt may result. The shame of being unable to demonstrate the self-control demanded by parents may become the basis for later difficulties; the experience of attaining adequate self-control in childhood may lead to feelings of autonomy in later life. Erikson (1963) says:

> This stage, therefore, becomes decisive for the ratio of love and hate, cooperation and willfulness, freedom from self-expression and its suppression. From a sense of self-control without loss of self-esteem comes a lasting sense of goodwill and pride; from a sense of loss of self-control and of foreign overcontrol comes a lasting propensity for doubt and shame. (p. 254)

Initiative versus Guilt

Initiative versus guilt is the last conflict experienced by the preschool child. It occurs during Freud's phallic stage. The child must learn to appropriately control feelings of rivalry for the mother's attention and develop a sense of moral responsibility. At this stage, children initially indulge in fantasies of grandeur, but they may actually feel meek and dominated. To overcome the latter feelings, the child must learn to take role-appropriate initiative by finding pleasure in socially and culturally approved activities. These include creative play and caring for younger siblings.

Industry versus Inferiority

The conflict between industry and inferiority begins with school life. If they are to emerge as healthy individuals, children at this stage must apply themselves to their learning, begin to feel some sense of competence relative to peers, and face their own limitations. Note that these important developments occur during the time when, from Freud's point of view, the child is in a period of latency.

Identity versus Role Confusion

With the advent of puberty, the adolescent must begin to develop a sense of identity. **Identity,** as used by Erikson, refers to confidence that others see us as we see ourselves. The selection of an occupation or career is particularly important for identity. If an identity is not formed, *role confusion* may occur. It is characterized by an inability to select a career or to further educational goals, and by overidentification with popular heroes or cliques. Role confusion can be overcome through interaction with peers or elders who, for example, know about various occupational opportunities or accept the adolescent's self-perception.

Intimacy versus Isolation

By young adulthood, people are expected to be ready for true intimacy. They must develop cooperative social and occupational relationships with others and select a mate. If they cannot develop such relationships, they will remain isolated. Erikson (1963, p. 265) notes that when Freud was asked what a healthy person should be able to do well, he curtly answered: *"Lieben und Arbeiten"* (love and work). Erikson says "we cannot improve on 'the professor's' formula."

Generativity versus Stagnation

A mature person must do more than establish intimacy with others, according to Erikson. The individual "needs to be needed" and to assist the younger members of society. *Generativity* is concerned with guiding the next generation; if it is not done, the individual may feel stagnant and personally impoverished.

Ego Integrity versus Despair

Unless the preceding conflicts are suitably handled, despair may result in later life. Disgusted with themselves and correctly realizing that it is too late to start another life, such individuals live their last years in a state of incurable remorse. To become psychosocially adjusted and have a lasting sense of integrity, the person must develop each of the adaptive qualities of the other seven stages. Erikson believes that everyone, regardless of capabilities, can achieve such adjustment.

OBJECT RELATIONS

Object relations is an important idea within psychoanalysis which addresses the essence of social relations. **Object**, in this context, refers to other people. **Object relations** concern how we relate to others. A number of psychoanalysts have proposed object relations theories that differ in the degree to which they adopt Freud's theory as the basis of object relations. The theories range from those that build on traditional Freudian theory (e.g., Kernberg, 1975, 1976; Mahler, 1968) to those that replace it with a whole new view of development (e.g., Fairbairn, 1952; Guntrip, 1969; G.S. Klein, 1976; Kohut, 1977). There are also theories that accept Freudian theory with modifications (e.g., Kohut, 1971; Modell, 1975). We will examine two object relations theories. The first is consistent with Freud's theory; the second totally rejects it.

Mahler's Object Relations Theory

At birth, infants do not differentiate between what is "I" and what is "not I," between themselves and other people. Newborns appear, from their behavior, to view their mothers as part of themselves. The newborn is at the height of egocentricity. Margaret Mahler's (1897–1985) theory of development focuses on the process by which the infant assumes its own physical and psychological identity (Mahler, 1968; Mahler, Bergman, & Pine, 1975). A pediatrician, Mahler became interested in the very close relationship between mother and child. Her theory is based on both clinical

Margaret Mahler

Courtesy of the Margaret Mahler Foundation

and naturalistic observations. The latter were gathered in a large indoor playroom where children were free to use various toys. The room was divided by a low, fencelike barrier. Mothers sat and watched their children from the other side of the barrier. Participant-observers interacted with both children and mothers and later made detailed records of their observations (Bergman & Ellman, 1985).

Mahler divides the child's development into phases (stages) summarized in Table 4–4. In the first phase, the first few weeks of life, the infant is in a state of **normal autism**—completely within itself, oblivious to an external world. Any stimulation the infant receives is evaluated in terms of an instinctual concept: pleasurable/good versus painful/bad. Infants consider having their needs met by their mothers as part of their own " 'unconditional,' omnipotent, *autistic* orbit" (Mahler, 1968, p. 42).

TABLE 4–4
Mahler's stages of object relations development

Phase	Approximate Time Frame	Developmental Processes
Normal autism	Birth–1 month	Completely within self; unresponsive to external stimuli
Symbiotic phase	2nd–3rd month	Undifferentiated "I" and "not-I"; fusion with mother; vague awareness of need-satisfying objects
Separation-individuation phase		
Differentiation subphase	4th–8th month	Initial attempts at separation; sensory exploration of external environment; frequent checking back to mother
Practicing subphase	9th to 15th–18th month	Locomotion allows further exploration of world; increased temporary separation from mother
Rapprochement subphase	15th–18th to 24th month	Conflict between independence and dependence; child wants to be with mother yet fears being engulfed by her; critical period for future development
"On the way to object constancy" subphase	24 months on	Development of permanent sense of self and permanent emotional mental representations of others

During the second and third months, the infant enters the **symbiotic phase.** The child is vaguely aware of the need-satisfying object, its mother. Still, the infant is in an undifferentiated state, fused with its mother, and does not distinguish between "I" and "not-I."

The development of object relations takes place during the third and final phase of the developmental sequence—**separation-individuation.** This is divided into four subphases. The previous two phases are necessary precursors for the development of object relations; how the infant has fared in them affects the critical separation-individuation process. The infant must first pass from normal autism to the symbiotic phase. It is important that the infant derive satisfaction from its symbiotic relation with its mother; this serves as the basis for the differentiation to follow.

Beginning in the fourth or fifth month and lasting through about the eighth month, the infant begins the separation-individuation process in the first subphase, **differentiation.** Here "infants take their first tentative steps toward breaking away, in a bodily sense, from their hitherto completely passive. . . . stage of dual unity with the mother" (Mahler et al., 1975, p. 55). Infants who experienced optimal satisfaction in the symbiotic phase will freely explore their environment. This includes being curious and fascinated with other people, rather than experiencing anxiety around strangers. Children are not completely independent of their mother, however. They can be observed periodically checking to see whether mother is nearby as they tentatively venture into the external world.

The next subphase—**practicing**—encompasses from about the ninth month to about 15 to 18 months. Here, children expand their horizons even more. They become physically able to explore the external environment as they begin to locomote, first by crawling and climbing, and finally by walking upright. During this period, the child "appears to be at the peak point of his belief in his own magic omnipotence, which is still to a considerable extent derived from his sense of sharing his mother's magic powers" (Mahler, 1968, p. 20). The child still does not venture too far from its mother and occasionally returns to her for a boost of emotional support.

Rapprochement, the third subphase, begins at about 15 to 18 months and ends about 24 months. It is characterized by ambivalence about separating from the mother—a struggle between still wanting to be close to the mother but also being afraid of being engulfed by her. As the child becomes more aware of separation and experiences greater separation anxiety, he or she has an increased desire to be with the mother, share with her, and experience her love. The child alternately "shadows" the mother and flees from her. Mahler considers this subphase to be critical for future personality development. The child must develop a *rapprochement* between the need for independence and dependence. This requires that the mother continue to provide the child with needed emotional support while at the same time allowing the child to be independent. Failure to permit independence often results in the child remaining attached to the mother, unable to become interested in activities or other people (Eagle, 1984).

The fourth and final subphase of separation-individuation begins around the third year of life. To some degree, it continues during later development. It is referred to as *"consolidation of individuality and the beginnings of emotional object constancy"* (Mahler et al., 1975, p. 109). Here, the child develops a defined lifelong individuality and sense of object permanency that involve having mental representations of people (especially the mother) so that they are constantly with the child symbolically. This lets the child be away from the mother without giving up a healthy degree of emotional dependence on her love and approval; her love and approval have been internalized. For example, while at nursery school, a child may help another child and feel good about doing so. This good feeling comes from the mental image of the mother approving of such behavior.

Critics have argued that the infant is not totally undifferentiated and fused with the mother (Klein, 1981; Stern, 1983). Still, Mahler's ideas are important because they point out separation-individuation as a dimension of personality development. Indeed, the dimension appears to be important for all species (Eagle, 1984). A number of Mahler's concepts have been supported by nonpsychoanalytic empirical research. This adds to the breadth of empirical support. For example, studies have shown that children whose mothers provide a "safe base" to which the children can return will explore their surroundings more (Ainsworth, 1974; Ainsworth, Bell, & Stayton, 1971). Interestingly, this relationship also exists in birds (e.g., Wilson & Rajecki, 1974) and monkeys (e.g., Harlow & Harlow, 1972; Kaufman, 1974). Further, Mahler's position as well as that of other object-relations theorists (e.g., Winnicott, 1958, 1965) predicts that the closer the infant-mother attachment, the more independence and exploration the child will display (Eagle, 1984). Again, nonpsychoanalytic studies support Mahler's idea (Ainsworth, 1984; Ainsworth et al., 1971).

Fairbairn's Object Relations Theory

Mahler's object relations theory makes a basic assumption consistent with Freud's theory—namely, the infant is primarily motivated by pleasure seeking. Thus, the aim of object relations is to maximize pleasure. In contrast, Scottish psychoanalyst W. R. D. Fairbairn (1889–1964) developed a "pure" object relations theory. It assumes that people are motivated by object seeking, not pleasure seeking.

According to Fairbairn (1952), personality develops from a state of infantile dependence to a state of mature dependence. In the latter, the self is differentiated from the object. This is accomplished in three stages: (1) *infantile dependence,* (2) *transitional stage,* and (3) *mature or adult dependence.* Fairbairn's basic position is similar to Mahler's movement from symbiosis to separation-individuation. However, the end state is achieved by a different process.

In Fairbairn's system, there is a single personality structure. This is called the **central ego**. The central ego has its own libidinal energy which is directed toward establishing object relations (rather than reducing tension). If the relationships with real, external objects are satisfactory, the central ego stays whole and integrated. When relationships become unsatisfactory, the central ego compensates for this deprivation by internalizing objects. The process involves cathecting part of the central ego to the internalized objects. This results in *splitting the central ego*. Ego splitting is the central concept in Fairbairn's theory. It is shown schematically in Figure 4–2 (page 88), and you may want to refer to the figure as you read the description of ego splitting.

An infant's relationship to its mother is both good and bad, gratifying and ungratifying. Further, the ungratifying aspects involve two different kinds of experience. One involves rejection and deprivation. The other involves rejection with some hope or promise. Thus, infants view their mothers in three ways or parts: (1) *gratifying mother*, (2) *rejecting mother*, and (3) *enticing* (or promising) *mother*.

All infants feel deprivation and frustration with respect to their mothers. To cope, the real, external mother is *internalized* as a mental image. (Objects are easier to control in the infant's mental sphere than in the external world over which the infant has little control.) Corresponding to the three ways the infant views its mother, three objects are internalized: (1) **ideal object** (gratifying mother); (2) **rejecting object** (depriving mother); and (3) **exciting object** (enticing mother).

While internalizing the rejecting and exciting objects, part of the central ego splits off and is cathected to them. The ego bound to the exciting object is called **libidinal ego**. The part cathected to the rejecting object is called **antilibidinal ego**. The result is that the central ego is no longer an integrated whole. Some of the ego is now unavailable for healthy relations with real, external objects. (Here there is a definite parallel with Freud's concepts of a closed energy system, cathexis, and fixation.)

W. R. D. Fairbairn

Courtesy of Mrs. Marian Fairbairn

FIGURE 4–2
Schematic representation of Fairbairn's concept of ego splitting

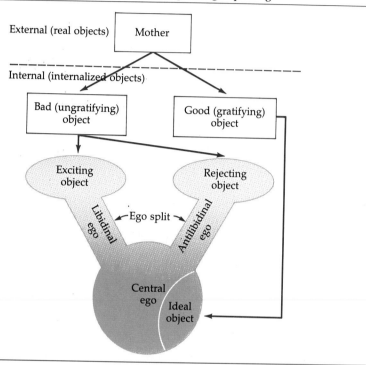

A somewhat different process occurs with the ideal object. It, too, becomes connected to the central ego, but as *part* of it. The ideal object does not split the central ego because it is consistent with it. As was true of the internal representation of the gratifying, comforting aspects of the mother, the ideal object serves as a goal toward which the central ego strives.

The state in which the central ego is split represents the height of infantile dependence on objects; the objects have become part of the person. There is no differentiation between "I" and "not I." Over the course of development, during the transitional stage, the internalized objects must be expelled for mature dependence on objects to emerge. The process may be likened to expelling foreign bodies that have been ingested and are not part of the person (Eagle, 1984). When the internalized objects are expelled, the cathected libido is free to be invested in the external world—that is, with actual people rather than internalized objects. This is characteristic of *mature dependence*. Mature dependence also involves a capacity to be a differentiated person and to maintain cooperative relationships with other differentiated people.

Fairbairn's theory primarily concerns defensive processes and the development of psychopathology. Ego splitting is a defensive process. To cope with the ungratifying aspects of its parents, the infant internalizes these aspects of the parents so that they are easier to deal with. When the child experiences "badness" in the external world, in the real parents, he or she is painfully aware of being unable to do anything about it. If the "badness" is internalized, however, the child has a chance of influencing it.

If a person does not grow out of infantile dependence, psychopathology develops. Psychopathology involves retaining old ties and hopes represented in internalized objects. This indicates disturbances and interferences in real relations with others. Normal behavior requires mature dependence, the state achieved as the individual relinquishes internal objects and exchanges them for real objects. Fairbairn's approach to psychoanalytic psychotherapy is aimed at restoring the patient's capacity to meaningfully relate to real human beings. As we shall see in Chapter 6, this sharply contrasts with Freud's classical psychoanalytic approach to therapy in which the goal is resolving intrapsychic conflicts concerned with pleasure seeking.

SUMMARY

1. Freudian theory holds that we are primarily motivated by the sexual drive and secondarily by the aggressive drive. For Freud, "sexual" is synonymous with pleasure.

2. People have a fixed amount of psychic energy that they cathect (invest) in the mental images of people, things, or activities. Psychic energy builds up within the personality and is experienced as tension that periodically must be released. Tension release is pleasurable, so that people engage in behaviors that release tension.

3. Many psychoanalysts disagree with Freud's emphasis on the sexual drive. Adler considers strivings for superiority to be the dominant human motive.

4. Personality development is a central issue in psychoanalysis, although psychoanalysts differ in the importance they place on biological versus social factors and early versus later experiences.

5. Freud describes four basic stages of psychosexual development. The stages are delineated by the erogenous zone that predominates at various ages and is the focus of the libido (sexual energy). Each stage has a conflict that must be successfully resolved in order to proceed to the next stage. When people have difficulty moving to the next stage (because of frustration or overindulgence in the present stage), they leave some libido fixated at that stage. Fixation results in adult character types.

6. In the oral stage (the first year of life), pleasure is derived from

sucking, eating, and biting. The conflict is weaning. The oral character centers around dependency and pessimism. Post-Freudians have broadened Freud's theoretical ideas about the oral stage to include more social aspects.

7. In the anal stage (second and third years), pleasure focuses on the retention and expulsion of feces. Toilet training is the conflict. The anal character involves three basic traits: orderliness, stinginess, and obstinacy.

8. In the phallic stage (ages four and five), pleasure focuses in the genital region. The Oedipus complex, the conflict in the phallic stage, involves the child's sexual attraction to the opposite-sexed parent. Freud considers resolution of this conflict to be critical for normal personality development. Horney, among other psychoanalysts, provides alternative (less sexual) explanations for the child-parental rivalries observed during the phallic stage.

9. Between the phallic stage and puberty, the child enters a period of latency that involves no psychosexual development. Post-Freudians have stressed important social developments that occur at this time.

10. The genital stage begins at puberty and lasts through adulthood. Again the libido is focused in the genital area, but now it is directed toward heterosexual rather than autoerotic pleasure.

11. Erikson's eight psychosocial stages provided an alternative to Freud's developmental scheme.

12. Object relations refer to interpersonal relationships. Post-Freudians have developed elaborate theories of object relations. Mahler assumes that pleasure-seeking is a primary motive, and her theory focuses on the process of the child's separation from its mother and subsequent development of a separate identity. In contrast, Fairbairn assumes that people are motivated by object-seeking, and his theory explains the separation-individuation process in terms of ego splitting and internalized objects.

THE ORGANIZATION OF PERSONALITY

OVERVIEW

It is a shattering experience for anyone seriously committed to the Western tradition of morality and rationality to take a steadfast, unflinching look at what Freud has to say. It is humiliating to be compelled to admit the grossly seamy side of so many grand ideals. . . . To experience Freud is to partake a second time of the forbidden fruit. (Brown, 1959, p. xi)

In the last chapter, we had a taste of "forbidden fruit": Freud's ideas about basic pleasure-seeking motives, in general, and infantile sexuality in particular. In this chapter we will continue our exploration of the irrational and even immoral aspect of human personality. We begin by discussing the central concept of unconscious motivation. Freud was not the first to suggest the unconscious (Whyte, 1960). But his emphasis on aspects of personality of which we are unaware has had a great influence on the scientific study of personality. It has also affected everyday conceptions about personality. Freud himself noted that humans suffered three blows to egocentrism. The first blow was dealt by Copernicus; this was the discovery that the Earth was not the center of the universe. Next, Darwin made the human being an animal among animals. Finally, Freud made us conscious of our unconscious; he made us aware of how much we are influenced by unknown internal forces that are frequently beyond our control.

THREE LEVELS OF CONSCIOUSNESS

Freud divides the mind into three levels of awareness: conscious, preconscious, unconscious. The **conscious** includes what we are aware of at a given point in time. This definition is close to our everyday use of the term. However, Freud contends that only a very small portion of our thoughts, images, and memories are conscious. The Freudian mind, like an iceberg, is nine tenths below the surface.

The **preconscious** includes thoughts we are not immediately aware (conscious) of; however, they can be easily brought to awareness. For example, as you read these words you are thinking about the material presented. However, unless a test on this information is imminent (and perhaps even then), you could begin to think about your plans for the weekend or the good time you had on your last vacation. These thoughts were in your preconscious.

Finally, Freud believes one part of the mind plays the dominant role in personality. This is the **unconscious.** According to Freud, most of our behavior is directed by forces we are totally unaware of. They are out of consciousness. Unlike preconscious thoughts, unconscious thoughts enter consciousness only in disguised or symbolic form.

JUNG'S DIVISION OF THE PERSONALITY

Jung divides the personality into three levels of consciousness. These are the conscious ego, personal unconscious, and collective unconscious. The **conscious ego** includes perceptions, thoughts, feelings, and memories we are aware of.

The **personal unconscious** contains mental images we are not immediately aware of; but these can readily become part of the conscious ego. We are not aware of some content of the personal unconscious because we are attending to other matters or because of disuse. Other images in the personal unconscious are actively repressed because they were threatening or unacceptable to the conscious ego.

In other aspects, Jung's views about the personal unconscious diverge from Freud's. Jung rejects the idea that the unconscious is "monsterous" (Roazen, 1975). In contrast to Freud, Jung believes that the personal unconscious not only stores past experiences, but also anticipates the future. In addition, the personal unconscious helps us compensate. It adjusts personality if a person's conscious attitudes lean too heavily in one direction. This is done by allowing the appropriate opposite tendency to occur in dreams or fantasy (Jung, 1969).

Archetypes and the Collective Unconscious

The **collective unconscious** is the dominant aspect of personality for Jung. It has no direct parallel in Freud's theory. In fact, it is Jung's most original and controversial idea.

Jung believes that we are not just a product of our own histories. We also think and act in ways shaped by experiences common to all humans throughout the evolution of the species. Such predispositions to form a common idea are called **archetypes.** "The archetype is a structure inferred from the fact that across individuals, throughout history, and in diverse cultures remarkable similarities in fantasy . . . are evident" (Steele, 1982, p. 300). Archetypes are primarily in the collective unconscious.

Four archetypes play a prominent role in personality. The **persona** is a person's public "mask"; this is the personality we show to others.

The **shadow** is the model for our animal instincts and for evil and unacceptable ideas. It functions like Freud's id. Jung, like Freud, believes we all have masculine and feminine qualities. In other words, humans are *bisexual*. Bisexuality involves two complementary archetypes. The **anima** is the feminine aspects of men. The **animus** is the masculine aspects of women. These and other archetypes are listed in Table 5–1.

The collective unconscious is the same in all people. But people do not all behave in the same way. Reactions to a situation are determined both by the relevant archetype and by individual experiences. The mother archetype, for instance, leads all children to react toward their mothers (and other mother figures, such as a grandmother or an older sister) in a characteristic way; this involves seeing her as nurturant and responding to her by being dependent. Children's perceptions of and reactions to their mothers usually follow the mother archetype. A mother could deviate from the universal image by neglecting her child. In this case, the child's reaction would also differ from the usual pattern of child-mother interaction.

Evidence for the collective unconscious and archetypes comes from Jung's extensive study of universal myths and symbols. Indirect support for the idea concerns the development of phobias (irrational fears). Seligman (1971) argues that certain phobias seem to be learned quickly and are very difficult to eliminate. Further, people are phobic about a limited number of things. They include fear of the dark, snakes, insects, high places, and open spaces (cf. Spiegler & Liebert, 1970). Each of these is not, under normal circumstances, objectively threatening. But people often report being afraid of them. In contrast, Seligman (1971) points out that "only rarely, if ever, do we have pajama phobias . . ., electric-outlet phobias, hammer phobias, even though these things are likely to be associated with trauma in our world" (p. 312). Possibly, the events which give rise to phobias are "related to the survival of the human spe-

TABLE 5–1
Examples of Jung's archetypes

anima
animus
birth
child
death
god
hero
magic
great mother
persona
shadow
wise old man
witch

cies through the long course of evolution" (p. 312). Humans may be *prepared* to fear such species-survival-based events. This conclusion bears directly on Jung's notion of a collective unconscious. "Does preparedness range beyond simple symbolic associations? Are there ways of thinking in which humans are particularly prepared to engage? . . . Are there stories that . . . [humans are] prepared to formulate and accept? If so, a *meaningful version of the . . . [collective unconscious] lurks close behind"* (pp. 317–18; italics added).

ID, EGO, AND SUPEREGO: THREE FUNCTIONS OF PERSONALITY

In his early theory, Freud organized personality in terms of levels of consciousness. The primary emphasis was on the unconscious. Later, around 1920, Freud revised his theory. He provided another division of personality: id, ego, and superego. Functions formerly relegated to the unconscious were primarily taken over by the id; the id operates totally at the unconscious level. The ego and superego function at all three levels of awareness. However, the ego and superego also operate mainly at the unconscious level. This is consistent with the predominant role Freud gives the unconscious. The three personality functions are shown schematically in Figure 5–1.

The id, ego, and superego can be viewed on several different levels. First, they are theoretical constructs; they do not physically exist within the brain. (Freud did believe that all mental functions would be ultimately

FIGURE 5–1
The relationship of the personality functions to the levels of awareness

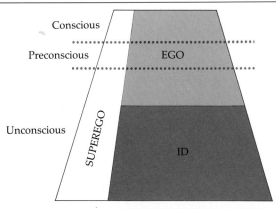

tied to neural structures; but his theory does not depend on discovering specific structures.) Second, the id, ego, and superego are often referred to as structures; but it may be more useful to think of them as *functions* or *aspects* of the personality. They represent the desiring, pleasure-seeking (id), realistic, rational (ego), and moral, ideal (superego) parts of human behavior. Finally, the three personality aspects are often discussed in psychoanalytic writing as if they had human capabilities. For example, they demand, mediate, and restrict. Psychoanalysts do not view the id, ego, and superego as little people inside us. Rather id, ego, and superego are convenient ways of conceptualizing complex psychological functions.

Id

The term **id** comes from the German word *es* meaning *it*. The id is the original system of personality; it contains all psychological aspects present at birth. The id is a reservoir for all drives; it derives power directly from bodily needs and processes. As bodily needs, like hunger and thirst, build up, they must be satisfied; the resulting increase in tension must be discharged. When the id governs this discharge, gratification cannot be delayed because the id is regulated by the pleasure principle. This guides the person toward immediate satisfaction—in other words, instant pleasure and no pain.

The id has two basic techniques to reduce tension: reflex action and primary process. At its most primitive level, the id works by reflex action. It reacts automatically and immediately to internal and external irritants to the body. Tension or distress from the irritants is thus quickly removed. Reflex actions include inborn mechanisms like sneezing, blinking, and coughing.

The id cannot tolerate any delay of gratification or any tension. So we would expect very young children to "cry" as soon as an appetite or need arises which they cannot satisfy. This seems to be exactly what happens. (Infants, of course, can satisfy some of their own needs, such as urination.) The child may need something tangible from the outside world, like food or water. If it is not immediately available, the id's **primary process** forms a memory image of the needed object. When the infant is hungry, for instance, an image of food is produced. This experience is called **wish fulfillment,** because, for the moment, the desire is fulfilled. There are remnants of wish fulfillment in adulthood. Most involve dreams in which a fond desire is met (e.g., a sexual encounter with an attractive person).

Primary process is a crude mechanism; it does not distinguish what is required to satisfy a need from a memory image of the object, such as between food and a mental picture of food. The id may be momentarily satisfied with a memory image. But primary process does nothing to actually reduce tension. Obviously, one cannot long survive on mental pictures of food. If the infant's needs were met immediately, as they were before birth, primary process would be satisfactory. But inevitably gratification must be delayed; a mother cannot be available constantly to feed her baby, for example. The infant must become able to tolerate some delay of gratification. This begins as the infant "realizes" there is an external world. The child grows aware of something which is "not me" that must be taken into account and considered apart from, but interrelated with, the infant. This comes with the development of the second aspect of personality, the ego.

Ego

The **ego** develops out of the id; that is, it uses some of the id's psychic energy for its own functions. At birth, all the child's psychic energy is in the id and is used for primary processes. Therefore, the energy for ego functions must come from the id. The energy system is a closed system. An important consequence is that as psychic energy is transferred to the ego, there is less energy left for id functions. So the child becomes more willing to wait for gratification.

In contrast to the id's pleasure principle, the ego is governed by the **reality principle**. This principle postpones the discharge of energy until an appropriate situation or object in the real world appears. The ego does not attempt to thwart the id's pleasure seeking. Instead it temporarily suspends pleasure for the sake of reality. According to Freud, the ego is the representative of the external world. The id's primary process indicates the object or situation necessary to satisfy a particular need (e.g., an image of food). In contrast, the **secondary process** of the ego creates a strategy for actual satisfaction (e.g., going to the cookie jar). The ego, then, is characterized by realistic thinking and problem solving. It is the seat of intellectual processes. Daydreaming is an example of a secondary process which illustrates the reality-bound nature of the ego. We enjoy the pleasurable fantasy of a daydream. But we do not mistake the fantasy for reality as we do in a nocturnal dream which is a primary process.

We function both as individuals and as members of society. To do this, we must learn not only to deal with the direct constraints of physical reality but also to follow social norms and prohibitions. Further, we must conform to society's "laws" even when there are no external monitors and no realistic fear of apprehension, punishment, or failure. Around age three or four, children begin to evaluate their own behavior independently of immediate threat or reward. This is the function of the third aspect of personality, the superego.

Superego

The **superego** is the internal representative of the values of parents and society. It strives for the *ideal* rather than the real. The superego judges an act as right or wrong, as being consistent or inconsistent with moral values, independent of its usefulness. The superego gives both rewards and punishments, depending on the nature of our behavior. When our actions and thoughts are acceptable, we experience pride, satisfaction, and worthiness. When our behaviors are unacceptable, we experience guilt.

The superego has three roles in adult life. First, whereas the ego postpones the impulses of the id, particularly if they are sexual or aggressive, the superego inhibits these impulses. Second, the superego persuades the ego to attend to moral rather than realistic goals. (This presumably accounts for various types of self-sacrifice and altruism.) Third, the superego directs the person toward the pursuit of perfection.

Until this century, ethical or moral behavior was generally presumed to come from a "still, small voice" provided by God (Brown, 1965). Freud argued that moral conscience is acquired after birth. The superego develops through the process of **incorporation;** this involves "taking in" the values of parents in a manner analogous to the way we take in food. Incorporation begins about the fourth year of life. It is closely related to resolution of the Oedipus complex. Through defensive identification, the child acquires the moral values of the same-sexed parent. Identification with both parents occurs through another process. This is **anaclitic identification;** children come to value their parents because of the love, warmth, and comfort the parents provide. By association, they also come to value their parents' standards and ideals.

The Interaction among the Id, Ego, and Superego

To summarize the development of personality, at birth only the id exists. Later, in response to the demands of reality, the ego develops from the id. Finally, the superego is an outgrowth of the ego. It is the societal representative in personality. When all three aspects have developed, the psychic energy that once belonged solely to the id is divided among the id, ego, and superego and fluctuates among them. The ego mediates among the three basic forces: (1) the demands of the id, (2) the requirements of reality, and (3) the limitations imposed by the superego (see Figure 5–2). The ego ensures that instinctual needs are met in a realistic and, at the same time, socially approved manner.

The aims of one aspect of the personality may be at odds with the aims of one or both of the other aspects. This is an **intrapsychic conflict.** Most often intrapsychic conflict erupts because of id demands pressing for immediate satisfaction. But the aims of all three aspects of the personality can be in conflict. This is shown in Table 5–2 (page 100).

How are intrapsychic conflicts resolved? Logically, three possibilities exist: (1) complete elimination of the drive, (2) direct expression of the drive, or (3) redirection of the drive. It is assumed that a drive can never be completely eliminated; a drive can be banished from consciousness

FIGURE 5–2
The ego as the mediator of personality

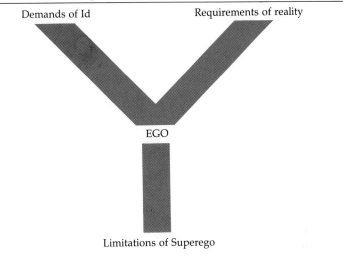

Demands of Id   Requirements of reality

EGO

Limitations of Superego

but not from the total personality. Direct expression rarely occurs; if an id drive were allowed total expression, the ego would be overwhelmed with excitation and the person would feel intense anxiety. (The defensive processes the ego uses to prevent this will be discussed shortly.) Therefore, most intrapsychic conflicts are dealt with by redirection of a drive. This entails a compromise between the personality functions involved. For instance, in an id-ego conflict over the desire to hit someone you are angry at, you may choose to say something nasty to the person.

Intrapsychic conflicts are part of normal personality functioning. Their resolution, however, is a defensive process performed by the ego, which requires psychic energy. The more successfully the ego minimizes intrapsychic conflicts, the more energy is "left over" for the ego's higher mental functions, such as problem solving and creative endeavors.

EGO PSYCHOLOGY: EXPANDING THE FUNCTIONS OF THE EGO

Freud (1940) always considered the id as the dominant force in the personality. A major role of the ego, and to some extent of the superego, is ensuring that id impulses are in control so the personality is not overwhelmed by instinctual desires. As psychoanalysis developed, it became clear that this view of the dynamics of personality was limiting. An id-dominated, conflict-ridden personality was a reasonable explanation of

TABLE 5–2
Possible conflicts among the aspects of personality

Conflict	Example
Id versus Ego	Choosing between a small immediate reward and a larger reward which requires some period of waiting (i.e., delay of gratification).
Id versus Superego	Deciding whether to return the difference when you are overpaid or undercharged.
Ego versus Superego	Choosing between acting in a realistic way (e.g., telling a "white lie") and adhering to a potentially costly or unrealistic standard (e.g., always telling the truth).
Id and Ego versus Superego	Deciding whether to retaliate against the attack of a weak opponent or to "turn the other cheek."
Id and Superego versus Ego	Deciding whether to act in a realistic way that conflicts both with your desires and your moral convictions (e.g., the decision faced by devout Roman Catholics as to the use of contraceptive devices).
Ego and Superego versus Id	Choosing whether to "act on the impulse" to steal something you want and cannot afford. The ego would presumably be increasingly involved in such a conflict as the probability of being apprehended increases.

the development of psychopathology, but it was an inadequate basis for a normal, adaptive personality. From this perceived deficit, **ego psychology** arose as a new branch of psychoanalysis (Blanck & Blanck, 1974). Ego psychology emphasizes (1) *adaptive controls* rather than defense, (2) *general motives*, such as mastery and competence, rather than limiting itself to sexual and aggressive drives, and (3) *conscious determinism* rather than unconscious determinism (Klein, 1976; Levine & Slap, 1985).

Heinz Hartmann (1894–1970) is considered the founder of ego psychology. He believes the ego both develops and remains partially independent of the id. Hartmann (1958, 1964) acknowledges the existence of and the necessity for conflict between the ego and the id. He also acknowledges the defensive operations of the ego. But he believes that there is a "conflict-free ego sphere." This part of the ego is not at odds with the id, the superego, or external reality. Ego psychology is concerned with how the ego adaptively deals with reality through perception, thinking, language, creative production, attention, and memory. In this regard, ego psychology comes closer to mainstream psychology than most psychoanalytic theory. It also provides a more complete theory of the full range of psychological processes (Loewenstein, Newmann, Schur, & Solnit, 1966).

Heinz Hartmann

Bettmann Newsphotos

Hartmann (1951) felt ego psychology should investigate "how psychological conflict and 'peaceful' internal development mutually facilitate and hamper each other" (p. 368). The emphasis in ego psychology is clearly on the *conscious, normal, coping* functions of personality. This contrasts with the emphasis in classical, id-dominated psychoanalysis on unconscious, abnormal functions. For example, fantasy (daydreaming) is a secondary process which can have definite adaptive features. Hartmann (1951) contends that "fantasy can be fruitful even in scientific thinking, which is the undisputed domain of rational thinking" (p. 372). Other ego psychologists, such as Ernest Kris (1950), argue that the role of fantasy in creative and artistic thinking can be fully explained only if the ego is considered an autonomous part of the personality that can freely make and relinquish its own cathexes.

Robert White (1963) also developed an ego psychology theory. In his view, *competence*, not drive reduction, is the major motivation. The classic drives of sex and aggression on which Freudian theory is based are satisfied through reduction. In contrast, competence drives are satisfied through *stimulation*. By **competence**, White (1960) means an organism's "fitness or ability to carry out those transactions with the environment which result in its maintaining itself, growing, and flourishing." White (1959) draws on a great deal of research that shows the importance of motives like exploration, manipulation, and curiosity.

The difference between White's ego psychology and Freud's "id psychology" is illustrated by White's reconceptualization of Freud's psychosexual stages. White (1960) traces the development of competence, in its various forms, instead of the development of the sexual drive. Table 5–3 summarizes White's view of development. You may note some similarities with the psychosocial stages described by Erikson, who is also considered an ego psychologist (see Chapter 4).

Object relations are another significant area of investigation for ego psychologists. Indeed, Fairbairn's object relations theory (see Chapter 4)

TABLE 5–3
White's reconceptualization of Freud's psychosexual stages

	Freud's Theme	White's Theme (Competency)	Example of Competency
Oral Stage	Feeding	*Coping with environment*	Infant playing with any and all objects it can come in contact with.
Anal Stage	Elimination	*Independence*	Two-to-three-year-olds' negativism: not wanting to do what they are told to do and wanting to do things on their own.
Phallic Stage	Oedipal situation	*Locomotion*	Moving about freely and at will.
		Language	Communicating one's needs verbally and influencing other people through language.
		Imagination	Taking on imaginary roles, especially those of adults.
Latency Period	No psychosexual development	*Social skills*	Making and keeping friends; coping with social rejection.
		Meeting realistic challenges	Doing well with school work and athletics.
Genital Stage	Heterosexual behavior	*Sense of identity*	Defining oneself in terms of strengths and weakness and developing self-confidence.
		Life skills	Developing intellectual skills that will be used in lifelong pursuits.

is one of the most extreme examples in ego psychology. The (central) ego is autonomous with its own source of psychic energy in Fairbairn's theory. It is also the only personality structure.

ANXIETY AND DEFENSE

Anxiety is all too familiar to each of us. In his early theorizing (in the 1890s), Freud suggested that repressed libido is transformed into anxiety. Some thirty years later he revised his theory to state the reverse. *Anxiety leads to repression.* Freud's later formulation (in the 1920s) holds that anxiety is a *signal* of impending danger. The source of the danger can be either external or internal. But Freud thinks it is usually the result of an id impulse seeking expression. Why is this dangerous?

When the infant is incapable of delaying gratification—before the ego develops—he or she is occasionally overwhelmed by the tension created by an id impulse. This may occur when there is no one around to satisfy the hunger drive. Such trauma is accompanied by intense stimulation called **primary anxiety.** Children later learn to anticipate the danger and to react with anxiety. However, now the anxiety is less intense than that which accompanied the actual traumatic experience (no food). This **signal anxiety** warns the ego to somehow prevent the recurrence of the trauma and the accompanying intense stimulation. The ego is "motivated" to deal with the danger because anxiety is unpleasant.

An alternative view was popularized by a contemporary of Freud's, Otto Rank. Rank (1929) argued that the **birth trauma,** the initial biological separation of child and mother, is the prototype for all separation, loss, and anxiety in later life. In fact, Freud (1961a) said the same thing somewhat earlier. But he never pursued the role of the birth trauma in his theory. Rank (1929, 1959) developed his own theory of personality development. Here, the trauma of birth is the prime motivation. He suggested that every enjoyable act is oriented toward regaining the pleasure of the womb. Thus, sexual intercourse, for the male, is a symbolic return to the womb.

Freud made a distinction among three types of anxiety that occur in adulthood.

1. **Neurotic anxiety** results from an id-ego conflict in which the id seeks to discharge an impulse, and the ego tries to place reality restraints on the impulse. For instance, the urge to urinate is held in check until one reaches a bathroom.

2. **Moral anxiety** is generated by an id-superego conflict in which the id impulse (e.g., to shoplift) is in opposition to the moral and ideal standards of society (e.g., "Thou shalt not steal") and is experienced by the individual as guilt or shame.

3. **Objective anxiety** is produced when a realistic, external threat is present, such as a fire or a mugger.

In each case, anxiety signals impending danger. In objective anxiety, the danger is external. It can be dealt with by taking realistic steps to eliminate or reduce the actual threat. Neurotic and moral anxiety are due to an impending *intrapsychic* danger. They must be coped with by internal means, namely, the defense mechanisms of the ego.

Ego Defense Mechanisms

Defense mechanisms are *unconscious* ego processes that keep disturbing and unacceptable impulses from direct expression. To learn about defense mechanisms, it is helpful to examine them separately. Bear in mind, though, that people rarely defend themselves against anxiety with a single mechanism. An individual typically combines different defense mechanisms. Further, as will become apparent, there is considerable overlap in the way defense mechanisms protect the ego from overwhelming anxiety.

Sublimation

Sublimation alters unacceptable impulses by changing them to completely acceptable, and even admired, social behaviors. Sublimation deprives an impulse of its unacceptable character. At the same time, the impulse is expressed. Creative endeavors, like painting and writing poetry, are common sublimations of the sex drive. Playing, or even watching, contact sports like football and boxing are common sublimations of aggression. Freud believes our highest virtues are sublimations of our lowest dispositions. The surgeon, for example, may be seen as having a socially acceptable outlet for aggressive impulses; the movie censor has sublimated sexual drives.

Sublimation is the only truly successful defense mechanism; it succeeds in permanently redirecting undesirable impulses. All other defense mechanisms are to some degree unsuccessful; they require continually warding off the threatening impulses.

Repression

With repression, a dangerous impulse is actively and totally excluded from consciousness. This does not mean that the impulse is no longer influencing the individual. Quite the contrary is likely to be true. The impulse affects behavior, as do all unconscious impulses. As a solution to conflict, repression is characterized by a continual struggle to contain primitive desires.

Repression, as all defense mechanisms, may occur in "healthy" or normal individuals. There is always a price paid, however. Psychic energy

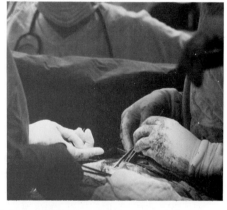

According to psychoanalytic theory, artistic work is a sublimation for the sexual drive and surgery is a sublimation of the aggressive drive. Both are socially acceptable ways of expressing id impulses. *Left, Photo by Christopher O'Keefe and Michael D. Spiegler. Right, Copyright © by J. Berndt, 1982.*

used to defend the ego is unavailable for more adaptive functions like intellectual and social pursuits. Further, in the case of repression, the price is particularly severe. Repressed impulses might be "healthy" or adaptive. But they are permanently excluded from the development of the personality. For example, exclusion of all aggressive impulses is likely to result in a very passive person.

Repression is the most fundamental defense mechanism. It is also the crudest. In Freud's early writings, *repression* was a general term, synonymous with ego defense. In a sense, other defense mechanisms could be construed as types of repression. Repression should not be confused with **suppression** which refers to *conscious* forgetting of unpleasant events or threatening thoughts. Suppression is not considered an ego defense mechanism.

Experimental Evidence for Repression. Repression has been the subject of numerous laboratory investigations (e.g., D'Zurilla, 1965; Worchel, 1955; Zeller, 1950, 1951). The typical experiment is outlined in Table 5–4. It can be divided into three phases. In the first phase, experimental and control subjects memorize a list of words. They are then tested for their recall of the words (Recall Test 1). Subjects have been treated in the same way to this point; no difference between the recall of experimental and control subjects is expected.

During the second phase, experimental subjects are exposed to an ego-threatening situation. An example is taking a personality test and getting negative feedback (e.g., "The test indicates that you may be prone to spells of anxiety"). The control subjects are exposed to a similar, but nonthreatening, situation. They may take a personality test but get neutral feedback (e.g., "The results are in the normal range").

Next, the subjects' recall of the words is reassessed (Recall Test 2). This time experimental subjects who were ego-threatened are expected to recall fewer words than control subjects. The words are assumed to be associated with the ego-threat for the experimental group, because both occurred at the same time and in the same situation. Consequently, the words that elicit anxiety due to the threat have been repressed.

According to the theory of repression, if the threat were removed and anxiety thus reduced, the repressed material would return to consciousness. In the third phase of the study, subjects are debriefed. That is, they are told that they were given *false* feedback. Then the subjects' recall of the words is tested once more (Recall Test 3). No difference in recall between the experimental and control subjects is expected.

In general, the results of the experiments using the design just described have been consistent with the predictions based on psychoanalytic theory. Ego-threat leads to lowered recall in Test 2; removal of the threat restores recall to prethreat levels in Test 3. These results have been interpreted as supporting the concept of repression.

TABLE 5-4
Experimental paradigm for demonstrating the existence of repression

Procedures				
	Experimental Subjects	**Control Subjects**	**Prediction**	**Interpretation**
Phase 1	Learn list of words Recall Test 1	Learn list of words Recall Test 1	No differences between experimental and control subjects	Groups have been treated identically
Phase 2	Ego-threatening task Recall Test 2	Neutral task Recall Test 2	Experimental subjects recall less than control subjects	Ego-threat and resultant anxiety lead experimental subjects to repress words associated with threat
Phase 3	Debriefing (threat removed) Recall Test 3	Debriefing Recall Test 3	No differences between experimental and control subjects	When threat is removed, repression is lifted and memory of repressed words become conscious again

Reaction Formation

One way of warding off an unacceptable impulse is to overemphasize its opposite in thought and behavior. A man may be threatened by his desire to dominate and be aggressive in social situations. So he thinks of himself as a timid and shy person and acts passively. Timidity and passivity would be a **reaction formation** against a strong aggressive drive.

It is often difficult to tell whether an act is a manifestation of an impulse or of its opposite. An important hallmark of reaction formation is the persistence or excess of the behavior ("going overboard"). As Shakespeare's Hamlet observed: "The lady doth protest too much." The apparently puritanical person, particularly one who responds to sexual advances with numerous gasps, may well be seething with erotic desire. Similarly, an individual's avowed love for a sibling or spouse may sometimes indicate profound, but disguised, hate.

Undoing

Undoing makes retribution for an unacceptable act committed or even contemplated. A person may be unscrupulous in business dealings. He or she may undo this by being very active in civic and charitable organizations. Undoing frequently involves a ritual act that symbolically compensates for an id impulse that is threatening the ego. A classic example is Lady Macbeth compulsively washing her hands as if to cleanse herself of the blood she had spilled.

Projection

Projection involves attributing unacceptable impulses or wishes to someone or something else. Freud used the example of the jealous husband who called his wife unfaithful. In fact, it was the husband who wanted to have an affair but could not face it in himself.

Experimental Evidence for Projection. Two types of projection have been studied (Holmes, 1978). **Classical projection** occurs when an individual is *unaware of* having a negative characteristic. To defend against becoming aware, the person attributes the characteristic to someone else. Usually this is someone the person dislikes. Scapegoating is an example of classical projection on a mass scale. **Attributive projection,** in contrast, is involved when a person projects a characteristic he or she is *aware of* onto another individual. Attributive projection is not a psychoanalytic concept.

Several experiments provide evidence that classical projection can and does occur in some circumstances. In one study, undergraduate men and women completed a questionnaire designed to tap their sexual defensiveness (Halpern, 1977). The questionnaire required true or false responses to simple statements like "I never have sexual fantasies" or "I never have dreams with sexual content." Sexual fantasies and dreams are experienced by most people. So subjects responding "true" to a large number of such statements were presumed to be relatively sexually defensive. Next, subjects looked at six photographs of college students. They ranked the photographs from most favorable to least favorable.

At this point, subjects assigned to the experimental group were shown a set of pornographic pictures to heighten sexual arousal. Control subjects were not shown any pictures. Then, as a final measure, all subjects rated themselves and the person they had picked from the photographs as least favorable on a personality scale. The scale included a rating of lustfulness.

Psychoanalytic theory would predict that subjects who were highly sexually defensive, when presented sexually stimulating material, would deny the feelings by projecting them onto the disliked other. Thus, in the experimental group, high-defensive subjects should project more lust onto the disliked other than would low-defensive subjects. In the control group, there should be no difference between high and low sexually defensive subjects. This is exactly what was found.

In another study, female undergraduates were given false feedback indicating that they had a tendency toward "neuroticism" (Sherwood, 1979). The women then rated both a favorable and an unfavorable target person on neuroticism. As the theory of projection would predict, women who denied the higher level of neuroticism in themselves tended to attribute neuroticism to the unfavorable target person; those who accepted the psychologist's claim that they were neurotic tended to attribute neuroticism to a favorable other. This study demonstrates the operation of both classical and attributive projection. It also indicates something about the different nature of the two forms of defense.

Displacement

Projection involves attributing an impulse to another person. **Displacement** involves shifting an impulse directed toward an unacceptable and threatening object to a more acceptable and less-threatening object. A common example involves the person who is bawled out at work by a superior. He or she then "takes it out" on family members. Expressing hostility toward the superior is obviously a threatening and unadaptive strategy. So instead the person redirects the anger toward family members who are less likely to retaliate.

According to psychoanalysis, displacement is the primary mechanism in phobias. A phobia starts with a realistic or unrealistic fear of someone or something that is difficult to avoid. Repeated contact with the feared stimulus induces intense anxiety. To reduce it, the person displaces the fear to another target that can easily be avoided and is symbolically related to the feared stimulus. Freud's (1957) famous case of "little

Hans" involved a four-year-old boy who became phobic of horses because he was actually afraid of his father, someone he could not avoid. Hans displaced his fear onto horses, a symbol for strong, masculine figures. This lowered Hans's anxiety because he could avoid horses, which had become the anxiety-evoking stimuli.

Regression

Escaping to a more satisfying and pleasant behavior is often used to cope with frustration and anxiety. **Regression** is a retreat to an earlier period of development. For adults, this is a pregenital psychosexual stage. Common examples of regression include dreaming, smoking, fingernail biting, talking baby talk, getting drunk, overeating, breaking the law, and losing one's temper.

The potential importance of regression as an adaptive mode in people with diseased kidneys has been discussed by psychoanalysts (Viederman, 1974; von Euen, 1975). Patients with kidney failure undergo a treatment called hemodialysis. They are attached to a machine that extracts

Fingernail biting is a example of the defense mechanism called regression. To deal with anxiety or frustration, the person reverts to a mode of behavior that was comforting at an earlier stage of psychosexual development—in this photograph, the oral stage. *Mark Antman/The Image Works*

waste products from their blood. Usually, hemodialysis must be done for five to eight hours, two or three times a week. Without such treatment (or a successful kidney transplant), the patient will die. The parallel between hemodialysis and the mother-child relationship during the oral stage is evident.

> The machine represents the mother through its life-giving potential, through its umbilical-like connections, through the bath and water which may symbolize the womb and birth processes. It is a demanding and restricting mother, permitting only brief periods of separation before reunion is required. It can easily be perceived as a bad mother since it frustrates orally, is always threatening to break down (ruptured coils occur with considerable frequency), and often leaves the patient feeling ill (weak, with muscle cramps, hypotension, etc.). (Viederman, 1974, p. 69)

Viederman (1974) compiled case studies of patients undergoing hemodialysis. He concluded that adapting to the highly stressful treatment depends on the patients' ability to regress to the oral stage and deal with their infantile oral conflicts. Similar reasoning was used in discussing the diet restrictions that are also part of kidney patients' treatment. Von Euen (1975) interpreted patients' failure to follow the prescribed diet as resisting being deprived of oral gratification; this is symbolic of early arbitrary parental demands.

Rationalization

A person may perform an unacceptable act or think a threatening thought. Afterward, he or she gets rid of the anxiety or guilt by finding a "perfectly reasonable" excuse for the behavior. This defense mechanism is called **rationalization.** It is often used to maintain self-esteem. If you are "stood up" by a date, you may tell yourself and friends that you "really" didn't want to go out with that loser. This rationalization has been labeled *sour grapes*, after the fable of the fox who, unable to reach some grapes, concluded that they must be sour. Rationalization is an *unconscious* process, as are all of the ego defense mechanisms; it is not the same as consciously making excuses.

Denial

Still another way to handle painful experiences and thoughts is to deny their existence. A person may refuse to believe that a loved one has died. He or she will behave as though the person were still alive. Severely overweight and underweight individuals tend to have distorted body images (Spiegler, 1981, 1982a). A more common form of **denial** involves fantasy or play. Most people do this from time to time. We find temporary relief from reality by daydreaming about how our lives might have been different if some unpleasant event had not occurred. Children deny their inferiority through play, as when a young boy becomes a strict father while playing "house."

Defense Mechanisms as Adaptive Functions

According to Freud, the main purpose of ego defense mechanisms is to defend the ego from id impulses. Ego psychologists believe that defense mechanisms can also play a more positive, adaptive role. Hartmann (1951) makes this point regarding denial and avoidance: "avoidance of the environment in which difficulties are encountered—and its positive correlate, the search for one offering easier and better possibilities for action—is also a most effective adaptation process" (p. 373). For example, putting off studying for a final examination indefinitely is far from adaptive. But it is often useful to *temporarily* forget the upcoming test (denial) and engage in some diverting activity (avoidance) before resuming studying.

The defense mechanism of rationalization involves finding a plausible reason or "excuse" for an unacceptable thought or action. In Aesop's fable, the fox could not reach the grapes it wanted and rationalized that the grapes must be sour. *The Bettmann Archive, Inc.*

TRENDS IN THE EVOLUTION OF PSYCHOANALYTIC THEORY

Psychoanalytic theory has been evolving ever since Freud and his early followers first charted its course. There are five broad directions in this evolution. All of them have been suggested in our discussion of psychoanalytic theory.

First, there has been increasing recognition of social determinants of personality. This contrasts with the predominant role assigned to biological drives and instincts in classical psychoanalysis.

Second, the time frame of personality development has been expanded. Many psychoanalysts view personality development as a lifelong process rather than one that is, as Freud believes, virtually completed by age five. "Whereas the formation of psychic structure in a child is like broad strokes painted on a bare canvas, the evolution of psychic structure in adulthood is equivalent to fine, nearly invisible strokes on a complicated background" (Colarusso & Nemiroff, 1979, p. 62). This broader concept of personality has implications for personality change (Gedo, 1979). "The analytic patient, regardless of age, is considered to be still in the

Denial is a powerful defense mechanism that protects us from becoming aware of disturbing events. *Photo © 1985, Jan Lukas*

process of ongoing development as opposed to merely being in possession of a past that influences . . . present conscious and unconscious life" (Shane, 1977, pp. 95–96).

Third, many psychoanalysts, particularly ego psychologists, consider conscious aspects of personality to be important. In contrast, one of the hallmarks of Freudian theory is the predominant role of the unconscious. Nonetheless, psychoanalysis still emphasizes unconscious motives and conflicts more than the other personality strategies.

Fourth, contemporary psychoanalysis emphasizes normal personality more than does classical psychoanalysis. This is true both in terms of devoting more study to normal personality functioning, as ego psychologists do, and in terms of viewing normal personality independent of abnormal personality. Classical theory focuses on intrapsychic conflict, anxiety and defense, and psychopathology. Ego psychologists examine the other side of the coin—the conflict-free part of personality that lets people remain relatively healthy by coping successfully with the inner and outer forces that shape their personalities. Still, most psychoanalytic theorists and researchers are psychotherapists by training and profession. As a result, psychoanalysis remains a strategy that tends to proceed from abnormal personality to normal personality.

Fifth, psychoanalysis has increasingly been related to basic theory and research in academic psychology. Psychoanalysis began outside of traditional academic circles, in the private sessions of psychoanalytic psychotherapy. The methods of psychoanalysis—dream analysis, free association, interpretation of mistakes and symbolism—are clearly not what academic and empirically-oriented psychologists typically consider legitimate and important. Since the 1930s, however, there have been numerous attempts to relate psychoanalysis to theories and research in the mainstream of academic psychology and to try to empirically validate psychoanalytic concepts.

Today, there is a major trend in academic psychology toward examination of cognitive processes. Many psychologists are vigorously pursuing the possible ties between cognitive psychology and psychoanalysis. The clearest link so far is in the conclusion of cognitive psychologists that humans systematically process and "edit" environmental input or stimuli through unconscious but nonetheless highly active processes (Erdelyi, 1974; Motley & Baars, 1978; Neisser, 1976; Nisbett & Wilson, 1977; Posner, 1973). Psychoanalysts have been insisting on the importance of unconscious processes for almost one hundred years.

SUMMARY

1. Freud divides the mind into three levels of awareness: conscious, preconscious, and unconscious. Personality functioning is dominated by the unconscious.

2. Jung proposes an alternative division: conscious ego, personal unconscious, and collective unconscious. Jung emphasizes the influence of the collective unconscious which contains archetypes that are universal predispositions to think and act in common ways.

3. Freud divides personality according to three basic functions. The id is concerned with pleasure-seeking and is the reservoir of biological drives. It operates through the pleasure principle that requires immediate gratification of needs. This is accomplished through primary process in which memory images of goals are formed.

4. The ego is the reality aspect of personality and operates according to the reality principle—the gratification of needs is delayed until an appropriate actual goal (i.e., not a mental image) can be obtained. This is accomplished through secondary process which involves problem solving and other intellectual functions.

5. The superego is the moral aspect of personality. It is the internal representative of the values of society and guides the individual toward ideals.

6. The ego serves as a mediator among the pleasure demands of the id, the moral limitations of the superego, and the requirements of the real world. Intrapsychic conflicts among the id, ego, and superego play a major role in determining behavior.

7. Ego psychologists emphasize ego functions including conflict-free adaptive functions, general motives (e.g., competency), and conscious determinism.

8. Anxiety is a central Freudian concept. Freud distinguishes three types: neurotic anxiety (from an id-ego conflict), moral anxiety or guilt (from an id-superego conflict), and objective anxiety (from actual external dangers).

9. Unconscious ego defense mechanisms keep us from being overwhelmed by unacceptable impulses that are the basis for neurotic and moral anxiety. Sublimation involves the channeling of unacceptable impulses into socially acceptable endeavors; it results in a permanent solution to dealing with unacceptable impulses. All other defense mechanisms require a continual defensive process to ward off unacceptable impulses.

10. Repression, in which unacceptable impulses are totally excluded from one's consciousness, is the most fundamental defense mechanism. Other defense mechanisms include reaction formation, undoing, projection, displacement, regression, rationalization, and denial.

11. Five ongoing trends in psychoanalytic theory can be identified: (1) recognizing social factors; (2) considering present influences on behavior; (3) emphasizing conscious personality functioning; (4) emphasizing normal personality functioning; and (5) relating psychoanalytic theory to basic psychological research and theory.

THE PSYCHOANALYTIC STRATEGY:

CHAPTER 6

ASSESSMENT AND PERSONALITY CHANGE

OVERVIEW

115

In the previous chapters we explored the major theoretical propositions of psychoanalysis. Now we will look at personality assessment and change from the psychoanalytic view. Unconscious processes cannot be directly observed. This means that psychoanalytic personality assessment must be *indirect* because many psychoanalysts assume that most of personality functions at the unconscious level. We will discuss two indirect methods of personality assessment: dream interpretation and projective techniques. Psychoanalytic psychotherapy is the final topic of the chapter. It may be considered a method both of personality change and of assessment, because much of psychoanalytic therapy involves uncovering what is in the patient's unconscious.

DREAMS: THE ROYAL ROAD TO THE UNCONSCIOUS

One third of our lives is spent sleeping, and as we sleep we often dream. People have probably always been intrigued by their dreams and wondered what they mean. One ancient view is that every dream has a secret meaning which can be interpreted by a sufficiently skilled person. Biblical Joseph's interpretations of fat calves and lean calves is an example. Other well-known ideas about the meaning of dreams include the belief that they represent wishes in disguised form and that they result from experiences and ideas in waking life.

What is a dream? Technically a dream is a mental experience during sleep that involves mainly visual images. The images are often vivid and are considered "real" when they occur (Hobson & McCarley, 1977, p. 1336). We only have access to another person's dreams by asking about them.

Freud's Dream Theory

Freud was not the first to call attention to the psychological meaning of dreams, but his theory was the first comprehensive account of dreaming (Freud, 1961a). Freud believes dreaming obeys the same underlying psychological laws as all other mental functions; his dream theory is an integral part of his overall theory of personality. *The Interpretation of Dreams* is the book that presents Freud's dream theory. He thought it was his most significant contribution, and many commentors agree with his evaluation. First published in 1900, Freud revised the book a number of times. The work is largely based on Freud's analysis of his own dreams. (The germ of many of Freud's ideas came from his self-analysis. He began self-analysis in 1897 by examining a dream; he continued self-analysis throughout his lifetime, usually as the last activity of the day [Jones, 1953].)

Freud believes dreams are highly significant mental products. They result from the interaction of unconscious wishes, the censoring mechanisms of the ego, and events in waking life. Although the dream itself occurs in sleep, the origins and preparation of the dream reflect all aspects of the dreamer's psychological experience. Dreams, for Freud, are carefully constructed camouflages; there is always a concealed wish and a true meaning. Dreams are subtle and profound reflections of intrapsychic processes. Freud likens a dream to a fireworks display "which takes hours to prepare but goes off in a moment." Freud called dreams "the royal road to the unconscious." This reflects his conviction that dreams are the single best source of information about a person's unconscious.

Manifest versus Latent Content of Dreams

Freud distinguishes two levels of dream content. **Manifest content** is what a person can remember about a dream. **Latent content** is the underlying intrapsychic events that led to the manifest content. The latent content of a dream is primarily unconscious thoughts, wishes, fantasies, and conflicts. These are expressed in translated or disguised form in the manifest content. Freud thought the relation of manifest and latent dream content is like a rebus. In these puzzles, pictures suggest the sounds of words or syllables they represent (see Figure 6–1). Latent meaning cannot directly enter consciousness because it is threatening. It can, however, be disguised. Manifest content is the "dressed-up" version of the disreputable determinants of the dream. Like the rebus symbols, the images in manifest content "stand for" something else. Latent content becomes manifest through two basic processes, dream work and symbolization.

Dream Work

Dream work refers to the ways latent dream content is transformed into manifest content. Freud believes condensation and displacement are the major processes in dream work. He also identifies two other processes, visual representation and secondary revision.

Condensation compresses and combines separate thoughts. The resulting manifest content is a much abbreviated version of the latent content.

An example would be a man dreaming of being affectionate with a woman who looked like his wife, who acted like his ex-wife, and whom he believed in the dream was his mother. The wife, ex-wife, and mother are condensed in a single person. One implication of condensation is that all elements in the dream result from more than one latent source. In other words, they are **overdetermined**. Condensation, like all forms of dream work, disguises threatening latent content; its threat is not apparent in the manifest dream.

Displacement involves shifting emphasis. An important element of the dream is changed to an unimportant element. Or an element of latent content is replaced by a remotely associated element in the manifest content. For example, a woman receives a telegram saying that her son was killed. She dreams of receiving a telegram without any reference to its contents. In this dream, a critical aspect of the latent content appears as a trivial aspect of the manifest content.

The abstract wishes, urges, and ideas that make up latent content would be extremely difficult to grasp. Thus, these abstract concepts are translated into concrete pictures or images. This is done by the dream-work process known as **visual representation**. The rebus in Figure 6–1 is a crude example of visual representation. A more sophisticated example would be presenting the concept of possession as *sitting on an object*, much as children actually do to maintain possession of an object and keep other children from having it. Note the similarity between displacement as dream work and displacement as a defense mechanism. Both dream work and defense mechanisms keep unacceptable and threatening material from becoming conscious.

FIGURE 6–1
An example of a rebus in which the pictures depict the syllables of a word*

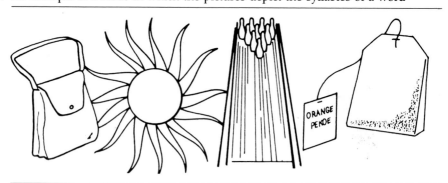

* A simpler rebus would be a picture of a coffee mug (cup) followed by one of a plank of wood (board) to represent the word *cupboard*. The reader who is unable to decipher the word that is visually represented above should see the first page of this book, on which the word appears.

When we awaken, we may try to reconstruct a dream. We often find that the parts of the dream do not fit together logically. This is not surprising. The meaning of the dream (latent content) has been distorted and disguised through condensation, displacement, and visual representation. After waking up, the dreamer tries to fill in the missing elements and otherwise create a coherent overall picture of the dream. The dream is thus further distorted by another type of dream work, **secondary revision.**

Symbolization

Dream work changes unacceptable latent content into acceptable manifest content. **Symbolization** allows latent content to become part of the manifest content. But this is done in an unrecognizable and therefore nonthreatening form. *Symbols* are objects or ideas that stand for something else. Freud believes that that some symbols have universal meanings. They therefore represent the same thing in all dreams. Examples of symbols and their meanings according to psychoanalytic theory are shown in Table 6–1. Symbols are not the exclusive domain of dreams. Freud and many others (e.g., Jung) examined symbolism in myths, fairy tales, literature, and everyday speech.

Table 6–1 shows that most of the symbols refer to sexual objects and activities. This is consistent with the central Freudian idea that human motivation is primarily sexual. Freud believes that although there are

TABLE 6–1
Common psychoanalytic symbols and their latent meanings

Symbol	Latent Meaning
House	Human body
Smooth-fronted house	Male body
House with ledges and balconies	Female body
King and queen	Parents
Little animals	Children
Children	Genitals
Playing with children	Masturbation
Beginning a journey	Dying
Clothes	Nakedness
The number three	Male genitals
Elongated object (e.g., snake, stick, gun, tree trunk, necktie, pencil)	Penis
Balloon, airplane	Erection
Woods and thickets	Pubic hair
Room	Woman
Suite of rooms	Brothel or harem
Box	Uterus
Fruit	Breast
Climbing stairs or ladder	Sexual intercourse
Baldness, tooth extraction	Castration
Bath	Birth

many symbols, only a few concepts are symbolized. What evidence exists for sexual symbolism? Do people connect sexual symbols with sexual objects, as psychoanalysis proposes?

One line of research in this area had people classify psychoanalytic symbols of male and female genitals as either masculine or feminine. In general, these studies have confirmed that adults, and sometimes children, can group sexual symbols according to the gender predicted by psychoanalytic theory at a better-than-chance level (Kline, 1972). However, people may use cultural associations to make the classification even though their responses are consistent with psychoanalytic theory. This would happen when psychoanalytic and cultural symbols are the same. For instance, a gun is a masculine symbol both in psychoanalysis and in our culture.

Lessler (1964) found that classifying so-called sexual symbols depended on the context. This was true whether psychoanalytic or cultural stereotypes were used. When the symbols had cultural referents, subjects used cultural stereotypes to assign gender. Where no cultural bias existed, subjects classified the symbols according to psychoanalytic theory. Lessler argues that these findings are consistent with psychoanalytic theory. Sexual objects are usually threatening. Thus, if a cultural gender referent for the symbol exists, people will choose it (because it is nonthreatening) over the psychoanalytic sexual meaning (e.g., calling a rolling pin feminine). If no cultural gender meaning is obvious, then people "must" use the psychoanalytic sexual meaning (e.g., classifying a cane as masculine).

As a further test of psychoanalytic theory, the dreams of men and women have been compared. An example is Hall and Van de Castle's (1963) study of the differences in the Oedipal symbolism in dreams of men and women described in Chapter 4 (page 75). That study provides indirect support for the sexual symbolism predicted by psychoanalytic theory.

Freud's approach to interpreting symbolism may be characterized as *analytic-reductive*. The interpretation proceeds backwards to the origin of the symbol, to its most basic form. Implicit in this method is the assumption that every symbol can ultimately be reduced to a single meaning. In contrast, Jung interprets symbols using a *constructive* method. Jung believes symbols can be understood both in terms of their historical origins and of their future significance. He maintains that the latter is more important. "The symbol carries an as yet to be realized significance for the person. The work of interpretation [according to Jung] is to create a subjective significance for the symbol and to identify typical symbolic motifs" (Steele, 1982, p. 233). Thus, Jung thinks that symbols may hold both universal and individual meaning.

Freudian Dream Interpretation

Freud's method of dream interpretation begins with the subject's report of the dream (the manifest content). The subject then gives associations to the dream. Dream reports are often relatively short. The associations are generally quite extensive. In the final step, the psychoanalyst interprets the latent meaning of both the manifest content and the associations. The interpretation is based on the principles of dream work and symbolization. It takes into account information the analyst has about the subject, such as events in the subject's life that appear to be related to the dream.

Freudian dream interpretation thus involves analysis of more than just the dream. The dream is viewed in the context of the dreamer's life and associations to the manifest dream. The interpretation is admittedly highly subjective; its validity cannot be judged against any objective standards of right or wrong. The validity of an interpretation is more a matter of how *useful* it is in providing the psychoanalyst with information about the subject's personality. This implies that there may be more than one "correct" (useful) interpretation of a dream.

A Dream Interpreted by Freud. The following dream interpretation by Freud (1961a) illustrates the use of condensation, displacement, and symbolization to understand the latent meaning of the dream. The dreamer was a patient of Freud's. The woman was still quite young but had been married for a number of years. She had recently received news that a friend, Elise L., who was about the same age, had become engaged. Shortly thereafter, she had the following dream.

> She was at the theater with her husband. One side of the stalls [theater boxes] were completely empty. Her husband told her that Elise L. and her fiancé had wanted to go too, but had only been able to get bad seats—three for one florin fifty kreuzers—and of course, they could not take those. She thought it would really not have done any harm if they had. (p. 415)

Freud began his interpretation of this rather brief dream report by analyzing the symbolic meaning of the monetary units. This particular symbol was partially determined by an unimportant event of the previous day. The dreamer had learned that her sister-in-law had recently been given a gift of 150 florins (exactly 100 times the amount dreamed of) and had quickly spent this gift on jewelry. Freud notes that *three* tickets are mentioned in the dream. Elise L. and her fiancé would only have needed two tickets for themselves. Examination of previous statements made by the dreamer revealed a connection: "her newly engaged friend was the same number of months—*three*—her junior" (p. 415).

That one side of the stalls was entirely empty is important. Recently, the patient had wished to attend a play. She had rushed out to buy tickets days ahead of time. In doing so, she had incurred an extra booking fee. When the patient and her husband arrived at the theater, they found that only half the seats were taken. This bit of information accounts in part for the appearance of the "empty stalls" in the dream. More important in terms of psychoanalytic theory is the underlying meaning of the empty stalls. The patient's actual experience with the theater tickets could clearly lead to the conclusion that she had been too hasty about running out to buy tickets and therefore had to pay an additional, unnecessary price. Freud assumed that she might have the same hidden *meaning* concerning her own marriage; in symbolic form, these feelings are revealed by the dream. Thus, Freud offered the following final interpretation of the dream.

> "It was *absurd* to marry so early. There was *no need for me to be in such a hurry*. I see from Elise L.'s example that I should have got a husband in the end. Indeed, I should have got one a *hundred times better*" (a *treasure*) "if I had only *waited*" (in antithesis to her sister-in-law's *hurry*). "My money" (or dowry) "could have bought *three* men just as good." (p. 416)

The Functions of Dreaming

Why do people dream? Freud discusses three interrelated functions of dreaming: (1) *wish fulfillment*, (2) *the release of unconscious tension*, and (3) *guarding sleep*. He believes that every dream is an attempt to fulfill a wish. The wish may be a conscious desire that is not fulfilled during the day (e.g., wishing to be out sailing rather than at the office working). Or it may be an unconscious desire that is a more direct expression of a repressed impulse (e.g., murdering a friend). Most dreams represent a combination of the two. Thoughts from the day, called **day residues,** combine with an unconscious impulse to produce the dream. In effect, the unconscious impulse provides the psychic energy for enactment of the day residues in the form of a dream. The result is that each of the three functions of dreaming is satisfied.

First, the wish is fulfilled in the dream. Dreams are primary processes. Therefore, the mental representation of the object or activity needed to satisfy a wish is not distinguished from the actual object. When a wish "comes true" in a dream, it is as if the wish were actually fulfilled. While dreaming, we usually believe that the events are really happening.

Second, the unconscious impulse is allowed expression. However, this is in a disguised and acceptable form, due to dream work and symbolization. Thus, dreams allow for the release of tensions that have built up in the unconscious.

Third, the individual remains asleep even though unconscious threatening impulses are becoming conscious in the manifest dream. When we are awake, if threatening impulses begin to enter consciousness, anxiety is generated. If such anxiety were present while dreaming, we would wake up. However, through dream work and symbolization, the threatening aspects of the latent material are removed. The result is that anxiety is not generated; the person can continue sleeping.

We will return to Freud's three functions of dreams and comment on their validity in the light of more recent evidence on dreaming, to which we now turn.

The Physiology of Sleep and Dreaming

Freud was well aware that his study of dreams was highly subjective. Even if he had wanted to use more objective methods, it would be more than fifty years from the publication of *The Interpretation of Dreams* to the advent of the remarkable techniques for objectively studying dreams that are employed today. Modern methods are based on continuously recording brain-wave patterns and the parallel eye movements of sleeping subjects. Research subjects volunteer to sleep in the laboratory and be observed. This includes having some of their physiological functions monitored while they sleep and occasionally being awakened and questioned.

Brain waves are recorded by an instrument called an **electroencephalograph** (e-LEK-tro-en-CEF-a-low-graph). It produces an **electroencephalogram** (EEG), a tracing, plotted against time, of the frequency and potential (voltage) of electric currents emitted by the brain. (See Figure 6–2.) The frequency of electric currents from the brain is measured horizontally on the EEG; the closer the tracings, the higher is the frequency. Electrical potential is measured vertically on the EEG; the greater the amplitude, or height, of the tracings, the greater is the electrical potential. EEG recordings are made by placing electrodes directly on the scalp. The procedure is painless and does not appear to disturb sleep.

FIGURE 6–2
Sample EEG patterns for the waking state and the four stages of sleep

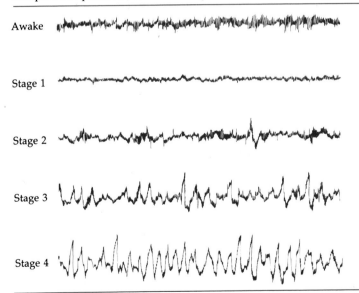

Awake

Stage 1

Stage 2

Stage 3

Stage 4

Source: "An Essay on Dreams: The Role of Physiology in Understanding Their Nature" by W. C. Dement, 1965, in *New Directions in Psychology* Vol. 2, New York: Holt, Rinehart & Winston.

Eye movements have been measured during sleep primarily by placing small electrodes around the orbits of the eyes. Differences in electrical potential produced by displacement of the eyeballs are measured. Figure 6–3 shows a subject wearing both brain-wave and eye-movement electrodes.

Stages of Sleep and Dreaming

Sleep is not a uniform state. Instead, it consists of various stages. EEG recordings reveal four basic stages of sleep that can be distinguished from the waking state. As sleep progresses from Stage 1 to Stage 4, high-amplitude, low-frequency waves develop. This is shown in Figure 6–2. Originally, these waves were thought to be correlated with reduction in neural activity and responsiveness as the person went from "light sleep" in Stage 1 to "deep sleep" in Stage 4. The stages of sleep can be roughly placed on a quantitative continuum of depth. But there is a very im-

FIGURE 6–3
A sleeping subject with EEG and eye-movement electrodes

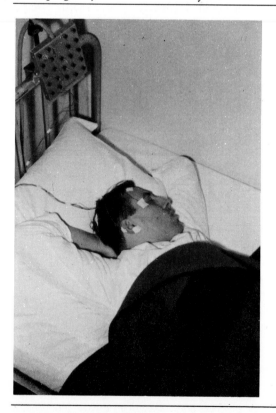

Courtesy of Dr. William Dement

portant exception. This exception occurs during Stage 1 sleep. It is so striking that it has been the primary focus of researchers.

In 1953, Eugene Aserinsky and Nathaniel Kleitman at the University of Chicago were studying the sleep patterns of infants. They inadvertently discovered occasional periods of very quick movements of the eyes during sleep. Such **rapid eye movement**, or **REM,** only occurs during Stage 1 sleep. REM occurs in all Stage 1 sleep with the exception of the initial period of Stage 1 when the person is first falling asleep.

Much research has examined the characteristics of REM sleep. During this phase, there is a considerable amount of neural activity, similar to that in the waking state, in the cerebral cortex of the brain. The autonomic nervous system is activated. Such activation is indicated by irregular heartbeat, irregular breathing, and genital arousal. (See Figure 6–4.) These physiological correlates of REM sleep give the impression of "light sleep." At the same time, REM sleep is associated with considerable muscular relaxation. People in REM sleep are relatively insensitive to external stimulation; when they are awakened, they frequently report having been in "deep sleep."

Is REM sleep "light" or "deep"? The best available answer seems to be that it is both and neither; it is a unique neurophysiological stage that is qualitatively different from the other sleep stages. It is sometimes called **paradoxical sleep.** It occurs in humans of all ages and in other mammals ranging from the opossum (Snyder, 1965) to the monkey (Weitzmann, 1961). In adults, REM sleep occupies slightly more than 20 percent of total sleep time (about 50 percent in infants). It usually occurs in regular cycles of approximately 90 minutes each. (See Figure 6–5.) Successive REM periods become progressively longer. The final period lasts from 25 to 45 minutes. Of course, these are only average figures; they vary somewhat from individual to individual and from night to night.

FIGURE 6–4
REM sleep is paradoxical in that it consists of elements of both light and deep sleep. There is rapid eye movement, irregular heart beat and breathing, and genital arousal. But there is also skeletal muscle relaxation, and it is difficult to awaken the sleeper.

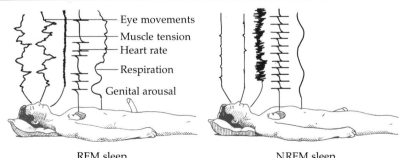

REM sleep   NREM sleep

Most dreaming occurs during REM sleep. This makes it important from a psychological viewpoint. When Aserinsky and Kleitman discovered REM, they believed that it might be related to dreaming. To test this, they woke up adults during REM and **nonrapid eye movement (NREM)** periods and asked whether they had been dreaming. Of the subjects awakened from REM sleep, 74 percent said that they had been dreaming. Only 7 percent of those awakened from NREM sleep said that they had been dreaming (Aserinsky & Kleitman, 1953). This finding was very important; for the first time, a reliable relationship had been found between an objective measure of a sleep variable (REM) and recall of dreams. The percentage of dream recall for REM and NREM has varied in different studies. But generally REM periods are associated with substantially more dreams than are NREM periods (Van de Castle, 1971).

If dreams actually occur during REM sleep, then the subjective duration of the dream should be proportional to the duration of REM observed before the subject wakes up. This hypothesis received strong support in studies by William Dement (1965).

In one series of trials, subjects were awakened either five minutes or fifteen minutes after the onset of REM and were asked to choose the correct interval on the basis of whatever dream material they recalled. A correct choice was made in 92 of 111 instances. In another series, high correlation coefficients were obtained between the number of words in the dream narratives and the number of minutes of . . . [REM] preceding the awakenings. (p. 172)

REM is an objective indication of a high probability that dreaming is occurring. Observation of REM also yields information about some general aspects of the content of dreams. We apparently scan our dream images in much the same way that we visually scan similar events when awake, and our eyes move accordingly. For example, more frequent eye movements are associated with reports of active dreams (e.g., running); less-frequent eye movements are related to reports of passive dreams (e.g., staring at a distant object) (Berger & Oswald, 1962; Dement & Wolpert, 1958). Further, when eyes move up and down, subjects tend

FIGURE 6–5
Sleep cycles as they relate to stages of sleep

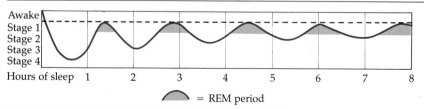

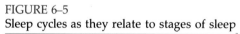

to report dreams of vertical movement, such as looking up and down a flight of stairs; when the eye movements go from side to side, dream reports tend to contain horizontal images, such as two people throwing a ball back and forth (Dement & Kleitman, 1957).

Freudian Dream Theory in the Light of Recent Evidence

To what degree does contemporary dream research support Freudian dream theory? To answer this question, we will look at the three functions of dreams that Freud identified and his view of the role of the manifest dream. Freud's dream theory concerns the psychological aspects of dreaming. As a result, modern physiological research is only indirectly related to it. Still, it is interesting to examine the correspondence between the two lines of inquiry.

Freud states that wish fulfillment is the basis for all dreams. However, it is quite possible that Freud actually meant that dreams portray unconscious impulses (Fisher & Greenberg, 1977). Freud (1953) said that "the reason why dreams are invariably wish fulfillments is that they are products of the . . . unconscious, whose activity knows no other aim than the fulfillment of wishes and which has at its command no other forces than wishful impulses" (p. 568). If we can assume that wish fulfillment and the expression of unconscious impulses are equivalent, then two of the three functions of dreaming Freud identifies—wish fulfillment and release of unconscious tension—also become one and the same.

Freud's hypothesis concerning the release of repressed psychic energy through dreaming can be extended: if this outlet is not provided, the individual should shows signs of abnormal behavior. Studies of dream deprivation have shed some light on this issue. The procedure involves depriving subjects in a sleep laboratory of REM sleep. They are awakened just as they are entering a REM period and then allowed to go back to sleep. Thus subjects are not deprived of all sleep. Two general findings have emerged from this research. First, there are large individual differences in responses to dream deprivation (Cartwright & Ratzel, 1972); any general statements about the effects of not dreaming must be viewed cautiously. Second, it appears that "the disturbance following dream deprivation is not of the extreme magnitude that the original investigators of this matter thought it to be [cf. Webb, 1975]. But there is a discernible average trend for signs of disturbance to a person following limitation of dreaming that fit in with the [Freudian] idea that dreams somehow serve as an outlet or channel for tension reduction" (Fisher & Greenberg, 1977, p. 61).

Contemporary physiological research generally does not support Freud's third function of dreaming—sleep preservation. As we have seen, dreaming occurs at regular intervals. It is therefore unlikely to be caused by threatening impulses that occur at irregular times. Further, more than half of all REM periods, when dreaming is known to occur, include short periods of wakefulness (Dement, 1964). The only way REM periods preserve sleep is that people are relatively insensitive to external stimulation during REM periods.

The final aspect of Freud's dream theory that we will evaluate is the insignificant role he gives manifest content. Freud considers manifest content important only insofar as it results in latent content. Contemporary psychoanalytic researchers do not deny the significance of the latent content. But they have found manifest content itself to be rich with psychological meaning. Dream reports clearly indicate that people tend to dream about matters that concern them. Consider just a few examples from a wide array of findings (reviewed by Fisher and Greenberg [1977, pp. 30–46]).

> Pregnant women are significantly more likely than other women to report dreams involving babies or children.
>
> Men are more likely than women to dream about aggression.
>
> Women are more likely to have dreams relating to sex or hostility during their menstrual periods than at other times.
>
> Older people (over 65) are more likely than younger individuals to report dreams involving loss of resources and strength or death-related topics.

Dreaming as Problem Solving

Some post-Freudian analysts think that dreaming can serve the important ego functions of solving problems, particularly interpersonal problems, and planning future actions (e.g., Adler, 1973; Erikson, 1954; French & Fromm, 1964). For example, dreaming may "integrate current stressful experiences with similar experiences from the past, thus enabling the individual to use . . . basic coping mechanisms (defenses) to deal with the current stressful situation" (Grieser, Greenberg, & Harrison, 1972, p. 281).

This idea was tested in an experiment. College students were asked to solve anagrams (forming words out of other words) (Grieser et al., 1972). The experimenters told the students which anagrams they had solved and which they had failed to solve. Failure was made ego threatening by telling the subjects the anagrams were a test of intelligence in which the average college student did quite well. It was predicted that subjects who were permitted to dream following the task would remember the failed anagrams better than subjects who were prevented from dreaming. This prediction follows from the view that dreaming is a period in which we cope with stressful situations, such as failure. Presumably, coping with failure makes the failure less ego threatening. This reduces the need to repress the events leading to the failure (the unsolved anagrams) and makes it more likely that the events will be remembered.

Subjects who were awakened during NREM periods recalled significantly more failed anagrams. This group presumably was able to dream during REM sleep. Subjects who were awakened during REM periods were presumably not able to dream. They recalled fewer anagrams. These results support the view that dreams have an adaptive function that enables the dreamer to cope with ego-threatening material.

PROJECTIVE TECHNIQUES

Dream analysis is one method of indirect personality assessment. The dream serves as a stimulus with which the subject associates and to which the analyst relates events from the subject's life. In this sense, dream analysis can be viewed as a projective technique. These techniques are another major method of indirect personality assessment used in the psychoanalytic strategy to uncover unconscious motives, ideas, and feelings.

The Nature of Projective Techniques

Projective techniques are based on the **projective hypothesis:** when individuals must impose meaning or order on an ambiguous stimulus, their responses will project or reflect their feelings, attitudes, desires, and needs. (This process has some obvious parallels with projection as an ego-defense mechanism.) Some projective techniques appear similar to a *test*. But *technique* or *method* is a more accurate term; most projective techniques do not meet the generally accepted technical psychometric criteria for tests (e.g., being standardized and having norms).

There is a variety of existing projective techniques; they involve a wide range of stimulus materials and responses from subjects. The most common types of responses are listed below.

1. *Association*, such as to inkblots or words.
2. *Construction* of stories about pictures that are open to a variety of interpretations (e.g., the Thematic Apperception Test).
3. *Completion* of sentences (e.g., "I often feel. . . .") or stories.
4. *Expression* as in drawings (e.g., Draw-a-Person Test) or by acting out a loosely specified role (e.g., in psychodrama).

Different techniques involve a diversity of stimuli and responses. However, projective techniques share five important characteristics.

1. The stimulus, be it an inkblot, a picture, or the first part of a sentence, is relatively unstructured and ambiguous. This forces the subject to impose order or structure.

2. The subject is usually not told the purpose of the test and how responses will be scored or interpreted.

3. The subject is told that there are no correct answers.

4. Each response is assumed to reveal something valid and significant about the subject's personality.

5. Scoring and interpretation are generally lengthy, relatively subjective procedures.

We will first describe the most common projective technique, Rorschach inkblots, and then contrast it with the Holtzman Inkblot Technique. Another projective technique, the Thematic Apperception Test, is discussed in Chapter 11.

The Rorschach Inkblots

The use of inkblots to reveal something about an individual, such as imagination, was not a new idea when Hermann Rorschach began his experiments in the early part of the twentieth century. But Rorschach, a Swiss psychiatrist, was the first to systematically use a standard set of inkblots to assess personality. In 1921 Rorschach published the results of his work. His monograph, *Psychodiagnostik*, bore the informative subtitle *Methodology and Results of a Perceptual-Diagnostic Experiment (Interpretation of Accidental Forms)*. A year later Rorschach died; it was left to others to elaborate on the basic procedures he had outlined.

Description of the Inkblots

There are ten nearly symmetrical Rorschach inkblots; five have some color and five are black and white. The blots are printed on white cardboard (about 7 × 10 inches). Figure 6–6 shows inkblots similar to the Rorschach

FIGURE 6–6
Inkblots similar to those employed by Rorschach

Source: From *Personality Measurement: An Introduction* by B. Kleinmuntz, 1967, Chicago, Ill.: Dorsey Press.

inkblots. The blots were originally made by spilling ink on a piece of paper and then folding the paper in half.

Administration

The Rorschach inkblot technique, or *the Rorschach* as it is commonly called, is administered individually. Administration involves two phases. The first is *performance proper*. It begins with simple instructions from the examiner: "I am going to show you a number of inkblots, and I want you to tell me what you see in each of them." The examiner records exactly what the subject says about each blot (e.g., "That reminds me of a rabbit running"). The examiner responds to the subject's questions (e.g., the subject asks "Do you want to know only one thing that I see?") so that the decision is left to the subject (e.g., the examiner answers "That's up to you").

When the subject has responded to all ten inkblots, the second phase begins. This is the *inquiry*. Starting with the first card, the examiner reminds the subject of each response made. The examiner also asks where the response was on the inkblot (e.g., "Where did you see a rabbit running?") and what determined the response (e.g., "What about the inkblot made it look like a rabbit running?").

Scoring and Interpretation

There are a number of different systems for scoring and interpreting Rorschach responses. In one system, each response is scored for five characteristics that focus on how the response was generated rather than what the response is (Klopfer & Davidson, 1962):

The Rorschach inkblots are the most frequently used projective technique. This subject is showing the examiner where on the inkblot she saw a particular concept. *Photo by Christopher O'Keefe and Michael D. Spiegler*

1. *Location*—where on the card the concept was seen.
2. *Determinant*—the qualities of the blot that led to the formation of the concept (e.g., shape, color, apparent movement).
3. *Popularity-originality*—the frequency with which particular responses are given by subjects in general.
4. *Content*—the subject matter of the concept.
5. *Form-level*—how accurately the concept is seen and how closely the concept fits the blot.

Interpretation is subjective. It requires extensive knowledge of underlying personality theory, usually psychoanalytic. The interpreter looks for patterns of responses or consistent themes rather than interpreting single responses. Table 6–2 presents examples of possible interpretations of re-

TABLE 6–2
Examples of scoring and interpretation of the Rorschach inkblots

Scoring Characteristic	Examples of Scoring Category	Sample Responses	Examples of Interpretations*
Location	Whole	Entire blot used for concept	Ability to organize and integrate material
	Small usual detail	Small part which is easily marked off from the rest of the blot	Need to be exact and accurate
Determinant	Form	"The outline looks like a bear"	Degree of emotional control
	Movement	"A flying hawk"	Level of ego functioning
Popularity-originality	Popular	Response which many people give	Need to be conventional
	Original	Response which few people give and which fits blot well	Superior intelligence
Content	Animal figures	"Looks like a house cat"	Passivity and dependence
	Human figures	"It's a man or a woman"	Problem with sexual identity
Form-level	High form-level	Concept fits blot well	High intellectual functioning
	Low form-level	Concept is a poor match to blot	Contact with reality tenuous

*Interpretations would be made only if the type of response occurred a number of times (i.e., not just once). See text for further precautions regarding interpretations of Rorschach responses.

sponses. To validate the interpretations, they are often compared with interpretations derived using other assessment procedures.

The Holtzman Inkblot Technique

Projective techniques do not adhere to the same psychometric standards as other personality assessment methods. They have been criticized on this account. Wayne Holtzman and his associates (Holtzman, Thorpe, Swartz, & Herron, 1961) were aware of this limitation. As a result, they developed "a completely new approach to inkblot testing, one which is designed from its inception to meet adequate standards of measurement while preserving the uniquely valuable projective quality of the Rorschach" (p. 10). They tested a large number of inkblots with samples of normal college students and psychiatric patients. Inkblots were then evaluated and selected on the basis of two additional criteria. These were: (1) the ability of an inkblot to reliably differentiate between the normal and abnormal samples, and (2) maximum **interrater reliability** (agreement among scorers) on the categories for which the inkblots were being scored.

Two equivalent sets of 45 inkblots were eventually selected. With equivalent sets of inkblots, it is possible to use the technique twice with the same subjects. This might be done before and after psychotherapy. Because there are two sets, the second responses are not "contaminated" by previous exposure to the same set of inkblots. **Retest reliability** measures the stability of a test over time. This can be assessed with the Holtzman inkblots because equivalent sets exist.

Subjects are asked to give *one* response to each of the 45 inkblots. The number of responses is therefore constant for all subjects. As a result, it is easier to compare subjects and to develop norms. Each response is scored for 22 variables. These include all the variables for which the Rorschach is scored and other variables like anxiety and hostility.

PSYCHOANALYTIC PSYCHOTHERAPY

Freud's practice of psychotherapy served a dual function. In addition to helping his patients, Freud's clinical cases provided both the data and the evidence for his theory of personality. Based on what he learned from his patients, Freud formulated his theory. He then gathered support for the theory from further clinical observations. The result is psychoanalytic personality theory and psychoanalytic psychotherapy. In the following discussion, the term *psychoanalysis* refers to therapy (as opposed to personality theory).

The Origin of Psychoanalysis

Most of Freud's patients suffered from *hysteria*. This is called *conversion disorder* today. It is characterized by a physical ailment, like paralysis of the legs, with no physiological cause. Hysteria was quite common at the end of the nineteenth century (more so than now). However, physicians had little success treating it. For example, Jean Charcot was a Parisian neurologist with whom Freud studied for a year. Charcot hypnotized his hysteric patients and then directly told them to renounce their symptoms. This hypnotic suggestion was generally effective as long as the patient remained hypnotized. But when the patient awoke, the symptoms almost always returned.

Shortly after studying with Charcot, Freud opened his private medical practice in Vienna and became associated with Josef Breuer, a prominent Viennese physician. Breuer also used hypnosis in treating hysteria. But Breuer did not directly will a patient's symptoms away. Instead, he asked his hypnotized patient to vividly recall the traumatic experiences that had first led to the hysterical symptoms. The patient's reenactment of the trauma that presumably produced the hysteria was accompanied by a great emotional release, which seemingly led to a cure. Breuer's therapy was called **hypnocatharsis** [hip-no-ka-THAR-sis]. (*Catharsis* is the Greek word for purification.) In contrast to Charcot, Breuer obtained changes that lasted after the patient awakened.

Breuer and Freud (1955) concluded that hysterical symptoms come from painful memories and emotions that have been repressed. This explains why the patient's symptoms go away when the repressed memories and associated painful emotions are expressed. Freud later generalized the theory to all neuroses. **Neuroses** (plural of *neurosis*) are psychological disorders characterized by anxiety with which the person has difficulty coping and by abnormal behavior, such as phobias, obsessions, and, as in hysteria, physical complaints. Freud came to believe that neuroses always reflect unresolved repressed conflicts. These must be resolved for the neuroses to be fully cured. If the symptoms go away but the conflict is not resolved, a new symptom will appear. This process is called **symptom substitution.**

The Process of Psychoanalysis

Psychoanalysis is meant to bring unconscious wishes, thoughts, and emotions and the conflicts that result from them into consciousness. The process involves four fundamental tasks: *free association, interpretation, overcoming resistances,* and *insight.* (See Figure 6–7.) What the patient says, especially free associations, is the material the analyst interprets. The patient is expected to gain insights about the causes of her or his behavior and problems from these interpretations. This is possible when various resistances (behaviors that impede therapy) to such insights (self-knowledge) are overcome.

Free Association

Initially Freud hypnotized his patients to help them recall events that might be related to the onset of their illnesses. Early in his practice, however, Freud began to urge nonhypnotized patients to try to recall past events that were repressed. He found that, given sufficient freedom, patients wandered in their thoughts and recollections; this resulted in a superior understanding of the patients' unconscious conflicts. This observation led Freud to the fundamental technique of psychoanalysis, free association.

In **free association,** the patient says whatever comes to mind regardless of social convention, logic and order, seeming importance, or feelings of embarrassment. To make free association easier, Freud had the patient lie down on a couch. (See Figure 6–8.) He sat behind the couch, out of the patient's view. The reclining position is reminiscent of sleep. It supposedly brings a person closer to unconscious primary processes and stimulates fantasy and memory. The therapist is out of sight. So the patient is not constantly reminded of the therapist's presence, which makes free association easier. (But free association is not easy. You can demonstrate this for yourself by trying to tell a friend or even just a tape recorder everything and anything that you think of over the course of a five to ten minute period.)

Interpretation

Free association is the initial step in penetrating the unconscious, but it is not sufficient. Unconscious material becomes conscious only in disguised or symbolic form during free association, just as it does in dreams. The analyst must translate the symbolism and offer **interpretations** of the underlying unconscious meaning. Interpretations are also made of dreams,

FIGURE 6–7
Steps in the process of psychoanalytic psychotherapy

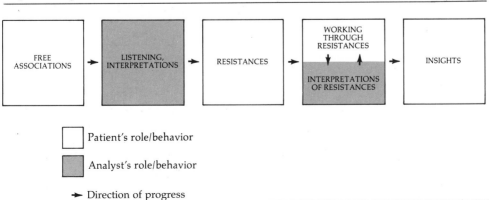

symptoms, past experiences, current behavior in and out of therapy, and the patient's relationship with the analyst. Interpretations help patients understand how their neurotic behavior developed by reconstructing childhood experiences that led to the conflict producing the neurosis. Freud likens this process to the excavation and reconstruction of an archaeological ruin. (Freud was fascinated by archaeology, as you might guess from the pictures in his consulting room seen in Figure 6–8.)

Insight

From the analyst's interpretations, the patient gains insight into the nature and origin of the neurosis. **Insight** is more than an intellectual under-

FIGURE 6–8
Freud's consulting room in Vienna, with his chair and patient's couch. Truly it may be said psychoanalysis was born here.

Edmund Engelman

standing. It is an *emotional* experience and acceptance of parts of the personality that were previously unconscious. The interpretation leading to an insight must seem right to the patient. Interpretations cannot be forced on a patient. It is important that the analyst does not advance an interpretation until the patient is "ready" to hear it. The patient must often work through inner resistances to be able to accept particular insights. This sort of understanding and acceptance develops gradually and often painstakingly.

Resistance

Freud's patients sought treatment for their neuroses. But they often seemed to resist being cured. **Resistance** is any impediment to successful treatment. It can be conscious or unconscious (Strean, 1985). Conscious resistance occurs when the patient is aware of impeding the progress of analysis. For example, a patient may have a disturbing dream and decide not to tell the analyst about it. Or a patient might deliberately miss a therapy session. In unconscious resistance, the patient is not aware of "fighting" the treatment. Examples include a patient's ego defense mechanisms preventing him or her from describing the disturbing dream or forgetting (unconsciously) a therapy session. Unconscious resistance is more difficult to overcome than conscious resistance. It is also more significant because it indicates the patient's unconscious strivings. In other words, unconscious resistance is another clue helping the analyst understand the patient.

Transference. The patient's inappropriate feelings toward the analyst are called **transference;** specifically, the feelings are *distorted displacements* from significant figures in the patient's life (usually in the past). For example, patients may act *as if* the analyst were their father or mother. Transference can be positive (e.g., love, respect, and admiration) or negative (e.g., hatred, jealousy, and disgust). Transference is the most important form of unconscious resistance.

Transference is an impediment to psychoanalysis because it is an inappropriate reaction. For instance, the analyst is not the patient's father. But a male patient who had a strict father may respond to the analyst's interpretations as if they were criticisms; this makes it more difficult for the patient to accept interpretations. Analysts can use such inappropriate behavior to point out to patients the nature of the patients' relationships to significant people in their lives. The interpretation of transference is an integral part of psychoanalysis. It is a form of resistance that must be overcome. It is also a valuable source of information about the patient's significant interpersonal relationships. Indeed, Freud holds that the patient has to experience transference toward the analyst and has to work through it if psychoanalysis is to be successful.

Psychoanalysts may also experience distorted displacements toward their patients. This is called **countertransference**. Not surprisingly, it may adversely affect the critical patient-analyst relationship (e.g., by reducing the analyst's objectivity). Two major controls have been established to deal with countertransference. First, psychoanalysts themselves must undergo psychoanalysis as part of their training. Having insight into their own unconscious processes and conflicts helps analysts recognize and deal with countertransference. Second, analysts periodically review their cases with a supervising analyst who may notice countertransference that the analyst missed and help the analyst manage it.

The Psychoanalytic Session

Freud saw his patients for 55-minute sessions five or six times a week. He generally thought that successful treatment required between six months and three years. If you were to observe a session of psychoanalysis you would, at the very least, see that the patient does most of the talking while the analyst listens and occasionally comments on what the patient says. That process does not sound extraordinary to us today; indeed, it is the basis of many verbal psychotherapies. When Freud developed this "talking cure," however, the idea of a physician *listening* to a patient was revolutionary. The existing model of doctor-patient interaction was that the doctor talked, prescribing treatment, and the patient listened. Freud reversed the roles and had the physician act as a compassionate but neutral observer.

At the beginning of the twentieth century, psychological problems were treated almost exclusively by physicians who usually specialized in neurology (as Freud did); psychiatry did not exist as a specialty. Freud believed that psychoanalysts need not have medical training. (Anna Freud, for one, did not.) Nonetheless, most early analysts were physicians. A majority of present-day analysts are physicians trained in the treatment of psychopathology (psychiatrists).

Post-Freudian Modifications of Psychoanalytic Psychotherapy

Post-Freudian psychoanalysts have made changes in psychoanalytic psychotherapy. These changes are consistent with post-Freudian modifications in personality theory. There are many forms of post-Freudian therapy. But it is possible to abstract some overall themes. In general, post-Freudian analysis is more *flexible* and *broader* than Freudian analysis.

In post-Freudian therapy the patient's present is considered as significant as his or her past. Post-Freudians consider it important to explore the ways the patient is functioning effectively as well as to analyze problem behaviors that bring the patient to therapy. The individual's strengths are used to devise a plan of therapy. The patient's object (interpersonal) relations are emphasized. Situational stresses are considered along with intrapsychic conflicts.

Interaction between therapist and patient is less formal and restrictive in post-Freudian analysis. The patient usually sits facing the therapist. The emphasis in therapy can be supportive as well as uncovering. The patient-therapist relationship is considered important independent of, but not excluding, transference. Post-Freudian analysts specifically attempt to foster a **therapeutic alliance**. This is a stable, cooperative relationship between patient and therapist. It is considered a necessary (but not sufficient) condition for effective therapy (Greenson, 1965, 1967; Hartley & Strupp, 1983; Zetzel, 1956). Fostering a therapeutic alliance is one example of the more active role of post-Freudian analysts. They tend to talk more and to be more directive. This includes giving advice to their patients, which Freudian analysts usually do not do.

There are still other ways that post-Freudian approaches to therapy are more flexible. The therapy is often individualized and less likely to follow standard procedures that guide the treatment of all patients. In Freudian analysis certain elements (e.g., experiencing and successfully working through transference) are assumed to be essential. Post-Freudian interpretations are likely to be psychosocial as well as psychosexual, and more concrete and practical and less abstract and theoretical. This contrasts with Freudian interpretations. Post-Freudian therapy can be briefer than Freudian psychoanalysis; it involves fewer sessions per week and/or fewer total sessions.

A Glimpse at a Post-Freudian Psychoanalytic Therapy Session

The following brief excerpt from a psychoanalytic session illustrates the type of verbal interchange that takes place. The patient is a woman in her mid-thirties, and the therapy is post-Freudian.

Patient (P): I feel scattered apart as it is. . . . Well, I don't know what to say about it really. (19-second pause)

P: Well, I just feel scattered. If I lost the last bit of control that I have, I might not stay together. (12-second pause)

P: It's true, also, that I have a vivid imagination, and most likely those things would not happen. (30-second pause)

P: You know sometimes, like even right now, I feel as though there is nothing for me to say. (11-second pause)

P: That's really honest. I just, um . . . I feel in order to convey messages to someone else you have to say words, and sometimes I am at a loss. (9-second pause)

P: Maybe we should play charades (laughs). You might get the idea. (15-second pause)

Analyst (A): You mean you know what kind of charade you would play?

P: Oh, no. I really don't. Yeah, sure. I might pick up my purse and throw it at you.

A: Hmm-mm.

P: Uh, I might pretend to scream a little bit, just to loosen things up. Maybe a dance. This is charming, isn't it? I hope you have a good imagination too. No, I hope you don't. And . . . I might be, I don't know . . . any kind of thing will come to my mind. I feel as though I have some pretty wild feelings in me, and pretty wild thoughts and . . . it wouldn't be civilized to let go.

A: Well, you recognize, I'm sure, I'm not asking you to do them.

P: No, I know you're not.

A: Neither am I asking you to do something that I don't think you can do. I think you can. And my point is that as a result you will not have less control, but more control. More natural control, not unnatural control.

P: And you feel that I have unnatural control?

A: You mean there is some doubt?

P: No. I just wanted you to say it.

Perhaps the most striking thing about this excerpt is how unstriking it is. The patient says nothing particularly extraordinary and the therapist makes no monumental interpretations that result in the patient making startling revelations about herself. Contrary to popular accounts of psychoanalysis in books and movies, uncovering the roots of the patient's problems is a long, slow process. Major breakthroughs come infrequently. The excerpt, as mundane as it might appear, is typical. The patient does most of the talking, much of which is more or less free association. There are a number of instances where she has trouble staying with her flow of thoughts. These are examples of resistance. After listening to the patient, the analyst comments on (interprets) what the patient said. From the comments, the patient gains some insight about her feelings. She is also reassured by the analyst's validating her thoughts. That is an example of the therapeutic alliance. The excerpt contains no clear indication of transference.

SUMMARY

1. Freud considers dreams to be the most revealing source of information about personality. He believes that the manifest content—what we recall of the dream—is determined by a latent content that involves unconscious desires and conflicts.

2. Socially unacceptable latent content is transformed into acceptable manifest content through dream work, including condensation, displacement, visual representation, and secondary revision. Through symbolism, latent content becomes manifest content in disguised and nonthreatening forms. Freud emphasizes sexual symbolism in dreams.

3. In Freudian dream interpretation, the manifest dream as well as the patient's free associations to it are analyzed. The psychoanalyst interprets both of these sources based on the principles of dream work and symbolism.

4. Freud posits three functions of dreaming: wish fulfillment, tension release, and sleep maintenance.

5. The physiology of sleep and dreaming has been studied in the laboratory by measuring brain waves (EEG) and eye movements. Four basic sleep stages have been identified. Most dreaming occurs in rapid eye movement (REM) sleep. REM sleep is paradoxical; the person is very relaxed as in deep sleep yet is mentally active as in light sleep. The physiology of dreaming provides some indirect support for Freud's dream theory.

6. Post-Freudians propose that dreaming serves other functions than those proposed by Freud, including problem solving and planning future actions.

7. Projective techniques present an ambiguous stimulus on which the subject must impose order or meaning; it is assumed that these projections are based on the subject's unconscious feelings, thoughts, and wishes. Projective techniques involve association (e.g., to words), construction (e.g., of stories), completion (e.g., of sentences), and expression (e.g., through drawing).

8. The Rorschach inkblots are the most common projective technique. The Holtzman inkblots provide a more standardized and somewhat more objective alternative.

9. In Freudian psychoanalytic psychotherapy the patient talks about his or her problems and is encouraged to free associate about them. The psychoanalyst makes interpretations of what the patient reveals, and the patient gains emotional and intellectual insight into the causes of the problems. Insight is possible only when the patient has worked through various resistances, especially transference, in which patients displace feelings about significant people in their lives onto the analyst.

10. Post-Freudian therapy places greater emphasis on the present and the therapeutic alliance between the patient and therapist. Besides making interpretations, post-Freudian analysts provide concrete suggestions for action. Post-Freudian analysis is often briefer than Freudian analysis (which tends to be quite lengthy).

CHAPTER 7

LIABILITIES

OVERVIEW

This is the first of four liabilities chapters that appear at the end of the presentation of each personality strategy. Each strategy has both its strengths and weaknesses. In the preceding chapters, we have tried to present the substance and flavor of the psychoanalytic strategy primarily in terms of its strengths. In this chapter we discuss several of its major weaknesses. Some may have already occurred to you. Bear in mind that the criticisms we will discuss have been made mainly by proponents of other strategies.

PSYCHOANALYTIC CONCLUSIONS ARE BASED ON LOGICAL FALLACIES

Psychoanalysts often commit three logical errors in presenting evidence for their theory. First, they often *do not distinguish between observation and inference*. The Oedipus complex is a prime example. Freud observed that at around age four, boys are affectionate toward and seek the attention of their mothers; to some degree, they also avoid their fathers. To explain these *observations*, Freud conjectures that the boy's feelings for his mother are due to sexual desires; his feelings for his father are related to the rivalry due to this sexual attachment and the implicit threat of castration. This *inference* has the status of a hypothesis. It is one alternative explanation, and nothing more. Thus, to say that four-year-old boys experience an Oedipus complex is, in effect, *replacing the observation with the inference*. It would be a different matter to say that four-year-olds show behavior consistent with the Oedipus complex. The fallacy is presenting inferences as observations when they represent only one possible explanation. This is an especially acute problem because nonpsychoanalytic theories can sometimes provide at least as good, and often better, explanations of the observed facts (e.g., Sears, 1943).

Second, psychoanalysts often *confuse correlation and causation*. For instance, it is legitimate to report that during the first year of life children engage in many behaviors involving the mouth (e.g., eating, sucking, crying); they are also dependent on others for most of their needs. Oral behavior and dependency occur together. Therefore they are *correlated*. However, based on this relationship, it is not legitimate to conclude that dependency is *caused by* orality. It is entirely possible that a third variable accounts for both dependency and orality. (See Chapter 2 for a discussion of correlation and causation.)

Psychoanalysts often use analogies to describe theoretical principles (e.g., troops left in battle, dammed-up libido). Herein lies a third logical error. *Analogy is not proof.* An analogy may help to describe a new or complex concept. But it cannot be considered verification of the concept. However, this is frequently done in psychoanalytic writing. It is true that military troops may be permanently lost for future battles in a difficult skirmish. This fact, however, does not in any way validate the claim that libido is fixated at a stage in which the child had trouble resolving the relevant conflict.

PSYCHOANALYTIC CASE STUDIES ARE UNDULY BIASED

Case studies are the main method of personality research in the psychoanalytic strategy. These studies are usually of patients undergoing psychoanalysis. The limitations of the case-study method were discussed in Chapter 2; here, some specific problems with psychoanalytic case studies will be addressed.

The psychoanalytic session is private. Yet it is during these sessions that the data for case studies are gathered. This raises some serious potential problems.

> First, there is the analyst's influence upon the patient's own statements, which remains a completely unassessable factor since verbatim records are not available. [One of the earliest criticisms of Freud's work was that the confessions of patients may have been responses to suggestions made by the analyst rather than reflections of the patient's private experiences.] Second, there is the selective nature of the analyst's recollections of the case and the possibility of . . . [the analyst's] reconstructing earlier materials in the light of later observations. Thus, the psychoanalyst's theoretical commitment can influence both the patient's utterances themselves and the manner in which they are organized, written up, and interpreted. (Sherwood, 1969, p. 71)

There is some evidence to suggest that analytically-oriented therapists may be more likely to succumb to observer bias than therapists of other persuasions (Langer & Abelson, 1974; Weiss, 1972). Langer and Abelson (1974) conducted an experiment involving psychoanalysts and behavioral therapists. Both groups interviewed people who were supposedly "patients" or "job applicants." The analysts were significantly more likely to vary their clinical observations based on the labels alone. They tended to find the "patients" more disturbed than the "job applicants."

The patient can also directly contribute to the distortion of psychoanalytic case material. Distortion may be produced by forgetting, secondary revision, condensation, and similar mental processes. The patient may consciously or unconsciously lie. Perhaps he or she does this to avoid particularly threatening thoughts. (The psychoanalyst's reply is that distortion is less of a problem in the psychoanalytic strategy than in other personality strategies.) This is because a basic assumption of psychoanalysis is that all behavior is determined and has meaning. Theoretically, then, it should be possible to uncover the truth in whatever the patient reports. Practically, however, this may not be done. Instead, the data may be seriously misinterpreted. Further, psychoanalysts rarely verify information gathered in psychoanalysis, such as by checking with parents about childhood recollections.

Psychoanalytic evidence is also biased in the sense that it is based on a small, atypical sample—that is, it comes from those undergoing psychoanalysis. A good deal of Freud's original theory is based on his own self-analysis. In all of his writings, Freud describes only twelve cases in detail. Psychoanalytic therapy is lengthy and time-consuming. As a result, each analyst can, in an entire career, see only a relatively small number of individuals. But size alone does not determine the suitability of a sample. Whether the sample is representative of the population to which generalization will be made is the critical criterion. Freud considers very few people suitable for analysis. Among Freud's requirements are: maturity, courage, education, and good character. He also requires the intellectual ability to understand and assimilate the complexities of their neuroses as revealed in analysis (Roazen, 1975, p. 137). Clearly, Freud's sample was severely restricted. Therefore, it is difficult to justify his making generalizations to other groups of people, including the vast majority of human beings.

Contemporary psychoanalytic cases present the same problem. The samples from which generalizations about human personality are made are not representative. Today, patients in psychoanalysis are typically young or middle-aged white adults; they are above average in intelligence, highly articulate, and have relatively high incomes. (Psychoanalysis can easily cost more than $15,000 per year.) They are typically Jewish or Protestant, almost never Catholic. They are also unusually psychologically minded. In a study of one hundred people applying for analysis, fully half were themselves workers in mental-health fields (Knapp, Levin, McCarter, Wermer, & Zetzel, 1960). Further, observation of this highly restricted sample is very limited. The subjects are observed in a psychoanalyst's office, sometimes stretched out on a couch, free associating about their dreams and early childhood memories for 50 minutes. How typical is that of human behavior?

Reliability of interpretations of data from psychoanalytic case studies is another problem. For instance, different analysts looking at the same data should reach similar interpretations. As it turns out, such agreement is rare. The same dream report is likely to be interpreted in different ways by independent, highly competent psychoanalysts (e.g., Lorand, 1946; Schafer, 1950). Psychoanalytic interpretations have low reliability partially because the data and interpretations are qualitative. If these were quantified, even in the basic sense of categorizing, greater agreement might be possible.

PSYCHOANALYTIC CONCEPTS ARE POORLY DEFINED

Many psychoanalytic concepts are poorly defined. They tend to be vague, nonspecific, and ambiguous. We need go no farther than the pivotal concept of the unconscious. Freud (1965) defines this as any mental event that we must assume exists but of which we have no knowledge. This definition tells us nothing. Some psychoanalytic concepts are defined more explicitly. But they still do not have guidelines that make it possible to tell when the phenomena occur. Reaction formation is one example. When does affection reflect underlying hate as opposed to love, for instance?

The vagueness of psychoanalytic terms is partly due to literary style. Most psychoanalytic cases are written in narrative form, much like stories. This style easily lends itself to the use of metaphor. In fact, psychoanalytic theory can be interpreted on at least two levels, the literal and the metaphorical. Consider Freud's description of the Oedipus complex. In his description, Freud apparently literally meant that every four-year-old boy wants to have sex with his mother. Many post-Freudians, however, take the Oedipal situation as metaphorical. They consider it an analogy to a complex rivalry between children and their parents (Mullahy, 1948).

The imprecise definitions characteristic of psychoanalytic theory make it difficult to measure important concepts. Further, some psychoanalytic concepts are said to occur in varying amounts. Fixated or cathected libido are examples. But these concepts are not actually quantified. As a result, it is not possible to answer critical questions such as: How much libido must be invested at the oral stage for a person to become an oral character? How much threat of castration must children experience to repress sexual desires for their opposite-sexed parent?

Psychoanalytic researchers have tried to make "elusive" concepts operational. This is to their credit. However, the task is extremely difficult. Vague terminology often results from these attempts, making it difficult to develop reliable and valid research definitions. In turn, this severely limits the extent that psychoanalytic theory can be tested objectively.

Reliable definitions are objective and unambiguous so that a number of observers would generally agree whether the phenomena had or had not occurred. Additionally, valid definitions must be closely related to the theoretical concept so that research findings will have a bearing on the theory. In practice, it is often difficult to meet both requirements with psychoanalytic concepts. The following study of penis envy illustrates the problem.

The study tested the straightforward prediction that more women than men would exhibit penis envy. Johnson (1966) defined penis envy as "keeping a borrowed pencil" (a phallic symbol). Johnson did find that significantly more women than men in the study failed to return pencils that had been loaned to them. "Keeping a borrowed pencil" is an objective and reliable measure; the researcher has only to count the number of pencils loaned to each sex and the number returned by each sex. It could be argued, however, that pencil hoarding is not a *valid* measure of penis envy. In other words, it is too remote from the theoretical concept of penis envy. Johnson's study shows how a reliable measure may not be a valid measure. It cannot be considered a serious test of the concept of penis envy.

Often measures that are closer to the theoretical concepts are highly subjective (e.g., rating symbolism in dreams or Rorschach responses). In these cases, interrater reliability tends to be low (Kline, 1972). Reliability is a prerequisite for validity. As a result, such measures are also not valid.

PSYCHOANALYTIC THEORY IS UNTESTABLE

Many aspects of psychoanalytic theory cannot be tested. We have already discussed the problems of providing adequate research definitions for many psychoanalytic concepts. This makes empirical testing of concepts difficult and requires ingenuity from researchers (cf. Masling, 1983, 1985a).

There is another, more serious impediment to testing some parts of psychoanalytic theory. A number of the theoretical propositions cannot be proved false (Popper, 1963). As a result, psychoanalysis has been called a "rubber-sheet theory"; it can be stretched to cover any outcome. Suppose we investigate the hypothesis that people fixated at the oral stage are dependent in their relationships. The results of the study may show that oral characters are dependent. Then the hypothesis is obviously supported. But suppose the study showed that oral characters are independent. In this case, the hypothesis would still be supported. Independence can be a defense—a reaction formation—against dependence. Finally, oral characters might be found to be both dependent and independent. The hypothesis is still supported, because the behavior is a compromise between the drive and its defense.

Similarly, Freud postulates that all dreams fulfill a hidden wish. Yet dreams are often unpleasant and disturbing. It is difficult to understand how such dreams can be wish fulfilling. Freud (1961a) explains that these are counterwish dreams. At the same time, they are wish fulfillments because they satisfy the person's masochism. This type of reasoning led an early critic to comment that psychoanalysis "involves so many arbitrary interpretations that it is impossible to speak of proof in any strict sense of the term" (Moll, 1912, p. 190).

Present-day psychoanalytic researchers are no less guilty of such logically indefensible practices. For example, Cooperman and Child (1971) could not reproduce findings of an earlier laboratory study of characteristics of oral and anal types. Yet they concluded: "Our finding . . . though *opposite* in direction to the findings of earlier studies, seems to be what the theory used in those studies would predict" (p. 59; italics added).

CLASSICAL PSYCHOANALYSIS IS SEX BIASED

Freud's theory is, without question, sex biased. This is also true of many traditional psychoanalysts. The theories are based on males and then extended to females. For example, Freud attempts to make the Electra complex fit the model of the Oedipus complex. The fit is none too snug. Similarly, Freud's concept of castration anxiety fits well with the notion that the little boy wants to have sex with his mother. What punishment would better fit the crime? Freud considers penis envy the female counterpart of castration anxiety. But penis envy is not directly parallel. Neither does it serve the same purpose as castration anxiety, namely, to prevent incest. This part of Freud's theory is poorly formulated because he used male personality development as the basis for female development. It is curious that Freud wasn't better at theorizing about females, since most of his early patients were women. It may be that Freud actually based much of his theory on his own self-analysis.

Freud uses male personality as a prototype. He also considers it the ideal. Quite bluntly, in Freud's view, women are inferior to men. The part of their personalities that is different from men's comes from defending against and overcompensating for their inferiority. Consider three of Freud's ideas about female sexuality and personality.

1. *Females are castrated.* Obviously this assumes that women once had a penis, which implies the superiority of the male sexual anatomy. In Freud's (1964b) words: "Her self-love is mortified by the comparison with the boy's far superior equipment" (p. 126). There is no evidence that women feel inferior because they have a vagina rather than a penis.

2. *Females have more difficulty establishing a sex role than males.* Freud derives this proposition from the view that the girl has a more complex Oedipal situation. Though the mother is the first object of love for

both sexes, the girl must switch her love to her father, whereas the boy continues with his mother as his primary love object. The additional step for the girl could potentially make her sex-role identification more troublesome. "But the empirical literature suggests that, if anything, the female has less difficulty than the male in the process of evolving a sex role" (Fisher & Greenberg, 1977, p. 220).

3. *Vaginal orgasm indicates sexual maturity.* Freud believes that a woman needs to relinquish her desire for a penis (penis envy) to successfully resolve her Electra complex and to function as a mature adult. According to Freud, the mature woman derives sexual pleasure primarily from penile stimulation of the vagina rather than the clitoris. Freud views the clitoris as a woman's penis. Therefore, "no longer deriving sexual pleasure from clitoral stimulation" means relinquishing penis envy. Although this is a minor aspect of Freud's theory, it has been widely accepted as fact. The existing evidence, however, contradicts it.

> Fisher (1973) obtained ratings from several different samples of married women with regard to the degree to which they prefer clitoral as compared to vaginal stimulation in the process of attaining orgasm. He found no indications that women with a clitoral orientation were especially inferior in their psychological adaptation. Surprisingly . . . it was not the clitorally-oriented woman who was most anxious, as would be expected within the Freudian framework, but rather the vaginally-oriented one. (Fisher & Greenberg, 1977, p. 212)

Many of Freud's views of women have not been substantiated. This is not, in itself, an indictment. Theories are developed to be tested. The telling criticism of classical psychoanalytic views of women is that they assume men are the model for all human personality and women should strive to be like men.

Classical psychoanalytic views of women have not gone unchallenged. *Feminist analysis*, although not new, is very much a contemporary approach within psychoanalysis (Steele, 1985). Early feminist analysis (e.g., Horney, 1939; Jones, 1927; Thompson, 1941, 1942, 1943, 1950) primarily involved critique and reformulation of classical psychoanalytic ideas. (An example is Horney's reinterpretation of the Oedipal situation, described in Chapter 4.) More recently, feminist analysis has gone beyond negative criticism of Freud's position. It now presents a more balanced view of female personality (e.g., Gilligan, 1982). Mitchell (1974a, 1974b), for example, used classic psychoanalysis as a starting point. She argued that classical psychoanalysis need not be viewed as "a recommendation *for* a patriarchal society," but as "an analysis *of* one. If we are interested in understanding and challenging the oppression of women, we cannot afford to neglect it" (Mitchell, 1974b, p. xv).

PROJECTIVE TECHNIQUES HAVE LOW RELIABILITY AND VALIDITY

Several thousand studies (Buros, 1965, 1972) have examined the reliability and validity of projective techniques. There is relatively little evidence from well-designed studies to support their reliability when they are used to generate global personality descriptions. The reliability is somewhat higher when projective techniques are used to measure specific personality characteristics (e.g., achievement motivation with the Thematic Apperception Test [TAT]; see Chapter 11). Interrater reliability and internal consistency (agreement among the items or stimuli used with a given technique) is usually low. Retest reliability (consistency over time) is equally poor when responses or the themes based on those responses are compared in two separate administrations. For example, Lindzey and Herman (1955) gave the same subjects the TAT twice. For the second administration they told subjects to write different stories. If the TAT were effective in assessing the subjects' personality dynamics, then the *themes* of the stories should be the same for each subject in the two administrations, even though the specific stories were different. There was no support for this hypothesis.

The validity of projective techniques is also largely unsubstantiated by empirical research. Validity studies of techniques like the Rorschach and the TAT have not been all negative, however. The case is similar to the reliability of projective techniques. Predictive accuracy is highest when they are used to measure a particular personality characteristic rather than to yield a general personality description. Nevertheless, results from most studies have been inconsistent and inconclusive. This is due to a host of methodological (e.g., Anastasi, 1968; Kleinmuntz, 1967) and statistical (e.g., Cronbach, 1949) problems. In one of the more common types of validity studies, experienced clinicians write personality descriptions about subjects based on responses to a projective technique such as the Rorschach. The judges are "blind" in terms of other information about the subjects. Agreement between the judges' descriptions has been low. Also, the descriptions are often so general as to apply to almost anyone. (The description would include statements like those appearing in Demonstration 1–1 on bogus personality testing.)

Another source of negative evidence casts doubt on the very basis of the techniques, namely, the projective hypothesis. According to the hypothesis, responses to ambiguous stimuli will be projections of a person's enduring personality characteristics. Rather than assessing underlying personality dynamics and motivational dispositions, projective techniques may be measuring individual differences in perceptual and cognitive factors. For instance, suppose we could demonstrate a relationship between responses to an inkblot and sexual activity. This would not necessarily mean that an underlying sexual drive is being measured and that it causes the sexual behavior. An equally plausible explanation of the relationship is that people who engage in more sexual behavior have more sexual thoughts (e.g., Epstein, 1966; Klinger, 1966).

Some problems with projective techniques stem from a lack of standardization of administration, scoring, and interpretation. Subtle changes in how a projective technique is presented to the subject, including the relationship between the examiner and the subject, can influence performance (e.g., Masling, 1960).

Subjectivity is another factor that may account for the low reliability and validity of projective methods. Scoring of projective techniques requires at least some subjective judgment, even when scoring involves placing responses in already designated categories. There is considerably more subjectivity in the interpretation of the responses. Interpretations of projective techniques vary widely with the skill and experience of the examiner. They also vary with examiners of comparable ability. Projective techniques may be as much a projection of the examiner's own biases, hypotheses, favorite interpretations, and theoretical persuasions as an indication of the characteristics of the subject (Anastasi, 1968). Well-developed standards for scoring and interpreting projective techniques would certainly help, but few adequate standards exist.

Despite their problems, projective techniques are used extensively in personality research and in applied clinical settings for assessment and diagnosis (Lubin, Wallis, & Paine, 1971). The theoretical basis for projective techniques is most often psychoanalytic. However, psychologists who adopt other strategies also use them in their research and clinical practice (e.g., Swan & MacDonald, 1978). What accounts for this popularity, given the negative evidence about reliability and validity?

The simplest explanation can be summarized in one word: *Tradition!* Compared to other methods of personality assessment, projective techniques have the longest history, and they have received the most attention. It is difficult to discard such a huge investment of time and effort. Moreover, projective techniques are used mainly to measure unconscious motives, conflicts, and thoughts. Few alternatives for assessing the unconscious have been developed.

Most of the negative evidence about projective techniques is based on the criteria for psychometric tests. Therefore, the fact that projectives are *techniques* rather than tests must be kept in mind. Related to this argument is evidence that some individual clinicians consistently use projective data and make accurate predictions about a patient's behavior. However, in these instances, the skill of the clinicians and not the techniques per se, account for the accuracy of the predictions (cf. Sarbin, Taft, & Bailey, 1960). Thus, the value of projectives "as clinical tools is proportional to the skill of the clinician and . . . cannot be assessed independently of the individual clinician using them" (Anastasi, 1976, p. 586).

PSYCHOANALYSIS AND SCIENCE

The criticism leveled against psychoanalysis in this chapter comes mainly from the standpoint of "mainstream (American) scientific psychology" which was originally modeled after nineteenth century physical sciences (e.g, physics). Its standards include studying behavior under controlled conditions, operationally defining concepts, and objectively assessing behavior using quantitative measures that are reliable and valid. This all boils down to *objectivity* and *repeatability* (Steele, 1986). Perhaps psychoanalysis cannot and should not be judged according to such criteria. After all, much of what psychoanalysts study—the unconscious, dreams, and wishes—are subjective and may not be repeatable. Investigating such phenomena may call for subjective methods. Psychoanalysts, as much as other personality psychologists, may care passionately for the truth, but their evidence is different from that of others.

Different is not necessarily less valid, however. Objectivity and repeatability appear to be logical and even "right." Still, they are in the end, as they were when they were adopted, arbitrary standards. Interestingly, contemporary mainstream psychology may be moving away from exclusive reliance on objectivity and repeatability to some degree. The emergence of cognitive psychology in the 1980s is an indication. Cognitive processes, like intrapsychic processes, are subjective phenomena. They do not lend themselves to scientific study that is exclusively objective and rigidly controlled (e.g., Erdelyi, 1985).

The goal of the psychoanalytic strategy is also different from the goal of mainstream psychology. Mainstream psychology emphasizes prediction and control. Psychoanalysis is mainly concerned with *understanding*. Understanding is subjective and often incomplete and ambiguous (Steele, 1979).

The issue of the relation of psychoanalysis to science is as old as psychoanalysis. Freud often considered calling psychoanalysis *metapsychology*—meaning that it goes *beyond* psychology—thereby removing it from psychology as the science of behavior. In 1900 Freud wrote:

> I am not really a man of science. . . . I am nothing but by temperament . . . an adventurer . . . with the curiosity, the boldness, and the tenacity that belongs to that type of being. Such people are apt to be treasured if they succeed, if they have really discovered something; otherwise they are thrown aside. And that is not altogether unjust. (quoted in Jones, 1953, p. 348)

Summary

1. Psychoanalysts often commit three logical errors in presenting evidence for their theories: (1) they fail to distinguish between observation and inference; (2) they confuse correlation and causation; and (3) they use analogy as proof.

2. Psychoanalytic case studies may be unduly biased due to the highly private nature of the observations. Also, psychoanalysts may be more biased in their observations than other therapists. Psychoanalytic case studies are based on a small, atypical sample of people. Finally, the reliability of psychoanalytic interpretations is generally low.

3. Many psychoanalytic concepts are defined in vague, nonspecific, and ambiguous terms. It is often unclear whether a concept is meant literally or metaphorically. The inadequate definitions make measuring the concepts problematic.

4. A number of psychoanalytic propositions are stated in a way that makes them incapable of being falsified.

5. Freud's theorizing is biased against women. He considers the male personality to be both a prototype and an ideal. The evidence does not support his views about female personality.

6. Projective techniques generally have low reliability and validity. Nonetheless, they continue to remain popular as personality assessment procedures.

7. Psychoanalysis has primarily been criticized as being unscientific. It may be that psychoanalysis should not be judged in terms of the standards of mainstream scientific psychology.

SECTION

III

THE DISPOSITIONAL STRATEGY

THE DISPOSITIONAL STRATEGY

CHAPTER 8

INTRODUCTION

OVERVIEW

"He had a special personal charm, a fine courage that dominated his physical weakness, great gifts as a conversationalist and a persistent gaiety that made for him warm friends" (Nisenson & DeWitt, 1949, p. 139). This description gives us the feeling that we know something about the man described. There is a hint of the enduring qualities that set him apart from others; it might help us identify him or predict what he might do in different situations. The man described is the nineteenth century Scottish author, Robert Louis Stevenson. The description might, of course, apply to many other people as well. There is also much that it does not tell us about Stevenson's personality. Still, we believe it tells us something about his basic characteristics and about the way he was usually *disposed* to behave in social interactions.

This section considers the dispositional strategy for studying and understanding human personality. The major idea behind the strategy is found in the definition of a **disposition.** It is an *enduring, stable personality characteristic within the person.*

According to this strategy, people differ in the way they are disposed to act. Put another way, people differ in what they are basically like. It should come as no surprise that most writers see this as the oldest of the strategies. Describing people, groups, and even nations in dispositional terms seems almost to "come naturally." Therefore, before proceeding further, you may wish to try Demonstration 8–1. In it, you will be able to explore some of your own dispositional notions about human behavior and personality.

DEMONSTRATION 8–1

DESCRIBING PEOPLE IN DISPOSITIONAL TERMS

We are all accustomed to using dispositional notions in describing and attempting to explain people's behavior. These usually take the form "So-and-so is a _____ person" or "So-and-so acts that way because he or she is _____." For example, we might say that "Harry is a *meek* person" or that "Susan acts that way because she is *proud.*"

The purpose of this Demonstration is to give you an opportunity to describe in dispositional terms people whom you know. It will allow you to compare the way in which you use dispositions to the way in which personality psychologists use the dispositional strategy. It will also serve as an introduction to some of the methods, predictions, and general findings of the strategy.

PROCEDURE

1. Take six sheets of lined paper and write one of the letters "A" through "F" at the top of each sheet. Then make a copy of the work sheet in Table 8–1 (this will be used later in the Demonstration).

2. You will need to designate a particular person of your *own sex* for each of the categories listed below. Write each of their names at the top of the appropriate sheet of paper.

TABLE 8–1
Work Sheet for Demonstration 8–1

| Rank | | Name | Number of Adjectives Used | Pervasiveness | | | | Percent of Similarity |
				Almost Always 4	Fre-quently 3	Occa-sionally 2	Rarely 1	
		Self						
Know best	1st							
	2nd							
	3rd							
	4th							
Know least	5th							
"Σ" = Sum (total) "M" = Mean			$\Sigma =$	$\Sigma =$	$\Sigma =$	$\Sigma =$	$\Sigma =$	
			$M =$	%	%	%	%	

A. Your same-sexed parent or, if you have never known this person, a close biological relative of the same sex (i.e., a "blood relative").

B. A close friend who is not related to you.

C. Someone (not related to you) with whom you are somewhat friendly (i.e., a more casual relationship than with person *B*).

D. Someone (not related to you) whom you know only in one specific context (e.g., a high school or college teacher).

E. A historical figure whom you admire.

F. Yourself.

3. Beginning with your same-sexed parent (i.e., person *A*), list all the adjectives you can think of that describe him or her. Write down as many or as few adjectives as seem necessary to describe the person fully. (The order of the adjectives does not matter.) Repeat this procedure for the persons in categories *B* through *F*, in that order.

4. Starting with person *A*, look over the adjectives to see whether any of them are similar or redundant. (For example, "clumsy" and "awkward" have similar meanings.) When you are unsure, double-check with a standard thesaurus. *Condense any redundant adjectives either by eliminating one or more of the adjectives or by combining them* (e.g., clumsy-awkward). Repeat this procedure for persons *B* through *F*, in that order.

5. Starting again with person *A*, now rate each of the adjectives or adjective combinations according to the degree to which each is characteristic of the person. Use the following scale:

4 = *Almost always* characterizes the person.
3 = *Frequently* characterizes the person.
2 = *Occasionally* characterizes the person.
1 = *Rarely* characterizes the person.

Write the scale number that is most applicable next to each of the adjectives or adjective combinations. Repeat this procedure for persons *B* through *F*, in that order.

6. *Rank* the people *A* through *E* (excluding yourself) in terms of how well you know them. The person whom you feel you know best should be given the "first" rank, the person whom you feel you know second best should be assigned the "second" rank, and so on until the person whom you feel you know least well has received the "fifth" rank. Write the rank in the upper right-hand corner of each sheet.

7. In the first column of the work sheet (which you copied in Step 1), write the names of the five people *other than yourself* (i.e., persons *A* through *E*) in order of the degree to which you feel you are familiar with them (see Step 6). The person whom you ranked "first" (i.e., the one you feel you know best) should be listed first, the person whom you ranked "second" should be listed next, and so on.

8. On the work sheet, in the "Number of Adjectives Used" column, put the total number of adjectives or adjective combinations you have used to describe each of the persons (A through F).

Then, at the bottom of the column, put the total number of adjectives or adjective combinations used to describe all of the people *other than yourself* (i.e., sheets A through E). Divide this total by 5 to obtain the mean number of adjectives you used to describe the other people, and enter this in the appropriate space at the bottom of the work sheet.

9. In the "Pervasiveness" columns of the work sheet, record the number of adjectives for each person (A through F) which fall in each of the four categories. These are the numbers you wrote next to the adjectives in Step 5.

Then, at the bottom of the column, put the total number of adjectives in each of the four pervasiveness categories for the five persons *other than yourself.*

Next, compute and record at the bottom of the work sheet the percentage of adjectives which fall into each of the pervasiveness categories. To do this, divide the total number of adjectives for each category by the total number of adjectives used to describe the other persons (i.e., combined across all categories) and then multiply by 100.

10. Looking at all of the sheets on which you have listed adjectives (i.e., A through F), check to see whether any of the adjectives are similar or redundant across persons. For example, if you described yourself as generous and your parent as giving, these should now be condensed into one adjective, either by changing "generous" to "giving" or vice versa or by hyphenating the two adjectives where they both appear (e.g., "generous-giving"). Note that this step is similar to Step 4, and a thesaurus may help you. On sheets A through E (i.e., every sheet except the one for yourself) *circle each adjective or adjective combination which is the same as one you used to describe yourself* (on sheet F).

11. Compute the *percentage* of adjectives used for each of the other people (A through E) which corresponds to your own, and record it in the "Percent of Similarity" column. (That is, divide the number of adjectives which are the same for yourself and the other person—the ones you have circled—by the total number of adjectives used to describe the other person, and then multiply by 100.)

DISCUSSION

You may have already noticed a number of interesting features and patterns in your use of dispositional descriptions for others and yourself. To add some further ideas, we will mention a few of the findings of dispositional psychologists which are related to the Demonstration.

Number of Descriptive Adjectives Used

Gordon Allport was one of the first to examine the range of dispositional terms, or "trait names," which people use to describe others. He found that we often use a large number of adjectives for this purpose, but that many of them are synonymous. The number can therefore be reduced. To the extent that your own experiences in this Demonstration parallel Allport's findings, you would have been able to substantially reduce the size of your initial lists of descriptive adjectives.

After condensing redundant adjectives, Allport found that most people actually use a fairly small number of adjectives in describing others they know, the usual range being between three and ten. Does your mean number of adjectives fall within this range? How does the number of adjectives you used to describe yourself compare with the mean number of adjectives you used to describe other people?

Dispositions and Genetics

Dispositional psychologists who take a biological view have found evidence suggesting that certain dispositions are transmitted genetically. Evidence of genetic dispositions might show up in this Demonstration in the degree of similarity between yourself and your parent ("Percent of Similarity" column of the work sheet). Is this similarity greater than the similarity between yourself and a close friend?

Relationship to People

Many people believe that the closer one's relationship to someone, the "better" they know that person. Yet there is some evidence from psychological studies that we often feel more comfortable assigning dispositional adjectives to people whom we know *less* well.

Examine the relationship between the number of adjectives you used to describe a person and how well you feel you know that person. The five people other than yourself are listed on the work sheet in descending order of familiarity, so you can look down the "Number of Adjectives Used" column to see whether a pattern emerges. Is "secondhand" information such as that which you used to describe the historical figure whom you admire sufficient to adequately characterize the person? How well were you able to describe the person you know in only a single context?

Pervasiveness

Allport and others have noted that dispositions vary in the degree to which they seem to pervade a particular personality. Not very many people have dispositions that pervade all that they do and dominate their entire personality ("almost always" category).

Other Issues

You should save the Demonstration materials and inspect them again as you read the chapters in this section. Even now, you might wish to consider some further analyses of your own. What are the qualitative differences among the adjectives you use to describe various individuals you know? What differences would you expect if you repeated the Demonstration, but described people of the *opposite* sex? Examining questions like these will help you to better understand the dispositional strategy.

Most people find Demonstration 8–1 easy; we often think of others in dispositional terms. One reason is that dispositional labels serve as organizing concepts that may explain a person's behavior in a variety of situations. Stagner (1976) gives this example:

> If a young man refuses an invitation to a party, drops a course that requires group discussion, and takes his vacation hiking alone in the mountains, we begin to get the idea that there is an inner consistency that involves the avoidance of situations that require close contact with other human beings. . . . The concept of a trait of seclusiveness, it seems to me, makes sense as a unifying concept here. . . . (p. 112)

EARLY DISPOSITIONAL CONCEPTS

Dispositional concepts in one form or another have been used to organize and explain the actions of others for thousands of years. It is interesting to examine some of the early dispositional ideas. We will therefore take a brief look backward before describing contemporary approaches to the dispositional strategy.

Early dispositional views assumed that people could be divided into a relatively small number of *types* according to their personalities. By knowing an individual's type, you might predict the way the person would behave in a variety of circumstances. The ancient Hebrews used this perspective for what may have been the first formal personality assessment. This is shown in the following quotation from the Old Testament. It is apparent that the perspective was dichotomous. The goal was identifying two types of people, those who could be ferocious fighters and those who could not.

And the Lord said unto Gideon, The people that are with thee are too many for me to give the Midianites into their hands. . . . Now therefore go to, proclaim in the ears of the people, saying, Whosoever is fearful and afraid, let him return and depart early from Mount Gilead. And there returned of the people twenty and two thousand; and there remained ten thousand.

And the Lord said unto Gideon, The people are yet too many; bring them down unto the water, and I will try them for thee there. . . . So he brought down the people unto the water: and the Lord said unto Gideon, Every one that lappeth of the water with his tongue, as a dog lappeth, him shalt thou set by himself; likewise every one that boweth down upon his knees to drink. And the number of them that lapped putting their hand to their mouth, were three hundred men: but all the rest of the people bowed down upon their knees to drink water. And the Lord said unto Gideon, By the three hundred men that lapped will I save you, and deliver the Midianites into thine hand: and let all the other people go every man unto his place. (Judges 7:2–7)

A second historic view is the *theory of the four temperaments.* It is close to several contemporary theories and quite a few everyday conceptions of personality. The position is based on the Greek idea that the universe can be described in terms of four basic elements: air, earth, fire, and water. The Greek physician Hippocrates, the "father of medicine," extended this argument to people. He suggested that the body is composed of four "humors": blood, black bile, yellow bile, and phlegm. These correspond to the four elements. The Roman physician Galen later suggested that an excess of any of these humors leads to a characteristic temperament. These "personality types" were: sanguine (hopeful), melancholic (sad), choleric (hot tempered), or phlegmatic (apathetic). This ancient theory of personality is no longer taken seriously. But the four temperaments have survived to this day as part of our language.

There are clearly more than four types of people. This was obvious even to the ancients. Thus, extensive catalogs of types emerged. Identifying types of people continued to be the popular conception of personality, with few changes, for thousands of years. The most striking addition was the idea that physical appearance indicated personality. In Shakespeare's play *Julius Caesar,* for example, Caesar advises Marcus Antonius:

Let me have men about me that are fat;
Sleek-headed men, and such as sleep o' nights.
Yond Cassius has a lean and hungry look;
He thinks too much: such men are dangerous. (act 1, sc. 2)

The belief advanced by Shakespeare's Caesar is still popular today; for instance, many people believe they can identify a "criminal type" by physical appearance.

Theoretical Assumptions of the Dispositional Strategy

Three major assumptions are common to all theories and viewpoints within the dispositional strategy: Dispositions are relatively stable and enduring within the individual; dispositions are consistent and general to some extent; and individuals differ in their dispositions.

Relative Stability of Dispositions

If persons are truly disposed to act or respond in particular ways, then personalities should be fairly stable over time. However, dispositional psychologists often caution that this assumption must be understood in the light of several further distinctions.

For one thing, most dispositional psychologists conceptualize an individual's enduring dispositions as *traits* and distinguish them from temporary dispositions, or *states*. The latter result from temporary conditions like fatigue, stress, or sudden changes in fortune. The difference can be seen with anxiety. Spielberger (1966) describes **trait anxiety** as "the disposition to respond [with anxiety] to situations that are perceived as threatening." This is different from **state anxiety,** "a condition of the organism characterized by subjective feelings of apprehension and heightened autonomic nervous system activity" (Spielberger & Gorsuch, 1966, p. 33). Trait anxiety is a predisposition to be anxious. A person high in trait anxiety will not necessarily be anxious all the time. A person low in trait anxiety may exhibit state anxiety under highly stressful conditions. Recent research suggests that the trait/state distinction is valuable for other dispositions as well. As would be expected, state measures vary much more than trait measures from situation to situation (Zuckerman, 1983).

Equally important, dispositional psychologists point out that a disposition is a general mode of functioning. The disposition may take different concrete behavioral forms as the individual matures. Thus, we must know what to look for before we can tell whether a person's behavior has been "stable" over time. Dispositions are not merely habits; they reflect instead an inner consistency. However, it often takes more than a simplistic analysis of overt acts to reveal this.

The point is well illustrated in an article by Lewis (1967) titled "The Meaning of a Response, or Why Researchers in Infant Behavior Should Be Oriental Metaphysicians." Briefly, Lewis was interested in the consistency of infants' responses to frustration, which he measured in a group of babies at one month of age and then again when his subjects were twelve months old. At one month, the frustration involved removing a nipple from the infants' mouths for thirty seconds; at twelve months, a physical barrier blocked the youngsters from reaching either their mothers or some attractive toys. Crying was the measure of frustration. Responses to the two situations were negatively related. The babies who cried at one month were *not* the ones who cried at twelve months. However, as Lewis points out, this should not mask a deeper consistency. Specifically, some of the babies were consistently *active* and others consistently *passive* in their responses. At one month motor skills are not yet developed. Thus, the active baby can do nothing but cry—which it does. But at twelve months, crying is a relatively passive response. At this age, the active babies did not cry; they took some physical action to change the situation.

Consistency and Generality of Dispositions

A second assumption of the dispositional strategy is related to the first. Dispositions have *some* consistency and generality within a person. *Consistency* and *generality* refer to the extent to which a disposition affects behavior. A man who is ambitious in his work is also likely to be ambitious and striving in his recreation. He will probably have high ambitions for his children as well.

No disposition is expected to appear all the time or in every situation. One reason is that a person has many dispositions. A somewhat different set may be brought into play, depending on demands and circumstances. Moreover, one disposition can be a "moderator" for another. Kipnis (1971), for example, examined the relationship between impulsiveness and academic performance. He found their relationship was moderated by the person's intellectual ability. Among those with above-average intelligence, impulsive people seemed to do less well academically because of their impulsiveness. But impulsiveness was not related to academic performance in those with below average intellectual ability.

Over the past twenty years, one of the most heated and controversial debates in personality psychology has involved consistency, generality, and stability of dispositions. Critics, such as Walter Mischel (1968), attacked the dispositional strategy by claiming "the behaviors which are often construed as stable personality trait indicators actually are highly specific and depend on the details of the evoking situations and the response mode employed to measure them" (p. 37). In reply, it was pointed out that many of the studies chosen by Mischel as showing inconsistency were flawed by inadequate research methods (e.g., Block, 1977). In the past few years, dispositional researchers have refined their methods. They have been able to show that some aspects of behavior are quite consistent across situations (e.g., Diener & Larsen, 1984; Woodruffe, 1985) and time (e.g., Conley, 1984; Staw & Ross, 1985). Woodruffe (1985), for instance, found a high degree of consistency across situations in how much people are outgoing or reserved. And Conley (1984) showed that introversion/extroversion and emotionality remain moderately consistent over a forty-five-year period. That would be over most of the adult life span!

Nonetheless, many characteristics studied by dispositional psychologists seem less consistent or stable. So the debate over dispositional consistency continues.

Individual Differences

We have all noticed clear differences in abilities, interests, and social responses among adults we know. Even from birth, infants differ in the vigor and tone of their responses to both frustration and reward (Buss & Plomin, 1984). Clearly, we are all unique individuals, different from others. The dispositional strategy accounts for individual differences by making a third major assumption: Individual differences arise from differences in the strength, amount, and number of dispositions a person has.

IDENTIFYING PERSONALITY DISPOSITIONS

Human behavior can be ordered and divided on a nearly infinite number of dimensions. We can speak of someone as a happy person, an aggressive person, a person who needs to be loved, a benevolent person, a stingy person, and so on. Which of these dimensions is important? Which is most likely to meet the theoretical assumptions of the dispositional strategy?

As Demonstration 8–1 reveals, most people describe themselves and others with a relatively small number of dispositions. But the total number of traits, types, motives, and needs suggested as human dispositions is truly vast. Modern dispositional psychologists have therefore been searching for a set of underlying personality dimensions from which all other trait-like characteristics of a person can be derived.

The search is like early efforts by psychologists interested in visual perception and color vision. These investigators wanted to identify the "primary colors" from which all others could be derived by appropriate combinations and mixtures. We now know that just three colors of light—red, green, and blue—can produce any one of the vast array of colors that can be seen by a normally sighted person. Many dispositional psychologists believe that personality can also be cast into a small set of primary or underlying dimensions from which all the others can be derived.

Dispositional psychologists must decide whether to look for (a) many narrow components of personality or (b) fewer broad dispositional clusters. The decision is primarily based on preference and intuition. The first approach gives rise to *trait* theories. The second generates *type* theories. (There is an easy way to think about the distinction: people can have a number of traits but fit only one type.) In either case, the disposition is an abstraction that is synthesized and inferred from diverse sources of information about people.

A major task of dispositional psychologists is to identify important dimensions, or dispositions, that describe and explain human behavior and personality. In this endeavor, it is essential that there are some fairly clear indicators, or criteria, that can be used to test whether a given dimension, a prospective psychological disposition, will be useful. One such indicator involves meeting the assumptions of consistency and generality. But consistency and generality are not sufficient. The dimension must also clearly discriminate between or among people. If everyone were happy (or aggressive or ambitious), then this dimension would be of little use as a psychological disposition; we could not use it to predict or explain any of the *differences* in people's behavior. Dispositional approaches are, in fact, very much psychologies of "amount." Dispositions that do not let us say that one person has more or less of some durable characteristic than another add little predictive power.

DISPOSITIONAL PERSONALITY ASSESSMENT

The dispositional strategy has employed almost all of the major personality assessment techniques. Interviews as well as projective and situational tests of various sorts have been used to identify various characteristics. However, *reporting* (as opposed to observing) has played a central role in most dispositional assessments. A wide range of "paper-and-pencil" self-report tests have been used. So have "reputational" reports in the form of descriptions given by friends, acquaintances, and, sometimes, biographers.

Dispositions are theoretical constructs. It is therefore not possible to measure them directly. Instead, dispositional researchers must devise measures of behavior that yield indicators of various underlying dispositions. Often these are self-report inventories or questionnaires. At the same time, it is presumed that there is no one "absolute measure" of a disposition; in fact, there should be several different indexes. The dispositional psychologist

> explains the behavior of an individual by the values assigned him on dimensions considered relevant to the behavior in question. These values may be expressed numerically as scores on a test, or they may be represented by labels that stand for different positions on the dimension. A psychologist might, for example, explain an individual's pattern of deference to certain people and hostility to others in terms of authoritarianism, by saying that he is an authoritarian type of person. Or the psychologist might predict a person's success as a business executive from his scores on measures of intelligence, aggressiveness, and sociability. The use of these and other dimensions implies that the values obtained on them by individuals have consequences over a fairly wide realm of behavior and that these

dimensions exist independently of any single method of measurement. Therefore, although a particular test may be the one most frequently used in the measurement of some dimension, it is assumed that there may be other, equally valid measures. Like other theoretical constructs, dimensions are inferred; their definition rests not on any single set of operations but on the *convergence* of a set of operations. (Levy, 1970, p. 200)

A related characteristic of dispositional personality assessment is the assumption of *additivity*. The strength of any disposition is assumed to be the "sum" of various individual response tendencies. Consider a person who likes to meet strangers, easily approaches teachers to dispute grades on examinations, *and* is often outspoken in class discussions. This person would be considered somewhat more extroverted (outgoing) than another person who likes to meet strangers and argue about grades but prefers not to take part in large-group discussions. In other words, the first person exhibits more behaviors indicating a disposition of extroversion.

A good example of what is meant by "adding" behaviors to infer a disposition can be seen in the work of Robins (1966). He used a combination of aggressive symptoms in childhood to predict adult criminal behavior. Robins found that adding up all the early signs and symptoms suggesting a disposition toward aggression predicted later criminal behavior considerably better than did any single aggressive or delinquent act during childhood.

Two formal criteria have been adopted for measuring the adequacy of a dispositional assessment procedure: **convergent validity** and **discriminant validity** (Campbell & Fiske, 1959). Measures of presumably the *same* disposition may be quite different in form, such as paper-and-pencil, projective, and situational. But they should *converge* and thus correlate highly with one another. In contrast, tests meant to measure *different* dispositions should *discriminate* between them. Thus, they should *not* be highly correlated.

Finally it should be noted that dispositional psychologists typically believe their tests are imperfect. All tests are assumed to include error, or "noise," as well as true information about the disposition being measured. So they probably *under*estimate the actual stability and generality of the underlying dispositions.

DISPOSITIONAL RESEARCH

Dispositional personality research is concerned with three major problems. One is to identify the underlying dimensions of personality. The second is to discover the source of various individual differences. (This especially relates to inherited characteristics or those stemming from early life experiences.) The third is to examine the reliability and validity of various personality and ability tests. They also attempt to determine the usefulness of such tests for description and prediction.

Recall that the psychoanalytic strategy dictates that the predominant method of research must be the case study. The dispositional strategy also dictates that one method of research will predominate—the correlational method. The dispositional researcher is always interested in how well various behaviors go together. Only when a number of different behaviors are related can we speak of an underlying personality disposition that may be influencing them.

DURABILITY OF DISPOSITIONS AND THE POSSIBILITY OF PERSONALITY CHANGE

The dispositional strategy has little to say about personality change. It is not associated with any form of psychotherapy. This distinguishes it from the other strategies discussed in the book. There are at least two reasons the dispositional strategy does not deal with change. First, the strategy emphasizes the stability of personality. It follows logically that personality change would be difficult, if not impossible. Second, many dispositional psychologists have strong links with academic psychology rather than clinical practice. The practical contributions of dispositional psychologists focus on measurement and prediction of behavior rather than on its change. At most, the dispositional psychologist finds a situation for which a person is already suited. This contrasts with psychotherapy which tries to change the person to fit the situation he or she is in. For example, suppose a person is disposed to be very aggressive. It may be wiser to keep that person away from aggression-provoking situations than to try to change him or her into someone who "turns the other cheek."

Although the dispositional strategy has not itself been associated with efforts to change personality, some of the psychologists discussed in this section have been actively interested in personality change techniques based on other strategies. David McClelland, for example, has developed an imaginative program for altering one disposition, the need to achieve (as we will see in Chapter 11).

SUMMARY

1. A disposition is an enduring, stable personality characteristic that resides within the person. Most people find it "natural" to think about others and themselves in dispositional terms.

2. The concept of personality dispositions goes back thousands of years. Most of the early dispositional viewpoints simply divided people up into a number of distinct types.

3. The major assumptions of the dispositional strategy are that dispositions are relatively stable over time and relatively consistent across situations. But dispositional psychologists do not expect a person's dispositions to manifest themselves all the time or in every situation.

4. The relative importance of dispositions and situations in determining behavior has been hotly debated by personality psychologists for many years.

5. A major task of the modern dispositional strategy is to identify the most important or central dispositions on which people can be compared.

6. The dispositional strategy relies heavily on self-reports and the reports of others to assess personality. Assessment is usually additive, in the sense that the strength of a disposition is assumed to be the sum of all the individual's responses that are related to the disposition in question. Because there is error or "noise" in every measure of personality, dispositional psychologists believe that estimates of the stability and generality of personality dispositions are often underestimated.

7. Dispositional personality research involves identifying dispositions, exploring individual differences, and evaluating tests.

8. The dispositional strategy has less to say about personality change than the other three strategies, partly because it views personality as stable and partly because relatively few dispositional psychologists have been concerned with clinical endeavors.

THE DISPOSITIONAL STRATEGY

CHAPTER 9

TRAIT AND TYPE APPROACHES

OVERVIEW

In this chapter, we consider various ways personality psychologists have tried to identify traits and types. We will discuss the work of several dispositional psychologists. All of them consider traits and types to be real psychological entities, not just convenient labels to summarize behavior. Allport described this approach as **heuristic realism.** *Heuristic* [your-IST-tick] has Greek and Latin roots and means "to find out or discover." Allport (1966) meant the term to convey that "the person who confronts us possesses inside his skin generalized action tendencies (or traits) and that it is our job scientifically to discover what they are" (p. 3). Allport did not believe that traits are physical entities, like glands or organs. He did believe that psychological traits are real attributes of persons; they serve to *explain* behavior rather than merely describe it.

Suppose, for example, that a five-year-old girl and a twenty-five-year-old woman are given a fifty-pound barbell to lift. Assuming that both subjects are motivated, it is a safe bet that the woman will succeed but the girl will fail. Why? Many would say the woman is stronger than the girl. The difference in strength does not only describe the fact that one individual could lift the weight. The difference in strength is an attribute of the persons involved. It explains *why* one succeeded and the other failed. In much the same way, trait and type theorists believe it is legitimate to say someone behaves aggressively *because* she has an aggressive trait or *because* he is an aggressive type.

THE SEARCH FOR IMPORTANT DISPOSITIONS

The problems facing the dispositional approach were recently analyzed by Buss and Craik (1985) who observed:

> One of the most fundamental theoretical tasks in personality psychology is to identify a subset of *important* dispositions from among the array of thousands available or imaginable. . . . A central function of conceptual frameworks is to establish explicit criteria for ordering dispositions by importance and priority. Without inclusion and exclusion criteria, personality research can appear directionless, with each investigator focusing on a favorite disposition or subset of dispositions. (p. 934)

Dispositional psychologists have tried to identify the most basic or important traits and types using three broad approaches: the lexical approach, the theoretical approach, and the statistical approach.

The *lexical approach* is based on the assumption that the more important a disposition is, the more often it will be referred to in natural language. (*Lexical* derives from the word *lexicon,* which means dictionary.) From the lexical approach, many researchers consider aggressiveness an important disposition. The word *aggressive* and its synonyms are common in everyday language when discussing and comparing people.

As the name suggests, the *theoretical approach* is a basis for studying dispositions suggested by theory. For example, psychoanalytic theory suggests ego strength and defensiveness as important dispositions on which people differ.

Finally, there is the *statistical approach.* Very large amounts of data about many people are analyzed using a statistical procedure designed to identify the basic factors that underlie the data. Factor analysis has been a favorite tool of those using the statistical approach. It will be discussed later in the chapter.

The three ways of identifying important dispositions are not mutually exclusive. As we shall see, some investigators have combined two or even all three of the approaches. This is done to justify the claim that a particular disposition is an important or central dimension of personality.

In the remainder of this chapter, each of the approaches will be illustrated as we consider some of the most influential dispositional theories. Our discussion begins with the theory of Gordon Allport (1897–1967). Allport is acknowledged as one of the founders of the modern dispositional strategy.

ALLPORT'S TRAIT APPROACH

Allport spent virtually his entire career trying to understand human personality. His significant writings span more than thirty-five years. Throughout this period, Allport adhered to the idea of heuristic realism.

Gordon Allport

Harvard University News Office

He insisted that finding out "what the other person is really like" should not be avoided even though difficulties are involved.

Traits as the Units for Studying Personality

Allport believes *traits* are the basic units of personality. His original statement of what traits are appeared in 1931. Allport still believed it was defensible in 1966. His eight assertions are:

1. *Traits have more than nominal existence.* They are not just summary labels of observed behavior. Rather, traits exist within the person.
2. *Traits are more generalized than habits.* Brushing one's teeth, Allport notes, may well be a habit, but it is not properly called a trait (although an underlying trait, such as cleanliness, might account for it).
3. *Traits are dynamic and determine behavior.* Traits direct action and are not mere structural artifacts. And unlike the intrapsychic structures posited by Freud, they do not require energizing from somewhere else.
4. *Traits may be established empirically.* Allport was steeped in the tradition of experimental psychology and unequivocally acknowledged that psychologists must finally defer to their data.
5. *Traits are only relatively independent of other traits.*
6. *Traits are not synonymous with moral or social judgments.*
7. *Traits may be viewed either in the light of the personality which contains them (i.e., idiographically) or in the light of their distribution in the population (i.e., nomothetically).*
8. *Acts, and even habits, that are inconsistent with a trait, are not proof of the nonexistence of the trait.* For example, if a person with a trait of assertiveness acts passively, this does not indicate that the person lacks the trait of aggressiveness. It simply means that, in this instance, the person's trait is not being expressed.

Allport's eight assertions have become the fundamental assumptions and guidelines followed by most trait psychologists.

The Dimensions of Traits: Pervasiveness within a Personality

Allport proposes that a person's traits may be classified by the extent that they pervade his or her personality. He calls the most pervasive traits **cardinal dispositions**. A cardinal disposition dominates the individual. It cannot stay hidden; it often makes its possessor famous. For example, Niccolo Machiavelli, the famous Italian political philosopher, is closely associated with the idea that the ends justify the means. The adjective

Machiavellian has come to be used to describe anyone who holds that idea. According to Allport, few people have cardinal dispositions.

Central dispositions are the relatively small number of traits that tend to be highly characteristic of a person. They might be thought of as the characteristics we would mention when writing a detailed letter of recommendation. According to Allport, everyone has a few central dispositions that characterize them; the typical number is between three and ten.

Secondary dispositions are characteristics that operate only in limited settings. A person's preferences for particular kinds of food, specific attitudes, and other "peripheral" or situationally determined characteristics would be included.

The Dimensions of Traits: Comparison with Other Personalities

Allport presents two views of traits. Traits can be characteristics that let us compare one person with another (as we might compare body weights). Or they can be a person's unique characteristics that need not invite, or even permit, comparison with others.

Common Traits

Trait comparisons across people presume that there are **common traits**. Life situations continually make us compare people. Business executives must choose among candidates for a secretarial job; colleges must identify the best applicants for higher education. In most cases where the job or role is fixed, someone must identify the personality or person who "fits." Most of us make such rough, approximate comparisons among people daily. The researcher committed to discovering common traits must formalize the criteria for identifying a common trait and must also specify the procedures for measuring it.

This task can be seen in a classic study by Allport and Allport (1928). The investigators were interested in the common trait of *dominance/submission*. This trait was selected based on lexical considerations; in everyday language we often categorize people according to the degree to which they tend to be dominant or submissive in their interactions. Allport and Allport began by developing a scale requiring responses to a variety of situations involving alternatives for action. The alternatives could be characterized as either dominant or submissive.

For Allport, part of the proof of a trait's existence lies in its reliability. The **reliability** of a measure or test is its consistency or repeatability, customarily expressed as a correlation coefficient. *Retest reliability* is the consistency between administrations of the test. In other words, the same test (or an equivalent form) is given to the same people more than once. If each person places about the same on the scale on each occasion, the test has high retest reliability. Here, the correlation is between test administrations. *Internal reliability* is the degree to which the items on a test measure the same thing. A high correlation between items or groups of items indicates high internal reliability.

Trait theory requires that an individual who is dominant in one situation should also tend to be dominant in other situations. Allport found this to be the case. The test for dominance/submission has a retest reliability of +.78 and an internal reliability of +.85. Both correlations are quite high.

Common traits, according to Allport, when scaled for the population at large, often have a *normal distribution*. That is, if the scores of a large sample are plotted on a graph they produce a bell-shaped curve. The majority of cases pile up as average scores in the middle; the high and low scores taper off at the more extreme positions. Allport's test for dominance/submission is distributed this way. Most people are slightly submissive; a few are very submissive or very dominant. The curve is shown in Figure 9–1.

"Patterned Individuality" and the Nature of Individual Traits

Allport acknowledges the merits of comparing personalities along common dimensions (the nomothetic approach). Yet he insists we can really understand others only by coming to grips with the uniqueness of personality. Each of us, Allport believes, has a unique inner organization of motives, traits, and personal style. The result is a "patterned individuality" that will never again be exactly repeated.

Some personality psychologists favor a nomothetic approach and seek general principles of behavior. These psychologists often argue that uniqueness merely reflects the combination of common traits in varying

FIGURE 9–1
The distribution of scores from a test measuring dominance/submission

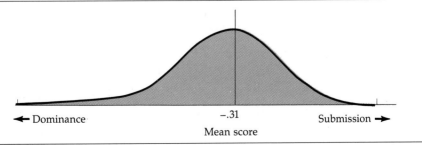

← Dominance   −.31   Submission →

Mean score

Source: From *Pattern and Growth in Personality* by G. W. Allport, 1961, New York: Holt, Rinehart & Winston.

strength. Allport takes issue with this line of reasoning. He claims that a person's traits always interact to form a unique pattern; that pattern cannot be fully explained by its separate parts. As an example, he invites us to compare a molecule of water with a molecule of hydrogen peroxide. They "have the same universals—hydrogen and oxygen; they differ only quantitatively (H_2O versus H_2O_2), but a small quantitative difference leads to totally unlike products. Try them on your hair and see" (Allport, 1961, p. 10).

Allport uses the term **individual traits** to refer to those important characteristics of the individual that do not lend themselves to comparison across persons. Most of Allport's research focuses on common traits and is nomothetic. But he believes that such studies only approximate what people are really like; *all* of an individual's behavior and thought is unique to that person. "Even the acts and concepts that we apparently 'share' with others," he wrote, "are at bottom individual. . . . It is true that some acts and concepts are more idiosyncratic than others, but none can be found that lacks the personal flavor" (Allport, 1961, p. 29). And elsewhere he insisted that "the key qualities which we seek must . . . be *personal*, not universal," adding:

> I am not repudiating the use of nomothetic factors, nor of test scales, ratings and dimensions. More of my own research and writing has been devoted to this type of approach to personality than to any other. The resulting "common traits," I find, have utility for *comparative* purposes, for approximations to the modes of adjustment that similarly constituted individuals in similarly constituted societies can be expected to acquire. . . . What I argue is that . . . we must acknowledge the roughness and inadequacy of our universal dimensions. Thereby shall we enhance our own ability to understand, predict and control. By learning to handle the individuality of motives and the uniqueness of personality, we shall become better scientists, not worse. (Allport, 1960, p. 148)

TYPOLOGIES

The idea that people can be categorized by a small number of types has been popular since ancient times. To show how twentieth-century personality psychology explores this idea, we will look at two quite different typologies. The first comes from the fact that people have noticeably different physiques or body types; the typology tries to relate these differences to differences in personality. The other typology began with the observation that people with a certain behavior pattern seem to be at high risk for heart attacks; this typology has been used to look at differences between people who do and do not display the behavior pattern.

Body Types and Personality: Kretschmer and Sheldon

In 1921, Ernst Kretschmer, a German psychiatrist, published a volume titled *Physique and Character*. It contained the basics of the first modern type approach to personality. From observations made in his clinical practice, Kretschmer investigated the relationship between physique and mental disorders. He proposed three fundamental types of physique: (1) the *asthenic*, a fragile, narrowly built physique; (2) the *athletic*, a muscular type; and (3) the *pyknic*, characterized by plumpness. More unusual types were lumped together as *dysplastic*. (See Figure 9–2.) After examining 400 psychiatric patients, Kretschmer concluded that pyknics are most likely to be diagnosed as manic depressive (i.e., to experience alternating periods of elation and sadness). The remaining types were most likely to be diagnosed as schizophrenic (i.e., to suffer from thought disorders). Some of Kretschmer's data are summarized in Table 9–1 (page 181).

Following Kretschmer's lead, an American psychologist named William Sheldon (1942) tried to relate physique to normal behavior. Sheldon first developed taxonomies of physique and temperament. As had Kretschmer, Sheldon identified three components of body structure; he called them *endomorphy* (plump), *mesomorphy* (muscular), and *ectomorphy* (frail). (See Figure 9–3.) Unlike Kretschmer, however, Sheldon did not classify people as one type or the other. Rather, Sheldon developed a system of **somatyping** using a seven-point scale. Each individual was rated for all three body types. In somatyping, the first number is endomorphy, the second, mesomorphy, and the last, ectomorphy. Thus, a muscular, powerful person might approach the somatype 1–7–1; an individual of average build might be somatyped 4–4–4.

Sheldon then correlated somatypes with personality. He somatyped 200 Caucasian males and followed their lives for five years. He found a clear pattern. Endomorphs tended to be relaxed, easygoing, and lovers of creature comfort. Ectomorphs were generally restrained, inhibited, and apprehensive. Finally, mesomorphs tended to be bold, assertive, and action-oriented.

Developments Following Sheldon's Work

Spurred by Sheldon's provocative findings, the search for relationships between body type and personality continued for many years. For example, a widely cited study compared the somatypes of delinquent and nondelinquent boys (Glueck & Glueck, 1950, 1956). A much larger percentage of mesomorphs than ectomorphs were delinquent. (See Figure 9–4, page 182.)

Other studies dealt with the relationship between physique and occupation. They produced much objective evidence that physique is related to the occupation one pursues; it also relates to success on the job. Students

FIGURE 9–2
The four body types identified by Kretschmer

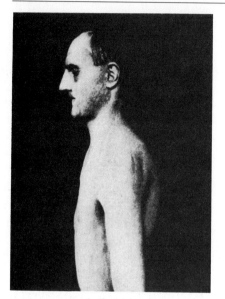

Asthenic

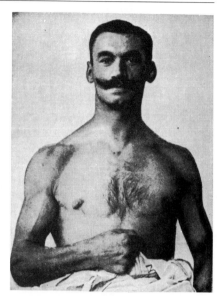

Athletic

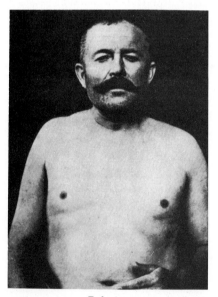

Pyknic

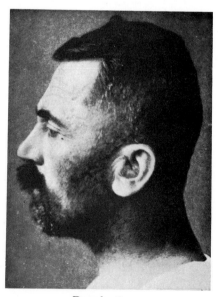

Dysplastic

Source: From *Physique and Character: An Investigation of the Nature of Constitution and of the Theory of Temperament* by E. Kretschmer (W. J. H. Sprott, Trans.), 1926, New York: Harcourt.

TABLE 9–1
The relationship between physique and psychiatric diagnosis

	Schizophrenic (%)	Manic-depressive (%)	Total (%)
Asthenic and athletic	91.2	8.8	100.0
Pyknic	6.5	93.5	100.0

Source: Adapted from *Physique and Character: An Investigation of the Nature of Constitution and of the Theory of Temperament* by E. Kretschmer (W. J. H. Sprott, Trans.), 1926, New York: Harcourt.

of engineering, dentistry, and medicine are more mesomorphic and less ectomorphic than physics and chemistry students (Parnell, 1953). Officer cadets are considerably more mesomorphic and less endomorphic than university students (Tanner, 1955). In one study, research workers were found to be more ectomorphic and less mesomorphic than factory workers in the same organization (Garn & Gertler, 1950). Civilian air pilots are more mesomorphic than the general population (McFarland, 1953); the most successful wartime aviators seem to be the most mesomorphic (Damon, 1955).

What accounts for these associations? Tanner (1955) concluded that a person's choice of a career and the criteria established by employers are probably the most important factors. A person may seem "cut out" for a particular occupation because of physical strength or even appearance; he or she may therefore be attracted to that type of employment. The person may also be seen as appropriate by relevant selection officers and employers.

FIGURE 9–3
Three views of the extremes of Sheldon's somatypes

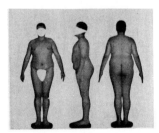
Endomorph

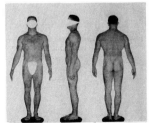
Mesomorph

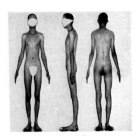
Ectomorph

Source: From *Atlas of Men: A Guide for Somatotyping the Adult Male at All Ages* by W. H. Sheldon, 1954, New York: Harper & Row.

How close is the association between body type and personality? Rees (1961) has summed it up this way:

> One might say that the evidence suggests that there are tendencies for different types of physique to be associated with certain psychological characteristics . . . but the majority of investigations do not report any correlations as high as those reported by Sheldon. . . . The available evidence suggests that the correlations between physical characteristics and personality traits . . . are nearly always too small to be trusted for the needs of [individual prediction]. (p. 377)

Thus, an individual cannot be psychologically "sized up" with any degree of accuracy by body type alone. Nonetheless, *on average*, people with different body types do tend to show recognizable patterns of personality characteristics.

FIGURE 9–4

A portion of Glueck and Glueck's comparison of the somatypes of matched pairs of delinquent and nondelinquent boys. Among the delinquents there are more mesomorphs and fewer ectomorphs than would be expected by chance, a finding consistent with Sheldon's constitutional theory.

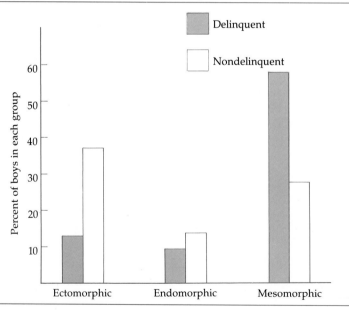

Source: From data published in *Unraveling Juvenile Delinquency* by S. Glueck and E. Glueck, 1950, New York: Commonwealth Fund.

Type A versus Type B Behavior Patterns

Physicians have long noted that the personalities of those with heart problems appear to differ from those without such problems. It wasn't until the late 1950s, however, that the contribution of psychological and behavioral variables to the development of coronary problems was examined systematically. At that time two cardiologists, Meyer Friedman and Ray Rosenman, sent a questionnaire to 150 businesspeople in San Francisco. It asked for information about the behavior of friends who had had heart attacks. More than 70 percent of those who responded said "excessive competitive drive and meeting deadlines" were the most prominent characteristics of the heart disease victims they had known. Friedman and Rosenman called this combination of characteristics the **Type A** behavior pattern. They hypothesized that it is a major cause of coronary artery and heart disease (Friedman & Rosenman, 1974).

Type A and Coronary Disease

An ambitious investigation examined the relationship between Type A behavior and heart disease. Over 3,500 men were followed over a fifteen-year period (Rosenman, Jenkins, Brand, Friedman, Straus, & Wurm, 1975). Incidence of heart problems in those who were unafflicted at the beginning of the study were obtained after periods of four, six, and eight years. The results strongly supported Friedman and Rosenman's hypothesis. Men with Type A behavior at the beginning of the study were several times more likely to have heart problems during the study. This contrasted with men having an easygoing and relaxed behavior pattern. Friedman and Rosenman called the latter group **Type B;** it is essentially the opposite of Type A.

How does Type A behavior lead to heart problems? Research paints a picture of a Type A as an individual who is constitutionally prone to biochemical and physiological overarousal. This is made worse by a tendency to seek out stressful situations; these people still persist in striving, competitive behavior even after symptoms of physical distress appear.

At the biochemical level, under pressure, the Type A has increased serum cholesterol (Friedman & Rosenman, 1974) and catecholamine levels (Glass, 1977b). Either substance may contribute, over time, to coronary problems. There is also evidence that Type A individuals differ from Type B individuals in certain glandular and metabolic responses that may result in increased risk of coronary difficulties (Williams, Friedman, Glass, Herd, & Schneiderman, 1978).

Physiologically, the Type A displays more arousal (e.g., increased blood pressure) than the Type B when working on challenging tasks (Holmes, McGilley, & Houston, 1984; Houston, 1983). The tendency to overrespond physiologically to difficult tasks is coupled with the fact that the Type A seems to go out of his or her way to seek very challenging tasks (Ortega & Pipal, 1984). This suggests that chronic, self-induced over-arousal may be an important link between Type A behavior and heart problems.

Finally, there is reason to believe that the Type A tends to ignore signs of physical distress while working intensely on tasks (Matthews & Carra, 1982; Weidner & Matthews, 1978). This may mean they ignore physical warnings from their bodies; they literally drive themselves into heart attacks.

Personality Characteristics and the Type A/Type B Distinction

Thus far, we have only discussed the relationship of Type A to physical responding and heart problems. Considerable research has looked at the Type A/Type B distinction as a personality typology, independent of its relationship to heart disease. Friedman and Rosenman's original studies used a structured interview to classify Type A or B. Later research relied mainly on a simple paper-and-pencil test, the Jenkins Activity Survey (JAS). The JAS consists of forty-four questions involving the pace and intensity of a person's life. There are several versions for various populations. Sample items from the student form of the JAS appear in Table 9–2.

TABLE 9–2
Sample items from the Jenkins Activity Survey*

Ordinarily, how rapidly do you eat?
1. *I'm usually the first one finished.*
2. I eat a little faster than average.
3. I eat at about the same speed as most people.
4. I eat more slowly than most people.

Would people who know you well agree that you enjoy "a contest" (competition) and try hard to win?
1. *Definitely yes.*
2. Probably yes.
3. Probably no.
4. Definitely no.

Do you ever set deadlines or quotas for yourself in courses or other things?
1. No.
2. Yes, but only occasionally.
3. *Yes, once per week or more often.*

Do you make yourself written lists of "things to do" to help you remember what needs to be done?
1. Never.
2. Occasionally.
3. *Frequently.*

---

*Italicized answers indicate a tendency toward the Type A disposition.

Source: Provided by G. Weidner.

In the decade following Friedman and Rosenman's work, research has established that high scorers on the JAS (which indicates Type A) are characterized by a hard-driving, competitive style; they always seem to be under great time pressure. In fact, they have been described as having "hurry sickness" (Glass, 1977a; Matthews, 1982). Type As are more likely than Type Bs to blame themselves rather than the situation when they fail (Musante, MacDougall, & Dembroski, 1984; Rhodewalt, 1984). They also express more hostility toward others than Type Bs when under pressure (Carver & Glass, 1978; Strube, Turner, Cerro, Stevens, & Hinchey, 1984). Thus, the classic picture of a Type A is a "tense, driven business executive who struggles for long hours at his desk, tapping his fingers and pencil, gulping down his lunch, and talking rapidly into two telephones at once while grimacing hostilely at his dallying assistant" (Friedman, Hall, & Harris, 1985, p. 1299).

Research also suggests that Type A behavior is motivated by a strong need to maintain control over events (Brunson & Matthews, 1981; Miller, Lack, & Asroff, 1985). Strube and Werner (1985), for example, had 160 undergraduate men complete the JAS. They were categorized as Type A or Type B on this basis. The subjects then participated in an experiment. The subject and a partner were to perform a reaction-time task. Each person first did the reaction-time task alone. Subjects were then given feedback on their performance. In fact, this feedback was manipulated; subjects were led to believe that their partners had faster reaction times than they actually had. Subjects were then told to work with their partners to achieve the fastest reaction times for the team over the next twenty trials. It was further explained that only one person could perform on any given trial; each subject was told he was to choose who would perform for their team in each trial. Type Bs willingly gave up control to their "faster" partners. In contrast, Type A subjects refused to give up control,

This executive is exhibiting one of the key characteristics of the Type A behavior pattern: a sense of time urgency that includes doing a number of tasks simultaneously. *Photo by Michael D. Spiegler*

even when they thought their partner's reaction time had been over-whelmingly faster than their own.

Type A: Hindrance or Help?

Type As seem irrational in overburdening themselves. Nonetheless, with their high achievement striving, they tend to be quite successful by society's standards. For example, research has shown that Type As are more successful in school (Waldron et al., 1980); they also reach higher job status (Mettlin, 1976; Waldron, 1978) and greater scientific distinction (Matthews, Helmreich, Beane, & Lucker, 1980) than Type Bs.

There is an interesting twist on the relative advantages of the Type A and Type B patterns. It has recently been noted that the Type A behavior pattern is well-suited to younger individuals; at their stage in life, an achievement-oriented competitiveness may be productive (Strube, Berry, Goza, & Fennimore, 1985). The more relaxed, easygoing style of the Type B is better matched to the slower pace of older ages. Based on this reasoning, Strube and his colleagues surveyed over 3,000 adults between the ages of 18 and 89. They obtained JAS scores and several measures of psychological well-being. As expected, younger Type As experienced greater well-being than Type Bs of their age group. However, older Type As experienced lower well-being than similarly aged Type Bs.

The Type A/Type B distinction is currently being refined. For example, Friedman, Hall, and Harris (1985) recently suggested that the Type A/Type B typology may encompass four distinct types rather than two. These workers point out that not all highly vigorous individuals are impatient, hostile, and tense. And not all slow-paced individuals are calm, contented, and relaxed. Friedman and his associates carefully studied sixty men at risk for heart disease. Based on this work, they believe the four distinct types depend on both activity level and emotional adjustment. (See Figure 9–5.) They also present tentative evidence suggesting that the quality of personal adjustment rather than activity level and pace may determine how illness-prone an individual will be. We must wait for more research to see whether this new, more refined distinction holds up.

THE GENETIC APPROACH

The concept that an individual's personality (as well as physical characteristics) can be transmitted "through the blood" is well known. Is there support for such a belief? Answering this question is fraught with difficulties.

Suppose a man who is very capable verbally *and* very aggressive has three children. If all three of the children were also verbal and aggressive, we might be tempted to conclude that they had inherited these dispositions from their father. Yet it is equally possible that the cause was social, not biological; the children may have been exposed to socially aggressive behavior as well as to a large vocabulary and books; thus, they could have *learned* these characteristics in the early years of life. To sort out the relative effects of heredity and environment, we would somehow have to hold one factor constant so the effects of the other could be seen. The *twin study method* does just this.

The Twin Study Method

One out of every 85 births produces twins. Approximately two thirds of all twins are *fraternal*, or *dizygotic*. This means they develop from separate ova and sperm. Fraternal twins share only a birthday with their "womb mates." Otherwise they are no more alike genetically than siblings born separately. The smaller remaining group are *identical*, or *monozygotic* twins. They develop from the same ovum and sperm. Consequently they have the same genetic endowment. On measures of personality identical twins may be more similar than fraternal twins. If this is so, it results from genetic contribution, as long as the twins are exposed to the same environment. The twin study method involves identifying and measuring a disposition that may be inherited. Then its degree of *concordance* or agreement among many pairs of either identical or fraternal twins is determined.

FIGURE 9–5
A more refined scheme for understanding the Type A/Type B distinction. According to Friedman, Hall, and Harris (1985), emotional adjustment may be as important as pace of life in determining the degree to which an individual is prone to illness.

		Good	Poor
	High	Fast-moving Charismatic Vigorous	Hostile Competitive Impatient
PACE	*Low*	Relaxed Calm Content	Tense Over-controlled Inhibited

EMOTIONAL ADJUSTMENT

Twin Studies of Abnormality and Deviance

In the 1940s, Franz Kallman, a German psychiatrist, examined large samples of persons diagnosed schizophrenic. He determined the percentage of twins who were also diagnosed schizophrenic (Jackson, 1960). Kallman found that concordance, or similarity, in diagnosis of schizophrenia was significantly higher for monozygotic than for dizygotic twins. Later researchers have replicated these findings (Fischer, 1973; Hoffer & Pollin, 1970; Nicol & Gottesman, 1983).

Twin studies suggest that, in addition to schizophrenia, there is a genetic component to manic depressive psychosis, alcoholism, juvenile delinquency, and adult crime (Rushton, Russell, & Wells, 1985). (See Table 9–3.)

Twin Studies of Personality within the Normal Range

Loehlin and Nichols (1976) conducted one of the most extensive twin studies of normal personality done to date. These investigators compared 514 pairs of monozygotic twins with 336 relatively comparable same-sexed dizygotic twins. The twin pairs were chosen from the almost 600,000 persons who, in high school, had taken the National Merit Scholarship test in 1962. Subjects included opposite-sexed and same-sexed pairs. Each subject was given a wide variety of personality, attitude, and interest tests and questionnaires. What is most impressive about the sample is that it was drawn from the entire United States, rather than a single geographic region or ethnic group. It also included more than 5 percent of the entire U.S. twin population in the age group studied.

Table 9–4 shows the major results of the study which support

TABLE 9–3

The percentage of monozygotic (MZ) and same-sex dizygotic (DZ) twins showing concordance for five deviant behavior patterns

Behavioral Category	Number of Studies	Number of Pairs			Percent Concordant	
		Total	MZ	DZ	MZ	DZ
Adult crime	6	225	107	118	71%	34%
Alcoholism	1	82	26	56	65%	30%
Manic-depressive psychosis	5	518	168	350	73%	12%
Juvenile delinquency	2	67	42	25	85%	75%
Schizophrenia	13	1,251	503	748	53%	11%

Source: From data summarized in "Personality and Genetic Similarity Theory" by J. P. Rushton, R. J. H. Russell, and P. A. Wells, 1985, *Journal of Social and Biological Structure, 8.*

numerous earlier studies. Monozygotic twins were more alike than dizygotic same-sexed pairs on a wide variety of measures of personality and ability. In addition, though this is not shown in Table 9–4, the same general pattern held for both male pairs and female pairs.

Aspects of Personality Most Susceptible to Genetic Influence

Evidence has been mounting that three broad aspects of personality—introversion/extroversion, emotionality, and activity level—may be genetically influenced. They show up as individual differences early in life; they are also impressively stable over the life span (Buss & Plomin, 1984).

Introversion/Extroversion (Sociability)

Introversion/extroversion or sociability encompasses opposite styles of dealing with the social environment. At one extreme, **introverts** are shy and anxious in new social situations; they prefer to withdraw from people rather than approach them. **Extroverts,** in contrast, show unusual ease among people, great friendliness, and a marked ability and willingness to introduce themselves to and seek out others.

What is the evidence that introversion/extroversion is inherited? Friendly infants tend to become friendly teenagers; unfriendly infants are likely to be unfriendly as adolescents (Schaefer & Bayley, 1963). In addition, a large and growing body of evidence suggests that monozygotic twins are considerably more alike than dizygotic twins on the sociability dimension (Buss, Plomin, & Willerman, 1973; Royce & Powell, 1983; Scarr, 1969). For example, one study dealt with almost 13,000 pairs of Swedish twins (Floderus-Myrhed, Pedersen, & Rasmuson, 1980). The correlations for monozygotic twins were .54 and .47 for females and males, respectively; the corresponding correlations for dizygotic twins were only .21 and .20.

TABLE 9–4
Resemblance of monozygotic and dizygotic twin pairs in Loehlin and Nichols' study of 1,700 twins

Area Measured	Monozygotic Twins*	Dizygotic Twins*
General ability	.86	.62
Special abilities	.74	.52
Personality scales	.50	.28
Self-concept clusters	.34	.10

*The data shown are correlation coefficients.

Source: From data reported in *Heredity, Environment, and Personality* by J. C. Loehlin and R. C. Nichols, 1976, Austin: University of Texas Press.

Similarly, Daniels and Plomin (1984) found that adopted infants tend to be more similar in sociability to their *biological* mothers, with whom they have had no contact, than to their adoptive mothers. This is taken as very strong evidence that sociability is largely a genetically determined trait (Plomin, 1985).

Emotionality

Considerable evidence suggests that the degree to which a person is emotionally reactive has a hereditary component. There is strong evidence that children differ in emotionality almost from birth (Birns, 1965; Thomas & Chess, 1977; Thomas, Chess, & Birch, 1970). For example, Thomas and his associates have been following the development of 141 children since 1956. They have interviewed each youngster's parents every three months during the first year, every six months until age five, and every year thereafter. Behavioral data were obtained from a variety of sources: teacher interviews; direct classroom observation; psychometric testing done when the children were three, six, and nine; and through a direct interview with each child between the age of sixteen and seventeen. The data showed that people have well-established emotional patterns by the time they are two or three months old. This is seen, for example, in responses to unfamiliar objects. These findings agree with earlier studies of newborns. The studies showed sizable individual differences in how intensely infants respond to various situations; this was true even in the first few days of life (Birns, 1965; Schaffer & Emerson, 1964).

Buss, Plomin, and Willerman (1973) demonstrated the genetic component in emotionality. These workers used the twin study method. They obtained extensive questionnaire information from the mothers of 127 pairs of twins. The twins included monozygotic and same-sexed dizygotic pairs of both sexes. At the time of the study, the age of the twins ranged from four months to sixteen years. A portion of the results are shown in Table 9–5. It can be clearly seen that ratings of similar emotionality were

TABLE 9–5
Similarity of emotionality in Buss, Plomin, and Willerman's study of monozygotic and dizygotic twin pairs as rated by their mothers*

Boys		Girls	
Monozygotic	**Dizygotic**	**Monozygotic**	**Dizygotic**
.63	.00	.73	.20

*The data are correlation coefficients.

Source: From data reported in "The Inheritance of Temperaments" by A. H. Buss, R. Plomin, and L. Willerman, 1973, *Journal of Persoanlity, 41*, pp. 513–24.

higher for monozygotic than for dizygotic twins; this was true for both males and females.

Activity Level

Buss and his associates (1973) referred to activity level as "the sheer amount of response output" of the individual. A person's activity level seems to be influenced by genetic factors. For example, two studies showed that hyperactive children may be as much as ten times more likely than non-hyperactive, control-group children to have had hyperactive parents (Cantwell, 1972; Morrison & Stewart, 1971). In addition, Willerman and Plomin (1973) found significant correlations between activity levels of normal children and activity levels of both parents when they were children.

A number of other studies support the conclusion that activity level is inherited and that the effect is present for both sexes (Plomin & Foch, 1980; Willerman, 1973). For example, in a recent study of fifty-three twin pairs, Torgersen (1985) found a correlation of .93 for the activity levels of monozygotic twins; in comparison, the correlation was only .14 for the dizygotic twins.

FACTOR ANALYSIS

Raymond Cattell (1905-), a prominent dispositional psychologist, quipped that "the trouble with measuring traits is that there are too many of them!" (1965, p. 55). To solve the problem, Cattell uses a statistical approach (as opposed to a lexical or theoretical approach). His intent is to discover empirically the natural personality structures that exist in people. Cattell (1965) explained the rationale behind his approach using the following analogy.

> The problem which baffled psychologists for many years was to find a method which would tease out these functionally unitary

Raymond B. Cattell

Courtesy of Raymond B. Cattell

influences in the chaotic jungle of human behavior. But let us ask how, in the literal tropical jungle, the hunter decides whether the dark blobs which he sees are two or three rotting logs or a single alligator? He watches for movement. *If they move together— come and disappear together—he infers a single structure.* (1965, p. 56; italics added)

In the "jungle" of human behavior, however, perfect covariation is rare. Psychological variables do not *always* go together. We may get a fleeting glimpse of some strong covariations but never the perfect data generated by Cattell's alligator. The correlational method lets us evaluate degrees of relationship that are not perfect. It also solves an additional problem. The number of variables to consider in trying to discover the basic structure of personality is very large. How do dispositional psychologists like Cattell deal with correlations between dozens, even hundreds, of psychological variables? The answer lies in a mathematical procedure known as **factor analysis.** Basically, this method reduces a large number of relationships (correlations) to a smaller, more manageable and comprehensible number of relationships. In essence, the smaller group summarizes the entire array of intercorrelations. Factor analysis was first developed in 1904 by Charles Spearman, a British statistician. Its popularity today results from the availability of high-speed computers; without them, much of the current work using the technique would be virtually impossible.

A Hypothetical Example of a Factor Analysis

Suppose that an investigator wants to learn something about college students' patterns of academic performance, to determine what underlying skills are involved. Factor analysis could be used in such research. If it were, the investigation would proceed through the five steps summarized in Figure 9–6.

Data Collection

The first step in factor analysis is data collection. In our example, the investigator gathered a large number of students (subjects) and gave them seven different tests (measures).

Determining the Relationship of Each Variable to Every Other: The Correlation Matrix

The next step involves producing a **correlation matrix.** This is a table showing the exact relationship between each measure and every one of the others. Consider the correlation matrix in Table 9–6. It contains the

FIGURE 9–6
The five steps involved in factor analysis. The purpose of the procedure is to reduce the information available about a large number of measures (variables) to manageable size, and to interpret the pattern that emerges.

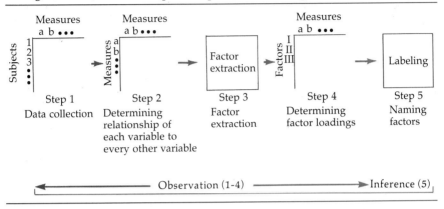

correlations of each of seven measures with every other measure. This matrix tells us that there is a high positive relationship between a and b (+.70), a and c (+.80), a and d (+.80), b and c (+.90), b and d (+.70), c and d (+.80), e and f (+.80), e and g (+.70), and f and g (+.70). There is virtually no systematic relationship (i.e., correlation coefficients in the vicinity of 0) between a and e (−.10), a and f (.00), a and g (.00), b and e (+.10), b and f (+.10), b and g (.00), c and e (−.10), c and f (−.10), c and g (−.10), d and e (.00), d and f (−.10), and d and g (.00).

TABLE 9–6
Hypothetical correlation matrix

Measure	a	b	c	d	e	f	g
a	+1.00	+.70	+.80	+.80	−.10	.00	.00
b		+1.00	+.90	+.70	+.10	+.10	.00
c			+1.00	+.80	−.10	−.10	−.10
d				+1.00	.00	−.10	.00
e					+1.00	+.80	+.70
f						+1.00	+.70
g							+1.00

Factor Extraction

Our example yielded a correlation matrix (Table 9–6) from a relatively small number of measures. However, it is not uncommon for 100 or more variables to be correlated in actual factor-analytic studies. Still, the complexities and sheer time needed to summarize and interpret the data should be apparent from the rather laborious enumeration of results just presented. A major function of factor analysis is to reduce large sets of data to manageable units. By means of complex mathematical formulas, the data are reduced to small numbers of relatively homogeneous dimensions; these are called **factors.** The factors are said to be *extracted* from the data.

Determining Factor Loadings

Factors extracted in the previous step are the "common denominators" of all relationships between the variables. In a less exact way, the factors are like the three primary colors from which all colors are composed. The next step is determining the relationship between each of the measures and each of the factors. The correlation of a measure with a particular factor is its **factor loading.** Thus, a variable is said to "load" on a factor to the extent that it is correlated with that factor.

Factor Naming

Factor naming is the last step in a factor analysis. It is the point at which inference and subjective judgment enter the picture.

Let us return to the correlation matrix in Table 9–6. Suppose that the measures were aptitude tests in academic areas, where a = English, b = fine arts, c = history, d = French, e = mathematics, f = physics, and g = engineering. The factor analysis reveals a distinct pattern among these seven measures (a through g). Specifically, a, b, c, and d seem to "go together." They are highly correlated with one another but show little or no relationship (i.e., near 0) to the other three measures. Similarly, e, f, and g are highly related to one another but not to the other measures. Thus, two units or *factors* emerge from the seven measures. One factor consists of English, fine arts, history, and French, and the other factor consists of mathematics, physics, and engineering. These factors might simply be labeled X and Y. We could also inspect the related measures for common qualities and give the two factors more meaningful names. However, the naming itself would be a *subjective* judgment; it is not a logical consequence of the mathematical factor analysis. Some people might insist that factor X represents a "literary" aptitude and factor Y a "scientific" aptitude; others might say that factor Y involves understanding inanimate forces, whereas factor X involves understanding people and their products. This is why we should remember that "there is nothing in the factor-analytic methods themselves that can demonstrate that one factor solution is more scientifically useful than another" and "the correctness of interpretations based on factor-analytic results must be confirmed by evidence outside the factor analysis itself" (Comrey, 1973, p. 11).

A number of dispositional psychologists rely on factor analysis to direct their research. We will discuss two of the more prominent of these dispositionalists, Cattell and Eysenck.

CATTELL'S TRAIT APPROACH

Cattell (1965; 1979; Cattell & Kline, 1977) proposes that there should be three broad sources of data about personality. He labels these *L*-data, *Q*-data, and *T*-data. **L-data** are information that can be gathered from a person's life records (e.g., school records and work history).

Q-data are gathered from questionnaires and interviews. The common feature of *Q*-data is that the individual answers direct questions about him- or herself, based on personal observations and introspection (e.g., "Do you have trouble making and keeping friends?").

T-data are obtained from objective testing situations. "The subject is placed in a miniature situation and simply acts . . . [and] *does not know on what aspect of his behavior he is really being evaluated*" (Cattell, 1965, p. 104). There are several hundred tests that meet these criteria of objectivity (Cattell & Warburton, 1967).

According to Cattell, the three sources of data can and must be integrated to capture the full complexity of human personality. Traditionally, psychologists have looked at only one slice at a time; their research has been *univariate*—that is, the experiments change one (independent) variable and examine its effects on one other (dependent) variable. In contrast, *multivariate* approaches have the advantage that "with sufficient analytical subtlety we can tease out the connections from the behavior of the man in his actual life situation—without the false situation of controlling and manipulating" (Cattell, 1965, p. 20). Cattell uses correlational studies in which existing characteristics of subjects are measured; these provide the more natural data-gathering process that Cattell advocates. Cattell (1965) asserts that

> The development of beautiful and complex mathematicostatistical methods like factor analysis has enabled us to take natural data, much as the clinician has long done—except that normals are now included—and to find laws and build sound theories about the structure and functioning of personality. (p. 23)

What is the evidence for this assertion?

Three Personality Traits Derived from *L*-data and *Q*-data

In one of Cattell's studies, several hundred young men and women were rated by people who knew them well. The rating was on fifty different **trait elements,** that is, elements from which the traits are derived using factor analysis. Four of these trait elements are listed in Table 9–7.

Correlations among ratings on the fifty trait elements were subjected to a factor analysis. Cattell found that twenty factors emerged.[1] Twenty factors summarize the personality ratings better than fifty trait elements do. But twenty bits of information are still not exactly an easily comprehensible summary. Therefore, the next step was determining the relative importance of each of the twenty factors. For this purpose, the factors

TABLE 9–7
Four (of fifty) trait elements on which young men and women were rated

1.	*Adaptable:* flexible; accepts changes of plan easily; satisfied with compromises; is not upset, surprised, baffled, or irritated if things are different from what he expected.	vs. *Rigid:* insists that things be done the way he has always done them; does not adapt his habits and ways of thinking to those of the group; nonplussed if his routine is upset.
2.	*Emotional:* excitable; cries a lot (children); laughs a lot; shows affection, anger, all emotions to excess.	vs. *Calm:* stable, shows few signs of emotional excitement of any kind; remains calm, even underreacts, in terms of dispute, danger, social hilarity, etc.
3.	*Conscientious:* honest; knows what is right and generally does it, even if no one is watching him; does not tell lies or attempt to deceive others; respects others' property.	vs. *Unconscientious:* somewhat unscrupulous; not too careful about standards of right and wrong where personal desires are concerned; tells lies and is given to little deceits; does not respect others' property.
4.	*Conventional:* conforms to accepted standards, ways of acting, thinking, dressing, etc.; does the "proper" thing; seems distressed if he finds he is being different.	vs. *Unconventional, eccentric:* acts differently from others; not concerned about wearing the same clothes or doing the same things as others; has somewhat eccentric interests, attitudes, and ways of behaving; goes his own rather peculiar way.

Source: From *The Scientific Analysis of Personality* by R. B. Cattell, 1965, Baltimore: Penguin Books.

---

[1]The number of factors that adequately summarize a given set of data depends upon the nature of the data and the specific type of factor analysis employed.

are arranged in terms of the degree to which each "explains" or "accounts for" all the trait elements as a group. At the top of this hierarchy is the factor that is the largest single summary of all the data. This factor is assigned the letter A; the letter B is assigned to the factor that accounts for the next most comprehensive summary of all the trait elements; and so on. Cattell (1965) suggests that this procedure lets us look at the patterns of results "without prejudice from earlier clinical notions or traditional popular terms." He noted, as an aside, that "the investigators of vitamins did just the same, in a parallel situation, where the entities could be identified in terms of their *effects* before truly interpretive chemical labels could be attached to them" (p. 65).

Cattell summarized his work in *The Scientific Analysis of Personality* (1965). In it, he indicated that 16 personality traits were scientifically derived with factor-analytic and related procedures. These represent the major dimensions of differences in human personality. The 16 traits are listed in Table 9–8.

We will consider the three most important factors (i.e., A, B, and C). As part of the factor analysis, the ratings for each of the fifty trait elements were correlated with each of the factors that had been found. The elements that correlated (loaded) most highly with factor A, both in a positive and a negative direction, are listed in Table 9–9.

TABLE 9–8
The sixteen major factors in Cattell's analysis of personality

Low-Score Description	Factor		Factor	High-Score Description
Reserved	$A-$	vs.	$A+$	Outgoing
Less intelligent	$B-$	vs.	$B+$	More intelligent
Emotional	$C-$	vs.	$C+$	Stable
Humble	$E-$	vs.	$E+$	Assertive
Sober	$F-$	vs.	$F+$	Happy-go-lucky
Expedient	$G-$	vs.	$G+$	Conscientious
Shy	$H-$	vs.	$H+$	Venturesome
Tough-minded	$I-$	vs.	$I+$	Tender-minded
Trusting	$L-$	vs.	$L+$	Suspicious
Practical	$M-$	vs.	$M+$	Imaginative
Forthright	$N-$	vs.	$N+$	Shrewd
Placid	$O-$	vs.	$O+$	Apprehensive
Conservative	Q_1-	vs.	Q_1+	Experimenting
Group-tied	Q_2-	vs.	Q_2+	Self-sufficient
Casual	Q_3-	vs.	Q_3+	Controlled
Relaxed	Q_4-	vs.	Q_4+	Tense

Source: From *The Scientific Analysis of Personality* by R. B. Cattell, 1965, Baltimore: Penguin Books.

TABLE 9–9
Elements (ratings) which load on factor *A:* Outgoing versus reserved

A+ (Positively Loaded)		A− (Negatively Loaded)
Good natured, easygoing	vs.	Critical, grasping
Cooperative	vs.	Obstructive
Attentive to people	vs.	Cool, aloof
Softhearted	vs.	Hard, precise
Trustful	vs.	Suspicious
Adaptable	vs.	Rigid

Source: From *The Scientific Analysis of Personality* by R. B. Cattell, 1965, Baltimore: Penguin Books.

Source Traits

Cattell calls factor *A* (as well as factors *B* and *C*) **source traits.** These are underlying variables that are sources or determinants of behavior. He views source traits as the building blocks of personality. Cattell maintains that they can be discovered only by factor analysis.

Surface traits are produced by interaction of source traits. They are clusters of overt behavior that seem to go together, even to the casual observer. However, the behaviors that make up a surface trait do not always vary together; the behaviors may not have a common cause. For example, success in politics and success in business sometimes occur in the same people; the relationship would constitute a surface trait. This surface trait, though, might be caused by a combination of independent source traits, such as being outgoing (factor *A*) and shrewd (factor *N*). Relative to surface traits, there are only a small number of source traits. Source traits tend to be more stable than surface traits. Also, surface traits are mainly descriptive; source traits are explanatory and causal.

Let us return to our discussion of factor *A*. If it is a source trait, we would expect the same pattern of results that emerged from the *L*-data (i.e., the ratings on the fifty trait elements) to appear in *Q*-data. That is, if the trait is really an underlying dimension of personality, it should be reflected in all measures of personality. Sample questionnaire responses that load high on factor *A* are given in Table 9–10. Considering these *Q*-data, and referring back to the *L*-data, Cattell (1965) concluded: "The warm sociability at one pole, and the aloofness and unconcern with people at the other are as evident here as in the observers' ratings" (p. 71).

With respect to the ratings on the fifty trait elements (i.e., *L*-data), Cattell (1965) concluded that the second largest source trait, factor *B*, "looks like nothing less than general intelligence, and correlates well with actual test results" (p. 72).

Cattell identified the third largest source trait, factor *C*, as "ego strength." The *L*- and *Q*-data in Table 9–11 illustrate the nature of this

TABLE 9–10
Factor *A* in questionnaire responses (*Q*-Data)

1. I would rather work as:
   (a) An engineer   (b) *A social science teacher*
2. I could stand being a hermit.
   (a) True   (b) *False*
3. I am careful to turn up when someone
   expects me.
   (a) *True*   (b) False
4. I would prefer to marry someone who
   is:
   (a) A thoughtful companion   (b) *Effective in a social group*
5. I would prefer to read a book on:
   (a) *National social service*   (b) New scientific weapons
6. I trust strangers:
   (a) Sometimes   (b) *Practically always*

Note: A person who selects all the italicized answers has a highly outgoing personality.

Source: From *The Scientific Analysis of Personality* by R. B. Cattell, 1965, Baltimore: Penguin Books.

TABLE 9–11
L- and *Q*-Data for source trait *C*

Behavior Ratings (*L*-Data) which Load on Factor *C*

C+ (Positively Loaded)		C− (Negatively Loaded)
Mature	vs.	Unable to tolerate frustration
Steady, persistent	vs.	Changeable
Emotionally calm	vs.	Impulsively emotional
Realistic about problems	vs.	Evasive, avoids necessary decisions
Absence of neurotic fatigue	vs.	Neurotically fatigued (with no real effort)

Factor *C* Questionnaire Responses (*Q*-Data)

Do you find it difficult to take no for an answer even when what you want to do is obviously impossible?
  (a) Yes   (b) *No*

If you had your life to live over again, would you
  (a) *Want it to be essentially the same?*   (b) Plan it very differently?

Do you often have really disturbing dreams?
  (a) Yes   (b) *No*

Do your moods sometimes make you seem unreasonable even to yourself?
  (a) Yes   (b) *No*

Do you feel tired when you've done nothing to justify it?
  (a) *Rarely*   (b) Often

Can you change old habits, without relapse, when you decide to?
  (a) *Yes*   (b) No

Note: A person who selects all the italicized answers has high ego-strength, whereas selection of all the nonitalicized responses indicates low ego-strength.

Source: From *The Scientific Analysis of Personality* by R. B. Cattell, 1965, Baltimore: Penguin Books.

source trait. Cattell noted the following about factor *C*:

> The essence of factor *C* appears to be an inability to control one's emotions and impulses, especially by finding for them some satisfactory realistic expression. Looked at from the opposite or positive pole, it sharpens and gives scientific substance to the psychoanalytic concept of "ego strength," which it [factor *C*] has come to be called. (1965, pp. 73–74)

TYPES AS DIMENSIONS OF PERSONALITY: EYSENCK'S VIEW

There are differences in the dispositional approaches of Cattell and of Hans Eysenck (1916–). Perhaps the main one is the level at which each looks for the basic dimensions of personality. Cattell's research revealed sixteen source traits. In contrast, Eysenck's investigations focus on a considerably smaller number of basic personality *types*.

In Eysenck's view, **types** are not categories that a few people fit; rather, types are dimensions on which all persons differ. They tend to be normally distributed, as do traits. (See Figure 9–7 on page 201.) Most people fall around the average mark. Eysenck conceives of types as continuous dimensions. This is different from ancient theories that considered traits to be discontinuous or dichotomous. Figure 9–7 illustrates the difference.

Eysenck developed a structural model of personality. Types are at the top of the personality structure; therefore, they exert the most com-

H. J. Eysenck

Courtesy of H. J. Eysenck

FIGURE 9–7
A graphic representation of the difference between ancient type theories (A) and Eysenck's view of types as continuous dimensions on which personalities differ (B)

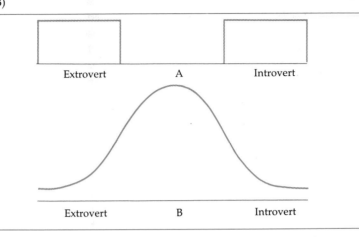

manding influence. Types are composed of traits; traits are composed of habitual responses. At the most particular level, specific responses are the elements from which we form habits. This overall view is shown in Figure 9–8.

Using factor-analysis, Eysenck and his colleagues have performed dozens of studies over more than forty years. (As far back as World War

FIGURE 9–8
Eysenck's hierarchical model of personality

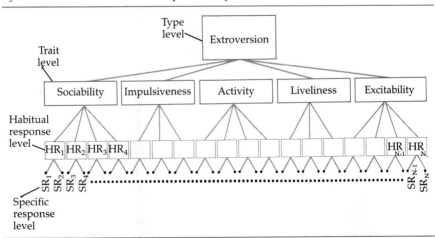

Source: Adapted from *The Biological Basis of Personality* by H. J. Eysenck, 1967, Springfield, Ill.: Charles C Thomas.

II, for example, Eysenck applied factor-analysis to ratings and classifications of approximately 10,000 soldiers.) In this time, he has gathered an impressive body of evidence that suggests there are two major personality dimensions: *introversion/extroversion* and *stability/instability*.

How are introversion/extroversion and stability/instability related? Eysenck's (1975) representation of personality appears in Figure 9–9. Each individual's personality is positioned somewhere within a circle bisected by each of the two dimensions; four quadrants result. Eysenck says of this model: "The trait names inside the circle may serve to give an idea of the behavior patterns characteristic of extroverts and introverts, labile and stabile people—remembering always that extremes in either direction are rare, and that most people are somewhere intermediate" (1975, p. 190). Eysenck (1975) points out, however, that forms of psychological deviance, such as criminal acts, can be understood in part as extreme cases

FIGURE 9–9

The two major dimensions of personality suggested by Eysenck's factor-analytic studies. An individual personality can fall in any of the four quadrants.

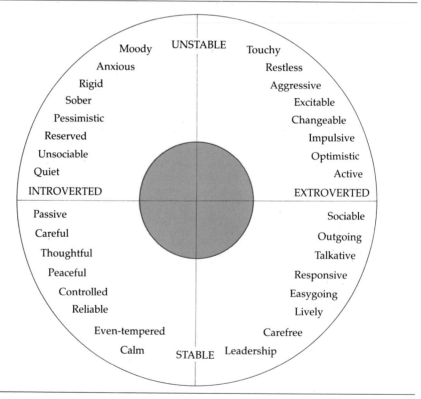

Source: Adapted from *The Inequality of Man* by H. J. Eysenck, 1975, San Diego, Calif.: Edit Publishers.

in the normal distribution of the two major personality dimensions. For example, he concluded that when high emotionality and high extroversion combine, they tend to produce criminality (Eysenck, 1977).

Eysenck (1975) identified a third underlying aspect of personality, called *psychoticism*. It plays a somewhat smaller role than extroversion / introversion and stability/instability. Psychoticism includes a disposition toward psychosis (a mental disorder characterized by poor contact with reality and inability to handle daily tasks). Psychoticism also includes a degree of psychopathy (characterized by an absence of real loyalties to any person, group, or code). Unlike extroversion/introversion and stability/instability, psychoticism is not a dimension with polar opposites; rather, it is an ingredient that is present to varying degrees in individual personalities. People who score high on psychoticism, according to Eysenck (1975, p. 197), are characterized by eleven dispositions:

1. Solitary, not caring for people.
2. Troublesome, not fitting in.
3. Cruel, inhumane.
4. Lack feeling, insensitive.
5. Sensation seeking, underaroused.
6. Hostile to others, aggressive.
7. Like odd, unusual things.
8. Disregard danger, foolhardy.
9. Like to make fools of other people, upsetting them.
10. Opposed to accepted social customs.
11. Engage in little personal interaction; prefer "impersonal" sex.

Eysenck (1975) reports that psychoticism is: higher in men than in women; heritable; higher in prisoners than in nonprisoners (and highest in those imprisoned for sexual or aggressive offenses); and lower in psychiatric patients who have improved than in those who have not.

Origins of Personality Differences

In his early writings (e.g., Eysenck, 1952), Eysenck did not discuss the causes of personality types. Later, Eysenck (1961, 1964) hypothesized that underlying all the differences that distinguish introversion from extroversion is a difference in *conditionability*—that is, the tendency to form stimulus-response associations on the basis of experience. Specifically, Eysenck believes that introverts condition much more rapidly than do extroverts. This explains, among other things, why introverts seem so "sensitive." He also believes that the brains of extreme introverts are too easily aroused so that they shy away from stimulation. In contrast, extreme extroverts must seek stimulation to maintain their brain activity levels and avoid boredom. "Extroverts," Eysenck wrote, "tend to have a level [of arousal] which is too low much of the time, unless environment can provide excitement and stimulation; hence they tend to be stimulus hungry and sensation seeking" (1975, p. 194).

In *Crime and Personality* (1977), Eysenck reviews the literature supporting a relationship between extroversion and antisocial behavior. Along these lines, Eysenck (1964) and other investigators (Lykken, 1957; Schachter & Latané, 1964) report that antisocial individuals do not easily form conditioned avoidance responses. That is, they do not learn to avoid unpleasant stimuli. For example, in Lykken's (1957) experiment, subjects included penitentiary inmates judged to have sociopathic personalities. (These people are characterized by selfishness, lack of guilt feelings, and inability to display loyalty.) Other subjects were inmates judged not to be sociopaths, and college students. The task involved learning through trial-and-error to avoid pressing a lever that produced electric shocks. Everyone learns this task with experience. But the college students learned to avoid shocks more quickly than the sociopaths. This suggests at least some relationship between personality and conditionability. Eysenck interpreted these and similar findings as showing an association between the need for stimulation and the difficulty in learning social inhibitions that characterize both extroversion and a tendency toward criminal behavior.

In his later writings, Eysenck (1975) went further. He suggested that much of personality is fixed and of a constitutional or genetic origin. "However we look at the facts," argues Eysenck (1975) after summarizing thirty-five years of research, "heredity plays a very important part in the cause of these many different types of conduct and . . . behavior, and is responsible for a good proportion of the individual differences observed in our type of society" (p. 201). Eysenck's conclusion converges with the conclusions of genetic researchers discussed earlier in the chapter. This suggests that sociability or introversion/extroversion and emotionality or stability/instability are important, heritable dimensions of personality.

SUMMARY

1. In their search for important dispositions, personality psychologists have used three different approaches. The lexical approach begins with the words that people use to describe others and themselves in everyday conversation. The theoretical approach relies on theory as a guide to identifying important dispositions. The statistical approach feeds large amounts of data about people into complex statistical procedures, especially factor analysis, to identify the most basic personality dimensions on which people differ.

2. Allport is generally acknowledged as the founder of the modern dispositional strategy. His basic philosophy is called heuristic realism, meaning that traits actually exist within the person (i.e., they are not just convenient fictions).

3. Allport acknowledged three levels of dispositions, varying in their pervasiveness. The most pervasive traits are cardinal dispositions, which dominate the personalities of those who have them. Central dispositions are the small set of traits that are highly characteristic of the individual. Secondary dispositions are those that operate only in limited settings.

4. Allport drew the distinction between individual and common traits. Common traits are the dispositions on which people can be compared; they are usually normally distributed. Individual traits are those characteristics of a person that do not lend themselves to comparison with other persons.

5. Kretschmer pioneered the modern type approach by showing that among mental patients there is a link between body type and psychiatric diagnosis. Sheldon studied the relationship between physique and normal personality. He reported that those with a plump body type (endomorphy) tend to be easygoing and to love comfort, whereas those of frail body type (ectomorphy) tend to be inhibited and apprehensive, and those with a muscular body type (mesomorphy) tend to be bold and action-oriented. Later studies have confirmed these relationships to some extent, but the correlations between physique and temperament are too small to allow individual personality predictions based merely on body type.

6. Friedman and Rosenman found that hard driving, competitive people who are always hurrying to meet deadlines (Type A individuals) are at considerably greater risk for heart attacks than more relaxed, easygoing individuals (Type B). Type As have been found to become psychologically overaroused and often hostile under stress; they also appear to be strongly motivated to maintain personal control over events in their lives. These characteristics often lead to greater academic and business success, but are poorly suited to the more relaxed and noncompetitive tempo of older adults.

7. The genetic approach begins with the assumption that some dispositions are inherited. Research comparing monozygotic (identical) and dizygotic (fraternal) twins suggests that several types of abnormality and deviance are partly heritable. Within the normal range of personality, introversion/extroversion (sociability), emotionality, and activity level all seem to have a significant heritable component.

8. Cattell pioneered the use of factor analysis to determine the underlying dispositions (source traits) on which people differ. Using a combination of questionnaires and interviews (Q-data), observations made in test situations (T-data), and information drawn from people's life records (L-data), Cattell concluded that the three most significant source traits are sociability, general intelligence, and ego strength (emotional control).

9. Eysenck has used factor analysis to search for underlying dimensions of personality. He also has found introversion/extroversion and emotional stability/instability to be two major dimensions on which people differ. Eysenck has identified a third dimension, psychoticism, which does not consist of polar opposites but serves instead as an ingredient that is present to a greater or lesser degree in all personalities. Psychoticism includes a tendency to be solitary, troublesome, insensitive, sensation-seeking, aggressive, and foolhardy. Over the years Eysenck has come to share the geneticists' view that the major dispositions are to a considerable extent heritable.

THE ASSESSMENT OF DISPOSITIONS

OVERVIEW

As we saw in the last chapter, many personality psychologists who adopt a trait or type perspective rely heavily on self-report inventories for their data. (Self-report inventories are also used in other personality strategies.) **Self-report personality inventories** are questionnaires. They contain a large number of statements or questions to which the subject responds with a limited number of fixed alternatives, such as "yes/no," "true/false," and "agree/disagree." (Occasionally there is a "cannot say" choice.) The following are typical items:

I often get mad when things don't turn out as planned.

I enjoy music and dancing.

Are you afraid of high places?

Do you have trouble falling asleep at night?

The items are usually printed in a booklet with separate answer sheets. The tests can easily be given to many subjects at once. The use of such procedures is extremely widespread; perhaps as much as two thirds of the American population will take some sort of self-report personality inventory at some time in their lives (cf. Fiske, 1971).

CONSTRUCTION OF PERSONALITY INVENTORIES

There are two basic ways of constructing self-report personality inventories: content validation and empirical keying.

Content Validation

Most dispositional psychologists see traits or types as composed of more specific habits, response tendencies, and ways of reacting to situations. Thus, if we specify what a person with a particular disposition should think, feel, and do, an adequate self-report inventory need only sample these thoughts, emotions, and behaviors. An example of an item that reflects the disposition toward depression might be: "I am often sad." If the habits and "symptoms" of the dispositions the inventory measures are adequately sampled, the inventory would have **content validity.** The content of the items relates to the disposition being measured.

The content validation approach to inventory construction has some problems. First, content validity does not tell us what a test actually measures. *External* validation is needed to determine if the test is successful in classifying people. For example, the classification using the test could be compared with that obtained from the independent clinical judgments of psychologists. If individuals cannot be classified properly from test responses, there is little solace in knowing that the test asked about the full range of behavior in every category. As we shall see later in the chapter, a test with high content validity can fail because examinees respond not to the content of the items but to some aspect of the test-taking situation.

There is a second problem with content validation. An inventory constructed on the basis of content validity may lack subtlety. The test items may clearly indicate what they are assessing. Psychologists who designed some of the early self-report inventories paid little attention to this problem (e.g., Woodworth, 1920). They felt a test item should "look like" it was measuring what it was intended to measure. More recently, psychologists have tended toward the other extreme. They maintain that the respondent should be unaware of what a test item is supposed to measure. A principal argument for the use of subtle test items is that obvious items let the subject fake answers, make a good impression, or otherwise distort his or her "real" personality.

Empirical Keying: An Alternative to Content Validation

Many research-minded test designers are sensitive to the limitations of content validation. Instead, they use **empirical keying** to design self-report inventories. This procedure makes no theoretical assumptions about the items needed for a test to be valid. To illustrate the procedure, we will describe the development of the Minnesota Multiphasic Personality Inventory (MMPI).

The MMPI was constructed by S. R. Hathaway, a clinical psychologist, and J. C. McKinley, a neuropsychiatrist, in 1942. It filled a need for a practical and valid test to classify patients according to diagnostic categories of abnormal behavior. Hathaway and McKinley began with a pool of 1,000 self-descriptive statements. The statements were collected from various psychiatric examination forms and procedures, psychiatric textbooks, and previous inventories. The 1,000 items were given to groups of diagnosed psychiatric patients. (The patients were classified based on clinical judgments.) It was also given to groups of normal subjects. How often subjects agreed with each item was tabulated. Only items that clearly differentiated between a diagnostic group and the normal group were retained. For instance, a statement might become an item on the depression scale if, and only if, patients with a depressive disorder agreed with the statement significantly more often than did normal persons. Thus, using empirical keying, it was possible for an item with little content validity (e.g., "I sometimes tease animals") to be included on the depression scale (or any other scale) of the MMPI.

THE MINNESOTA MULTIPHASIC PERSONALITY INVENTORY

The MMPI is probably still the most widely used personality inventory. It consists of 550 statements. These deal with such matters as attitudes, educational information, general physical health, sex roles, mood, morale, vocational interests, fears, and preoccupations. The MMPI is scored for four validity scales and ten basic clinical scales. The characteristics and labels of these scales are listed in Table 10–1. The validity scales provide information about the validity of responses on the clinical scales. For example, an elevated *Lie* (*L*) scale indicates that the respondent is trying to answer the items to present her- or himself in a favorable light.

Scoring the MMPI is straightforward. Scoring keys indicate the items on each scale and the direction of each item (i.e., true or false). The test can be scored by hand in less than ten minutes. Scoring is even faster with a computer. Interpreting the scores is not as simple. To reach a clinical diagnosis, the *pattern* of scores on the ten clinical scales is examined. This pattern is often graphed in a **personality profile.** An example is shown in Figure 10–1. MMPI atlases help in interpreting profiles (e.g.,

TABLE 10–1
The validity and clinical scales of the MMPI

Scale Name	Symbol	Sample Item	Interpretation
CANNOT SAY	?	No sample. It is merely the number of items marked in the "cannot say" category or left blank.	This is one of four validity scales, and a high score indicates evasiveness.
LIE	L	I get angry sometimes. (*False*)*	This is the second validity scale. Persons trying to present themselves in a favorable light (e.g., good, wholesome, honest) obtain high L-scale scores.
FREQUENCY	F	Everything tastes the same. (*True*)	This is the third validity scale. High scores suggest carelessness, confusion, or "fake bad."

TABLE 10–1 (*Concluded*)

CORRECTION	K	I have very few fears compared to my friends. (*False*)	An elevation on the last validity scale, K, suggests a defensive test-taking attitude. Exceedingly low scores may indicate a lack of ability to deny symptomatology.
HYPOCHONDRIASIS	Hs	I wake up fresh and rested most mornings. (*False*)	High scorers have been described as cynical and defeatist.
DEPRESSION	D	At times I am full of energy. (*False*)	High scorers are usually shy, despondent, and distressed.
HYSTERIA	Hy	I have never had a fainting spell. (*False*)	High scorers tend to complain of multiple symptoms.
PSYCHOPATHIC DEVIATE	Pd	I liked school. (*False*)	Adjectives used to describe some high scorers are adventurous, courageous, and generous.
MASCULINITY/ FEMININITY	Mf	I like mechanics magazines. (*False*)	Among males, high scorers have been described as esthetic and sensitive. High-scoring women have been described as rebellious, unrealistic, and indecisive.
PARANOIA	Pa	Someone has it in for me. (*True*)	High scorers on this scale are characterized as shrewd, guarded, and worrisome.
PSYCHASTHENIA	Pt	I am certainly lacking in self-confidence. (*True*)	Fearful, rigid, anxious, and worrisome are some of the adjectives used to describe high Pt scorers.
SCHIZOPHRENIA	Sc	I believe I am a condemned person. (*True*)	Adjectives such as withdrawn and unusual describe Sc high scorers.
HYPOMANIA	Ma	At times my thoughts have raced ahead faster than I could speak them. (*True*)	High scorers are called sociable, energetic, and impulsive.
SOCIAL INTROVERSION/ EXTROVERSION	Si	I enjoy social gatherings just to be with people. (*False*)	High scorers: modest, shy, and self-effacing. Low scorers: sociable, colorful, and ambitious.

*The true or false responses within parentheses indicate the scored direction (high/low) of each of the items.

FIGURE 10–1
Sample MMPI profile

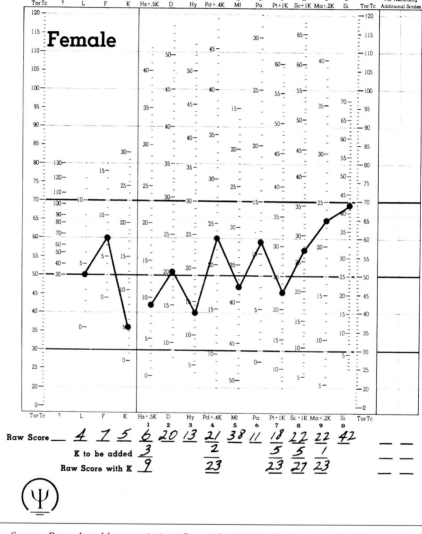

The Minnesota Multiphasic Personality Inventory

Starke R. Hathaway and J. Charnley McKinley

Marks & Seeman, 1963). These books contain typical profiles and descriptive information about samples of subjects producing each profile. For example, they give a list of typical and atypical symptoms and behaviors for people with a given profile; the atlases may provide information about the most common diagnostic category of these people, their personal histories, courses of treatment, and so on. It is rare to find a perfect match of profiles (i.e., identical scores on all the scales). However, there are criteria for two profiles to be considered similar. These help the examiner find the profile in the atlas which is most like that of the respondent.

The MMPI was designed to aid in the diagnosis of psychiatric patients. It still serves this function. The inventory has also been used extensively in personality research. For the latter purpose, several hundred additional experimental scales have been developed using subsets of the basic 550 items. For example, there are scales for anxiety, depression, and hostility.

Several studies show that MMPI scores can be used to predict people's long-range performance. Hathaway and Monachesi (1952), for example, were able to predict delinquent behavior using a combination of subjects' scores on the Psychopathic Deviate and the Hypomania scales. Harrell (1972) found that speed of advancement in business and income ten years later could be predicted at well above chance level.

THE CALIFORNIA PSYCHOLOGICAL INVENTORY

The California Psychological Inventory (CPI) is another example of an empirically keyed self-report personality inventory. It was devised by Harrison Gough (1956) as an MMPI-like scale. The CPI was intended for use with a normal population. Careful research went into its construction, including a validation sample of 13,000 normal subjects.

The CPI contains almost 500 true/false items. About half of these come from the MMPI. It is administered, scored, and profiled in much the same way as the MMPI. The CPI contains three validity scales and scales for fifteen personality traits, including dominance, tolerance, self-control, self-acceptance, sense of well-being, responsibility, socialization, and flexibility. The scales discriminate well on *non*psychiatric criteria, such as leadership. There is much favorable evidence for their validity (Cronbach, 1959; Kleinmuntz, 1967).

The CPI Socialization Scale

We will illustrate the validation research that underlies the CPI with an example. The socialization (*So*) scale is based on the assumption that people differ in their ability to sense and interpret the behavior of others.

Thus, they differ in the degree that they control their own behavior in social situations. Below are a few of the items on the CPI that are "diagnostic" for *So.* You will probably be able to guess the direction of the more socialized "answer."

> Before I do something I try to consider how my friends will react to it.
>
> I have often gone against my parents' wishes.
>
> If the pay was right, I would like to travel with a circus or carnival.
>
> I find it easy to "drop" or "break with" a friend.
>
> I often think about how I look and what impression I am making upon others.

Gough (1960) demonstrated the validity of the *So* scale in a massive study involving forty-one research samples and over 20,000 subjects. These subjects represented three groups: (1) "exemplary," or socialized to a supernormal degree, such as individuals nominated as "best citizens" of their high schools; (2) "asocial," such as those with records of high school delinquency or, more seriously, prison inmates; and (3) "socialized more or less within the normal range," including high school students, graduate students in psychology, airline hostesses, and machine operators. If the scale is valid, the supernormals should score higher than the normals who, in turn, should score higher than those considered asocial. A portion of Gough's (1960) actual findings is shown in Figure 10–2. As expected, the more "socialized" the group, the higher its mean *So* score. Note, too, that virtually the same pattern was found for both females and males.

PERSONALITY INVENTORIES AND PERSONNEL SELECTION: CURRENT CONTROVERSIES

Personality inventories may be used for personnel selection to determine whether a candidate's personality structure or attributes fit the profile believed to be important for success in the job in question. More often, however, they are used to screen out individuals from highly stressful or responsible positions because of poor mental health or adjustment difficulties. The MMPI is inadequate for selecting ideal candidates. But studies have shown that it detects psychopathology in job applicants fairly reliably. It is therefore sometimes used as an exclusion criterion for critical occupations. These are jobs requiring a strong sense of responsibility and personality stability, such as nuclear power plant operators (Butcher, 1979).

Use of the MMPI for screening out possible deviants has generated considerable controversy and even litigation (Dahlstrom, 1980). In the

FIGURE 10–2
Mean scores on the CPI sociability scale in Gough's (1960) study

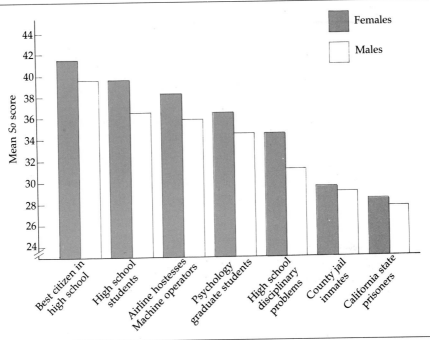

summer of 1977, five men sued two officials of the Jersey City, New Jersey government and the Laboratory of Psychological Studies (part of the Stevens Institute of Technology), which conducted psychological screening of the emotional fitness of aspiring fire fighters. This suit was later joined by several civil-liberties organizations. It involved two firemen, two applicants for a position in the fire department, and one unsuccessful candidate. They charged that the use of psychological tests such as the MMPI requires applicants to disclose personal information. (Some of the items from the MMPI allude to sexual practices and religious and political beliefs.) It therefore was an invasion of privacy. The men further charged that the testing violated their rights of freedom of belief as protected by the First and Fourteenth Amendments to the Constitution.

After an extremely lengthy trial, presiding Judge Coolahan issued his opinion (*McKenna v. Fargo*, 451 F. Supp. 1355 [1978]). He said the heart of the case involved the "involuntary disclosure" that accompanied responding to the MMPI and the projective techniques in the test battery. The job applicant did not always know exactly what his responses to specific items were revealing about his personality. Therefore, his privacy was being invaded on some level. Nevertheless, Judge

Coolahan dismissed the allegation that the applicants' constitutional right of freedom of belief was violated. It did not appear that the applicants were being tested for their beliefs or values; the fire department received only a testing summary. They never received the raw scores of the tests, which would be needed to find out how applicants responded to specific items. Further, the judge thought the job of fireman entailed life-threatening risks to the applicant and the public. He therefore recognized the need for the state to protect its interests by hiring only those who were emotionally fit.

Judge Coolahan decided "that the constitutional protection afforded privacy interests is not absolute. State interests may become sufficiently compelling to sustain State regulations or activities which burden the right to privacy." He further determined that psychological evaluation is an acceptable selection procedure, largely because psychological factors play a major role in fire fighting. This decision was later upheld by the Circuit Court of Appeals in Philadelphia.

DEMONSTRATION 10–1

FIRSTHAND EXPERIENCE WITH A SELF-REPORT PERSONALITY INVENTORY

We have been talking about self-report personality inventories, and it's time to try one out firsthand. Most of the major inventories (e.g., the MMPI and the CPI) would be inappropriate for this sort of trial because special training and a technical manual are required to interpret personality profiles meaningfully. But Willerman (1975) has published a short inventory that can yield some interesting insights.

PROCEDURE

1. Before reading further, answer the items at the top of page 217 by selecting the number from 1 to 5 that best describes how true each item is of you. List the numbers 1 through 15 on a separate piece of paper and write down your numerical answer as you read each item.

2. Before you can score the inventory, items 2, 4, 5, and 10 (which have an R after them) need to be reversed. In other words, if you indicated "5," change it to "1." Similarly, change "4" to "2," "2" to "4," and "1" to "5." ("3" remains unchanged.)

3. To score the inventory, group your answers into three clusters: items 1–5, 6–10, and 11–15. Sum your answers to obtain a total score for each of the three clusters.

4. You are now ready to evaluate the inventory. Items 1–5 pertain to *sociability*, items 6–10 to *activity level*, and items 11–15 to *emotionality*.

Item	How True Is This of You?				
	Hardly at All				A Lot
1. I make friends easily.	1	2	3	4	5
2. I tend to be shy. (R)	1	2	3	4	5
3. I like to be with others.	1	2	3	4	5
4. I like to be independent of people. (R)	1	2	3	4	5
5. I usually prefer to do things alone. (R)	1	2	3	4	5
6. I am always on the go.	1	2	3	4	5
7. I like to be off and running as soon as I wake up in the morning.	1	2	3	4	5
8. I like to keep busy all of the time.	1	2	3	4	5
9. I am very energetic.	1	2	3	4	5
10. I prefer quiet, inactive pastimes to more active ones. (R)	1	2	3	4	5
11. I tend to cry easily.	1	2	3	4	5
12. I am easily frightened.	1	2	3	4	5
13. I tend to be somewhat emotional.	1	2	3	4	5
14. I get upset easily.	1	2	3	4	5
15. I tend to be easily irritated.	1	2	3	4	5

(You may recall from Chapter 9 that some psychologists believe these three dispositions to be partly inherited.)

5. Most self-report personality inventories can only be understood with respect to group norms, and this one is no exception. Willerman (1975) reported that 68 percent of University of Texas at Austin students score within the ranges given below, and adds: "If your score falls below or above these ranges, you may regard yourself as . . . high or low [in that disposition]" (p. 35).

	Males' Average Range	Females' Average Range
Sociability	13–19	15–20
Activity	13–19	13–20
Emotionality	9–16	11–18

6. Several other considerations regarding the Demonstration have to do with the utility of the measure. For example, did you think that you knew what the questions were "getting at" as you answered them? Do you think you purposely (or unwittingly) biased your answers in any way? Could someone else use a copy of your answers to actually predict your *behavior* from them? Somewhat more technically, were your responses influenced by the form of the question (reversed or not)? Were

they affected by possible social judgments of its content (e.g., our culture does not admire those who are easily frightened)? We will look at these issues later in the chapter.

ALTERNATIVES TO TRADITIONAL SELF-REPORT INVENTORIES

Self-report inventories are not the only way to assess dispositions. In the pages that follow, we will consider three other alternatives: ratings, nominations, and composite profiles.

Ratings

Perhaps the most obvious alternative to self-reports of personality is to observe the person directly in many situations. Whether he or she "gets mad often," "tires easily," and so on can be determined objectively. However, in most assessment efforts, it is impractical to observe the person over a range of situations and for enough time for an adequate rating. One practical alternative is to obtain data through the reports of those who know the person well. Assessment data obtained in this way are given the general name **ratings.**

Ratings of one kind or another enjoy extremely wide use. Almost everyone has been a rater and been rated by others. Ratings are often used, for example, in letters of recommendation from former employers and teachers. They may also be used in reports by mental-health workers of a client's behavior or progress. Formal rating scales are used in personality assessment and research. Typically, the psychologist will ask a person who knows the subject well (such as a teacher, friend, or mate) to indicate *whether or not* the subject has a particular characteristic. Or the person assigns a number (say, from 0 to 10) that indicates *how much* of a given characteristic the subject has.

A strong word of caution needs to be injected about ratings. Unless rating scales are designed very carefully, they are open to a number of serious biases and distortions. These biases come from the rater; they distort the picture he or she gives about the subject of the assessment. Several major types of bias are shown in Table 10–2.

Nominations

In contrast to evaluations by one or two raters, nominations involve a variety of people and situations. **Nominations** are based on observations made over extended periods of time by a number of observers who see the subject from a variety of perspectives and with whom the subject has had different relationships. Neale and Weintraub (1977), for example, collected peer nominations for a large number of children of schizophrenic parents. The subjects were assessed in part using a 35-item peer nomination procedure developed by Pekarik and his associates (Pekarik, Prinz, Liebert, Weintraub, & Neale, 1976). The procedure involves distributing the 35-item Pupil Evaluation Inventory to all of the children in the subject's classroom. The inventory asks the children to name (nominate) other children in the class who have various characteristics (e.g., "Those who can't sit still," "Those who are liked by everyone," and "Those who make fun of people"). A subject's score for any category is his or her percentage of the possible nominations in that category; thus, a child in a class of 50 who was nominated by 10 classmates as among "those who can't sit still" would receive a score of 20

TABLE 10–2
Possible sources of bias in personality rating scales

Source of Error	Explanation
ERROR OF LENIENCY	When raters know a person well, as they must to offer an informed evaluation, they tend to rate the person higher (or sometimes lower) than they should.
ERROR OF CENTRAL TENDENCY	Raters are often reluctant to use the extreme ends of a rating scale even when these are appropriate, preferring to stick closer to the middle range of descriptions. (We all do this when we describe a very ugly person as "not being that attractive.")
HALO EFFECT	Raters tend to permit their *general* impression of a person to influence their ratings for most of the person's specific characteristics, just as a halo casts a pleasant, diffuse light over an angel or a cherub.
CONTRAST ERROR	Raters often describe others as being less like themselves than is actually the case. A relatively submissive rater, for example, may see others as being considerably more dominant than they really are.
"LOGICAL" ERROR	Raters often assume that two characteristics should be related ("it seems logical") and bias their evaluations accordingly. For example, a rater who believes that *hostility* and *abrasiveness* go together may rate people who are abrasive as being more hostile than they really are.
PROXIMITY ERROR	When a standard rating form is used, characteristics that are near one another on the list often receive similar ratings just because they are close together. This is a type of response set problem.

Source: Based on the analysis offered in *Psychometric Methods*, 2nd ed., by J. P. Guilford, 1954, New York: McGraw-Hill.

(10/50 = 20 percent); a child in a class of 25 who was nominated by 20 classmates would receive a score of 80. The usefulness of the procedure has been clearly demonstrated (Pekarik et al., 1976). But the cost is high because the inventory must be administered to an entire classroom to assess a single child. In fact, to assess a single individual, gathering data through an adequate nomination technique is often out of the question except in the case of school children.

The "Composite Profile" Approach to Assessment

Rather than rely on one method of personality measurement, some investigators propose a multimethod approach to ensure that the findings are valid (Campbell, 1960; Campbell & Fiske, 1959). As many different measures of the same trait as possible are used. It is assumed that the measurement error associated with any one method will be less likely to distort the final measure. An example is measuring generosity. People may want to present themselves in a favorable light. So they may overestimate their generosity in a self-report questionnaire, in which case the results will differ from their "true" generosity. However we could also ask peers to rate these individuals for the trait in question. When the two different measures are combined, a more accurate picture will emerge.

Following this rationale, Harris (1980) proposed employing three methods of assessment to approximate an individual's "true" personality profile. He suggested starting with a carefully constructed personality inventory that objectively assesses formally defined variables (e.g., the MMPI or CPI). Then both peer ratings and self-report ratings on the variables assessed by the inventory should be obtained. The three separate assessments should be averaged to produce a composite profile.

Harris (1980) demonstrated that such composite profiles are considerably more stable over time than are single-method profiles. Further, they provide quite valid measures of personality. So long as one's time and budget are sufficient, Harris' three-method approach may offer an alternative that is better than the single-method approach to personality assessment.

PROBLEMS WITH SELF-REPORT AND RATING DATA

In 1934 Richard LaPiere, a sociologist, wrote letters to 250 hotels and restaurants across the United States asking: "Will you accept members of the Chinese race as guests in your establishment?" A majority of the proprietors answered LaPiere's letter. More than 90 percent replied that they would *not* serve Chinese guests. Perhaps this should not have been surprising. There was a good deal of anti-Chinese sentiment in the United States in the mid-1930s. What was surprising was that the proprietors didn't mean it, as LaPiere well knew. Six months earlier, he had toured the country with a Chinese couple. They had stopped at each of the 250 establishments to which LaPiere had written. And the Chinese couple had in fact been served in 249 of them, for the most part with very pleasant treatment.

More recent studies have repeatedly confirmed LaPiere's basic finding. People's stated attitudes or intentions may tell us little or nothing about how they will behave. A "law-and-order" political attitude does not go along with adherence to certain municipal laws (Wrightsman, 1969); church attendance cannot be predicted from expressed attitudes toward church (Wicker, 1971); and it is almost impossible to predict how often individual students will cut classes from their attitudes toward their professors (Rokeach & Kliejunas, 1972).

The attitudes that people express do not always correspond to or predict their behavior. *Photo by Christopher O'Keefe and Michael D. Spiegler*

There is a general point underlying these findings. The "answers" we get in personality assessment will often depend on the method of inquiry or test we use. Many innkeepers might have been labeled harsh bigots based on their written sentiments; they would have been perceived as fair-minded and unbiased on the basis of their observed actions. There certainly are people who follow a pattern opposite to the one shown by LaPiere's innkeepers. Although these people express egalitarian attitudes, their private lives are filled with racially or ethnically biased actions. Of course, we might still believe that some innkeepers are more prejudiced than others, regardless of the method of assessment used. But the burden of proof regarding the validity of both the disposition we are trying to measure ("prejudice") and the method of measurement used lies with the researcher. It is never "obvious" enough to be taken on faith. This is why many investigators have tried to identify the weaknesses in personality inventories.

Faking on Personality Inventories

People taking tests such as the MMPI have devised various schemes for faking their answers. They may want to make a good impression when applying for a job. Or they may want to give a bad impression when being tested for sanity in connection with a murder trial. How successful are these conscious efforts to achieve a desired impression?

Some "fakers," particularly those who overdo it, will be detected by one or more of the validity scales that are part of most self-report personality inventories. Still, on the average, people seem to get "better scores" on self-report personality inventories when told to simulate a "nice personality"; there are also wide individual differences in the degree to which people succeed in "faking good" or "faking bad" (Edwards & Abbott, 1973). And there are also other kinds of test-taking attitudes, known as *response sets*, which may distort the personality picture presented by self-report inventories.

Response Sets

Psychologists often assume that a person's response to any given personality inventory item is a reaction to the *content* of the item. For example, we assume that a person who responds "true" to the statement "I like parties" often attends social functions. Is this a valid assumption? The answer is frequently "no." People with particular test-taking attitudes may not be answering the items in terms of content. **Response sets** are characteristic and consistent ways of responding to a test regardless of what the items say. For instance, **response acquiescence** is the tendency to agree with items, no matter what their content.

Response deviation is the tendency to answer items in an uncommon direction.

Social Desirability as a Response Set

The response set that has received the most attention is **social desirability.** This involves answering items in the most socially accepted direction, irrespective of whether such answers are correct for the respondent. For example, an individual who prefers to be alone and dislikes social gatherings might answer "true" to the statement "I like parties." The response is given because he or she feels that it is socially desirable to enjoy parties.

Several methods have been devised for controlling the influence of social desirability. One is to measure the respondent's tendency to answer items on a self-report inventory in the socially desirable direction. The person's score on the inventory is then adjusted to take the degree of this tendency into account.

Another approach involves employing neutral items with respect to social desirability. These statements are rated in the middle of the social desirability/undesirability scale. An example is "I am easily awakened by noise." However, it is often difficult to find or rewrite items that meet the requirement of neutrality and simultaneously convey the necessary content. It is hard to imagine how one could rewrite the statement, "Most of the time I wish I were dead" to make it more socially desirable without changing the meaning substantially. (This is an MMPI item that is rated as extremely undesirable [Hanley, 1956]).

A third approach for controlling the effects of social desirability is to use a **forced-choice inventory.** Respondents must choose which of two statements is more characteristic of them. All of the statements in the inventory are first scaled for social desirability and then paired according to their scale values. The choices in each pair have approximately the same social desirability scale value but different content. Therefore, when respondents choose the statement in each pair that is more characteristic of them, the choices cannot be based on social desirability. Edwards (1953) constructed his Personal Preference Schedule in this way to control for social desirability. The Personal Preference Schedule is a self-report personality inventory developed for counseling and research with nonpsychiatric individuals. Examples of items appearing on it are given in Table 10–3.

Response Styles: An Alternative View of the Data

Fiske and Pearson (1970) noted that people can judge the intention of a personality test rather accurately. They pointed to the complex implications of this fact. "Like other reactions, reactions to tests and to test tasks have

TABLE 10–3
Examples of items from the Edwards Personal Preference Schedule

Alternatives	Items	
A B	A:	I like to tell amusing stories and jokes at parties.
	B:	I would like to write a great novel or play.
A B	A:	I like to have my work organized and planned before beginning it.
	B:	I like to travel and see the country.
A B	A:	I feel like blaming others when things go wrong for me.
	B:	I feel that I am inferior to others in most respects.
A B	A:	I like to avoid responsibilities and obligations.
	B:	I feel like making fun of people who do things that I regard as stupid.

Source: From *Manual for Edwards Personal Preference Schedule* by A. L. Edwards, 1953, New York: Psychological Corporation.

their personality correlates" (p. 68). In other words, responding to the fact that you are taking a test may itself be a personality disposition. And this may alter responses to the items on the test. Some psychologists have tried to rid self-report inventories of the distorting influence of response sets. Other psychologists have observed that these characteristic ways of responding might not be sources of error at all. The latter group suggests looking at test-taking attitudes as personality traits rather than as situation-specific reactions. The salient measures of personality in self-report inventories might be *how* someone responds rather than *what* they respond to (i.e., the content of the items).

Response tendencies can be viewed either as a source of distortion or as an indication of personality dispositions. It is useful to assign different terms to describe each situation. *Response sets,* as we said, are sources of distortion. **Response styles** are personality dispositions (Jackson & Messick, 1958). We have already examined social desirability as a response set; now, we will consider it as a response style—that is, a personality disposition.

Social Desirability as a Response Style: Edwards' Approach

Edwards (1953) developed a measure of the inclination to respond to self-descriptive statements in the socially desirable direction. He chose 150 items from the MMPI and asked ten judges to respond to each in the socially desirable direction. The judges agreed perfectly on 79 of the 150 items; these 79 items formed the first *Social Desirability (SD) scale.* Later, Edwards reduced the SD scale to 39 items by selecting those items that showed the greatest differentiation between subjects who had high and low total scores.

Edwards hypothesized: "If the SD scale does provide a measure of the tendency of subjects to give socially desirable responses to statements in self-description, then the correlations of scores on this scale with other personality scales, given under standard instructions, should indicate something of the extent to which the social desirability variable is operating at the time" (1957, pp. 31, 33). A number of studies by Edwards and other investigators (e.g., Edwards, 1953, 1957; Merrill & Heathers, 1956) support this hypothesis. Scales measuring socially desirable traits, such as dominance, responsibility, status, cooperativeness, agreeableness, and objectivity, correlate positively with the SD scale. In contrast, scales measuring socially undesirable traits, such as social introversion, neuroticism, hostility, dependency, insecurity, and anxiety, are negatively correlated with the SD scale (cf. Edwards, 1970).

One possible implication of the correlations between Edwards' SD scale and other personality scales is that the traits these scales measure are, despite their names (e.g., dominance and introversion), only different aspects of social desirability. It might be more fruitful from the standpoint of prediction and explanation as well as parsimony to view the traits that correlate strongly with the SD scale as measures of social desirability. For example, Edwards believes that the trait measured by the Taylor Manifest Anxiety (MA) Scale (Taylor, 1953) should be interpreted as social desirability/undesirability.

The MA scale is negatively correlated with the SD scale. This means that high anxiety tends to be associated with low social desirability; low anxiety tends to be associated with high social desirability. This finding is not surprising if we look at the items that make up the MA scale. Statements like "I am a very nervous person," "I am certainly lacking in self-confidence," and "I cry easily" appear on the MA scale. They are unquestionably socially undesirable characteristics in our society. Thus, high scores on the MA scale can be viewed as endorsing socially undesirable statements. Low scores on the MA scale can be seen as denying socially undesirable characteristics. (It is interesting that for certain subgroups of our culture—such as residents of psychiatric hospitals or homes for the aged—these characteristics are less undesirable and may even be construed as socially desirable because they lead to attention and care.)

The MA scale has been used in numerous studies to select subjects with high and low anxiety. One finding is that, for certain kinds of verbal learning, low-anxiety subjects make fewer errors and learn faster (in fewer trials) than do high-anxiety subjects (e.g., Montague, 1953; Ramond, 1953; Taylor & Spence, 1952). Edwards (1957) explains these results in terms of social desirability:

> I believe it possible . . . to describe the low group on the Taylor scale as those who desire to make a good impression on others and

the high group as those who are less interested in what others may think of them. I would predict that the group desiring to make a good impression on the Taylor scale, that is to say, those with low scores, might also desire to make a good impression in terms of their performance on the learning task. They are, in other words, perhaps more highly motivated by the desire to "look good," not only in their responses to the Taylor scale, but also in their performance in the learning situation itself. Surely, to be able to learn fast is, in our society, a socially desirable characteristic. If a subject has a strong tendency to give socially desirable responses in self-description, is it unreasonable to believe that he may also reveal this tendency in his behavior in a learning situation where he is aware of what would be considered socially desirable, namely to learn fast, to do his best? The high group, on the other hand, being less interested in making a good impression, showing less of a tendency to give socially desirable responses in self-description, caring less about how others may value them, does not have equal motivation with the low group in the learning situation. (p. 89)

Evaluation of Response Sets and Response Styles

The arguments favoring a response-style or response-set interpretation of self-report inventories are impressive. They have certainly not gone unchallenged, however. In fact, several psychologists argue that the tendency to respond to items on the basis of characteristics other than content may be minimal. Block (1965) went so far as to develop an MMPI scale that consisted of only those items that were rated as neutral in social desirability. The scale was given to nine diverse samples of subjects. The influence of social desirability on MMPI responses was insignificant.

Polarization has tended to characterize the debate between the content and response-style interpretations of self-report inventories. This is typical of many controversies in personality psychology. Theorists often take extreme stands on issues rather than seek a middle ground. (As a result, it is possible to classify approaches to personality into opposing strategies, as we have done in this book for heuristic purposes.) Yet personality psychologists would no doubt agree that behavior is multiply determined. Therefore, on purely logical grounds, it would seem more enlightening to search for interactions among the multiple sources of personality. In other words, we should look at traits *and* situational influences, rather than traits *versus* situational influences. The approach taken by Henry Murray, described in the next chapter, is a partial attempt to view personality as an interaction of enduring dispositions within the person and external situational forces that press in from the environment.

SUMMARY

1. The two basic approaches to the construction of personality inventories are content validation and empirical keying. Content validity involves including in personality inventories a wide sample of items bearing on the thoughts, feelings, and actions that presumably comprise each disposition being measured. Empirical keying involves screening a large number of items to identify those that differentiate between criterion groups irrespective of the content of the items.

2. The MMPI, which was developed mainly by empirical keying, consists of ten clinical scales and four validity scales. The scale scores of each individual are often graphed as a personality profile that can be matched with the personality descriptions of others with similar profiles published in MMPI atlases.

3. The CPI is similar to the MMPI in form, but focuses more on assessing normal personality dispositions.

4. There has been long and heated controversy over the legitimacy of using personality inventories for personnel selection. Recent court decisions acknowledge that submitting to such tests involves an invasion of privacy at some level, but have found that the tests do not violate the fundamental constitutional right of freedom of belief. So, personality inventories are now held to be a legitimate selection procedure and will probably continue to enjoy wide use in personnel screening and selection.

5. Ratings, nominations, and composite profiles are the major alternatives to self-report inventories. Ratings involve asking people who know the assessees well to rate them on the degree to which they display the characteristics of interest. Such ratings are open to a number of biases, including a tendency for raters to be too lenient or to allow their general opinions to color their ratings of specific characteristics (halo effect).

6. Nominations, unlike ratings, are based on the impressions of many people rather than just a few. The information they yield tends to be highly reliable, but the cost is high.

7. The composite-profile approach involves combining information from several different assessment sources, such as self-report personality inventories, self-report ratings, and peer ratings.

8. The major limitation of self-report and rating data is that the written responses they obtain from a person may not correlate very well with the person's actual behavior. This may result from deliberate faking or from a variety of unintentional factors that distort the way we describe and evaluate ourselves and others.

9. Self-report inventories may be biased by response sets which are characteristic ways of responding to inventory items regardless of what the items say. Response sets include response acquiescence (agreeing with statements irrespective of their content), response deviation (answering

many items in an uncommon direction), and social desirability (answering in the most socially approved direction).

10. Social desirability may be controlled to some extent by measuring it and then removing its influence statistically; by developing personality inventories in which all the items are socially neutral; or by using a forced-choice procedure in which the respondent must choose between items equivalent in social desirability.

11. Some psychologists believe that social desirability and other factors that have been shown to influence responses to self-report inventories should be considered personality dispositions in their own right. These researchers use the term response styles rather than response sets. Edwards considers social desirability to be an important and stable response style. He argues that various personality characteristics, such as the tendency to report or deny symptoms of anxiety, may be explained largely by individual differences in social desirability.

THE DISPOSITIONAL STRATEGY

CHAPTER 11

NEEDS AND MOTIVES

OVERVIEW

The idea that we can understand people and their behavior if we know "what drives them"—that is, their motivation—has enormous appeal. However, the motivational forces behind personality entail many specific questions. Is there a set of common human motives that can be measured? Do these motives have a general influence on behavior? Do things we say, such as our favorite verbal metaphors and the kinds of stories we tell, reflect our motivations? The dispositional psychologists to whose work we now turn would answer "yes" to each of these questions. In their view, people's needs differ in both kind and amount. In turn, these differences motivate people to think about different things and take different actions. Thus, needs supply motives that lead to thought and action. This is shown in Figure 11–1.

In this chapter, we will discuss research and theory concerning motives. This work differs in some very basic ways from the dispositional theories in Chapter 9. One difference is that motivational theorists were greatly influenced by several psychoanalytic ideas. These include the importance of driving, impelling forces for explaining a person's behavior and the belief that projective responses and elicited fantasies reveal something about the individual's personality. Thus, need and motive theories have ties with the psychoanalytic strategy. However, the theorists

FIGURE 11–1
The relationship between needs and motives, showing how the motive influences both thought and action

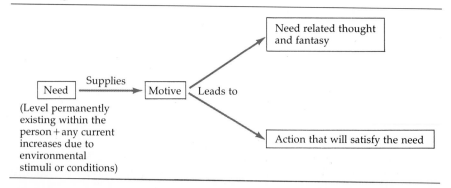

discussed in this chapter remain within the dispositional framework. They assume that (1) there are measurable individual differences between people (in this case, in their needs and motives); (2) these individual differences manifest themselves in a wide range of actions and are relatively stable over time; and (3) motives and needs, as dispositions within the person, are the basis for predicting, explaining, and understanding behavior. Whereas the psychoanalytic strategy emphasizes the *similarity* of motivations of all people, motive theories emphasize the dispositional strategy's basic approach: identifying and elaborating the *differences* between individuals in terms of the strength of their motives and the ways those motives are manifested.

THE CONCEPT OF MOTIVE

David Winter (1973) suggests that the modern concept of *motive* involves six related points.

First, motive is used to explain changes in behavior. Motivational issues arise when we ask "why" questions, such as "Why did John cross the street?" Some answers refer to external causes (e.g., a barricade blocked the sidewalk). Most refer to explanations that are *within the person.* For instance, the answer may be "John crossed the street because he wanted to get a newspaper." This is a motivational explanation of John's behavior. So is "John crossed the street to keep from slipping on the ice ahead." Thus, Winter (1973) observes that " 'motive' is a way of explaining those changes in behavior that cannot readily be explained by external forces alone" (p. 21).

Second, a motive-based explanation typically connects a specific behavior to a more general disposition. If John wants a newspaper today, he has probably wanted one in the past. He will probably want one in the future, as well. So we say that John "likes to," "tends to," or "often does" buy the newspaper.

Third, a motive explanation of behavior usually implies a *goal.* It also indicates knowledge about certain means-ends relationships. John must know that newspapers exist, what they are, and how and where to buy one.

Fourth, and very important, the motive explanation gives rise to predictions of how the person will behave in other situations. It also defines the limits of the behavior that has been observed. If John has already bought or read the newspaper today, we can predict that he probably will *not* cross the street again to buy another one. (This is assuming, of course, that he usually reads only one newspaper.)

Fifth, under some circumstances, a motive explanation lets us anticipate an entire sequence of behaviors. John may find that the newspaper stand is out of papers. He may then "go out of his way" to find another newsstand. Or he may be more likely to tune in the news on his car radio that evening.

Sixth, a motive explanation leaves out habit and stylistic factors. "We do not know whether John will walk, run, jump, or perhaps even use a pogo stick to get across the road. We do not know whether he will cross the road at a right angle or take a diagonal course directly to the front of the newsstand. To answer those questions, we would ask about his *habits*" (Winter, 1973, p. 22).

Approach and Avoidance: The Two Faces of Motivation

One component of motivation is the positive, or *approach tendencies* associated with need or motive. For instance, a person may strive for achievement or power. He or she may seek the approval of others or affiliation with them. But, as we shall see later in this chapter, *avoidance tendencies* may also dominate a person's motivation. Some people are driven by success; others are motivated to avoid failure (Atkinson & Litwin, 1960). Some people hope for power; others fear it (Winter, 1973).

MURRAY'S NEED THEORY

The father of modern need theory is Henry A. Murray (1893–   ). The approach of Murray and his associates involves "directional forces within the subject, forces that seek out or respond to various objects or total situations in the environment" (1962, p. 24). Positing such forces has a long history in personality psychology. Impelling passions and drives were suggested by many early writers. The dynamic aspects of Freud's theory were already well known. But Murray wanted to do more than

Henry A. Murray

Harvard University News Office

acknowledge these forces. He wished to identify and catalog them. He also wanted to assess them in persons and to determine their relationship to one another. Finally, he wanted to take the bold step of writing a comprehensive need theory.

Primary Constructs

Murray believes that the individual and the environment must be considered together—a person/environment interaction. However, to analyze this interaction, forces within the individual and environmental forces must first be separated. The former are referred to as *needs*. The latter are *press*. (Note: The plural of "press" is *press*, not presses.)

Needs

A **need (n)** is a theoretical construct. It refers to "a readiness to respond in a certain way under given conditions. . . . it is a noun which stands for the fact that a certain trend is apt to recur" (Murray, 1962, p. 61). So defined, needs are identified with particular effects or temporary end states (e.g., satisfying the need for sex is identified with orgasm).

Murray believes that there are 39 human needs in all. They can be divided into primary and secondary needs. **Primary needs** are biological in origin. They represent the person's physical requirements. There are 12 of them, including the need for air, water, food, sex, and physical safety. It is relatively easy to agree on the external or internal conditions that will arouse one of these needs (e.g., a seductive mate for sex, or thirst for water). There is less agreement about Murray's 27 **secondary needs** which are learned. (See Table 11–1.)

Press

Murray believes needs are only half of the process that determines behavior. **Press (p)** are the complementary, and equally important, directional forces provided by objects, situations, or events in the environment. Some common examples of press appear in Table 11–2. Murray distinguishes two types of press. **Alpha press** are objective descriptions of environmental situations (e.g., a certain grade-point average is required for admission to medical school). **Beta press** are how the person sees significant environmental influences (e.g., "If I don't make the required grade-point average for medical school, I have been a total failure"). To function adequately, a person's alpha press (objective experience) and beta press (subjective experience) in the same situation should be fairly similar. If alpha press and beta press sharply diverge, the result is what we call *delusion*.

TABLE 11–1
Murray's list of secondary needs

Major Category	Need	Behavioral Example
Ambition	n Achievement	Overcoming obstacles
	n Recognition	Boasting
	n Exhibition	Making efforts to shock or thrill others
	n Acquisition	Acquiring things by work or stealing
	n Conservance	Repairing possessions
	n Order	Tidying up
	n Retention	Hoarding
	n Construction	Organizing or building something
Defense of status	n Inviolacy	Maintaining psychological "distance"
	n Infavoidance	Concealing a disfigurement
	n Defendance	Offering explanations or excuses
	n Counteraction	Engaging in acts of retaliation
Response to human power	n Dominance	Dictating to or directing others
	n Deference	Cooperating with others
	n Similance	Imitating others
	n Autonomy	Manifesting defiance of authority
	n Contrariance	Taking unconventional or oppositional views
	n Aggression	Assaulting or belittling others
	n Abasement	Apologizing, confessing, or surrendering
	n Blamavoidance	Inhibiting unconventional impulses
Affection between people	n Affiliation	Joining groups
	n Rejection	Discriminating against or snubbing others
	n Nurturance	"Mothering" a child
	n Succorance	Crying for help
	n Play	Seeking diversion by "having fun"
Exchange of information	n Cognizance	Asking questions
	n Exposition	Lecturing to, or interpreting for, others

Source: Adapted from *Explorations in Personality* by H. A. Murray, 1962, New York: Science Editions.

TABLE 11–2
Common examples of press

Press	Example
p Achievement	Others getting good grades
p Order	A messy desk
p Counteraction	Being attacked (verbally or physically)
p Autonomy	Overprotective parents
p Abasement	Doing something wrong
p Affiliation	Friendly companions
p Play	Saturday night
p Cognizance	Not understanding a lecture

Murray's Approach to Personality Assessment

Murray assumes that needs are sometimes *manifest* (observed in overt behavior) and sometimes *latent* (inhibited, covert, or imaginal). The strength of a need must be measured in both forms.

The Assessment of Manifest Needs

There are four major criteria for estimating the strength of manifest needs from overt action. These are: (1) frequency of action, (2) duration of action, (3) intensity of action, and (4) readiness to act. Frequency is measured by counting. Duration is measured by reference to a clock or watch. Intensity can be measured by grading responses to a situation. For example, Murray (1962) suggested this grading for *n* Aggression (need for aggression): "criticism given with a smile, a laugh at the other's expense, a mild insult, a severe accusation, a violent push, a blow in the face, murder" (p. 254). Finally, readiness to act may be measured by the speed of a response ("I was asleep as soon as my head touched the pillow").

The Assessment of Latent Needs

It is more complicated to deal with latent needs. Consider the theoretical nature of these needs:

> The chief differences between an imaginal need and an overt need is that the former enjoys in reading, or represents in fantasy, in speech or in play what the latter objectifies in serious action. Thus, instead of pushing through a difficult enterprise, a subject will have visions of doing it or read books about others doing it; or instead of injuring an enemy, he will express his dislike of him to others or enjoy playing an aggressive role in a play. . . . The term "imaginal need" is convenient for the expression "the amount of need tension that exhibits itself in thought and make-believe action." (Murray, 1962, p. 257)

Assessment of latent needs follows from this description. A strong latent need "is apt to perceive . . . what it 'wants'. . . . A subject under the influence of a drive has a tendency to 'project' into surrounding objects some of the imagery associated with the drive that is operating" (Murray, 1962, p. 260). This reasoning led to the development of a widely used projective technique, the **Thematic Apperception Test (TAT).**

The TAT consists of a set of 20 pictures. There are separate sets for men, women, and children. Most of the pictures show at least one person, thereby providing someone the respondent can presumably identify with. Figure 11–2 is an example of a TAT picture. The subject is given the following instructions:

This is a test of your creative imagination. I shall show you a picture and I want you to make up a plot or story for which it might be used as an illustration. What is the relation of the individuals in the picture? What has happened to them? What are their present thoughts and feelings? What will be the outcome? Do your very best. Since I am asking you to indulge your literary imagination, you may make your story as long and detailed as you wish. (Murray, 1962, p. 532)

Stories are scored for various needs and press. Scoring is based on the explicit or implicit themes in the stories. For example, a story that focuses on a character's concerns with a business failure might be scored as reflecting a need for achievement.

FIGURE 11–2
Example of a TAT picture

THE NEED TO ACHIEVE

Murray's dispositional approach stimulated a great deal of research. A prime example is the work of David McClelland (1917–   ) and his colleagues. For more than twenty-five years, McClelland investigated the need to achieve (i.e., Murray's *n* Achievement). His viewpoint was both theoretical and extremely practical. Murray and McClelland share a common bias concerning the nature of human personality. However, they differ in their basic approach. Murray chose to catalog and study a large number of needs. McClelland focused his attention on a single need. McClelland has justified his approach this way.

> Concentration on a limited research problem is not necessarily narrowing; it may lead ultimately into the whole of psychology. In personality theory there is inevitably a certain impatience—a desire to solve every problem at once so as to get the "whole" personality in focus. We have proceeded the other way. By concentrating on one problem, on *one motive*, we have found in the course of our study that we have learned not only a lot about the achievement motive but other areas of personality as well. (McClelland, Atkinson, Clark, & Lowell, 1953, p. vi)

The McClelland-Atkinson Approach to Defining and Measuring Motives

The first step in studying achievement, or any motive or personality variable, is finding a way to define and measure it. The approach devised by McClelland and his colleague John Atkinson is the basis for most of the research discussed in the rest of this chapter (Atkinson, 1958; Atkinson & McClelland, 1948; McClelland, Atkinson, Clark, & Lowell, 1953).

In brief, the McClelland-Atkinson approach involves the following

David McClelland

Harvard University News Office

steps. First, subjects are exposed to a motive-arousing experience. They might be told they are taking an important examination to arouse the achievement motive. Or they might watch a stirring political film to arouse the power motive. Control subjects are exposed to a comparable "neutral" experience that presumably does not arouse the motive in question. Subjects in both groups then write TAT-type stories about standard pictures. The difference in the imagery produced by the motive-aroused and motive-nonaroused group is taken as evidence of the motive.

An early experiment measured the strength of a primary need, n Food. Sailors deprived of food for varying lengths of time could be reliably differentiated on the basis of their responses to Murray's TAT (Atkinson & McClelland, 1948). Following this success, the same technique was used to measure a secondary need, n Achievement.

Students were exposed to either achievement-arousing situations (e.g., they were given success or failure experiences) or situations that did not arouse achievement (e.g., the experimental tasks were presented in a casual, relaxed way). They were then asked to write stories about four TAT-type pictures that were especially pertinent to n Achievement. The instructions were similar to those Murray used with the TAT. Stories were scored for a number of different categories related to achievement. Categories that differentiated subjects exposed to varying degrees of achievement arousal were defined as measures of n Achievement. The logic behind this approach is shown in Figure 11–3. The figure also suggests how the individual's n Achievement score is multiply determined.

Research on Achievement Motivation

McClelland and his associates demonstrated the validity of using imagery reflecting achievement as a measure of achievement motivation. When they compared people with high and low achievement imagery scores, they found:

> In general, people with a high achievement imagery index score complete more tasks under achievement orientation, solve more simple arithmetic problems on a timed test, improve faster in their ability to do anagrams, tend to get better grades, use more future tenses and abstract nouns in talking about themselves. . . . and so on. (McClelland et al., 1953, p. 327)

The basic technique of measuring achievement motivation was later used by McClelland and others in a wide variety of investigations. From this research it appears that the origins of n Achievement (abbreviated n Ach) are

> rooted in early training for independence, . . . support of the n Ach by warm but demanding parental models, and considerable

FIGURE 11–3
Determinants of the *n* Achievement score derived from a single story

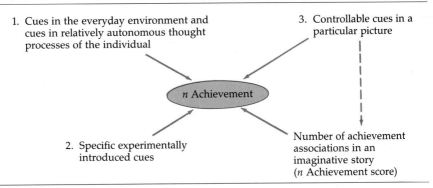

1. Cues in the everyday environment and cues in relatively autonomous thought processes of the individual

3. Controllable cues in a particular picture

n Achievement

2. Specific experimentally introduced cues

Number of achievement associations in an imaginative story (*n* Achievement score)

Source: From *The Achievement Motive* by D. C. McClelland, J. W. Atkinson, R. A. Clark, and E. I. Lowell, 1953, New York: Appleton-Century-Crofts.

experience with emotional satisfaction in achievement situations. Certainly such a pattern does suggest that the *n* Achiever should be experienced in maximizing payoffs, relatively free from anxiety about failure, and therefore, efficient at those tasks he chooses to attempt. (Birney, 1968, p. 878)

The TAT measure of the achievement motive made possible a unique type of psychological investigation. The scoring system for TAT stories can be used with any written material. McClelland could therefore study *n* Achievement in historical people and groups from written records of their lives. For example, McClelland and his associates studied the relationship between independence training and achievement motivation in North American Indian tribes by scoring their folktales for *n* Achievement (McClelland et al., 1953).

An even more ambitious task involved McClelland's (1967) attempt to "search for the broadest possible test of the hypothesis that a particular psychological factor—the need for Achievement—is responsible for economic growth and decline" (p. vii). Specifically, McClelland tried to "predict" the economic growth of twenty-three countries over the period 1929–1950. Prediction was based on the amount of achievement imagery in children's stories in those countries in the preceding decade (1920–1929). He found a moderately high positive correlation (+.53) between achievement emphasis in children's stories and economic growth. The evidence suggests that a society's aspirations may well be found in the stories that it offers its children. And the stories seem to influence children who heard them. The latter possibility is supported by a more recent experimental study (McArthur & Eisen, 1976). Preschool children tried harder to finish an achievement-related task after they heard a story describing the achievement-related behavior of another child of their own sex.

There has been an impressive array of practical applications of the concept of achievement motivation (McClelland, 1978). We know, for example, that high achievement motivation is positively related to job satisfaction (Reuman, Alwin, & Veroff, 1984). Various programs have been aimed at increasing achievement motivation. As a result, psychologists

Achievement motivation may be manifested in different ways. Academic excellence is one way, but so too is being a skilled aircraft mechanic and winning road races. *Top left, Photo by Christopher O'Keefe. Top right, Photo by Michael D. Spiegler. Bottom, Courtesy of Bobby Doyle.*

have helped raise the standard of living of the poor (McClelland, 1965), increase benefits of an education program (DeCharms, 1976), control alcoholism (McClelland, 1977), and make business management more effective (McClelland & Burnham, 1976).

A Program for Developing Achievement Motivation

McClelland (1965; McClelland & Winter, 1969) developed a formal course to increase achievement motivation of businesspeople. It was based on evidence that entrepreneurs need high n Achievement to function successfully. Most psychologists consider acquiring motives in adulthood difficult or impossible. Acknowledging this, McClelland (1965) wrote:

> We were encouraged by the successful efforts of two quite different groups of "change agents"—operant conditioners and missionaries. . . . The operant conditioners [see Chapter 19] have not been encumbered by any elaborate theoretical apparatus; they do not believe motives exist anyway, and continue demonstrating vigorously that if you want a person to make a response, all you have to do is elicit it and reward it. . . . Like operant conditioners, the missionaries have gone ahead changing people because they have believed it possible. . . . commonsense observation yields dozens of cases of adults whose motivational structure has seemed to be quite radically and permanently altered by the educational efforts of the Communist party, Mormon, or other devout missionaries. (p. 322)

Changing participants' motivational structure is the major goal of McClelland's achievement motivation program.

The Program

McClelland's (1965) courses for developing n Achievement are typically taught to groups of from nine to twenty-five businesspeople. They are given over a short time, but the sessions are lengthy. (The optimal period is somewhere between six and fourteen days, twelve to eighteen hours per day.) Most of the courses have been taught in India; they have also been held in the United States, Japan, Mexico, and Spain. Based on experience in these courses, McClelland (1965) proposed twelve guidelines for motive change. Although these principles evolved from a program designed to increase a particular motive, McClelland believes they are applicable to the development of motives in general.

The first thing one must do in any motivational development program is create confidence that the program will work. Proposition 1 states: *"The more reasons an individual has in advance to believe that he can, will, or should develop a motive, the more educational attempts designed to develop that motive are likely to succeed."* McClelland used the scientific authority of research, the prestige of Harvard University (where he was chairman of the Department of Social Relations), and the suggestive power of experimenter enthusiasm in "selling" the program and setting high expectations for the participants, even before training began.

Proposition 2 stresses the importance of rational arguments in introducing the purpose of the course. *"The more an individual perceives that developing a motive is consistent with the demands of reality (and reason), the more educational attempts designed to develop that motive are likely to succeed."*

Proposition 3 provides the first hint of what the program itself entails. *"The more thoroughly an individual develops and clearly conceptualizes the associative network defining the motive, the more likely he is to develop the motive."* With this in mind, it is easy to see why McClelland explains the meaning of achievement motivation to participants early in training. Participants are asked to take the fantasy test of *n* Achievement at the beginning of the program. They are taught to score it for themselves. "We point out that if they think their score is too low, that can be easily remedied, since we teach them how to code and how to write stories saturated with *n* Achievement; in fact, that is one of the basic purposes of the course: to teach them to think constantly in *n* Achievement terms" (McClelland, 1965, p. 325).

The next step is to tie changes in thought to changes in action. According to Proposition 4: *"The more an individual can link the newly developed network to related actions, the more the change in both thought and action is likely to occur and endure."* Earlier work by McClelland showed that those high in achievement motivation: (1) like challenges in their work and prefer moderate risk; (2) want concrete feedback on how well they are doing; and (3) like to take personal responsibility for meeting work goals. To develop these characteristics, McClelland uses a specially designed business game. The game lets participants learn achievement-oriented actions both by playing the game and by seeing others play.

> The game is designed to mimic real life: they must order parts to make certain objects (e.g., a Tinker Toy model bridge) after having estimated how many they think they can construct in the time allotted. They have a real chance to take over, plan the whole game, learn from how well they are doing (use of feedback), and show a paper profit or loss at the end. While they are surprised often that they should have to display their real action characteristics this way in public, they usually get emotionally involved in observing how they behave under pressure of a more or less "real" work situation. (McClelland, 1965, p. 326)

Behavior developed in the game situation must be generalized to actual business situations. Proposition 5 states: *"The more an individual can link the newly conceptualized association-action complex (or motive) to events in his everyday life, the more likely the motive complex is to influence his thoughts and actions outside the training experience."* Actual case studies of career development are discussed by the group in order to facilitate generalization.

Participants may realize that achievement orientation applies to actual business experience. But they must be convinced that this pertains to them. The point is made in Proposition 6: *"The more an individual can perceive and experience the newly conceptualized motive as an improvement in his self-image, the more the motive is likely to influence his future thoughts and actions."* Candid self-appraisal is emphasized by telling participants about an incident in one of the courses in which a participant decided he did not want to be an achievement-oriented person. This honest self-evaluation led him to leave the course. He quit his management job and became a chicken farmer. (This case is the exception rather than the rule, however. Most participants come to see achievement motivation as desirable.) Participants evaluate the influence of increased achievement motivation on their self-images. They are helped by such techniques as individual counseling, group-dynamics sessions, and silent group meditation.

Participants must also come to feel that increased *n* Achievement is consistent with, or an improvement on, the existing cultural values of their own country. According to Proposition 7: *"The more an individual can perceive and experience the newly conceptualized motive as an improvement on prevailing cultural values, the more the motive is likely to influence his future thoughts and actions."* After examining their own values concerning achievement motivation, participants analyze the values of their culture toward achievement. This is done by looking at children's stories, myths, popular religion, and customs. In the United States, for example, participants discuss how high achievement motivation can affect popularity. Role playing is used to help participants understand and accept their new motivational orientation in relation to their cultural values.

At the end of the course, participants write an essay outlining their aspirations and plans for the next two years. Describing one's future realistically is emphasized. So is setting moderate (rather than high) goals. The essay helps participants use the practical implications of the course. It is also a basis for further evaluation of participants and the program. Over a two-year follow-up, questionnaires are sent to participants every six months. This reminds participants of the goals they set and assesses their progress. These procedures led to Propositions 8 and 9: *"The more an individual commits himself to achieving concrete goals in life related to the newly formed motives, the more the motive is likely to influence his future thoughts and actions,"* and *"The more an individual keeps a record of his progress toward achieving goals to which he is committed, the more the newly formed motive is likely to influence his future thoughts and actions."*

McClelland found that it helped if instructors were warm, rewarding, and somewhat nondirective. This finding is consistent with results of a study that showed that fathers of boys with high *n* Achievement were warmer, more encouraging, and less directive than fathers of boys low on this measure (Rosen & D'Andrade, 1959). Proposition 10 states: *"Changes in motives are more likely to occur in an interpersonal atmosphere in which the individual feels warmly but honestly supported and respected by others as a person capable of guiding and directing his own future behavior."*

The achievement motivation course is structured as a retreat for self-study. Whenever possible, the sessions are held in an isolated resort hotel. This increases concentration and lessens outside interference. There is considerable evidence that opinions, attitudes, or beliefs are changed more easily if people join new reference groups. The course encourages a new reference group by having participants study and live together. Signs of identification with the group are built into the course; these include knowledge of the *n* Achievement coding system and membership certificates. Moreover, it is beneficial if participants come from the same community. In this way, after the course, the new reference group will remain physically intact and will help maintain the newly acquired motivation. These procedures are reflected in Propositions 11 and 12: *"Changes in motives are more likely to occur the more the setting dramatizes the importance of self-study and lifts it out of the routine of everyday life,"* and *"Changes in motives are more likely to occur and persist if the new motive is a sign of membership in a new reference group."*

Results of the Program

How successful have McClelland's courses been? Based on a number of concrete, economic measures, course participants increased their achievement motivation substantially more than businesspeople who applied for the course but were not accepted (i.e., control subjects). As can be seen in Table 11–3, course participants and controls were similar in the

TABLE 11–3
Examples of the economic effects of McClelland's achievement motivation courses

		Before Course (1962–1964)	After Course (1964–1966)
1. Rated at highest business activity level*	Participants	18%	51%
	Controls	22%	25%
2. Working longer hours	Participants	7%	20%
	Controls	11%	7%
3. Starting new business	Participants	4%	22%
	Controls	7%	8%
4. Employing more people at end of two-year period	Participants	35%	59%
	Controls	31%	33%

* Subjects' business activity was rated on a four-point scale, with the highest level being exemplified by an action which directly resulted in an improvement in a business venture (e.g., increased profit).

Source: Data from *Motivating Economic Achievement* by D. C. McClelland and D. G. Winter, 1969, New York: Free Press.

two-year period before the course. Following the course, however, significantly more participants than controls engaged in actions that directly improve business, worked longer hours, started new businesses, and employed more workers (McClelland & Winter, 1969). Here is one case study that illustrates the potential impact of the course.

> A short time after participating in one of our courses in India, a 47-year-old businessman rather suddenly and dramatically decided to quit his excellent job and go into the construction business on his own in a big way. A man with some means of his own, he had had a very successful career as employee-relations manager for a larger oil firm. His job involved adjusting management-employee difficulties, negotiating union contracts, etc. He was well-to-do, well thought of in his company, and admired in the community, but he was restless because he found his job increasingly boring. At the time of the course, his original *n* Achievement score was not very high and he was thinking of retiring and living in England where his son was studying. In an interview, eight months later, he said the course had served not so much to "motivate" him but to "crystallize" a lot of ideas he had vaguely or half consciously picked up about work and achievement all through his life. It provided him with a new language (he still talked in terms of standards of excellence, . . . moderate risk, goal anticipation, etc.), a new construct which served to organize those ideas and explain to him why he was bored with his job, despite his obvious success. He decided he wanted to be an *n*-Achievement-oriented person, that he would be unhappy in retirement, and that he should take a risk, quit his job, and start in business on his own. He acted on his decision and in six months had drawn plans and raised over $1,000,000 to build the tallest building in his large city, to be called the "Everest Apartments." He is extremely happy in his new activity because it means selling, promoting, trying to wangle scarce materials, etc. His first building is part way up and he is planning two more. (McClelland, 1965, p. 332)

Achievement Motivation in Women

Unfortunately, there is neither a systematic theory nor a consistent body of data about achievement motivation in women. Until quite recently, there were few studies of achievement among women. For example, McClelland's research on achievement motivation deals exclusively with men. We will review findings that seem to shed some light on achievement motivation in women. One of the consistent themes is that, from childhood, males and females have very different experiences regarding the cultivation and expression of achievement.

Maternal Attitudes and Achievement Motivation

A repeated finding is that mothers of girls high in n Achievement tend to be hostile toward their daughters. Kagan and Moss (1962) found one of the best predictors of child and adult intellectual achievement in girls was early (up to age three) maternal hostility. In contrast, maternal protectiveness predicted achievement in boys. Mothers of achieving girls tended to be aggressive and competitive and were critical of their daughters. Another study found that mothers of academically successful elementary school girls were less affectionate and less nurturant toward their daughters than were mothers of less competent girls (Crandall, Dewey, Katkovsky, & Preston, 1964). Completing the negative picture with high school subjects, Pierce (1961b) described the mothers of high-achieving girls as more strict, authoritarian, and controlling than the mothers of low-achieving girls.

The consequences of different home backgrounds were studied nationwide. Veroff, Atkinson, Feld, and Gurin (1960) found different results for women and men. Their results are shown in Figure 11–4. They indicate

FIGURE 11–4

Relationship of various home backgrounds to the frequency with which men and women show above-average n Achievement

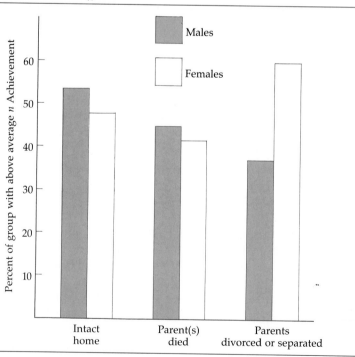

Source: Data from "The Use of Thematic Apperception to Assess Motivation in a Nationwide Interview Study" by J. Veroff, J. W. Atkinson, S. C. Feld, and G. Gurin, 1960, *Psychological Monographs, 74.*

that women whose parents were divorced or separated are more likely to have high *n* Achievement scores than are women from intact homes or women whose parents had died. The reverse is true for men. Veroff and his associates (1960) interpret the findings and the differences between men and women as follows:

> A boy, having lost his masculine model for achievement, may become highly involved in avoiding failure. In doing so, his achievement motivation, his positive motivations for success, become weakened. On the other hand, girls living with a divorced mother have a readily available model for achievement identification. Resentment of the father can reinforce the need for feminine independence and self-reliance in a masculine world. The fact that her mother is apparently self-sufficient further enhances an image of the achievement orientation of women. (p. 27)

Social Acceptability as a Factor in Women's Achievement Motivation

Another clear theme in studies of women is that *n* Achievement seems more closely tied to social acceptability in women than in men. Two studies found that the achievement needs of girls in elementary school are directly related to girls' desire for adult approval and affection; this pattern did not hold for boys (Crandall, Katkovsky, & Preston, 1962; Sears, 1962).

Anxiety about Achievement: The Motive to Avoid Success

Evidence has been available for some time suggesting that women, more than men, experience conflict over the role of striving for achievement in their lives (French & Lesser, 1964; Lesser, 1973; Lesser, Krawitz, & Packard, 1963). Possible negative consequences of success for women—competition with men, loss of femininity, the threat of social rejection by peers—are discussed in some of the classic writings of Freud (1965) and the noted anthropologist Margaret Mead (1949).

Horner (1973) theorized that conflict causes anxiety for women in achievement-oriented situations. This anxiety about success may also be a major factor underlying sex differences in achievement motivation and performance. Horner (1973) calls anxiety about the negative consequences of success the **motive to avoid success.** She views it as "a stable personality predisposition within the person acquired early in life in conjunction with sex-role standards" (p. 224).

In an often cited study, Horner (1973) asked women and men to write a story in response to a written lead. The lead was designed to elicit a motive to avoid success. The women in Horner's study were given the lead:

> *After first-term finals, Anne finds herself at the top of her medical school class.*

The lead for males was identical, except that the name of the story character was changed:

> *After first-term finals, John finds himself at the top of his medical school class.*

Scores for the motive to avoid success were based on negative imagery related to success, including concern about success or the consequences of success, denial of success, and bizarre responses to the situation. As Horner predicted, the responses of the women were strikingly different from those of the men. More than 65 percent of the women in the sample had high fear of success; this was true of less than 10 percent of the men.

In Horner's study, the most common responses of women emphasized negative social consequences of success. These included rejection, loss of friendship, reduced chances for marriage, and loneliness. The second-largest category of responses from women involved remarkable denials. Here are some examples:

> Anne is a code name for a nonexistent person created by a group of med students. They take turns taking exams and writing papers for Anne.

> Anne is really happy she's on top, though Tom is higher than she—though that's as it should be. . . . Anne doesn't mind Tom winning.

> Anne is talking to her counselor. Counselor says she will make a fine nurse. She will continue her med school courses. She will study very hard and find she can and will become a good nurse.

> It was luck that Anne came out on top of her med class because she didn't want to go to med school anyway. (Horner, 1973, p. 226)

Another common response that occurred quite frequently was to propel Anne out of the conflict situation—and out of medical school. Here is one that Horner (1973) describes as a "typical female story."

> Anne has a boyfriend Carl in the same class and they are quite serious. Anne met Carl at college and they started dating around their soph year in undergraduate school. Anne is rather upset and so is Carl. She wants him to be higher scholastically than she is. Anne will deliberately lower her academic standing the next term, while she does all she subtly can to help Carl. His grades come up and Anne soon drops out of med school. They marry and he goes on in school while she raises their family. (p. 227)

Finally, some of the stories that Anne's situation elicited from otherwise normal women are bizarre. Below is an excerpt from one such response.

She starts proclaiming her surprise and joy. Her fellow classmates are so disgusted with her behavior that they jump on her in a body and beat her. She is maimed for life. (Horner, 1973, p. 226)

Times have unquestionably changed since Horner's data were actually collected in the mid-1960s. It is possible that women may experience less anxiety about success than was true over twenty-five years ago. Still, her findings remain quite provocative.

POWER: THE ANATOMY OF A MOTIVE

David Winter (1939–   ) is the leading theorist and researcher on the need for power. Winter (1973) views "the striving for power as one important motive or disposition in individuals" (1973). He defines **power** as a person's ability or capacity to produce intended effects on the behavior or emotions of someone else. Winter's (1973) research tries "to determine whether there are differences in the extent to which people want power, or strive to affect the behavior of others according to their own intentions; to measure these differences; and to determine their further consequences and associated characteristics" (p. 5). In fact, Winter (1967, 1968, 1972, 1973) and other investigators have gathered an enormous amount of evidence indicating that there are individual differences in power motivation (or *n* Power).

The Measurement and Meaning of Power Motivation

According to Winter (1973), the goal of the power motive is the *status of having power*. He writes:

> By the power motive, I mean a disposition to strive for certain kinds of goals, or to be affected by certain kinds of incentives. People who

David Winter

Courtesy Wesleyan University

have the power motive, or who strive for power, are trying to bring about a certain state of affairs—they want to feel "power" or "more powerful than. . . ." Power is their goal. We would expect that they tend to construe the world in terms of power and to use the concept of "power" in categorizing human interaction, but they do more than that. Not only do they categorize the world in terms of power, but they also want to feel themselves as the most powerful. (p. 18)

Winter used six TAT-like pictures to measure *n* Power; each picture covers one or more general themes related to power motivation. In one picture, for example, soldiers are pointing to a map or chart. The pictures, and a fairly sophisticated scoring system, were chosen and developed along the same broad lines used by McClelland and Atkinson in their studies of achievement motivation. That is, the sample consisted of two otherwise comparable groups. One was aroused by power-related experiences (e.g., by viewing power-inspiring films). The other group responded to the pictures without prior arousal. Differences in the imagery generated were used to identify themes "diagnostic" of naturally high levels of *n* Power.

What responses indicate a high power motive? According to Winter (1973), there are three types: (1) responses containing imagery of strong, vigorous actions expressing power; (2) responses containing imagery of actions that produce strong emotional reactions in others; and (3) responses containing statements expressing concern about a person's reputation or position.

The Hope and Fear of Power

The use of power-related themes in projective stories does not always imply a hope of power. Sometimes the reaction expressed in such themes seems riddled with conflict or doubt. Winter believes that there are two aspects to the power motive. These are Hope of Power and Fear of Power. **Hope of Power** and the overall power motive are positively correlated. (See Table 11–4.) Therefore, Hope of Power and *n* Power are treated as roughly equivalent in our discussion. Hope of Power and Fear of Power show a slight negative correlation. People with high Hope of Power tend to have low Fear of Power, and vice versa.

Fear of Power: A Closer Look

Fear of Power is simultaneous interest in and worry about power, especially when the individual wants to avoid power. For example, Winter (1973) investigated the relationship between Fear of Power and attitudes toward academic work among college students. He gave over 200 freshmen an extensive questionnaire that included the following questions:

Would you prefer to have your academic work organized to allow:

TABLE 11–4
The correlations between Hope of Power and total *n* Power in five samples. The data show that the two scores can be considered almost interchangeable for many research purposes.

Sample	Correlation Coefficient
Total sample of Wesleyan students (*n* = 325)	.80*
Upper middle-class American executives (*n* = 22)	.71*
Harvard class of 1964 students (*n* = 225)	.91*
Oxford University students (*n* = 58)	.86*
German engineering students (*n* = 96)	.80*

* $p < .01$.

Source: Data reported in *The Power Motive* by D. G. Winter, 1973, New York: Free Press.

> A predominance of class work, class assignments, regular examinations, etc.
>
> *A predominance of independent reading, writing, and research.*
>
> In the average humanities or social sciences course, do you generally prefer:
>
> Objective examinations (e.g., true-false, multiple choice).
>
> *Essay examinations.*
>
> If class size permitted, which type of instruction would you prefer?
>
> All or mostly lectures.
>
> *All or mostly discussions.* (Winter, 1973, p. 150)

Most students showed some preference for the less-structured alternatives (printed in italics). But students high in Fear of Power were significantly more likely to select the less-structured alternative. Winter believes this reflects a desire for autonomy.

> One interpretation of these results is that the autonomy concerns of men high in Fear of Power derive from a fear of structure, especially structure that is imposed by someone else of high status or power (e.g., a professor or university administrator). Specified programs, assigned work, lectures, and "objective" examinations are all constraints on behavior that originate from the "outside." Fearing the structure that someone else imposes is thus one manifestation of a fear of the potential power of other people. (Winter, 1973, p. 149)

This interpretation was supported by two further studies. These showed that students high in Fear of Power were more likely than others to be late with major term papers, even in the face of warnings (e.g., the papers would be graded down for lateness). They were also more likely to take "incompletes" in their courses.

A clear implication of these findings is that Fear of Power is often unadaptive. Winter has other evidence pointing in this direction. For example, those high in Fear of Power tend to have more automobile accidents than do other students. They are also relatively more inefficient when playing a competitive bidding game. When their power is threatened, those with high Fear of Power seem to become debilitated.

Action Correlates of the Power Motive

A major part of Winter's research is looking for what he calls the *action correlates* of those who are high in *n* Power. These correlates are the overt manifestations of the power motive.

Presentation of Self

Two studies show that people with high *n* Power tend to have more "prestige possessions" than do those with low *n* Power (Winter, 1968, 1972). This is true even when income or spending money is held constant. Students high in *n* Power are more likely to put their names on the doors of their dormitory rooms. And they tend to report their college grades in a "favorable" light. For example, Winter (1973) asked students to indicate the lowest final grade they had received thus far in college. Those high in *n* Power tended to report their lowest grade as higher than it really was.

There is a bit more to the picture, though. Winter (1973) asked middle-class business executives and college students what automobile they would most like. He found that those high in *n* Power did *not* want the most expensive cars. They chose cars that handled best. This was true of both the students and the executives. It held for both those who chose American cars and those who chose foreign cars.

Apparently, *control*—of people, possessions, and situations—is a central concern of those motivated by *n* Power. Such control may be gained through force, prestige possessions, or the embellishment of one's products. Here is an interesting example:

> At Wesleyan University as elsewhere, students submit term papers in a great variety of formats, bindings, and conditions of neatness. Some hand in a few ragged sheets of paper full of typing mistakes and bound precariously with a paper clip. Others submit neatly typed, carefully proofread papers which are impressively bound in colored plastic covers with plastic grips running along the left margin. To the extent that professors judge a paper by its cover—a misleading but human tendency—the paper that is neatly and impressively bound will fare a little better or at least get a favorable first reaction. In a small way, such bindings use prestige to enhance reputation—they are an "impressive show." In one introductory psychology course, those thirteen students who bound their term papers in colored plastic or colored paper binders were significantly higher

in Hope of Power than those fifty students who turned in ordinary papers. (Winter, 1973, p. 133)

In a related study, Veroff (1957) found that college men high in n Power tended to be argumentative in class. They were also eager to convince their instructors or fellow students of their point of view. This may be why men high in n Power do well in college courses that require classroom participation (McKeachie, 1961).

Selection of Friends

Winter (1973) discovered that students high in n Power tend to prefer friends who are not popular or well known. Winter (1973) explains:

> To a power-motivated person, such friends are attractive because they are presumably not a threat, since they do not compete for power and prestige. Being less well known, such friends are also more disposed to form strong ties of friendship, regard, and support for the power-motivated "leader." (p. 114)

One of the most remarkable characteristics of individuals high in n Power is that they gather a group of followers to whom they are both generous and understanding. At the same time, they display a competitive stance toward those outside the circle. Winter (1973) asked students: "Do you generally like to do things in your own way and without regard for what other students around you may think?" Most of those *low* in power motivation answered "yes." A majority of those high in power motivation answered "no." To be powerful you must have a following; to maintain a following you must show consideration toward those who follow you. Or so it seems.

People high in n Power have a rough-and-ready attitude toward those who oppose them. For example, Winter (1973) asked students: "If you could say one sentence—any sentence—to *anyone,* anywhere in the world, in person and without fear of reprisal, what would you say?" Students high in n Power were significantly more likely to say something with a strong negative effect, usually something obscene, than were those low in n Power.

Relative Indifference to Time and Risk

Winter believes people high in n Power are relatively indifferent to time and risk. In the autumn of 1967, most college men in the United States faced the serious likelihood of being drafted into the Army. Winter asked 145 men whether they would enlist after college. (This would ensure admission to the branch of their choice, but commit the students to some form of military service.) The other choice was waiting to be drafted and thus taking their chances. Men high in n Power were significantly more likely to take their chances. "Thus they are prepared to gamble about military conscription," observes Winter, "just as they also like to gamble when they play ordinary games" (1973, p. 181).

In another study, Winter examined the n Power scores of thirty-five undergraduates who kept calendars of some sort in their rooms. Their scores were significantly lower than the n Power scores of an otherwise comparable group of thirty-five students who had no calendar. It is unclear whether the latter students felt that they didn't need to know what day it was, or felt that they didn't need to be reminded by an "external" source. In either event, though, the message is clear. "I'm not worried," thinks the person with high power motivation. "I have it all under control."

Reactivity to Power Stresses

McClelland (1982) hypothesized that individuals high in n Power would react more to "power stresses." He predicted that in situations that arouse power motivation but do not allow power to be exercised, the power-motivated individual will experience a high degree of emotional arousal. Fodor (1984) tested this hypothesis. He created an industrial simulation with college students who were either high or low in power motivation acting as "supervisors" of a work crew. During the experiment, members of the work crew either expressed no work concerns or expressed increasing concerns about their performance. (They were told what to do by the experimenter.) The concerns were expressed in comments made to the supervisor. "We're trying to outdo the other groups but we're getting all upset because we're not doing well." "What stress! I never realized money could mean so much to people." "I think we're not really making the grade. Bad scene." (Fodor, 1984, p. 855). The supervisors could do little to change the attitudes or performance of the crew. Supervisors were monitored for emotional arousal as they got feedback from their crews. Supervisors high and low in power motivation had almost identical levels of arousal when their groups expressed no concern about performance. However, consistent with McClelland's prediction, when the crew did express performance concerns, supervisors high in power motivation became much more aroused. The pattern of results is shown in Figure 11–5.

Sexual Behavior and Power

Sexual behavior and power have been closely related both in literature and in psychology. Winter's (1973) research indicates that the suggested link has some basis in fact. Male students who report having had sexual intercourse before entering college have appreciably higher n Power scores than do those who did not have sex before entering college; the trend is the same through the sophomore year but not thereafter. Power-motivated men either have had sex at an earlier age than other men, or say that they did. Winter's findings are shown in Figure 11–6.

FIGURE 11–5
Degree of arousal displayed by supervisors high and low in *n* Power in Fodor's experiment, as a function of whether their work crews were or were not expressing concern about how the work was going

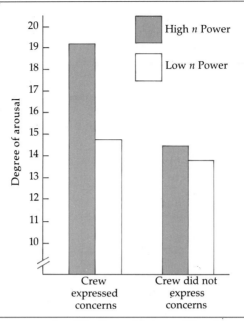

Source: From data presented in "The Power Motive and Reactivity to Power Stresses," by E. M. Fodor, 1984, *Journal of Personality and Social Psychology, 47*, pp. 853–59.

FIGURE 11–6
Mean *n* Power scores of men reporting that they did and did not have sexual intercourse at various periods. The data suggest that a desire for early sexual experience is associated with power motivation.

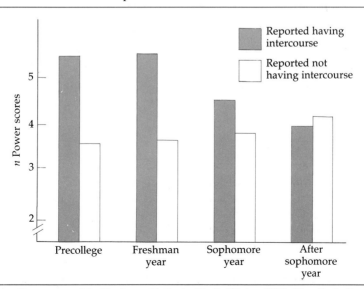

Source: Data reported in *The Power Motive* by D. G. Winter, 1973, New York: Free Press.

Winter also found that college men high in *n* Power were more likely than other men to say that they considered an "ideal wife" to be a woman who was dependent. Winter (1973) explains:

> While a dependent wife may interfere with her husband's power, she probably enhances his *feelings* of power; presumably he then thinks that *he* is not dependent on *her*. Thus this combination of qualities is attractive to high *n* Power men because it gives them . . . feelings of superiority. (p. 178)

Alcoholism and Power

McClelland and co-workers have proposed that the need for power plays a major role in problem drinking (McClelland, Davis, Kalin, & Wanner, 1972). In a ten-year research program, these investigators found that men's feelings of power increased after drinking alcohol. In addition, men with an intense need for power drank even more to satisfy that need, particularly if they were low in self-control. The investigators concluded that dependence on alcohol to satisfy the need for power distinguishes alcoholics from nonalcoholics.

Indirect support for this came from an investigation of the use of a power-motivation training program in combination with standard therapy for alcoholism (McClelland, 1977). The program gave participants feedback on their need for power and the way alcohol satisfied that need (Cutter, Boyatzis, & Clancy, 1977). They also received training in more appropriate ways of satisfying their need for power. Only 25 percent of the alcoholics given just the standard treatment stayed rehabilitated one year after treatment. In contrast, nearly 50 percent of the alcoholics given standard therapy and power-motivation training remained rehabilitated at the one-year follow-up. This supports the idea that need for power plays a role in alcoholism.

SUMMARY

1. Psychologists interested in needs and motives as dispositions have been influenced by psychoanalytic theory in that they view behavior as determined by guiding, impelling forces within the individual. They also believe that information about personality can be extracted from projective responses and other elicited fantasies. The dispositional need and motive theorists share with other dispositional psychologists the view that there are stable and relatively generalized individual differences that allow us to predict, control, and understand behavior.

2. Approach and avoidance tendencies are the two faces of motivation. A motive may be important to someone because of what one wants to get (e.g., hope of success) or because of what one wants to avoid (e.g., fear of failure).

3. Murray is the father of modern need and motive theories. His theory states that behavior is determined both by needs within the individual and by environmental pressures (press).

4. Murray argues that needs may be either manifest or latent. Manifest needs can be assessed by observing overt behavior, but latent needs must be assessed by probing the individual's fantasies, which Murray does with the Thematic Apperception Test (TAT). Subjects are shown pictures and asked to make up stories about them.

5. McClelland picked up on Murray's broad scheme but focused his attention on an in-depth analysis of one motive, the need to achieve. Using his own variation of the TAT, McClelland found that individuals scoring high in need achievement fantasy tend to perform better than those scoring low in need achievement on a variety of measures, such as getting better grades. Achievement motivation appears to be fostered by early training in independence and by warm but demanding parents. In one study, McClelland demonstrated that individuals exposed to achievement-saturated stories as children tended to become achieving adults, as measured by their country's economic growth.

6. McClelland developed a formal course to increase achievement motivation. The course runs from one to two weeks, twelve to eighteen hours a day, and has been found to significantly increase the entrepreneurial efforts and accomplishments of participants.

7. Achievement motivation in women appears to develop under somewhat different conditions than it does for men. For example, maternal hostility and criticism are linked to achievement striving in girls, while for boys having a relatively protective mother is associated with high achievement striving. Divorce, too, seems to increase achievement striving in girls but to decrease it in boys. Finally, there is reason to believe that whereas men fear achievement failure, women often fear achievement success, apparently because they think success makes them less attractive to men.

8. Winter has studied the need for power which he measures using TAT-like pictures. College students who fear power prefer more freedom in choosing course-related work than those who do not fear power (e.g., preferring discussions over lectures and essay examinations over objective examinations).

9. People high in the need for power tend to cultivate a group of followers toward whom they are generous and understanding, while taking a competitive stance toward outsiders. Individuals with a high need for power become emotionally aroused when they feel powerless.

10. Alcohol appears to provide a temporary inner feeling of power. Thus a high need for power, especially when it is unsatisfied, is associated with alcoholism.

THE DISPOSITIONAL STRATEGY

CHAPTER 12

LIABILITIES

As we did with the psychoanalytic strategy, we now turn to the major problems facing the dispositional strategy. We will discuss six broad liabilities pointed out by critics.

THE DISPOSITIONAL STRATEGY LACKS ITS OWN THEORETICAL STRUCTURE

Theory plays a central role in all science. However, the dispositional strategy has operated without any clear theoretical guidelines. Instead, dispositional psychologists have borrowed theoretical ideas from other strategies to explain and make sense of patterns uncovered in their research. We saw, for instance, that Cattell used the term *ego strength.* It was borrowed from psychoanalytic theory and used to both label and help describe what he found in "source trait C." Even the term *trait* was borrowed from genetics. How much similarity there is between the biological and the psychological concept is still unclear in most dispositional discussions.

When terms like *ego strength* and *introversion* are used, empirical findings are, in effect, given a "theoretical home"; the findings can be theoretically associated with other personality variables. The theory employed, however, is not dispositional; rather, the data have been placed in a "foster home." Dispositional psychologists use theoretical notions in their work. For the most part, though, they have not developed their own theories of personality. Therefore, they depend on other strategies for theoretical progress.

THE DISPOSITIONAL STRATEGY RELIES TOO HEAVILY ON SELF-REPORT INVENTORIES

Each strategy discussed in this book uses some form of self-report measure. However, self-report measures in the form of personality inventories are relied on most heavily in dispositional assessment. There is evidence that such reliance may not be justified. Self-reports are clearly useful to some extent, but they are more limited than dispositional psychologists recognize.

Faking

In any personality assessment, a person can probably succeed in faking to some extent. The person can present himself or herself in a more favorable light than "the truth" would justify. Self-report inventories, however, are particularly susceptible to faking. The absence of an examiner makes the evaluation impersonal and distant. The assessee need not fear, for example, that facial expressions or other signs of "nervousness" will give him or her away. Instead, the inaccurate or misleading response is made by simply checking a category or circling a number.

There have been numerous demonstrations that such faking can be quite successful (e.g., Anastasi, 1968; Noll, 1951; Wesman, 1952). Further, the problem is compounded because those at lower educational or intellectual levels may be less able to fake (Anastasi, 1968). Various corrections, such as the Lie scale on the MMPI, may not detect faking by brighter or more insightful assessees. However, these corrections generally improve an instrument's validity.

The Test-Trait Fallacy

Tryon (1979) has argued that dispositional theorists make faulty assumptions about personality testing. He labeled the problem the *test-trait fallacy*. Tryon sees the mistake as assuming that test scores are trait measures. He claims that tests are only *performance* measures. As such, test scores may let the tester predict how the individual will respond to similar, but naturally occurring, stimuli. However, there is no reason to believe that they provide a magical "X ray" of the inner person. Dispositional psychologists reify measures derived from self-report inventories and give them the status of causal factors. Tryon concludes that dispositionalists misinterpret the measures and go dangerously beyond the information that the test scores actually provide.

THE DISPOSITIONAL STRATEGY INVOLVES MANY SUBJECTIVE DECISIONS

Factor analysis involves sophisticated mathematical procedures. It therefore has an aura of precision and objectivity. In discussing factor analysis, we mentioned that naming factors is invariably a subjective decision.

Additionally, the number and kinds of factors extracted will depend on the mathematical procedure chosen—another subjective decision. Thus, Eysenck finds two factors and Cattell finds sixteen. In part, this is due to the statistical analysis each selected. Obviously, then, Eysenck did not discover a small number of types. Cattell did not discover sixteen personality traits. Both investigators made subjective decisions that forced their data into the patterns that emerged.

The preconceptions of raters, as well as of researchers, can influence factor analyses. For example, Cattell conducted his research without stating preconceived notions about the nature of the traits that would emerge. But his findings are by no means free of subjective distortion. There is evidence that Cattell's findings were largely determined by the preconceptions and stereotypes regarding personality organization that his raters held. This is illustrated in the research of Norman (1961, 1963) and his colleagues.

Norman used factor analysis to look at peer ratings across a number of diverse groups of people. He consistently found a stable set of the same five factors. Passini and Norman (1966) then showed that very similar factors emerged when students rated classmates with whom they were unacquainted. Passini and Norman concluded that ratings do not reflect the "true" organization of traits in the rated persons. Instead, they reflect the concepts of raters about personality (e.g., about what traits seem to go together).

The dispositional strategy, then, confuses subjective impression with objective discovery. This problem is by no means limited to factor analysts. There are endless arguments about the definition of achievement, power, aggression, and other traits in the dispositional literature. Consider, for example, the striking difference between Murray and McClelland's ideas of n Achievement. They both use the same term (and it is a novel and technical-sounding term at that). But they are referring to very different concepts. By n Achievement, Murray means a permanent characteristic set down in childhood and operating almost unconsciously. McClelland, in contrast, has in mind a conscious attitude and orientation that can be readily taught to adults. Both researchers use the same basic measuring instrument, the TAT, but for different ends. For Murray, a person writing achievement-saturated stories in response to a TAT picture displays the latent need for n Achievement. The person was probably not even aware of this need. The value of the TAT, Murray (1951) wrote, "is its capacity to reveal things that the . . . [subject] is unwilling to tell or unable to tell because he is unconscious of them" (p. 577). In contrast, McClelland used the TAT to teach people to become achievement-oriented by making them consciously aware of achievement strivings. McClelland did not do this because he discovered that Murray was wrong about the difference between latent and manifest needs. He changed the meaning of n Achievement because he subjectively decided that the new concept would be more "fruitful" than the old one.

THE DISPOSITIONAL STRATEGY CANNOT PREDICT INDIVIDUAL BEHAVIOR

The dispositional strategy has discovered many reliable and intriguing relationships. The link between physical appearance and personality is an example. And no one doubts that there is consistency in the way people behave. But the dispositional strategy provides almost no basis for predicting the behavior of a single individual with a high degree of accuracy. For example, many people with delicate builds love action and adventure, despite the general tendency for this group to be somewhat introverted. Many powerful leaders refrain from alcohol or sexual exploits and drive cars that would hardly be found at a grand prix.

To illustrate the problem, let us consider an exaggerated hypothetical example. Suppose that an investigator informally observes that some people seem to be more intrusive than others. To reflect this idea, he defines intrusiveness as "a tendency to provide unsolicited information or advice, to show up uninvited, and to examine and use the belongings of others without asking." Next, the investigator devises a broad assessment procedure to measure intrusiveness. It includes peer ratings, self-report measures, and fantasy measures. The procedure produces reliable intrusiveness scores and shows considerable individual differences among people.

At this point, the investigator begins to compare the backgrounds of those who are high (above average) and low (below average) in intrusiveness. He finds high intrusives tend to report that their parents used to leave the doors to their rooms—and even their homes—unlocked. Apparently they worried little about privacy. Individuals low on intrusiveness, in contrast, report that their parents locked their doors and emphasized everyone's "right to privacy."

Suppose that, given this information, you meet someone who mentions that his or her parents always left their doors unlocked. You would certainly be tempted to think that your new acquaintance is likely to be intrusive. However, that is not sound logic. There is a decent chance that your assumption will be wrong.

Part of the reason can be seen in Figure 12–1. The figure shows our hypothetical intrusiveness data. We have assumed that intrusiveness is normally distributed. (Modern dispositionalists commonly assume normal distributions.) We also show a difference between the "locked door" and the "unlocked door" group that is large enough to be reliable (statistically significant). Thus, Figure 12–1 represents the usual magnitude of difference between "trait-high" and "trait-low" people in typical dispositional research.

Three areas of the figure deserve comment. The colored portion indicates *overlap*. It accounts for more than half of the area under the curves.

FIGURE 12–1
Hypothetical distributions of scores for the disposition "intrusiveness," showing that a significant difference between the average trait scores of two groups (here, "locked-door" versus "unlocked-door" backgrounds) does not ordinarily provide the basis for predicting what any specific individual will be like

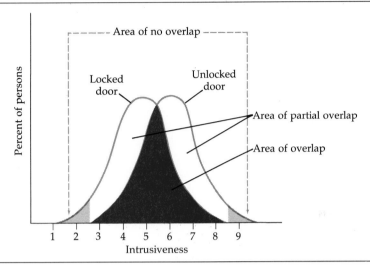

This shows that most people will tend to get an average intrusiveness score, whether or not the doors in their homes were locked. The two white areas indicate *partial overlap*. Some members of both groups obtain scores in this range, but one group predominates in each area. Notice, for example, that some persons from "locked-door" and "unlocked-door" backgrounds obtained an intrusiveness score of "4." However, most of those with this score were in the "locked-door" group. Finally, the grey areas indicate *nonoverlap*. Only one group is represented. In the figure, the only people with intrusiveness scores as low as "2" came from homes where the doors were locked. The only people with intrusiveness scores as high as "9" came from homes where the doors were unlocked. The most important thing to note about the areas of nonoverlap is how small they are; only a small percentage of people fall in these extreme ranges.

With this analysis in mind, we can ask: What conclusion can we draw about an individual person's intrusiveness knowing she or he comes from a home where the doors were never locked? We certainly do not want to conclude that the person must be highly intrusive. (Even among people from "unlocked-door" homes, the majority are only about average in intrusiveness.) As a matter of fact, our new acquaintance could be less intrusive than average—maybe even very *un*intrusive—and still come from a home where the doors were left unlocked. In this case at least, to reach any other conclusion would be stereotyping the person.

Of course, this does not mean that the data in the preceding chapters were wrong. Rather, it means that the dispositional strategy has, to date, given us assessment procedures that improve our guessing (above chance) as to what other people will be like or do. But they do not elevate us above the level of still *guessing*.

Mischel (1968), in a now-classic critique of the dispositional strategy, made the point this way:

> It is important to clearly distinguish between "statistically significant" associations and equivalence. A correlation of .30 easily reaches statistical significance when the sample of subjects is sufficiently large, and suggests an association that is highly unlikely on the basis of chance. However, the same coefficient accounts for less than 10 percent of the relevant variance [i.e., what the variables share in common]. Statistically significant relationships of this magnitude are sufficient to justify personality research on individual and group differences. It is equally plain that their value for making statements about an individual are severely limited. Even when statistically significant behavioral consistencies are found, and even when they replicate reliably, the relationships usually are not large enough to warrant individual assessment and treatment decisions except for certain screening and selection purposes. (p. 38)

Underestimation of the Importance of Situational Factors

A related liability is that the dispositional strategy underestimates—sometimes overlooks entirely—the influence of the situation and circumstances in determining behavior. For example, for years psychologists sought to determine what traits make a person a leader. Ultimately, however, it was recognized that, in most groups, a leader is selected based on how well he or she can facilitate attainment of the group's goals.

> What was overlooked . . . in the view that leaders are uniquely endowed . . . was the actual fact of daily life, that is, that persons function as leaders in a particular time and place, and that these are both varying and delimiting conditions; that there are several pathways to leadership, sometimes from higher authority, other times from group consent. . . . Indeed, if any point stands forth in the modern day view of leadership it is that leaders are made by circumstances. . . . The leader's emergence or waning of status is . . . inextricably linked to the prevailing situation. (Hollander, 1964, pp. 4–5, 15)

Failure to Specify When Dispositions Will Be Manifested in Behavior

The last of Allport's eight assumptions about traits is: "Acts, and even habits, that are inconsistent with a trait are not proof of the nonexistence of the trait." The intent of this assumption is clear. People do not always act consistently, and Allport does not want that fact to invalidate a trait approach. At some point, though, the argument is stretched to absurdity. If *all* of a person's acts are inconsistent with a trait, surely that is proof that the person does not possess the trait. Otherwise, we can describe people in any dispositional way we like, without regard to their behavior. An example would be to say that a minority group has the trait of dishonesty even though you have always known its members to behave honestly. How much inconsistency can a dispositional approach endure?

Critics have repeatedly challenged the assumption that human behavior is consistent enough across situations to justify a dispositional view of personality (e.g., Bandura & Walters, 1963; Mischel, 1968; Rotter, 1954). They have gathered empirical evidence from psychological investigations and compelling everyday examples to support their argument. It is clear, for instance, that someone who is aggressive at the office may be a Milquetoast at home, completely dominated by his family. Overstated, the criticism becomes unfair. Allport's point was that a person with the trait of hostility will not be hostile in every situation. But if a person is not hostile in every situation, it is essential to know *when* the characteristic will appear. The dispositional strategy has failed to provide useful ways of describing or predicting when a person's disposition will or will not show up. This is a fundamental deficit.

THE DISPOSITIONAL STRATEGY IGNORES PERSONALITY DEVELOPMENT AND CHANGE

As much as any other strategy, the dispositional view has examined *longitudinal data*. The characteristics of people have been measured at various points in time (e.g., in childhood and again as adults), and similarities and differences have been noted. These data certainly indicate some consistency in behavior. But changes over time are also apparent for most people. The dispositional strategy has paid little attention to these changes. It has hardly concerned itself with the *processes* underlying development or changing complexion over time of a person's traits, types, or needs. When and how do source traits develop? Why does one behavior pattern emerge and not another? Such questions are not simply unanswered from the dispositional perspective. The strategy does not even call on the investigator to ask them.

A closely related point is that the dispositional strategy has contributed almost nothing to personality-change techniques. Individual dispositionalists, such as Murray, Eysenck, and McClelland, have been involved in personality-change work. However, their approaches, like many of their basic theoretical concepts, are borrowed from other strategies. Murray's approach to personality is based on needs. He practiced as a therapist in the Harvard Psychological Clinic using procedures influenced primarily by psychoanalysis. Eysenck is a major advocate of the type approach based on factor analysis. He is also one of the most ardent proponents of personality-change procedures associated with the behavioral strategy. McClelland's program to increase achievement motivation is based on principles derived from the psychoanalytic, phenomenological, and behavioral strategies, as well as social psychology.

In sum, the dispositional strategy tries to capture and describe a *static* person. It ignores the dynamics of development, growth, and change although these are obviously important aspects of personality.

THE DISPOSITIONAL STRATEGY FAILS TO PROVIDE ADEQUATE EXPLANATIONS

When consistencies or regularities occur in behavior, it is convenient to summarize them with a descriptive label. Thus, "introversion" is a label for an observed pattern of behavior or set of relationships. This labeling process is perfectly legitimate if our purpose is description. But the label obviously does not *explain* our observations. Yet the error of confusing description with explanation is repeatedly made by dispositionalists.

Below is a related argument made by Skinner (1953) many years ago. By substituting appropriately, you can see how Skinner's argument applies to introversion, achievement motivation, or any of the other labels that have been invented to describe behavior.

> When we say that a man eats *because* he is hungry, smokes a great deal *because* he has the tobacco habit, fights *because* he has the instinct of pugnacity, behaves brilliantly *because* of his intelligence, or plays the piano well *because* of his musical ability, we seem to be referring to causes. But on analysis, these phrases prove to be merely redundant descriptions. A single set of facts is described by the two statements: "He eats" and "He is hungry." A single set of facts is described by the statements "He smokes a great deal" and "He has the smoking habit." A single set of facts is described by the two statements: "He plays well" and "He has musical ability." The practice of explaining one statement in terms of the other is dangerous because it suggests that we have found the cause and therefore need search no further. (p. 31)

Finally, it should be noted that failing to provide adequate explanations cannot be escaped by dispositional psychologists who claim that dispositions are only meant as descriptions. In that case, the dispositional strategy, by its own admission, does not provide an *explanation* of behavior.

Summary

1. The dispositional strategy lacks its own theoretical structure. When theoretical ideas are used, they are borrowed from one of the other strategies.

2. The dispositional strategy relies too heavily on self-report data, even though it is clear that such data can be faked or distorted by a variety of biases. Moreover, it is a logical fallacy to simply equate test scores with the dispositions themselves.

3. Many subjective decisions are made by dispositional psychologists, including the naming of traits and types in factor analysis and the often inconsistent ways in which motivational terms such as the need to achieve are used.

4. The dispositional strategy cannot accurately predict the behavior of individuals. One reason is that situational factors often exert considerable influence over how we behave. Dispositional psychology tends to minimize or completely ignore the influence of situational factors.

5. The dispositional strategy fails to explain personality development and provides few hints as to how personality can be changed. The therapies used by dispositional psychologists are borrowed from other strategies.

6. The dispositional strategy fails to provide adequate explanations for the causes of behavior. To explain a behavior by saying it is caused by a disposition and then to turn around and claim that the presence of the disposition is proved by the occurrence of the behavior is a completely circular argument.

SECTION

IV

THE
PHENOMENOLOGICAL
STRATEGY

THE PHENOMENOLOGICAL STRATEGY

CHAPTER 13

INTRODUCTION

OVERVIEW

A tree falls in a forest, but no one is there to hear it fall. Does it make a sound as it falls? This philosophical question involves the issue of whether physical phenomena have reality of their own, or whether they must be perceived to be real. Psychology is interested in the reality of physical events from the point of view of the perceiver. In fact, questions about subjective human experience were among the first asked by psychologists (James, 1890).

How people react to events in their physical or interpersonal world depends to some degree on the *meaning* that various events have for them. Suppose someone were standing close to the proverbial tree as it fell and heard the loud cracking that precedes the fall. If the person were a lumberjack, the sound would be familiar. The lumberjack would hastily retreat to a safe distance. However, the same sound might have no special meaning to a lawyer from the "big city" who had never heard it before. The lawyer might not react to the sound (other than to look around curiously for its source). Note that, in fact, the lumberjack reacts not to the sound itself, but to an *interpretation* of the sound. The lawyer fails to react because the lawyer has no interpretation of the sound.

PHENOMENOLOGY AND THE PHENOMENOLOGICAL STRATEGY

The reality of phenomena lies solely in the way they are perceived. This is the essence of phenomenology. It is also the basis for the phenomenological approach to personality. What is real to an individual is what is in the person's **internal frame of reference,** or subjective world. This includes everything the person is aware of at a particular point in time.

For centuries, the phenomenological view was in disrepute, especially among philosophers of science. It seemed to deny the possibility of establishing "objective facts." But modern philosophers and contemporary scientists have recently begun to show a new respect for the phenomenological claim that all experiences, and thus all knowledge, depend on subjective interpretation (Heelan, 1983; Manicas & Secord, 1983; Rock, 1983). At the heart of this new acceptance is the growing recognition that *perception is an interpretive act.* To see what this means, look at the *wine goblet* in Figure 13–1 on the next page; then continue reading. Now look at the *two faces in silhouette* in the same figure. Look at the figure for a while. You may see it flip back and forth between a goblet and faces. (Some people can make it look like a goblet or like two faces at will.) Is the figure a wine goblet or two silhouettes? It is both and neither. It depends on how you, the perceiver, interpret the figure. What we see is more than a simple mirroring of the "world out there." The figure doesn't change at all when our perception shifts from a goblet to faces; the change is only in our minds!

The phrase *only in our minds* does not mean that subjective perception is unimportant. Nor does it mean that subjective phenomena, such as the change between a goblet and faces, do not exist. Phenomenologists consider subjective reality as real as external reality. This position has important practical implications. For instance, it is now being applied to city planning.

> In a sense, social scientists find, the city does not exist. There is no such single entity, but rather many cities, as many as there are people to experience them. And researchers now believe that the subjective reality is every bit as important to understanding and fostering successful urban life as the concrete and asphalt of objective measurement.
>
> Although most earlier approaches to assessing the quality of city life led researchers to consider such factors as noise levels and density, the new work shows that how people actually perceive their

FIGURE 13–1
Reversible figure-ground pattern

environments is as important as the environments themselves. (Goleman, 1985, p. C1)

From the standpoint of predicting behavior, phenomenological psychology says that effective reality is *reality as it is perceived*. Two people observing the "same" circumstances may perceive two very different things. (This is so often the case with "eyewitnesses" in traffic accidents.)

The importance of the way things are perceived and experienced subjectively is illustrated in an experiment by Geer, Davison, and Gatchel (1970). These investigators hypothesized that stress is determined not only by the objective characteristics of the situation—such as the person's ability to influence what happens—but also by whether the person *believes* he or she can control what is happening. In the experiment, all subjects received a series of identical electric shocks. No subjects had any control whatsoever over the shocks. But some of them believed they could control the shocks; whereas others believed they could not.

The experiment was presented to the subjects as a study of reaction times. It was conducted in two phases. In Phase I, all subjects were treated alike. They were given painful electric shocks, each lasting six seconds. They were asked to press a switch as soon as the shock began. This was the measure of reaction time. During this period, levels of physiological arousal were recorded as a measure of stress. During Phase II, half the subjects were assigned to a *perceived control* condition. They were told that they could cut the duration of the next ten shocks in half if they pressed the switch "quickly enough." (The necessary speed was left undefined.) The remaining subjects were assigned to a *perceived noncontrol* condition. They were just told that the next ten shocks would be shorter. Actually, all of the subjects received shocks of three seconds' duration, while their physiological arousal was again measured.

If stress is partially determined by the belief that one can control the situation, perceived control subjects should have experienced less arousal during Phase II than perceived noncontrol subjects. As seen in Figure 13–2, this is what occurred. The two groups did not differ in arousal in Phase I; they did differ in the predicted direction in Phase II. Geer and his associates (1970) noted the following implication of their finding: "Man creates his own gods to fill in gaps in his knowledge about a sometimes terrifying environment, creating at least an illusion of control which is presumably comforting. Perhaps the next best thing to being master of one's fate is being deluded into thinking he is" (pp. 737–38).

A phenomenological approach to personality implies that behavior can only be understood from the person's own point of view. The strategy focuses on subjective experiences. It is these experiences that direct behavior. Subjective experience may or may not coincide with **objective reality.** We can define the latter as something a number of observers agree on. Consider the following somewhat whimsical example.

A man construes [views] his neighbor's behavior as hostile. By that he means that his neighbor, given the proper opportunity, will do him harm. He tries out his construction [view] of his neighbor's attitude by throwing rocks at his neighbor's dog. His neighbor responds with an angry rebuke. The man may then believe that he has validated his construction of his neighbor as a hostile person.

The man's construction of his neighbor as a hostile person may appear to be "validated" by another kind of fallacy. The man reasons, "If my neighbor is hostile, he will be eager to know when I get into trouble, when I am ill, or when I am in any way vulnerable. I will watch to see if this isn't so." The next morning the man

FIGURE 13–2

The effects of perceived control on the amount of arousal subjects experienced while awaiting electric shocks in Geer et al.'s experiment. During Phase I, all subjects received shocks of six seconds' duration. During Phase II, all subjects received shocks of three seconds' duration. Subjects in the perceived control group believed that the shorter shocks were a result of their own quick reaction times, whereas subjects in the perceived noncontrol group believed that shock duration was unrelated to their responses and therefore not within their control.

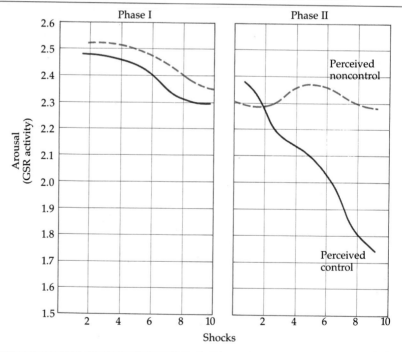

Source: Adapted from "Reduction of Stress in Humans through Nonveridical Perceived Control of Aversive Stimulation" by J. H. Geer, G. C. Davison, and R. I. Gatchel, 1970, *Journal of Personality and Social Psychology, 16*, pp. 731–738.

meets his neighbor and is greeted with the conventional, "How are you?" Sure enough, the neighbor is doing just what was predicted of a hostile person. (Kelly, 1955, pp. 12–13)

In many instances, external reality is much less clear than in the preceding example. For all practical purposes, what a person perceives, subjective experience, determines the ultimate reality of a situation for the person. Consider eight-year-old Beth. Her family has just moved to a new city. After her first day at the new school, Beth's parents ask, "How was school today?" Beth replies:

I hated it. The kids are really unfriendly. When I came into the class, all the kids stared at me. They were grinning and thought I was funny looking. Only two kids in the whole class talked to me at lunch.

Now consider how Beth might have *perceived* the same situation differently and reported a very different experience.

I liked it. The kids are really friendly. When I came into the class, they were all interested in me. The kids were looking at me and smiling. And two kids, who I didn't even know, came over to talk to me at lunch!

The same situation could have led Beth to have either of these two very different subjective experiences. Beth's reactions, of course, would vary with her perceptions. (It is also likely that Beth's reactions would influence how her classmates react to her and changes the nature of the situation in later interactions.)

From a philosophical standpoint, no practical problems are presented by phenomenology's exclusive concern with subjective knowledge. But when phenomenology enters the realm of psychology, a dilemma arises. Psychology is a scientific endeavor. It tries to deal with objective knowledge. Objective knowledge comes from observations on which others can agree. Subjective knowledge involves only a single person's experiences. Phenomenological psychologists solve this problem by seeking what Carl Rogers (1964) calls **phenomenological knowledge.** This involves understanding a person from the person's own internal frame of reference.

The importance of subjective experience is often acknowledged in everyday psychology. We use expressions such as "Beauty is all in the eye of the beholder," "One person's meat is another person's poison," and "Try stepping into the other person's shoes." These common sayings emphasize the role of subjective knowledge in determining actions. They also show that phenomenological knowledge is important in understanding and predicting someone else's behavior. We may not see things as other people see them, and this may get us into interpersonal difficulties. For example, we make a joke about an incident that another person takes seriously.

We will examine two somewhat different approaches to phenomenological personality theory. First we discuss the self-actualization approaches of Carl Rogers and Abraham Maslow. Both emphasize understanding personality and behavior in terms of each person's unique biological and learned inclinations to develop and change in particular directions. Then we consider George Kelly's psychology of personal constructs. Kelly's theory deals with how people interpret and interact with the events in their lives and in doing so, develop unique personalities. These positions differ in basic assumptions about the nature of human personality, but they share fundamental suppositions about personality theory, assessment, research, and change. These suppositions are the basis of the phenomenological strategy for studying personality.

PHENOMENOLOGICAL PERSONALITY THEORY

Rogers and Kelly propose comprehensive theories of personality. They try to account for the full range of human behaviors. Their theories grew, in part, out of the clinical experiences each had in dealing with abnormal behavior; thus, they are interested in both the "sick" and "healthy" sides of personality.

In contrast, Maslow's theory is narrower. It is not a comprehensive theory of personality. Instead, Maslow focuses on theoretical explanations of several specific aspects of human behavior. As a personality theorist, Maslow is almost alone in focusing on the positive, healthy side of personality. For example, he believes every individual has a vast potential for growth. So Maslow explored the optimal or fully functioning person—someone who is close to all he or she can become.

The theories of Rogers, Maslow, and Kelly focus on "higher" human functions. Rogers' and Maslow's work deals with self-actualization; Kelly's personal construct theory involves how people interpret their experiences. In contrast, the other three strategies all focus on "lower" functions, like drives and reflexes. Each of the phenomenological positions we discuss takes into account basic biological needs, but its theory of human personality begins at the point where these have been satisfied.

Another common theme in phenomenological approaches is that humans are naturally *active beings*. In making this assumption, phenomenological psychologists partially avoid the basic problem of explaining motivation. If humans are inert objects that must be compelled to action, then we must invent some special force, like a drive or a motive, to account for behavior. Phenomenological personality theories view human beings as active organisms, not passive objects. These theories assume humans react *with* their biological makeup and immediate environment; they are not compelled to action *by* these factors.

Phenomenological psychologists are concerned with the *direction* of behavior. On a broad scale, they answer questions such as why some people spend their lives accumulating money while others want prestige and fame. In the more narrow sphere of day-to-day endeavors, they must account for observations such as the fact that Janette always studies at the last minute while her roommate Cindy always gets her studying done early. To explain the direction that one's behavior takes, a general principle is advanced. Rogers posits that behavior is directed by people's unique *self-actualizing tendencies*. Maslow proposes that behavior is determined by a hierarchy of needs. Kelly theorizes that people act to maximize their ability to accurately anticipate events in their lives. How these broad principles operate to direct a person's behavior varies with each individual.

Phenomenological approaches not only view people as active but also see people as being in a general state of flux. As Rogers (1961) put it: "Life, at its best, is a flowing, changing process in which nothing is fixed" (p. 27). This dynamic conception of the person is related to the phenomenological emphasis on the **here-and-now**, or momentary experience. In contrast to the *present*, which may mean this hour or day or even the current year, *here-and-now* refers to what is occurring at this very moment.

Phenomenological psychologists acknowledge that past experiences influence present behavior. But they view the past only in terms of how it affects present perceptions. Phenomenological theories pay little attention to stable, enduring characteristics (the focus of the dispositional strategy) or to lifelong patterns that originated in early childhood (central to the psychoanalytic strategy).

The theories of Rogers, Maslow, and Kelly are **holistic**. That is, they view and explain specific acts in terms of an individual's entire personality. For example, Rogers stresses the importance of consistency between how people view themselves and how they would like to be. Kelly does not differentiate between thoughts, feelings, and actions; he considers them all to be psychological processes governed by the same principles.

The Concept of Self

Self or **self-concept** is a theoretical construct used by phenomenological psychologists to represent and sometimes explain the consistency, organization, or pattern in personality.

Wylie (1968) suggested that the self can be seen as a complex structure of interrelated aspects. In Wylie's view, we can speak of a *generic self-concept*. This is an all-inclusive concept that incorporates all of the following features:

1. The person's experiencing himself or herself as a distinct entity which can be differentiated from others.
2. A sense of continuing to be the same person over time.
3. A person's physical characteristics *as experienced by the person.*
4. A person's past behaviors as experienced and remembered, especially those that are perceived as having been executed voluntarily or as having been under the control of the person.
5. The experiencing of a degree of organization or unity among the various aspects of the generic self-concept.
6. Evaluations, thoughts, and memories.
7. Varying degrees of consciousness or unconsciousness.

As Figure 13–3 shows, the generic self-concept can be subdivided. The subdivisions are the *actual self-concept* (what we are) and the *ideal self-concept* (what we would like to be). The actual self-concept also has two subdivisions. There is an important difference between the way we see ourselves, *private self-concept,* and the way we present ourselves to others, *social self-concept.* And the ideal self-concept has two subdivisions. These correspond to the way we would like to be, *own-ideal self-concept,* and *concepts of others' ideals for one.*

Existential Psychology and the Phenomenological Strategy

The phenomenological approach to personality has close ties with the existential movement in psychology. Rollo May (1967) is a prominent champion of existential psychology. He describes the movement as "an

FIGURE 13–3
Wylie's analysis of the self-concept

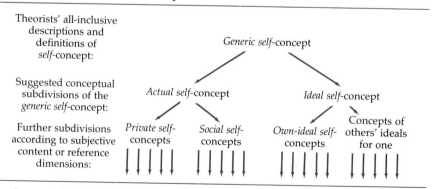

Source: Adapted from "The Present Status of Self Theory" by R. C. Wylie, 1968, in E. F. Borgatta & W. W. Lambert (Eds.), *Handbook of Personality Theory and Research,* Chicago: Rand McNally.

attitude, an approach to human beings, rather than a special school or group. . . . it is not a system of therapy but an attitude toward therapy, not a set of new techniques but a concern with the understanding of the structure of the human being and his experience" (p. 245). This existential attitude requires an intimate understanding or experiencing of what someone else is going through. It suggests that psychologists should try to *know* people rather than merely *know about* them.

Two themes in existential psychology are central to the phenomenological strategy: the individual's *free will* and his or her opportunity for *choice.* In different ways, we will see the related themes of free will and choice repeatedly in the phenomenological theories discussed in the next three chapters. Both Rogers and Maslow assume that individuals are capable of directing their own lives. Rogers' formula for personality change involves establishing conditions conducive to self-growth. Kelly's personality theory is based on the assumption that people can choose to view events in their lives in a variety of ways.

A final distinguishing characteristic of the phenomenological strategy is that humans are *rational.* Their actions represent "sensible" responses to the world as each person perceives it. This implies that people are aware of their psychological processes. The phenomenological strategy therefore emphasizes *conscious* experience.

PHENOMENOLOGICAL PERSONALITY ASSESSMENT

Personality assessment presents difficulties for the phenomenological strategy. How can person A know how person B is perceiving the world when all that person A truly can know is what person B describes? Ignoring issues of trust and accuracy, how can you be sure the experience another person describes is even remotely like the one that the person has in mind? Think of all the different possible meanings of a simple statement such as "I'm tired." This gives you a hint of what the odds are against your knowing exactly what people mean when they say "I'm scared" or "I love you."

The phenomenological strategy concerns subjective experiences. Phenomenological personality assessment must therefore involve gaining knowledge of private events. This is also the essential task of psychoanalytic personality assessment. In both the phenomenological and psychoanalytic strategies, behavior is neither the basic unit of personality nor the exclusive means of getting at personality.

Consider the student who does not speak up in class. What can we infer from this behavior? Would it be a good hunch that the student has not read the assignment for the day and therefore is not prepared to participate? Or is the student familiar with the reading but afraid of being considered a show-off in class? The student's behavior on any given day will not answer these questions; the same behavior can have vastly different *meanings*.

Within broad limits, behavior can yield information about someone's personality; but for more specific information, we must find the meaning of the behavior for the person. In fact, all of phenomenological personality assessment is aimed at discovering *meaning*. It is the meaning of experiences for people that constitutes their personalities and determines their actions.

Often we confuse our *own* view of things with those of another. Consider the case of a college student named Jim. He told his parents that he wanted to drop out of school because he wasn't learning anything worthwhile. Jim's parents told Jim that they "understood exactly how he felt. When they were in college there were times that they were tired and depressed and wanted to quit." His parents went on to suggest that Jim take a few days off and relax. What Jim's parents "understood" was how *they* had felt in a similar situation. They did not know how their son was feeling. Phenomenological knowledge is a matter of *what the experience means for the person.* It does not involve what the experience means for the assessor or for people in general.

The essence of phenomenological personality assessment is the assessor's attempt to understand subjective experiences from the internal frame of reference of the person relating the experiences. This primarily involves **empathy**—understanding a person's experiences in terms of what they mean for that person. It necessitates abandoning our connotations for the words and phrases the other person uses, our interpretation of the experiences, and our preconceived ideas about such experiences. Instead, we try to grasp the idiosyncratic meaning of the other person's verbal descriptions of the experience.

Phenomenological assessment focuses on the present, often on the here-and-now. An individual's past experiences are important only insofar as they clarify present perceptions. For example, in practice, Rogerian personality assessment almost completely ignores the past; Kellian assessment techniques deal with the past sparingly.

Phenomenological personality assessment is relatively straightforward; this contrasts with the largely inferential tack of the psychoanalytic and dispositional strategies. Most phenomenological personality-assessment techniques involve self-report measures, especially verbal self-report. These descriptions of subjective experiences are accepted more or less at face value. They are not considered signs or indications of some inferred psychological state (e.g., an intrapsychic conflict). Neither are they used to indicate some underlying disposition (e.g., a trait). The assessment remains on the level of phenomenological knowledge.

Conscious experiences are taken as direct evidence of important personality functions. They are not necessarily viewed as indicators of underlying unconscious processes. A basic assumption of the phenomenological strategy is that people are generally aware of their subjective experiences. In fact, it is this awareness that is presumed to direct behavior. The phenomenological strategy acknowledges experiences outside awareness (i.e., unconscious), but does not consider them major determinants of normal behavior. Unconscious processes are assumed to play a greater role in determining abnormal behavior.

DEMONSTRATION 13–1

PERCEIVING FROM ANOTHER'S INTERNAL FRAME OF REFERENCE

This Demonstration will give you a chance to try to understand another person's subjective experiences from his internal frame of reference. Below are a series of statements made by a thirty-year-old man at the beginning of a psychotherapy session. Your task is to assume the role of the therapist by *commenting on the man's statements so that you let him know that you understand what he is saying from his perspective (internal frame of reference)*. Respond to each of the client's statements by writing down a sentence or two that meet this goal.

1. "I thought I'd have something to talk about—then it all goes around in circles. I was trying to think of what I was going to say. Then coming here it doesn't work out. . . . I tell you, it seemed that it would be much easier before I came."

2. "I tell you, I just can't make a decision; I don't know what I want. I've tried to reason this thing out logically—tried to figure out which things are important to me."

3. "I thought that there are maybe two things a man might do; he might get married and raise a family. But if he was just a bachelor, just making a living—that isn't very good."

4. "I find myself and my thoughts getting back to the days when I was a kid, and I cry very easily. The dam would break through."

5. "I was in the Army four and one-half years. I had no problems then, no hopes, no wishes. My only thought was to get out when peace would come."

Now compare your responses to the client with the responses in Table 13–1 to see what success you had at adopting the client's internal frame of reference. If you responded from the client's internal frame of reference, your responses will be similar to those in the left-hand column. If you responded from your own external frame of reference, your responses will more closely resemble the responses in the right-hand column. Rogers (1965) explained why the responses in the right-hand column are

TABLE 13–1
Attitudes and thoughts representing internal and external frames of reference*

Internal Frame of Reference	External Frame of Reference
1. It's really hard for you to get started.	1. Should I help you get started talking? Is your inability to get under way a type of dependence?
2. Decision making just seems impossible to you.	2. What is the cause of your indecisiveness?
3. You want marriage, but it doesn't seem to you to be much of a possibility.	3. Why are you focusing on marriage and family? You appear to be a bachelor. I didn't know that.
4. You feel yourself brimming over with childish feelings.	4. The crying, the "dam," sound as though you are repressing a great deal.
5. To you the Army represented stagnation.	5. You're a veteran. Were you a psychiatric patient? I feel sorry for anybody who spent 4½ years in the service.

*Statements quoted or paraphrased from *Client-Centered Therapy* by C. R. Rogers, 1965, Boston: Houghton Mifflin, pp. 33–34.

representative of an external frame of reference by noting that "these are all attitudes which are basically sympathetic. There is nothing 'wrong' with them. They are even attempts to 'understand,' in the sense of 'understanding about,' rather than 'understanding with.' The locus of perceiving is, however, outside of the client" (p. 33).

PHENOMENOLOGICAL RESEARCH

The three basic methods of personality research—experimental, correlational, and case study—have all been used in the phenomenological strategy; however, correlational and case studies have predominated. Rogers and Maslow in particular are interested in examining people as they exist; this involves using correlational and case studies rather than experiments. The existential approach involves gaining knowledge *of* people rather than *from* them. Consistent with this perspective, Rogers (1973) advocates a research approach that does not view the person as an *object* (of study) and does not "push the individual into some contrived situation to investigate some hypothesis we have imposed" (p. 380). Instead he suggests that psychologists study personality by learning *from* people by being open to "hearing" what they are "saying."

Phenomenological research focuses on subjective experiences and the way people perceive events. This means that the phenomenological strategy emphasizes idiographic research. Such research most frequently utilizes the case-study method. Maslow's investigations of the self-actualizing person are a prime example. The data from these studies are detailed, qualitative descriptions of subjective, intensely personal experiences. They yield rich, in-depth portraits of single personalities. By studying subjects with a particular characteristic, such as self-actualization, the researcher can combine data to produce a composite of that personality characteristic. Thus, what begins as a series of idiographic investigations can also yield nomothetic information applicable to a great many people.

Like psychoanalytic research, phenomenological research is often related to and done in conjunction with psychotherapy. Rogers and Kelly began their careers as clinical psychologists; they developed their theories and approaches to personality while actively practicing psychotherapy. Phenomenological approaches also tend to emphasize application of theory to practical human problems. This is another reason the research often has an applied bent. For example, Rogers' and Kelly's theories have been applied to a vast array of human endeavors besides psychotherapy. These include education, politics, and environmental planning.

PHENOMENOLOGICAL PERSONALITY CHANGE

In the phenomenological strategy, personality is considered a product of perceptions and subjective evaluations. Therefore, to change personality, these private experiences must be modified. Among other things, this involves helping people to become more aware of their subjective experiences and the influence of these experiences on their behavior.

In phenomenological personality change, the client (as the "patient" is called) takes major responsibility for modifying his or her personality. It is assumed that people can change their own behaviors and personalities. The specific procedures vary with each approach. However, the basic theme of self-determination runs through all phenomenological personality-change procedures. Further, clients know themselves and their own subjective experiences far better than anyone else could. Therefore, the client, rather than the therapist, must direct the change process.

Phenomenological personality change is primarily present-oriented. Often the locus of time is here-and-now. This means events happening in therapy become the focus. This includes all of a client's thoughts and feelings during the therapy hour. For example, the client's immediate anxiety in the therapy situation may be the focus of discussion. Phenomenological personality change also deals with the future. Expectations, beliefs, and predictions about the future (although these are obviously occurring in the present) are frequent topics in therapy.

SUMMARY

1. The phenomenological strategy is based on the notion that the reality of events rests solely with the way they are perceived. Thus, the same objective event may be perceived and/or interpreted in subjectively different ways. It is people's subjective experiences or their internal frames of reference that make up their personalities and determine their behavior.

2. The phenomenological strategy's interest in subjective knowledge is problematic for a scientific study of personality that emphasizes objective knowledge. Phenomenologists deal with this problem by attempting to gain an understanding of a person's views of events (phenomenological knowledge.)

3. The theories of Rogers, Maslow, and Kelly illustrate the phenomenological strategy and share several features. They deal with "higher" human functions (e.g., self-actualization, cognitions) and view people as active, reacting beings who are constantly changing.

4. The focus of the phenomenological strategy is in the present, often the immediate experience (here-and-now).

5. Phenomenological theories are holistic in that they view personality as consistent and involving an interrelationship among its various aspects. This approach is exemplified by Rogers' concept of self and Kelly's view that thoughts, feelings, and actions are all psychological processes governed by the same principles.

6. The phenomenological strategy is related to existential psychology in that it emphasizes free will and rationality.

7. Phenomenological personality assessment is difficult because it deals with private, subjective experiences that people may be unable or unwilling to reveal accurately. Various self-report measures must be used, and the assessor attempts to understand the individual's experiences from that person's perspective (empathy).

8. Consistent with an interest in subjective experience, phenomenological research is often idiographic and primarily uses correlational and case studies. The research is frequently related to psychotherapy.

9. Phenomenological personality change involves changing subjective experience (e.g., self-concept, personal construct). It is primarily presented-oriented, and clients are given major responsibility for change.

THE PHENOMENOLOGICAL STRATEGY

CHAPTER 14

ROGERS' SELF-ACTUALIZATION THEORY

OVERVIEW

*E*ach *of us has a unique potential to develop, grow, and change in healthy and positive directions; given a psychological climate that is essentially free of external influences or constraints, that potential will guide all of a person's behavior.* This central theme is the principle of *self-actualization.* It has directed Carl Rogers' (1902–   ) theorizing, research, and therapy for more than fifty years. It has had a major impact on the field of personality psychology (Rogers, 1974).

Rogers began his career in 1927. At the time, personality psychology was essentially the psychoanalytic strategy. Rogers' theory was the first major alternative to psychoanalysis. In contrast to psychoanalysis, self-actualization theory offers an optimistic outlook of our ability to develop and enhance ourselves in positive and healthy ways. Clearly, Rogers' ideas were developed, in part, as a reaction to psychoanalytic concepts.

There are many striking differences between the theories of Rogers and Freud. There are also a number of interesting parallels. Like Freud, Rogers began as a psychotherapist. He also used his experiences in therapy both as a source of ideas about personality and as an arena for testing, refining, and revising these ideas. Rogers developed a new form of personality change. It became the first significant alternative to psychoanalytic psychotherapy. Also, as in Freud's case, Rogers' theories were innovative and were initially considered heretical. Finally, Rogers' ideas, like Freud's, have been widely adopted and expanded to diverse human endeavors,

Carl Rogers

Courtesy of Carl Rogers, photo by Nozizwe S.

including interpersonal relations, education, and the development and survival of cultures.

NORMAL PERSONALITY DEVELOPMENT AND FUNCTIONING

Rogers' personality theory is based on two major assumptions: (1) human behavior is guided by each person's unique self-actualizing tendency and (2) all humans need positive regard. We will examine these concepts in terms of normal personality development and functioning. Then we will see how they can become distorted and result in abnormal behavior.

The Actualizing Tendency

Rogers believes that all behavior is governed by the **actualizing tendency:** "the inherent tendency of the organism to develop all its capacities in ways which serve to maintain or enhance the organism" (Rogers, 1959, p. 196). At the most basic level, this inborn tendency maintains the individual by meeting fundamental needs (e.g., for oxygen, water, and food) and governing physical maturation, continued growth, and regeneration. More important to human personality is the motivation the actualizing tendency provides for increased autonomy and self-sufficiency, for expanding one's repertoire of experiences, and for personal growth.

The actualizing tendency guides the person toward generally positive or healthy behaviors rather than toward negative or unhealthy behaviors. Rogers (1980) notes that "the organism does not tend toward developing its capacity for nausea, . . . for self-destruction, nor . . . to bear pain. Only under unusual or perverse circumstances do these potentialities become actualized. It is clear that *the actualizing tendency is selective and directional—a constructive tendency*" (p. 121; italics added).

How does the actualizing tendency lead us to act in positive ways? According to Rogers, we evaluate our experiences in terms of whether they *maintain* or *enhance* us. He termed this process the **organismic valuing process.** *Experiences* include all that is going on at a given moment that the person can potentially be aware of (Rogers, 1959). Experiences perceived as maintaining or enhancing the individual are evaluated positively and are sought. Such positive experiences result in feelings of satisfaction. In contrast, experiences perceived as opposing maintenance or enhancement are evaluated negatively and are avoided.

The actualizing tendency can be thought of as having two aspects. One consists of shared biological tendencies—inclinations that result in behaviors that keep organisms (including nonhumans) alive. The other aspect involves unique tendencies toward increased autonomy, self-sufficiency, and personal growth. This **self-actualization** is most germane to personality. It involves maintenance and enhancement of the *self*, a central construct in Rogers' theory.

The Self

An infant does not distinguish what is "me" and what is "not me." The self develops as the child begins to distinguish what is directly part of him or her and what is external. Rogers uses the terms *self* and *self-concept* synonymously. They both refer to the organized, consistent, and whole perceptions that each of us has of ourselves. This is what we consider "I" or "me," separate from "you" (Rogers, 1959). The self includes the values associated with these perceptions. (Note the similarities between Rogers' *self* and Fairbairn's *central ego* discussed in Chapter 4.)

According to Rogers, the self must stay a cohesive whole. This means that our various self-perceptions must be relatively compatible. For example, a woman could think of herself as being both organized and sloppy, but only if these two contrasting characteristics could be reconciled. For instance, she could see herself as organized in terms of her ideas and schedule but messy in how she keeps her belongings.

The self has two aspects: (1) how we actually see ourselves and (2) how we would like to see ourselves. The latter is the **ideal self.**

Assessment of the Self

Knowledge of another person's self-concept is always incomplete. However, it is possible to gain some understanding of how others view themselves. One method is the **Q-sort**. It lets people make comparative judgments of statements about themselves (e.g., "I am lazy"; "I don't like to be with other people"; "I am a domineering person"). The statements are printed on cards that subjects place in piles according to how characteristic each statement is of them. In other words, the cards are sorted based on the degree to which the statement fits the person's self-concept. Usually, the subject sorts the statements according to some fixed distribution. He or she places a specific number of statements in each pile. This is illustrated in Figure 14–1. Depending on the instructions, subjects will sort the statement in terms of *perceived self* (how they actually see themselves) or *ideal self* (how they would like to see themselves).

The Q-sort is particularly useful for assessing changes in these judgments over time. Rogers and Dymond (1954), for example, had clients do perceived-self and ideal-self Q-sorts before and after psychotherapy. They found that clients at the beginning of therapy typically showed considerable divergence between the way they actually viewed themselves and how they would have liked to be. Following therapy, these two aspects of the self were closer together.

FIGURE 14–1

Example of the distribution of self-referent statements in a Q-sort. Subjects must sort the statements so that the specified number is put in each pile.

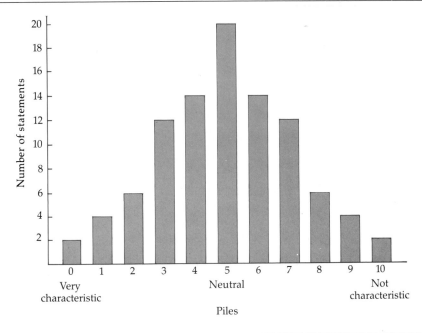

DEMONSTRATION 14–1

THE Q-SORT

To get a better understanding of the Q-sort, you are invited to perform two Q-sorts of your interests.

PREPARATION

1. First, write the name of each of the interests or activities listed in Table 14–1 along with its number on separate 3 × 5 index cards (or any small pieces of paper).

2. Next, referring to Table 14–2, number nine cards (1–9). On each card, write the description of the corresponding degree of interest and the required number of activities that must be sorted into the pile. (The first three columns of Table 14–2 provide descriptions of the information for these nine cards.) On a desk or other flat surface, place these cards in numerical order (from left to right), thereby forming a nine-point scale. You are now ready to perform the first Q-sort.

TABLE 14-1
List of activities for Q-sort in Demonstration 14-1

1. Basketball	14. Sewing or knitting
2. Camping or hiking	15. Shopping
3. Card games	16. Singing
4. Dancing	17. Social drinking
5. Dining out	18. Swimming
6. Drawing or painting	19. Talking with friends
7. Going to movies	20. Tennis
8. Going to parties	21. Travel
9. Hunting or fishing	22. Visiting museums or art galleries
10. Listening to music	23. Walking
11. Playing a musical instrument	24. Watching television
12. Politics	25. Writing letters
13. Reading for pleasure	

FIRST Q-SORT

3. To help you sort the activities into nine piles, first divide the twenty-five activity cards into three broad categories: (1) *definitely interested* at present, (2) *definitely not interested* at present, and (3) *ambivalent* at present.

4. You have just sorted the activities into the three gross categories of definitely interested, ambivalent, and definitely not interested. The Q-sort involves sorting or categorizing the activities on the nine-point scale that you have set up. Start with the "definitely interested" category, and distribute these cards where you feel they belong (i.e., according to how interested you are in the activities *at the present time*). Be sure you do not exceed the number of activities for each pile. Next, do the same with the "definitely not interested" category. Finally, sort the "ambivalent" category.

5. Check each pile to see that it contains the correct number of cards.

6. Check the Q-sort to be sure that each activity is in the pile you think it belongs in.

TABLE 14-2
Piles for Q-sort in Demonstration 14-1

Pile Number	Degree of Interest	Required Number in Each Pile	Rank
1	Very strong interest	1	1.0
2	Strong interest	2	2.5
3	Moderate interest	3	5.0
4	Slight interest	4	8.5
5	Ambivalent (neutral)	5	13.0
6	Slight lack of interest	4	17.5
7	Moderate lack of interest	3	21.0
8	Strong lack of interest	2	23.5
9	Very strong lack of interest	1	25.0

TABLE 14–3
Sample recording sheet for Q-sort in Demonstration 14–1

Activity Number	First Sort Rank	Second Sort Rank	Difference	Difference Squared
1				
2				
3				
4				
5				
6				
7				
8				
9				
10				
11				
12				
13				
14				
15				
16				
17				
18				
19				
20				
21				
22				
23				
24				
25				
Sum of difference squared =				

7. It is now possible to rank the activities from the ones you are most interested in to the ones you are least interested in. The ranks for each pile are given in the last column of Table 14–2. Make a copy of the "Recording Sheet" in Table 14–3 on a piece of lined paper and record the rank of each activity in the column designated "First Sort Rank."

By examining the Q-sort you have just produced, you can get an idea of what your present interests are, just as a therapist can gain some understanding of a client's self-concept by looking at the client's Q-sort of self-referent statements.

SECOND Q-SORT

8. To have a comparison Q-sort, repeat steps 2 through 7, but now sort the activities with respect to your interests sometime *in the past*, say, five years ago. (An alternative would be to have a friend perform the Q-sort of her or his present interests.) Record the rank of each activity in the column designated "Second Sort Rank" on your Recording Sheet.

COMPARISON OF Q-SORTS

9. You are now ready to compare the two Q-sorts. Although this can be done by visual inspection alone, correlating the rankings of the activities on the two sorts is a more exact and potentially more meaningful method of comparison. This is easily done by means of the *rank-order correlation* method, which is outlined in simple, step-by-step fashion below.[1]

a. For each pair of ranks (i.e., for each activity), calculate the difference between the ranks. (The smaller value can always be subtracted from the larger, disregarding algebraic signs, because these values will be squared.) Record the differences in the "Difference" column on your Recording Sheet.

b. Square each difference and record the squared differences in the last column of the Recording Sheet.

c. Add all the squared differences found in Step b.

d. Multiply the sum obtained in Step c by 6.

e. Divide the product obtained in Step d by 15,600.

f. Subtract the quotient obtained in Step e from 1.00. This number is the rank-order correlation coefficient, which is designated by the Greek letter *rho*.

If *rho* is positive, your interests have tended to remain the same. The closer *rho* is to +1.00, the greater is the similarity between your interests in the two sorts. If *rho* is negative, then your interests now tend to be different from those you had in the past. The closer *rho* is to −1.00, the more dissimilar your present interests are from your past interests.

The Need for Positive Regard

The second major assumption in Rogers' theory is that all people have a **need for positive regard**. This is a basic need for acceptance, respect, sympathy, warmth, and love. At first these feelings of worthiness come from other people. As the self-actualization tendency directs the person toward more autonomy, **positive self-regard** develops from the positive attitudes shown by others. Positive regard can come directly from the self as well as from others. (See Figure 14–2.)

---

[1]Lest the reader think that the steps in calculating the rank-order correlation coefficient (*rho*) have been magically rather than mathematically determined, the formula is:

$$rho = 1 - \frac{6\Sigma d^2}{N(N^2 - 1)}$$

where D = differences in ranks of each pair and N = number of pairs of ranks (in the present example $N = 25$).

FIGURE 14–2
The need for positive regard is first met exclusively from others. Positive self-regard develops out of the positive regard shown toward oneself by others. Positive regard can be conditional or unconditional.

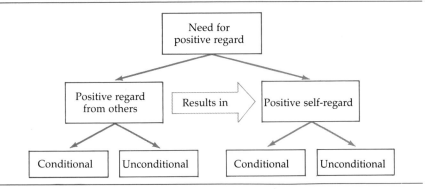

The need for positive regard may be inborn or learned. (Rogers favors the latter explanation; however, he believes the origin is irrelevant to his theory.) An important characteristic of positive regard is its reciprocal nature. When a person knows he or she is satisfying another's need for positive regard, the person's own need is also satisfied. (This is similar to the popular idea that we experience love by loving another person.)

Most often, we receive and give positive regard for specific behaviors. This is **conditional positive regard**. It is similar to rewarding someone for doing something well. It is possible, however, to give someone positive regard independent of the worth or value you place on the person's specific actions. This involves accepting and respecting the person as an unanalyzable whole. The person is valued not for specific behaviors but because he or she is worthy of positive regard as a human being. Such **unconditional positive regard** is most likely to be seen in parents' love for a child. Regardless of the child's specific behaviors, the child is loved and accepted "because it is . . . their child, not because the child has fulfilled any specific condition, or lived up to any specific expectation" (Fromm, 1963, p. 35). Unconditional positive regard involves valuing all of what a person does equally and positively. This may mean accepting a person's objectively negative behaviors as positive because the behaviors are part of the individual and you are accepting the whole person. Thus, the parent who disapproves of a child's misbehavior can still give the child unconditional positive regard. In effect, the parent feels: I do not approve of what you did, but I approve of you.

Both conditional and unconditional positive regard may come from others or from oneself. (See Figure 14–2.) In terms of self-actualization, **unconditional positive *self*-regard** is most important; the individual relies on the self rather than others for overall feelings of worth and esteem.

Whether from others or ourselves, unconditional positive regard is highly desirable. It allows us to be guided by our self-actualizing tendency. In contrast, the specific value judgments that constitute conditional positive regard may interfere with the self-actualizing tendency.

Conditions of Worth

The need for positive regard is extremely powerful. It can come to supersede the organismic valuing process. That is, independently of whether an experience is in any way maintaining or enhancing the person, it may be valued as positive or negative and either approached or avoided. The values that others and people themselves place on specific behaviors are called **conditions of worth.**

Conditions of worth develop "when the positive regard of a significant other is conditional, when the individual feels . . . in some respects . . . prized and in others not" (Rogers, 1959, p. 209). Conditions of worth are an inevitable part of living. It is hard to conceive of significant others regarding all of a person's behavior equally. It is also highly unlikely that anyone values all of his or her own behaviors equally.

Conditions of worth may adversely affect one's personality growth. They substitute for and interfere with the organismic valuing process, thereby preventing the person from functioning freely and with maximum effectiveness. When conditions of worth become more influential than the organismic valuing process in directing behavior, nature is being tampered with, so to speak. We turn next to the problems that arise when this occurs.

IMPEDIMENTS TO SELF-ACTUALIZATION

Optimally, the self is governed exclusively by the organismic valuing process. The process uses as criteria of evaluation the principles of self-actualization (maintenance and enhancement of the individual). When unconditional positive regard exists, the person can accurately perceive all experiences. If no experience is more or less worthy of positive regard than any other, there is no reason to exclude any experience from awareness. Under these circumstances, the self remains consistent and whole.

The Experience of Threat

In the course of development, positive regard becomes important to the individual and conditions of worth become part of the self. As this happens, conflicts inevitably arise between the self-concept and experiences.

The conflict consists of the person's self-concept being at odds with some experience. For instance, failing an exam would conflict with our self-concept of being a competent student. Conflicts occur because externally imposed values arising from conditions of worth are different from internally imposed values arising from the organismic valuing process. What is significant about such conflicts is that they threaten to fragment the self.

Rogers defines **threat** as a person perceiving, consciously or unconsciously, an incongruity between experience and his or her self-concept. This is threatening because the individual's personality is no longer a consistent whole; it is no longer regulated by a unitary process, the actualizing tendency; instead, more than one standard is operating. Rogers (1959) described this division in the following way.

> This . . . is the basic estrangement in man. He has not been true to himself, to his own natural organismic valuing of experience, but for the sake of preserving the positive regard of others has now come to falsify some of the values he experiences and to perceive them only in terms based upon their value to others. Yet this has not been a conscious choice, but a natural—and tragic—development. . . . [In contrast,] the path of development toward psychological maturity, the path of therapy, is the undoing of this estrangement in man's functioning, the dissolving of conditions of worth, the achievement of a self which is congruent with experience, and the restoration of a unified organismic valuing process as the regulator of behavior. (pp. 226–27)

We experience threat emotionally as a vague uneasiness and tension. We commonly call it *anxiety*. Anxiety is a signal that the unified self-concept is in danger of being disorganized. This will happen if the person becomes fully aware of the discrepancy between the self-concept and the threatening experience. The anxiety leads to defensive processes that reduce the incongruity and consequently lower the unpleasant feelings of anxiety.

The Process of Defense

Defensive processes maintain consistency between the self and experience. Rogers (1959) theorizes two basic ways this goal can be met: perceptual distortion and denial. Through **perceptual distortion**, people change (distort) how the experience is perceived to make it compatible with their self-concept. For example, the teenage girl who considers herself popular becomes aware that no one asks her to do things on weekends. She may distort this by telling herself that her peers don't ask her because they think she must be busy on weekends (because she is so popular). From the phenomenological perspective, perceptual distortion changes the experience itself. Experiences have only subjective reality. An experience is the *person's perception of it.*

Perceptual distortion changes the experience so it is more compatible with one's self-concept. **Denial** is the other basic defensive process. It prevents us from becoming aware of the experience that is incongruent with our self-concept. In one way or another, we convince ourselves that the experience does not exist. We can use the previous example of the teenager who viewed herself as popular. She could deny the threatening experience by thinking that her peers invited her but she chose not to accept. Phenomenologically, if you deny the experience, it does not exist.

Examples of the defensive processes that result from perceptual distortion and denial, separately and in combination, are presented in Table 14–4. The table also points to some parallels with psychoanalytic ego defensive mechanisms. The two theories posit quite different sources of threat and anxiety: sexual and aggressive impulses in psychoanalysis and experiences incompatible with the self-concept in Rogers' theory. Still, the basic ways that people defend themselves appear similar.

Psychological Adjustment

Rogers views psychological adjustment in terms of the congruence between the self and experience. Psychologically well-adjusted people perceive themselves and their relation to people and objects in their environ-

TABLE 14–4
Examples of defensive processes resulting from perceptual distortion and denial and their parallel with ego defense mechanisms

---

SITUATION: A wealthy man who spends 12 to 14 hours every day working at his job views himself as being a devoted husband and father.

Perceptual Distortion

Rationalization: "I have to work so hard to provide for my family's needs."

Fantasy: "I am always doing things with my family."

Perceptual Distortion and Denial

Reaction Formation: "I spend so much time with my family that I am neglecting my work."

Projection: "I think it is horrible that some men work so hard that they have no time for their families."

Denial

Denial: "I spend as much time with my family as I do at work."

Repression: The man is totally unaware of how little time he spends with his family.

---

ment as they "really" are—as other people would see them. At first glance, this may appear inconsistent with the phenomenological emphasis on subjective experience. Subjective experience is critical in Rogers' theory. But psychological adjustment requires a close correspondence between subjective experience and external reality. When such a correspondence exists, a person is *open to experience,* rather than threatened by it. Experiences are consistent with one's self-concept. Consider a professor with a reputation as "tough." Her self-concept includes the perception of maintaining high standards for students. Thus, the professor would not be threatened by finding that students' course evaluations indicated "difficult to get an A." In contrast, when an experience conflicts with the self-concept, the person uses perceptual distortion or denial to prevent the experience from being accurately symbolized. If the professor's self-concept involved being very lenient, she would have to distort or deny the course evaluation indicating "difficult to get an A" to maintain consistency within her personality. (She could also change her self-concept, but this alternative is less likely because one's self-concept does not usually change as a result of a single contradictory experience.)

Chodorkoff (1954) provided experimental support for Rogers' theory of adjustment as it relates to self-perception and defensive processes. Male undergraduates were used as subjects. Chodorkoff tested the following hypotheses derived from Rogers' theory.

1. The greater the agreement between the individual's self-description and . . . [others'] description of him, the less perceptual defense he will show.

2. The greater the agreement between the individual's self-description and . . . [others'] description of him, the more adequate will be his personal adjustment.

3. The more adequate the personal adjustment of the individual, the less perceptual defense he will show. (1954, p. 508)

The subjects first performed a Q-sort. The resulting *self-descriptions* were compared with Q-sorts of the same statements made for each subject by two clinically experienced judges. The judges' Q-sort descriptions served as the *description by others.* These descriptions were based on information from a biographical inventory of subjects and projective techniques they completed.

One projective technique was a word-association test. It presented subjects with fifty emotional words (e.g., whore, bitch, penis) and fifty neutral words (e.g., house, book, tree). For each subject, the ten emotional words resulting in the longest reaction time and the ten neutral words resulting in the shortest reaction time were used in the perceptual defense test. These twenty words were flashed on a screen in random order for very brief times (e.g., 1/100 of a second). Exposure time for each word was increased until the word was accurately reported; this time was the subject's *recognition threshold* for each word. **Perceptual defense** is a theoretical construct; it refers to an unconscious mechanism that keeps a person from recognizing threatening material (cf. Erdelyi, 1974). In Chodorkoff's study it was operationally defined as the difference between the recognition thresholds for emotional and neutral words. The greater this difference, the greater was the perceptual defense.

The third variable of interest in Chodorkoff's study was *personal adjustment*. This was rated by the clinically experienced judges based on the projective techniques.

All three of the hypotheses were supported.

1. When accuracy of self-description was compared with recognition thresholds, the two variables were negatively correlated. High accuracy of self-description tended to be associated with low recognition thresholds for threatening words.

2. When accuracy of self-description was compared to personal adjustment, the two variables were positively correlated. High accuracy in self-description was associated with good psychological adjustment.

3. Personal adjustment and recognition thresholds were negatively correlated. Greater psychological adjustment was associated with lower thresholds of recognition.

Chodorkoff's (1954) conclusions are consistent with Rogers' theory.

> In a group of subjects who show varying degrees of adjustment and defensiveness, one finds that the more inaccurate and faulty the individual's perception of his environment, the more inaccurate and faulty is his perception of himself; and the more inaccurate and faulty the individual's perceptions of himself and his environment, the more inadequate is his personal adjustment. (p. 511)

The Process of Breakdown and Disorganization

Even the most psychologically well-adjusted individuals are occasionally threatened by an experience that is inconsistent with their self-concept. People use defensive processes to keep themselves from becoming totally aware of the inconsistency. Their resulting anxiety is moderate because the inconsistency between self and experience is also moderate. The individuals' defenses are adequate to deal with it.

Experiences may become highly incongruent with the self-concept. Or moderately incongruent experiences may occur frequently. In such cases, the person feels a level of anxiety that is distinctly unpleasant and may actually interfere with daily activities. Some form of psychotherapy may be needed to reduce this anxiety. However, usually the person's defenses are still able to keep incongruent experiences out of conscious awareness. This allows the self to continue to function as a whole, if somewhat tenuous, process.

When the inconsistency between self and experience becomes very great, the individual's defenses may be incapable of distorting or denying the experience. In this defenseless state, the person becomes fully aware of the threatening incongruent experience. As a result, the consistent, whole self is shattered. The individual's behavior seems "disturbed" to relatives and friends. In fact, these behaviors may be congruent with experiences the person was never fully aware of because the experiences were distorted or denied. The behaviors are odd only insofar as they are incongruent with how the person is seen by *others*. For example, a woman has rigidly controlled her aggressive tendencies, denying they are part of her self. She may begin to display hostility toward people. The woman's friends may see the hostility as alien to her personality. In fact, it was very much a part of her personality, albeit an aspect of which she and they were unaware.

Personality disorganization can occur because the person, behaving in "uncharacteristic" ways, feels she or he is not understood. There is no consensual validation (affirmation from other people) for the person's view of the world. Rogers (1980) believes that when a person tries

> to share something that is very personal with another individual and it is not received and not understood, this is a very deflating and a very lonely experience. I have come to believe that such an experience makes some individuals psychotic. It causes them to give up hoping that anyone can understand them. Once they have lost that hope, then their own inner world, which becomes more and more bizarre, is the only place where they can live. They can no longer live in any shared human experience. I can sympathize with them because I know that when I try to share some feeling aspect of myself which is private, precious, and tentative, and when this communication is met by evaluation, by reassurance, by distortion of my meaning, my very strong reaction is, "Oh, what's the use!" At such a time, one knows what it is to be alone. (p. 14)

The Process of Reintegration

People who regularly distort or deny certain experiences are more or less constantly defending themselves against accurately perceiving these experiences. Such individuals are "always on the defensive." Their behavior illustrates the potential negative consequences of defensive processes. They question the meaning and sincerity of even the most innocent comments made by other people. They are quick to respond as if the comments were negative. But from their internal frame of reference, the innocent remark *is* negative, because it was perceived in distorted form.

People who inaccurately perceive experiences are not able to function fully; they are closed to (defended against) many experiences. Thus, they miss or must avoid potentially threatening aspects of life. Consider the case of Jane Y., a college senior. Due to a self-concept that permitted only success, she was threatened by any situation in which she might fail. Jane distorted her view of such an event from one that *could* lead to failure to one that is undesirable. She thereby successfully avoided it. Rather than apply to graduate school, she "decided" she could do just as well with a B.A. (Anyhow, she might as well be making money while her friends in graduate school took out loans.)

Discrepancies between one's self-concept and experiences can be reduced by a process of reintegration within the personality. **Reintegration** restores consistency by reversing the process of defense. In other words, the individual becomes clearly aware of distorted or denied experiences. For example, reintegration for Jane Y. could mean, first, realizing that she might not be admitted to graduate school. She could make this possibility acceptable by integrating it into her self-concept. Her self-concept would then include the idea: "It is not necessary for me to succeed at everything I try." This would make her less likely to find such situations threatening.

Rogers maintains that reintegration is possible only when there is *a reduction in the person's conditions of worth and an increase in unconditional positive self-regard*. This can happen if the person is exposed to and perceives the unconditional positive regard of someone else. In a state of unconditional positive regard, our existing conditions of worth lose both their significance and their power to direct behavior. We become open to more experiences because without conditions of worth, all experiences are consistent with the self. Consider the case of a man who values restraint positively and aggression negatively. He cannot accurately perceive his need to be aggressive on some occasions. Aggressive behavior is inconsistent with his self-concept, which tells him that restraint is good. If this condition of worth were dissolved, restraint and aggression could exist harmoniously within a unified self. Sometimes the man would behave with restraint and at other times aggressively. There would be, in effect, no value placed on either mode of behavior in the sense that neither would be valued more or less than the other.

Due to the unconditional positive regard of others, we experience an increase in unconditional positive *self*-regard. This lets us be open to experience and nondefensive when other people are not present. Increased unconditional positive self-regard and the resulting decrease in conditions of worth are the prerequisites for personality reintegration.

Receiving unconditional positive regard is not the only situation in which personality reintegration can occur. Minor personality reintegrations occur in our daily lives. They are possible without experiencing unconditional positive regard *if there is no threat to the self*. Rogers believes that when we are left alone, we can face minor, inconsistent experiences and restructure our self-concept to assimilate them. For example,

> the child who feels that he is weak and powerless to do a certain task, to build a tower or repair a bicycle, may find, as he works rather hopelessly at the task, that he is successful. This experience is inconsistent with the concept he holds of himself, and may not be integrated at once; but if the child is left to himself he gradually assimilates, upon his own initiative, a revision of his concept of self, that while he is generally weak and powerless, in this respect he has ability. This is the normal way in which, free from threat, new perceptions are assimilated. But if this same child is repeatedly told by his parents that he is competent to do the task, he is likely to deny it, and to prove by his behavior that he is unable to do it. The more forceful intrusion of the notion of his competence constitutes more of a threat to self and is more forcefully resisted. (Rogers, 1965, p. 519)

Rogers (1965) maintains that reintegration in the absence of threat is only possible when the inconsistency between the self and experience is minor. When the inconsistency is great, reintegration is only possible in a relationship with another in which the person is sure of being accepted. This relationship occurs in client-centered therapy.

Client-Centered Therapy

In addition to his comprehensive theory of personality, Rogers (1942, 1965) developed a new method of personality change.

The Meaning of "Client-Centered"

The essence of client-centered therapy is contained in its name. Rogers (1965) explains the term *client* in the following way:

> What term shall be used to indicate the person with whom the therapist is dealing? "Patient," "subject," "counselee," "analysand," are terms which have been used. We have . . . used the term client . . . because, in spite of its imperfections . . . it seems to come closest to conveying the picture of this person. . . . The client, as the term has acquired its meaning, is one who comes actively and voluntarily to gain help on a problem, but without any notion of surrendering . . . responsibility for the situation. It is because the term has these connotations that we have chosen it, since it avoids

the connotation that . . . [the person] is sick, or the object of an experiment, and so on. (p. 7)

Thus, Rogers considers clients as ultimately responsible for their own behavior. This includes, as we will see, solving their own problems, albeit with the help of a therapist.

In keeping with Rogers' phenomenological position, psychotherapy is *centered* on the client. Therapy deals with the client's unique problems, feelings, perceptions, attitudes, and goals. In short, client-centered therapy proceeds from the client's internal frame of reference. One person can never fully understand another person's subjective experiences. But the therapist tries to learn as much as possible about how the client views his or her particular experiences.

The Necessary and Sufficient Conditions for Personality Change

Rogers and Truax (1967) hypothesized that there is a set of six necessary and sufficient conditions for personality change in therapy.

1. *The client and therapist must be in "psychological contact."* Minimally, *psychological contact* requires face-to-face interaction. This implies, for example, that any form of psychotherapy that does not involve human contact (e.g., computerized psychotherapy) would not be effective. The remaining five conditions spell out the nature of the client-therapist relationship. If each of the next five conditions is met, then this first condition is assumed to be met as well.

2. *The client must be in a state of incongruity.* The incongruity is a result of inconsistencies between a client's self-concept and experiences. In this state, the client is likely to be vulnerable and anxious. An indirect source of evidence for this hypothesis is the finding that less anxious clients have difficulty becoming involved in therapy and consequently tend to drop out (Gallagher, 1953).

3. *The therapist must be in a state of congruity in relation to the client.* The therapist need not be open to all experiences, but while in the therapeutic relationship, the therapist should be relatively free of threatening experiences. In other words, although the therapist may have some personal problems, they should not be relevant to the client and the relationship with the client. This allows the therapist to be genuine with the client and to experience unconditional positive regard and empathic understanding for the client; by doing so the essential conditions for personality reintegration are established (Rogers, 1959).

4. *The therapist must experience unconditional positive regard for the client.* By valuing positively and equally all of the client's experiences and

thereby not judging the client, the therapist establishes conditions that are nonthreatening and thus conducive for personality reintegration.

5. *The therapist must experience empathic understanding for the client.* **Empathy** is the process of understanding another person from that person's perspective—from the person's internal frame of reference. To be empathic, one must feel as if he or she were the individual, but without losing the "as if" quality.

> To be with another in this way means that for the time being, you lay aside your own views and values in order to enter another's world without prejudice. In some sense it means that you lay aside your self; this can only be done by persons who are secure enough in themselves [i.e., congruent] that they know they will not get lost in what may turn out to be the strange or bizarre world of the other, and that they can comfortably return to their own world when they wish. (Rogers, 1980, p. 143)

6. *The client must perceive, at least to some degree, the therapist's congruity, unconditional positive regard, and empathic understanding.* It would not matter how congruent the therapist was or how much unconditional positive regard or empathic understanding the therapist experienced for the client if the client was not aware of it. This last condition reemphasizes the importance of viewing the client through the client's internal frame of reference.

There is evidence for the importance of some of Rogers' six basic conditions for therapeutic change. Presently, however, there is no evidence supporting Rogers' contention that the *set* of six criteria are responsible for therapeutic change. To date, psychologists have not performed studies specifically testing that proposition. Some studies have been correlational, and thus have not tested causative hypotheses. Or all six conditions have not been examined in the same study (Watson, 1984). Thus, Rogers' minimal conditions remain hypotheses to be tested.

Empathy

Rogers (1975) believes that empathy is the most potent factor in creating personality change. He considers empathy a prerequisite for unconditional positive regard (which establishes the nonthreatening atmosphere necessary for personality change). Rogers (1959) explains why empathy is necessary for unconditional positive regard.

> If I know little or nothing of you, and experience an unconditional positive regard for you, this means little because further knowledge of you may reveal aspects which I cannot so regard. But if I know you thoroughly, knowing and empathically understanding a

wide variety of your feelings and behaviors, and still experience an unconditional positive regard, this is very meaningful. It comes close to being fully known and fully accepted. (p. 231)

Much research has addressed the role of empathy in a variety of types of psychotherapy; some of the more important findings are summarized below.

1. *The ideal therapist is, first of all, perceived as empathic.* For example, Raskin (1974) asked eighty-three practicing psychotherapists of at least eight different orientations to describe the ideal therapist (i.e., the type of therapist they would like to be). Empathy was considered the most important quality.

2. *Empathy is positively correlated with client self-exploration and progress in therapy* (e.g., Bergin & Strupp, 1972; Kurtz & Grummon, 1972).

3. *Empathy early in the therapeutic process predicts later success in therapy* (Barrett-Lennard, 1962; Tausch, 1973). The degree of empathy a therapist shows for a client can be identified very early in therapy, and such early measurements are positively correlated with later success in therapy.

4. *Therapists offer more empathy than caring friends* (van der Veen, 1970), a finding which reinforces the notion that empathy is a skill acquired with training and experience (see number 7 below).

5. *Experienced therapists tend to offer more empathy than inexperienced therapists* (Barrett-Lennard, 1962; Mullen & Abeles, 1972). In an early study, Fiedler (1950) compared the relationship established between expert and novice therapists and their clients in three different types of psychotherapy: client-centered, traditional psychoanalytic, and post-Freudian. Four judges listened to recordings of the therapy sessions, and, for each session, they sorted seventy-five statements descriptive of the therapeutic relationship (e.g., "Therapist treats patient with much deference"; "Therapist is sympathetic with patient") on a seven-category Q-sort ranging from "most characteristic" to "least characteristic" of the session. The results showed that experienced therapists of all three orientations tended to create a relationship in which they demonstrated an understanding of the client's communications from the client's point of view.

6. *Therapists who are better integrated (well adjusted) show a higher degree of empathy for their clients* (Bergin & Jasper, 1969; Bergin & Solomon, 1970). Not surprisingly, being relatively free of personal problems and feeling confident in interpersonal relationships is associated with the ability to empathize with another person.

7. *Empathy can be learned, especially from empathic persons* (Aspy, 1972; Aspy & Roebuck, 1974; Goldstein & Michaels, 1985). This is an important finding because it means that therapists can acquire empathic

understanding and need not be born with it. Having this skill modeled by one's parents, teachers, and supervisors appears to be the prime way in which people learn to be empathic.

The Process of Client-Centered Therapy

To review, Rogers believes three primary factors account for personality change. (1) *Therapist congruence* which allows the therapist to experience (2) *empathic understanding* and consequently (3) *unconditional positive regard* for the client. How do these conditions facilitate personality change?

> Briefly, as persons are accepted and prized, they tend to develop a more caring attitude toward themselves. As persons are empathically heard, it becomes possible for them to listen more accurately to the flow of inner experiencings. But as a person understands and prizes self, the self becomes more congruent with the experiencings. The person thus becomes more real, more genuine. These tendencies, the reciprocal of the therapist's attitudes, enable the person to be a more effective growth enhancer for himself or herself. There is a greater freedom to be the true, whole person. (Rogers, 1980, pp. 116–17)

The Practice of Client-Centered Therapy

In client-centered therapy, the major responsibility for the therapeutic process falls to the client. Rogers believes clients can resolve their own problems, given the right circumstances. This is consistent with Rogers' view of how disorders develop. Behavioral disorders stem from conflict between the two sets of criteria we use to evaluate experiences. These are (1) the organismic valuing process (based on the self-actualization tendency) and (2) conditions of worth (based on other people's values). Rogers holds that people would not develop behavioral disorders if they were guided solely by their organismic valuing process. Thus, client-centered therapy creates a situation in which clients feel free from conditions of worth and which allows them to be guided by their organismic valuing process. This can occur in a nonthreatening situation. The client feels understood (empathic understanding) and accepted as a whole person (unconditional positive regard). Under these conditions, clients can accurately examine experiences inconsistent with their self-concepts. Clients were previously unaware of these experiences because the experiences were perceived in a distorted fashion or denied. How does the therapist create these necessary conditions?

Client-centered therapy involves a verbal interchange between the client and the therapist. Therapy focuses on the here-and-now—the client's experiences during the session. The therapist listens to the client and accepts equally and without evaluation all of the client's feelings and behaviors. In other words, the therapist shows unconditional positive regard for the client. Clients certainly talk about *objectively* negative experiences. After all, they have problems, are feeling emotions such as anxiety and depression, dislike themselves and their behaviors, and so on. But these "negative" experiences are genuinely part of the client at the time. The client already has conditions of worth associated with these experiences. The goal of client-centered therapy is to remove the conditions of worth and replace them with unconditional positive self-regard.

From what the client says, the therapist tries to understand the client from her or his internal frame of reference. To do this, the therapist "checks out" with the client whether the picture of the client's experiences the therapist is forming is accurate. The therapist reflects back to the client what the therapist believes the client is feeling and thinking. **Clarification of feelings** is synthesizing or reorganizing the feelings the client has expressed, directly or indirectly. **Restatement of content** is rephrasing the cognitive or intellectual aspects of what the client has expressed, explicitly or implicitly. The major difference between these two basic responses is whether the focus is on the clients' emotions (clarification of feelings) or thoughts (restatement of content). Since the emphasis in client-centered therapy is on the client's feelings, clarification of feelings is considered more important than restatement of content. For either type of response to be considered empathic, the therapist must experience the affect or cognition from the client's internal frame of reference.

Clarification of feelings and restatement of content give therapists feedback on the accuracy of their impressions of the client. They also serve two other important functions. First, such responses, when they are accurate, indicate that the therapist is empathizing with the client. Second, they reflect back what the client has just said. Such "reflection" often leads to understanding and insights that they might not have reached by merely listening to their own words. (You are likely to have had this experience when another person repeats, in a slightly different way, something you've just said.)

Both types of responses are seen in the following excerpt from a client-centered therapy session. The excerpt also illustrates the nature of the client-therapist interaction. The client is a twenty-year-old college woman whose right hand is malformed. (See whether you can identify which of the therapist's comments involve clarification of feelings and which involve restatement of content; footnote 2 on page 307 contains the correct identification.)

Client (C): After I left here last time—that night during dinner the student dean in our house asked to speak to my roommate. My roommate told me about it afterwards—Miss

> Hansen asked if I would be embarrassed as hostess at the table. She said she didn't want to hurt me! These darn student deans who think that they must guard us! The other student dean I had before never raised the issue. It makes me so mad!

Therapist (T): You feel that this incident helped to accentuate the difficulty.

C: That was the first time with a student dean. Really though, it struck me very funny. She watches us like a hawk. We can't make a move but she knows it.

T: You resent her activity.

C: I just don't like it on general principles. Oh, I suppose that she was trying to save me embarrassment.

T: You can see why she did that.

C: I think that she is really afraid of us—she's queer. I don't know, but so far as I am concerned, I'm pretty indifferent to her.

T: You feel that she doesn't affect you one way or the other. (Snyder, 1947, p. 278)[2]

Client-centered therapists do not interpret clients' statements, behaviors, or displays of emotion. Interpretations are inappropriate because they come from an external frame of reference; the meaning of a client's behavior is only relevant from the perspective of the client's internal frame of reference. Client-centered therapists also do not offer advice; the therapist assumes the client's organismic valuing process is the client's best source of guidance. Instead of advice, the therapist provides an accepting and nonthreatening atmosphere that allows the client's organismic valuing process to operate.

New Developments in Client-Centered Therapy

In recent years, client-centered therapy has diverged somewhat from Rogers' theory (e.g., Levant & Shlien, 1984; Lietaer, 1981). The techniques used in client-centered therapy have been expanded. This is consistent with the current general trend in psychotherapy toward eclecticism and integration of therapies (e.g., Garfield & Bergin, 1985).

One new development in client-centered therapy is that therapists have become somewhat confronting (e.g., Lietaer, 1984). For instance,

---

[2]The therapist's first, third, and fourth comments are restatement of content, while the second is clarification of feelings.

client-centered therapists may interject their own here-and-now experiences. This obviously diverges from the traditional practice of letting the client dictate the flow of therapy. The rationale for this new practice is that the therapist's impressions of the client and the feelings the client evokes in the therapist may be important for the client to hear; they may stimulate the client's further self-explorations. Confrontation differs from interpretation if therapists clearly state their reactions as their own and do not impose them on clients. To maintain unconditional positive regard, the therapist must communicate that her or his reactions are toward specific, concrete behaviors rather than toward the client as a person. Further, to remain *client*-centered, the therapist must continuously be in touch with how the client experiences the confrontation and respond to that experience (Lietaer, 1984).

Another important development in client-centered therapy involves how therapists show empathy (e.g., Bozarth, 1984). Traditionally, therapists have demonstrated their empathic understanding primarily by reflecting the client's feelings. Another way to communicate empathy involves the therapist's attending to and interacting with the client in an intuitive and idiosyncratic manner; the goal is entering the client's world as if the therapist were the client. One example is a therapist's participating in a client's idiosyncratic thought processes. Bozarth (1984) describes joining in the homicidal fantasies of a client several times in a session by extending the client's imagery with a comment like "Maybe a shotgun would be better."

A Case Example of Personality Growth and Change

The following letter was written to Rogers (1980) by a young woman who was in therapy; Rogers did not know either the woman or her therapist.

Dear Dr. Rogers,

I don't know how to explain who I am or why I am writing to you except to say that I have just read your book, *On Becoming a Person*, and it left a great impression on me. I just happened to find it one day and started reading. It's kind of a coincidence because right now I need something to help me find *me*. I do not feel that I can do much for others until I find me.

I think that I began to lose me when I was in high school. I always wanted to go into work that would be of help to people but my family resisted, and I thought they must be right. Things went along smoothly for everyone else for four or five years until about two years ago. I met a guy that I thought was ideal. Then nearly a year ago I took a good look at us, and realized that I was everything that *he* wanted me to be and nothing that *I* was. I have always been emotional and I have had many feelings. I could never sort them out and identify them. My fiancé would tell me that I was just mad or just happy and I would say okay and leave it at that. Then when I took this good look at us I realized that I was angry because I wasn't following my true emotions.

I backed out of the relationship gracefully and tried to find out where all the pieces were that I had lost. After a few months of searching had gone by, I found that there were many more than I knew what to do with and I couldn't seem to separate them. I began seeing a psychologist and am presently seeing him. He has helped me to find parts of me that I was not aware of. Some parts are bad by our society's standards, but I have found them to be very good for me. I have felt more threatened and confused since going to him, but I have also felt more relief and more sure of myself.

I remember one night in particular. I had been in for my regular appointment with the psychologist that day and I had come home feeling angry. I was angry because I wanted to talk about something but I couldn't identify what it was. By eight o'clock that night I was so upset I was frightened. I called him and he told me to come to his office as soon as I could. I got there and cried for at least an hour and then the words came. I still don't know all of what I was saying. All I know is that *so much hurt* and *anger* came out of me that I *never really knew existed.* I went home and it seemed that an *alien* had taken over and I was hallucinating like some of the patients I have seen in a state hospital. I continued to feel this way until one night I was sitting and thinking and I realized that this alien was the *me* that I had been trying to find.

I have noticed since that night that people no longer seem so strange to me. Now it is beginning to seem that life is just starting for me. I am alone right now, but I am not frightened and I don't have to be doing something. I like meeting me and making friends with my thoughts and feelings. Because of this I have learned to enjoy other people. One older man in particular—who is very ill— makes me feel very much alive. He accepts everyone. He told me the other day that I have changed very much. According to him, I have begun to open up and love. I think that I have always loved people and I told him so. He said, "Were they aware of it?" I don't suppose I have expressed my love any more than I did my anger and hurt.

Among other things, I am finding out that I never had too much self-respect. And now that I am learning to really like me, I am finally finding peace within myself. Thanks for your part in this. (pp. 208–210)

Rogers (1980) commented on this letter by paraphrasing what he considers to be the critical statements concerning the woman's feelings and attitudes. His remarks provide a good summary of his view of personality development, growth, and change.

I was losing me. Her own experiences and their meanings were being denied, and she was developing a self that was different from her real experienced self, which was becoming increasingly unknown to her.

My experience told me the work I wanted to go into, but my family showed me that I couldn't trust my own feelings to be right. This phrase shows how a false concept of self is built up. Because she accepted her parents' meanings as her own experience, she came to distrust her own organismic experience. . . . As she distrusted more and more of her own experience, her sense of self-worth steadily declined until she had very little use for her own experience or herself.

Things went along smoothly for everyone else. What a revealing statement! Of course things were fine for those whom she was trying to please. This pseudoself was just what they wanted. It was only within herself, at some deep and unknown level, that there was a vague uneasiness.

I was everything he wanted me to be. Here again she was denying to awareness all her own experiencing—to the point where she no longer really had a self and was trying to be a self wanted by someone else.

Finally my organism rebelled and I tried to find me again but I couldn't, without help. Why did she finally rebel and take a good look at her relationship with her fiancé? One can only attribute this rebellion to the actualizing tendency that had been suppressed for so long but that finally asserted itself. However, because she had distrusted her own experience for such a long period and because the self by which she was living was so sharply different from the experiences of her organism, she could not reconstruct her true self without help. The need for help often exists when there is such a great discrepancy.

Now I am discovering my experiences—some bad according to society, parents, and boyfriend, but all good as far as I am concerned. The locus of evaluation that formerly had resided in her parents, in her boyfriend, and others, she is now reclaiming as her own. She is the one who decides the values of her experience. She is the center of the valuing process, and the evidence is provided by her own senses. Society may call a given experience bad, but when she trusts her own valuing of it, she finds that it is worthwhile and significant to her.

An important turning point came when a flood of the experiences that I had been denying to awareness came close to the surface. I was frightened and upset. When denied experience comes close to awareness, anxiety always results because these previously unadmitted experiences will have meanings that will change the structure of the self by which one has been living. Any drastic change in the self-concept is always a threatening and frightening experience. She was dimly aware of this threat even though she did not yet know what would emerge.

When the denied experiences broke through the dam, they turned out to be hurts and angers that I had been completely unaware of. It is impossible for most people to realize how completely an experience can be shut out of awareness until it does break through into awareness. Every individual is able to shut out and deny those experiences that would endanger his or her self-concept.

I thought I was insane because some foreign person had taken over in me. When the self-concept is so sharply changed that parts of it are completely shattered, it is a very frightening experience, and her description of the feeling that an alien had taken over is a very accurate one.

Only gradually did I realize that this alien was the real me. What she was discovering was that the submissive, malleable self by which she had been living, the self that had been guided by the statements, attitudes, and expectations of others, was no longer hers. This new self that had seemed so alien was a self that had experienced hurt and anger and feelings that society regards as bad, as well as wild hallucinatory thoughts—and love. As she goes further into self-discovery, it is likely that she will find out that some of her anger is directed against her parents. The hurts will have come from various sources; some of the feelings and experiences that society regards as bad but that she finds good and satisfying are experiences and feelings that probably have to do with sexuality. In any event, her self is becoming much more firmly rooted in her own gut-level experiences. Another person put something of this in the phrase "I am beginning to let my experience *tell me* what it means instead of *my* trying to *impose* a meaning on it." The more the individual's self-concept is rooted in the spontaneously felt meanings of his or her experiencing, the more he or she is an integrated person.

I like meeting me and making friends with my thoughts and feelings. Here is the dawning of the self-respect and self-acceptance of which she has been deprived for so long. She is even feeling affection for herself. One of the curious but common side effects of this change is that now she will be able to give herself more freely to others, to enjoy others more, to be more genuinely interested in them.

I have begun to open up and love. She will find that as she is more expressive of her love, she can also be more expressive of her anger and hurt, her likes and dislikes, and her "wild" thoughts and feelings (which will turn out to be creative impulses). She is in the process of changing from psychological maladjustment to a much healthier relationship to others and to reality.

I am finally finding peace within myself. There is a peaceful harmony in being a whole person, but she will be mistaken if she thinks this reaction is permanent. Instead, if she is really open to her experience, she will find other hidden aspects of herself that she has denied to awareness, and each such discovery will give her uneasy and anxious moments or days until it is assimilated into a revised and changing picture of herself. She will discover that growing toward a congruence between her experiencing organism and her concept of herself is an exciting, sometimes disturbing, but never-ending adventure. (pp. 211–14)

THE PERSON-CENTERED APPROACH: BEYOND CLIENT-CENTERED THERAPY

Carl Rogers' career as a psychologist spans more than half a century; he is still professionally active in his mid-80s. He has broadened his interests and professional endeavors considerably in the past two decades. But his basic view of personality has remained essentially unchanged. He has a deep faith in *the inherent capability of each person to develop, grow, and change in basically healthy ways when the person is guided by her or his unique self-actualizing tendency.*

Much of Rogers' career has been devoted to discovering the conditions in which a person's unique resources can be freely expressed. Rogers has found three basic conditions necessary for growth. A person must experience:

1. *Congruence, genuineness, or realness*—an openness or transparency in which another person is being totally what he or she is in the relationship, with no holding back and no façades.
2. *Unconditional positive regard*—a nonpossessive caring, acceptance, or prizing of the person no matter what he or she is doing or feeling at the time (including objectively negative actions or emotions).
3. *Empathic understanding*—being accurately perceived by the other person.

These conditions are required for effective client-centered therapy. But Rogers believes they are not restricted to therapy. They "apply whether we are speaking of the relationship between therapist and client, parent and child, leader and group, teacher and student, or administrator and staff. The conditions apply, in fact, in any situation in which the development of the person is a goal" (Rogers, 1980, p. 115). Rogers (1980) even boldly asserts that these conditions might be effective in situations now dominated by the exercise of raw power—in politics, for example, especially in our dealings with other nations. I challenge . . . the current American belief, evident in every phase of our foreign policy, and especially in our insane wars, that "might makes right." That, in my estimation, is the road to self-destruction. I go along with Martin Buber and the ancient Oriental sages: "He who imposes himself has the small, manifest might; he who does not impose himself has the great, secret might." (p. 45)

In recent years, Rogers and his followers have turned their attention to discovering and creating psychological climates that facilitate growth and enhancement in diverse human endeavors. These include: general education (Rogers, 1983); higher-education administration (W. Rogers, 1984); humanizing medical treatment and education (Barnard, 1984; Rogers, 1980); psychological research (Mearns & McLeod, 1984); the psychology of secrecy (Shlien, 1984); interracial and intercultural harmony, including an attempt to ease tensions between Catholics, Protestants, and the English in Northern Ireland (McGaw, Rice, & Rogers, 1973); and alternatives to nuclear holocaust (Rogers & Ryback, 1984). Rogers (1979) uses the term **person-centered approach** when principles originally discovered and used in client-centered therapy are extended to people who would not be labeled *clients* and to problems beyond the boundaries of psychotherapy.

The Future of Humankind: A Person-Centered Perspective

Rogers' most far-reaching speculations concern the future of humankind. He is keenly aware of a number of contemporary trends that he believes are *counter* to human beings' self-actualizing. They include:

advances in computer intelligence and decision making; "test-tube" babies . . . ; new species of . . . life being created through recombinant work with the genes; cities under domes, with the whole environment controlled . . . ; completely artificial environments permitting human beings to live in space: these are some of the new technologies that may affect our lives. They have in common the fact that each removes humankind further from nature, from the soil, the weather, the sun, the wind, and all natural processes. (Rogers, 1980, pp. 342–43)

Despite these grave indications, Rogers (1980) continues to be optimistic about the future of humankind. He believes there are "many new developments today that alter our whole conception of the potentialities of the individual; that change our perceptions of 'reality'; that change our ways of being and behaving; that alter our belief systems" (p. 343). As examples he cites: increased interest in various forms of meditation that utilize our "inner energy resources"; growing apprecia-tion and use of intuition; experiencing altered states of consciousness (e.g., hypnosis) that may increase human capabilities; the potential of bio-feedback training; holistic health concepts and practices, which include the increasing recognition that we may be able to cure or alleviate physical diseases, such as cancer, through the "intentional use of our conscious and nonconscious minds."

Rogers believes that to survive in a world characterized by increasing technology and artificiality, human beings will have to become inter-personally oriented and natural—that is, more person centered. Rogers (1980) enumerates twelve qualities that he thinks will be characteristic of the "survivors" in our future: (1) openness to experience; (2) desire for authenticity; (3) skepticism regarding science and technology; (4) desire for wholeness; (5) wish for intimacy; (6) being process persons (always changing); (7) caring for others; (8) feeling of closeness to nature; (9) being anti-institutional; (10) trust in inner authority and distrust of exter-nal authority; (11) an indifference to material things; and (12) a yearn-ing for spirituality. Obviously, no single individual will have all of these qualities. These hypothesized optimal characteristics of the persons of tomorrow parallel the qualities that Abraham Maslow identified as charac-teristic of self-actualizing individuals, as we will see in the next chapter.

SUMMARY

1. Rogers' theory of personality was the first major alternative to psychoanalysis. It is based on the principle of self-actualization which holds that each person has a unique potential to develop, grow, and change in basically positive ways.

2. The self-actualizing tendency operates through the organismic valuing process which evaluates experiences in terms of whether they maintain or enhance the person.

3. The self or self-concept embodies all of an individual's percep-tions of him- or herself, including both how the individual sees him- or herself and how the individual would like to be seen (ideal self).

4. The Q-sort is one means of gaining information about a person's self. Clients make comparative judgments of statements about them-selves by sorting the statements in terms of how self-descriptive they are. Repeated Q-sorts are used to show changes in the self over time.

5. Rogers makes the basic assumption that all people have a need for positive regard—that is, a need to experience acceptance, love, and respect from others. Conditional positive regard is given for specific behaviors whereas unconditional positive regard is independent of the person's specific behaviors. Both forms of positive regard first come from others and later from oneself.

6. Conditions of worth are positive or negative values placed on specific behaviors by others and oneself. They often supersede the organismic valuing process in evaluating experiences and thus interfere with self-actualization. Conditions of worth come from conditional positive regard.

7. The presence of conditions of worth inevitably leads to some conflict or incongruity between self and experience. This is threatening to the wholeness of the personality and is experienced as anxiety. To prevent such incongruity and decrease anxiety, people use two defensive processes: perceptual distortion and denial.

8. Psychological adjustment results from congruence between self and experience, and psychopathology results from incongruence between self and experience. For personality reintegration to occur (i.e., reducing incongruity), one must experience a reduction of conditions of worth and an increase in unconditional positive regard to allow the self-actualizing tendency to predominate.

9. Client-centered therapy provides the optimal conditions for personality reintegration because the therapist gives the client unconditional positive regard. To do this, the therapist must show empathy for the client, which involves understanding the client from the client's internal frame of reference. The therapist empathizes with the client by restating what the client says and clarifying the client's feelings. New developments in client-centered therapy have expanded its process but still remain client-centered.

10. Rogers' person-centered approach has extended the principles of client-centered therapy to diverse human endeavors and problems.

MASLOW'S THEORY OF HUMAN MOTIVATION

OVERVIEW

Abraham Maslow (1908–1970) was a leading spokesperson for the psychology of health and strength. He shares with Rogers a distinctly optimistic outlook about human nature. He believes people are inherently good and that they are fully capable of developing in healthy ways if circumstances allow expression of their innate potential. In contrast to Rogers, Maslow did not develop a comprehensive theory of personality. Instead, Maslow's theory and research primarily involve the factors that motivate behavior. Additionally, Maslow explored in depth the role of self-actualization motives. This includes how such motives are manifest at the highest levels of human functioning.

Before reading any further, take a few minutes to complete Demonstration 15–1. It relates directly to Maslow's hierarchy of needs. You may find it useful to briefly examine some of your own needs before learning what Maslow had to say about human motivation.

Abraham Maslow

Courtesy of Bertha G. Maslow. Photo by Marcia Roltner

DEMONSTRATION 15–1[1]

AN ASSESSMENT OF YOUR PRESENT NEEDS

As we saw in previous chapters, personality psychologists have identified various basic needs that motivate our behavior. Table 15–1 lists five catego-

---

[1] Adapted from Grasha (1978).

TABLE 15–1
Maslow's categories of needs with examples (for Demonstration 15–1)

Self-actualization needs
Examples:
    Living up to your potential
    Accepting your strengths and limitations
    Accepting other people for whom and what they are
    Being spontaneous
    Acting creatively
    Acting independently (of others' opinions)

Esteem needs
Examples:

Self-esteem	*Esteem from others*
Achievement	Recognition
Confidence	Appreciation
Mastery	Attention
Strength	Status
	Reputation

Social needs
Examples:
    Love
    Affection
    Belonging (to family, group)
    Friendship
    Spending time with other people

Safety needs
Examples:
    Physical security
    Dependence
    Stability, order, structure
    Freedom from fear

Physiological needs
Examples:
    Food and water
    Rest and sleep
    Exercise
    Health

ries of needs which Maslow believes are essential for all individuals, along with specific examples of each. After reading over the list, *write down three significant examples of activities in which you have engaged in the past month that fit into each category.* The activities can be either overt actions or covert behaviors, such as thoughts or fantasies. Make a copy of the worksheet in Table 15–2 to record your examples.

Using the recent activities you listed for each category, consider how satisfied you are that you have been able to meet those needs. This will be very much an individual matter. Using the scale below, *rate the degree to which you are satisfied that your needs have been met in each category.* Write

TABLE 15-2
Sample worksheet for Demonstration 15-1

Need Category	Examples of Recent Behavior	Satisfaction Rating
Self-actualization	1. 2. 3.	
Esteem	1. 2. 3.	
Social	1. 2. 3.	
Safety	1. 2. 3.	
Physiological	1. 2. 3.	

the scale number in the appropriate box on your copy of the worksheet in the column titled "Satisfaction Rating."

1 = totally unsatisfied

2 = generally unsatisfied

3 = slightly unsatisfied

4 = slightly satisfied

5 = generally satisfied

6 = totally satisfied

As you read about Maslow's theory regarding the five categories of needs, you will have a chance to observe how well your individual behavior with respect to these needs fits with his theory. Maslow arranged the five categories of needs in a hierarchy of importance. Needs lower in the hierarchy are satisfied before higher needs are satisfied. The need categories in Table 15-1 are listed in descending order. Self-actualization needs are the highest and last to be fulfilled; physiological needs are the lowest and first to be fulfilled. Generally, the higher the need the more our satisfaction in meeting it decreases; we tend to be most content with how we meet our physiological needs and least content with how we meet our self-actualization needs (e.g., Graham & Balloun, 1973).

Obviously, this Demonstration may have some personal implications. Assessing how well you are fulfilling various needs can be revealing and may suggest changes you'd like to make in your priorities. Keep in mind that this assessment of your needs is very broad and superficial. Therefore it should only be used as a rough guideline to point to *possible* personal implications that should be checked out further.

A HIERARCHICAL THEORY OF MOTIVATION

Maslow conceptualizes motivation in terms of needs that are common to all of us. We will first discuss the specific nature of these needs. Then we will examine the hierarchical order in which Maslow theorizes that we meet them.

Instinctoid Needs

Instinctoid is a term coined by Maslow to differentiate human needs with a biological basis from biologically based needs of other species. This is an important distinction. Maslow (1970) firmly believes that humans are only minimally influenced by biological instincts; instinctual motivation lessens as animals proceed up the evolutionary scale. "Thus, if we examine the sexual life of the human being we find that sheer drive itself is given by heredity but that the choice of object and the choice of behavior must be acquired or learned in the course of the life history" (p. 27).

Everyone is born with identical instinctoid needs. However, behaviors motivated by and that fulfill instinctoid needs are idiosyncratic for each person. They depend on our unique biological makeup and environmental experiences.

There are some important ways that Maslow's (1970) conception differs from the dispositional needs discussed in Chapter 11. Needs as dispositions are relatively stable (sometimes even permanent) personality characteristics; they are not expected to change very much over time or in different situations. In contrast, Maslow's instinctoid needs are likely to vary in their influence on behavior at different periods in one's life. Further, instinctoid needs are *processes* rather than static entities. Maslow's theory of human motivation views humans as active and striving rather than passive and reactive. This is consistent with the assumptions of the phenomenological strategy. Maslow believes that people are continually trying to satisfy their needs. When they are successful in satisfying one set of needs, they turn to the next set of unfulfilled needs.

The Content of the Need Hierarchy

Maslow postulated five levels of basic human needs. They are depicted in Figure 15–1. These levels, in order of decreasing strength, are as follows:

Basic physiological needs (e.g., food).

Safety needs (e.g., shelter).

Belongingness and love needs (e.g., companionship).

Esteem needs (e.g., feeling competent).

Self-actualization needs (e.g., creativity).

Maslow (1967) also identifies two other levels of needs: cognitive and aesthetic. *Cognitive needs* are desires to know and to understand. They include inquisitiveness, exploration, and novelty. *Aesthetic needs* involve an awareness of beauty, order, symmetry, and artistic endeavors (e.g., music, poetry). Less is known about these two needs than about the other five. Therefore, Maslow has relatively little to say about them. It is also unclear from Maslow's writings where these needs fit in the hierarchy.

The lower a need is in the hierarchy, the more basic it is in terms of survival. Thus, for adaptive reasons, lower needs exert a more powerful influence on our behavior. The higher a need is in the hierarchy, the

FIGURE 15–1
Schematic representation of Maslow's hierarchy of instinctoid needs. The higher the need in the hierarchy, the weaker is the need in terms of motivating human behavior.

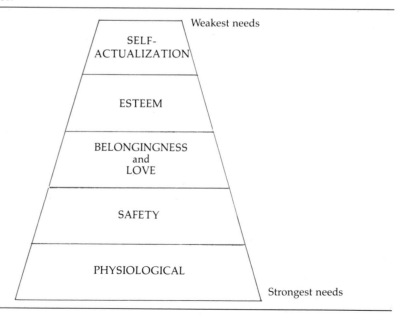

less basic it is and thus the weaker it is in its potential influence. Also, the higher a need in the hierarchy, the more distinctly human it is. Humans definitely share physiological and safety needs with other animals; we may share belongingness and love needs with higher animal species; but it is assumed that humans alone have esteem and self-actualization needs.

Movement within the Need Hierarchy

As we satisfy needs at one level in the hierarchy, we progress to the next level. A set of needs does not have to be *totally* satisfied before we can deal with the next set of needs. In general, however, we are not concerned with meeting higher needs until lower needs have been at least partially satisfied. There are some well-known exceptions to this rule, though.

One exception is relatively rare. It occurs among individuals who defy "normal" social customs. For example, some very creative people ignore physical needs. They may eat poorly and live in squalor in order to pursue their creative interests (e.g., writing). Another exception is some dedicated political activists. They may ignore personal safety (and some basic physiological needs) to protest social injustice. For example, Irish militants have gone on hunger strikes to protest British policies in Northern Ireland.

The normal progression up the need hierarchy can also be temporarily reversed in unusual circumstances. Consider the example of a successful, unmarried business executive in his early thirties. His life was dominated by esteem needs. He described an experience that he had one night while working late.

> I was very much enjoying my work, going over the draft of a marketing report I had written the previous week. I liked what I had written and so it was gratifying to put the finishing touches on it before it was to be typed and distributed. I felt good working—the work was going well and I was enjoying doing it. I felt very content to be working at my desk late at night, a kind of "all's well with the world" sensation except . . . except that something was missing to make it complete, to make it perfect. At first I couldn't figure out what could be missing. I had a good, secure job that I enjoyed, and I had been getting a lot of the right kind of exposure in the field. My boss openly expressed his pleasure about what I had been doing, and my co-workers seemed to like me and seemed to respect my abilities. I was making good money, I was healthy, and I had interests to keep me occupied when I wasn't working. What more could I want? Finally I realized that all this good life was solely mine and that I did not share it with

anyone else. I apparently was missing sharing good things with a close loved one. I had not had much social life recently but did not miss it since I was very much into my work. But the more I thought about it, the more I realized that I would have felt more content—more full—if there were a woman in my life with whom I could have shared my otherwise very positive life.

How would this man's feelings be explained in terms of Maslow's hierarchy? The man was primarily functioning at the esteem level. This involves needs that are satisfied when other people recognize our accomplishments as well as when we acknowledge our self-worth. From his own report, the man's esteem needs appeared to have been well met. However, his needs relating to belongingness and love, which are at a lower level, were not being satisfied. These lower needs must have been gratified at one time in his life for him to have progressed to a higher level. Apparently his single-minded devotion to his work (esteem needs) created a temporary void in his life. It called for a return to a lower level to satisfy his now-unmet social needs.

At various times in our lives, some of our basic needs will inevitably be frustrated. When this occurs, we must temporarily engage in behavior that will satisfy the more basic needs before the higher needs can once again be attended to. A common example occurs when we are too sick to perform normal daily functions, including work and social obligations. Until we have recovered, our life focuses on basic physiological needs. Higher social and esteem needs (and even some safety needs) are, of necessity, placed "on a back burner." (At such times, we become aware that there are few things in this world that we *must* do. However, under normal circumstances, we often live as if certain commitments, such as work, cannot be put aside.)

Physiological Needs

Our most basic needs are physiological. They include food, water, oxygen, elimination, and rest. They relate most directly to survival, so they are the most powerful needs we have. When a basic need is not met, it consumes a person's life until it is satisfied. An individual in a chronic and extreme state of hunger "knows" that Utopia is a place where food is always available. Food becomes the central focus of the hungry person's life; it pervades actions, thoughts, and fantasies. Such a person would be said to "live by bread alone" (Maslow, 1970). However, at least in much of our own society and the Western world, people are rarely in such a situation with respect to hunger or any other physiological need. Thus, under normal circumstances, physiological needs play a small role in human motivation. Higher, less-potent needs dominate most people's lives.

Safety Needs

Safety needs include security, protection, dependency, stability, order, structure, limits, and freedom from fear, anxiety, and chaos. When our safety needs are met, we feel secure and free from danger. The safety needs of most adults in our culture are largely satisfied. "The peaceful, smoothly running, stable, good society ordinarily makes its members feel safe enough from wild animals, extremes of temperature, criminal assault, murder, chaos, tyranny, and so on" (Maslow, 1970, p. 41). Thus, for adults under ordinary circumstances, safety needs are not active motivators. The dominance of safety needs is most easily seen in children's behavior and adult abnormal behavior.

"Infants," for example, "will react in a total fashion and as if they were endangered, if they are disturbed or dropped suddenly, startled by loud noises, flashing light, or other unusual sensory stimulation, by rough handling, by general loss of support in the mother's arms, or by inadequate support" (Maslow, 1970, p. 39). The urgency of safety needs can be readily seen when a child suffers illness or injury.

> At such a moment of pain, it may be postulated that, for the child, the whole world suddenly changes from sunniness to darkness, so to speak, and becomes a place in which anything at all might happen, in which previously stable things have suddenly become unstable. Thus, a child who because of some bad food is taken ill may for a day or two develop fear, nightmares, and a need for protection and reassurance never seen . . . before. (Maslow, 1970, p. 40)

Still another indication of children's heightened safety needs is their preference for predictable, undisrupted routine, such as having meals at a set time.

Adult abnormal behavior is often similar, in many respects, to the child's desire for safety. The adult may see the world as hostile, threatening, and overwhelming. He or she may behave "as if a great catastrophe were almost always impending . . . usually responding as if to an emergency" (Maslow, 1970, p. 42). This is most clearly seen in obsessive-compulsive behavior.

> Compulsive-obsessives try frantically to order and stabilize the world so that no unmanageable, unexpected, or unfamiliar dangers will ever appear. They hedge themselves about with all sorts of ceremonials, rules, and formulas so that every possible contingency may be provided for and so that no new contingencies may appear. (Maslow, 1970, p. 42)

For most of us, safety needs are generally well satisfied in normal existence; they take a backseat to higher needs. Common examples of how adults meet their safety needs include buying insurance, having savings accounts, and preferring secure jobs.

Belongingness and Love Needs

When physiological and safety needs are substantially gratified, needs related to affiliation, affection, and love emerge. We experience deep feelings of loneliness when friends, family, and loved ones are absent. We long for affectionate relationships and a secure place in primary groups, such as a family. When belongingness and love needs predominate, people are keenly aware of and upset by feelings of ostracism, rejection, friendlessness, and rootlessness.

Maslow and other personality psychologists (e.g., Fromm, 1963) believe that unsatisfied belongingness and love needs are a major problem in contemporary Western societies. The popularity of personal-growth groups (e.g., encounter groups, EST) in the 1960s and early 1970s may have been in part due to

> this unsatisfied hunger for contact, for intimacy, for belongingness and by the need to overcome the widespread feelings of alienation, aloneness, strangeness, and loneliness, which have been worsened by our mobility, by the breakdown of traditional groupings, the scattering of families, the generation gap, the steady urbanization and disappearance of village face-to-faceness, and the resulting shallowness of American friendship. . . . *Some* proportion of youth rebellion groups . . . is motivated by the profound hunger for groupiness, for contact, for real togetherness in the face of a common enemy, *any* enemy that can serve to form an amity group simply by posing an external threat. The same kind of thing was observed in groups of soldiers who were pushed into an unwonted brotherliness and intimacy by their common external danger, and who may stick together throughout a lifetime as a consequence. Any good society must satisfy this need, one way or another, if it is to survive and be healthy. (Maslow, 1970, p. 44)

Esteem Needs

If needs in the first three levels of the hierarchy are adequately satisfied, the person becomes concerned with meeting esteem needs. Maslow (1970) distinguishes two types of esteem needs: self-esteem and esteem from others. **Self-esteem** involves a desire for competency, mastery, achievement, strength, adequacy, confidence, independence, and freedom. When these needs are met, we feel worthwhile, confident, capable, useful, and necessary. If these needs are frustrated, we may feel inferior, weak, and helpless. **Esteem from others** includes desire for recognition, appreciation, attention, prestige, reputation, status, and fame. In short, we need to feel respected by other people for what we can do and want others to recognize our worth.

Maslow considers self-esteem more essential than esteem from others, although the former is partially a result of the latter. (Note the parallel with Rogers' concepts of positive regard and positive self-regard.) Maslow emphasizes that enduring and healthy self-esteem is based on the *deserved* respect of others—recognition earned through a person's efforts—rather than on status or fame.

Self-Actualization Needs

Most people spend their lives trying to fulfill physiological, safety, belongingness/love, and esteem needs. And they never completely accomplish this task. A small number of individuals, however, substantially gratify their needs in the first four levels of the hierarchy. They then become motivated by self-actualization needs. Maslow (1970) defined **self-actualization** as "the desire to become more and more what one idiosyncratically is, to become everything that one is capable of becoming" (p. 46). (This definition is essentially the same as Rogers'.) Only by being all that one is "destined for" can a person's needs ever be truly satisfied and can the person feel truly content.

Self-actualization is a goal that is never fully attained by any person. A few people—Maslow estimated about one percent of the population—come close to reaching it. For several reasons, movement toward self-actualization is neither automatic nor easy. This is so even for people successfully fulfilling their lower needs.

First, self-actualization needs are at the top of the hierarchy, which means they are the weakest of the instinctoid needs. "This inner nature is not strong and overpowering. . . . It is weak and delicate and subtle and easily overcome by habit, cultural pressure, and wrong attitudes toward it" (Maslow, 1968, p. 4).

Second, Maslow believes people are often afraid of the self-knowledge necessary for self-actualization. Accurate self-knowledge can be threatening; it may change our self-concept. It involves giving up the certainty of what we have long known, believed, and trusted for new concepts, the unknown, and uncertainty. This course of action is more readily chosen by people who feel secure. Maslow observed, for example, that children from secure, nurturing families are more likely to select experiences that result in personal growth than are children from insecure, cold families.

Third, self-actualization requires an environment where people are free to express themselves and to explore. People must be free to act without restriction (within the normal bounds of not harming others) and to pursue such values as truth, justice, and honesty. Few of us are lucky enough to live in such ideal circumstances, even in open democratic societies. For instance, our culture, through established social customs about the proper expression of one's feelings, generally inhibits the genuine spontaneity that tends to characterize self-actualizing individuals.

The specific nature of self-actualization needs varies considerably from person to person. This contrasts with lower needs that are relatively uniform. It is important to note, however, that self-actualization does not necessarily involve special talent or creative and artistic endeavors. One does not have to be an Einstein, a Bach, or a Picasso to be self-actualizing. Self-actualization may be manifest in any human activity (e.g., farming, athletics, mechanics, parenting).

GROWTH MOTIVATION

Maslow places self-actualization needs at the top of the hierarchy of human motives. But, in a sense, self-actualization needs do not fit in the hierarchy. They are fundamentally different from the basic needs in the first four levels. For one thing, most people never satisfy their lower needs sufficiently to be motivated by self-actualization. A more telling difference is that physiological, safety, belongingness/love, and esteem needs motivate us in terms of *deficit*. Self-actualization needs motivate us in terms of *growth* (Maslow, 1955).

We are all familiar with **deficit motivation.** An individual's behavior is energized by and directed toward reducing tension or filling a temporary lack. We drink because we are thirsty. We seek company when we are lonely. Needs in the first four levels of Maslow's hierarchy operate through deficit motivation. However, this tends to be more the case for physiological and safety needs and somewhat less for belongingness/ love and esteem needs. A deficit motive is characterized by five criteria (Maslow, 1968):

1. When it is absent, illness occurs (e.g., in the case of the need for food, a person who does not eat may get sick).

2. When it is present, illness is prevented (e.g., eating well prevents certain illness).

3. When it is restored, illness is cured (e.g., illness caused by malnutrition is often cured by proper eating).

4. In special complex situations, a deprived individual will prefer gratification of a deficit motive to other gratifications (e.g., a starving person is more likely to be interested in eating food than in appreciating its attractive appearance on the plate).

5. It is essentially inactive in a healthy person (e.g., healthy people tend to be sufficiently well fed so that hunger is not an active motive for them).

Growth motivation, in contrast to deficit motivation, is oriented toward enhancing life in line with the person's unique self-actualizing tendencies. Growth motives are a step beyond basic (deficit) motives. Growth motives are the self-actualization motives. They involve "intrinsic values" such as beauty, truth, and self-sufficiency. Other examples of growth motives are listed in Table 15–3.

Maslow believes that growth needs are of equal value. Thus, they are not arranged in a hierarchy. Further, growth needs all involve intrinsic values; their fulfillment involves the common goal of enhancement or growth. Thus, growth needs can be readily substituted for one another depending on circumstances in a person's life.

When people are motivated by growth needs, even their routine work is on a higher plane. Maslow (1971) gives some examples.

> "The law" is apt to be more a way of seeking justice, truth, goodness, etc., rather than financial security, admiration, status, prestige, dominance, masculinity, etc. When I ask the questions: Which aspects of your work do you enjoy most? What gives you your greatest pleasures? When do you get a kick out of your work? etc., such people are more apt to answer in terms of intrinsic values, of transpersonal, beyond-the-selfish, altruistic satisfactions, e.g., seeing justice done, doing a more perfect job, advancing the truth, rewarding virtue and punishing evil, etc. (p. 310)

Growth Motivation versus Deficit Motivation

To understand growth motivation, we must contrast it with deficit motivation. The two basic forms of motivation differ in numerous ways.

Satisfying growth motives often results in an increase in tension. A decrease in tension is generally associated with satisfying deficit motives. For example, satisfying the growth motive for beauty by hiking through the mountains is likely to lead to increased wonder and awe as vistas

TABLE 15–3
Examples of growth motives identified by Maslow

Truth	Justice
Goodness	Order
Beauty	Simplicity
Unity, wholeness	Richness, totality, comprehensiveness
Aliveness; process	Effortlessness
Uniqueness	Playfulness
Perfection	Self-sufficiency
Necessity	Meaningfulness
Completion; finality	

open up along the trail. In contrast, we can satisfy the deficit motive for security by staying in the valley rather than climbing in the mountains. This will most likely result in diminished anxiety about the dangers of traversing narrow, precipitous trails.

Jourard (1974) distinguishes two styles of perceiving associated with deficit and growth motivation. *Deficit perception* resembles "a highly focused searchlight darting here and there, seeking the objects which will satisfy needs, ignoring everything irrelevant to the need." *Growth perception* is "a more passive mode of perceiving. It involves letting oneself be reached, touched, or affected by what is there so that the perception is richer" (p. 68).

Maslow (1968) differentiates growth love (unneeding, unselfish love) from deficit love (needing, selfish love). The following are characteristics of growth love, which implicitly contrast it to deficit love.

1. Growth love is completely enjoyed and is nonpossessive.
2. Growth love can never be satisfied, and it usually increases rather than decreases over time. The opposite is true for deficit love.
3. Growth love is often likened to an aesthetic or mystic experience.
4. Growth love can have a deep, therapeutic effect.
5. Growth love is a richer, higher, and more valuable experience than deficit love.
6. Growth love involves no anxiety/hostility component such as is always present to some degree with deficit love.
7. Growth lovers are less dependent on each other, less jealous, less needful, less invested in the other person than are deficit lovers. At the same time, growth lovers are more eager to help their partner self-actualize and tend to be prouder of the other's accomplishments than are deficit lovers.
8. Growth love involves the truest, most penetrating perception of the other, whereas deficit love is often "blind."
9. Receiving growth love fosters personal growth, self-acceptance, and feelings of self-worth.

Growth Needs in Everyday Life

Growth needs play a minor role in most people's day-to-day lives. Although most people remain at one of the need levels below self-actualization, occasionally people who are not predominantly self-actualizers are motivated by intrinsic growth values. This may occur in circumstances that demand some extraordinary behavior, such as in a crisis. The individual temporarily postpones gratification of basic deficit needs and rises above them to the realm of growth needs. Usually, feats of courage or self-sacrifice are examples.

MASLOW'S STUDY OF SELF-ACTUALIZING PERSONS

More often than not, theories of normal personality are based, at least at first, on observations of abnormal behavior. There has been relatively little theorizing and research on optimal functioning and the healthy personality. However, there are exceptions. Rogers (1963) theorizes that **fully functioning people** are guided by their organismic valuing processes; they are open to all experiences; their self-concepts are whole and consistent with their experiences; they are free of threat and anxiety, and therefore have no defenses. In short, the fully functioning person epitomizes psychological health or adjustment. Actually, the type of person Rogers describes is an ideal—such a (living) specimen has yet to be found. However, some individuals come close to the goal of being fully functioning or self-actualizing.

Maslow's (1954) research on the self-actualizing person is well known, and other psychologists have also studied self-actualizers (e.g., Seeman, 1984). Maslow (1972a) described the origin of his studies this way.

My investigations on self-actualization were not planned to be research and did not start out as research. They started out as the effort of a young intellectual to try to understand two of his teachers whom he loved, adored, and admired and who were very, very wonderful people. It was a kind of high-IQ devotion. I could not be content simply to adore, but sought to understand why these two people were so different from the run-of-the-mill people in the world. These two people were Ruth Benedict and Max Wertheimer.[2] They were my teachers . . . and they were most remarkable human beings. My training in psychology equipped me not at all for understanding them. It was as if they were not quite people but something more than people. My own investigation began as a prescientific or nonscientific activity. . . . When I tried to understand them, think about them, and write about them . . . I realized in one wonderful moment that their two patterns could be generalized. I was talking about a kind of person, not about two noncomparable

---

[2]Ruth Benedict was an anthropologist at Columbia University who studied Native Americans, and Max Wertheimer was a psychologist at the New School for Social Research and was one of the founders of Gestalt psychology.

individuals. There was wonderful excitement in that. I tried to see whether this pattern could be found elsewhere, and I did find it elsewhere. . . . (pp. 41–42)

Selection of Subjects and Methods

Maslow primarily used the case-study method in his investigations of self-actualizing persons. For the most part, he gathered biographical data from interviews with a relatively small, select group of subjects and from the written accounts of historical figures (total of sixty). Ethical considerations prevented giving the names of his living subjects. The historical persons are known and include those shown in Figure 15–2.

Maslow selected his subjects using a negative and a positive criterion. The negative criterion was absence of psychopathology. The positive criterion was evidence of self-actualization. Maslow (1970) defined this as

> the full use and exploitation of talents, capacities, potentialities, etc.
> . . . [Self-actualizing] people seem to be fulfilling themselves and
> to be doing the best that they are capable of doing, reminding us
> of Nietzche's exhortation, "Become what thou art!" They are people
> who have developed or are developing to the full stature of which
> they are capable. . . . These potentialities may be either idiosyn-
> cratic or species-wide. (p. 150)

This criterion also implies gratification, past or present, of the needs in the first four levels of the need hierarchy as well as the cognitive needs for knowledge and understanding. Thus, all of Maslow's subjects "felt safe and unanxious, accepted, loved and loving, respectworthy and respected, and . . . they had worked out their philosophical, religious, or axiological bearings" (Maslow, 1970, pp. 150–51). Whether this basic gratification is a sufficient condition or a prerequisite for self-actualization remains unanswered.

Maslow was aware that his research on the self-actualizing person was unorthodox and therefore felt compelled to justify his approach.

> I consider the problem of psychological health to be so pressing,
> that *any* suggestions, *any* bits of data, however moot, are endowed
> with great heuristic value. This kind of research is in principle so
> difficult . . . that if we were to wait for conventionally reliable data,
> we should have to wait forever. It seems that the only manly thing
> to do is not to fear mistakes, to plunge in, to do the best that one
> can, hoping to learn enough from blunders to correct them even-
> tually. At present the only alternative is simply to refuse to work
> with the problem. Accordingly, for whatever use can be made of it,
> the following report is presented with due apologies to those who

insist on conventional reliability, validity, sampling, etc. (Maslow, 1963, p. 527)

The Characteristics of Self-Actualizing Persons

Maslow's research on self-actualizing persons focused on forming impressions from observations rather than on testing hypotheses. With this type of qualitative data, it is essential that investigators accurately and graphically summarize their *impressions*, which are the basic units of data. Fortunately, Maslow had a distinct talent in this regard. We will rely heavily on direct quotations of Maslow's (1963) highly expressive and communicative impressions.

Maslow's investigations yielded fifteen key characteristics of self-actualizing persons. Three important points should be kept in mind as you read about them. First, self-actualization is a process and not an end state. No one is ever self-actualized; the people we are discussing here are in the process of self-actualiz*ing*. Second, there is overlap among the characteristics, but each characteristic contributes to an understanding of the self-actualizing person. Third, none of Maslow's subjects, and probably no person, exhibits every one of these characteristics. However, self-actualizing individuals exhibit a large number of them.

Efficient Perception of Reality

Self-actualizers are able to easily and accurately judge themselves and others. Their judgments are not distorted by personal needs, fears, or beliefs.

> The first form in which this capacity was noticed was an unusual ability to detect the spurious, the fake, and the dishonest in personality, and in general to judge people correctly and efficiently. . . . As the study progressed, it slowly became apparent that this efficiency extended to many other areas of life—indeed *all* areas that were tested. In art and music, in things of the intellect, in scientific matters, in politics and public affairs, they seemed as a group to be able to see concealed or confused realities more swiftly and more correctly than others. Thus an informal experiment indicated that their predictions of the future from whatever facts were in hand at the time seemed to be more often correct, because [they were] less [likely to be] based upon wish, desire, anxiety, fear, or upon generalized, character-determined optimism or pessimism. (Maslow, 1963, p. 531)

Figure 15–2 Some of the historical figures whom Maslow identified as self-actualizing. *(A)* Jane Addams (1860–1935), peace activist, *The Bettmann Archive*; *(B)* William James (1842–1910), psychologist, *The Bettmann Archive*; *(C)* Ralph Waldo Emerson (1803–1882), writer, *The Bettmann Archive*; *(D)* Martin Buber (1878–1965), theologian, *UPI/Bettmann Newsphotos*; *(E)* Pablo Casals (1876–1973), musician, *Photo Researchers, Inc.*; *(F)* George Washington Carver (1864–1943), agricultural chemist, *The Bettmann Archive*; *(G)* Abraham Lincoln (1809–1865), politician, *The Bettmann Archive*; *(H)* Eleanor Roosevelt (1884–1962), humanitarian, *Photo Researchers, Inc.*

(I) *Albert Einstein (1879–1955)*, physicist, *The Bettmann Archive;* (J) Thomas Jefferson (1743–1826), political philosopher, *The Bettmann Archive;* (K) Sholom Aleichem (1858–1916), author, *Spertus College of Judaica, Chicago;* (L) Harriet Tubman (1821–1913), abolitionist, *Library of Congress;* (M) Albert Schweitzer (1875–1965), medical missionary, *The Bettmann Archive;* (N) Benjamin Franklin (1706–1790), inventor, *The Bettmann Archive;* (O) Walt Whitman (1819–1892), poet, *Photo Researchers, Inc.;* (P) Adlai Stevenson (1900–1965), diplomat, *Photo Researchers, Inc.*

Acceptance (of Self, Others, and Nature)

Self-actualizers accept themselves, others, and nature without chagrin or complaint and without thinking much about it.

> They can accept their own human nature in stoic style, with all its shortcomings, with all its discrepancies from the ideal image without feeling real concern. It would convey the wrong impression to say that they are self-satisfied. What we must say rather is that they can take the frailties and sins, weaknesses, and evils of human nature in the same unquestioning spirit with which one accepts the characteristics of nature. One does not complain about water because it is wet, or about rocks because they are hard, or about trees because they are green. As the child looks out upon the world with wide, uncritical innocent eyes, simply noting and observing what is the case, without either arguing the matter or demanding that it be otherwise, so does the self-actualizing person look upon human nature in himself and in others. (Maslow, 1963, p. 533)

Spontaneity, Simplicity, and Naturalness

Self-actualizing persons are relatively spontaneous in their overt behavior, but they are not the stereotyped unconventional people in society.

> Their behavior is marked by simplicity and naturalness, and by lack of artificiality or straining for effect. This does not necessarily mean consistently unconventional behavior. . . . It is his impulses, thought, consciousness that are so unusually unconventional, spontaneous, and natural. Apparently recognizing that the world of people in which he lives could not understand or accept this, and since he has no wish to hurt them or fight with them over every triviality, he will go through the ceremonies and rituals of convention with a good-humored shrug and with the best possible grace. Thus I have seen a man accept an honor he laughed at and even despised in private, rather than make an issue of it and hurt the people who thought they were pleasing him. (Maslow, 1963, p. 535)

Problem-Centered

Self-actualizers have a sense of mission or purpose in life, and they efficiently go about fulfilling it. Their problems tend to be broad and outside the narrow sphere of themselves. They are

> ordinarily concerned with basic issues and eternal questions of the type that we have learned to call philosophical or ethical. Such people live customarily in the widest possible frame of reference. They

seem never to get so close to the trees that they fail to see the forest. They work within a framework of values that is broad and not petty, universal and not local, and in terms of a century rather than the moment. In a word, these people are all in one sense or another philosophers, however homely. (Maslow, 1963, p. 537)

Detachment

Self-actualizers tend to enjoy solitude and privacy more than the average person. They are often able to remain undisturbed, even aloof, from events that generally lead to turmoil in most people. Their detachment allows them to concentrate to an extraordinary degree. A by-product is "absent-mindedness, the ability to forget and to be oblivious to outer surroundings. Examples are the ability to sleep soundly, to have undisturbed appetite, to be able to smile and laugh through a period of problems, worry, and responsibility" (Maslow, 1970, p. 161). Self-actualizers make decisions themselves, based on their own inclinations; they are "self-starters."

Independence from Culture and Environment

Self-actualizing people do not depend much on the external environment or other people for meeting their needs.

> Deficit-motivated people *must* have other people available, since most of their main need gratifications (love, safety, respect, prestige, belongingness) can come only from other human beings. But growth-motivated people [i.e., self-actualizers] may actually be *hampered* by others. The determinants of satisfaction and of the good life are for them . . . inner-individual and *not* social. They have become strong enough to be independent of the good opinion of other people, or even of their affection. The honors, the status, the rewards, the popularity, the prestige, and the love they can bestow must have become less important than self-development and inner growth. (Maslow, 1970, p. 162)

Continued Freshness of Appreciation

Self-actualizing persons continually appreciate even the most ordinary events in their lives. They have

> the wonderful capacity to appreciate again and again, freshly and naively, the basic goods of life, with awe, pleasure, wonder, and even ecstasy, however stale these experiences may have become to others. . . . Any sunset may be as beautiful as the first one, any flower may be breathtaking, even after . . . seeing a million flowers. . . . For such people, even the casual workaday, moment-to-moment

business of living can be thrilling, exciting, and ecstatic. These intense feelings do not come all the time; they come occasionally rather than usually, but at the most unexpected moments. (Maslow, 1963, pp. 539–40)

In essence, continued fresh appreciation of life events can be considered "counting one's blessings." Maslow points out that most people realize the worth of others, their health, their economic well-being, and the like only after these aspects of life are lost. Self-actualizers value them as they are experienced.

Peak Experiences

Self-actualizing persons tend to have more peak experiences than most people. A **peak experience** refers to feelings of

limitless horizons opening up to the vision, the feeling of being simultaneously more powerful and also more helpless than one ever was before, the feeling of great ecstasy and wonder and awe, the loss of placing in time and space with, finally, the conviction that something extremely important and valuable had happened, so that the subject is to some extent transformed and strengthened even in his daily life by such experiences. (Maslow, 1963, p. 541)

This definition says nothing about what the person is doing when the peak experience occurs. Peak experiences may be a consequence of almost any activity or event. The peak experience itself consists of feelings that are more or less independent of the circumstances. Peak experiences transcend immediate, concrete occurrences. There are, however, precipitating events that many people cite as sometimes leading to peak experi-

"Freshness of appreciation" is one of the characteristics that Maslow found typified self-actualizing individuals. It involves repeatedly experiencing the wonder of the world *as if* it were being experienced for the first time. *Photo by Mary Puckett and Stephen Puckett*

ences. Being in love and doing something as well as one can—close to perfection—are two common themes.

Maslow believes peak experiences are always growth producing; they have some effect on the individual beyond the peak experience itself. However, the peak experience itself is transitory. It lasts only a brief time (a few seconds to a few minutes). Peak experiences are spontaneous. They cannot be created or anticipated. We may expect some event to be special, but that is no guarantee that it will result in a peak experience. In fact, expecting a peak experience will almost guarantee that it will not occur, at least not in the form anticipated.

Examples of Peak Experiences. The content of the events leading to peak experiences is almost limitless. Here are two rather different personal accounts of peak experiences. The first involved a successful struggle to overcome a difficult situation.

> It was to be the last and most difficult climb of our brief climbing trip. Because I was the novice of the group, Richard and Christopher briefed me on what lay above, giving special attention to the overhang in the third and last pitch [segment of the climb]. Some fifty feet below the summit there was a five-foot horizontal outcropping (at a right angle to the face of the cliff and parallel to the ground). Quite simply, to proceed to the summit, a climber would, for a brief time, be in a position where his or her back was parallel to the ground as the overhang was negotiated. I had never done anything like that before, but my more experienced team members assured me that it was within my capabilities.
>
> The first two pitches were relatively uneventful, as was most of the third. Then there was a short traverse to the left along a narrow ledge, and I found myself directly below the overhang. I was being belayed [protected from a fall by a rope] from above by Christopher who, because of the overhang, was out of sight and sound. Fortunately, Richard was below me and gave me detailed instructions as to how to negotiate the overhang. It would involve jamming [wedging] both feet in a large crack in the vertical wall while my right hand gripped the underside of the overhang at about the position of my right knee and my left hand made a small but secure finger jam in a crack on the underside of the overhang at about the level of my shoulder. In fact, it was easier to get into this position than the description might sound, and because it was a secure position, I felt relatively safe to rest in it for the moment. However, the next and critical move would require me to let go of my secure right grip, straighten my legs, and reach up and around the overhang to blindly feel for a large handhold on the top side of the overhang.

That was easier explained than done. My right hand must have started its assigned journey a dozen times in the next five minutes, only to quickly retreat to its secure hold each time. Finally, it was time to risk. My right hand quickly found the crack on the top, and it was not difficult to then move my left hand into the same crack, release my legs from their supports, and mantle [raise oneself by pressing downward with the arms] to the top of the overhang.

I was exhilarated, triumphant, almost giddy with joy. As I climbed the last bit to the top, I had to keep reminding myself that I'd better pay attention lest I fall on this relatively easy final ascent.

Safely on top, I told Christopher, "Off belay," and we proceeded to embrace each other. I asked him if he wanted me to belay Richard to the top; he said no, that he was fine and that I should rest. So I walked along the summit and shortly came to a magnificent overlook, displaying the entire lush green valley to the southeast. As I stood there, glowing in the warmth of the afternoon sun and my own energy, I had the following thoughts, which I will never forget.

I was surely not ready to die. I may never have felt more alive—that life was so full and worth living—than at that moment. But, if I had to die, I was more ready to—because I had lived.

The events that result in peak experiences are generally pleasant. They may also be unpleasant. The peak experience itself, however, is always enriching and growth producing. This can be seen in the following description of an intensely unpleasant event that led to a peak experience.

We took a ferry to another island that day, and so we had a limited time to explore. In the early afternoon I found myself without any energy. I told my friend Dennis to go off on his own for a while; I was content just to sit down in a comfortable chair. When Dennis returned an hour later, I was still sitting where he had left me, and I had become still more lethargic. Reluctantly we headed back early for the main island.

I began to feel quite sick on the trip back, and by the time we reached our hotel, I had a high fever and every part of my body ached. I must have been somewhat delirious because I recall rambling on about early childhood experiences, in a not too coherent fashion. I tried to sleep. Although I was exhausted and quite sleepy, I would doze for only a few minutes at a time because I could not find a comfortable sleeping position.

I remember noting that the clock read 1:30 in the morning. Then I fell back to sleep. When I awoke forty-five minutes later— the longest I had slept—I was immediately aware that the fever had broken. I was cool, without having chills; I was thinking straight;

my body was still sore but it no longer ached as it had. I could not get over the sudden, drastic change. I may never have been more aware of my physical self than at that moment.

I told myself then that I would be willing to go through the intense pain and discomfort that I had had for fourteen hours to experience the dramatic change that had occurred. I still feel the same way twelve years later.

The two people whose peak experiences were just described were not self-actualizers. Fortunately, all people have occasional peak experiences, just less often than self-actualizers. Maslow considered these experiences *transient moments of self-actualization of ordinary people* (Chiang & Maslow, 1977).

DEMONSTRATION 15–2

BECOMING AWARE OF YOUR PEAK EXPERIENCES

We all occasionally have peak experiences, although we may not be aware that they are peak experiences when they occur. Having learned something about the nature of peak experiences, you might want to explore your own.

To identify your peak experiences, think of the most wonderful experiences of your life. These may be happiest moments, ecstatic moments, moments of rapture. They may have come from being in love, from listening to music, from suddenly "being struck" by a book or painting, from some creative moment, from suddenly having a profound insight. They may have arisen from doing something—even a minor task—extremely well, nearly perfectly. These special moments will be unique to you; it does not matter whether anyone else would consider them special. To qualify as a peak experience, the moment should meet the following two requirements.

1. It was relatively *brief*, ranging from a few seconds to several minutes. Often we feel special for some time (several hours or even days) after a peak experience because it is generally very pleasant and always growth producing. But the actual peak experience is a brief, momentary event.

2. It is an *actual experience* you have had, not one that you think you might have or should have. (There are many events that are *supposed* to be special, such as winning a race or contest, graduation, and making love, but they may not result in peak experiences. Furthermore, peak experiences rarely, if ever, can be anticipated; they are, by nature, spontaneous.)

This Demonstration involves three simple steps. You will need three pieces of paper and a pencil.

1. First, using the description of peak experiences given above, write a brief description of several peak experiences in your life.

2. Second, using a separate sheet of paper, write in a few words, the general nature of each peak experience (e.g., "finally getting something to work," "being in love," "getting an 'A' "). In other words, put a label on each experience.

3. Finally, considering all the peak experiences you have listed, write on a separate piece of paper a description of how you felt in those special moments. In particular note how you felt *differently* from the way you generally feel—how you were at the moment a different person in some ways.

Exploring your peak experiences and how you felt during them can be enlightening. You may find, for example, that some of your happiest, most special moments have come at times that you would not have predicted, perhaps in the midst of rather ordinary activities or events. By discovering the circumstances in your life that are most likely to result in peak experiences, you may choose to do them more often merely because they have, at times, led to peak experiences for you.

You might also find it interesting to compare your peak experiences with those of others who have done this Demonstration. It is not necessary to reveal the intimate details of your peak experiences if you choose not to. You can share what you have written in Steps 2 and 3.

Genuine Desire to Help Humankind

Self-actualizing people have "a deep feeling of identification, sympathy, and affection" for human beings in general (although they occasionally may be angry, disgusted, or impatient with a particular person). Self-actualizers have a genuine desire to help the human race. They tend to treat all people as most people usually treat a family member. This attitude may come close to unconditional positive regard for all humankind.

Deep Interpersonal Relations

Self-actualizers have deeper, more profound interpersonal relations than do most other adults. "They are capable of more fusion, greater love, more perfect identification, more obliteration of the ego boundaries than other people would consider possible" (Maslow, 1970, p. 166). Becoming close to another person in this profound way takes considerable time. As a consequence, they tend to have deep ties with relatively few individuals. Their circle of friends is small. As one of Maslow's subjects noted: "I haven't got time for many friends. Nobody has, that is, if they are to be *real* friends" (Maslow, 1963, p. 542).

Although self-actualizers have few close relationships, they tend to attract admirers. Such relationships are apt to be one-sided; the admirer expects more from the self-actualizing person than she or he wants to give. But self-actualizers are likely to act kindly toward their unwanted admirers while trying to gracefully avoid such relationships.

Democratic

Maslow describes self-actualizers as democratic in the deepest sense. They are free of prejudice regarding characteristics such as race or ethical background; they tend to respect all persons. For example, they are willing to learn from anyone who can teach them something. At the same time, self-actualizers do not indiscriminately equalize all human beings. Rather, self-actualizers, "themselves elite, select for their friends elite, but this is an elite of character, capacity, and talent, rather than of birth, race, blood, name, family, age, youth, fame, or power" (Maslow, 1963, p. 544).

Discrimination between Good and Bad, Means and Ends

Self-actualizing people have a sustained and coherent set of ethical standards. This tends to result in their doing the "right" thing. At one time they would have been described as "walking in the path of God." Very few of Maslow's subjects were religious, however, in the sense of observing institutionalized rituals.

Self-actualizers can discriminate between means and ends. While they usually focus on ends rather than means, their ends are often what most of us consider means. That is, they are "somewhat more likely to appreciate for its own sake, and in an absolute way, the doing itself; they can often enjoy for its own sake the getting to some place as well as the arriving. It is occasionally possible for them to make out of the most trivial and routine activity an intrinsically enjoyable game or dance or play" (Maslow, 1963, p. 545).

Philosophical Sense of Humor

Self-actualizers tend to have an unhostile, philosophical sense of humor. The average person often enjoys humor that pokes fun at someone's inferiority, that hurts someone, or that is "off-color." The self-actualizing person finds humor in the foolishness of humans in general. Such thoughtful, philosophical humor typically elicits a smile rather than a laugh. The humor is pervasive in self-actualizers' lives. They may place a serious endeavor in perspective so that without minimizing its importance, they are able to see its absurdities and make light of it.

Creativeness

Without exception, Maslow found that self-actualizers are characterized by originality and inventiveness and by a fresh perception of the environment. This creativeness is different from unusual talent or genius. It is more like the

> naive and universal creativeness of unspoiled children. It seems to be more a fundamental characteristic of common human nature—a potentiality given to all human beings at birth. Most human beings lose this as they become enculturated, but some few individuals [self-actualizers] seem either to retain this fresh and naive, direct way of looking at life, or if they have lost it, as most people do, they later in life recover it. (Maslow, 1963, p. 546)

This special creativeness need not be manifest in art, music, writing, and the like. It can show up in the mundane; a fabulous pizza would be considered more creative than an average poem!

Resistance to Enculturation

Self-actualizing persons fit in with their culture in a variety of ways. But they maintain an inner detachment from it. Outwardly—in dress, speech, and behavior—they are within the limits of convention. They are not among those in the forefront of social action. But they are likely to challenge authority when necessary, especially in the face of injustice. And they are committed to social change. For example, one of Maslow's subjects

> who was a hot rebel in his younger days, a union organizer in the days when this was a highly dangerous occupation, had given up in disgust and hopelessness. As he became resigned to the slowness of social change (in this culture and in this era) he turned finally to education of the young. All the [other self-actualizers] . . . show what might be called a calm, long-time concern with culture improvement that seems to me to imply an acceptance of slowness of change along with the unquestioned desirability and necessity of such change. (Maslow, 1963, p. 548)

The Imperfections of Self-Actualizing People

Despite the idealistic nature of the fifteen characteristics of self-actualizing people, Maslow makes it clear that such individuals are not perfect.

> They too are equipped with silly, wasteful, or thoughtless habits. They can be boring, stubborn, irritating. They are by no means free from a rather superficial vanity, pride, partiality to their own produc-

tions, family, friends, and children. Temper outbursts are not rare. Our subjects are occasionally capable of an extraordinary and unexpected ruthlessness. It must be remembered that they are very strong people. This makes it possible for them to display a surgical coldness when this is called for, beyond the power of the average man. The man who found that a long-trusted acquaintance was dishonest cut himself off from this friendship sharply and abruptly and without any pangs whatsoever. Another woman who was married to someone she did not love, when she decided on divorce, did it with a decisiveness that looked almost like ruthlessness. Some of them recover so quickly from the death of people close to them as to seem heartless. (Maslow, 1963, pp. 550–51)

Besides having their share of human frailties, self-actualizing people need not be highly intelligent (at least in the traditional sense) or educated. Neither need they be famous for their contributions. Self-actualizers may be quietly and privately living to their full potential—undistinguished in the public eye, but distinctive in being as fully human as members of our species are capable of being.

Self-Actualizing by Chance?

The main character in the movie *Being There* (based on Jerzy N. Kosinski's 1970 novel by the same name) might be considered a self-actualizing person. Chance (played by the late Peter Sellers) would be labeled a "simpleton." He is not very intelligent and is illiterate and uneducated. His life consists of watching television and gardening. (He apparently is fairly competent at the latter.) His basic needs are provided for by virtue of his being a permanent "guest" of a rich old man. When his benefactor dies, Chance, by a quirk of fate, becomes the temporary guest of another rich and influential man, Ben Rand. Ben is quickly taken by Chance's fresh appreciation of life, his complete candor and spontaneity, his genuineness and total lack of pretense, and his acceptance of his life for what it is. Chance has undoubtedly become everything that he is capable of becoming (and, in some sense, even more). The irony, and the source of the story's humor, is that intellectually Chance's potential appears very limited; but most people he meets find him profound. In fact, his advice is sought by the great and powerful. Even the president of the United States, whom he meets through Ben, interprets Chance's objectively very simple pronouncements about the inevitable change of seasons (made in the context of gardening) as having some deep significance concerning a change in the nation's economy. In fact, given Chance's minimal intellectual skills, his ideas about seasonal changes might well be considered extremely insightful from a phenomenological viewpoint (i.e., looked at from Chance's internal frame of reference).

ASSESSING SELF-ACTUALIZATION: THE PERSONAL ORIENTATION INVENTORY

Not surprisingly, a major criticism of Maslow's research on self-actualizing individuals is that the criteria for identifying self-actualizers are highly subjective; they are based almost entirely on the clinical impressions of Maslow and his co-workers. One response to this criticism has been the development of an objective test of values and behaviors related to self-actualization.

The **Personal Orientation Inventory (POI),** devised by Everett Shostrom, consists of 150 forced-choice items (Knapp, 1976; Shostrom, 1963, 1964, 1974; Shostrom, Knapp, & Knapp, 1976). The POI is self-administered; respondents merely record which of two statements for each item more consistently applies to them. Table 15-4 contains several examples of the type of items found on the POI.

The items are scored twice, first for two scales that measure fundamental personal orientations: (1) *time ratio* indicates the degree that a person is present oriented versus past and future oriented; (2) *support ratio* assesses the degree that an individual is inner- or self-oriented versus other-oriented. Then the 150 items are scored again for ten subscales measuring important elements of self-actualization. A brief description of these scales and subscales appears in Table 15–5. The time ratio and support ratio scores will be discussed in some detail to show how subjective, abstract, and even esoteric concepts related to self-actualization have been operationally defined in the POI.

TABLE 15–4
Items and instructions similar to those appearing on the Personal Orientation Inventory

Instructions: After reading each pair of statements, decide which one is most consistently true for you.

1. *a.* I enjoy listening to dirty stories.
   b. I rarely enjoy listening to dirty stories.
2. *a.* When I get something new, I like to use it right away.
   b. When I get something new, I like to save it for a special time.
3. *a.* I am afraid of expressing my emotions.
   b. I am not afraid of expressing my emotions.
4. *a.* Daydreaming about the future can be harmful.
   b. Daydreaming about the future is always good.
5. *a.* I have a lot of bad memories.
   b. I have very few bad memories.
6. *a.* People are naturally friendly.
   b. People are naturally hostile.

TABLE 15–5
The scales of the Personal Orientation Inventory

	Scale Name	**Description**
I. Ratio scores	*Time ratio*	The ratio of time incompetence to time competence indicates the degree to which a person lives in (is oriented toward) the past and future versus the present, respectively.
	Support ratio	The ratio of other to inner indicates the degree to which a person relies primarily on social or external factors versus internalized factors, respectively, to guide behavior.
II. Subscales* Valuing	*Self-actualizing value*	Measures extent to which person holds values of self-actualizing people.
	Existentiality	Measures degree of flexibility in applying principles to one's life.
Feeling	*Feeling reactivity*	Measures sensitivity to one's own feelings and needs.
	Spontaneity	Measures one's ability to express feelings behaviorally, to be oneself, to be uninhibited.
Self-perception	*Self-regard*	Measures ability to like oneself because of one's strengths and worth.
	Self-acceptance	Measures ability to like oneself in spite of one's limitations and weaknesses.
Awareness	*Nature of man*	Measures the extent to which a person views people as essentially good.
	Synergy	Measures the ability to view opposites in life as meaningfully related (e.g., viewing work and play as not really different).
Interpersonal sensitivity	*Acceptance of aggression*	Measures ability to accept one's anger or aggression as natural and to not deny such feelings.
	Capacity for intimate contact	Measures the ability to make meaningful, close relations with other people.

* The subscales can be grouped into complementary pairs—valuing, feeling, self-perception, awareness, and interpersonal sensitivity—representing the balancing which is important for self-actualization.

Time Orientation

The time-ratio scale measures the extent to which a person focuses on the present (as opposed to the past and future). Scores on this scale are a ratio (proportion) between time incompetence (past and future focus) and time competence (present focus). A ratio is used because time orientation is relative. (No one is entirely oriented in one time frame.) *Time competency* involves living "primarily in the present with full awareness." *Time incompetency* is characterized by living "primarily in the past, with guilts, regrets, and resentments, and/or in the future, with idealized goals, plans, expectations, predictions and fears" (Shostrom, 1974, p. 4).

Self-actualizing people are primarily time competent. Their focus is on the present. Time-competent individuals are not oblivious to or independent of the past and future, however. They are "able to tie the past and the future to the present in meaningful continuity" (Shostrom, 1974, p. 13). They can usefully reflect on the past as it relates to the present and realistically relate long-range aspirations to current, ongoing goals. Time-competent individuals are optimistic about the future without being overly idealistic.

In contrast, non-self-actualizers tend to be relatively time incompetent. Their current lives are based on regrets and guilt about their past and unrealistic goals and pessimism about the future. People who are primarily time incompetent have essentially split off their past and future from their present. They have difficulty using what they have done and can potentially do at some later time in their current lives. These two contrasting styles are illustrated in Figure 15–3.

Support Orientation

The support-ratio scale measures the extent to which a person is characteristically other-oriented as compared to self- or inner-oriented (cf. Reisman, Glazer, & Denney, 1950). The scale's score is a ratio of other-orientation

FIGURE 15–3
Schematic representation of the difference between *time competence* (living in the present), which is characteristic of self-actualizers, and *time incompetence* (living in the past and future), which is characteristic of non-self-actualizers.

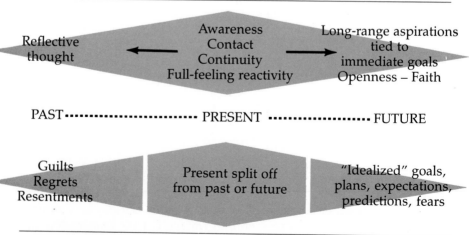

Source: Adapted from *Manual for the Personal Orientation Inventory* by E. L. Shostrom, 1974, San Diego: EdITS.

to self-orientation. As with the time scale, the ratio indicates that people use both orientations in their lives; it is most meaningful to view their support orientation as the extent to which they are other-oriented relative to self-oriented. A *self-orientation* is characterized by behavior governed primarily by internalized principles and motives. It is associated with autonomy, self-support, individuality, and freedom. An *other-orientation* is characterized by behavior primarily influenced by social norms and pressures and other external factors. It is associated with dependence, conformity, and desire for approval and acceptance.

Self-actualizers tend to have a mixture of both support orientations. However, as would be expected, they tend to be more self-directed than other-directed, in a ratio of about 3:1. Non-self-actualizers tend to have approximately a 1:1 ratio; this indicates an even balance between self- and other-orientation.

Interpreting the POI

Interpretation of POI involves examining the pattern of scores obtained on the twelve scales and subscales. A profile is plotted on a psychogram, as is done for many self-report inventories (see Figure 10–1, page 212). The subscales are often grouped into complementary pairs for interpretation. These pairs are identified in Table 15–5. They represent complementary characteristics of self-actualization, a balance critical to self-actualization. For example, acceptance of aggression and capacity for intimate contact can be complementary qualities. "It is possible to be either assertive and aggressive or warm and loving in human contacts. Both are expressions of good interpersonal contacts and both may be considered to reflect the general area of interpersonal sensitivity" (Shostrom, 1974, p. 18). Interpretation of the POI requires understanding the inventory and its rationale as well as the theoretical concepts of self-actualization.

SUMMARY

1. Maslow developed a general theory of motivation. He is especially noted for his investigations of the role of self-actualization motives.

2. Maslow believes that people are motivated by a common set of instinctoid needs that have a biological basis.

3. These needs are arranged in a hierarchy of levels which are, in order of increasing strength: self-actualization, esteem, belongingness and love, safety, and basic physiological needs. People progress up the hierarchy, beginning with the strongest needs. In general, when needs at a particular level are met, the individual can then work on meeting needs in the next level, but there are exceptions.

4. In most Western cultures, people's physiological and safety needs

are generally met as a matter of course, and thus they are not strong motivators.

5. For most people, love and belongingness and esteem (both self-esteem and esteem from others) needs are primary motivators.

6. Self-actualization needs are concerned with a person fulfilling his or her unique potential. They are the weakest of our needs and are only goals toward which people strive. Most people's behavior is only minimally motivated by self-actualization needs.

7. Self-actualization needs motivate in terms of growth, and they are qualitatively different from the other four levels of needs which motivate in terms of deficit.

8. Maslow identified people who are substantially motivated by self-actualization needs and studied them intensively to discover the common characteristics of self-actualizing people. The fifteen characteristics are: efficient perception; acceptance; spontaneity; problem-centered; detachment; independence from culture; freshness of appreciation; peak experiences; desire to help others; deep interpersonal relations; democratic; discrimination between good and bad, means and ends; philosophical sense of humor; creativeness; resistence to enculturalization. Self-actualizers are not perfect human beings, nor are they always highly intelligent or famous.

9. The Personal Orientation Inventory is a forced-choice self-report inventory that assesses values and behaviors related to self-actualization. Two important scales derived from it concern one's time orientation (present versus past and future) and support (self versus other).

KELLY'S THEORY OF PERSONAL CONSTRUCTS

OVERVIEW

There are always alternative ways of viewing the world. No one need be completely the victim of present circumstances or history. George A. Kelly (1905–1967) called this philosophical position **constructive alternativism**. It is the basis for his *theory of personal constructs*.

Kelly began his career in 1931. He started, like many other personality theorists, as a clinician doing psychotherapy. As was true of most clinicians at that time, he practiced psychoanalysis. In the course of his practice, he realized that the accuracy of his interpretations was less important in helping clients change than the fact that the interpretations let his clients see themselves and their problems in a different way. And so, Kelly (1969) tried an informal experiment that he describes as follows:

> I began fabricating "insights." I deliberately offered "preposterous interpretations" to my clients. Some of them were about as un-Freudian as I could make them—first proposed somewhat cautiously, of course, and then, as I began to see what was happening, more boldly. My only criteria were that the explanation account for the crucial facts as the client saw them, and that it carry implications for approaching the future in a different way. (p. 52)

Eventually Kelly concluded that clients had their own interpretations of events in their lives; these interpretations were ultimately responsible for their abnormal behaviors. He came to believe that clients would change

George A. Kelly

National Library of Medicine

their abnormal behaviors if he could help them change their interpretations so that they saw themselves and their worlds somewhat differently.

THE PERSON AS A SCIENTIST

Kelly (1955) found a paradox in the way personality psychologists studied people.

> It is customary to say that the *scientist's ultimate aim is to predict and control.* . . . Yet curiously enough, psychologists rarely credit the human subjects in their experiments with having similar aspirations. It is as though the psychologist were saying . . . "I, being a *psychologist,* and therefore a *scientist,* am performing this experiment in order to improve the prediction and control of certain human phenomena; but my subject, being merely a human organism, is obviously propelled by inexorable drives welling up within . . . or else is in gluttonous pursuit of sustenance and shelter." (p. 5)

Besides being elitist, this position assumes that scientists are the only ones interested in prediction and control. Actually, everyone needs to predict events and have some control over them.

Consider the case of Bud, a four-year-old who wants a second helping of ice cream. He tearfully cuddles up to his grandfather. Bud is acting on the implicit theory that grandparents will be more sympathetic and lenient than parents with respect to such "plights." His hypothesis might be: "I have a better chance of getting that ice cream if I play on grandpa's sympathy." He tests this prediction by acting sad with his grandfather. If grandpa gets the ice cream for Bud, the hypothesis is confirmed, and the theory receives some support. In the future, Bud will be more confident in using the theory. If grandpa is not the "softy" his grandson thought he was, the hypothesis is not supported. In this case, Bud may very well try a new theory the next time ice cream is served.

People are constantly involved in prediction and control of events in their lives. This observation led Kelly to view people *as if they were scientists.* Like scientists, each of us has theories about the world. These theories guide our behavior in dealing with people and events. Kelly assumes that just as events in the real world actually exist, people's theories about them also exist. Thus, these theories can also be studied scientifically.

PERSONAL CONSTRUCTS: THE BASIC UNITS OF PERSONALITY

Kelly (1955) suggests that we view the world through *transparent patterns* or *templets.* We create these patterns and then attempt to fit them over the realities of which the world is composed. Kelly calls these templets

constructs. A construct is a representation or interpretation of an event; it is a way of viewing something. Constructs are not abstracted from existing realities; rather, they are imposed *on* real events. *A construct comes from the person, not from the event it is being used to interpret.*

Examples of constructs include: just versus unjust, stable versus changing, liberal versus conservative, healthy versus sick, flexible versus dogmatic, warm versus aloof, and friendly versus hostile. Kellian constructs always take the form of one characteristic *versus* another (usually opposite) characteristic. We will discuss the bipolar nature of constructs later.

Everyone has a unique set of *personal constructs*. Constructs often seem to be the same for many different people when they are described verbally. This is because we cannot express subtle nuances of meaning through language. For example, most of us use a construct that we would label *good versus bad*. But this construct has a slightly different meaning for each person. Thus, it is necessary to understand a person's constructs from his or her unique perspective. This is the crux of the phenomenological strategy.

Constructs are used to **construe,** or place an interpretation or meaning on, events. Kelly uses the term **event** for anything going on in a person's life. In construing an event, a person predicts that a particular construct will adequately fit the event. Then the person tests this hypothesis by behaving as the construct dictates. Bud, our four-year-old ice cream lover, acted in accord with his construct *sympathetic versus unsympathetic*. He predicted that his grandpa would be sympathetic to a request for more ice cream; he then acted on the prediction to test its validity.

Constructs that predict events well are retained; those that fail to predict events adequately are revised or discarded. In this way, we develop and amend our system of personal constructs. The validity of a construct is measured by its **predictive efficiency.** The more successful a construct is in anticipating events, the greater is its predictive efficiency.

We continually change our constructs. It is inevitable that our constructs sometimes fail to anticipate future events. This makes revision necessary if we are to construe the world with high predictive efficiency. Constructs involving events in the near future are revised more often. That is because feedback concerning their ability to anticipate is quickly obtained.

No event is associated with any particular construct. According to constructive alternativism, any event can be viewed from a variety of different perspectives. As we change the constructs we use to construe an event, our behavior changes. This is strikingly illustrated by the case of a psychiatric patient we will call Sally (Neale, 1968). Sally's behavior was among the most deviant on the ward. Her speech was unintelligible. She had extremely poor personal habits. Her behavior in the presence of other patients and visitors was ludicrous. And Sally was prone to violent outbursts. One day the aides dressed Sally in an attractive outfit, including stockings, high heels, and lipstick. They also took her to the beauty parlor to have her hair done. When Sally returned to the ward several hours later, she no longer behaved in the bizarre ways that had been her trademark. Yet, she was still a patient in a psychiatric hospital. In every other respect, her *circumstances* were the same. It seemed, however, that she had changed the *way she construed herself* (e.g., not as a "crazy"), if only temporarily. Her new construct resulted in new behavior.

Properties of Constructs

Constructs differ on three important dimensions: their range of convenience, their focus of convenience, and their degree of permeability.

Range of Convenience

The **range of convenience** of a construct refers to the set of events for which the construct is applicable. Each of our constructs is useful for construing a particular set of events. The range of convenience puts a limit on the usefulness of the construct. The construct *religious versus not religious*, for example, is applicable to construing a variety of human endeavors, but it is hardly applicable for predicting the behavior of one's pets. Applying a construct outside of its range of convenience lowers its predictive efficiency. The construct *religious versus not religious* will not likely predict whether Daphne the dog will sit on command.

All constructs have a limited range of convenience. But the breadth of the range may vary substantially from one construct to another. The construct *good versus bad* ordinarily has a wider range of convenience than *brave versus cowardly* because the former can be used to construe a larger range of events than the latter.

Focus of Convenience

Each construct also has a **focus of convenience.** This is the maximally predictive point in the construct's range of convenience. For example, the focus of convenience of *religious versus not religious* might be the customs and ceremonies of a church. Cheating on an exam could be construed as *not religious;* but it would be more efficiently construed by the construct *honest versus dishonest*. Cheating lies within the *range* of convenience of both constructs, but it is the *focus* of convenience of only the latter construct.

Permeability

Permeability is the degree that a given construct can be used to construe new events. The more open the construct, the more permeable it is. A relatively permeable construct can be used to construe many new events;

357

this widens the construct's range of convenience. A relatively impermeable construct has already been used to construe most of the events in its range of convenience; therefore, it is relatively closed to construing new experiences. One person's construct of *good versus bad symphonic music* might be sufficiently permeable to account for any new piece of music heard. For example, on hearing music produced by a Moog synthesizer for the first time, the person could construe it as either *good* or *bad*. Another person's construct of *good versus bad symphonic music* might be impermeable to any sounds other than those made by traditional orchestral instruments; therefore, it could not be used to construe Moog-synthesized music.

There are relative degrees of permeability; constructs range from those that very easily construe new events to those that virtually exclude any new event. However, permeability is relevant only to events in the range of convenience of the construct. By definition, a construct is impermeable to any event outside its range of convenience. For instance, the range of convenience of *intelligent versus stupid* includes animals, ideas, and perhaps computers. Thus, the construct is potentially permeable to animals, ideas, and computers. However, rocks and trees are not in the construct's range of convenience, which means that it is impermeable to rocks and trees.

THE FUNDAMENTAL POSTULATE AND ITS COROLLARIES

The theory of personal constructs is presented as a single basic postulate and eleven corollaries describing the details of the theory.[1] Like many other personality theorists, Kelly uses some common terms in unique ways. But the terms are rich in meaning and therefore worth "translating."

The Fundamental Postulate

"A person's processes are psychologically channelized by the ways in which he anticipates events" (Kelly, 1955, p. 46). The major point of the Fundamental Postulate is that psychological processes, including personality, are aimed at predicting events. Kelly thereby specifies the direction of human behavior. He says nothing about what energizes behavior toward

---

[1] We will discuss all but the Fragmentation Corollary which states: "A person may successively employ a variety of construction subsystems which are inferentially incompatible with each other" (Kelly, 1955, p. 83).

anticipation of events, however, because he sees humans as active organisms. They do not need to be pushed by needs or drives, or pulled by incentives. The Fundamental Postulate also shows that Kelly's theory is concerned with active "processes" rather than static personality structures.

The Construction Corollary

"A person anticipates events by construing their replications" (Kelly, 1955, p. 50). We make predictions about events by viewing them in terms of *recurrent themes* (replications). These are characteristics of events that are relatively stable over time and circumstances. No two events are ever exactly the same. But our construction (interpretation) of events can be the same (Kelly, 1970). If this were not so, our daily lives would be chaotic; we would have no basis for predicting even the most minor events. We would have to "start from scratch" in dealing with hundreds of events each day. For example, each class a student attends is (hopefully) different; but there are enough similarities, such as the general roles played by students and teacher, so that students can predict what will happen in each new class and thus know how to act.

Construing Similarities and Differences

To construe events, we must identify themes that are both similar and different. Differences provide the contrast necessary to comprehend any concept. A "delicious meal," "dry wine," and "stimulating companion" mean something to us only because we can refer to contrasts: "tasteless meal," "sweet wine," and "boring companion." Without the contrasts, we could enjoy the meal, wine, and companion, but we would not be able to refer to them as "delicious," "dry," and "stimulating." As another illustration of this important point, the next time you are sick, think about how your temporary pain and discomfort is made all the worse by knowing how you feel when you are well.

The contrast may only be implicit when we use a construct. But it must be capable of being made explicit. The contrast is necessary to define the construct. Consider the constructs *happy versus sad* and *good versus bad* in relation to *happy versus euphoric* and *good versus non-Christian*. It is not enough to state one of the construct's poles, as the examples demonstrate. This is why Kellian constructs always have two poles—they are *bipolar*.

Labeling Constructs

To communicate our constructs to others, we use verbal labels. These labels should not be confused with the constructs themselves. Two constructs with the same label are not necessarily identical. Furthermore, all of us have many nonverbal constructs to which verbal labels are not or cannot be applied. This may be because the constructs are not well specified. More often, it is due to the lack of precision of our language or our ineptitude in using language. Children's constructs are frequently preverbal, though they may be as predictively efficient as those of adults.

The Individuality Corollary

"Persons differ from each other in their construction of events" (Kelly, 1955, p. 55). Each person has a unique set of personal constructs. No two people will have exactly the same interpretation of an event. (See Figure 16–1.) All qualities, not just beauty, are in the eyes of the beholder. One consequence of contruing events differently is that we often disagree about "the way things are." For example, "what is popularly called the 'generation gap'—the fundamental differences of viewpoint between parents and their offspring—[is] a situation which, in Kelly's theory, might more properly be labeled a 'personal construct gap'" (Hjelle & Ziegler, 1981, p. 333).

FIGURE 16–1
The same life events are viewed somewhat differently by different persons because they are perceived through unique individual constructs which are analogous to different colored glasses.

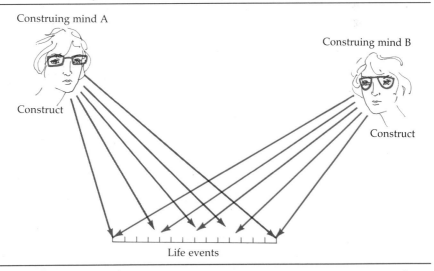

Source: Adapted from "The Psychology of Personal Constructs" by George A. Kelly, 1973, in J. Rychlak (Ed.), *Introduction to Personality and Psychotherapy*, Boston: Houghton Mifflin.

The Dichotomy Corollary

"A person's construct system is composed of a finite number of dichotomous constructs" (Kelly, 1955, p. 59). Personal constructs are *bipolar* and *dichotomous*. And we have a limited number of constructs.

A construct always indicates how some events are both similar to and different from other events. Thus, to construe an event, at least three things are needed: (1) the event being construed; (2) a second event that is similar to it (i.e., that it replicates); and (3) a third event that is different from the first two. For example, Ernest dives into a swimming pool and screams, "It's freezing." To construe the water as *freezing*, Ernest must be comparing it to water he previously construed as *freezing.* He also must be contrasting it to water that was some other temperature, such as *warm.* His concept of *freezing* would have no meaning without both the comparison (replication) and the contrast. If he had only been in water that he considered *freezing*, then he could not make any comparison with *warm* water. In that case, Ernest could only have used a construct such as *water versus not water.*

One pole of a construct specifies similarity; the other specifies difference. The **emergent pole** designates similarity; it is used directly or explicitly to construe an event. The **implicit pole** designates difference; it is used indirectly as a contrast. In the previous example, *freezing* was the emergent pole and *warm* was the implicit pole of *freezing versus warm.* Which pole is emergent and which is implicit depends on the situation. If Ernest was a penguin he might have considered the water *warm.* Then the poles would be reversed. *Warm* would be the emergent pole and *freezing* the implicit pole.

The poles of a construct are *discrete and mutually exclusive.* A construct is *not* a continuum—but it is bipolar. If an event is in a construct's range of convenience, then it must be construed at *either* one pole *or* the other—not somewhere in between.

Constructs are composed of mutually exclusive alternatives. Kelly (1955) explains how they can be used relatively: "Dichotomous constructs can be built into scales, the scales representing superordinate constructs which are further abstractions of the separate scalar values. Thus, *more grayness versus less grayness* is a further abstraction of the construct *black versus white"* (p. 66).

The implicit pole of a construct consists only of contrasting events. It does *not*, as in classical logic, include irrelevant events as well. In other words, events that are placed at the implicit pole must be in the construct's range of convenience. Suppose one were using the construct *friendly versus unfriendly. Friendly* is the emergent pole. The implicit pole *unfriendly* could be used to construe people, pets, and some places (e.g., a friendly atmosphere). But it would not make sense to use it to construe luggage, linen, or lollipops; the latter are not within the range of convenience of the construct.

The Range Corollary

"A construct is convenient for the anticipation of a finite range of events only" (Kelly, 1955, p. 68). A construct's range of convenience is finite. This implies that people may encounter events they are not able to construe. We cannot construe an event because either (1) we have no construct to interpret the event, or (2) our existing constructs are too impermeable to admit the new event.

Anxiety

When we cannot construe an event, we experience anxiety. Anxiety typically includes *vague* feelings of danger and helplessness. We cannot "put our finger" on why we feel that way. Kelly's definition of **anxiety** explains these feelings. They are a consequence of not being able to interpret (construe) an event. We must be able to construe an event before we can behave with respect to it. From Kelly's perspective, psychotherapy for abnormal anxiety would help the client (1) develop new constructs that will successfully predict the troublesome events or (2) modify existing constructs so that they are more permeable and therefore capable of construing the new events.

The Organization Corollary

"Each person characteristically evolves, for his convenience in anticipating events, a construct system embracing ordinal relationships between constructs" (Kelly, 1955, p. 56). For Kelly, constructs are the units of personality. The structure of personality is the relation of constructs to one another. People differ not only because they use different constructs, but also because their constructs are organized in different ways. Two people can have similar personal constructs yet have extremely different personalities because their constructs are ordered differently.

Constructs are arranged in a *hierarchical structure.* Thus, most constructs are both subordinate to some constructs and superordinate to others. This allows us to move from one construct to another in an orderly fashion and to resolve conflicts and inconsistencies among constructs. Consider the relationships among three of David's constructs depicted in Figure 16–2. The construct *loving versus unloving* is superordinate to the constructs *giving versus selfish* and *pleasant versus unpleasant,* which are on the same level. David has planned to spend the day at the beach with his friends. He is faced with the dilemma of deciding whether to take along his younger brother. If he takes his brother, David would construe himself as *giving* but the day at the beach as *unpleasant.* If he chooses not to take his brother, David would construe himself as *selfish* but the day as *pleasant.* Thus, using the two

FIGURE 16–2
An example of a hierarchical structure among three personal constructs

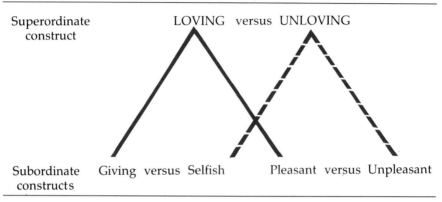

Superordinate construct — LOVING versus UNLOVING

Subordinate constructs — Giving versus Selfish   Pleasant versus Unpleasant

subordinate constructs, David is in a no-win situation. To resolve this conflict, David uses the superordinate construct *loving versus unloving* to construe taking his brother to the beach. Now David can view his magnanimous act as both *giving* and *pleasant* because both of these poles are subsumed under *loving*.

A **construct system** is all of a person's constructs in a particular hierarchical order. It is generally more permanent than individual constructs. But it can change. We modify our construct systems when they fail to accurately predict events. The usefulness of a construct system, like a construct, is judged by its predictive efficiency.

The Choice Corollary

"A person chooses for himself that alternative in a dichotomized construct through which he anticipates the greater possibility for extension and definition of his system" (Kelly, 1955, p. 64). To predict a person's behavior, we must know: (1) the construct the person will use and (2) which is the emergent pole. The person chooses as the emergent pole—used to directly construe the event—the pole that will result in greater predictive efficiency. The predictive efficiency of a construct can be enhanced by defining it more precisely and by extending its range of convenience to new events.

Definition involves choosing the pole of the construct that has been more accurate in anticipating events in the past. It therefore has the higher probability of predicting the present event. If the prediction is accurate, the construct becomes more precise (or more defined) because it has successfully predicted another event.

Extension involves choosing the alternative that is more likely to expand or extend the construct—the one that will increase its range of convenience. In extension, the construct is used either to anticipate a new event or to anticipate a familiar event in a new way. This makes extension riskier than definition, but it also has a greater payoff. If the prediction is correct, the construct becomes more comprehensive. Definition can be thought of as a relatively safe wager with a modest payoff; extension is a riskier bet with a more substantial payoff.

Kelly (1955) spoke of the difference between definition and extension as being between security and adventure. "One may anticipate events by trying to become more and more certain about fewer and fewer things [definition] or by trying to become vaguely aware of more and more things on the misty horizon [extension]" (p. 67).

The difference between definition and extension can be seen with respect to Linda's use of the construct *need versus want*. Linda uses this construct whenever she must decide whether to spend money. For Linda, *need* usually is the emergent pole. (This choice is consistent with her parents' conservative spending habits.) Linda tends to buy items and services she considers necessities; she avoids spending money on things that would be nice to have but which she can do without. Suppose Linda were looking for a new car, and she narrowed down her choices to two cars of the same make. One is the standard model and the other the deluxe model. She would like the air-conditioning, four-way stereo, sun roof, and leather interior on the deluxe model. But she does not need those features. Let us assume that she successfully predicts the event; in this case, that means being satisfied with the car she bought. Deciding on the standard model would lead to definition of her construct, taking the safer wager in the sense that she is more likely to feel good about her choice. Picking the deluxe model would result in extension, making the bet that is riskier but also is more likely to expand her horizons (as she experiences the pleasure of being cool on a hot summer day, for instance).

Kelly (1955) does not specifically address the issue of when people choose to define and when to extend their construct systems. Several possible factors may influence the choice. First, the state of the construct being used may affect the choice. Some constructs may be "in need" of either extension or definition. For example, Vander Goot (1981) suggests that women today may find themselves in a liberation gap, the

> puzzling state that a woman finds herself in when she thinks that she has made up her mind about the status of women in general and then discovers that she does not yet understand what this means for her in particular. In Kelly's terms we might say that the system of new constructs which these women are assembling has extension (i.e., it is comprehensive) but it lacks definition (i.e., it is not explicit and clear-cut). (p. 261)

Second, the choice between extension and definition may be related to the circumstances surrounding the event to be anticipated. Extension may be more likely when prediction of future events has been relatively successful. Definition is likely when prediction has been relatively unsuccessful. For example, "a young man is more likely to consider asking the new girl in town for a date when he has been relatively successful in his experiences with the old ones" (Sechrest, 1963, p. 221).

A third hypothesis is that when people are anxious, they are more likely to define; when people are bored, they are more likely to elaborate (Sechrest, 1977).

Fourth, extending or defining constructs may be due to personal styles in construing. One person may typically prefer the conservative definition route. Another may choose the riskier extension approach in most situations. It is possible that the same person will prefer definition in construing some aspects of his or her life (e.g., finances) but choose extension in other areas (e.g., recreation).

As with any choice, deciding between definition and extension involves anticipating events to estimate the consequences of each alternative. This is done with a superordinate construct, *definition versus extension*, which, like all constructs, has personal meaning. In other words, each time we choose a pole of a construct, we implicitly refer to our *definition versus extension* construct to select the pole that will increase the construct's predictive efficiency.

The Experience Corollary: How a Construct System Changes

"A person's construct system varies as he successively construes the replications of events" (Kelly, 1955, p. 72). The Experience Corollary deals with the way our construct system changes. Like hypotheses derived from scientific theories, predictions made using constructs are tested to see how well they anticipate events. Constructs that make accurate predictions are typically retained in their existing form. Those that fail to predict accurately are modified or eliminated. Life is full of novel events that must be anticipated. Therefore, minor changes in our construct system occur all the time.

Kelly (1955) defines **experience** as successively construing events. Experience involves more than exposure to a succession of events. To gain experience, we must do something with events as they occur. Specifically, we must interpret them. Kelly says that if we passively observe events, we do not gain experience. To gain experience, we must actively construe and reconstrue events. Contrary to the usual meaning of the term, Kelly (1980) maintains that events do not change people; rather, people change themselves through experience—that is, by reconstruing events.

Kelly's view of experience has many intriguing implications. For one thing, we must be precise when we state the level of experience in a particular instance. A professor who gives the same lectures for ten years can only claim one year of teaching experience. Another implication of the Experience Corollary is that learning is an active process rather than a static outcome. Learning occurs as long as we are reconstruing events, as long as we are experiencing. For Kelly, learning is not a special process; instead, like motivation, it comes with the person, so to speak.

The Modulation Corollary: When a Construct System Changes

"The variation in a person's construction system is limited by the permeability of the constructs within whose range of convenience the variants lie" (Kelly, 1955, p. 77). The Modulation Corollary specifies when a construct system can change. First, constructs will change only if they are permeable. The more permeable a person's constructs, the greater the change possible within the construct system.

Second, we must be able to construe the change itself. Changing a construct or a group of constructs is an event. Thus, for the change to have any influence on our behavior, we must already have a superordinate construct that can construe the change. We need a construct that can make sense of the change. Kelly (1955) provides the following illustration:

> Suppose a person starts out with a construct of *fear versus domination* and shifts to a construct of *respect versus contempt*. Whereas once he divided his acquaintances between those he was afraid of and those whom he could dominate, he may, as he grows more mature, divide his acquaintances between those whom he respects and those whom he holds in contempt. But, in order for him to make this shift, he needs another construct, within whose range of convenience . . . *fear versus domination* . . . lies and which is sufficiently permeable to admit new ideas of *respect versus contempt* . . . [for example,] *maturity versus childishness.* (pp. 81–82)

Emotion: Awareness of Construct Change

Kelly wanted to formulate a comprehensive theory of personality, one that would encompass all of human behavior. His theory of personal constructs is therefore very abstract. Rather than viewing thoughts, actions, and feelings as separate processes, Kelly construes them in the same psychological terms.

Emotions are defined in personal construct theory as *awareness of change or the need for change in one's construct system*. The change (1) may be comprehensive (major) or incidental (minor), (2) may involve validation (i.e., successful prediction) or invalidation (i.e., unsuccessful prediction) of constructs, and (3) may occur in core role constructs (i.e., constructs central to the person) or in noncore role constructs (i.e., constructs peripheral to the person) (McCoy, 1981). Table 16–1 provides examples of common emotions defined according to personal construct theory.

The Commonality Corollary

"To the extent that one person employs a construction of experience which is similar to that employed by another, his processes are psychologically similar to those of the other person" (Kelly, 1970, p. 20). Differences between people are due to differences in how they construe events. It follows that

TABLE 16–1
Emotions as defined by personal construct theory

Threat*	Awareness of imminent comprehensive change in one's core role structure
Fear*	Awareness of imminent incidental change in one's core role structure
Bewilderment	Awareness of imminent comprehensive change in one's non-core role structure
Doubt	Awareness of imminent incidental change in one's noncore role structure
Love	Awareness of validation of one's core role structure
Happiness	Awareness of validation of part of one's core role structure
Satisfaction	Awareness of validation of part of one's noncore role structure
Complacency	Awareness of validation of a small part of one's noncore role structure
Sadness	Awareness of the invalidation of implications of a part or all of one's core role structure
Guilt*	Awareness of deviating from one's core role structure
Self-confidence	Awareness of one's self-concept fitting with one's core role structure
Shame	Awareness of one's self-concept deviating from another person's construing of one's role
Contempt (Disgust)	Awareness that a core role of another person is comprehensively different from one's own and/or does not meet norms of social expectation
Anxiety*	Awareness that events lie outside the range of convenience of one's constructs
Contentment	Awareness that events lie within the range of convenience of one's constructs
Surprise	Sudden awareness of a need to construe an event
Anger	Awareness of invalidation of one's constructs which leads to hostility

* These definitions are Kelly's (1955); the others are derived from his theory.

Source: Adapted from "A Reconstruction of Emotion" by M. M. McCoy, 1977, in D. Bannister (Ed.), *New Perspectives in Personal Construct Theory,* London: Academic Press.

similarity between people is due to similarity in construing events. Two people are likely to behave similarly to the extent that they construe events in similar ways. Kelly (1955) emphasizes

> that we have not said that if one person has experienced the same events as another he will duplicate the other's psychological processes. . . . One of the advantages of this position is that it does not require us to assume that it would take identical events in the lives of two people to make them act alike. Two people can act alike even if they have each been exposed to quite different . . . [external] stimuli. It is in the similarity in the construction of events that we find the basis for similar action, not in the identity of the events themselves. (pp. 90–91)

Take the example of Mary and Steve trying to decide whether to eat at a Mexican restaurant. They look at the menu in the window. Mary notices the reasonable prices. Steve sees that they have some of his favorite dishes. Independently, each decides to have dinner in the restaurant. Their decisions were made by construing two separate events (i.e., menu prices and menu selection). They construe them similarly (i.e., worth eating there). The result is the same behavior (i.e., deciding to eat there).

A *culture* generally refers to a group of people who exhibit similar behaviors that are considered the result of similarities in upbringing and environment. Kelly (1955) adds to this concept: "People belong to the same cultural group, not merely because they behave alike, nor because they expect the same things of others, but especially because they construe their experience in the same way" (p. 94).

The Sociality Corollary

"To the extent that one person construes the construction processes of another, he may play a role in a social process involving the other person" (Kelly, 1955, p. 95). The Sociality Corollary sets forth the basic requirement for an interpersonal relationship. For Kelly, *playing a role* in relation to another person involves construing how the other person views events. The role player must attempt to understand part of the other's construct system. Specifically, the role player is interested in how the other person views the role being played. Suppose a woman wants to play the role of "student" in relation to her professor. She must predict how the teacher construes "student" and then act accordingly. For example, if the student thinks her teacher considers asking a lot of questions part of the student role, she will presumably ask questions.

For Kelly, it is critical that the role player *attempts* to infer the other's viewpoint. The role player need not necessarily be successful. Of course, the more accurately the role player understands the other's constructs, the more effective the role player will be in enacting the role. The role player need not construe events as the other person does; the role player must only understand the other's outlook (constructs). Furthermore, people need not have the same constructs to be able to subsume the other's constructs within their own systems.

An interpersonal relationship requires that at least one person construes the other's perspective. That is, one person plays a role with respect to the other person. Role playing need not be reciprocal. Nonetheless, an optimal relationship usually involves mutual understanding. This understanding may be limited in scope, as with a student and a teacher. Or it may be extremely broad, covering most of each person's construct system, as in a good marriage (e.g., Neimeyer & Hudson, 1985).

Guilt

Most of the roles we play in our lives are peripheral in that they are not very important to us in the long run; they are **noncore roles.** For instance, we often assume the role of "customer." With the exception of professional buyers, how well we play that role generally makes little difference. Each of us plays a few roles that are central to our lives. These roles are at the core of our identity. They are essential to our self-concept. Kelly called these **core roles.** How well we perform them does have important consequences.

When people realize they are straying from one of their core roles, they experience **guilt.** Think about times that you have felt guilty. What made you feel guilty? Your answer is apt to be that you were doing something "wrong." "Wrong behavior" may be viewed as contrary to expectations (yours or others') about how you should act. We experience guilt when we stray from expectations for performing our core roles. A young woman considers herself a "good daughter." She experiences guilt when she does not write to her parents or when she brings home a male friend they will not approve of. These behaviors deviate from her parents' expectations about how a "good daughter" should act.

Kelly's definitions of concepts such as guilt and anxiety differ markedly from usual definitions. One characteristic that makes them different is that they are independent of value judgments. Kelly defines guilt in terms of deviation from a core role. This contrasts sharply with conventional views of guilt involving evil and punishment. The latter are absolute, value-laden concepts. Absence of evaluation is one of the hallmarks of the phenomenological strategy. What is more, Kelly's unique definitions exemplify the principle of constructive alternativism that is the essence of the strategy. We may assume that for Kelly the definitions represent his most efficient ways of predicting behavior.

DEMONSTRATION 16–1

GUILT IS ALL IN THE ROLE OF THE BEHAVER

There are two purposes of this Demonstration. First, it should enhance your understanding and appreciation of the usefulness of Kelly's definition of *guilt*. Second, it may help you reconstrue your view of guilt and perhaps deal with your feelings of guilt somewhat differently (Spiegler, 1985).

1. *Think about instances in the recent past when you have felt guilty and about which you still feel guilty.* Write a brief description of three of these.

2. Consider the first description and answer the question, *"What important role that I was expected to play in the situation did I not play (or did I play poorly)?"* The expectations may have come from others or from yourself (although the former is more likely). Write down the role. (Examples of roles would be "loyal friend," "competent worker," and "stimulating conversationalist.")

3. Ask yourself the question, *"Was it important for me to be playing that role at the time?"* You should answer this question independently of the expectations you or others had regarding the appropriateness of the role.

If your answer is "yes," continue to Step 4.

If your answer to the question is "no," then you should think about the fact that your guilt is unwarranted, according to Kelly's definition. *Guilt* is the awareness that you are not performing a role that is important to you. Thus, if the role is not important to you, perhaps you have no reason to feel guilty. (Suppose you believe that "voter" is an expected role, but you do not consider it an important role for you. In this case, there is no reason for you to feel guilty if you do not vote in an election.) Having thought about this issue, return to Step 2 and examine the remaining situation(s) you described in Step 1.

4. Ask yourself the question, *"Approximately what proportion (or percent) of the time do I play the role satisfactorily (when, of course, it is appropriate to be playing the role)?"* For instance, you might conclude that about 80 percent of the time when *you are in class,* you play the role of "attentive student."

If you believe that the proportion is relatively high, then you should think about the implications of this fact. If you often play the role satisfactorily, then you may be doing as well as you can (or want to) and still remain a fallible human being. No one fully plays a role 100 percent of the time that the role is appropriate. If you are playing the role most of the time, that may be perfectly acceptable.

If you believe that the proportion is relatively low, then you can use this as worthwhile feedback and work at performing the role more when it is expected.

5. Return to Step 2 for the remaining situation(s) you described in Step 1.

THE ASSESSMENT OF PERSONAL CONSTRUCTS

Personal constructs determine behavior. But observing behavior may not yield valid information about how people construe the relevant events. People may behave quite similarly although they construe events in very different ways. Take the example of three men who play golf together on Saturday mornings. One sees golf as a competitive sport. Each week, he looks forward to improving his score and beating his two opponents. For the second man, the game of golf is more a means of socializing than an athletic event. The third man construes Saturday morning golf as an opportunity to be outdoors and get some exercise. It would be difficult to accurately predict each man's construction of the events from observing his behavior.

If our interest were only in predicting what each man in the example would be doing next Saturday morning, merely observing his behavior might serve us well. However, knowing how each man construes the Saturday golf game may also let us predict how he would behave in other situations. For instance, we might predict that the first man would be competitive in his work as well as on the golf course if he uses the same construct for work and golf.

Aside from observing behavior, we can learn about someone's constructs by asking about them. But constructs cannot always be communicated in words. Even when they can be, the meanings of the words are often too broad to give us much specific information. Further, people are usually not accustomed to communicating their personal constructs. So direct questions may not be effective in eliciting contructs.

The Role Construct Repertory Test (Rep Test)

Kelly devised a technique to assess personal constructs that surmounts some of the problems associated with behavioral observation and direct inquiry. The **Role Construct Repertory Test (Rep Test)** elicits the constructs we use to construe important people in our lives. A **role construct** is a construct someone uses to understand another's views (i.e., another's constructs). To elicit role constructs, research subjects or therapy clients compare and contrast important people in their lives. The process is called **sorting.**

In the *grid form* of the Rep Test a grid, or matrix, is constructed. Significant people in the subject's life, called *figures,* are listed on one axis. The constructs used to construe them are listed on the other axis. Figure 16–3 is an abbreviated version. We will use it to illustrate how the technique works. The following steps are involved in completing the grid.

1. First, the subject provides the name of a person to fit each of the role descriptions at the top of the grid.
2. Next, the subject considers the three people designated by the circles in the boxes under the names in the first sort (in Figure 16–3 these are Terry, Stephen, and Harry). The subject decides in what important way two of the people are alike and different from the third. An "X" is placed under the names of the two alike people (Stephen and Harry) and the characteristic that makes them alike becomes the emergent pole of the construct (*organized*). The characteristic that makes the third person (Terry) different becomes the implicit pole of the construct (*spontaneous*).
3. Next, the subject considers the remaining people (i.e., those not compared and contrasted in the sort) and places an "X" under the names of those persons who also would be described by the emergent pole (Anne and Martin).
4. Steps 2 and 3 are repeated for each of the sorts.

FIGURE 16–3
Example of part of a completed grid form of the Rep Test

Sort No.	1. Self Al	2. Mother Anne	3. Spouse Terry	4. Admired person Martin	5. Happy person Barbara	6. Successful person Stephen	7. Ethical person Harry	(Constructs) (Similar) Emergent Pole	 (Different) Implicit Pole
1		X	○	X		⊗	⊗	Organized	Spontaneous
2	○	⊗	⊗				X	Feminine	Masculine
3		X		⊗	○	X	⊗	Rigid	Flexible
4	⊗	○			⊗	X		Intellectual	Emotional

The Rep Test elicits constructs subjects use to construe important people in their lives. The pattern of "Xs" indicates the similarity of the constructs. For example, independent of the verbal labels assigned to the constructs (i.e., the emergent and implicit poles), constructs with identical patterns are assumed to be equivalent. (In Figure 16–3, *organized versus spontaneous* is equivalent to *rigid versus flexible*.) The grid form is frequently used in personal construct research (e.g., Fransella & Bannister, 1977; Rathod, 1981).

DEMONSTRATION 16–2

THE ROLE CONSTRUCT REPERTORY TEST

This Demonstration will allow you to explore your own personal constructs using the grid form of the Rep Test.

DESIGNATING FIGURES

Figure 16–4 is a grid form. First, draw on a large sheet of paper the grid form exactly as it appears in Figure 16–4. Note that each row of the grid has three circles; check to be sure that you have placed the circles for each row in the correct columns.

Table 16–2 on page 374 contains 15 role definitions. Read each definition carefully and then write, in the appropriate diagonal space at the top of your grid form, the first name of the person who best fits that role in your life. If you cannot remember the name of the person, put down a word or brief phrase that will bring the person to mind. Do *not* repeat any names; if some person has already been listed, simply make a second choice.

Next to the word *Self* write your own name. Then next to the word *Mother* put your mother's name (or the name of the person who has played the part of a mother in your life). Continue until all 15 roles have been designated with the name of a specific individual.

SORTING FIGURES

Now look at Sort No. 1, which is the first row of the grid form. Note that there are circles in the squares under columns 9, 10, and 12. These circles designate the three people you are to consider in Sort No. 1 (i.e., Rejecting Person, Pitied Person, and Attractive Person). Think about the three people you have designated for these roles. Decide how *two of them are alike* in some important way that *differentiates them from the third person*. When you have decided the most important way in which two of the people are alike but different from the third person, put an "X" in each of the two circles that correspond to the two people who are alike. Do *not* place any mark in the third circle.

Next, in the column marked *Emergent Pole,* write a word or short phrase that tells how the two people are alike. Then, in the column marked *Implicit Pole,* write a word or short phrase that explains the way in which the third person is different from the other two.

Finally, consider each of the remaining 12 people. Which of them also have the characteristic you have designated as the emergent pole? Place an "X" in the square corresponding to the name of each of the other people who has this characteristic.

When you have finished the procedures outlined above for Sort

FIGURE 16–4
Sample grid form of the Rep Test for Demonstration 16–2

Role / Figure — Sort No.	1. Self	2. Mother	3. Father	4. Brother	5. Sister	6. Spouse	7. Pal	8. Ex-Pal	9. Rejecting Person	10. Pitied Person	11. Threatening Person	12. Attractive Person	13. Accepted Teacher	14. Rejected Teacher	15. Happy Person	(Similar) Emergent Pole	(Different) Implicit Pole
1									○	○		○					
2		○	○	○													
3					○								○		○		
4		○						○					○				
5	○									○		○					
6					○				○					○			
7				○				○			○						
8						○					○				○		
9							○	○				○					
10	○			○	○												
11		○	○								○						
12							○			○					○		
13	○					○	○										
14	○	○	○														
15				○					○					○			

No. 1, begin again with Sort No. 2. The process should be repeated for each of the 15 sorts. The steps are summarized below.

1. Consider the three people who are designated by circles under their names. Decide how two of them are alike in an important way, and different from the third.

2. Put an "X" in the circles corresponding to the names of the two people who are alike and leave the remaining circle blank.

3. In the *Emergent Pole* column, write a brief description of the way in which the two people are *alike*.

4. In the *Implicit Pole* column, write a brief description of the way in which the third person is *different* from the two who are alike.

5. Consider the remaining 12 persons and place an "X" in the squares corresponding to those who can also be characterized by the description in the *Emergent Pole* column.

TABLE 16–2
Definition of roles for Demonstration 16–2

1. *Self:* Yourself.
2. *Mother:* Your mother or the person who has played the part in your life.
3. *Father:* Your father or the person who has played the part in your life.
4. *Brother:* Your brother who is nearest your own age or, if you do not have a brother, a boy near your own age who has been most like a brother to you.
5. *Sister:* Your sister who is nearest your own age or, if you do not have a sister, a girl near your own age who has been most like a sister to you.
6. *Spouse:* Your wife (or husband) or, if you are not married, your closest present girlfriend or boyfriend.
7. *Pal:* Your closest present friend of the same sex as yourself.
8. *Ex-pal:* A person of the same sex as yourself whom you once thought was a close friend but in whom you were badly disappointed later.
9. *Rejecting person:* A person with whom you have been associated who, for some unexplained reason, appeared to dislike you.
10. *Pitied person:* The person whom you would most like to help or for whom you feel most sorry.
11. *Threatening person:* The person who threatens you the most or the person who makes you feel the most uncomfortable.
12. *Attractive person:* A person whom you have recently met whom you would like to know better.
13. *Accepted teacher:* The teacher who influenced you most.
14. *Rejected teacher:* The teacher whose point of view you have found most objectionable.
15. *Happy person:* The happiest person whom you know personally.

Source: From *The Psychology of Personal Constructs* by G. A. Kelly, 1955, New York: W. W. Norton.

DISCUSSION

By the time you have completed the Demonstration Rep Test, a number of its characteristics should be apparent. Think about how the Rep Test has elicited your constructs. What is the range of convenience of the constructs? Which of your constructs are relatively permeable, and which are relatively impermeable? What relation do these constructs have with one another? Do the sorts compare people randomly, or is there a rationale behind each sort? Finally, you should think about what you have learned from doing the Rep Test about the way you construe important people in your life.

The particular sorts that the examiner asks the subject or client to make will depend upon the purpose of the assessment procedure. Several of the sorts used in the Demonstration are briefly described below (Kelly, 1955, pp. 275–76).

> *Valency sort.* [Sort No. 1] The client is asked to compare and contrast a person whose rejection of him he cannot quite understand, a person whom he thinks needs him, and a person whom he does not really know well but whom he thinks he would like to know better. All three of these are somewhat phantom figures, and one may expect that in interpreting them the client relies heavily upon projected attitudes.
>
> *Sister sort.* [Sort No. 3] This is an invitation to construe a Sister figure. It provides an opportunity to see the Sister as like the Accepted Teacher and in contrast to the Happy Person, like the Happy Person and in contrast to the Accepted Teacher, or in contrast to both of them.
>
> *Need sort.* [Sort No. 5] The Self is compared and contrasted with the Pitied Person and the Attractive Person. This gives the clinician an opportunity to study the relative subjective and objective reference which the client gives to personal needs.
>
> *Threat sort.* [Sort No. 7] The client has an opportunity to construe threat in the context of the Brother, Ex-Pal, and Threatening Person.

Several limitations of the Rep Test should be noted. First, the constructs elicited are used to construe the behavior of others. If we want to predict the behavior of the person taking the test, we must find out if these constructs also apply to his or her own behavior.

Second, the Rep Test requires that constructs be set down in words. But it may not be possible to verbalize some constructs. Therefore, we cannot assume that the constructs elicited represent all, or even the most important, constructs the person uses to construe individuals in her or his life.

Third, even when people make their constructs explicit, we cannot assume that the labels refer to accepted meanings. Constructs such as *successful versus unsuccessful, attractive versus unattractive,* and *difficult versus easy* have highly personal meanings. It is critical to examine how the person uses constructs. The pattern of "Xs" in the grid form is an indication.

Applications of Personal Construct Theory

Personal construct theory has been applied to a wide variety of topics in psychology and other fields. Examples include: problems of mentally handicapped children (McConachie, 1983, 1985); marital relationships and marital therapy (McCoy, 1980; Neimeyer & Hudson, 1985); suicide (Kelly, 1961; Stephan & Linder, 1985); juvenile delinquency (e.g., D. Kelly & Taylor, 1981; Miller & Treacher, 1981); psychology of death (Warren & Parry, 1981); student teaching (Diamond, 1985); experiential learning (Harri-Augstein, 1985); architecture and urban design (e.g., Honikman, 1976; Hudson, 1974); aesthetic judgment (O'Hare & Gordon, 1976; Rosenberg, 1977); and political events (DuPreez, 1977). As with most other theories of personality, psychotherapy is the major application of personal construct theory (e.g., Bannister, 1985; Landfield & Leitner, 1980).

Personality Change

Constructive alternativism, the philosophical basis of the theory of personal constructs, states that people can always reconstrue events. This means that people can always change their personalities (construct systems). Thus, personality change is part and parcel of personal construct theory.

Clients' Problems Construed by Personal Construct Theory

According to personal construct theory, abnormal or problem behavior, like all behavior, is caused by how people construe events. Specifically, individuals showing abnormal behavior have difficulty anticipating events in ways that lead to responding adaptively. This may take several forms: (1) not having appropriate constructs; (2) having constructs that are too impermeable; and (3) having constructs that are too permeable.

The Personal Construct Approach to Personality Change

The overall goal of personal construct psychotherapy is helping clients develop construct systems that allow them to follow their own natural development. This is similar to what Rogers advocates in client-centered therapy. Personality change is conceived of as a continuing *process*. It is not a terminal state of well-being or an optimal static construct system. The therapist sets the stage for the client's ongoing construct revision. The therapist directly and indirectly models the role of a scientist who formulates hypotheses about future events, tests them, and then revises the theory (constructs) that led to the hypotheses in order to increase its predictive efficiency.

Personal construct therapy changes personal constructs indirectly. Specifically, the client is encouraged to change *behaviors*. In turn, this results in reconstruing events and a modified construct system. New behaviors indicate that the client is viewing events differently. The basic principle of changing behavior to modify constructs is evident in Kelly's fixed-role therapy.

Fixed-Role Therapy

In **fixed-role therapy,** the client plays the role of a fictitious person whose behavior is consistent with a construct system that would be beneficial for the client. By playing this **fixed role,** the client behaves in ways that will modify his or her existing construct system.

The client writes a detailed self-description and completes a number of self-descriptive personality tests. Using this information and knowledge of the client's problems, several therapists write a **fixed-role sketch.** It describes the fixed role the client will enact. The fixed-role character is assigned a name. This makes the role more credible and facilitates reference to the fixed role as distinct from the client's customary role.

The following is a fixed-role sketch written for a male client who characterized himself as *passive, self-conscious, shy, occasionally interpersonally boring, and having difficulties with his sex-role identity.*

> Dick Benton is probably the only one of his kind in the world. People are always just a little puzzled as to how to take him. About the time they decide that he is a conventional person with the usual lines of thinking in religion, politics, school, etc., they discover that there is a new side to his personality that they have overlooked. At times, they think that he has a brand-new way of looking at life, a really *fresh* point of view. Some people go through an hour of conversation with him without being particularly impressed; while others find that afterwards they cannot get some of his unusual ideas out of their minds. Every once in a while he throws an idea

into a discussion like a bomb with a very slow fuse attached. People don't get it until later.

At times he deliberately makes himself socially inconspicuous. Those are the times when he wishes to listen and learn, rather than to stimulate other people's thinking. He is kindly and gentle with people, even on those occasions when he is challenging their thoughts with utterly new ideas. Because of this, people do not feel hurt by his ideas, even when they seem outrageous.

He is devoted to his wife and she is the only person who always seems to understand what is going on in his mind.

His work in college is somewhat spotted and the courses are interesting to him only to the extent that they give him a new outlook.

All in all, Dick Benton is a combination of gentleness and intellectual unpredictability. He likes to take people as they are but he likes to surprise them with new ideas. (Kelly, 1955, p. 421)

The fixed role deals with only a few of the client's constructs. It is aimed at creating minor personality changes. The fixed role often includes some of the client's positive attributes or strengths. This bolsters the client's most efficient constructs and makes the role easier and more realistic to enact.

Clients are not asked to *be* the person described in the fixed-role sketch or even to adopt the role as their own. They are merely told to play the role for a period of time (e.g., a week or two). However, clients often stop thinking of their new behaviors as a role. They begin to consider the role as their own, "natural" way of behaving. Clients often adjust their fixed role so that it is more consistent with their other behaviors and styles. Clients who can "get into" the fixed role begin to adopt the constructs that underlie the fixed-role behavior. This is the ultimate goal of fixed-role therapy.

Demonstration 16–3 will let you engage in a process analogous to fixed-role therapy and will give you an experiential view of the therapy.

DEMONSTRATION 16–3

FIXED-ROLE THERAPY: A DEVIL'S ADVOCATE ANALOG

Formal debating involves supporting arguments that are either for or against a particular statement. Debaters must be able to defend a position whether they agree with it or not, and frequently they are assigned to argue for a statement that is quite alien to their own views. This situation is analogous to what a client is asked to do in fixed-role therapy—namely, behave in a manner consistent with a *new* set of constructs. The following exercise will give you an idea of how the therapy works.

1. *Write down on index cards five statements about important social issues you* strongly agree *with.* Choose statements with which you strongly agree and in which you have a personal investment (e.g., as shown by your actions regarding them). Each statement should be written so that your position on the issue is clear. For example, if you believe that 18-year-olds should be allowed to drink legally, you should write a statement such as "The drinking age should be 18" and *not* just "drinking age" (which does not specify your position on the issue).

2. *Shuffle the cards and "blindly" pick one of them.*

3. *Write down as many arguments as you can think of* against *the statement you picked.* This may not be easy, particularly if you feel very positively about the statement. But keep trying to think of negative arguments. You may find yourself countering each of the negative arguments you wrote down; avoid this temptation. Instead, make every effort to assume a "devil's advocate" position and argue as strongly *against* the idea as you would argue for it.

An alternative way of doing this Demonstration is to actually debate the issue—arguing forcefully against it—with a friend who strongly agrees with the position (as you actually do).

To get a good "feel" for what a client experiences in fixed-role therapy, you should "blindly" select at least one more of the remaining issues you have written down for the Demonstration and list arguments against it. Keep in mind that, in contrast to a client in fixed-role therapy, you are only verbalizing, not acting, in accord with new constructs. And you are doing this for only a brief time, rather than consistently over the course of a week or more.

SUMMARY

1. Kelly's theory of personal constructs is based on constructive alternativism, the position that there are always different ways of viewing the world.

2. Kelly believes that all people behave as scientists in that they predict events by advancing theories about the nature of the events and then testing the theories.

3. Kelly calls the "theories" through which people view the world constructs. Each person has a unique set of personal constructs that is continually revised to enhance prediction. Constructs with high predictive efficiency tend to be more stable.

4. Each construct has a range of convenience that specifies the events to which it is applicable and a focus of convenience that indicates the events it predicts best. Constructs differ in their permeability which refers to how open they are to construing new experiences.

5. Kelly's theory is presented in the form of a basic postulate and eleven corollaries.

6. Kelly believes that human behavior is directed toward anticipating events. Personality consists of active processes rather than static structures.

7. We predict events by looking for the recurrent themes in them (how they are similar to other events we have encountered) and by considering how the event is both similar to and different than other events.

8. Kelly's constructs are bipolar (a similarity versus a difference) and dichotomous (not a continuum).

9. Anxiety results from not being able to construe an event (i.e., not having an appropriate construct).

10. Constructs are arranged in a hierarchial construct system.

11. The predictive efficiency of a construct can be enhanced by either defining or extending it.

12. Experience involves successively construing events, not just being exposed to events.

13. Emotions are an awareness of change or the need for change in one's construct system.

14. People behave similarly if they have similar constructs.

15. We play roles with respect to other people by trying to construe the constructs of others. We experience guilt when we deviate from a core role (one that is central to our identity).

16. The Role Construct Repertory Test is a major means of assessing one's constructs used to predict other people's behavior.

17. Personality change ultimately involves changing one's constructs, but this is done by changing behaviors that, in turn, result in viewing events differently. In fixed-role therapy, the client temporarily plays the role of a person who uses constructs that the client would benefit from using.

THE PHENOMENOLOGICAL STRATEGY

LIABILITIES

OVERVIEW

In the preceding four chapters we presented the phenomenological strategy in a generally favorable light. We presented it as phenomenological personality psychologists would. Now we turn a critical eye on the strategy. We will discuss five of the most frequently voiced liabilities of the phenomenological approach to personality. Most of the criticisms are germane to the strategy as a whole. Some are aimed mainly at one of the theoretical perspectives we have covered.

THE PHENOMENOLOGICAL STRATEGY IS LIMITED IN SCOPE

The phenomenological strategy is seriously restricted by two of its basic assumptions—namely that both conscious and present experience is sufficient for understanding personality.

The phenomenological strategy focuses on conscious experiences. In this emphasis, the strategy comes close to dealing with aspects of behavior that laypersons most often think should be the focus of psychological investigations—namely, personal, subjective experiences. Thus, the phenomenological strategy "makes sense intuitively." It is consistent with "commonsense" notions of personality. However, this focus excludes from study events of which a person is not immediately aware. Can behavior be predicted accurately if we know only what is in the person's immediate awareness? Many personality psychologists would say "no." Psychoanalysts, for instance, argue strongly that events which are unconscious, even permanently, form the core of personality and play a crucial role in determining behavior.

Can actions be explained without reference to past experiences? Again, many personality psychologists would say "no." They argue that knowledge of past experiences is essential for predicting and understanding someone's present behavior and personality. The phenomenological strategy is limited by almost totally ignoring the influence of the past. It focuses, instead, on immediate, subjective experiences. Obviously, this is an extreme point of view. It sharply contrasts, for example, with the traditional Freudian approach that relies almost totally on a person's past. Neither perspective seems viable. Each clearly disregards important variables in other time frames. Of course, phenomenologists real-ize that the past does affect a person's immediate experiences. But they do not account for it. Neither do they explain the nature and extent of the influence. Further, they do not attempt to examine an individual's past experiences. This is true even when the experiences might directly relate to that person's present experiences. It is assumed that if a past experience is important in the present, it will be manifested in the per-son's present experiences. This implies that there is no need to examine past experiences. Phenomenological psychologists further believe that the form the past experience assumes in the present is all that is rel-evant to an understanding of current personality functioning. These assumptions are largely unsubstantiated.

Two of the major phenomenological approaches we considered have specific gaps in coverage. The gaps result from the particular emphases of Rogers and Kelly. Rogers' approach focuses on the emotional aspects of human functioning. It largely ignores the intellectual, thinking aspects. Kelly's bias is exactly opposite; the theory of personal constructs empha-sizes cognitive processes. It pays relatively little attention to emotions. Bruner (1956) remarked that Kelly is so perturbed by psychoanalytic, dispositional, and behavioral psychologists who regard humans as ir-rational (emotional) animals that he overreacts and turns *Homo sapiens* into a species of superrational college professors.

> Here is an example of the folly: "No matter how obvious it may be that a person would be better off if he avoided a fight . . . , such a source of action would seem to him personally to limit the definition and extension of his system as a whole." *I rather suspect that when some people get angry or inspired or in love, they couldn't care less about their "system as a whole."* (Bruner, 1956, p. 356)

Phenomenological Analysis Offers a Simplistic View of Personality

Phenomenological theorists often criticize other personality theories as being oversimplified. Yet in many ways, phenomenologists themselves have been narrow and simplistic. As an alternative to the positions they consider limited, phenomenologists present a single, overriding principle. The principle—such as the self-actualizing tendency or the anticipation of future events—accounts for all human behavior. "Such an alternative, if taken literally, provides too few parameters to account for complex behaviors. Some *ad hoc* way must be found to stuff many diverse obser-vations into one or two pigeonholes, yielding serious distortions and omissions" (Wylie, 1968, pp. 731–32).

The fundamental premises of the three phenomenological ap-proaches we examined can be easily stated in a sentence or two. This is especially true for the theories of Rogers and Kelly. Each of them had a single core idea about the nature of personality, and they based an entire comprehensive theory of personality on it. This may make it easier to understand their positions. It also gives their theories internal consistency. But it may result in a simplification that is inappropriate for the study of a topic as complex as human personality.

The phenomenological strategy does not deal with the complexity of one of its central concepts, the self. Analysis of the self using assessment procedures such as the Q-sort and the Rep Test only provides pale reflections of the underlying experience these procedures seek to explain.

> An individual's conception of himself is ordinarily many-sided and internally contradictory. To determine and interrelate its many facets is no small undertaking. We need to know which facets of the self-conception are unconscious; which facets are conscious and how they are regarded (for example, with pride, resignation, guilt, or casual acceptance); what the person thinks he is, what he would like to be, and what he expects, eagerly or anxiously, to become. Pervading the overall conception of self will be the individual's concepts of masculinity and femininity; his values, in the form of both moral prohibitions and ideals; and his modes of dealing with inner dispositions and with external opportunities and demands. (Inkeles & Levinson, 1969, p. 450)

Phenomenological psychologists also tend to dismiss as unimportant some psychological processes that a majority of personality psychologists consider essential in studying personality. A prime example is the concept of motivation. Motivation is central to most personality theories. But it is casually passed over by Rogers and Kelly. They assume that people are inherently motivated and that this "fact" requires no explanation.

PHENOMENOLOGICAL PERSONALITY THEORY DOES NOT ADEQUATELY EXPLAIN PERSONALITY DEVELOPMENT

Kelly's theory of personal constructs contains little discussion of how personality develops. The discussion that does exist is too general to be of much use. Kelly certainly does not believe that people are born with constructs. According to Kelly, constructs develop in order to predict one's experiences. It is reasonable to assume that these experiences do not begin until birth. Kelly asserts that constructs are acquired beginning early in life. But there is little in Kelly's theory that specifically outlines how constructs develop. The psychology of personal constructs is essentially applicable only to an already-construing person. It applies to a person who has developed a set of templets through which experiences are viewed.

In contrast, Rogers' theory includes some discussion of the development of personality, such as in relation to the self-concept and conditions of worth. However, the developmental *process* is not explicit. For example, the self-concept develops as part of the actualizing tendency's process of differentiation. But other than indicating that the actualizing tendency is responsible for differentiating psychological functions, Rogers' theory says little about how the process operates.

A more serious problem with Rogers' concepts of personality development is that there is no empirical evidence to support his notions. Rogers conducted and inspired a large body of research concerning personality change. There have been no parallel efforts to accumulate evidence regarding personality development. In sum, Rogers' theory of personality development is vague or unspecified and remains untested.

The needs in Maslow's hierarchy are inborn. However, they do develop and change as the individual attempts to satisfy them. Maslow's theory does not specify what leads to changes in either the needs themselves or how a person satisfies them. Presumably, how we satisfy our needs becomes more sophisticated and complex as we grow older and have more experience with them. However, Maslow's theory does not address such developmental issues.

PHENOMENOLOGISTS RELY TOO HEAVILY ON SELF-REPORTS

The goal of phenomenological personality assessment is knowledge about a person's subjective experiences. The intent is understanding behavior from a person's internal frame of reference. By definition, the individual alone has direct knowledge of subjective experiences. Thus, phenomenological personality assessment relies almost entirely on self-reports. It is assumed that we are both willing and able to accurately describe phenomenological experiences. There are, however, factors that raise doubt about the validity of these two assumptions and therefore indicate that phenomenologists rely too much on self-reports.

People are not always willing to reveal their personal experiences. To begin with, this may be the case when private experiences are intimate or reveal less favorable aspects of someone's personality. The subject may only reveal highly personal experiences after he or she trusts the examiner. Building rapport between the subject and the examiner takes time, and personality assessments are often a "one-shot deal."

Both psychological research and everyday observations suggest that self-reports are often intentionally distorted. People tend to report what they want others to know about them. Usually this means they will distort their personality picture in a favorable light. Occasionally, people may find it more profitable to distort their responses so they are seen unfavorably, as in a court-ordered assessment for ability to stand trial. People may also distort their self-reports in ways they are not even fully aware of. Response sets such as social desirability and acquiescence (Chapter 10) are examples.

People may be unwilling to completely reveal their own private experiences. This is a problem for any strategy that uses self-report data. Psychoanalytic and dispositional methods of personality assessment try to get around this problem by using indirect procedures—such as projective techniques and empirically-keyed personality inventories. With indirect methods, the respondent is not fully aware of what is being assessed. Such an indirect approach implicitly involves some deception, and this is contrary to the basic theme of straightforwardness or openness that permeates the phenomenological strategy. The behavioral strategy handles peoples' reluctance to reveal subjective experiences by emphasizing public events—that is, overt behavior. However, this is not a viable option in the phenomenological strategy. Overt behavior is only indirectly related to the subjective experiences that are the basic units of personality. Thus, the effectiveness and validity of phenomenological personality assessment is limited by the extent that people are fully open about their subjective experiences.

Even if a person were willing to honestly report his or her experiences, there is still the problem of whether the person *can* report them accurately. Phenomenological personality assessment assumes that people are aware of all the private experiences that directly influence their behavior. Psychoanalysts who believe in the importance of unconscious motivation would disagree. They argue that people are often *un*aware of the determinants of their behavior.

Can someone describe their subjective experiences in a way that is both meaningful and useful to the assessor? We have all experienced frustration in trying to tell someone else how we feel. We struggle with words like: "I'm kind of depressed but not really depressed. It's more like I'm . . . Oh, I don't know . . . I just can't describe it." This inability to describe feelings to others, or even specify them for ourselves, is partly due to the limitations of language. It may also be because Western societies place a higher value on rationality and thought than on irrationality and emotion.

For language to convey information to another person, the meanings of words and phrases must be commonly agreed on and understood. However, it is often difficult to "translate" private experiences into words that fully describe them and, at the same time, communicate them to another person. Often the words are understood but the meaning is lost. When language is too imprecise and general, observers can only base their understanding of the words on their own experiences and perspective. This does not result in phenomenological knowledge.

PHENOMENOLOGICAL PERSONALITY THEORY IS MORE DESCRIPTIVE THAN EXPLANATORY

Phenomenological approaches to personality provide more of a description than an explanation of behavior. This is a major criticism of the strategy. Key theoretical concepts such as the self and personal constructs are seen by some critics as only partial explanations. We may say that George behaves in a certain way because of the construct he uses to construe the relevant events. Or Carla acts as she does because of her self-actualizing tendency. This does not explain the person's actions unless the construct or the self-actualizing tendency is, in turn, accounted for. *Personal constructs* and *self-actualizing tendencies* are theoretical constructs. They only have the status of what Skinner (1964) calls "mental way stations." They do not answer the crucial question: What conditions are responsible for someone's personal constructs or self-actualizing tendency?

A theory may provide behavioral descriptions without specifying the conditions that determine the behavior described. Or it may not designate the variables that influence the theoretical constructs hypothesized to be most directly responsible for the behavior. In such cases, prediction is difficult, if not impossible. The self-actualization approaches of Rogers and Maslow are particularly vulnerable in this regard. Aside from sustaining physical life, the self-actualizing tendency differs from person to person. Each of us has a different basic nature, and our behavior is guided by it. Given this theoretical orientation, "explanations" of behavior take the form of a tautology—A = A or "Barbara is what she *is*"—which tells us nothing. The causal chain of "explanation" goes like this.

1. Why does Barbara read books (a behavior)?
2. Barbara reads books because that is an activity that is consistent with her self-actualizing tendency.
3. How do we know that reading is part of Barbara's self-actualizing tendency?
4. We know because we observe Barbara reading books.

By now the argument has become circular because we have simply returned to our starting point.

In studying self-actualizing individuals, Maslow ran headlong into this problem. He never adequately solved the basic dilemma of definition. A priori, he defined certain individuals as self-actualizing; then he studied such people; finally, from what he learned about them, he further described the characteristics of self-actualizers. This strategy would be acceptable as a starting point. It would then be necessary to see whether the new information gathered about self-actualizers could be used to predict other characteristics and behavior—especially using additional, independent samples of people. Unfortunately, Maslow never got beyond the starting point in his investigations.

To a lesser degree, Kelly's theory of personal constructs also suffers from the limitation of being more descriptive than explanatory. Knowing that people constantly strive for accurate prediction of events tells us little about the *direction* of behavior. As Kelly fully acknowledges, a person has available many alternative ways of anticipating events.

The Phenomenological Strategy Posits Arbitrary Inborn Tendencies

Let us examine a concrete example of the phenomenological strategy's failure to provide real explanations for personality phenomena. Various inborn tendencies—to actualize one's potentialities or to construe events— are introduced as "explanations" of behavior. However, phenomenological psychologists do not specify the origins of these tendencies; they are simply said to exist. For example, Rogers (1965) categorically states: "The organism has one basic tendency and striving—to actualize, maintain, and enhance the experiencing organism" (p. 487) and Kelly (1955) says in his Fundamental Postulate: "A person's processes are psychologically channelized by the ways in which he anticipates events" (p. 46). Having stated that these natural, inborn tendencies exist, the tendencies become all-purpose "explanations" of behavior. Research has not directly sought evidence for the existence of these tendencies. However, hypotheses derived from the assumption that they exist have been supported.

Maddi (1976) points out that neither Maslow nor Rogers, for example, "gives us enough formal theoretical basis for determining what the assumed inherent potentialities are so that we can avoid the circular position of deciding that everything that the person has done must have stemmed from some potential of his" (p. 104). Indeed, we often have the impression that the constructs phenomenological theorists favor were not so much discovered through systematic research or logical deduction as revealed by some unspecified process of insight or inspiration.

Phenomenological personality theories relegate the problem of explanation to a freewheeling "self" or similar entity within the personality. The self is portrayed as a *homunculus*—a miniature person within the person, that can feel, think, distort, evaluate, accept and reject facts, and so on. These capacities are simply assigned to the self by pronouncement. In the last analysis, explaining personality on the basis of hypothesized self-tendencies is reassuring double-talk, not explanation.

THE PHENOMENOLOGICAL APPROACH IS ROMANTICALLY NAIVE

A frequent criticism of the phenomenological strategy is that it expresses a naive and rather romantic notion of human beings. For example, Millon (1967) criticizes phenomenological psychologists' idealistic conception of our inherent natures.

> The notion that man would be a constructive, rational, and socially conscious being, were he free of the malevolent distortions of society, seems not only sentimental but invalid. There is something grossly naive in exhorting man to live life to the fullest and then expecting socially beneficial consequences to follow. What evidence is there that one's inherent self-interest would not clash with the self-interests of others? There is something as banal as the proverbialism of a fortune cookie in the suggestion "be thyself." Conceiving man's emotional disorders as a failure to "be thyself" seems equally naive and banal. (p. 307)

To their credit, both Rogers and Maslow presented an optimistic view of human personality, emphasizing positive, creative aspects. (This contrasts, for example, with the psychoanalytic focus.) But in their zeal to focus on the positive, they have, to a large extent, presented an idealistic view of human beings. Their views say more about how humans *should* be (from Rogers and Maslow's perspectives) than about how they actually are. Such romanticism has no place in the scientific study of personality. In fact, Rogers' theory sometimes seems more philosophical and even religious than psychological.

There is another way in which phenomenology cannot meet the requirements of scientific psychology. The subject matter of the phenomenological strategy is subjective experience. By definition, it can only be fully known by one person, the subject. Scientific psychology requires agreement among observers and the repeatability of findings. Obviously, it is not possible to objectively agree about subjective experience. Indeed, objectivity, the basis of science, is antithetical to the phenomenological approach. Requiring agreement about observations and repeatability distinguishes the psychological approach to the human condition from philosophical, religious, and literary approaches. Those who insist on abandoning scientific criteria in favor of plausibility, common sense, or a romanticized vision of what human beings can become, propel themselves out of science entirely. The phenomenological strategy, like the psychoanalytic strategy, appears to violate the basic tenets of scientific psychology.

SUMMARY

1. The phenomenological strategy is limited in its scope, especially in assuming that conscious and present experience is sufficient for understanding personality. Psychoanalysts and other psychologists argue that we need not be aware of factors that influence our behavior, and that one's past is essential to understanding present personality functioning.

2. Limitations of specific approaches include Rogers' largely ignoring cognitive experiences and Kelly's paying little attention to emotional experiences.

3. Phenomenological analyses of human personality may be too simplistic. They present a single principle (e.g., self-actualization) that is postulated to account for diverse behaviors.

4. Phenomenological theories do not adequately explain personality development. They are most useful in explaining "already developed individuals."

5. Phenomenologists rely too heavily on self-reports. Self-report measures are problematic because people may be unwilling or unable to reveal private information, and they may choose to distort their reports.

6. Phenomenological approaches provide more description than explanation. Phenomenological explanations are often circular in nature. Various inborn tendencies are invoked as explanations, but empirical evidence supporting them is at best indirect.

7. Phenomenological approaches express naive and romantic views of personality that are more ideals of how humans should be than how they are. These approaches are more philosophical than scientific. Dealing with subjective experience presents problems for a science based on agreement among observers and repeatability of findings.

SECTION

V

THE BEHAVIORAL
STRATEGY

THE BEHAVIORAL STRATEGY

CHAPTER 18

INTRODUCTION

OVERVIEW

Personality psychologists of all theoretical persuasions begin their study of personality by examining behavior. In most strategies, however, the psychologist is not ultimately interested in behavior. A psychoanalyst may collect a subject's *dream reports*, which are behaviors. But the psychoanalyst is not concerned with the dream reports themselves. Instead, the interest is in what the dream reports reveal about the individual's unconscious processes. A dispositional psychologist may study a person's *MMPI responses*. But these responses are not examined for their own sake. Instead, they are taken as signs of various traits. A phenomenological psychologist will examine how a person sorts *self-referent statements* in a Q-sort but is most interested in the congruence between the person's perceived and ideal self.

THE PREEMINENCE OF BEHAVIOR

In contrast to the other three strategies, the behavioral strategy is often directly and ultimately concerned with *behavior* for its own sake. Behavioral psychologists use observations of behavior as *samples* (rather than signs) of a general class of behaviors. (For example, tutoring another student without charge is a sample of helping behavior.) The aim of such assessment is predicting future behavior from present or recent past behavior. In principle, a dream report *could* be used to predict the types of dreams the person is likely to have; MMPI responses *could* be used to predict responses on other inventories; and the way someone sorts statements *could* be used to predict similar categorizing behavior. However, only a behavioral psychologist *would* treat these observations simply as behavior. Put another way, the basic unit of personality in the behavioral strategy is *behavior*. Indeed, behavioral psychologists often do not use the term *personality*. For them, personality is the *sum and organization of an individual's behaviors*. Personality and behavior are closer to being synonymous in the behavioral strategy than in any of the other three strategies.

The Distinction between Overt and Covert Behavior

Behavior can be **overt**—external and more or less directly observable by others—or **covert**—internal, private, and not directly observable by others. Consider what you are doing right now. Your overt behavior may include sitting at a desk, underlining the words in this book, and turning the pages; your covert behavior may include reading, thinking, memorizing, and daydreaming. Overt behaviors can be observed directly by other people; covert behaviors are private and known directly only to the person engaging in them. Covert behaviors are often inferred from overt behaviors. Reading might be inferred from a student's answers to questions on a test on the material in the book. You might *say* you were fantasizing about being at the beach. Your verbal report, an overt behavior, could be taken as an indication of daydreaming, a covert behavior. In fact, verbal self-reports are the overt behaviors most often used to assess covert behaviors.

RADICAL AND METHODOLOGICAL BEHAVIORISM

Historically, the behavioral strategy grew out of the school of psychology called *behaviorism*. It was founded by John Broadus Watson (1878–1958) in the early years of the twentieth century. Watson distinguished two forms of behaviorism: radical and methodological. The former deals with both the subject matter and research methods of psychology. The latter deals only with methods of inquiry.

Radical behaviorism earned its name because of the extreme nature of its propositions. It defines the phenomena that are and are not appropriate topics for psychological study. Watson (1914, 1919) believed that psychology was the science of *behavior*—and he most emphatically meant

John Broadus Watson

The Ferdinand Hamburger, Jr., Archives, The Johns Hopkins University

only *overt* behavior. Watson was suspicious of covert behavior because it could only be studied subjectively by introspection (i.e., by subjects' reporting their thoughts, feelings, and perceptions). Radical behaviorism also specifies the legitimate ways in which overt behavior may be studied. This is through carefully controlled research based on objectively verifiable observations. (Obviously introspection is excluded.) A few excerpts from Watson's (1914) writings provide the flavor of radical behaviorism as its founder saw it.

> Psychology as the behaviorist views it is a purely objective experimental branch of natural science. Its theoretical goal is the prediction and control of behavior. . . . The behaviorist attempts to get a unitary scheme of animal response. He recognizes no dividing line between man and brute. The behavior of man, with all of its refinements and complexity, forms only a part of his total field of investigation. . . . It is possible to write a psychology, to define it as . . . the "science of behavior" . . . and never go back upon the definition: never to use the terms consciousness, mental states, mind, content, will, imagery, and the like. . . . Certain stimuli lead . . . organisms to make . . . responses. In a system of psychology completely worked out, given the responses the stimuli can be predicted; given the stimuli the responses can be predicted. (pp. 1, 9, 10)

When Watson speaks of "a purely objective experimental branch of natural science," he is alluding to **methodological behaviorism.** Methodological behaviorism emphasizes objectivity, direct observation of phenomena, precise definitions, and controlled experimentation in the study of human behavior. In a sense, it is one "half" of radical behaviorism. In contrast to radical behaviorism, methodological behaviorism does *not* specify what are legitimate topics to investigate. It merely indicates the legitimate ways of conducting research in psychology.

Three Basic Behavioral Approaches

Since Watson's time, virtually all behavioral psychologists have followed the basic ideas of methodological behaviorism. Until relatively recently, most have also more or less subscribed to radical behaviorism. In the 1950s, some behavioral psychologists began to study phenomena that do not meet the requirements of radical behaviorism. *Social learning approaches* include social phenomena that are distinctly human. *Cognitive-behavioral approaches* deal with covert events such as cognitions and mental images. These approaches are concerned with the role of overt behavior in determining covert events (e.g., our actions toward someone influence our attitudes about that person). They also deal with the role of covert events in influencing overt behavior (e.g., mentally rehearsing how we will perform in a difficult situation affects our actual performance).

Social learning and cognitive-behavioral approaches represent a break from radical behaviorism. But they remain true to methodological behaviorism. For example, two important factors distinguish how covert events are studied in the behavioral and in other strategies (Spiegler, 1983). First, covert events are defined explicitly and unambiguously in terms of how they are measured. Second, the covert events are often defined or anchored in terms of observable behaviors. For example, *learning* is a covert response. It is frequently defined as *performance on an examination,* an overt, directly observable behavior.

We will distinguish among three approaches within the behavioral strategy. They are the *radical behavioral, social learning,* and *cognitive-behavioral* approaches. Some behavioral psychologists consider themselves strong adherents of one approach. In practice, however, these approaches—particularly contemporary social learning and cognitive-behavioral positions—often overlap. We turn next to two fundamental issues that distinguish the behavioral strategy: the importance of learning and the situational specificity of behavior. All three behavioral approaches emphasize these issues.

BEHAVIOR IS LEARNED

Behavior develops and is modified primarily by learning and experience rather than through heredity and biological factors. This is a basic assumption of the behavioral strategy. Behavioral approaches differ from one another, however, with respect to the form of learning that is emphasized: namely, classical conditioning, operant conditioning, or observational learning.

In *classical conditioning,* behavior is learned through *association* between stimuli and responses. For example, a male college professor wears jeans to a faculty party at which most of his male colleagues wear suits. He may have learned to do so because he has come to associate the look and feel of tight jeans with very pleasant experiences in the past, like being out with attractive women.

In *operant conditioning,* behavior is learned primarily from the *consequences* of actions (i.e., reinforcement and punishment). From this perspective, the college professor might wear jeans to parties because wearing jeans often brings him compliments and seems to attract attention (which he likes).

In *observational learning,* as the name implies, we learn behaviors by observing others (models) perform and also from observing the consequences of their actions. Our professor may have learned to wear jeans to parties by seeing that his students did so and by noting that the students appeared to be more comfortable than men in business suits, starched collars, and ties.

These three explanations reflect different but not necessarily incompatible accounts of how behavior is learned and maintained. Most human behavior is acquired and sustained by a combination of learning processes. For example, the professor may wear jeans because he observed his students wearing them, because he felt good when wearing them, and because people complimented him on his casual attire—in other words, a combination of all three forms of learning.

BEHAVIOR IS OFTEN SITUATION SPECIFIC

Behavior is more or less consistent in the sense that each person tends to behave in similar ways or patterns. This is not to say that people do not vary in their behavior. But human behavior does not appear to be random. Accordingly, any theory of personality must account for the apparent consistency of behavior. Psychoanalytic theories posit that lifelong patterns of behavior are developed early. Dispositional positions speak of relatively stable and enduring personality characteristics that result in consistent behavior. Phenomenological theories attribute behavioral consistency to how people view themselves, others, and events in their lives.

Behavioral personality theories hold that the consistency of behavior depends on the *situation*. People behave in response to cues in the particular situation in which they find themselves at the moment. The cues tell us which behaviors are expected. They tell us what is likely to meet with approval and/or be adaptive in that particular circumstance. Behavioral personality theories say that people's behavior is consistent in the same or similar situations; it varies in different situations. In other words, behavior is **situation specific.**

Consider a college student named Greg. He sits quietly in lectures, is mildly animated in casual conversation at the cafeteria, and vigorously expresses his support for his college athletic teams. In each case, Greg's behavior is determined by the requirements and restrictions of the situation. This means that Greg's behavior will tend to be consistent *within* each situation; he will show about the same level of activity in a given circumstance as it occurs again and again. But Greg's behavior is quite variable *across* situations; he yells and jumps up and down at basketball games and doesn't make a sound in class. Thus, Greg's behavior is *consistent within a given situation, but not across different situations.* He behaves passively in some situations, actively in others, and somewhere in between in still other situations. This situation-specific viewpoint should be contrasted with the generality-consistency assumptions of the dispositional strategy. According to the latter, Greg might be a passive or an active *type.*

What constitutes the *situation* differs somewhat among the behavioral approaches. Within radical behavioral approaches, the situation consists of objective stimuli in the external environment, including other people. In social learning and cognitive-behavioral approaches, the individual's perception and interpretation are also considered part of the situation, and may provide important cues that influence behavior.

BEHAVIORAL PERSONALITY THEORY

Of the four aspects of the study of personality, theory is given the least attention in the behavioral strategy. It is not that theory is ignored, as it tends to be in the dispositional strategy. Rather, personality assessment, research, and change are given relatively more emphasis than theory. Further, the different behavioral approaches vary in the amount of theory they engender. Social learning and cognitive-behavioral approaches involve considerably more theorizing than do radical behavioral approaches. However, there are some common characteristics of behavioral personality theory. These include its being relatively parsimonious and its minimizing the use of theoretical constructs and of inferences.

Parsimony

Behavioral theories of personality tend to be parsimonious, or simple. Often a single set of principles is used to explain a variety of different behaviors. As an example, consider the behavioral explanation of unexpressed or inhibited behavior. *Unexpressed behavior* refers to acts that a person can perform but is not performing at the moment. An example is failure to recall a fact that you clearly know (as evidenced by its being recalled when the appropriate cues are available). Have you ever "blocked" on someone's name and then recalled it the moment you see the person?

In the psychoanalytic strategy, *unexpressed behavior* is explained by making two assumptions. First, there are levels of awareness (consciousness). Second, conscious responses are made unconscious by a defensive process, such as repression. Behavioral approaches deal with unexpressed behavior without making *additional* assumptions—that is, assumptions over and above those used to explain expressed behavior. Similarly, behavioral psychologists postulate that normal and abnormal behaviors develop, are maintained, and change according to identical principles of learning (e.g., Ullmann & Krasner, 1975). In effect, there is nothing special about abnormal behavior from the standpoint of understanding its basic nature. (What is distinctive about behavior labeled *abnormal* are its social consequences, such as the negative reactions of others and the legal ramifications of exhibiting some abnormal behaviors.)

Minimum of Theoretical Constructs

Compared with the other three personality strategies, the behavioral strategy uses relatively few theoretical constructs. Note that this is a *relative* statement. Behavioral personality theory is by no means free of theoretical constructs. However, behavioral theories specifically avoid explanations that involve special *entities* within the person. For example, behavioral theories do not posit any kind of unifying force or structure for personality. There are no behavioral equivalents of an ego or self. Instead, each aspect of personality is viewed semi-independently of all other aspects.

Theoretical constructs often serve as shorthand summaries of personality phenomena. Behavioral psychologists use theoretical constructs sparingly. As a result, behavioral descriptions of personality phenomena tend to be lengthy and complex. For instance, it is simpler to use the theoretical construct *repression* than to describe a person as *avoiding talking about painful past experiences*. At the same time, a detailed description of an individual's behavior is more precise.

Minimum of Inferences

Personality psychologists make inferences when they deduce something about one event based on information from another event. Thus, inferences always provide *indirect* information. However, the extent of an inference—that is, the degree of indirectness—depends on the similarity of the two events. Positing *repression of an unacceptable desire* from observing hysterical paralysis involves a series of inferential steps and hence a high degree of inference. In contrast, predicting a person's *future overt behavior* from similar past overt behavior involves only one inferential step and hence, little inference.

Consider the following example. We predict that Mary will arrive at work at 8:00 A.M. on Friday because she arrived at that time on Monday through Thursday. Mary's arrival time on Friday is inferred from her previous behavior in the same situation. In this case, what is inferred is on the same level of abstraction as the data from which it is inferred. Future *behavior* is being predicted on the basis of recent past *behavior*. This one-level inferential process should be contrasted with predicting (inferring) future *behavior* from a *nonbehavioral* source. This would be the case if Mary's arrival on Friday were predicted from assuming that Mary was a compulsive type. The behavioral strategy is not restricted to one-step inferences. However, behavioral psychologists tend to make smaller inferential leaps than do psychologists in the other three strategies (cf. Mahoney, 1974).

BEHAVIORAL PERSONALITY ASSESSMENT

Assessment of personality in the behavioral strategy can be characterized as direct, present oriented, and circumscribed.

Direct

The difference between the indirect and direct approaches to personality is illustrated by a tongue-in-cheek contrast. A psychoanalyst and a behavioral psychologist are trying to determine whether or not a man hates his mother. The analyst examines the man's dreams and interprets his responses to projective stimuli. The behavioral psychologist asks the man straight out, "Do you hate your mother?"

It is not the method of assessment per se that distinguishes behavioral from nonbehavioral approaches. Rather it is the way the method is employed. Consider the use of self-report inventories to *directly* assess personality. The Fear Survey Schedule is an example of a self-report instrument used to assess fear (Wolpe & Lazarus, 1966); subjects rate how much they fear a number of different situations and objects (see Figure 18–1). The Fear Survey Schedule directly *samples* the subject's fears. The examiner takes the subject's answer at face value and does *not* use them as *signs* indicating a fear of something else. If Myrna reports being afraid to climb ladders, the behavioral psychologist assumes that is her fear. In contrast, a psychoanalyst might assume that her fear of climbing ladders was a sign (symbol) of sexual intercourse and that it is sex that she actually fears.

As with all self-report measures, subjects' responses to the Fear Survey Schedule may be influenced by response sets and other extraneous variables. And the responses are, at best, only moderately correlated with actual overt behavior. Nevertheless, direct self-reports are often more valid measures of actual behavior than indirect assessment methods, such as projective techniques (e.g., Mischel, 1982).

The clearest example of direct assessment involves watching someone perform the very behavior the psychologist wants to assess. For instance, to learn how someone is likely to act in a stressful situation, the behavioral psychologist observes the person in several stressful situations. When this is not possible, the psychologist asks how the person has behaved in stressful circumstances in the recent past.

FIGURE 18–1
A portion of a fear survey schedule

Instructions: The items in this questionnaire are objects, experiences, or ideas that may cause fear, anxiety, or other unpleasant feelings. Using the scale below, write the appropriate number after each item to describe the degree to which the item causes you to feel fear, anxiety, or other unpleasant feelings.

1 = Not at all
2 = A little
3 = A moderate amount
4 = Much
5 = Very much

1. Open wounds	25. Blood
2. Being alone	26. Enclosed places
3. Speaking in public	27. Flying in airplanes
4. Falling	28. Darkness
5. Automobiles	29. Lightning
6. Being teased	30. Doctors
7. Dentists	31. Losing control
8. Thunder	32. Making mistakes
9. Failure	33. Older people
10. High places	34. Going blind
11. Receiving injections	35. Drowning
12. Strangers	36. Examinations
13. Feeling angry	37. Cancer
14. Insects	38. Fog
15. Sudden noises	39. Being lost
16. Crowds	40. Police
17. Large open spaces	41. Talking on the telephone
18. Cats	42. Death of a loved one
19. Being watched while working	43. Pain
20. Dirt	44. Suicide
21. Dogs	45. War
22. Sick people	46. Going insane
23. Fire	47. Violence
24. Mice	48. Psychologists

Source: Developed in "Some Correlates of Self-Reported Fear," by M. D. Spiegler and R. M. Liebert, 1970, *Psychological Reports, 26,* pp. 691–95.

Present-Oriented

To predict future behavior, the behavioral psychologist relies most on the individual's present and *recent* past behavior. This is consistent with the concept of situational specificity. There is little reason to explore an adult's childhood to assess her or his present personality. Events in the remote past (e.g., childhood for an adult) no doubt influence present personality. But this influence is considered minimal for two important reasons. First, the influence is, at the present time, indirect. For instance, crying as a reaction to frustrating events may have been learned by observing one's mother react in this way. But the habit will persist in adult life only if it continues to be reinforced (e.g., by friends' sympathy). Second, the influence of events in one's remote past is obscure. There is no way to accurately assess these events and the nature of their influence. At best, correlations between past and present personality variables can be obtained, and such relationships are not likely to yield clear-cut information about causation. For example, adult obsessive behavior may be correlated with severity of toilet training. The relationship does not tell us whether early difficulties with bowel control in childhood result in running business affairs in a precise and orderly fashion as an adult. It is possible that a third variable, such as parents' modeling fastidiousness, is responsible for both behaviors.

Direct observation of overt behavior provides an important source of data about personality for behavioral psychologists. It is often carried out in naturalistic settings where subjects are engaged in their normal activities. © *Alice Kardell, 1977*

Circumscribed

Behavioral personality assessment proceeds by examining relatively small aspects of an individual's total personality. For instance, it would be feasible within the behavioral strategy to study the interpersonal relationships of individuals without delving into their sexual relationships. Sometimes two or more aspects of personality are closely related. It is therefore necessary to consider them together to fully understand one of them. However, the behavioral approach does not assume that there is a necessary interdependence among different aspects of personality. The behavioral position contrasts with the holistic approach of the phenomenological strategy which maintains that each component of personality must be viewed in relation to one's total personality. The assumption that a person's behaviors are semi-autonomous also has implications for behavioral research and personality change. In research, specific personality phenomena are studied in depth. In behavioral psychotherapy, efforts are made to change particular behaviors rather than to modify the client's total personality.

DEMONSTRATION 18–1

THE OBSERVATION AND RECORDING OF BEHAVIOR

Direct observation and recording of behavior are important aspects of behavioral personality assessment. In doing this Demonstration you will learn about these two tasks experientially. You will observe and record your own behavior. (The instructions can be easily adapted to observing and recording another person's behavior.) Clients in behavioral therapy are often asked to self-record their problem behaviors to provide a baseline before therapy begins and then to provide continuous assessment of their progress during treatment.

SELECTING A RESPONSE AND RECORDING UNIT

1. The first step is *choosing a response* to observe and record. Table 18–1 contains examples of behaviors you might select, but you can choose any response that meets the following two requirements.
   a. You should be able to define the response precisely so that there will be no doubt as to when it has and has not occurred.
   b. The response should occur at a frequency that makes recording reasonable. If the response occurs at a very high rate (e.g., eye

TABLE 18–1
Example of target behaviors to observe and record (Demonstration 18–1)

Behavior	Unit of Behavior	Unit of Time
Reading	Pages	Day or hour
Writing	Lines	Day or hour
Jogging	¼ miles	Day
Swimming	Laps in a pool	Day
Tardiness	Times late for an appointment	Day
Daydreaming	Minutes spent	Day or hour
Talking on the telephone	Minutes spent on phone calls	Day or hour
Swearing	Curse words	Day or hour
Foreign language vocabulary	Words learned	Day
Studying	Minutes spent	Day
Bull sessions	Minutes spent	Day
Drinking		Day or hour
(a) Coffee	(a) Cups	
(b) Beer	(b) Ounces	
Smoking	Cigarettes	Day or hour

blinks), recording may be too difficult. Yet the response should occur often enough so that you will have something to record. (Buying a new car or getting married would, for most people, not occur often enough to be used in this Demonstration!)

2. After choosing a response, *select a unit of behavior* that is appropriate for it, as suggested by the examples in Table 18–1. No matter what the response, you will be simply counting the number of behavioral units that occur in a specified time period.

3. Next, decide on a *unit of time* that is appropriate for the response and that is practical for recording. A behavior that you engage in many times a day would most likely be recorded in hours or even parts of hours, whereas a less-frequent behavior would probably be recorded per day. In the case of a frequent behavior, it may be more feasible to **time sample**—that is, to record only in certain time periods that you have defined ahead of time, such as the first five minutes of every hour.

OBSERVING AND RECORDING

4. You will need a *convenient means of recording* the frequency of occurrence of the response. For example, this can easily be done by marking off a 3 × 5 index card in time intervals, and then simply making a tally mark each time you perform the behavior, as is shown in Figure 18–2. At the end of each day (or other unit of time you are using), the total number of tally marks is calculated, and this becomes your rate for the day (e.g., 26 pages read per day). Other possible ways of recording re-

sponses include making tally marks on a piece of masking tape on your watch band, wallet, or purse, or using an inexpensive golf or knitting counter. Whatever means of recording you choose, it should be available whenever you are observing the behavior and should be very easy to use (otherwise you may forget to record or decide it's too much of a hassle).

You should also make brief notes about special events that may have affected the frequency of the response (see Figure 18–2).

GRAPHING THE RESULTS OF OBSERVATIONS

5. The final step is to *graph your observations,* which will help you inspect and interpret the data you've collected. As an example, the data recorded in Figure 18–2 have been graphed in Figure 18–3. The horizontal axis of the graph should be marked off in time intervals, such as days or hours. The vertical axis should represent the number of responses per unit of time.

The sample graph (Figure 18–3) shows that the person read approximately the same number of pages for the first three days. On Thursday, the number of pages nearly doubled, and it remained the same on

FIGURE 18–2

Example of an index-card record of pages read in a week (Demonstration 18–1)

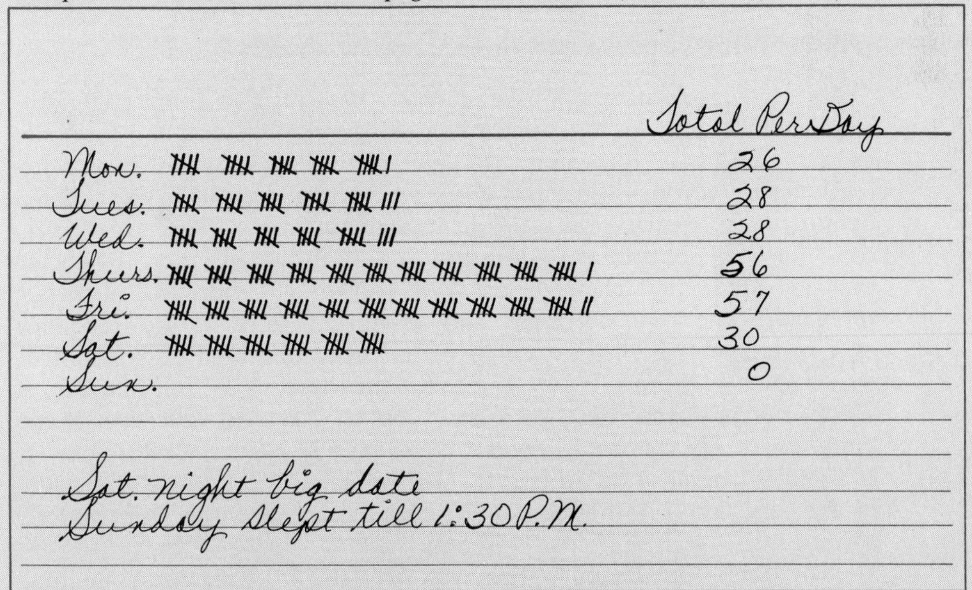

	Total Per Day
Mon.	26
Tues.	28
Wed.	28
Thurs.	56
Fri.	57
Sat.	30
Sun.	0

Sat. night big date
Sunday slept till 1:30 P.M.

FIGURE 18–3
Graph of a week's reading behavior (Demonstration 18–1)

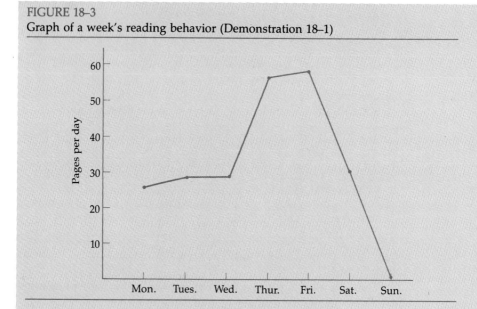

Friday. On Saturday, the number of pages dropped to approximately the Monday-through-Wednesday rate, perhaps because of the interference of the Saturday evening social engagement. And on the seventh day no pages were read (perhaps the person rested).

DISCUSSION

There are a variety of things you could have gained from doing this Demonstration, including some firsthand experience with the problems encountered in self-recording. Examples might be: (1) difficulty in knowing whether you made the response, which would occur if you did not define your response precisely and unambiguously; (2) forgetting to record the behavior and/or finding it a "pain" to record; and (3) noticing that the frequency changed as your recording proceeded. The last problem is known as **reactivity** and specifically refers to the frequency of a response changing by virtue of its being observed and recorded. For instance, if you were trying to cut down on the number of snacks you ate, recording each time you take a snack may make you more aware of your behavior and consequently reduce it. Reactivity is a problem because it interferes with obtaining a "pure" measure of the behavior—one not confounded by the act of observation and recording.

By doing the Demonstration, you may also have learned something about the particular behavior you were observing. The data may give you information about how often and when (e.g., time of day or day of the week) you perform the behavior and may lead to ideas about modifying the behavior, if you are interested in doing so.

BEHAVIORAL RESEARCH

In the tradition of methodological behaviorism, behavioral research emphasizes studying of personality phenomena through well-controlled experiments. Experiments are often carried out in the psychology laboratory where strict control of conditions is possible. The research is predominantly nomothetic. It intensively investigates small aspects of personality (e.g., the study of goal setting or delay of gratification), rather than examining personality as a single entity. Idiographic, single-subject studies are sometimes used to evaluate the effectiveness of personality-change techniques. These studies, too, focus on specific behaviors (e.g., assertive behavior, fear, overeating) as opposed to total personality or global dispositions.

Dependent variables in behavioral experimentation tend to be *samples* of the actual behavior of interest. For example, in behavioral experiments dealing with aggression, the measures of aggression are direct samples of aggressive behavior, such as giving an electric shock to another person.

Research within radical behavioral approaches is almost exclusively experimental. The experimental method is also the preferred method of research in social learning and cognitive-behavioral approaches. However, correlational studies, and occasionally case studies, are also employed in the latter approaches.

BEHAVIORAL PERSONALITY CHANGE

Behavioral therapy generically refers to behavioral personality-change procedures. These are also called *behavior therapy, behavior modification,* and *cognitive-behavior therapy.* Behavioral therapy is not a single method of personality change, like client-centered therapy. Rather, there are a variety of behavioral therapies. But they all share three common characteristics: dealing with target behaviors, treating maintaining conditions, and being action-oriented.

Target Behaviors

Behavioral therapies modify specific, well-defined behaviors called **target behaviors.** Typically, clients describe their difficulties in vague, general terms, such as feeling "anxious and uptight." A behavioral therapist first helps the client define these presenting problems as behaviors. Then, using behavioral assessment techniques, the therapist and client identify the *overt behavioral referents* of the client's report of anxiety and "uptightness." For one client, the subjective experience of anxiety may result in avoiding certain situations (e.g., dates). For another, it may lead to poor performance (e.g., on examinations).

The fact that behavioral therapies treat specific target behaviors does *not* mean that they ignore complex and multifaceted problems. Target behaviors are the components of complex difficulties. For instance, complicated marital problems may necessitate working on target behaviors like anxiety about sex, interpersonal skills, emotional sensitivity, and dependent behavior. Behavioral therapies proceed by dealing with one or two target behaviors at a time; when the initial target behaviors have been successfully treated, therapy turns to other target behaviors. Multiple problems are treated sequentially rather than simultaneously. This approach is partially validated by the fact that behavioral therapies work relatively quickly, especially as compared to other types of therapy.

Treating Maintaining Conditions

Behavioral therapy involves two major tasks. First, the factors that are *currently* maintaining or causing the target behavior must be assessed. Second, these **maintaining conditions** are altered in order to modify the target behavior. Behavioral therapists look for the maintaining conditions of a target behavior in the current antecedents and consequences of the behavior.

Antecedents are the stimuli present *before* the target behavior occurs. They include situational cues (e.g., where the target behavior occurs and what is going on at the time), temporal cues (e.g., time of day), and interpersonal cues (e.g., who is present and what they are doing). *Consequences* are events that happen *after* the target behavior is performed. This includes both the immediate and the long-range outcomes for the individual performing the behavior, as well as for other people and even the physical environment. Table 18–2 lists the antecedents and consequences of one client's target behavior, overeating.

Action-Oriented Techniques

Behavioral therapies are not traditional verbal psychotherapies. Personality change is not achieved primarily through a verbal dialogue, as in psychoanalysis, for example. Clients in behavioral therapies are actively engaged in such tasks as observing and recording their target behaviors, practicing adaptive behaviors, and setting up conditions (antecedents and consequences) in their lives to elicit and reinforce adaptive behaviors. In brief,

TABLE 18–2
The antecedents and consequences of *overeating* for a client

Antecedents	Consequences
At home alone	Enjoys eating
In the evening	Feels guilty
Bored	Gains weight
Frustrated	Clothes do not fit
Snacks in the house	Called "chubs" by friends

clients *do* things—often as *homework assignments*—rather than merely talking and thinking about their feelings and problems.

BEHAVIORAL APPROACHES AND THE LEARNING/ COGNITIVE PROCESSES CONTINUUM

The three basic approaches in the behavioral strategy—radical behavioral, social learning, and cognitive-behavioral—differ in the relative emphasis placed on learning and cognitive processes. Learning is a common theme in the behavioral strategy. But specific approaches within the strategy vary both (a) in terms of the kind of learning emphasized, and (b) in the overall emphasis on learning in their theoretical accounts of personality. Radical behavioral approaches (Chapter 19) deal with classical and operant conditioning. These forms of learning involve environmental stimuli and observable responses; there is no discussion of internal processes, which is consistent with the principles of radical behaviorism. Social learning approaches (see Chapter 20) acknowledge the importance of classical and operant conditioning, but they also include observational learning because learning from others is a social phenomenon. Social learning theorists study the underlying processes of learning and other phenomena using scientifically rigorous methods that are characteristic of methodological behaviorism. Although cognitive-behavioral psychologists (see Chapter 21) acknowledge the importance of learning, they do not focus on it. Rather, they deal with thoughts and images that are both the causes and products of overt behavior, while adhering to the standards of methodological behaviorism.

Thus, one of the major ways the three behavioral approaches differ is in terms of the stress placed on learning versus cognitive processes. The three approaches can be roughly aligned on a continuum that has *learning* at one end and *cognitive processes* at the other end, as seen in Figure 18–4. Radical behavioral approaches that emphasize learning and cognitive-behavioral approaches that stress cognitive processes are at

FIGURE 18–4
The three basic behavioral approaches can be roughly placed on a continuum indicating the relative emphasis placed on learning and cognitive processes.

Emphasis:	LEARNING		COGNITIVE PROCESSES
Approach:	Radical-behavioral	Social-learning	Cognitive-behavioral

opposite ends of the continuum. Social learning approaches that deal with both learning and cognitive processes lie somewhere between the two poles.

SUMMARY

1. The behavioral strategy is concerned with behavior per se, which distinguishes it from the other three strategies.

2. Behavior can be overt or covert. Overt behavior is public and can readily be observed by others; covert behavior is internal, private, and not directly observable by others.

3. Watson distinguished between radical and methodological behaviorism. Radical behaviorism deals only with overt behaviors, studying it through objectively verifiable observations and tightly controlled research methods. Methodological behaviorism uses the same methods of investigations but allows covert events to be studied as well.

4. Today we can identify three basic behavioral approaches to personality. Radical behaviorism holds a hard line against the inclusion of private events. Social learning theories acknowledge the importance of covert as well as overt behavior, but are concerned with firmly "anchoring" covert events in overt ones. The cognitive-behavioral approach goes even further, with the position that covert events are of central importance in determining behavior.

5. A central concept of all three behavioral approaches is that behavior develops and changes primarily through learning and experience.

6. Three types of learning have been identified. Classical conditioning refers to the learned association between stimuli and responses. Operant conditioning refers to learning that occurs as a result of consequences (i.e., rewards and punishments). Observational learning refers to learning by observing others and noting the consequences that they receive for their actions.

7. Behavioral theorists agree that what we do is determined to a

considerable extent by the immediate situation in which we find ourselves. For the radical behavioral approach, the situation consists of the
various stimuli present in the environment at any moment. The social
learning and cognitive-behavioral approaches also include the individual's perception and interpretation of these stimuli as part of the
situation.

8. Behavioral personality theories are distinguished by their parsimony, relatively few theoretical constructs, and minimum of inferences.

9. Behavioral assessment is direct, present-oriented, and circumscribed.

10. The behavioral strategy strongly favors the experimental method
of research. These experiments typically emphasize the importance of
obtaining direct samples of behavior as their dependent variables.

11. Behavioral therapy encompasses a wide variety of specific techniques. All identify specific target behaviors to be modified, focus on the
current maintaining conditions of these target behaviors, and are action-
oriented rather than just verbal.

12. The three approaches that comprise the behavioral strategy
form a continuum between a heavy emphasis on learning at one end
(radical behavioral) to a heavy emphasis on cognition at the other (cognitive-behavioral), with social learning in between.

THE RADICAL BEHAVIORAL APPROACH

OVERVIEW

The radical behavioral approach to personality emphasizes the importance of *overt behavior*. It pays little or no attention to thoughts, feelings, or other inner states. Radical behaviorists also maintain that *conditioning* (learning) is a primary mechanism of personality development and change. Within this broad perspective, radical behaviorists follow somewhat different paths, depending on whether their interest is in *classical conditioning* or *operant conditioning*. We will discuss each type of conditioning separately.

CLASSICAL CONDITIONING

In the late nineteenth century, Russian physiologist Ivan Pavlov (1849–1936) studied the digestive processes of dogs. (See Figure 19–1.) He noticed

FIGURE 19–1
Pavlov (center) with research assistants and subject (far left) at the Soviet Military Medicine Academy

The Bettmann Archive

that dogs which had been in the study for some time salivated even before food was put on their tongues. Pavlov recognized the potential importance of his accidental discovery, and spent much of the rest of his career studying and elaborating this phenomenon which came to be called *classical conditioning*.

Pavlov's first approach was introspective. It involved trying to imagine the situation from the dog's point of view. This strategy led up blind alleys. (His assistants could not agree on what the dog ought to think or feel.) Pavlov subsequently banned introspection from his laboratory (Hyman, 1964). He turned next to a more objective and verifiable approach. Pavlov reasoned that the animal's natural, or reflexive, tendency to respond to the food in its mouth with salivation had somehow also come to be evoked by the mere sight of food. The latter reaction was not innate. It had to be *conditioned* by environmental events. And it could be studied experimentally. This is just what Pavlov set out to do.

The order of events in a typical classical conditioning experiment is illustrated in Figure 19–2. First, a **conditioned stimulus (CS)**, such as a light, is presented; the CS does not initially produce the relevant response (salivation in Pavlov's work). Very shortly thereafter (a fraction of a second to no more than a few seconds), a stimulus that reflexively produces the response is introduced. This is the **unconditioned stimulus (UCS)**; the response that it produces is the **unconditioned response (UCR)**. In Pavlov's studies, the food was the UCS and salivary flow was the UCR. The CS and UCS are repeatedly presented together. Finally, the CS (light) produces salivary flow even before the UCS (food) is presented. The salivary flow in the latter condition is the **conditioned response (CR)**.

Classical Conditioning of Emotional Reactions

Watson was inspired by Pavlov's conditioning experiments. The conditioning process, Watson argued, had vast implications for understanding and managing human behavior. Watson was more of a spokesman than a researcher, though. His most cited study is the (in)famous case of "little Albert" (Watson & Rayner, 1920). Albert, an eleven-month-old apathetic child, appeared to be afraid of nothing except the loud sound made by striking a steel bar. To classically condition another fear in Albert, Watson and Rayner placed a white rat (CS) in front of him. At the same time, they produced the loud sound he feared (UCS). After seven such presentations, the rat, which had not previously elicited an emotional response in Albert, aroused a definite fear reaction (CR), including crying or attempting to escape from the situation.

Watson and some of his followers saw the case of Albert as a clear demonstration that emotional reactions could be conditioned in human beings. Later, critics found methodological flaws in this case study (Harris,

FIGURE 19–2
Schematic diagram of the classical conditioning process

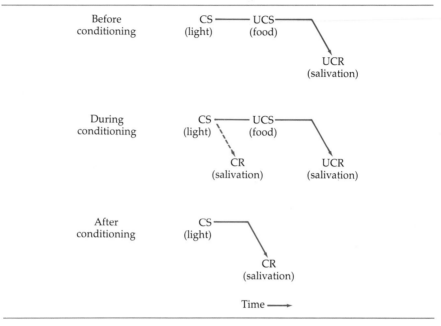

1979; Marks, 1981). But Watson's basic idea inspired many psychologists to study the role of classical conditioning in developing emotional reactions (cf. Eysenck, 1985). Geer (1968), for example, showed color photographs of victims of violent and sudden death (UCS) to college students. They were shown the photos five seconds after the presentation of a tone (CS) that initially elicited no emotional response. After twenty such pairings, the previously neutral tone produced galvanic skin responses (changes in skin conductance) indicating emotional arousal (CR).

Anxiety as a Classically Conditioned Response

A number of behavioral psychologists theorize that anxiety is an inappropriate fear response to situations and events that carry no objective threat and that it is learned through classical conditioning (e.g., Levis, 1985; Öst & Hugdahl, 1985). Specifically, a neutral cue (CS) is present when another stimulus (UCS) elicits a fear or anxiety response (UCR). The CS comes to elicit a similar response (CR) on future occasions. This conditioning analysis and the central role it could play in developing and maintaining emotional behavior is illustrated in the following example.

The child places his hand on the big, black, hot coal stove. He quickly withdraws the painful hand, tearful and fearful. His mother comforts him, but later notes that he keeps away from the stove and seems afraid of it. Clearly, the child has developed a beneficial habit of fearing and avoiding an actually harmful object.

But in some cases the experience also has another and less favorable consequence. Suppose in the mother's bedroom there is a large black chest of drawers. The child may have become afraid of this too—purely on the basis of its *physical resemblance* to the stove. . . . [This is known as] generalization. Fear of the chest of drawers is neurotic because there can be no harm in touching it. It can have several undesirable implications. In the first place, the very presence of an unpleasant emotion like fear is objectionable where it is not appropriate. Secondly, the child is now forced to make a detour if the chest of drawers is in his path; and thirdly, he no longer has easy access to any delectable contents of the drawers, such as candy. In these features of this child's case, we have the model of all neurotic fear reactions. (Wolpe & Lazarus, 1966, pp. 17–18)

CLASSICAL CONDITIONING THERAPIES

A variety of behavioral therapies use classical conditioning. Basically, they substitute an adaptive behavior for a maladaptive behavior. This is done by changing CS-UCS pairings that have led to the emotional problem. We will look at several examples.

Systematic Desensitization

Joseph Wolpe (1958) developed a technique for alleviating anxiety called **systematic desensitization.** The client is gradually exposed to increasingly more anxiety-evoking stimuli while making a response that is incompatible with anxiety. To accomplish this, the client first learns and/or practices an *incompatible response* to anxiety (e.g., relaxation). Second, the stimuli that make the client anxious are assessed and ordered in an *anxiety hierarchy.* Third, the client is gradually exposed to successively more anxiety-evoking stimuli while performing the incompatible response. This *desensitizes* the client to fear-evoking stimuli. The objective, in classical conditioning terms, is substituting a more adaptive response (CR) for the anxiety (UCR) elicited by particular stimuli. Before therapy, the stimuli are UCSs that lead to anxiety; after therapy, the same stimuli become CSs that lead to the incompatible response (CR).

Deep Muscle Relaxation

Deep muscle relaxation is incompatible with anxiety. It is difficult to be tense and relaxed at the same time. Training in deep muscle relaxation proceeds systematically, covering each skeletal muscle group—arms, head, face, neck, shoulders, trunk, abdomen, hips, thighs, legs, and feet. Clients first learn to differentiate between muscular relaxation and tension by tensing and relaxing each set of muscles. The following excerpt from relaxation training instructions illustrates the process.

> Settle back as comfortably as you can. Let yourself relax to the best of your ability. . . . Now, as you relax like that, clench your right fist, just clench your fist tighter and tighter, and study the tension as you do so. Keep it clenched and feel the tension in your right fist, hand, forearm . . . and now relax. Let the fingers of your right hand become loose, and observe the contrast in your feelings. . . . Now, let yourself go and try to become more relaxed all over. . . . Once more, clench your right fist really tight . . . hold it, and notice the tension again. . . . Now let go, relax; your fingers straighten out, and you notice the difference once more. (Wolpe & Lazarus, 1966, p. 177)

During relaxation training, clients usually sit in a reclining armchair, close their eyes, and follow the therapist's instructions. Eventually clients learn to relax muscles without first tensing them. Practice with the therapist is supplemented with practice at home.

Deep muscle relaxation is the response most often used to counteract anxiety (cf. Levin & Gross, 1985). We will refer to it as we describe desensitization. Other incompatible responses used in systematic desensitization include humor and laughter, pleasant thoughts, eating, assertive behavior, and sexual arousal (Spiegler, 1983).

Construction of Anxiety Hierarchies

Sometimes a person will come to a therapist with a well-defined fear of a particular class of stimuli or stimulus situations. Fear of driving or of going to the dentist are examples. More often, however, people feel anxious at various times. However, they are not aware of the specific conditions that give rise to the feeling. In such cases, the therapist must help the client discover the situations that cause anxiety. This is usually done through detailed questions in an interview. Self-report inventories like the Fear Survey Schedule (see Figure 18–1, page 403) are also used.

When the stimuli that elicit anxiety are identified, they are ranked in terms of the increasing amounts of anxiety they evoke. Often there is a common theme among the stimuli (e.g., fear of being alone). Table 19–1 (page 421) provides examples of such **anxiety hierarchies**.

Desensitization: Exposure to Anxiety-Evoking Stimuli

When the client has become proficient at deep muscle relaxation and has constructed one or more anxiety hierarchies, the desensitization process can begin. The client is exposed to the anxiety-evoking stimuli while he or she is relaxed. The aim is associating the stimuli that provoked anxiety with relaxation. This "breaks" the previous maladaptive association between the stimuli and anxiety.

Specifically, the therapist tells the client to relax his or her muscles and then to imagine scenes from the anxiety hierarchy. The client starts

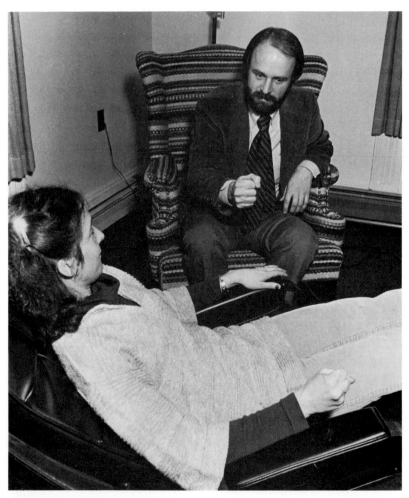

Deep muscle relaxation is the most frequently used response to counter anxiety in systematic desensitization. Clients learn deep muscle relaxation by first tensing and then relaxing various muscle groups. The aim is to learn to discriminate between tension and relaxation, which helps the client achieve the latter. © *Barbara Alper*

TABLE 19–1
Examples of anxiety hierarchies

Examination Series
1. On the way to the university on the day of an examination.
2. In the process of answering an examination paper.
3. Before the unopened doors of the examination room.
4. Awaiting the distribution of examination papers.
5. The examination paper lies face down before her.
6. The night before an examination.
7. On the day before an examination.
8. Two days before an examination.
9. Three days before an examination.
10. Four days before an examination.
11. Five days before an examination.
12. A week before an examination.
13. Two weeks before an examination.
14. A month before an examination.

Discord between Other People
1. Her mother shouts at a servant.
2. Her young sister whines to her mother.
3. Her sister engages in a dispute with her father.
4. Her mother shouts at her sister.
5. She sees two strangers quarrel.

Source: From *Behavior Therapy Techniques: A Guide to the Treatment of Neurosis* by J. Wolpe and A. A. Lazarus, 1966, New York: Pergamon Press.

with the least anxiety-provoking stimulus (i.e., the lowest item on each anxiety hierarchy). Each scene is repeated before going on to the next scene in the hierarchy until the client reports virtually no disturbance while visualizing the scene. Clients can also be exposed to the actual hierarchy stimuli instead of imagining them; this is called **in vivo desensitization** (e.g., Beck, 1985; Last, 1985).

Aversive Counterconditioning

Systematic desensitization neutralizes threatening events by associating them with pleasant experiences, such as deep muscle relaxation. In other instances, just the opposite effect is called for—namely, creating a negative emotional reaction to a pleasurable event. Such **aversive counterconditioning** has been used primarily in the treatment of addictive behaviors (e.g., drug addiction) (Miller, 1980) and sexually deviant behaviors (e.g., exhibitionism) (Maletzky, in press). These behaviors are immediately gratifying to the individual, but they have long-range negative consequences. They are socially inappropriate, culturally prohibited, or physiologically harmful.

Aversive counterconditioning pairs a UCS that normally produces an unpleasant, distasteful, or otherwise negative reaction (UCR) with the CS associated with the behavior to be reduced. This counterconditioning continues until the CS elicits a similar negative reaction (now a CR). The process is illustrated in the treatment of transvestic behavior (cross-dressing) (Lavin, Thorpe, Barker, Blakemore, & Conway, 1961).

The client was a twenty-two-year-old married truck driver. He reported wanting to dress as a woman since the age of eight. From age fifteen and through his military service and marriage, he derived erotic satisfaction from dressing in women's clothes and then looking at himself in a mirror. At the same time, he had a good sexual relationship with his wife.

The therapist photographed the client in various stages of female dress. The client made an audio tape describing the activities in the pictures. As expected, he became sexually aroused while looking at the pictures and listening to the tape.

The treatment involved pairing wearing women's clothes with nausea, produced by injection of a drug. As soon as the injection took effect, the pictures and tape were presented. These stimuli were removed only after the client began vomiting. After six days of treatment involving aversive counterconditioning, the client no longer wanted to wear women's clothes. Systematic follow-up over a six-month period, including interviews with both the client and his wife, suggested that recovery was complete.

The Treatment of Enuresis

Enuresis is the inability of persons older than three to control urination; it most often occurs during sleep, in which case it is called *nocturnal enuresis* or simply bed-wetting. Normally, bladder tension is a UCS that wakes us before urination (UCR) begins; but bladder tension does not "automatically" wake enuretics. Fifty years ago, Mowrer and Mowrer (1938) developed a therapy using classical conditioning called the **bell-and-pad method.** It conditions awakening by pairing bladder tension (a CS for enuretics) with an alarm (UCS), a stimulus that inevitably wakes up (UCR) the person and permits him or her to reach the toilet in time.

The treatment requires a special apparatus. The child sleeps on a specially prepared pad, consisting of two pieces of screening separated by heavy cotton. (See Figure 19–3.) When urination occurs, the urine seeps through the cloth and closes an electrical circuit. In turn, this sounds an alarm. Through repeated pairings, bladder tension (CS) alone comes to wake (CR) the child before urination. A similar classical conditioning procedure was developed to treat constipation (Quarti & Renaud, 1964).

The bell-and-pad technique is an effective treatment for enuresis (Yates, 1970). But there is some doubt that Mowrer and Mowrer's origi-

FIGURE 19–3
A schematic diagram of the bell-and-pad apparatus used to treat nocturnal enuresis

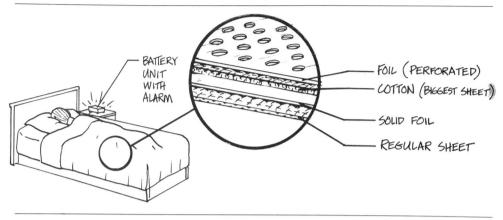

nal explanation in terms of classical conditioning is viable (Liebert & Fischel, 1986). Moreover, potentially more efficient treatments currently exist (e.g., Azrin & Thienes, 1978).

OPERANT CONDITIONING

Classical conditioning focuses on the conditions that come before and elicit behavior. **Operant conditioning** deals primarily with the *consequences* of behavior on future performance. In operant conditioning, we learn to *operate* on the environment by engaging in behaviors that produce certain effects or consequences. When the consequences are pleasant, the behavior tends to be repeated; when they are aversive, the behavior tends not to be repeated. Much of our everyday behavior is learned and maintained by operant conditioning. Operant conditioning is also known as **instrumental conditioning**; the person is *instrumental* in producing the effects.

Skinner and the Skinnerian Tradition

B. F. Skinner's (1904–) views concerning the scientific study of behavior set the ground rules for the operant conditioning approach. Skinner (1971) believes behavior is primarily determined by *external* environmental influences, particularly the consequences of our acts. He challenges the notion that we are autonomous beings in the sense that our behavior is influenced by internal factors (e.g., unconscious impulses, traits, self-

B. F. Skinner

Courtesy of B. F. Skinner, photo by Christopher S. Johnson

actualizing tendencies), which is the model used by the other three personality strategies.

Skinner's approach to personality is not theoretical. Skinner (1953) rejects explanations of behavior in terms of theoretical constructs, which he views as *convenient but redundant fictions.*

> The practice of looking inside the organism for an explanation of behavior has tended to obscure the variables which are immediately available for a scientific analysis. These variables lie outside the organism, in its immediate environment and in its environmental history. . . . The objection to inner states is not that they do not exist, but that they are not relevant. . . . (pp. 31, 35)

In place of theory, Skinner advocates discovering empirical relationships between behavior and the conditions that influence or control it. He is concerned only with observable characteristics of the environment *(stimuli)* that influence overt behavior *(responses)*. In a sense, Skinnerian psychology deals with an "empty organism." Variables that come between, or mediate, stimulus and response, and cannot be explained in terms of stimulus or response, are outside the domain of the operant approach. It should be noted, however, that this position can deal with many phenomena that are the basis for positing internal events in other personality approaches. Skinner (1956) believes in the maxim: "Control your conditions and you will see order." Prediction and control are all that is needed for a thorough understanding of personality.

Reinforcement

At the heart of operant conditioning is the concept of reinforcement. **Reinforcement** occurs whenever an event that follows a behavior (i.e., a consequence) increases the likelihood that the behavior will be repeated.

A **reinforcer** refers to the event that is a consequence of the behavior and has increased its probability of recurring. Note that we have defined reinforcement *empirically*. It depends on increasing the likelihood of the behavior and *not* on subjective desirability. In most cases, however, reinforcers are pleasurable or desirable events we typically call *rewards*.

Two broad categories of reinforcement have been distinguished, positive and negative. With **positive reinforcement,** a stimulus is *presented* following a behavior (e.g., a father praising a son for cleaning his room); with **negative reinforcement,** a stimulus is *removed* following a behavior (e.g., a father stops yelling at his son after the boy has cleaned his room). In both cases, if the stimulus increases the likelihood of repeating the behavior, reinforcement has occurred. Reinforcement always refers to *increasing* (or strengthening) behavior. The designation *positive* or *negative* merely indicates the *addition* or *subtraction* of the stimulus.

Negative reinforcement should not be confused with *punishment*. Punishment has the opposite effect of negative reinforcement. **Punishment** is defined empirically as a situation in which the event following a response *reduces* the probability that the response will recur.

The role of reinforcement in operant conditioning will be illustrated by describing procedures instituted to increase a young boy's studying. The treatment was evaluated by research that employed a **single-subject reversal design.** This research design, which is often used by operant psychologists, compares a subject's behavior in periods in which a treatment is presented and then withdrawn (reversed).

The Case of Robbie

Robbie was an elementary school boy who frequently disrupted class activities and spent almost no time studying (Hall, Lund, & Jackson, 1968). In the first phase of the study, Robbie was observed during seven 30-minute *baseline* periods. At these times, students were supposed to be working in their seats. Figure 19–4 presents a record of Robbie's study behavior. The behavior was defined as his having his pencil on paper for at least half of a ten-second observation. As can be seen in the figure, during the baseline observation, Robbie engaged in study behavior an average of 25 percent of the time. The remaining 75 percent of the time was taken up with behavior like "snapping rubber bands, playing with toys from his pocket, talking and laughing with peers, slowly drinking the half pint of milk served earlier in the morning, and subsequently playing with the empty carton" (Hall et al., 1968, p. 3). Observers also noted that during the baseline period Robbie's teacher paid attention to much of his nonstudy behavior. The attention included urging Robbie to work and to put away his toys.

Following the baseline period, the *conditioning phase* of the study was begun. Now, every time Robbie engaged in one minute of continuous

FIGURE 19–4
A record of Robbie's study behavior

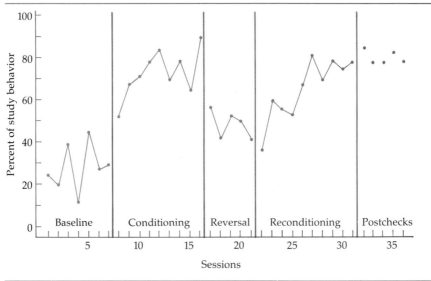

Note: Postcheck observations were made during the fourth, sixth, seventh, twelfth, and fourteenth weeks after the completion of reinforcement conditioning.
Source: Adapted from "Effects of Teacher Attention on Study Behavior," by R. V. Hall, D. Lund, and D. Jackson, 1968, *Journal of Applied Behavior Analysis, 1,* pp. 1–12.

studying, an observer signaled the teacher. The teacher then promptly reinforced the behavior with attention. The teacher ignored Robbie at all other times. The results of this procedure were striking, as can be seen in Figure 19–4. When Robbie received attention only if he studied, the amount of studying increased markedly in the first session. It continued to rise in subsequent sessions. Robbie spent an average of 71 percent of his time studying during the conditioning phase of the study.

It appeared, then, that introducing reinforcement, in the form of the teacher's attention for study behavior, was responsible for the increased rate of studying. Without the baseline to which the conditioning rate can be compared, no such statement could be made. However, it is still possible that some other factor, which occurred in the conditioning phase but not in the baseline period, led to Robbie's increased studying. For example, Robbie's parents might have begun to praise him when he said he studied at school. Thus, a *reversal phase* was instituted. The teacher stopped reinforcing Robbie with attention for his study behavior. This reinstated (reversed) the conditions before the conditioning phase (Cavell, Frentz, & Kelley, 1986). This period was also an *extinction phase;* **extinction** is the withdrawal of reinforcement. If study behavior had been controlled by reinforcement, when the reinforcement was withdrawn, we would expect the amount of study behavior to drop off. As Figure 19–4 clearly shows, Robbie's study behavior did decline during the reversal period to a mean of 50 percent.

The investigation had the practical purpose of increasing Robbie's study behavior. Therefore, a *reconditioning phase* was included. Specifically, teacher attention was reinstated as a reinforcer for studying. The result was an increase in Robbie's study rate. The rate stabilized at a level between 70 and 80 percent (see Figure 19–4). To determine the effectiveness of the operant conditioning procedures in maintaining Robbie's studying, periodic checks (*postchecks*) were made for the rest of the school year. The last check was made in the 14th week. These checks indicated that Robbie's studying was maintained at an average rate of 79 percent (see Figure 19–4). Further, Robbie's teacher reported that the quality of his studying had also improved; he was now completing written assignments and missing fewer words on spelling tests.

Eliciting Behaviors: Prompting and Shaping

For a behavior to be reinforced, the behavior must occur in the first place. This obvious point is important. When the behavior to be increased occurs at least occasionally, like Robbie's studying, we can reinforce it—although we may have to wait some time for the behavior to occur. But suppose the baseline level for a particular behavior is at or near zero. In such cases, two procedures are used to elicit infrequent behaviors so they can be reinforced, prompting and shaping.

Prompting involves reminding or telling someone to perform the behavior. Prompting cues may be *verbal*, as when a parent reminds a child to say "thank you." They may be *physical*, as when a coach moves a student's arms to prompt a swimming stroke. Or they may be *environmental*, as when a green traffic light prompts a driver to go. Once the behavior occurs often enough to be reinforced, the prompts may be gradually withdrawn. This procedure is called **fading.**

Prompting and subsequent fading of prompts are often used to teach language to children with severe mental handicaps. To teach the name of an object, the teacher points to it and says, "What is this? *Cup.*" As the child begins to say "cup," the teacher fades the prompt. The teacher does this by saying "cup" at successively lower volumes, whispering, then only mouthing, and finally withdrawing the prompt entirely so the child is only asked, "What is this?"

Another way to elicit behavior is to shape it. **Shaping** involves reinforcing progressively closer approximations of the behavior. First the desired behavior is broken down into its component parts. Then each component is reinforced until the entire behavior occurs. The logic of shaping is illustrated schematically in Figure 19–5. A common example of shaping is the children's game of "hot and cold." One child has to find an object in a room. A playmate directs the child by saying

FIGURE 19–5
A diagram representing the principle of shaping

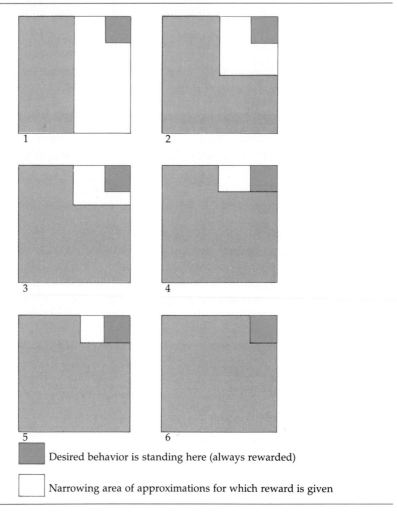

◼ Desired behavior is standing here (always rewarded)

☐ Narrowing area of approximations for which reward is given

"hot" when the child gets closer to the object and "cold" when the child moves farther away. Prompting and shaping are often used together to elicit behavior.

The following excerpt is from a case study of a forty-year-old male psychiatric patient. He had been completely mute during nineteen years of hospitalization. The case illustrates the use of shaping and prompting. To elicit the word *gum*, the experimenter first reinforced eye movement indicating attention. Then lip movements, next vocalizations, and finally successive approximations of the word were reinforced.

The S [subject] was brought to a group therapy session with other chronic schizophrenics (who were verbal), but he sat in the position in which he was placed and continued with withdrawal behaviors that characterized him. He remained impassive and stared ahead even when cigarettes, which other members accepted, were offered to him and were waved before his face. At one session, when E [experimenter] removed cigarettes from his pocket, a package of chewing gum accidentally fell out. The S's eyes moved toward the gum and then returned to their usual position. This response was chosen by E as one with which he would start.

The S met individually with E three times a week. The following sequence of procedures was introduced in the private sessions.

Weeks 1, 2. A stick of gum was held before S's face, and E waited until S's eyes moved toward it. When this response occurred, E as a consequence gave him the gum. By the end of the second week, response probability in the presence of the gum was increased to such an extent that S's eyes moved toward the gum as soon as it was held up.

Weeks 3, 4. The E now held the gum before S, waiting until he noticed movement in S's lips before giving it to him. Toward the end of the first session of the third week, a lip movement spontaneously occurred, which E promptly reinforced. By the end of this week, both lip movement and eye movement occurred when the gum was held up. The E then withheld giving S the gum until S spontaneously made a vocalization, at which time E gave S the gum. By the end of this week, holding up the gum readily occasioned eye movement toward it, lip movement, and a vocalization resembling a croak.

Weeks 5, 6. The E held up the gum, and said, "Say gum, gum," repeating these words each time S vocalized. Giving S the gum was made contingent upon vocalizations increasingly approximating gum. At the sixth session (at the end of Week 6), when E said, "Say gum, gum," S suddenly said, "Gum, please." (Isaacs, Thomas, & Goldiamond, 1960, pp. 9–10)

Schedules of Reinforcement

A **schedule of reinforcement** is the sequence or pattern in which reinforcement is received. In a **continuous reinforcement schedule,** the individual is reinforced every time he or she performs the behavior to be increased. Continuous reinforcement is generally used to initially condition a response, as in the examples of Robbie and the mute psychiatric patient. However, reinforcement for each response is rare in everyday life. Most of our behavior, once learned, is *maintained* by **intermittent** or **partial**

schedules in which only some instances of the desired response are rein-forced.

There are four basic schedules of intermittent reinforcement. They are produced by the combination of two dimensions: (1) the number of responses versus the period of time since the last reinforcement and (2) fixed versus variable quantity. (See Figure 19–6.) With **ratio schedules,** reinforcement occurs after a certain *number of responses* have been made. That number can be fixed (e.g., after every fifth response) or variable (e.g., after the third response, then after the seventh response, and so on). With **interval schedules,** reinforcement occurs if the response occurs (at least once) after a specified *period of time* since the last reinforce-ment; the time interval can be fixed (e.g., after five minutes) or variable (e.g., three minutes, then seven minutes, and so on). The four schedules of intermittent reinforcement are compared in Figure 19–7.

Fixed-Interval Schedules

In a **fixed-interval schedule,** reinforcement is given for the first response made after a set period of time has elapsed, such as every two minutes. (See Figure 19–7.) Many behaviors are maintained by fixed-interval schedules, including studying for college examinations, salaried work, and sometimes babies' feeding. Figure 19–8 shows that a fixed-interval schedule produces a reliable pattern of responding that looks "scal-loped" when graphed cumulatively.[1] With this schedule the person makes few responses immediately after reinforcement. The pace of re-sponse accelerates until the time for the next reinforcement. Consider,

FIGURE 19–6
The four basic schedules of intermittent reinforcement

	Interval (time since last reinforcement)	Ratio (number of responses)
Fixed (set time period or number)	FIXED-INTERVAL	FIXED-RATIO
Variable (changing time period or number)	VARIABLE-INTERVAL	VARIABLE-RATIO

---

[1]In a *cumulative record*, the steeper the slope or angle of the curve, the greater the rate of responding. Near-vertical curves indicate very high rates of responding and near horizontal curves indicate very low rates. A totally horizontal (flat) curve means no responding.

FIGURE 19–7
Comparison of fixed versus variable interval and ratio schedules of reinforcement
(arrows indicate reinforcement)

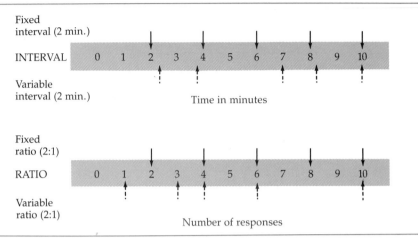

as an example, your own study behavior following an exam. You are least likely to study right after an exam and most likely to study right before one. And you have company in your habit. Even members of the U.S. Congress operate on a fixed-interval schedule (Weisberg & Waldrop, 1972). Bills are passed at a very low rate for the first few months of each session. As adjournment draws closer, the number of bills passed increases sharply, thereby producing the "scalloped" cumulative record in Figure 19–9 (page 433).

Many workers are paid on an hourly basis. This is an example of a fixed-interval schedule of reinforcement. *Photo by Michael D. Spiegler*

Fixed-Ratio Schedules

In **fixed-ratio** schedules, reinforcement is administered after a set number of responses. For example, a fixed ratio of 4:1 is a schedule in which every fourth response is reinforced. Fixed-ratio schedules generally produce considerably higher rates of responding than either continuous reinforcement or fixed-interval schedules. As Figure 19–8 shows, the slope of the cumulative curve for a fixed-ratio schedule is steeper than the slope for a fixed-interval schedule. This indicates a higher response rate. If fixed-ratio schedules are gradually built up, subjects will continue to respond on extremely "lean" schedules in which

FIGURE 19–8
Stylized records of responding under basic schedules of reinforcement

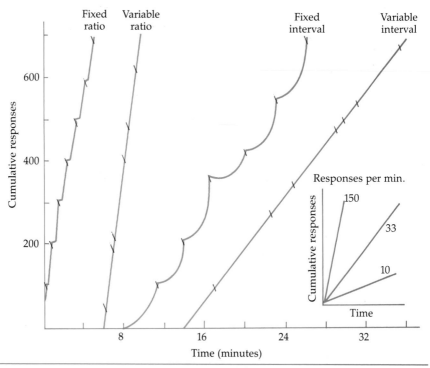

Note: Diagonal marks indicate reinforcement; the slope of various response rates is indicated at lower right. *Fixed ratio:* high rate, with brief pause following reinforcement and abrupt change to terminal rate. *Variable ratio:* high sustained rate; no pausing after reinforcement. *Fixed interval:* low overall response rate due to pause following reinforcement; length of pause increases with length of interval; gradual increase to high final rate as interval ends. *Variable interval:* low sustained rate; no pausing after reinforcement.

Source: Adapted from "The Analysis of Human Operant Behavior" by E. P. Reese, 1966, in J. A. Vernon (Ed.), *Introduction to Psychology: A Self-Selection Textbook*, Dubuque, Iowa: Brown.

the ratio of unreinforced to reinforced responses is very high (e.g., 1,000:1). A fixed-ratio schedule is common in education

> where the student is reinforced for completing a project or a paper or some other specific amount of work. It is essentially the basis of professional pay and of selling on commission. In industry it is known as piecework pay. . . . A limiting factor . . . is simple fatigue. The high rate of responding and the long hours of work generated by this schedule can be dangerous to health. This is the main reason why piecework pay is usually strenuously opposed by organized labor.
>
> Another objection to this type of schedule is based upon the possibility that as the rate rises, the reinforcing agency will move to a larger ratio. . . . the employee whose productivity has increased as the result of a piecework schedule may receive so large a weekly

FIGURE 19–9

Cumulative number of bills passed during the legislative sessions of Congress from January 1947 to August 1954

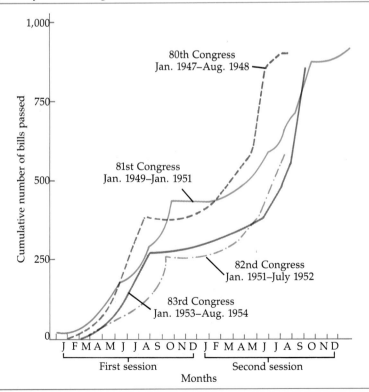

Source: From "Fixed-Interval Work Habits of Congress" by P. Weisberg and P. B. Waldrop, 1972, *Journal of Applied Behavior Analysis, 5,* pp. 93–97.

wage that the employer feels justified in increasing the number of units of work required for a given unit of pay. (Skinner, 1953, pp. 102–3)

Variable-Interval Schedules

In everyday life there is often variability in our schedules of reinforcement. In **variable-interval schedules,** the interval between reinforcements is randomly varied around a specified time. The result is that, *on the average,* the individual is reinforced, say, every two minutes. (See Figure 19–7 on page 431.)

> Some kinds of sports activities operate on this schedule, such as hunting and fishing. A fisherman drops in his line, and then he must wait. He does not know precisely when the fish will bite (maybe not at all) . . . even though through past conditioning history he has found certain areas to be situations in which the reinforcements occur. Although these reinforcements of catching the fish . . . are a function of his skill, the aspects of the availability of the reinforcements to him are a function of some undetermined schedule. The enthusiastic sportsman has a regularity of behavior that has had a past history of reinforcement, even though variable. (Lundin, 1961, p. 88)

Variable-interval schedules produce steady but relatively low response rates, rather than the "scalloped" ones of fixed-interval schedules. (See Figure 19–8 on page 432.)

Variable-Ratio Schedules

With a **variable-ratio schedule** the number of responses required for reinforcement is varied randomly around a particular ratio. The stated ratio

Piece work is an example of reinforcement based on a fixed-ratio schedule. *Photo by Michael D. Spiegler*

is the average of the number of required responses. (See Figure 19–7.) Variable-ratio schedules are among the most potent for inducing very high, steady rates of responding, as shown in Figure 19–8. The potentially powerful effect of variable-ratio schedules can be seen in compulsive gambling (e.g., Greene, 1982).

> Even though the returns are very slim, he never gives up. Families are ruined and fortunes lost; still the high rates of behavior are maintained, often to the exclusion of all alternate forms of activity. Witness the "all night" crap games in which a single person will remain until all his funds and resources are gone. . . . Although gambling may involve other auxiliary reinforcements, social and personal, the basic rate of behavior is maintained by the schedule itself. The degree of control exercised by such a schedule is . . . almost absolute. . . . The degree of control is often unfortunate and dangerous to the individual and his family, and the paradoxical thing about it is that the controlling agency (unless the gambling

Fishing is reinforced on a variable-interval schedule. The time between catches is variable and often the person will continue fishing even though a long time has passed since catching the last fish. © *William J. Jahoda from National Audubon Society*

devices are "fixed") is the simple factor of chance. (Lundin, 1961, p. 91)

Stimulus Control

Learning always involves two aspects. We learn *how* to perform a behavior. We must also learn to discriminate *when* and *where* the behavior is appropriate. (*Appropriateness* in this context refers to the likelihood of reinforcement.) **Discriminative stimuli** are environmental cues that tell us when a response is likely to be reinforced. Operant responses are primarily maintained by their consequences. However, discriminative stimuli play a role in maintaining behavior by setting the occasion for the behavior, which allows it to be reinforced. Behavior that is cued by discriminative stimuli is said to be under **stimulus control.**

Prompts are examples of discriminative stimuli that are introduced to establish stimulus control. In our everyday lives, we frequently encounter "naturally occurring" discriminative stimuli; in fact, most operant behaviors are under stimulus control in one way or another. The ringing

Gambling pays off on a variable-ratio schedule. The number of bets between winning is quite variable, and gamblers continue to bet even though many preceding bets have not paid off. This is one explanation of the lure of and even the addiction to gambling. *Photo by Dave Bellak/ Jeroboam*

telephone signals us to pick up the receiver and say hello. We are more likely to smile at someone who smiles rather than frowns at us. A police car up ahead is often a sufficient discriminative stimulus for decreasing our speed.

The same response may be controlled by different discriminative stimuli for different people. For example, in countries where food is scarce, people eat when their stomachs "tell" them that they are hungry. In more affluent societies, such as our own, people tend to eat when the clock "tells" them that they are "hungry."

The right amount of stimulus control is necessary for functioning efficiently. Too much or inappropriate stimulus control leads to rigidity. For example, parents of young children sometimes discover that bedtime is likely to be observed only when they are home and not when the children are left with grandparents or babysitters. The parents have become the discriminative stimuli for observing bedtime; the children have not learned to *generalize* the behavior to other discriminative stimuli.

More often, problems arise from too little appropriate stimulus control. Insomnia, for instance, may be due to the fact that sleeping is not under appropriate stimulus control. One behavioral-therapy treatment for insomnia involves establishing appropriate stimulus control (e.g., Bootzin, 1985). The client is asked to follow a basic set of rules, like those in Table 19–2, to establish the cues of bed and feeling tired as the discriminative stimuli for sleep and to acquire a consistent sleep rhythm.

TABLE 19–2
Rules clients follow in stimulus-control treatment of insomnia

Rule	Rationale
1. Go to sleep only when sleepy.	Establish feeling sleepy as a discriminative stimulus for sleeping.
2. Use bed only for sleeping.	Establish bed as discriminative stimulus for sleeping and not for any other behaviors (e.g., reading, eating). Sexual activity is the one exception.
3. If unable to fall asleep (within ten minutes) get out of bed.	Establish bed as discriminative stimulus for falling asleep quickly.
4. If unable to fall asleep after returning to bed, repeat Rule 3.	Same as above.
5. Get up at same time every morning.	Helps establish consistent sleep rhythm.
6. Do not nap.	Napping disrupts sleep rhythm and decreases chances of being sleepy at bed time.

Source: Based on "Behavioral Treatments for Insomnia" by R. R. Bootzin and P. M. Nicassio, 1978, in M. Hersen, R. M. Eisler, and P. M. Miller (Eds.), *Progress in Behavior Modification*, Vol. 6, New York: Academic Press.

DEMONSTRATION 19–1

OPERANT CONDITIONING OF HUMAN BEHAVIOR[2]

By doing this Demonstration, you will see a number of the principles of operant conditioning actually work. You will need to enlist the aid of a friend as a subject. Be sure that the friend has at least forty-five minutes of free time. The only equipment needed are a watch or clock that reads minutes and seconds, and pencil and paper.

THE RESPONSE

The first step is to select the response you will teach your subject. The procedures to be outlined will work with complex motor or verbal responses. For this Demonstration, we suggest you choose a relatively simple response; Table 19–3 contains suggestions. Other than simplicity, the response you choose to condition should meet three additional requirements.

1. The response should be *relatively brief.*

2. The response should *end where it began.* When the response is completed, the subject should be able to immediately perform the same response without having to rearrange the situation. (For example, you would not want to condition "opening a book" because you would have to close the book before the subject can open it again. Such rearrangement would be a salient cue for the subject and thus would confound the exercise.)

3. The response should normally *occur at a speed that makes recording feasible.* (Finger tapping, for example, would be a poor choice.)

SHAPING

If the response you select is one your subject makes frequently, then all you have to do is wait until it occurs to reinforce it. If, however, it oc-

TABLE 19–3
Examples of responses suitable for operant conditioning in Demonstration 19–1

Motor Responses	Verbal Responses
Opening and closing a book	Criticizing
Taking top off a pen and replacing it	Talking about the future
Standing up and sitting down	Talking about schoolwork
Nodding head	Using plural nouns

[2]The procedures used in this Demonstration are, in part, adapted from Verplanck (1956).

curs infrequently, you may have to shape it. This requires breaking down the total response into logical component parts and then successively reinforcing each one. For example, the components of "opening and closing a book" might be as follows.

1. First movement made; this will start the subject moving about. *The first movement the subject makes should be the initial component of any motor response.*

2. Movement of either hand.

3. Movement of either hand toward the book.

4. Touching the book.

5. Opening the book partway.

6. Opening it fully.

7. Closing the book.

Similarly, the steps to be reinforced for "verbal criticism" might be:

1. Any verbal utterance (e.g., a word or even a sound). *The subject's first verbal utterance should be the initial component of any verbal response.*

2. Any statement (i.e., as opposed to a question).

3. Any negative statement.

4. Any negative statement that is a criticism.

Keep in mind that the steps suggested above are examples only; they will not work in all cases. It may be necessary to create more steps in the sequence by breaking down some of the existing steps into additional components. It is also possible that your subject will combine some of the approximations you established. Shaping is very much an art, and it is only through practice that you will "get a feel" for the procedure. Figure 19–10 is a cumulative record of a response that was initially shaped.

REINFORCEMENT

Each time the subject makes a correct response (or an approximation of it, if shaping is being used), say the word *point.* (Earning points, like receiving grades, provides feedback that one is performing correctly. It is an example of a **token reinforcer,** so-called because the reinforcer itself has no actual value.)

The subject should be able to see a record of the points earned. This can be conveniently done by instructing the subject to make a tally mark on a sheet of paper each time you say "point." Or you can mark the points on a record sheet that is clearly visible to the subject.

The prompt and accurate administration of reinforcement is essential for operant conditioning. If reinforcement is not administered

FIGURE 19–10
Cumulative record of "hand raising" shaped by operant conditioning

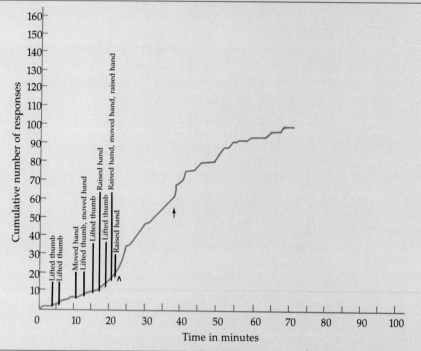

Note: Following the caret (∧), only the complete response was reinforced. Following the arrow (↑) no responses were reinforced (i.e., extinction).
Source: From "The Operant Conditioning of Human Motor Behavior" by W. S. Verplanck, 1956, *Psychological Bulletin, 53,* pp. 70–83.

promptly, then it is likely that one or more other responses will occur between the termination of the target response and the reinforcement. This will make it difficult for the subject to discriminate the response for which reinforcement is contingent. Thus, the reinforcement should be given *immediately* after the correct response (or an approximation of it) occurs. Careful observation of the subject's behavior is necessary to determine whether the response, as you have defined it, has been made.

PROCEDURE

Preparation

Before your subject arrives, arrange the room so that the subject will be sitting facing you. Place any props that are part of the response (e.g., a book for "opening and closing a book") near where the subject will be.

If you are using a room with which the subject is familiar, be sure that the physical arrangement does not appear out of the ordinary lest this "give away" the correct response.

Instructions to the Subject

When your subject arrives, explain that you are doing a project for one of your classes. Then give the following instructions:

"*Your job is to earn points. I will tell you each time you earn a point, and you (I) will record it immediately on this sheet of paper by making a tally mark for each point you receive. Try to get as many points as you can.*"

Do not give any further instructions to the subject. If the subject asks you a question, merely say: "*I'm sorry, but I'm not permitted to answer any questions. Just work for points and earn as many as you can.*"

After hearing your instructions, your subject may sit motionless and say nothing for several minutes. Sooner or later, however, your subject will make a response that you will be able to reinforce. Although this initial period of inactivity may be awkward for both of you, it should not affect the success of the conditioning. Do *not* try to break the silence or awkward social situation.

OBSERVATION AND RECORDING

Once you have instructed your subject as described above, your task is to (1) observe your subject's behavior very carefully, (2) record the frequency with which the correct response (or an approximation of it) is made, and (3) reinforce correct responses.

Prepare a record sheet similar to Figure 19–11. (Do not confuse the subject's record of the points earned with the record you keep of the subject's behavior and the procedures employed.) Your record sheet should *not* be visible to the subject. Three types of information should be recorded.

1. When the subject makes a correct response, note the 30-second interval in which it occurred. Your watch should be placed so that you can easily see it without indicating to your subject that you are checking the time.

2. Indicate on the record sheet whether a reinforcer was given for a response by circling the check mark (see Figure 19–11). This procedure is essential when the subject is shifted to a partial reinforcement schedule.

3. Indicate on the record sheet all procedural changes, such as a shift in reinforcement schedule. This can easily be done by making a dark, vertical line at the point of change in procedure. As illustrated in Figure 19–11, a small lowercase letter is placed adjacent to this line,

FIGURE 19-11
Model record sheet for Demonstration 19-1

Response = *looking out the window and then looking back*

✓ = Response   ⊘ = Reinforced response

30-second time interval	Total For each interval	Cumu-lative	30-second time interval	Total For each interval	Cumu-lative
1.	0	0	25. ✓✓✓	3	66
2.	0	0	26. ✓⊘✓	3	69
3. ⊘/a	1	1	27. ✓✓✓	3	72
4.	0	1	28. ⊘✓✓✓	4	76
5. ⊘⊘	2	3	29. ✓⊘✓✓	4	80
6.	0	3	30. ✓✓⊘	3	83
7. ⊘⊘	2	5	31. ✓✓✓✓	4	87
8. ⊘⊘	2	7	32. ⊘✓✓	3	90
9. ⊘⊘⊘	3	10	33. d/✓✓✓	3	93
10. ⊘⊘⊘⊘	4	14	34. ✓✓✓✓	4	97
11. ⊘⊘⊘	3	17	35. ✓✓✓	3	100
12. ⊘⊘⊘⊘	4	21	36. ✓✓	2	102
13. ⊘⊘⊘⊘	4	25	37. ✓✓	2	104
14. ⊘⊘⊘⊘	4	29	38.	0	104
15. ⊘⊘⊘⊘	4	33	39. ✓✓	2	106
16. b/✓✓✓/c	3	36	40. ✓✓	2	108
17. ✓⊘	2	38	41. ✓	1	109
18. ✓✓	2	40	42.	0	109
19. ✓✓	2	42	43. ✓	1	110
20. ⊘✓✓✓✓	5	47	44.	0	110
21. ⊘✓✓✓✓	4	51	45.	0	110
22. ✓⊘✓✓	4	55	46.	0	110
23. ✓✓⊘✓	4	59	47.	0	110
24. ✓✓✓⊘	4	63	48.	0	110

Comments:

a = Subject asks why a point was earned
b = start of fixed-ratio 5:1
c = Subject asks why I stopped giving points
d = start of extinction

and it is defined at the bottom of the record sheet in the space provided for comments.

CONDITIONING

The Demonstration involves three phases of conditioning: acquisition, partial reinforcement, and extinction.

Acquisition: Continuous Reinforcement

During acquisition, *every correct response* (or approximation of it) *is given a point.* Continuous reinforcement is the most efficient and effective way to initially establish a response. Continuously reinforce your subject until the *complete* response (not just a component of it) has been reinforced a minimum of 10 times.

If, after a number of continuous reinforcements, the subject's rate of responding begins to decrease noticeably, you should simply say: *"Keep earning points."* This will usually restore the previous response rate. Indicate on your record sheet when you gave this additional instruction to your subject.

Shift to Partial Reinforcement

Once the response has been well established—after a minimum of 10 continuous reinforcements—you will be able to shift your subject to a partial reinforcement schedule with little difficulty. Use a *"fixed-ratio 5:1"*; that is, reinforce every fifth response. This means that, although you will continue to *record* every response your subject makes in the 30-second interval in which it occurs, only after every five responses will you say, "Point." However, the five consecutive responses required for reinforcement need *not* occur in the same 30-second interval. Under this fixed-ratio schedule, you should observe that your subject's rate of responding will increase and that there will be a brief pause after each reinforcement (see Figure 19–8). Continue on the 5:1 fixed-ratio schedule for a minimum of 8 reinforcements (i.e., 40 responses).

When you shift to the partial reinforcement schedule, you may find that the subject will begin to emit other responses. The subject may also begin counting responses aloud or making statements to the effect that points are being earned for every five responses. Do not let such behavior changes bother you; just continue with the operant procedures.

Extinction

The final phase of the conditioning involves extinction of the response. This is done by completely withdrawing reinforcement for the response. Continue to record the number of responses that the subject makes in each thirty-second interval, but do *not* give points for any of these responses. Continue the extinction phase until the subject has failed to emit the response *during five successive thirty-second recording intervals.*

PLOTTING A CUMULATIVE RECORD

Once you have collected the data for the three phases of conditioning, you can plot the frequency of responding on a cumulative record similar to that in Figure 19–12 (which is a graph of the data in the record sheet

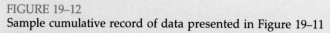

FIGURE 19–12
Sample cumulative record of data presented in Figure 19–11

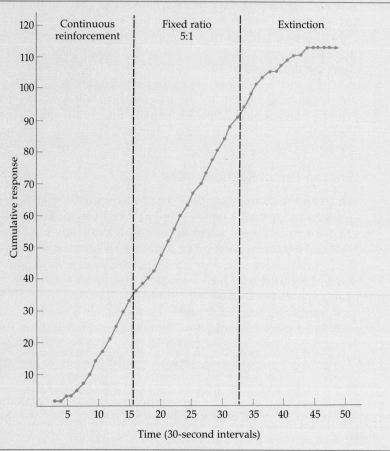

in Figure 19–11). Be sure to use graph paper that will accommodate the total (cumulative) number of responses for the entire recording period on the vertical axis. Draw dashed verticle lines to separate phases (as in Figure 19–12). Additionally, you may wish to note, with small vertical lines, any special changes in procedure and, in the case of shaping, the response component made (see Figure 19–10). You can do this either by writing directly on the cumulative record or with a lowercase letter that refers to a statement written at the bottom.

BEHAVIOR MODIFICATION: OPERANT BEHAVIORAL THERAPY

The principles of operant conditioning have been extensively applied to personality change. Operant behavioral therapy is often called **behavior modification.** It primarily changes the *consequences* of a behavior (i.e., reinforcement and punishment) in order to modify it. We will discuss the process in this section. Stimulus control procedures, which deal with the antecedents of a behavior, are also part of behavior modification; we have already presented the example of treating insomnia through stimulus control.

Behavior modification deals with overt behaviors. When clients' problems involve covert behaviors, such as feelings or thoughts, specific overt behaviors that are associated with the covert behaviors become the targets of change. Fear, for example, is often defined in terms of *avoidance behavior*. The person stays away from fear-evoking situations, as by avoiding interacting with strangers. Therapy might increase the client's approach behaviors by shaping closer and more intimate contact with strangers.

In behavior modification, desirable (adaptive) behaviors are *accelerated*, or increased. Undesirable (maladaptive) behaviors are *decelerated*, or decreased. Often therapy will combine these two basic goals to alleviate a client's problems.

Accelerating Adaptive Behaviors

Therapies that use reinforcement to accelerate adaptive behaviors, such as social skills, are often highly potent techniques. Unlike many verbal, insight-oriented psychotherapies (e.g., psychoanalysis and client-centered therapy), reinforcement therapies can be used with almost any client. This includes clients who have very low IQs, who do not speak, and who are suffering from serious abnormal behaviors, such as schizophrenia (Spiegler, 1983).

In a **token economy,** clients' adaptive behavior is systematically motivated (Spiegler, 1986). Clients earn token reinforcers (e.g., points, poker chips) for performing desirable behaviors. They exchange the tokens for tangible rewards that are referred to as **backup reinforcers.** Token economies are often used with groups of clients, such as patients on a psychiatric ward or school children. Standard lists describe the desirable behaviors and the number of tokens earned for performing each. The backup reinforcers that can be purchased and the specific token cost for each are also listed. Thus, clients know ahead of time exactly what they have to do to earn tokens and how they can spend them (Spiegler & Agigian, 1977). Token economies have been successfully used in a variety of settings. These include treatment programs for psychiatric patients, intellectually handicapped individuals, and predelinquent adolescents, as well as in classrooms (Fernandez, 1983).

In recent years, behavioral therapy techniques have been used increasingly to treat and prevent medical disorders and health-related problems. This is a relatively new discipline known as **behavioral medicine.** Seizures, pain, headaches, hypertension, cardiovascular disease, ulcers, insomnia, and obesity are among the disorders that have been treated using behavior modification. Additionally, reinforcement procedures have been successful in motivating patients to comply with medical procedures (e.g., taking medication and doing rehabilitative exercises) and to practice health care behaviors (e.g., regular checkups) that may prevent medical and dental problems.

Decelerating Maladaptive Behaviors

One way to decelerate maladaptive behaviors is to accelerate adaptive behaviors that will substitute for the maladaptive ones (e.g., Hogan & Johnson, 1985; Pfiffner, Rosén, & O'Leary, 1985). For instance, a man who was being treated for "violent outbursts" toward his family was reinforced for responding to disagreements at home with problem solving and appropriate assertive behavior.

Sometimes it is desirable to decelerate a problem behavior directly (e.g., Rosén, O'Leary, Joyce, Conway, & Pfiffner, 1984). This is done by making the consequences of the undesirable behavior aversive in some way. The person will therefore be less likely to engage in it. Technically, such procedures are forms of *punishment* because they *decrease* the likelihood that the behavior will recur. However, the common usage of the term *punishment* connotes physically aversive consequences which actually are seldom used in behavior modification (Franks, 1984; Spiegler, 1983). Instead, most operant procedures that decelerate maladaptive behavior eliminate the reinforcers maintaining the behavior. These procedures, especially when combined with accelerating substitute adaptive behaviors, are effective with a wide array of maladaptive behaviors (Matson & DiLorenzo, 1984).

Extinction, as a therapy procedure, involves withdrawing or withholding the reinforcers maintaining the maladaptive behavior. It is often used when the reinforcer is social attention. Take the case of four-year-old Cindy (Piacentini, Schaughency, & Lahey, 1985). Her severe temper tantrums appeared to be reinforced by her mother's attention. The therapist told Cindy's mother to ignore the tantrums. To deal with tantrums involving verbal or physical aggression, another deceleration procedure known as **time out from positive reinforcement** (**time out** for short) was suggested. Time out involves withdrawing a client's access to positive reinforcers for a brief, preset time period immediately after the maladaptive behavior occurs. In Cindy's case, when the aggressive tantrum occurred, Cindy was put in her room for five minutes. (This removed the many potential reinforcers outside her room.) Cindy was allowed out of the room after five minutes if she was not having a tantrum during at least the last minute of the time-out period. Extinction and time out were supplemented with positive reinforcement of appropriate behaviors. The combined treatments successfully eliminated Cindy's temper tantrums.

Response cost is a deceleration technique in which some valued item or privilege is removed when the maladaptive behavior is performed. For example, a college student wanted to eliminate dropping clothes all over her room. She instituted a response cost procedure. Any article of clothing not in its proper place (e.g., drawer, closet, hamper) when she woke up in the morning was put in a box and could not be removed until the end of the week (Spiegler, 1987). This relatively simple procedure substantially reduced the student's messy behavior. In many instances, the threat of response cost is a powerful incentive and prevents the client from engaging in the undesirable behavior. For example, a woman addicted to amphetamines gave her therapist ten fifty-dollar checks. The therapist would forward the checks as a donation to the Ku Klux Klan if the client (who was black) took drugs. This response-cost procedure had to be used only once during the three months of treatment. The client was drug-free at a fifteen-month follow-up (Boudin, 1972).

SUMMARY

1. Pavlov described the process of classical conditioning in nonhuman animals, and Watson extended the idea to humans.

2. Some radical behaviorists view anxiety as a classically conditioned response. To deal with such anxiety, Wolpe developed systematic desensitization. It involves pairing anxiety-provoking stimuli with incompatible responses (such as deep muscle relaxation).

3. Aversive counter conditioning involves association of an unpleasant stimulus with a response to be eliminated. It has been used primarily with addictive and sexually deviant behaviors.

4. Nocturnal enuresis (bed-wetting) has been successfully treated with the bell-and-pad method, which activates an alarm when clients begin to wet the bed.

5. Operant conditioning is closely associated with the Skinnerian tradition, which holds that the best way to explain the occurrence of any behavior is through analysis of the conditions that maintain it.

6. Positive reinforcement occurs when the contingent presentation of a stimulus increases the future likelihood of the response that immediately preceded it. Negative reinforcement occurs when the contingent

removal of a stimulus increases the future likelihood of the response that immediately preceded it.

7. Prompts are used to elicit infrequently occurring behaviors so they can be reinforced. Prompting involves showing or reminding someone how to perform a behavior. In shaping, progressively closer approximations of the desired behavior are reinforced.

8. Schedules of reinforcement describe the pattern or sequence in which reinforcers are administered. The four basic schedules of reinforcement are fixed-interval, fixed-ratio, variable-interval, and variable-ratio.

9. Discriminative stimuli are environmental cues that tell us when or where a particular response will be reinforced. Behavior that is cued by discriminative stimuli is said to be under stimulus control.

10. Behavior modification (operant behavioral therapy) has been used both to accelerate adaptive behaviors and to decelerate maladaptive behaviors. Accelerating adaptive behaviors has come to play an important role in the treatment and prevention of many health-related problems. Decelerating problem behaviors can be done indirectly by accelerating alternative adaptive behaviors or directly with such procedures as extinction and response cost.

THE BEHAVIORAL STRATEGY

CHAPTER 20

THE FAMILY OF SOCIAL LEARNING THEORIES

OVERVIEW

The radical behavioral approach was discussed in the previous chapter. Its roots are in ideas developed in the first half of this century. During this period, the phenomenon that most concerned behaviorists was conditioning. Conditioning was considered a relatively automatic process. It invariably occurred if the appropriate environmental conditions were established.

In the 1960s, psychologists turned their interest to *cognition,* or thought processes. This shift was dramatic; many historians consider the past two decades a "cognitive revolution" in psychology. The cognitive revolution was fueled by experiments showing that people are not affected by objective experiences per se, but rather by the way they interpret and remember these experiences (Neisser, 1967).

As explained in the previous chapter, psychologists espousing the radical behavioral approach to personality took their lead from the mechanistic tradition in experimental psychology. Similarly, many personality psychologists in the past decade were influenced by the new cognitive approach. This is true for both the social learning approaches discussed in this chapter and even more so for the cognitive-behavioral approaches discussed in Chapter 21.

The phrase *social learning* is appealing to personality psychologists because it weds learning—one of the most basic psychological processes— to the idea that personality always develops in a social context. There is no one social learning theory. Rather, the name is given to a family of theories. In this chapter, we describe three specific social learning theories.

MILLER AND DOLLARD'S SOCIAL LEARNING THEORY

Neal Miller (1909–   ) and John Dollard (1900–1980) were the first to use the term *social learning theory.* In their 1941 book, *Social Learning and Imitation,* they applied the learning theory of Clark Hull to personality phenomena. Hull's theory says that behavior is learned through a sequence of four events: drive, cue, response, and reinforcement.

Drive is the motivation behind all behavior. **Primary drives** come

Neal Miller

Courtesy Rockefeller University, Public Information Office, New York

John Dollard

Courtesy Yale University Library

from the biological needs of the individual. **Secondary drives** develop by association with primary drives. Hunger, for example, is the primary drive for all food seeking. The desire to find a fast-food restaurant would be an example of a secondary drive.

Cues determine when, where, and how we respond to a drive state. According to Miller and Dollard, learning to notice and interpret cues is of central importance to social learning. Among the most important cues are the responses we observe others, our **social models,** making in particular situations. For instance, a young man attending his first formal dinner will probably be motivated to show appropriate table manners—such as knowing which fork to use for salad, which for the main course, and which for dessert. But he may not know how to respond. By watching more experienced guests and "taking his cues from them," the young man can respond appropriately, even though he has never been in the situation before. Miller and Dollard's concept of **modeling cues** and the need to interpret them correctly remains a central concept in social learning theories today.

The most important element in the learning sequence is the *response.* Miller and Dollard paid a good deal of attention to how responses are initially produced and then modified. They concluded that learning to make appropriate responses typically involves much trial and error—until the appropriate cues are learned.

A good part of the trick of animal training, clinical therapy, and school teaching is to arrange the situation so that the learner will somehow make the first correct response. A bashful boy at his first dance cannot begin to learn either that girls will not bite him or how to make the correct dance step until he begins responding by trying to dance. (Dollard & Miller, 1950, p. 35)

The assumption that trial and error plays a major role in the early phases of social learning was perhaps the greatest limitation of Miller and Dollard's theory. They failed to see that social learning can often be a much more cognitive process. It lets people identify an appropriate response without direct experience. Contemporary social learning theories, as we shall see, emphasize how much can be learned without trial and error.

Reinforcement is the final element in the learning sequence. Reinforcement plays a central role in most learning theories. But these theories differ on the critical question, "What is reinforcing?" Miller and Dollard answered along the lines of Hull's learning theory. They assumed that reinforcement always involved *drive reduction* (cf. Freud's theory, Chapter 4). Later social learning theorists have not agreed with this assumption. They cast the concept of reinforcement in a very different light, as we will see.

Little, if any, personality theory, research, or psychotherapy today is based directly on Miller and Dollard's social learning theory. Nonetheless, their work is important because it defined many of the issues for the modern social learning theories to which we now turn.

ROTTER'S SOCIAL LEARNING THEORY

Julian B. Rotter (1916–   ) provided the next major development in social learning theory. In 1954, his book, *Social Learning and Clinical Psychology*, was published. Rotter, like Miller and Dollard, had an early interest in integrating laboratory psychology and clinical insights about human behavior into a comprehensive personality theory. Unlike Miller and Dollard, however, Rotter included cognitive elements in his formulations.

Julian Rotter

Courtesy University of Connecticut

Rotter's Four Basic Constructs

Rotter uses four basic constructs in his theory: behavior potential, reinforcement value, expectancy, and the psychological situation.

Behavior Potential

Behavior potential is the likelihood that a given behavior will occur in a particular situation. In any situation, there are usually different ways of responding. Each response has a probability of occurrence. Suppose I want vanilla fudge ice cream for dessert. I can drive to the store, use my bicycle, or walk. If I have plenty of time and the weather is nice, I'll walk. If it is daytime and bike-riding weather, I may take my bicycle. But if neither of these conditions hold, I will drive. Thus, the same behavior has a different probability of occurring in different situations. The behavior potential of a particular response is always relative to the possible alternative responses in the situation.

Reinforcement Value

Reinforcement value in Rotter's theory is a person's subjective preference for a given reinforcer relative to other possible reinforcers. Generally, people act to bring about their most preferred outcome. Assuming that you could spend an evening going to a movie, attending a concert, or playing poker at home, which would you prefer? Obviously, people differ in the value they place on various rewards. Your choice of a fun evening may be different from a friend's. (Hopefully not the friend with whom you are going to spend the evening.) Now suppose that you had a fourth choice: flying to Paris on the Concorde for dinner. Which of the four would you choose? Unless you are afraid of flying or don't like plush Parisian restaurants, you are likely to choose the evening in Paris. This illustrates that reinforcement value is not only an individual matter, but is also relative to the reinforcers available.

Expectancy

Besides preferences for various reinforcers, people have expectations about the chances that a particular behavior will result in a given reinforcer. In other words, each potential outcome or reinforcer is assigned a probability level. Rotter (1982) calls this an **expectancy.** Expectancy is independent of reinforcement value. You may have a high preference for spending your evening in Paris. But you may believe that the odds are near zero that you'll be able to. Or going to the movies may be your last choice, but that activity is the one that you are most likely to be able to do.

Expectancy, like reinforcement value, is subjective. What matters is how the person sees the chances of getting a particular reinforcer rather than any objective probabilities. Tricia may believe that she is more likely to obtain the night in Paris than the night at the movies. Even though most people would say the opposite, it is her expectancy that will influence her choice.

Rotter (1982) distinguished two types of expectancies. **Specific expectancies** are our subjective expectancies in a given situation. An example is the probability that asking your father for a loan will get you the money you need. Through learning, some expectancies come to be applied to a variety of related experiences. Such **generalized expectancies** are the person's subjective expectancies in a variety of situations. The probability that asking favors will get you what you want is an example. We use generalized expectancies when we perceive an important psychological similarity in a range of situations. We thus come to respond to them in similar ways. One of Rotter's major contributions to social learning theory has been identifying two particular generalized expectancies—locus of control and interpersonal trust. He also developed reliable tests to measure them as individual differences among people. We will discuss each of these two generalized expectancies later in the chapter. For the present, our discussion will deal only with specific expectancies.

Expectancy and Reinforcement Value: The Predictive Formula

Expectancy and reinforcement value are independent. Therefore, behavior can only be predicted by taking both factors into account simultaneously. This is shown in Rotter's "formula" for predicting behavior:

$$\text{Behavior Potential} = f(\text{Expectancy and Reinforcement Value})$$

In words, the formula says: *behavior potential is a function of expectancy and reinforcement value*. The formula can help us predict which response someone will make in a particular situation. Consider, for example, a college student named Kathie who wants to go to medical school. She must choose between an advanced and a basic math course to fulfill the requirements for an undergraduate degree. The perceived value of an "A" in the advanced course is higher than the value of an "A" in the basic course. So, if reinforcement value were the only determinant, Kathie would choose the advanced course. But clearly reinforcement value is not the only consideration. Kathie's expectancy of getting an "A" would almost certainly be greater for the basic course. Suppose Kathie believes that she has an 80 percent chance of earning an "A" in the basic course and only a 20 percent chance of getting an "A" in the advanced course. She might then choose to take the basic course, even though an "A" in the advanced course, if obtained, would be worth considerably more to her.

It is Kathie's *subjective perception*, not objective reality, that determines her behavior. If, for instance, Kathie actually had a high math aptitude, she might in fact have a 90 percent chance of getting an "A" in the advanced course. Nonetheless, it is her perceived (subjective) expectancy (20 percent) and not the "real" (objective) chance (90 percent) that determines her behavior. Similarly, medical schools might consider a "B" in the advanced course to be worth even more than an "A" in the basic course. But if Kathie is unaware of this or chooses to ignore it, the fact will play no part in her choice.

The Psychological Situation

Rotter (1981) believes that it is never appropriate to speak of behavior in the abstract. All behavior, he argues, occurs in a context. This context is the psychological situation from the vantage point of the person responding. The reinforcement value a person assigns to various outcomes and his or her expectancies regarding reinforcement always depend on the situation. Earning twenty dollars is likely to be more reinforcing if we have been laid off from work than if we have just gotten paid. And the chances of getting a date with someone we have known for a while may be greater than the chances of getting a date with someone we have never met.

The issue of the importance of the situation in determining behavior was first raised by Rotter (1954) more than thirty years ago. It has become a central debate in personality theory and research in the past few years, as we will see in Chapter 21.

We now turn to two generalized expectancies that Rotter identified as important: locus of control and interpersonal trust.

Locus of Control

When a person receives a desired outcome, such as a high grade on a test, a bonus at work, or a good hand in a card game, the question can be raised: *Why* did the outcome occur? Similarly, when a person receives an undesirable outcome, such as a low grade on a test, a notice of layoff at work, or a poor hand in a card game, the same question may arise. One answer is that the outcome resulted from the person's own effort, ability, merit, or skill. Another answer is that it was due to luck, chance, or fate. These alternatives capture what Rotter means by **locus of control.** It refers to the generalized way a person perceives the source of his or her outcomes, positive or negative. **Internal locus of control** is the view that our reinforcements and punishments are the result of our own resources and efforts. **External locus of control** is the view that our reinforcements and punishments are due to forces outside of ourselves and over which we have no control.

Are the outcomes we receive due to internal or external factors? The answer, of course, is that it depends. Getting three "As" in a row in a physics class is almost certainly the result of a considerable amount of ability and/or effort. Getting dealt three good poker hands in a row is certainly luck (unless you are cheating). But things are not always so clear-cut. In many situations, it is a matter of opinion whether a given reward or punishment comes our way because of internal or external factors. Furthermore, the source of an outcome may be objectively internal or external. But what determines our locus of control is how we perceive the source. And it is our (subjective) locus of control that affects how we behave.

Assessing Locus of Control: The I-E scale

Rotter (1966) and his colleagues developed a simple self-report inventory to assess locus of control. The **I-E Scale** contains 29 forced-choice items, 23 tapping locus of control and six filler items that partially disguise the purpose of the test. Two of the items are shown below. Respondents are asked to choose the alternative that better describes them in each case. See if you can identify the alternative in each item that suggests an internal locus of control.

   a. In the long run people get the respect they deserve in this world.
   b. Unfortunately, an individual's worth often passes unrecognized no matter how hard he tries.

   a. Many times I feel that I have little influence over the things that happen to me.
   b. It is impossible for me to believe that chance or luck plays an important role in my life.

The internal response was *"a"* in the first item and *"b"* in the second item.

The I-E Scale has good internal consistency and retest reliability. Its correlation with social desirability is quite low, and the scale is unrelated to intelligence or sex. The I-E Scale is the most widely used measure of locus of control in adults. Other scales have been developed for children and to tap more specific aspects of locus of control, such as related to health (e.g., Lefcourt, 1981, 1982; Strickland, 1977).

Correlates of Locus of Control

Much research has shown that people differ in terms of whether they believe reinforcement and punishment is generally controlled by internal or external factors. In turn, individual differences in perceived locus of control appear to be related to a variety of behaviors. Table 20–1 summarizes some of the correlates of locus of control.

Research has consistently shown that internals are more likely to seek information than externals (Phares, 1984). This would be predicted from the theoretical concept that internals consider themselves responsible for their outcomes. They therefore want information that improves their chances of desirable outcomes. For example, one study showed that internal students consulted with their instructor before a classroom examination more than did external students (Prociuk & Breen, 1977).

Another consistent finding is that internals have higher achievement than externals, especially in intellectual and performance tasks (Lefcourt, 1982). For instance, from elementary school to college, students with an internal locus of control tend to do better academically than their external peers (Findley & Cooper, 1983).

Internals tend to be more resistant to social pressure in that they are less likely to be persuaded by others (Phares, 1978). Internals have greater confidence in their own abilities. They can thus afford to be more independent. Additionally, they seem to prefer being in control of their lives. This means they are more likely to resist being influenced by others.

Internals also seem to have the advantage over externals when it comes to health. Strickland (1978, 1979) found that internals seek more general information about health maintenance, engage in more precautionary health practices, have more positive attitudes about exercise, and are less likely to have cardiac problems. The mental health of internals also appears to be generally better than that of externals. Internals have been found to be less anxious and less likely to be diagnosed as having psychiatric illnesses (Phares, 1976).

It would seem, then, that it is advantageous to have an internal locus of control. This may be generally true. But there are exceptions. Consistent with Rotter's emphasis on viewing behavior in context, under some circumstances, an external orientation can be more adaptive. In situations where there is little opportunity for personal control, it may be more adaptive to have an external orientation. One study examined a group of elderly people who were institutionalized and therefore had little

TABLE 20–1
Some correlates of locus of control

Internals tend to be higher than externals on:
Information seeking
Achievement
Resistance to social influence
Health-promoting behaviors
Psychological adjustment

control over their circumstances. In this group, external locus of control was associated with better adjustment and feelings of satisfaction than was internal locus of control (Felton & Kahana, 1974). The reverse was found in a group of noninstitutionalized elderly individuals (Wolk & Kurtz, 1975).

Despite their striking contrast with internals, externals are by no means a uniform group. There seem to be two quite different subtypes (Phares, 1979). **Congruent externals** are individuals whose belief that most outcomes are simply out of their hands is consistent (i.e., congruent) with their own behavior and experiences. Often they grew up in deprived socioeconomic conditions or their childhoods were chaotic and unpredictable. **Defensive externals,** in contrast, are individuals whose reported beliefs on the I-E scale are *not* consistent with their experiences and behavior. By claiming that the world is beyond their control, defensive externals can take credit for their successes without having to accept responsibility for their failures (Lloyd & Chang, 1979).

None of what we have said means that locus of control is completely stable. Rotter (1966) hypothesized that generalized expectancies such as locus of control may change as a person's life circumstances change. The evidence suggests that this is so. For example, Doherty (1983) found that shortly after divorce, many women become less internal; they tend to return to predivorce levels as they learn to deal with their new circumstances.

Interpersonal Trust

Rotter believes people differ in their general expectation that the word of others can be relied on. This is a function of the extent that parents, teachers, peers, and the media suggest that promises are generally kept or generally broken. Rotter (1967) formally defines **interpersonal trust** as a generalized expectancy "held by an individual or group that the word, promise, verbal or written statement of another individual or group can be relied upon" (p. 651).

To measure interpersonal trust, Rotter (1967) developed a 40-item self-report inventory consisting of 25 items measuring trust and 15 filler items. Below are four of the items; see whether you can pick out the low and high trust items.

In dealing with strangers one is better off to be cautious until they have provided evidence that they are trustworthy.

Parents can usually be relied upon to keep their promises.

Parents and teachers are likely to say what they believe themselves and not just what they think is good for the child to hear.

> Most elected public officials are really sincere in their campaign prom-
> ises. (Rotter, 1967, p. 654)

The first item is indicative of low trust; the remaining three are indicative
of high trust.

Rotter's Interpersonal Trust Scale provides evidence consistent with
what might be expected on common sense grounds. For example, students
who claim to be religious show more trust than those who claim to be
agnostics, atheists, or to have no religion. Rotter (1967) interprets this
result by saying: "Since it is clear that [nonreligious] students are already
expressing less faith in one currently accepted institution, it is not surprising that they show a generalized lower degree of trust in others"
(p. 658). Likewise, trust tends to be associated with socioeconomic status.
Students from higher socioeconomic groups are generally more trusting.
Here, Rotter's interpretation is that the poorer an individual is, the less
reason he or she has to accept either the status quo or the authorities
who define and defend it.

Among college students, interpersonal trust scores are related to the
scores of their parents. This is presumably because the attitudes modeled
and encouraged by parents are most likely to be adopted by their children (Katz & Rotter, 1969). Rotter (1971) also found a strong relationship
between trust and trustworthiness. That is, people who are more trusting
are less likely to lie to others or to cheat them.

A consistent finding in Rotter's (1980) research is that people who
are high in interpersonal trust tend to be happier and better liked than
those low in interpersonal trust. High trusters are also more likely to
give people a second chance and to respect the rights of others.

This does not mean that the highly trusting individual is unusually
gullible. High trusters believe what they are told when there is no good
reason to disbelieve. However, when circumstances warrant being suspicious, they are no more likely to be taken in than low trusters. On the
contrary, there is some evidence that the low-trust person is the easier
mark for con games that capitalize on greed (Rotter, 1980).

BANDURA'S SOCIAL LEARNING THEORY

About a decade after Rotter's theory was presented, Albert Bandura's
(1925–   ) social learning theory was introduced in a book titled *Social
Learning and Personality Development* (Bandura & Walters, 1963). Bandura
acknowledges the role of classical and operant conditioning in accounting
for the acquisition, maintenance, and modification of human behavior.
But he insists they are insufficient to account for the full range and variety
of responses that people display. He believes that we also learn by merely
observing what others do and what happens to them. This **observational**

Albert Bandura

Courtesy of Albert Bandura

learning plays a uniquely important role in personality development. During the 1960s and early 1970s, Bandura and his students conducted dozens of studies that demonstrated the impact of observing social models on an enormous range of human activities, social skills, fears, aggression, and sex-role behavior. These studies were designed to identify the mechanisms and processes underlying observational learning.

By the mid-1970s Bandura (1977b; 1986b) had revised and extended his theoretical analysis to encompass a much wider range of cognitive factors. In Bandura's (1983b) theory, personality develops through a process of **reciprocal determinism.** Personal, behavioral, and situational factors are in a state of continuing mutual interaction to determine what we do and think. (See Figure 20–1.) Bandura's theory also emphasizes people's self-regulatory processes. Bandura believes, consistent with his concept

FIGURE 20–1
A schematic diagram of Bandura's concept of reciprocal determinism in which person, situation, and behavior mutually influence each other

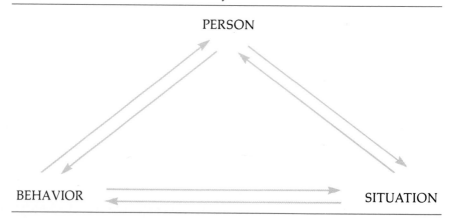

of reciprocal determinism, that personal goals and self-evaluations can have considerable influence on what people do. A third major area of Bandura's theory and research is the concept of *self-efficacy*. This is the conviction that we can successfully perform the behavior needed to produce a desired outcome.

Observational Learning

Observational learning is the process through which the behavior of one person, an **observer,** changes as a result of merely being exposed to the behavior of another, the **model.** Specific components of a model's behavior are called *modeling cues.* Such cues are available almost continually in real life, and they can be live or symbolic. **Live modeling** refers to observing models "in the flesh"—that is, models that are physically present. **Symbolic modeling** involves being exposed to models indirectly, such as in movies, by reading, and through oral descriptions of a person's behaviors.

Observational Learning as a Three-Stage Process

Observational learning can be usefully conceptualized as a three-stage process: (1) being exposed to modeling cues, (2) acquiring them, and (3) subsequently accepting them as a guide for behavior (Liebert, 1973). This is depicted schematically in Figure 20–2.

Exposure to (observation of) the modeling cues is the obvious first step in the observational sequence. **Acquisition** (learning) of modeling cues is the second stage of observational learning. It does not necessarily follow from adequate exposure. In addition to exposure, acquisition requires that we both pay attention to the modeling cues and store them in memory. Acquisition is measured by the observer's *recall* of the model's behavior. Notice that acquisition is a cognitive process, a covert behavior. However, it is defined operationally in terms of an overt behavior: recall. This has an obvious advantage in that acquisition is therefore made objectively and publicly verifiable.

When both exposure and acquisition have occurred, the third and final step in observational learning becomes relevant. **Acceptance** refers to whether or not the observer uses (accepts) the modeling cues as a guide for her or his own actions. To measure acceptance, the person is observed in a situation in which he or she is free to use the model's behavior as a guide. If the observer uses the model's behavior, acceptance has occurred.

Acceptance can take one of four forms: imitation or counterimitation, either of which can be direct or indirect. **Imitation** is acting as the model did. **Counterimitation** is acting in the opposite way. Modeling has a *direct* influence when the observer engages in the same behavior as the

FIGURE 20–2
The three stages of observational learning

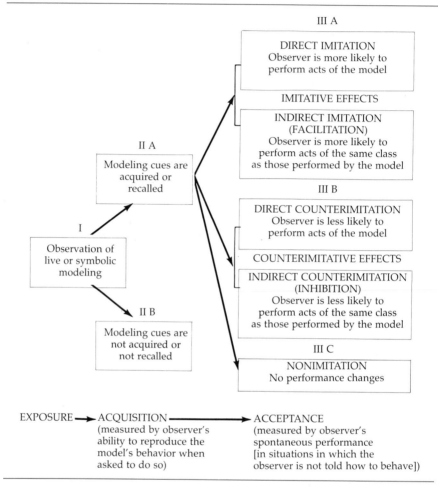

model (i.e., matching or copying). This is **direct imitation.** When the observer does exactly the opposite of what the model did, this is **direct counterimitation.** Modeling cues may also indirectly affect observers by suggesting acceptance of a *general* class of behaviors, of which the modeling cues are perceived as a specific instance. **Indirect imitation** involves behaving similarly to the model. **Indirect counterimitation** involves behaving differently than the model. Table 20–2 provides examples of each of the four possible types of acceptance of modeling cues.

The three-stage scheme of observational learning makes it clear that exposure and acquisition are necessary but not sufficient conditions for imitation or counterimitation. Simply stated, there is a distinction between what we "see" and remember, on the one hand, and what we eventually

TABLE 20–2
Forms of acceptance of modeling cues

Situation: *Five-year-old Doug often sees his parents donate money to charities*

Type of Acceptance	Examples
DIRECT IMITATION	Doug puts a coin in the collection box at church
INDIRECT IMITATION	Doug shares his toys with his friends
DIRECT COUNTERIMITATION	Doug walks past the collection box at church without donating
INDIRECT COUNTERIMITATION	Doug does not allow his friends to play with his toys
NONIMITATION	Doug's behavior is unaffected by observing his parent's behavior

do, on the other. This is why acceptance is an important theoretical construct for understanding the process of observational learning.

One factor that influences the particular outcome in the acceptance stage is the consequences the model receives for his or her actions. These are **vicarious consequences.** The importance of distinguishing between acquisition and acceptance as well as the role of vicarious consequences in determining the degree of acceptance was first demonstrated in a classic experiment by Bandura (1965). It is often referred to as the "Bobo doll study."

Bandura's "Bobo Doll Study"

In this experiment, nursery school children were the observers. The modeling cues were provided symbolically in a five-minute film.

> The film began with a scene in which [an adult male] model walked up to an adult-size plastic Bobo doll and ordered him to clear the way. After glaring for a moment at the noncompliant antagonist the model exhibited four novel aggressive responses each accompanied by a distinctive verbalization.
>
> First, the model laid the Bobo doll on its side, sat on it, and punched it in the nose while remarking, "Pow, right in the nose, boom, boom." The model then raised the doll and pommeled it on the head with a mallet. Each response was accompanied by the verbalization, "Sockeroo . . . stay down." Following the mallet aggression, the model kicked the doll about the room, and these responses were interspersed with the comment, "Fly away." Finally, the model threw rubber balls at the Bobo doll, each strike punctuated with "Bang." This sequence of physically and verbally aggressive behavior was repeated twice. (Bandura, 1965, pp. 590–91)

The major independent variable was the consequences that the model in the film received as a result of his aggressive behavior. One group of children simply watched the film, as described above. For them, the model received *no consequences*. A second group of children saw the same film, but a final scene was added in which the model was rewarded for aggressive behavior.

> For children in the *model-rewarded* condition, a second adult appeared with an abundant supply of candies and soft drinks. He informed the model that [the model] was a "strong champion" and that his superb aggressive performance clearly deserved a generous treat. He then poured [the model] a large glass of 7-Up, and readily supplied additional energy-building nourishment including chocolate bars, Cracker Jack popcorn, and an assortment of candies. While the model was rapidly consuming the delectable treats, his admirer symbolically reinstated the modeled aggressive responses and engaged in considerable positive social reinforcement. (Bandura, 1965, p. 591; italics added)

A third group of children also watched the basic film, but in the added final scene, the model was punished rather than rewarded.

> For children in the *model-punished* condition the reinforcing agent appeared on the scene shaking his finger menacingly and commenting reprovingly, "Hey there, you big bully. You quit picking on that clown. I won't tolerate it." As the model drew back he tripped and fell, and the other adult sat on the model and spanked him with a rolled-up magazine while reminding him of his aggressive behavior. As the model ran off cowering, the agent forewarned him, "If I catch you doing that again, you big bully, I'll give you a hard spanking. You quit acting that way." (Bandura, 1965, p. 591; italics added)

After seeing the film, each child was taken to a room containing a plastic Bobo doll, three balls, a mallet, a pegboard, plastic farm animals, and other toys. The subject was left alone with the toys for ten minutes. But the subject was observed by judges who were behind a one-way vision screen. The aggressive behavior the children performed in this situation was the *acceptance* measure.

Following the acceptance test, the degree to which children could demonstrate or reproduce the modeled behaviors was assessed. This constituted the *acquisition* measure. The experimenter reentered the room well supplied with sticker pictures and an attractive juice dispenser. The experimenter gave the child a small treat of fruit juice. The child was then told he or she would get more juice and a sticker for each of the model's responses that he or she could reproduce. Incentives for reproducing the model's behavior were provided to minimize possible reluctance to demonstrate the model's aggressive acts. Such reluctance was especially expected among children in the model-punished condition.

The results are shown in Figure 20–3. They provide clear support for the view that acquisition and acceptance (spontaneous performance) must be distinguished. In every comparison, the children tended to perform fewer aggressive behaviors than they had acquired through observation; this was particularly true of children in the model-punished condition.

It is noteworthy that the children showed a high degree of direct imitation of the model's aggressive acts when the children were being tested (with incentives) for acquisition. This can be seen in the comparison of the model's acts and the children's acts in Figure 20–4. This finding demonstrates the powerful influence of modeling, in this case a negative influence.

FIGURE 20–3

Results of Bandura's Bobo doll study of the *acquisition-acceptance* distinction in observational learning

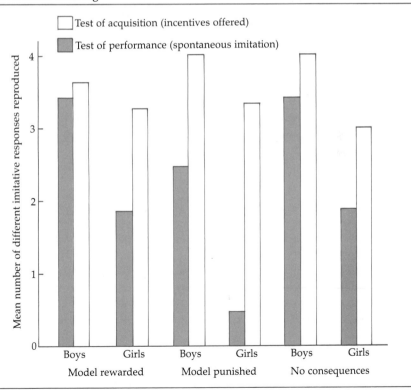

Source: Adapted from *Social Learning and Personality Development* by A. Bandura and R. H. Walters, 1963, New York: Holt, Rinehart & Winston.

FIGURE 20-4
Examples of the model's aggressive acts (top row) and children's imitation
of the model's acts (middle and bottom rows) in Bandura's Bobo doll study

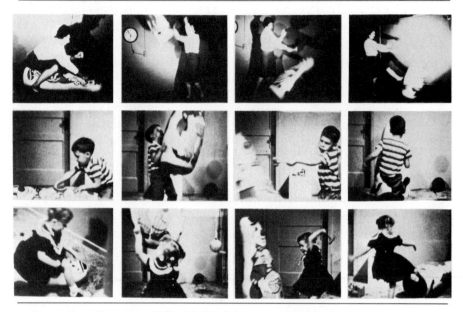

Source: From "Imitation of Film-Mediated Aggressive Models" by A. Bandura, D. Ross,
and S. A. Ross, 1963, *Journal of Abnormal and Social Psychology*, pp. 3–11. Copyright 1963 by
the American Psychological Association. Reprinted by permission.

Vicarious Consequences

As we just saw, the consequences that models receive for their actions
influence observers' behaviors. There are two classes of vicarious consequences. **Vicarious reward** is an outcome that will presumably be perceived by the observer as positive or desirable. **Vicarious punishment** is
a consequence that is likely to be seen as negative or undesirable.

Vicarious consequences give information about the effect of an action,
especially whether the effect will be desirable or undesirable. Vicarious
consequences let observers infer the outcomes they will likely receive for
similar actions. Vicarious reward produces direct and indirect imitation;
vicarious punishment produces direct and indirect counterimitation (e.g.,
Bandura, 1969b; Liebert & Fernandez, 1970a; Liebert, Sobol, & Copemann,
1972).

Vicarious consequences serve another function besides telling the
observer the *type* of reaction a particular behavior will probably elicit.
They also indicate that actions are likely to elicit *some reaction* from others.
Such information may signal the importance of the model's behavior. This
increases the likelihood that the observer will attend to and remember
what the model did. The *attention-focusing* function of vicarious conse-

quences has been confirmed in a number of experiments. Children who see a model *either* rewarded *or* punished for some behavior show better acquisition of that behavior than those who see the same behavior performed without consequences (e.g., Cheyne, 1971; Liebert & Fernandez, 1969, 1970a).

The effects of vicarious consequences on both acquisition and acceptance are illustrated in an experiment that presented the modeling cues in writing (Spiegler & Weiland, 1976). College students read a brief story about events involving a high school class president, the school principal, and other students. The new principal had made several changes in school policy that disturbed the students. The class president initiated actions in an attempt to change the new policies. Depending on the experimental condition, subjects read that the class president received positive, negative, or neutral consequences for each action she took. The only difference among the stories was the type of vicarious consequences. The excerpt below from the modeling story illustrates the three types of vicarious consequences.

> Janet Halloran, the newly elected president of the senior class at Jefferson, decided that her new job was to inform both the high school administration and the local community about the attitudes and interests of her class of 428 students. She wrote an editorial for the school newspaper, *The Unicorn*, explaining the dismay of the students at the new principal's policies.
>
> [*Positive Consequences*] The principal was pleased that Ms. Halloran had chosen to go through proper channels and commended *The Unicorn* staff for allowing discussion of controversial topics.
>
> [*Negative Consequences*] The principal was so enraged that he halted publication of *The Unicorn* for the next month and severely reprimanded Ms. Halloran.
>
> [*Neutral Consequences*] The principal acknowledged Ms. Halloran's letter and told *The Unicorn* staff that he would take the editorial comments into consideration. (Spiegler & Weiland, 1976)

After reading the story, the subjects answered written questions. They were asked what they would have done in a similar situation (a measure of acceptance). They were also asked to recall the (*a*) modeled behaviors, (*b*) vicarious consequences, and (*c*) details of the story (measures of acquisition).

Looking first at acceptance, positive as well as neutral vicarious consequences resulted in more imitation than did negative consequences. This is consistent with the view that vicarious consequences give observers information about the acceptability of modeled acts. Obviously, positive vicarious consequences indicate more acceptability than do negative vicarious consequences. In this situation, the modeled behaviors—actively defying the policies of people in authority in a high school—typically result in negative consequences. Thus, absence of negative sanctions in the neutral vicarious consequences version would be interpreted to mean that the modeled behaviors were acceptable.

Turning to the acquisition measure, subjects who read about a model who experienced positive or negative consequences recalled more of the total modeling cues than did subjects who read about models whose actions resulted in neutral consequences. This finding confirms the attention-focusing function of vicarious reward and punishment. Positive and negative vicarious consequences were equivalent in enhancing recall. It seems that the strength of the consequences, and not whether they are positive or negative, affects acquisition of modeled responses.

The most intriguing results of the experiment come from an examination of the three separate measures of recall. This is shown in Figure 20–5. Subjects who observed negative consequences had high recall of the details of the situation and the modeled behavior. But they had the lowest recall of the *consequences*. Recalling vicarious consequences (but not the model's acts or the details of the situation) depends on whether the consequences are positive or negative.

We can conclude that positive vicarious consequences enhance both acquisition and acceptance. In contrast, negative vicarious consequences decrease the likelihood of immediately imitating the model but increase the chances that the observer will remember the model's actions and related details. At the same time, the observer is apt to forget the vicarious punishment. The net result appears to be that negative vicarious consequences inhibit immediate imitation but not necessarily future imitation; the observer remembers the model's actions and the associated details, but forgets that they led to negative consequences.

This finding has practical implications. News reports of spectacular crimes like skyjacking and kidnapping usually contain both positive and negative vicarious consequences. The former are more likely to appear in the initial coverage of the crime, before the criminal is caught. This is when the criminal is receiving the rewards of the crime, such as success, ransom money, and publicity. Obviously, such reports could inspire imitation. When the criminal is caught or killed, negative vicarious consequences predominate in the news coverage. Yet, potential imitators would be more likely to remember the details of the crime, while forgetting that the criminal did not get away with it. They would therefore be more likely to imitate the criminal than if the consequences of the crime had been neutral or unreported.

Modeling Therapies

The basic principles of modeling have been extensively applied to personality change (e.g., Decker & Nathan, 1985; Perry & Furukawa, 1986). Two features of modeling therapies should be noted. First, they generally

FIGURE 20–5

The relative amount of recall of details of the modeling story, of the modeled behavior, and of the vicarious consequences by subjects exposed to negative, positive, and neutral vicarious consequences in Spiegler and Weiland's (1976) study. Note that for the negative vicarious consequences condition, recall of story details and of the modeled behavior is high but recall of vicarious consequences is lower than that of the other two groups.

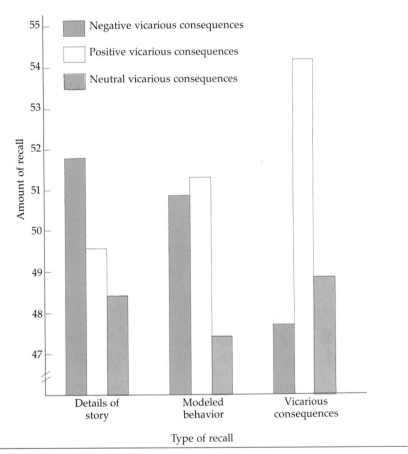

Source: Data from "The Effects of Written Vicarious Consequences on Observers' Willingness to Imitate and Ability to Recall Modeling Cues" by M. D. Spiegler and A. Weiland, 1976, *Journal of Personality, 44,* pp. 260–73.

are extremely efficient, often requiring relatively brief exposure to models who are successfully coping with the problems clients are experiencing. In addition, modeling sequences can be presented symbolically, as on videotape. Thus, many clients can be exposed to the therapy at the same time, and a professional therapist does not even have to be present. Second, modeling therapies are often used with other behavioral procedures. (We will see examples of modeling components in cognitive-behavioral therapies in Chapter 21.)

We will briefly describe the three major functions of modeling therapies: (1) teaching new adaptive behaviors; (2) facilitating the practice of previously learned adaptive behaviors; and (3) activating previously learned behaviors that are currently inhibited, such as by fear.

Clients' problems are often maintained by a *skill deficit*—that is, by not knowing how to perform appropriate and adaptive skills. Modeling, for example, has been used to instruct socially inept or withdrawn clients in both basic social skills (e.g., making simple requests of others) and complex social skills (e.g., problem-solving behavior), to teach language to intellectually handicapped and autistic children, and to help hospitalized psychiatric patients develop the social and daily living skills they need when they return to community living. In the last example, some of the skills taught to psychiatric patients may be new to them. Or the patients may have the skills but may not be presently using them. In the latter case, modeling facilitates performing the skills. Adaptive skills have been taught to clients using both live and symbolic modeling (Spiegler, 1983).

The other major use of modeling therapies has been to help clients perform behaviors that are inhibited, usually by fear or anxiety. Generally, clients have already learned the appropriate responses, but are reluctant to perform them (e.g., talking to a potential date). Occasionally, clients can learn an adaptive response (e.g., dancing) only if they can overcome their apprehensions about the behavior.

Vicarious consequences are essential in modeling therapies that deal with fear and anxiety. Clients are exposed to live or symbolic models who successfully deal with anxiety-evoking situations without incurring negative consequences. Thus, clients learn, vicariously, that it is "safe" to perform the dreaded behavior. This process is called **vicarious extinction.** Vicarious extinction has been used with both children and adults to treat such problem behaviors as fear of commonly encountered animals, test anxiety, and fear of medical and dental treatment and hospitalization. Reducing fear of health-related procedures is important not only because it lessens clients' emotional upset, but also because it increases the chances that they will seek regular checkups and obtain necessary treatment. Thus, modeling procedures can serve preventive as well as ameliorative functions (Spiegler, 1980, 1983).

Participant modeling is an especially potent therapy for treating fears. It combines the therapist's live modeling of the feared behavior with closely supervised practice of the feared behavior by the client. (Live modeling is generally more effective, although less efficient, than symbolic modeling in treating fear and anxiety.) Participant modeling involves three basic steps.

1. The therapist models the fear-evoking behavior.

2. The client performs the same behavior with the therapist's verbal and, if necessary, physical prompts. For example, the therapist

holds the client's arm and accompanies the client up an escalator (the feared situation).

3. Gradually, the therapist fades the prompts so that eventually the client is performing the feared behavior alone.

The behaviors that are modeled and practiced are arranged in a hierarchy. Therapy proceeds from the least to the most fear-evoking behavior, as in systematic desensitization (Chapter 19).

Modeling has also played a significant role in teaching therapy skills

Participant modeling is a potent behavioral therapy for fears. A model demonstrates the feared behavior and then physically assists the fearful person in imitating the nonfearful behavior. *Photo © 1983 Susan Rosenberg*

to both professional therapists and nonprofessionals who administer therapy, such as parents, spouses, teachers, and clients themselves (e.g., Webster-Stratton, 1984).

The Theory of Perceived Self-Efficacy

When we are faced with a task involving any difficulty or skill, we generally have some idea about whether we can succeed at it. How do our beliefs about our capabilities affect our behavior? This question has become the focus of Bandura's *theory of perceived self-efficacy*. **Self-efficacy** is our conviction that we can successfully execute the behavior necessary to produce a desired outcome. Self-efficacy is always personal; it is how we, and not others, perceive our ability to deal with the situation.

According to self-efficacy theory, whether we undertake a task depends on our perceived level of efficacy for that task. People willingly and even enthusiastically undertake tasks they feel they are capable of managing successfully, but they shy away from activities they believe exceed their abilities. Bandura further posits that, once a task is undertaken, the amount of energy we expend and the extent we persist in the face of difficulties is also governed by perceived self-efficacy. The stronger the perceived self-efficacy, the more vigorous and persistent are our efforts in the face of obstacles and setbacks (e.g., Cervone & Peake, 1986).

Whether we attempt a task is not just due to our **efficacy expectations**—the degree to which we believe we are capable of performing the required behavior. We also consider **outcome expectancies**—how likely we think the desired outcome is obtainable. "People can give up trying because they seriously doubt that they can do what is required [efficacy expectations]" or "because they expect their efforts to produce no results due to the unresponsiveness, negative bias, or punitiveness of the environment [outcome expectancies]" (Bandura, 1982, p. 140). Studies support this distinction in that the two kinds of expectancies are often aroused and altered by different conditions (e.g., Manning & Wright, 1983; Rosenbaum & Hadari, 1985).

Bandura theorizes that efficacy expectations stem from four major sources of information.

1. *Performance accomplishments* are a powerful source of efficacy information in that they provide direct experiences of personal mastery. Through successful performance, efficacy expectations are strengthened and the threat of occasional failure is likely to be reduced, which may increase persistence.

2. *Vicarious experience* can generate expectations in observers that they too can "do it."

3. *Verbal persuasion* is the most common source of self-efficacy expectations because it is easy to provide and generally available. By being

told that they can "do it," people come to believe that they can (i.e., their efficacy expectations are increased).

4. Finally, efficacy expectations can be influenced by *emotional arousal*, as in threatening situations. People often rely on their state of physiological arousal (e.g., heart rate, breathing) to judge their level of fear or anxiety. Feeling calm and relaxed (or even moderately aroused if some arousal is necessary for effective performance) may serve as positive feedback that increases efficacy expectations.

Self-Efficacy as a Mechanism in Personality Change

Bandura has hypothesized that *all forms of personality change are effective because they create and strengthen a client's perceived self-efficacy*. Various therapeutic procedures are postulated to be mediated by one of the four sources of efficacy expectations. This is shown in Figure 20–6. During the past decade, dozens of studies have examined the implications of Bandura's (1984) idea that self-efficacy is the common cognitive mechanism in psychotherapy, especially in reducing anxiety and fear through behavioral therapies.

For example, one study tested the hypothesis that the more effective a treatment is, the more it will enhance clients' efficacy expectations (Bandura, Adams, & Beyer, 1977). The subjects in this experiment were adults whose fear of snakes restricted their lives. They avoided any situation in which snakes could possibly be encountered. Before and after treatment, the subjects were given a behavioral avoidance test. In a **behavioral avoidance test,** people are asked to perform a series of tasks requiring increasingly more threatening interactions with a feared object or situation. In this experiment, there were twenty-nine tasks. The first was looking at a boa constrictor in a glass cage. The last was allowing the snake to crawl freely in their laps. To assess changes in self-efficacy, subjects rated their

In a behavioral avoidance test, subjects are asked to perform a series of steps involving increasing contact with a feared object or situation. This woman was being tested for her fear of snakes before treatment; the purpose of the test was to provide a baseline for assessing the effects of subsequent therapy. *Photo by Michael D. Spiegler*

FIGURE 20–6

The major sources of efficacy expectations and examples of psychotherapeutic procedures that induce efficacy expectations

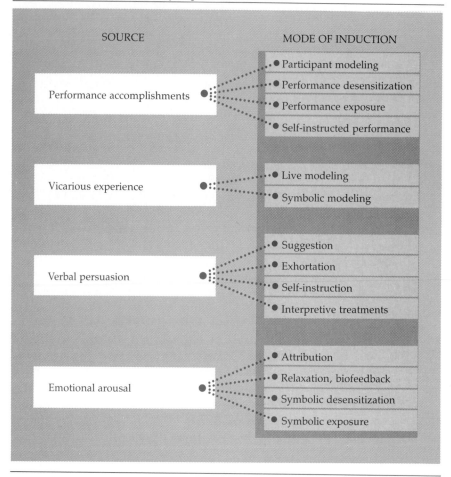

Source: Adapted from *Social Learning Theory* by A. Bandura, 1977, Englewood Cliffs, N.J.: Prentice-Hall, p. 80.

expectations for performing each of the steps in the behavioral avoidance test on a 100-point probability scale.

The subjects were assigned to one of three conditions. Those in the *participant modeling* condition observed a female therapist perform a series of increasingly more threatening interactions with the snake. Then they practiced the same behavior with the therapist's assistance. Subjects in the *modeling* condition merely observed the modeling sequences. A third group of subjects served as untreated controls. They were just given the assessment procedures.

Note that participant modeling gave subjects two sources of efficacy information (i.e., vicarious experience and performance accomplishments). Modeling gave them only one source of efficacy information (i.e., vicarious experience). Thus, we would predict that participant modeling would be a more effective treatment than modeling alone because participant modeling would lead to higher efficacy expectations. The results are consistent with these predictions.

Subjects' efficacy expectations were markedly enhanced by participant modeling, were moderately increased by modeling, and were unaltered in the control condition. The changes in self-efficacy were paralleled in the subjects' overt behavior, as self-efficacy theory would predict. Participant modeling produced slightly more approach behavior in the behavioral avoidance test than did modeling. The close correspondence between level of perceived self-efficacy and behavior can be seen in Figure 20–7.

FIGURE 20–7
Level of self-efficacy and approach behavior displayed by subjects after receiving participant modeling, modeling, or no treatment in Bandura et al.'s (1977) experiment

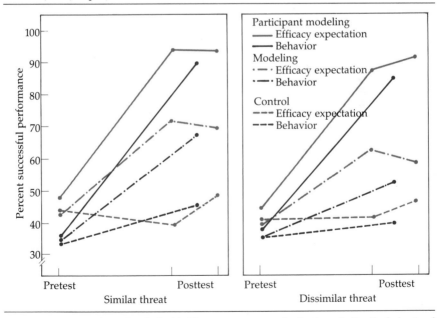

In the post-test phase, level of self-efficacy was measured prior to and after the behavioral avoidance tests with two snakes—one similar to the snake used in treatment and one different.
Source: Adapted from "Cognitive Processes Mediating Behavioral Change" by A. Bandura, N. E. Adams, and J. Beyer, 1977, *Journal of Personality and Social Psychology, 35,* pp. 125–39.

The figure shows these two measures for a snake similar to the one used in treatment (similar threat) and a snake unlike the one used in treatment (dissimilar threat).

The generality of self-efficacy theory has also been demonstrated. How well people will perform on a wide variety of tasks can be predicted from their level of perceived self-efficacy. For example, in the practical area of health behavior (O'Leary, 1985), higher self-efficacy is associated with: (*a*) successfully stopping smoking (e.g., Colletti, Supnick, & Payne, 1985; DiClemente, Prochaska, & Gilbertini, 1985); (*b*) increasing pain tolerance (e.g., Barrios, 1985; Manning & Wright, 1983); (*c*) successfully losing weight (e.g., Weinberg, Hughes, Critelli, England, & Jackson, 1984); and (*d*) complying with medical regimens, such as rehabilitative exercise (e.g., Kaplan, Atkins, & Reinsch, 1984).

Self-efficacy is considered to be situation specific. It varies depending on the *particular* behavior called for, rather than operating as a global personality trait or motive that would influence behavior in diverse circumstances. For example, with health behaviors that were enhanced by self-efficacy, efficacy expectations were directly related to the specific health-relevant behavior, such as stopping smoking and pain tolerance. A person's efficacy expectations concerning the ability to stop smoking would not predict that individual's ability to tolerate pain.

Self-Efficacy and Fear Arousal

Bandura (1983a, 1986b) argues that fear is largely a product of perceived *in*efficacy. We are afraid in situations that we feel we are incapable of handling. Therefore, as efficacy increases, fear is expected to diminish. To see whether this is indeed so, Bandura, Reese, and Adams (1982) first pretested people with severe fear of snakes using a behavioral avoidance test. During this pretest, subjects rated the intensity of the fear they experienced as each of the tasks was described to them. This was a measure of *anticipatory fear*. As a measure of self-efficacy, the subjects were also asked to indicate how certain they were that they could perform each task.

Subjects were then brought to either low, medium, or high levels of perceived self-efficacy. This was done by the experimenter first modeling each of the tasks and then helping the subjects to perform each task (i.e., participant modeling). Subjects in the low-efficacy group were treated until they felt they could put their hand in the cage but not touch the snake; those in the medium-efficacy group were treated until they felt they could lift the snake inside the cage; and those in the high-efficacy group were treated until they felt they could perform the entire set of threatening interactions with the snake.

As soon as the subjects achieved their assigned level of perceived self-efficacy, they were tested on both their fear arousal and their actual ability to perform the threatening tasks. The results are shown in Figure

20–8. As self-efficacy increased, both anticipatory and actual performance fear decreased, whereas performance increased. Moreover, level of fear was related to the strength as well as the level of perceived self-efficacy; the more confident subjects were in their efficacy judgments, the less fear they experienced.

Self-Regulation and Goal-Setting

Bandura's (1986b) theory places considerable importance on self-regulation in motivating and guiding behavior. Goal-setting is an especially powerful source of self-motivation. For goals to serve as effective motivators, they must be specific rather than vague; they must also be set at an appropriate level. When goals are long term, as they often are, then *subgoals* must be set. Students, for instance, are well advised to decide how much reading they will do tonight rather than focus on how much reading they must do by the end of the semester. "Proximal subgoals provide immediate incentives and guides for performance, whereas distal goals are too far removed in time to effectively mobilize effort or to direct what one does in the here and now" (Bandura & Schunk, 1981, p. 587).

Bandura and Schunk (1981) demonstrated the power of subgoals.

FIGURE 20–8
The effect of self-efficacy on fear and performance. As self-efficacy increased, both anticipatory and actual performance fear decreased while performance increased.

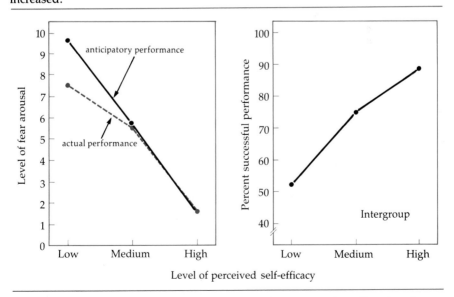

Source: Adapted from "Microanalysis of Action and Fear Arousal as a Function of Differential Levels of Perceived Self-Efficacy" by A. Bandura, L. Reese, and N. E. Adams, 1982, *Journal of Personality and Social Psychology, 43*, pp. 5–21.

They worked with elementary school children who had gross deficits in arithmetic and little interest in it. After a pretest of their mathematical ability and perceived mathematical efficacy, the children all participated in a self-directed learning program. This consisted of instructional materials and forty-two pages of subtraction problems, which they worked on for seven 30-minute sessions. The learning program was identical for all children, but the goal-setting procedures were systematically varied.

In the *proximal-goal* condition, the experimenter suggested that the children set themselves the goal of doing at least six pages of problems during each session. For those in the *distal-goal* condition, the experimenter suggested the goal of completing all forty-two pages of problems by the end of the seventh session. Children in the *no-goals* condition received no suggestion as to what goals, if any, they should set for themselves. Finally, a *no-treatment* control group received no mathematical instruction or goal-setting suggestions.

The dependent variables in the study were: mathematical skill, perceived mathematical efficacy, and interest in arithmetic. Change in mathematical skill was measured by giving children a set of subtraction problems after the instruction program was completed. This post-test was compared with their pretest performance. As seen in Figure 20–9, children who were given proximal goals improved the most. They gained almost twice as much as those in the distal goal and no-goal groups. Control children who received no mathematical instruction, not surprisingly, showed no increase in mathematical skill.

Perceived self-efficacy was measured three times: (1) at the pretest, (2) after training but before the mathematical skills assessment (Post-test 1), and (3) after the mathematical skills assessment (Post-test 2). The results are shown in Figure 20–10. As with the measure of mathematical skill, perceptions of efficacy increased the most for those who set proximal goals; the distal goal and no-goals groups did not differ in how much their self-efficacy increased. Control children who had been given no goal-setting instructions showed no increase in perceived self-efficacy.

On the day after the post-tests, the children's intrinsic interest in mathematics was assessed. They were given two tasks, subtraction problems and nonmathematical problems. The children were told to work on the problems of their choice, from either or both types. The number of subtraction problems they attempted during the 25-minute period was taken as the measure of intrinsic interest in mathematics. As seen in Figure 20–11, children in the proximal-goals group attempted far more subtraction problems than those in any of the other groups. This suggests that their interest in mathematics, like their perceived self-efficacy and actual competence in mathematics, had been enhanced by establishing proximal goals. In sum, then, proximal goal-setting served (1) to foster actual mastery, (2) to heighten self-efficacy, and (3) to increase interest in an activity that previously held almost no interest for the children.

FIGURE 20–9

Level of mathematical achievement in Bandura and Schunk's (1981) experiment as a function of type of goal setting

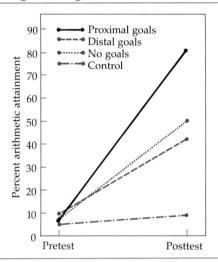

Source: Adapted from "Cultivating Competence, Self-Efficacy, and Intrinsic Interest through Proximal Self-Motivation" by A. Bandura and D. H. Schunk, 1981, *Journal of Personality and Social Psychology, 41,* p. 592.

FIGURE 20–10

Perceived self-efficacy for subtraction problems in Bandura and Schunk's (1981) experiment, as a function of type of goal setting

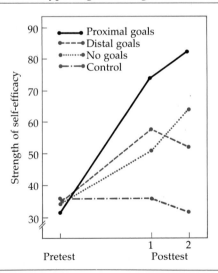

Source: Adapted from "Cultivating Competence, Self-Efficacy, and Intrinsic Interest through Proximal Self-Motivation" by A. Bandura and D. H. Schunk, 1981, *Journal of Personality and Social Psychology, 41,* p. 592.

FIGURE 20–11

Average number of subtraction problems children chose to solve in Bandura and Schunk's (1981) experiment, when given free choice of activities, taken as a measure of interest in mathematics

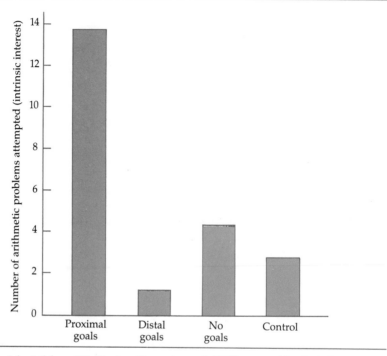

Source: Adapted from "Cultivating Competence, Self-Efficacy, and Intrinsic Interest through Proximal Self-Motivation" by A. Bandura and D. H. Schunk, 1981, *Journal of Personality and Social Psychology, 41,* p. 593.

SUMMARY

1. During the past few decades much of psychology has undergone a transformation from a science focusing on conditioning and learning to one focusing on cognitive processes. This is reflected in social learning theories.

2. Miller and Dollard advanced the first social learning theory, which emphasized the role of imitation. Their theory also posited that learning involves a sequence of drive, cue, response, and reinforcement.

3. Rotter's social learning theory employs four basic constructs. Behavior potential is the likelihood that a given behavior will occur in a particular situation. Reinforcement value is the degree of subjective preference a person has for various reinforcers. Expectancy is the subjective likelihood that a given behavior will result in reinforcement. The psychological situa-

tion is the immediate environmental context as seen from the person's viewpoint. In any given situation, behavior potential is a joint function of expectancy and reinforcement value.

4. According to Rotter, not all expectancies are situation-specific. Locus of control is a generalized expectancy regarding the degree to which people believe that the reinforcements they get result from their own efforts (internal locus of control) or from outside forces over which they have no influence (external locus of control). People with an internal locus of control tend to do better academically, to be more resistant to social pressure, and to have greater confidence in themselves.

5. Interpersonal trust, another generalized expectancy advanced by Rotter, refers to the degree to which we perceive the promises of others as generally kept or generally broken. Those high on interpersonal trust tend to be more religious, happier, and more trustworthy than those low in interpersonal trust.

6. Bandura's social learning theory emphasizes the role of observational learning in personality development and change. Observational learning is a three-stage process, involving exposure to modeling cues, acquisition of the information contained in them, and subsequent acceptance of these cues as a guide for our actions. Acceptance may take the form of either imitation or counterimitation and may be direct or indirect.

7. Observational learning is greatly influenced by vicarious consequences—that is, the rewards and punishments that models are seen to get as a result of their behavior. Vicarious reward informs us that modeled behaviors are appropriate and therefore increases acceptance; vicarious punishment informs us that modeled behaviors are inappropriate and therefore decreases acceptance. Both vicarious reward and vicarious punishment indicate that modeled behaviors are important and therefore enhance acquisition.

8. Modeling therapy can be used to teach new adaptive behaviors, to facilitate the practice of previously learned adaptive behaviors, and to activate behaviors that are currently inhibited by fear. Participant modeling is an especially powerful technique for reducing fear-inhibited behavior because it combines a therapist's live modeling with closely supervised practice.

9. Bandura's theory of perceived self-efficacy states that the decision to undertake various tasks depends upon a person's perception of his or her ability to perform the task successfully. Self-efficacy expectations may stem from performance accomplishments, vicarious experience, verbal persuasion, or emotional arousal. Changes in self-efficacy appear to be closely correlated with changes in actual performance. Bandura believes that perceived self-efficacy is the cognitive process that underlies all psychotherapeutic change.

10. Bandura considers self-regulation and goal-setting to be important determinants of behavior. Setting proximal goals fosters skill acquisition, heightens self-efficacy, and increases interest in the skill itself.

THE BEHAVIORAL STRATEGY

CHAPTER 21

THE COGNITIVE-BEHAVIORAL APPROACH

OVERVIEW

In this chapter we will discuss the cognitive-behavioral approach. Our discussion begins with the theory and research of Walter Mischel, the most prominent cognitive-behavioral theorist. We will then describe the application of the cognitive-behavioral approach to personality change.

MISCHEL'S COGNITIVE-BEHAVIORAL THEORY AND RESEARCH

Walter Mischel (1930–   ) studied with both George Kelly and Julian Rotter while earning his Ph.D. at Ohio State University. Later he was Henry Murray's colleague at Harvard; Murray convinced him of the importance of taking both personal and environmental variables into account when predicting behavior. Thus, his cognitive-behavioral theory owes a debt to all three of them. You will also notice parallels between Mischel's and Bandura's conceptualizations. They were colleagues at Stanford University for more than twenty years and did some collaborative research. However, Mischel went on to formulate a distinctive position of his own, one that typifies the cognitive-behavioral approach.

We will examine four of Mischel's contributions: (1) a comprehensive critique of traditional dispositional and psychoanalytic personality assessment; (2) the identification and investigation of critical *person variables* that

Walter Mischel

Courtesy of Walter Mischel

affect personality; (3) an explanation of the *consistency paradox;* and (4) the investigation of the interaction of emotion and cognition.

Critique of Traditional Personality Theories

In his 1968 book, *Personality and Assessment,* Mischel identified and challenged the assumptions underlying dispositional and psychodynamic personality assessment. Both of these approaches, according to Mischel, assume that a subject's responses on a personality test are a *sign* of an individual's true underlying personality. For example, a person's score on the MMPI Social Introversion scale shows how introverted or extroverted the person "really is." Thus, it is commonly inferred that a person who scores high on this scale will tend to be modest, shy, and self-effacing. This will be true across a wide range of situations in which the person has to deal with others. However, the average correlation between Social Introversion scale scores and actual behavior in various situations is quite modest: typically about +.30. Correlations between test scores and actual behavior are similar for most dispositional dimensions. Mischel (1968) coined the phrase **personality coefficient** "to describe the correlation between .20 and .30 which is found persistently when virtually any personality dimension inferred from a questionnaire is related to almost any conceivable criterion involving responses sampled in a *different* medium— that is, not by another questionnaire" (p. 78).

Relationships between personality test scores and everyday behavior are generally of the magnitude of a personality coefficient. Nonetheless, it was common in the 1960s to use such tests scores to make important decisions about a person's life and future. Mischel (1968) attacked such practices. He argued that assessment should involve obtaining *samples of behavior* (rather than *signs*). The samples should be taken in situations as similar as possible to actual performance situations. For example, suppose an employer wanted the best candidates to do telephone interviews. It would be better to observe the candidates doing mock telephone interviews than to use their MMPI Social Introversion scores.

On the surface, Mischel's critique seemed to indicate that behavior is mainly influenced by situational variables and that personality dispositions, such as traits or types, have little influence on behavior. But Mischel (1986) believes that the true picture is much more complex.

> Obviously behavior is not entirely situation specific; we do not have to relearn everything in every new situation, we have memories, and our past predisposes our present behavior in critically important and complex ways. Obviously people have characteristics and overall "average" differences in behavior between individuals can be abstracted on many dimensions and used to discriminate among persons for many purposes. Obviously knowing how a person behaved

before can help predict how he will behave again in similar contexts. Obviously the impact of any stimulus depends on the organism that experiences it. No one suggests that the organism approaches every new situation with an empty head. (Mischel, 1973b, pp. 261–62)

Thus, Mischel (1986) acknowledges the importance of **person variables.** These are a person's relatively enduring cognitive and behavioral attributes. Which person variables are important for predicting behavior and understanding personality? We turn next to Mischel's answer.

Person Variables

Mischel (1973b) theorizes that five broad person variables are central to personality.

1. *Competencies.* Each person has a set of behavioral and cognitive skills, overt and covert behaviors the person is capable of engaging in when the circumstances call for them.

2. *Encoding strategies and personal constructs.* People have specific ways of sorting out and categorizing the interpersonal and physical events they encounter. These include the personal constructs that Kelly considered the basis of personality (Chapter 16).

3. *Expectancies.* Each of us has individual probability estimates about the outcomes of particular courses of action in specific situations. For instance, the amount of studying a student will do for an examination is partially dependent on the student's estimate of the chances that increased studying will result in a higher grade.

4. *Values.* People place a specific value or worth on each of the outcomes of various courses of action. Two people with identical expectancies about the outcome of a particular behavior will behave differently if they place different values on the outcome. Consider two men who both expect a hangover the morning after a night of heavy drinking. One may consider that a "price" worth paying for the "pleasures of the night," whereas the other may think the "price" is too high.

5. *Self-regulatory systems and plans.* People are not influenced only by extrinsically imposed conditions. Our behavior is also influenced by self-imposed goals (standards of acceptable performance we establish for ourselves) and self-produced consequences (rewards we give ourselves for reaching our goals).

Person Variables versus Dispositions

It is important to differentiate between Mischel's person variables and the broad and general personality dispositions identified by dispositional psychologists. Person variables *vary* with the specific situation. Traditional personality dispositions are *constant* across situations. The way we choose to view events or our expectancies about the outcomes of courses of action are likely to be different in different situations.

To predict a behavior, we must have information about three factors: (1) the demands and restrictions of the situation; (2) the individual's person variables; and (3) how these situation and person variables interact. To put it another way, we need to know the specific way that the person variables mediate the effects of the situation. Generally, we have many ways of responding to a particular type of situation. But in a specific situation, we decide how to act based on our assessment of the specific nature of the situation as well as on the range of competencies we possess. For example, say we are lost in a strange area. If it is a city, we may ask for directions. Being lost in the woods may necessitate using a map and compass.

Delay of Gratification as a Basic Competency

Mischel has extensively studied one particular person variable. This is the ability to **delay gratification,** or foregoing small immediate rewards for larger rewards that will only become available later. Mischel devised a simple test of delay of gratification for children. The test involves giving children a choice between rewards of different value. They must choose either a small, immediately available reward or a larger reward for which they have to wait. Mischel (1966) found that the ability to delay gratification increases with age and is also associated with higher intelligence, greater social responsibility, and higher achievement strivings.

Mischel's research has revealed some of the conditions that can influence delay of gratification. In an early study, Bandura and Mischel (1965) provided evidence that observing social models could influence delay of gratification. Fourth- and fifth-grade children were given a delay-of-reward test. The test involved a series of fourteen choices between a small immediate reward and a larger postponed reward. (For example, children could have a small candy bar immediately or a larger one a week later.) On the basis of this assessment, the children were classified as preferring *high delay of reward* or *low delay of reward.* Next, Bandura and Mischel tried to change the children's delay preferences (i.e., from high to low and vice versa). This was done by exposing them to an adult model who made choices between immediate and postponed rewards. The model chose between items that are appropriate rewards for adults (e.g., chess sets, magazines). These rewards were different from the items that were offered to the children. Thus, subjects would have to imitate the *principle* behind the model's behavior (i.e., choosing immediate or postponed rewards). They could not merely copy the model's choices.

Children who preferred high delay of reward were exposed to a model who consistently chose the immediate-reward item. Children who preferred low delay of reward were exposed to a model who selected the postponed-reward item in each case. The model also briefly summarized his or her philosophy of life, which included the attitude toward delay of reward that was modeled. For instance, one of the choices was between having a plastic chess set right then and waiting two weeks for a more expensive wooden set. The model in the low-delay-of-reward condition commented, "Chess figures are chess figures. I can get as much use out of the plastic ones right away" (Bandura & Mischel, 1965, p. 701).

Subjects were assigned to one of three conditions. In the *live modeling* condition, the model was actually present. In the *symbolic modeling* condition, the subjects read about the model's choices. Subjects in the *no-model-present* condition were merely shown the series of paired objects. This group served as controls for the possible effects of simple exposure to rewards on subsequent delay of gratification. At the end of the modeling sequence, all children were given a second delay-of-reward test. To assess the stability of changes in delay-of-reward behavior as a result of modeling, the subjects were also given a third delay-of-reward test one month later.

The results of this experiment are presented in Figure 21–1. It can be seen that, for both high- and low-delay preference children, modeling produced a marked and moderately stable change in behavior. Initially high-delay children made more immediate choices after observing a low-delay model; initially low-delay children became more high delay in their choices after observing a high-delay model.

Similar findings were reported by Stumphauzer (1972). His work involved eighteen- to twenty-year-old prison inmates who had shown low delay of gratification. In Stumphauzer's study, the prisoner subjects were exposed to two older inmates who modeled high-delay behavior. These subjects markedly increased their delay behavior. The prisoners' increased willingness to delay gratification was still present at a four-week follow-up test. Additionally, the effect generalized to saving money.

Strategies for Maintaining Delay

Theoretically it was important to show that delay of gratification could be modified in either direction, as Bandura and Mischel (1965) did. In practice, we are generally interested in increasing delay of gratification. In Western cultures, high delay is considered desirable and a sign of maturity. Mischel and his colleagues have studied the strategies children use to postpone immediate rewards in order to get larger ones in the future. This research shows the operation of several person variables, including the way children set goals and use plans and strategies to increase the likelihood that their goals will be met.

Self-Distraction. Freud theorized that delay of gratification depends on the ability to create mental images of the desired object, thereby producing temporary substitute gratification. Using Freud's idea as a starting point, Mischel and Ebbesen (1970) predicted that children looking at the reward they were waiting for would increase delay of gratification.

FIGURE 21–1
Mean percentage of immediate-reward choices by children who initially preferred high delay and mean percentage of delayed-reward choices by children who initially preferred low delay in Bandura and Mischel's (1965) experiment

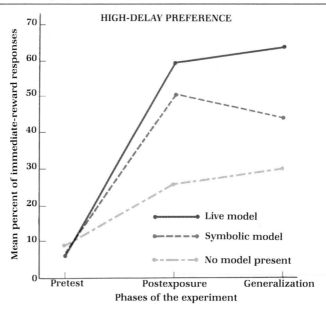

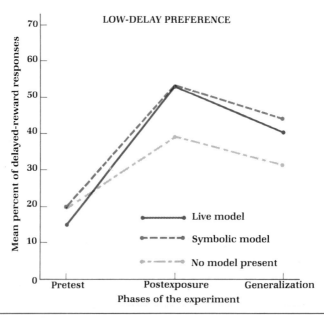

Source: From "Modification of Self-Imposed Delay of Reward through Exposure to Live and Symbolic Models" by A. Bandura and W. Mischel, 1965, *Journal of Personality and Social Psychology*, 2, pp. 698–705.

To test this hypothesis, children aged three to five were first asked whether they preferred cookies or pretzels. Each youngster was then asked to wait alone in a room until the experimenter returned, at which time the child would be given the preferred food. The children were told that they could also call the experimenter back to the room at any time. If they called the experimenter back, however, they would be given their *non*preferred food. The experimenter then left. Depending on the experimental condition, the child waited in full view of (a) both foods, (b) the preferred food only, (c) the nonpreferred food only, or (d) neither food. The experimenter returned in fifteen minutes (or earlier if called by the child).

The results were opposite to the hypothesis. This is shown in Figure 21–2. Children who waited without either food delayed significantly longer than those exposed to both foods or either one of them. The children

FIGURE 21–2
Average amount of time children were able to wait for the delayed but preferred reward in Mischel and Ebbesen's (1970) study. Note that children were able to wait longest when no foods were present in the room, and least able to control themselves when both foods were present. Which of the foods (delayed or immediate) was present did not seem to matter.

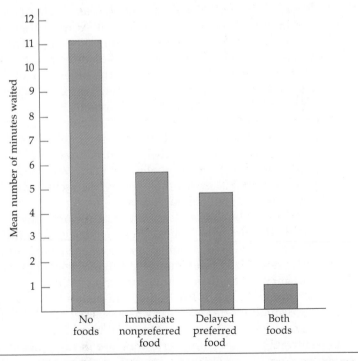

Source: Adapted from "Attention in Delay of Gratification" by W. Mischel and E. Ebbesen, 1970, *Journal of Personality and Social Psychology, 16,* pp. 329–37.

in the condition where no food was present sat alone for an average of 11 minutes. And 75 percent of them successfully waited the entire 15 minutes.

What strategies did the children use to delay gratification? Observation through a one-way mirror provided a clue. Many children spontaneously designed their own distraction techniques; they sang, talked to themselves, and invented games. Moreover, many of the children who successfully waited when the rewards were present avoided looking at the rewards, such as by covering their eyes.

This suggested that children might be taught to distract themselves to increase their delay of gratification. Thus, in a subsequent experiment, some children were told to think about "fun things" or "sad things" while waiting for the larger reward; other children were given no instructions (Mischel, Ebbesen, & Raskoff, 1971). Children who thought about "fun things" waited the longest; those who thought about "sad things" were the least able to wait.

But what happens if children think about the rewards themselves? Do such thoughts increase delay of gratification? Or do they arouse appetites and decrease the ability to wait, as the presence of the "real thing" did in the original study? The answer to these questions suggests that subtle and complex mental processes are involved in delay of gratification.

"Hot" versus "Cool" Thinking. Mischel and Baker (1975) gave nursery school children brief instructions meant to have them think about the reward they were waiting for in two different ways. One involved focusing on the *consummatory* or "hot" qualities of the reward (e.g., how marshmallows are sweet, soft, and chewy). The other way of thinking involved focusing on *nonconsummatory*, abstract, or "cool" qualities (e.g., how marshmallows look like white, puffy clouds). When the children thought about the reward they were waiting for in consummatory or "hot" ways, delay was very difficult. Presumably this is because "hot" ideation increases arousal and frustration (Mischel, 1979). Conversely, thinking about the nonconsummatory or "cool" qualities of the reward made waiting relatively easy. In fact, it was easier than totally distracting themselves from the reward by not thinking about it at all.

Although the presence of the real rewards decreases delay time, *pictures* of the rewards (slides) increase delay time (Mischel & Moore, 1973). The actual versus symbolic presence seems to lead children to think about the rewards in fundamentally different ways. Specifically, the actual rewards may be arousing enough to trigger the motivation to consume or take a reward; this is frustrating and makes delay more difficult. Symbolic presentations are not nearly as arousing; for one thing, "one cannot consume a picture" (Mischel & Moore, 1980, p. 212). Nonetheless, symbolic presentations can be arousing if they are thought about in a "hot" way. Mischel and Moore (1980) found that symbolic representation only helps children delay gratification if they think about the rewards in "cool" ways.

The Stability of Delay of Gratification

Delay competency in childhood is correlated with cognitive and social competence years later. Mischel (1984) obtained parent ratings of seventy-seven adolescents (average age 16 years, 8 months) who had been in his delay of gratification experiments a dozen years before (average age 4 years, 6 months). Some of the correlations between childhood delay of gratification and cognitive and social behaviors in adolescence are shown in Table 21–1. Subjects who tolerated relatively long delays as preschoolers tended, as adolescents, to be able to think and plan ahead. They also tended to act self-confidently, resourcefully, and in a trustworthy manner. In contrast, low delay in childhood predicted a later tendency to be immature, unpredictable, and stress prone. Mischel argues that ability to delay gratification is an important person variable. It is a basic positive social competence that remains reasonably stable throughout life.

Mischel's research on factors that account for delay of gratification illustrates the interaction between situation and person variables. For example, situational variables are important in that whether the actual reward or a picture of it is present can affect attempts to delay gratification. Person variables are also important. People can improve their delay of gratification by the way they *think* about the reward.

The Importance of Plans

Plans of action are another important person variable. Mischel (1979) has studied the development of personal plans in children. He and his colleagues used structured interviews to find out what plans mean to children

TABLE 21–1
Correlations between adolescent ratings and preschool delay time

Item	Correlation Coefficient	Item	Correlation Coefficient
Positive		*Negative*	
Is attentive and able to concentrate	.49	Tends to go to pieces under stress, becomes rattled	−.49
Is verbally fluent, can express ideas well	.40	Reverts to more immature behavior under stress	−.39
Uses and responds to reason	.38	Appears to feel unworthy, thinks of himself as bad	−.33
Is competent, skillful	.38		
Plans, thinks ahead	.35	Is restless and fidgety	−.32
Is self-reliant, confident, trusts own judgment	.33	Is shy and reserved, makes social contacts slowly	−.31
Is curious and exploring, eager to learn, open	.32	Tends to withdraw and disengage himself under stress	−.30

Source: From data presented in ''Convergences and Challenges in the Search for Consistency'' by W. Mischel, 1984, *American Psychologist, 39,* pp. 351–64.

and how children define and use them. It appears that children as young as eight can discuss their plans explicitly. They can provide concrete examples of how they use plans to structure and organize their behavior. One eight-year-old spontaneously told an interviewer: "Tomorrow I'll clean up my room. . . . Next week I'm gonna have a birthday party—if Mommy helps me" (p. 749). By age ten or eleven, children have a surprisingly good grasp of the nature, organization, and function of plans in their lives. They appreciate that plans have an intention or purpose (e.g., "I'm going to clean up my room tomorrow because I'm planning to have a friend over"); they also explicitly know the purpose a plan serves (e.g., "A plan tells you what to do and when and where and how to do it").

Further, most grade school children realize having a plan is useless unless it is carried out. A ten-year-old explained: "You have to make yourself do it when the time comes; planning is the part you do beforehand, but then doing it is the actual right-there part" (p. 749). Some children are so good at planning that they seem to do it automatically. One eleven-year-old saw himself as an expert planner. He explained:

> If I had to teach a plan to someone who grew up in the jungle— like a plan to work on a project at 10 A.M. tomorrow—I'd tell him what to say to himself to make it easier at the start for him. Like "if I do this *plan* on time I'll get a reward and the teacher will like me and I'll be proud." But for myself, I know all that already, so I don't have to say it to myself—Besides, it would take too long to say, and my mind doesn't have the time for that, so I just remember that stuff about why I should do it real quick without saying it—It's like a method that I know already in math; once you have the method you don't have to say every little step. (Mischel, 1979, p. 749)

Children increasingly use plans and strategies as they get older. This is revealed by what they have to say about how to delay gratification (Yates & Mischel, 1979). The youngest children incorrectly believe that seeing and thinking about the rewards will help them endure the delay. As they grow older, however, they realize they must avoid thinking about the rewards or think about them in ways that make them less, rather than more, tempting. One child explained that someone could more easily wait for two pretzels by imagining they had gum stuck all over them!

The Consistency Paradox

Ask yourself the following question. Do you think it is useful to characterize people you know by placing them in broad dispositional categories, such as honest, outgoing, or confident? In other words, do you believe that people are generally consistent in their behavior in various situations? At an intuitive level, most people would answer "yes." They would mention the "fact" that some people just do seem to be generally more honest than others. Certainly this is a widely held belief. However, it is contrary to research data showing that behavior is often quite variable from situation to situation. A person who is honest in one situation is *not* necessarily honest in another. This marked difference between our impressions of individual consistency and the actual data is called the **consistency paradox**. How can the paradox be explained? Mischel's answer draws on two main ideas: (1) the distinction between cross-situational and temporal consistency and (2) the concept of cognitive prototypes.

Cross-Situational Consistency versus Temporal Consistency

Cross-situational consistency is the extent that a person behaves the same way in different circumstances. It is consistency *across situations*. Consider nine-year-old Herbie. He is aggressive with smaller children on the playground. He is *also* aggressive with his brothers and sisters at home and with peers at school. Herbie's aggressiveness shows substantial cross-situational consistency. This contrasts with **temporal consistency**, which refers to someone behaving the same way in the same basic situation at different times. It is consistency *within situations across time*. Herbie's aggressiveness would be considered temporally consistent if he were aggressive with smaller children on the playground today as well as tomorrow, next week, and next month.

Mischel (1984) argues that there is little reason to expect broad cross-situational consistency. But temporal consistency is likely. Both claims are based on the contingencies in real life. Herbie's aggression with smaller, younger children on the playground probably pays off. Smaller, younger children are likely to be intimidated by a playground bully. In turn, his aggression is reinforced because it gets him what he wants, such as first choice of toys or recreational activities. If Herbie's aggression is successful today, it will likely be successful tomorrow and the following day, too. Thus, aggression becomes a stable mode of responding *in this situation*. Now suppose Herbie is playing with bigger, older children. Here the contingencies are quite different. Bigger, older playmates may respond to aggression with counter-aggression. Clearly, then, aggression in the first situation (with younger children) would not predict aggression in the second (with older children). Not, at least, if our young bully can distinguish one situation from the other. Thus, Herbie's behavior has temporal consistency but not cross-situational consistency.

Cognitive Prototypes

Basic research on how people categorize everyday objects shows that whether people place an object in a particular category depends on how "typical" it is of the category. We readily classify cows or rabbits as mammals. We are less likely to place whales and dolphins in the mammal category. The former are viewed as more typical of mammals than the latter. We seem to categorize objects using **cognitive prototypes**—that is, the "best" examples of the concept (e.g., Tversky, 1977).

Mischel (1984) believes that people also use cognitive prototypes to categorize some behaviors as more typical of a dispositional category than others. For example, college students believe that attending class regularly is more typical of a *conscientious student* than taking neat notes or coming to study sessions on time, even though the latter two behaviors have some relevance for conscientiousness.

We tend to see behaviors as more or less typical of a disposition. This gives us some understanding of the consistency paradox. As we indicated, the general impression of consistency in behavior is likely to be of temporal consistency rather than cross-situational consistency. This impression may be because we see the consistency in *prototypic* behaviors rather than in all behaviors in a disposition's domain. In other words, for us to see someone as having a particular disposition, say a trait of *courage*, the person must be consistent across time in exhibiting certain prototypic examples, such as rescuing someone from a burning building or making a solo ascent of an unclimbed mountain. However, the person may not exhibit certain behaviors that are examples of courage but are not *prototypic* examples, such as admitting lying to a friend. Such a nonprototypic example is likely to be overlooked in forming the general impression that the individual is courageous.

Mischel believes that we form our impressions from the temporal consistency of the most prototypic behaviors without being aware that this is the basis for our impressions. These and related theoretical ideas have received support in a study carried out at Carleton College.

The Carleton College Study. Mischel (1984) studied one particular trait—conscientiousness—in sixty-three undergraduates at Carleton College in Minnesota. Parents and a close friend rated each student on conscientiousness. In this study, students also rated themselves on how consistent or variable they were in conscientiousness. The students were observed in a variety of actual situations related to conscientiousness. They were assessed on such measures as class attendance, assignment neatness, assignment punctuality, room neatness, and personal appearance. (Students considered all of these measures to be indicative of conscientiousness.)

Raters agreed much more about the overall conscientiousness of students who rated themselves consistently conscientious than about those who rated themselves as inconsistently conscientious. However, students who rated themselves as consistent on the trait were *not* actually more consistent than those who rated themselves as inconsistent or variable. This can be explained with reference to cognitive prototypes. Specifically, the cognitive prototype approach suggests that people do not judge their consistency on a trait by averaging their behavior across all relevant behaviors. Instead, they take into account only their consistency on a few behaviors that seem most relevant to the trait.

Mischel and Peake (1982b) tested this theoretical prediction. They divided the behavioral measures from the Carleton College study into those judged by the students as more relevant (i.e., prototypic) or less relevant to conscientiousness. As expected, students who saw themselves as highly conscientious were much more temporally consistent on the most prototypical conscientious behaviors than students who considered themselves as variable. Next, Mischel and Peake examined *all* behaviors related to conscientiousness (not just prototypic behaviors). In this case, students who rated themselves as highly consistent were *not* in fact any more cross-situationally consistent in their actual behavior than those who saw themselves as variable in conscientiousness. The results are shown in Table 21–2. The data strongly support the idea that our perceptions about our consistency on a disposition come from *temporal consistency of prototypical behaviors.* They are not based on cross-situational consistency across all relevant behaviors.

When Are People Consistent?

Mischel believes that people are generally consistent in their behavior in the same situation. In other words, they show temporal consistency. Under normal circumstances, behavior is not consistent from one situation to another (i.e., cross-situational consistency) because people discriminate, adapt, and are flexible. In other words, people note that different behaviors are called for in different situations, and they change their behavior accordingly. However, there are times when cross-situational consistency is more likely. Specifically, it may be expected in abnormal circumstances, such as highly stressful situations and/or those that call for behaviors beyond a person's competency. In such situations, people tend to act in a rigid fashion. They use "tried and true" means of coping.

TABLE 21–2
The link between self-perceived consistency and actual behavior. Students who view themselves as highly consistent on conscientiousness are *not* more cross-situationally consistent than those who rate themselves as low in consistency, but they are more temporally consistent (stable) in their display of the behaviors most prototypical for conscientiousness. The data are correlation coefficients.

Behavioral Data	Self-Perceived Consistency	
	High	Low
Cross-situational consistency		
More prototypical	.15	.13
Less prototypical	.09	.14
Temporal stability		
More prototypical	.71	.47
Less prototypical	.65	.64

Source: Adapted from "Beyond Deja Vu in the Search for Cross-Situational Consistency" by W. Mischel and P. K. Peake, 1982, *Psychological Review, 89,* pp. 730–55.

Wright and Mischel (1986) were able to test this hypothesis by studying the behavior of emotionally disturbed children at a summer camp. The camp staff observed the children in twenty-one distinct situations (e.g., music, athletics, and group cabin meetings) over a forty-day period. The staff rated each child's aggressive and withdrawal behaviors.

The cognitive and self-regulatory demands of each situation were categorized according to the demand they placed on the child. *Low demand* situations were within the children's capacity; *high demand* meant they were beyond the children's capacity. The cross-situational consistency of the children's behavior in low- and high-demand situations was compared. Some of the results are shown in Table 21–3. As predicted, there was much more consistency across situations requiring a high degree of competency. The children showed more variability (i.e., less cross-situational consistency) when they had sufficient competence to alter their behavior as the situation required.

Thus, cross-situational consistency does occur under certain predictable conditions, namely, those in which consistency is likely to result from rigid or incompetent functioning. Good adjustment and competence requires "context sensitivity." It involves choosing the specific responses that are likely to produce desirable results in the situation at hand. This is why most people show a good deal of situational variability (i.e., little cross-situational consistency). The generally observed consistency in behavior is temporal. People have learned particular ways of behaving successfully in specific situations, and they tend to respond in the same situation-specific ways. Thus, consistency in human behavior is not paradoxical. *Consistency occurs over time but, under normal circumstances, not across situations.*

TABLE 21–3
Mean cross-situational consistency coefficients for two years as a function of a situation's cognitive and self-regulatory requirements. When the situation's requirements are high (and thus exceed the children's competencies) consistency was high, but when the situations were less demanding, there was considerably less cross-situational consistency.

Behavior Category		Situation Competency Requirements	
		Low	High
	1981		
Aggression		.37	.73
Withdrawal		.27	.69
	1982		
Aggression		.32	.61
Withdrawal		.06	.37

Source: From data reported in "Convergences and Challenges in the Search for Consistency" by W. Mischel, 1984, *American Psychologist, 39,* pp. 351–64.

The Interaction of Emotion and Cognition

For the most part, the behavioral strategy has paid little attention to emotion as a determinant of behavior. Mischel's position is an exception. He believes cognition and emotion constantly interact and influence each other in life situations.

In one experiment, Wright and Mischel (1982) induced a positive (happy), neutral, or negative (sad) mood in college students through imagery. Then the students performed a perception task which was set up so that they either "succeeded" or "failed." To assess the results of mood and success experience, the subjects were asked a series of questions related to their performance on the perception task.

Being in a positive mood resulted in higher expectations about future success, higher estimates of past performance, and higher overall self-evaluation of ability on the task. These results held both for subjects who had succeeded and those who had failed. Success or failure came into play in two areas. Mood had little effect on the self-evaluations of the success group. But those in the failure group were much less satisfied with their performance if they were in a bad mood. When subjects were asked to set minimal goals for future trials on the task, the combination of failure and a bad mood was particularly devastating. Subjects in this group were the only ones to set minimal goals that they did not expect to meet.

How does mood influence thought? Wright and Mischel (1982) suggest that people have a **mood-congruent bias.** This leads them to selectively process information about past experience in a way that is consistent with their mood. In broad terms, people in a positive mood tend to selectively attend to and recall success and other positive experiences. Conversely, people in a negative mood tend to selectively attend to and recall failure and other negative experiences.

The idea of a mood-congruent bias would explain Wright and Mischel's (1982) finding that subjects in a positive mood tended to recall their performance as more successful than it actually was. Specifically, the positive mood led to selective attention to and recall of success. The same mechanism appears to operate in depression. In one study, the social competence of depressed and nondepressed individuals was rated by observers and by the individuals themselves (Lewinsohn, Mischel, Chaplin, & Barton, 1980). Contrary to expectations, depressed subjects rated themselves as they were seen by others, so that they were quite accurate. The nondepressed patients rated themselves more positively than they were actually seen. Moreover, as the depressed subjects' mood became more positive over the course of psychotherapy, their self-perceptions also changed.

> In the course of treatment, the depressed not only rated themselves more positively, but . . . began to increase the discrepancy between

how they rated themselves and how they were rated. Indeed, during treatment their self-perceptions became more unrealistic in the sense that they began to see themselves more positively than the observers rated them. It is tempting to conjecture that a key to avoiding depression is to see oneself less stringently and more favorably than others see one. If so, the beliefs that unrealistic appraisals are a basic ingredient of depression and that realism is the crux of appropriate affect may have to be seriously questioned. To feel good about ourselves we may have to judge ourselves more kindly than we are judged. (Lewinsohn et al., 1980, pp. 211–12)

The relationship of emotion and cognition within the cognitive-behavioral approach has only begun to be explored. Still, it is a welcomed trend; no comprehensive theory of personality can ignore the important role of our emotional states. Cognitive-behavioral therapists have been dealing with the relationship of cognitions and emotions for some time. It is this important practical application of the cognitive-behavioral approach to which we turn next.

COGNITIVE-BEHAVIORAL THERAPY

From the perspective of the cognitive-behavioral approach, personality change requires modifying cognitions. **Cognitive-behavioral therapy** helps clients change the cognitions that are influencing their problem or abnormal behaviors (Meichenbaum, 1986). Theoretically, this can be done (1) by changing overt behaviors to indirectly change cognitions or (2) by directly changing the relevant cognitions. Whether cognitions are modified directly or indirectly depends on the emphasis of the particular cognitive-behavioral therapy as well as the client's problem behavior (e.g., Kendall, 1984). Most cognitive-behavioral therapies involve a combination of both tactics.

Cognitive Restructuring

Many cognitive-behavioral therapies are based on a fundamental principle called **cognitive restructuring,** which involves modifying the thoughts, ideas, and beliefs maintaining the client's problem behaviors (Spiegler, 1986). These cognitions may take the form of self-deprecating thoughts, illogical ideas, or irrational beliefs. Through cognitive restructuring, the person learns to recognize such maladaptive cognitions and replace them with adaptive cognitions.

The cognitions of greatest interest to cognitive-behavioral therapists are the client's **self-talk** or **self-statements**—the "soundless, mental speech, arising at the instant that we think about something, plan or solve problems in our mind. . . . we think and remember with the aid of words which we articulate to ourselves" (Sokolov, 1972, p. 1). Generally, it is more productive to ask a client, "What are you saying to yourself when you begin to feel anxious?" than to ask, "What are you thinking when . . . ?" because the former is easier to put into words.

DEMONSTRATION 21–1

COGNITIVE RESTRUCTURING[1]

In cognitive restructuring, a basic procedure in most cognitive-behavioral therapies, clients must first recognize that they are making negative or maladaptive self-statements and then substitute positive and adaptive self-statements. In this Demonstration, you will practice modifying negative self-statements. The primary purpose of the Demonstration is to familiarize you with the most frequently used cognitive-behavioral therapy procedure. Secondarily, you will be learning a coping skill that you may find useful in dealing with stressful events in your life.

Below are brief descriptions of some common stress-evoking situations and one possible negative or maladaptive self-statement a person might make when encountering the situation. The self-statements are maladaptive because they interpret the situation so that nothing can be done to cope with it. In fact, each situation is undesirable but not as disastrous as the negative self-statement implies.

PROCEDURE

1. For each negative self-statement below, write down several alternative self-statements that are positive, optimistic, and adaptive. Your positive self-statements should be directly related to the situation, should be realistic, and should point to some constructive course of action. For instance, if your brand-new car were stolen, it would be unrealistic to respond with, "I don't need the car."

Situation	Negative Self-Statement
1. Having a long, difficult assignment due the next day	1. "I'll never get this work done by tomorrow."
2. Having an accident with the family car	2. "Oh no, my father will 'kill' me."
3. Losing one's job	3. "I'll never get another job."

---

[1]Adapted from Spiegler (1983).

4. Moving away from friends and family

4. "My whole life is left behind."

5. Breaking up with a person you love

5. "I have nothing to live for. He/she was all I had."

6. Not getting into graduate school

6. "I guess I'm really dumb. I don't know what I'll do."

7. Having to participate in a class discussion

7. "Everyone else knows more than I do, so what's the use of saying anything."

2. After you have provided alternative positive self-statements for each of the negative self-statements, compare them with the examples of positive self-statements listed in Table 21–4 (page 502).

Rational-Emotive Therapy (RET)

Rational-emotive therapy (RET) was originated by Albert Ellis (1962). RET uses cognitive restructuring to change the faulty or irrational thoughts that result in negative emotions, like anxiety, depression, anger, and guilt (Huber, 1985). As Figure 21–3 shows, RET is based on the assumption that negative emotions and accompanying maladaptive behaviors result *directly* from maladaptive thoughts. They are only an indirect product of precipitating external events. (However, people often attribute their emotional upset to the external events.) Moreover, Ellis (1970) believes that certain common irrational beliefs are the root of most emotional disturbance (e.g., "I must be loved by everyone" and "I have to do things perfectly").

FIGURE 21–3

Ellis's rational-emotive model. Negative emotions (1) are a direct product of maladaptive thoughts and (2) are only an indirect product of external events that precipitated the maladaptive thoughts.

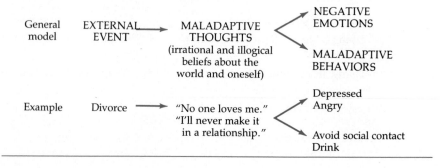

In RET, the therapist helps the client identify the specific maladaptive self-statements he or she is making with regard to some external precipitating event. Then the therapist points out the irrational or illogical beliefs on which the self-statements are based. For instance, Joe V. was a forty-year-old businessman who felt guilty and depressed whenever he went off his diet. The therapist asked Joe to monitor what he was saying to himself whenever he deviated from his diet. His self-statements included "I'll never be able to lose weight" and "I am going to be fat the rest of my life." The therapist showed Joe that his self-statements were based on the irrational belief that he must be perfect and the illogical idea that he could never stay on his diet just because he occasionally went off it. After several therapy sessions, Joe began to see the connection between his thoughts and his feelings. The therapist then taught him, through modeling and role playing, to identify why his thoughts were irrational (i.e., to find the underlying irrational beliefs). Finally, Joe learned to substitute rational thoughts for irrational thoughts (e.g., replacing "I'll always be fat" with "Just because I went off my diet today, doesn't mean I can't stay on it tomorrow").

Cognitive Therapy

Cognitive therapy was developed by psychiatrist Aaron Beck (1976). It is similar to RET. Cognitive therapy has been primarily used to treat depression and is one of the most successful treatments for that common disorder (e.g., Boffey, 1986; Rush, Beck, Kovacs, & Hollon, 1977; Shaw, 1977). In analyzing the thoughts of depressed patients, Beck (1976, 1984) identified three common themes: (1) negative interpretation of external events, (2) pessimistic view of the future, and (3) self-dislike. Beck attributes these distorted views to a common set of logical errors. One such error is *arbitrary inferences*. These are conclusions drawn without sufficient evidence or in the face of contradictory evidence. An example is believing you were laid off from a job because of incompetence, although the company has gone out of business. Another logical error is *overgeneralization*. This involves drawing a general conclusion from a single incident. For instance, you conclude that you will never succeed after failing on the first attempt.

In cognitive therapy, patients are taught (1) first to identify their logical errors, (2) then to challenge the basic premises of the illogical thoughts, and (3) finally to reinterpret events more accurately. The ultimate aim is to change depressed patients' cognitions—illogical thoughts and negative views. Techniques include both cognitive and behavioral components. One technique is **mastery and pleasure therapy.** Patients rate their success with and pleasure derived from daily activities; inevitably, patients find they are more successful at and get more pleasure from their activities than they realized. **Graded task assignments** involve shaping. Patients engage in a series of brief, simple behaviors that gradually

Examples of positive self-statements that could be substituted for negative self-statements (see Demonstration 21-1)

Situation	Negative Self-Statement	Positive Self-Statement
1. Having a long, difficult assignment due the next day	1. "I'll never get this work done by tomorrow."	1. "If I work real hard I may be able to get it all done for tomorrow." "This is going to be tough but it is still possible to do it." "It will be a real challenge finishing this assignment for tomorrow." "If I don't get it finished, I'll just have to ask the teacher for an extension."
2. Having an accident with the family car	2. "Oh, no, my father will 'kill' me."	2. "What's done is done; I'll just have to make the best of it." "I'll just have to figure out a way that I can pay for this." "This is going to cost me, but thank God no one was injured." "Maybe my father will understand if I explain it to him calmly."
3. Losing one's job	3. "I'll never get another job."	3. "I'll just have to look harder for another job." "There will be rough times ahead, but I've dealt with rough times before." "Hey, maybe my next job will be a better deal altogether." "There are agencies that can probably help me get some kind of a job."
4. Moving away from friends and family	4. "My whole life is left behind."	4. "I'll miss everyone, but it doesn't mean we can't stay in touch." "Just think of all the new people I'm going to meet." "I guess it will will be kind of exciting moving to a new home." "Now I'll have two places to call home."

Situation		
5. Breaking up with a person you love	"I have nothing to live for. He/she was all I had."	"I really thought our relationship would work, but it's not the end of the world." "Maybe we can try again in the future." "I'll just have to try to keep myself busy and not let it bother me." "If I met him (her), there is no reason why I won't meet someone else someday."
6. Not getting into graduate school	"I guess I'm really dumb. I don't know what I'll do."	"I'll just have to reapply next year." "There are things I can do with my life other than going to grad school." "I guess a lot of good students get turned down. It's just so damn competitive." "Perhaps there are a few other programs that I could apply to."
7. Having to participate in a class discussion	"Everyone else knows more than I do, so what's the use of saying anything."	"I have as much to say as anyone else in the class." "My ideas may be different, but they're still valid." "It's OK to be a bit nervous; I'll relax as I start talking." "I might as well say something; how bad could it sound?"

Source: From *Contemporary Behavioral Therapy* (pp. 403–404) by M. D. Spiegler, 1983, Palo Alto, Calif.: Mayfield.

become lengthier and more complex. The aim is to counter patients' views that they cannot competently perform various behaviors. The gradual shaping procedure allows patients to succeed and thus prove to themselves that they can perform behaviors competently.

Self-Instructional Training

Donald Meichenbaum (1985, 1986) is one of the architects of the cognitive-behavioral approach. He has designed a cognitive-behavioral procedure that teaches clients cognitive restructuring through modeling and cognitive behavior rehearsal. **Self-instructional training** begins by identifying the habitual cognitions (self-statements, images) present when the client experiences stress. Next the role of these cognitions in creating and increasing stress is explored. Finally, alternative adaptive cognitions are generated, modeled by the therapist, and practiced by the client. We will illustrate self-instructional training by describing its initial use to decrease children's impulsive behavior (Meichenbaum & Goodman, 1971).

Children who act impulsively do not think before acting. This often has undesirable consequences for them as well as for other people. The general goal of self-instructional training for impulsive behavior is teaching children to think and plan before they act. In simple terms, they are taught to "stop, look, and listen." (See Figure 21-4.) Self-instructional training for impulsive behavior involves five steps.

1. *Cognitive modeling*: an adult model performs a task while verbalizing an adaptive, counterimpulsive strategy. For example, an adult model might say while copying line patterns:

FIGURE 21-4
Cue cards used to prompt children to use self-instructions in solving problems

| What is my problem? | How can I do it? | Am I using my plan? | How did I do? |

Source: From *Think Aloud: Increasing Social and Cognitive Skills—A Problem-Solving Program for Children (Primary Level)* by B. W. Camp and M. A. S. Bash, 1981, Champaign, Ill.: Research Press. Reprinted by permission.

Okay, what is it I have to do? You want me to copy the picture with the different lines. I have to go slowly and carefully. Okay, draw the line down, down, good; then to the right, that's it; now down some more and to the left. Good, I'm doing fine so far. Remember, go slowly. Now back up again. No, I was supposed to go down. That's okay. Just erase the line carefully. (Meichenbaum & Goodman, 1971, p. 117)

2. *Cognitive participant modeling*: the child performs the task as the model verbalizes the instructions.

3. *Overt self-instruction*: the child performs the task while verbalizing the instructions out loud.

4. *Fading the overt self-instruction*: the child performs the task while whispering the instructions.

5. *Covert self-instruction*: the child performs the task while saying the instructions silently.

Using the sequence just described, the child first practices with brief and simple perceptual motor tasks, like coloring figures within boundaries.

I think I can—I think I can—I think I can—I think I can.

As in the children's story *The Little Engine That Could*, clients in self-instructional training tell themselves what they must do and repeatedly tell themselves that they can succeed.

Source: *The Little Engine That Could*, retold by Watty Piper, illustrated by George and Doris Hauman, New York: Platt & Munk, 1985.

Gradually the length and complexity of the tasks are increased (e.g., a complex task might be solving concept-formation problems).

Self-instructional training has been used to treat a wide variety of problems with a number of different populations. The problems include anxiety (Meichenbaum, Gilmore, & Fedoravicius, 1971) and lack of creativity in college students (Meichenbaum, 1975), deficits in problem solving among children (e.g., Camp & Bash, 1981) and the elderly (Labouvie-Vief & Gonda, 1976), pain in adults (Turk, Meichenbaum, & Genest, 1983), and schizophrenic speech (e.g., Meyers, Mercatoris, & Sirota, 1976). Self-instructional training has also proved helpful in teaching academic skills to children, especially those with behavioral or emotional problems that interfere with learning (e.g., Davis & Hajicek, 1985; Swanson, 1985).

Problem-Solving Therapy

Solving problems is ubiquitous in daily life. The ability to solve problems is related to competence and adjustment. For example, the more consistently children generate effective solutions to social problems, the more socially competent they appear to be (Hopper & Kirschenbaum, 1985). And college students who consider themselves effective at solving personal problems have higher levels of psychological adjustment than those who consider themselves ineffective problem solvers (e.g., Heppner & Anderson, 1985).

Solving personal problems is, in one way or another, part of all psychotherapies. Cognitive-behavioral therapists have specifically taught general problem-solving skills to clients with two aims: (1) to alleviate the particular personal problems for which clients have sought therapy (e.g., D'Zurilla & Nezu, 1982; Wasik, 1984) and (2) to provide clients with a general coping strategy for personal problems (e.g., Heppner, Neal, & Larsen, 1984). Problem-solving therapy involves clients' learning a series of basic steps that can be used to solve problems. Direct instruction, modeling, and practice are used to teach the steps. The steps are as follows:

1. *Problem identification.* First, it is necessary to define the dilemma as a problem to be solved.

2. *Goal selection.* What does the person want the ultimate outcome to be?

3. *Generation of alternative solutions.* Here the person lists many different possible solutions, without evaluating their potential merit (i.e., a kind of brainstorming).

4. *Evaluation of alternative solutions.* Now the person evaluates the pros and cons of each alternative in terms of (*a*) the probability that it will meet the goal selected (Step 2) and (*b*) its practicality, which involves considering the potential consequences to the person and others of each solution. The alternative solutions are ranked in terms of desirability and practicality, and the highest one is selected.

5. *Implementation.* The individual tries the solution chosen.

6. *Evaluation.* Did the solution alleviate the problem and meet the goal? If not, what went wrong? In other words, which of the steps in problem solving needs to be redone?

Problem-solving therapies have been used to treat a variety of target behaviors with a wide range of clients. Examples include peer relationship difficulties among children and adolescents (e.g., Pellegrini & Urbain, 1985), examination and interpersonal anxiety among college students (Mayo & Norton, 1980), relapse following a program to reduce smoking (Supnick & Colletti, 1984), harmony among family members (e.g., Robin & Foster, in press), and the ability of chronic psychiatric patients to cope with interpersonal problems (Hansen, St. Lawrence, & Christoff, 1985).

Stress Inoculation Training (SIT)

The final cognitive-behavioral therapy we will discuss incorporates several of the specific therapies we have already described. **Stress inoculation training (SIT)** was also developed by Meichenbaum (1985). It is a broadly applicable cognitive-behavioral therapy that is analogous to being inoculated against disease. It prepares clients to deal with stress-inducing events by teaching them self-control coping skills. Clients then rehearse these skills while gradually being exposed to stressors. SIT involves three phases: conceptualization, skill acquisition and rehearsal, and application and follow-through (West, Horan, & Games, 1984).

Conceptualization Phase

In the first phase, clients are given an adaptive way of viewing and understanding their negative reactions to stressful events. Basically, the rationale offered clients is that negative emotions associated with a stressful situation are caused by the way they see the situation and the actions they take in relation to it, rather than by the situation itself. (This is the general rationale of all cognitive-behavioral therapies.) Clients are told that they can learn coping skills that will let them reconceptualize and deal with such situations without becoming emotionally upset.

Skills Acquisition and Rehearsal Phase

In the second phase of SIT, clients learn coping skills appropriate to the type of stress they are experiencing. With interpersonal anxiety, the client might develop skills that would make the feared situation less threatening (e.g., learning to initiate and maintain conversations). The client might also learn deep muscle relaxation to lessen tension. To control anger, clients learn to view potential provocations as problems that require a solution rather than as threats that require an attack. They are also taught to rehearse alternative strategies for solving the problem at hand. For example, one coping skill clients learn in order to tolerate pain is refocusing their attention by imagining scenes unrelated to the pain-producing experience. Problem-solving therapy and self-instructional training are also often used in SIT to provide clients with coping skills. Examples of possible coping self-statements are listed in Table 21–5. (Note that many of these statements are general enough to be used with almost any type of stressful situation.)

Some clients already have adequate coping skills but are not using them to deal with their reactions to stressful events. In such cases, the second phase of SIT involves eliminating the factors that are keeping the client from using the coping skills. These factors may reside within the person (e.g., irrational beliefs) or in the external environment (e.g., being punished by a spouse for acting assertively).

Clients practice coping skills and receive feedback and reinforcement from the therapist. The aim of the second phase of SIT is for clients to become competent at using coping skills and to feel comfortable in doing so.

Application and Follow-Through Phase

When clients have mastered coping skills, they are ready to practice applying them in the third and final phase of SIT. Initially clients are exposed to stressful situations in the therapy situation. They rehearse applying

TABLE 21–5

Examples of coping self-statements used in stress inoculation to reduce fear or anxiety, anger, and pain

Fear or Anxiety[a]	Anger[b]	Pain[c]
What is it I have to do?	What is it I have to do?	What is it I have to do?
Just think about what I can do about it. That is better than getting anxious.	This is going to upset me, but I know how to deal with it.	I have lots of different strategies I can call upon.
One step at a time. I can handle this situation.	Think of what you want to get out of this.	Don't think about the pain, just what I have to do.
This anxiety is what the therapist said I would feel. It's a reminder to use my coping skills.	I'm not going to let him get to me.	This tenseness can be a help, a cue to cope.
I didn't handle that as well as I could have, but I'll get better.	I have a right to be annoyed, but let's keep the lid on.	When the pain mounts, I can switch to a different strategy; I'm in control.
	Can I laugh about this? It's probably not so serious.	That's better than before I used coping skills, so I'm making some progress.

Source: Adapted from (a) *Cognitive Behavior Modification* by D. Meichenbaum, 1974, Morristown, N.J.: General Learning Press; (b) *Anger Control* by R. Novaco, 1975, Lexington, Mass.: Heath; and (c) "Cognitive Control of Pain" by D. Turk, 1977, in D. Meichenbaum (Ed.), *Cognitive Behavior Modification*, New York: Plenum.

their coping skills to handle them. Clients may imagine encountering and coping with stress-inducing circumstances that have been arranged in a hierarchy. Clients also overtly role play dealing with stressful events. Next, the client is given homework assignments that involve gradual exposure to actual stressful events in his or her everyday life. To help prevent relapses, clients discuss and rehearse dealing with situations that are most likely to result in a relapse. Recent evidence indicates that such efforts toward long-term maintenance of treatment gains are successful (e.g., Long, 1985).

Finally, clients may be given *booster sessions* at periodic intervals (e.g., three-, six-, and twelve-months). These sessions provide incentives to continue using their coping skills when needed. They also help clients fine-tune their coping skills and deal with unanticipated difficulties they may experience in handling stress in their lives.

Uses of SIT

SIT is a broad-spectrum approach to coping with stress. Thus, it is not surprising that it has been applied to many types of problems (Meichenbaum, 1985). SIT has helped individuals cope with anger, anxiety, fear, pain, Type A behavior, health-related problems (e.g., cancer, hypertension), and the aftereffects of rape and terrorist attack. SIT appears to be suitable for all age levels. Various groups have received SIT to help cope with the stresses inherent in their work; these include nurses, teachers, police and probation officers, soldiers, and athletes. Additionally, consistent with the idea of inoculating people against stress, SIT has been used to prevent adverse reactions to medical and dental procedures.

SUMMARY

1. Mischel's first major contribution was a comprehensive critique of traditional dispositional and psychoanalytic personality assessment. He coined the term "personality coefficient" to refer to the generally low correlations typically found between personality test scores and actual behavior.

2. Mischel has identified five broad person variables: competencies, encoding strategies and personal constructs, expectancies, values, and self-regulating systems and plans. Person variables are unlike general personality dispositions in that person variables are not assumed to be constant across situations.

3. Mischel considers the ability to delay gratification to be an important person variable. Delay of gratification increases with age and is associated with higher intelligence, higher social responsibility, and higher achievement strivings. Delay of gratification is increased by exposure to delay-

oriented models and by the ability to distract oneself from immediate temptations (especially by thinking about immediately available rewards in "cool" ways).

4. Plans are another important person variable. Mischel has found that children as young as eight are able to explicitly formulate plans.

5. The consistency paradox refers to the fact that we think of people as being quite consistent in their behavior when in reality most people's behavior tends to vary a good deal from situation to situation. Mischel has concluded that behavior is temporally stable; that is, we react in similar ways when the same or similar situations recur in our lives. However, he argues that behavior is not very consistent across different situations because people are normally context-sensitive.

6. Mischel's solution to the consistency paradox invokes the concept of cognitive prototypes. When asked to think about a broad behavioral category, we usually call to mind the more typical members of the category while paying little attention to the less typical members. The impression of cross-situational consistency derives mainly from the fact that people are temporally consistent on a few behaviors that are most typical of a dispositional category, which gives the (false) impression of general consistency. People are sometimes cross-situationally consistent, but primarily when the demands of the situation exceed their own personal competencies.

7. According to Mischel, emotion and cognition interact to control behavior. People appear to have a mood-congruent bias—that is, a tendency to selectively recall and interpret experience in the direction of the mood they are in.

8. Cognitive behavioral therapy relies heavily on cognitive restructuring, which involves modifying how clients think about themselves and their lives. Ellis makes use of cognitive restructuring in his rational-emotive therapy, which involves showing people that their negative beliefs and opinions about themselves are irrational or illogical.

9. Cognitive therapy was developed by Beck to treat depression. Beck also believes that other human problems are rooted in illogical thoughts and negative self-perceptions. Cognitive therapy consists of a variety of specific techniques to identify, challenge, and finally reinterpret ways in which patients view themselves.

10. Self-instructional training involves teaching clients to talk to themselves in more adaptive ways.

11. Problem-solving therapy involves teaching clients to solve their own problems through five steps: problem identification, goal selection, generation of alternatives, evaluation of alternative solutions, and implementation of the best available solution.

12. Stress inoculation training is a psychological procedure analogous to being inoculated against disease. It involves preparing people to deal with stress through problem conceptualization, acquisition and rehearsal of relevant skills, and application of the skills.

THE BEHAVIORAL STRATEGY

CHAPTER 22

LIABILITIES

OVERVIEW

We conclude our presentation of the behavioral strategy as we concluded our discussions of the other three strategies, by looking at some problems and limitations. The first six liabilities are germaine to the behavioral strategy as a whole. The remainder are specific criticisms of two basic approaches within the strategy: the radical behavioral and the cognitive-behavioral approach.

EXCESS RELIANCE ON EXPERIMENTAL LABORATORY RESEARCH

The favored method of research in the behavioral strategy has been the controlled laboratory experiment. This is most conducive to drawing conclusions regarding cause-and-effect relationships. (See Chapter 2.) The strength of the experimental method notwithstanding, experiments in the field of personality have limitations.

Studying Multivariate Phenomena

To achieve precision, actual experimental situations are often narrow and simplified. Experiments generally involve the effect of one or two independent variables on one or two dependent variables. "Real life" experiences tend to be much more complex than this. In particular, behavior is almost always multiply determined. And the many factors influencing people generally affect a number of different response modalities (e.g., overt behavior, cognitions, emotions, physiological reactions). The experimental method is not suited to studying such complex interactions, at least not simultaneously. Experiments are also limited by the conditions the investigator can set up. Many factors that influence human behavior and personality cannot be dealt with in such artificial situations. This is due to both practical and ethical limitations. Conducting experiments in the artificial confines of the psychological laboratory also restricts the dependent variables that can be studied. Thus, although behavioral psychologists may conduct rigorous, carefully controlled research, the results may have low *external validity*. In other words, the experiments may reveal little about the phenomena as they occur in everyday life.

Experimental Analogs

Studying personality in the psychological laboratory entails another problem. We may be able to set up and measure the variables of interest in the laboratory. But the artificiality of most laboratory experiments limits the confidence we can have in generalizations drawn from our findings. The laboratory situation often restricts the form and content of subjects' responses. This differs from the free responding characteristic of "natural" situations. The motivation of subjects in experiments and of people in actual situations is also different. Often laboratory subjects are asked to perform tasks in which they have no personal interest or investment.

There is ample direct evidence that various personality phenomena, like delay of gratification or aggressive behavior, can be created and modified in the laboratory. But these demonstrations may not tell us much about how these responses are typically acquired and changed in the natural environment. Convincing evidence that any particular set of principles accounts for the acquisition and modification of complex human behavior requires more than *laboratory analogies* to real-life circumstances (Wilson, 1982, 1984).

NARROWNESS OF THE BEHAVIORAL VIEW

By its very nature, each strategy emphasizes some aspects of personality and devotes little or no attention to other aspects. Like each of the other three strategies, the behavioral strategy has "blind spots." Radical behavioral approaches have the most glaring limitation. They focus on "public," overt behavior and ignore "private," covert behavior. Social learning and cognitive perspectives are broader in the phenomena they study. They include covert events, most notably cognitions, to varying degrees. Still, for the most part, the covert behaviors are measured by reference to overt behaviors. Thoughts are often assessed by asking subjects to report what they are saying to themselves (i.e., self-talk). These overt behavioral referents (of the covert behaviors) allow objective verification by more than one observer. Yet the overt behavioral referents are not the same as the covert behaviors. Thus, the behavioral psychologist is not studying the covert events directly; it is likely that at least some information is lost along the way.

All behavioral approaches essentially ignore the effects of biological and hereditary factors on personality. It is not that behavioral psychologists deny these influences; even the most radical behaviorists, like Skinner (1974), acknowledge their role. But behavioral psychologists choose to focus on other factors. In doing so, they can only present a partial conceptualization of personality.

ABSENCE OF A COMPREHENSIVE THEORETICAL BASE

Behavioral approaches range from the essentially nontheoretical stance of Skinner to so-called social learning "theories." Between these extremes are more narrow theoretical *positions* like classical conditioning and Mischel's cognitive-behavioral theorizing. The social learning theories of Rotter and Bandura are broader than most behavioral approaches. But none of these conceptualizations is truly a comprehensive account of personality, such as exists in the psychoanalytic and phenomenological strategies. Contemporary social learning theories allude to general principles. But they actually only deal with a few narrow, selected areas of personality functioning (e.g., locus of control, perceived self-efficacy, and delay of gratification).

In the area of personality change, it has been argued that no specific theory or theories underlie behavioral therapies (Spiegler, 1983). Rather, behavioral therapists may only employ a "nontheoretical amalgamation of pragmatic principles" (Weitzman, 1967, p. 303) from which their procedures derive strength. For example, the effectiveness of systematic desensitization can be explained in terms of a variety of behavioral and nonbehavioral theories, including psychoanalysis.

Critics have pointed out that behavioral theories of personality did not really generate the change techniques with which they are associated. In fact, most behavioral change techniques were in use long before behavioral personality theories were formulated (cf. Wilson, 1986). Consider the comments of two early critics of behavioral therapy (Breger & McGaugh, 1966).

> It is clear that the techniques in question were in existence long [ago]. . . . Pfaundler described an apparatus for treating enuresis in 1904 that greatly resembled Mowrer's conditioning technique, and Nye, a pediatrician, outlined a proposed method for treating enuresis in 1830 that included all of the elements of "conditioning" therapy. . . . Circus animal trainers used "operant" and "shaping" techniques for centuries. (p. 171)

Bandura's theory of perceived self-efficacy does present a theoretical explanation of behavioral personality change procedures. However, Bandura's (1977a) claim that self-efficacy theory is "an integrative theoretical framework to explain and predict psychological changes achieved by different modes of treatment" (p. 191) may be too broad (e.g., Eastman & Marzillier, 1984; cf. Bandura, 1984). Critics argue that application of self-efficacy theory may be limited to a particular class of problems, notably fear and anxiety, and to a particular class of treatment procedures, such as performance-based therapies (e.g., participant modeling).

OVERCONFIDENCE IN SITUATIONAL TESTS

Behavioral psychologists often use situational tests to assess personality. For instance, if we wanted to learn how people respond to failure, we might place subjects in a situation in which they fail at some task. We would then observe and measure their reactions. (This should be contrasted with personality assessment procedures that have subjects respond to written questions about reactions to failure, that measure the need to achieve and avoid failure by having subjects write stories in response to TAT cards, and the like.) Situational tests make sense "intuitively." Measuring what a person does today is an "obvious" way of determining what the person will do tomorrow. Thus, situational tests typically have high **face validity,** they look like they measure what is being tested. This is partially the reason there has been little systematic evaluation of such techniques of personality assessment.

A classic application of situational tests occurred during World War II. American and British armed forces had to rapidly select suitable officer candidates (Morris, 1949) and individuals for military intelligence assignments (OSS Assessment Staff, 1948). Extensive situational tests were developed for this purpose. One test, for example, required subjects to assemble a wooden construction. They were "helped" by two other people who, although the subjects didn't know it, were supposed to impede progress. Observers rated candidates' performance and emotional reactions to the situation. In general, the reliability of these tests was not very high. Predictive validity—the ability to identify candidates who subsequently performed well on assignments—was not nearly as high as had been hoped (Anastasi, 1976). This disappointing performance of situational tests in these examples is, no doubt, partially attributable to factors that were independent of the techniques themselves. It is less than ideal to develop mass assessment procedures very quickly, which was necessitated by war-time conditions. Still, some of the failure appears to be due to the general problems of situational tests.

Two conditions that are part of most situational tests alter assessees' behavior to an unknown degree. One is merely being observed by psychologists, and the other is the stresses of being "on the spot" to perform in a test situation. Some people may "flub" a demonstration of a behavior they know how to do very well, just because they are asked to perform. Others may perform more competently or diligently than they are likely to in the actual situation because they know they are being observed and evaluated. For instance, professors who lecture enthusiastically when their chairperson is sitting in their classroom show that they *can* put forth an impressive effort; whether they *will* be as conscientious when only their students are present cannot be judged on this basis alone.

There is a related problem with situational tests involving role playing. The tests may involve somewhat different abilities than are called for in real life. For example, a soldier may be able to *pretend* to be a strong leader under test conditions but may not be an effective leader in the field when faced with real, rather than hypothetical, enemies.

Finally, situational tests may not be "lifelike" enough for adequate predictive validity. A person who can pick up a harmless snake in the laboratory and reports no longer being afraid of snakes may still show considerable fear when unexpectedly encountering a reptile on a solitary country lane. Indeed, such a possibility could be considered all the more likely given the emphasis on situational specificity in the behavioral strategy.

BEHAVIORAL THERAPY AND THE ERROR OF AFFIRMING THE CONSEQUENT

Behavioral psychologists take great pride in the success of their therapy techniques. They often claim or imply that these successes demonstrate the validity of behavioral personality theory. The logic of this assumption can be questioned. For instance, an unrealistic fear may be eliminated by counterconditioning. This does not prove that it was *acquired* through conditioning.

The logical fallacy at issue here is called *the error of affirming the consequent*. It involves assuming that "because behavior is generated under one set of circumstances, every time this or similar behavior occurs in nature, it had developed because of the same set of controlling conditions" (Davison & Neale, 1974, p. 28). The situation is similar to that of a person who takes aspirin for a headache. Generally, the medicine will relieve the pain and "cure" the ailment. Still, the fact that taking aspirin eliminated the pain hardly means that the pain was caused by a lack of aspirin in the first place. Likewise, the fact that a behavioral treatment eliminates a psychological problem does not logically tell us anything about how the problem originated.

THE BEHAVIORAL STRATEGY IS LOSING ITS IDENTITY

The behavioral strategy has changed significantly in less than two decades (cf. Liebert & Spiegler, 1970). Radical behavioral approaches are still part of the strategy. But their predominance has diminished with the growth of social learning and cognitive-behavioral approaches.

This trend is partially a response to criticism from supporters of other strategies. They point to the narrowness of the radical behavioral perspective. Change in the strategy is also due to growing recognition among behavioral psychologists that cognitive variables cannot be ignored in any comprehensive account of human personality.

This trend is viewed as progress by many. But it can be argued that including various cognitions and person variables in the behavioral strategy has diluted it. The result has been a loss of the behavioral strategy's unique identity. Cognitions like mental images, introjected objects, and dreams are central to the psychoanalytic strategy. Personal constructs and the self-concept are cognitive variables that are at the heart of the phenomenological strategy. And there is a distinct similarity between dispositional types and Rotter's dividing people into internals and externals.

The recent trend within the behavioral strategy to incorporate or integrate fundamental aspects of other strategies is not just restricted to theory. "Behavioral" personality assessment and change have also been looking less uniquely behavioral in recent years. There has been an increased use of self-report inventories, such as those used to measure perceived self-efficacy. Self-report measures are needed to assess cognitions like efficacy expectancies because only the subject has direct access to the cognitions.

Behavioral personality change is also becoming less distinct from the change procedures used by other strategies. This is in part due to the proliferation of cognitive-behavioral therapies (e.g., Haaga & Davison, 1986; Kanfer & Hagerman, 1985). For example, cognitive-behavioral therapies attempt to change cognitions that are maintaining problem behaviors. In a similar way, Kellian therapy tries to alter the constructs that result in abnormal behavior. Some behavioral therapists advocate broadening therapeutic techniques to include traditionally nonbehavioral procedures. Arnold Lazarus (1981) was at one time a strict radical behaviorist. He has since developed *multimodal therapy*, which involves analyzing clients' problems in terms of seven different modalities: behavior, affect, sensation, imagery, cognition, interpersonal relationships, and drugs. (Curiously enough, the therapy is known by the acronym *BASIC ID*.) Moreover, a number of behavioral therapists have abandoned a systematic behavioral approach in favor of one that freely borrows concepts from other strategies, most notably psychoanalysis (e.g., Goldfried & Wachtel, 1985; Messer, 1985).

PROBLEMS CONCERNING ACCEPTANCE OF RADICAL BEHAVIORAL APPROACHES

Radical behavioral approaches to personality have often been attacked as dehumanizing. Sperry (1976) made the following argument.

What remains of the human psyche and the mind of man in the [radical behavioral] scheme of objective science seems to boil down essentially to a complex system of electrophysiochemical interactions, all causally determined and physically controlled. The resultant view of human nature and the kind of values that emerge are hardly uplifting. The color, quality, and higher meaning of life seem to be lost or destroyed; and the long-standing separation between the material world of science on the one hand and the world of the humanities and inner experience on the other becomes increasingly wide and irreconcilable. The scientific renunciation of conscious mind and free will, flying as it does in the face of common experience and common aspiration, does little to counter the recent waning of intellectual confidence in science and opportunely feeds, instead, various sentiments of antiscience. (p. 12)

Sperry himself championed a view of the mind in which the "phenomena of inner experience become active causal determinants in brain activity and are given a functional role and a reason for having been evolved in a physical world."

The radical behavioral view of personality can easily be seen as simplistic. For example, at a basic level, there are only two essential variables: stimulus and response. People are often reluctant to view their own behavior and that of others, or human personality in general, in such simple terms. Each of the other personality strategies has some attractive and/or compelling aspects that make it "seem" more right or palatable than the radical behavioral perspective.

We consider ourselves to be highly complex organisms. Explanations of personality offered by the psychoanalytic strategy present humans as being governed by extremely complex processes. Although it may be difficult for us to accept some psychoanalytic concepts, such as infantile sexuality, other concepts, like the existence of an unconscious part of personality, seem helpful in providing us with reasons for many phenomena that otherwise appear to defy explanation.

The dispositional approach to personality is easy to accept. It presents scientific evidence for the way we typically describe and think of ourselves and others and "explain" behavior—that is, in terms of relatively enduring personality characteristics that influence behavior in diverse settings.

The phenomenological perspective is consistent with our predominantly self-centered view. There are countless everyday examples and demonstrations of the importance of subjective viewpoints. Further, more than any other strategy, the phenomenological strategy emphasizes self-determination, which certainly adds to its appeal.

Social learning and cognitive-behavioral approaches also present a more balanced and appealing view of personality than radical behavioral approaches. For example, Bandura's principle of reciprocal determinism acknowledges the mutual influence and dependence of person, situation, and behavior. Mischel's theorizing and research provide a picture of a decidedly complex organism. Behavior is determined by competencies, encoding strategies, personal constructs, expectancies, values, self-regulatory systems, and plans—in addition to situational variables.

In contrast, radical-behavioral approaches have a more difficult "product" to sell. How can complex human beings be explained by what seem to be comparatively simple principles (e.g., reinforcement and punishment)? Moreover, the proposition that personality is a function of environmental factors strikes deep at the heart of the time-honored and sacred notion of free will and self-determinism. Research on locus of control indicates that internals (who presumably believe they have free will) generally are healthier and more successful than externals (who presumably believe they are the pawns of external circumstance). Humans may, in fact, not have free will. But at least they seem to have a need to think they do.

Acceptability is one criteria by which theories are judged. Thus, to the extent that both psychologists and laypeople have difficulty accepting radical behavioral approaches, these approaches have an added burden to "prove" themselves.

COGNITIVE-BEHAVIORAL APPROACHES MISTAKENLY CAST THOUGHTS AS CAUSES OF BEHAVIOR

Many supporters of cognitive-behavioral approaches, like Mischel and Meichenbaum, are former adherents of strict radical behaviorism. They discovered the need to consider cognitive processes as a result of their research or clinical work. Not surprisingly, radical behaviorists have expressed serious reservations about cognitive-behavioral approaches (e.g., Eysenck, 1982; Rachlin, 1977; Skinner, 1974; Wolpe, 1978a).

Radical behaviorists do not deny that thoughts occur, or that they are "real." But they do not consider thoughts to operate as independent causes of behavior. Rather they hold that thoughts are the *effect* of our reinforcement histories and biological conditions. Thoughts are not a *cause* of behavior. For example, radical behaviorists would reply to Bandura that favorable experiences such as exposure to appropriate models lead us both to perform better and to feel that we have personal efficacy. The feeling of self-efficacy is thus an effect of experience and not a mental way station between experience and performance.

In the practice of behavioral therapy, radical behaviorists argue that very much the same principles of treatment apply regardless of whether or not the therapist has a cognitive orientation.

> [Cognitive-behavioral] therapy does not stop after the irrational idea is uncovered and the rational idea presented. If ideas themselves

could control behavior [as cognitive behaviorists assert] then one would expect the change of ideas to result simply in a change of behavior, as when a general orders his army to advance or retreat. But far from ending after the client's ideas are changed, therapy barely begins at that point. The therapy consists of homework assignments that to all intents and purposes are identical with the sorts of things noncognitive behavior therapists do as a matter of course. [The use of *mastery and pleasure therapy* and *graded task assignments* in Beck's cognitive therapy (Chapter 21) is a good example.] (Rachlin, 1977, pp. 372–73)

SUMMARY

1. The behavioral strategy has been accused of relying too heavily on laboratory research. Research is often carried out in artificial environments in which subjects' responses are constrained by tight situational control. The results of such research may not be generalizable to real-life settings.

2. The behavioral strategy is narrow. Radical behaviorists insist on ignoring private events such as thoughts and feelings, and all behavioral personality psychologists minimize the role that biological and hereditary factors play in shaping and controlling behavior.

3. Though the behavioral strategy encompasses many theoretical ideas, in actuality it lacks a comprehensive theoretical base. Behavioral therapists, for example, rely on a set of pragmatic principles rather than on a systematic theory of behavior change.

4. The behavioral strategy relies heavily on situational tests, which are often contrived. Such assessment procedures, especially when conducted in a laboratory setting, may not predict behavior in the natural environment very well.

5. Behavioral therapy commits the logical error of affirming the consequent. Demonstrations that a behavioral treatment eliminates a psychological problem do not tell us anything about how the problem originated.

6. The behavioral strategy appears to be losing its identity. Behavioral psychologists are increasingly blending their theory, assessment, and change procedures with concepts from other strategies.

7. People have a difficult time accepting the radical behavioral approach because it seems to present an overly simplistic view of personality. We like to think of ourselves as complex organisms, and other personality strategies present more complex (and therefore more attractive) pictures of human personality.

8. Cognitive-behavioral approaches have been criticized for mistakenly considering cognitions to be causes of behavior. These criticisms have come from outside the strategy as well as from radical behaviorists.

GLOSSARY

Note: Italics in the definitions indicate terms that are defined elsewhere in the Glossary.

acceptance In observational learning, the stage at which the model's behavior is accepted as a guide for one's own actions.

acquisition In observational learning, the stage at which the model's behavior is cognitively organized and stored in memory.

anal eroticism (anal compulsive) In the *anal stage*, pleasure from retaining feces; in later life, pleasure from being orderly and stingy.

anal sadism (anal expulsive) In the *anal stage*, pleasure from expelling feces; in later life, pleasure from being messy and disorderly.

anal stage Freud's second *psychosexual stage* of development (ages 2 to 3) when the *libido* is centered in the anal area.

anxiety Generally, the emotional experience of threat or danger; precise definition varies with the personality theory.

anxiety hierarchy List of situations that make a person anxious, ordered in terms of the amount of anxiety engendered; used in *systematic desensitization*.

archetype (Jung) Predisposition to form a common idea that may direct behavior; part of the *collective unconscious*.

aversive counterconditioning In behavioral therapy, the pairing of an aversive stimulus and a gratifying but dangerous or disapproved stimulus; used mainly with addictive or deviant behaviors (such as alcoholism or fetishism).

behavioral medicine The use of *behavioral therapy* techniques to prevent and treat health-related disorders.

behavioral therapy Any psychotherapy technique or combination of techniques derived from the behavioral approach.

behavior modification *Behavioral therapy* using the principles of operant conditioning.

behavior potential (Rotter) The likelihood that a given behavior will occur in a given situation.

cardinal disposition (Allport) A trait which dominates a person's entire existence; very few people have cardinal dispositions.

case study Research method involving detailed qualitative descriptions of the behavior of a single individual.

castration anxiety (Freud) Male's fear of loss of his penis, usually considered the probable retaliation for unacceptable sexual desires (such as incest with mother). It is the impetus for resolving the *Oedipus complex.*

cathexis The investment of *psychic energy* in the mental image of an activity or person. "Cathect" is the verb form.

central disposition (Allport) A trait which manifests itself in many aspects of personality; most individuals have between three and ten central dispositions.

central ego In Fairbairn's object relations theory, the single personality structure which has its own libidinal energy that is directed toward establishing *object relations* (rather than reducing tension).

character type (psychoanalytic) Adult personality characteristics resulting from *fixation* at a childhood *psychosexual stage.*

clarification of feelings (Rogers) *Client-centered therapy* technique in which the therapist reflects the emotions that the client is expressing (cf. *restatement of content*).

classical conditioning Learning process in which a stimulus comes to elicit a response because the stimulus is associated with another stimulus that already elicits the response.

client-centered therapy (Rogers) Therapy in which the client assumes responsibility for working out the solutions to problems, and the therapist primarily restates the content of what the client has said and clarifies the client's feelings.

cognitive behavioral therapy *Behavioral therapy* which focuses on changing a person's thoughts and perceptions in order to change their behavior.

cognitive prototypes (Mischel) The "best examples" of a trait concept, from which people draw inferences about the degree to which a trait is generally present in themselves or another person.

cognitive restructuring In *cognitive behavioral therapy*, teaching clients to think about themselves in positive and adaptive rather than negative and maladaptive ways.

cognitive therapy (Beck) Techniques for helping depressed patients to think about themselves in more positive ways.

collective unconscious (Jung) Level of awareness or division of the mind that is the product of the combined experiences of humans through their evolution.

conditioned response (CR) A response acquired through pairing an initially neutral stimulus with one that already elicits the response in question.

conditioned stimulus (CS)   An initially neutral stimulus which acquires the ability to elicit a response after it has been paired with an unconditioned stimulus.

conditions of worth (Rogers)   Differential values others place on particular behaviors; counterforce to *self-actualization*.

conscious (Freud)   Part of the mind containing all that we are immediately aware of.

consistency paradox (Mischel)   The fact that we tend to see people's behavior as quite consistent across situations when, in fact, there is a good deal of cross-situational inconsistency.

construct (Kelly)   A concept used to interpret events.

constructive alternativism (Kelly)   Philosophical position that any event can be viewed in a variety of ways.

construct system (Kelly)   The hierarchical order of one's *constructs*.

construe (Kelly)   To place an interpretation on an event.

content validity   The adequacy with which a test samples the domain it is intended to measure.

continuous reinforcement schedule   A reinforcement schedule in which the individual is reinforced every time the behavior to be strengthened is emitted.

control group   In an experiment, the group that does not receive the treatment being examined but is like the treated group in every other respect (cf. *experimental group*).

core role (Kelly)   A role a person plays that is central to his or her life.

correlation coefficient   A statistical index of the strength of a relationship, most often expressed as the Pearson product-moment correlation (r).

correlation matrix   The array of correlations between each variable and every other variable in a set of variables of interest.

correlational method   Research method that examines quantitative relationships between two or more variables for a group of people observed under the same conditions.

counterimitation   Behaving in a way opposite to the way a model has behaved.

countertransference   Feelings a psychoanalyst has for a patient that are inappropriate *displacements* from the analyst's past.

covert behavior   Behavior that occurs inside the person and thus is not directly observable by others (cf. *overt behavior*).

cross-situational consistency   The degree to which a person behaves in a consistent fashion from one situation to another.

day residues   Elements of actual external events in waking life that appear in dreams.

debriefing   The systematic explanation of the purpose of research, given to a subject after his or her participation is completed.

defense mechanism *Unconscious* psychological process for reducing *anxiety*; primarily a psychoanalytic term.

defensive identification A defensive process that involves becoming like a threatening person; follows the unconscious "reasoning": "If I cannot beat the person, I'll join the person."

deficit motivation (Maslow) Energizing and directing behavior to satisfy an unmet need (cf. *growth motivation*).

definition (Kelly) Choosing the pole of a *construct* that previously has been more successful at predicting events (cf. *extension*).

delay of gratification The ability to forego a small immediate reward for a large reward that requires waiting.

denial Defensive process in which the person does not acknowledge a threatening experience.

dependent variable In an *experiment*, the subjects' behavior that is measured; it is expected to be influenced by (depend on) the *independent variable*.

direct counterimitation Avoiding the specific behavior which one has seen a model perform.

direct imitation Copying the specific behavior which one has seen a model perform.

discriminative stimulus A stimulus that sets the occasion for a response.

displacement As a *defense mechanism*, shifting an impulse from a threatening or unacceptable event or person to something less threatening or unacceptable. In a dream, shifting the emphasis from an important element to a seemingly trival element.

disposition A tendency to behave in a particular way over time and across situations (e.g., a trait).

dream work (Freud) Process of transforming *latent content* into *manifest content*.

drive (psychoanalysis) An inborn, intrapsychic force that, when operative, produces a state of excitation or tension.

efficacy expectations (Bandura) The belief that one can perform the behaviors necessary to achieve a desired outcome.

ego (Freud) The reality-oriented aspect of personality; also mediates the demands of the other aspects of personality (*id* and *superego*).

ego psychology Post-Freudian psychoanalysis emphasizing ego and conscious aspects of personality.

Electra complex The female *Oedipus complex*.

electroencephalogram Tracings of brain waves made by an electroencephalograph.

emergent pole (Kelly) Pole of a construct used to directly interpret an event by noting its similarity to other events (cf. *implicit pole*).

empathy Experiencing how another person is feeling from the other person's viewpoint.

empirical Relating to or obtained by objective methods so that observations and results can be independently confirmed.

erogenous zone Area of the body especially sensitive to erotic stimulation (e.g., mouth, anus, genitals).

experience (Kelly) Interpreting an event in new ways (not just repeated exposure to the event).

experimental group In an *experiment*, subjects who are exposed to the *independent variable* (cf. *control group*).

experimental method (experiment) Research method that examines the quantitative cause-and-effect relationships between one or more variables that are systematically varied (*independent variables*) on one or more behaviors (*dependent variables*).

explicit pole (Kelly) Pole of a *construct* used to directly interpret an event (cf. *implicit pole*).

extension (Kelly) Choosing the pole of a *construct* that is more likely to expand the construct's ability to view new events (cf. *definition*).

external locus of control (Rotter) The belief that the reinforcements we get in life are due to chance factors or factors that are out of our control.

extinction Cessation of responding when a learned response is no longer reinforced; also, cessation of reinforcement for a previously reinforced response.

factor analysis A family of mathematical procedures for sorting personality measures and other variables into groupings such as factors or clusters.

factor loading In factor analysis, the correlation of a particular measure with a particular factor.

fading In operant *behavioral therapy*, the gradual removal of prompts so that the person finally performs the response without cues.

fixation Leaving a portion of *libido* permanently invested in an early psychosexual stage. The more difficult it is for a person to resolve the conflict, the more libido will remain fixated at the stage.

fixed-interval schedule A *reinforcement schedule* in which the individual is reinforced for the first response made after a predetermined, set period of time has elapsed.

fixed-ratio schedule A *reinforcement schedule* in which the individual is reinforced after a set number of responses has occurred.

fixed-role therapy (Kelly) Therapy in which a client temporarily adopts the behavior of someone whose behavior is consistent with *constructs* that would be helpful for the client to adopt.

focus of convenience (Kelly) The events that a particular *construct* is best able to predict.

free association In psychoanalytic psychotherapy, the patient's saying whatever comes to mind without any censoring.

Freudian Psychoanalyst who closely follows Freud's theory and practices (cf. *post-Freudian*).

Freudian slip Generic, lay term for mistakes that Freud believed had definite *unconscious* causes and meanings.

generalized expectancies (Rotter) Expectations that apply across a range of situations.

genital stage Freud's fourth and final *psychosexual stage* of development (puberty through adulthood) in which *libido* is centered in the genital region.

growth motivation (Maslow) Energizing and directing behavior by following one's *self-actualization tendency*.

guilt (Kelly) Awareness of not adequately playing an important role in one's life.

here-and-now Immediate experience—what is going on for the person at the moment.

heuristic realism (Allport) The belief that people really have traits.

holistic Approach in which all aspects of one's personality are related and must be viewed together as a whole; important position of the phenomenological strategy.

id (Freud) Biological, instinctual, pleasure-oriented aspect of personality (cf. *ego, superego*).

ideal self (Rogers) How we would like to see ourselves.

identity As used by Erikson, the confidence that others see us as we see ourselves.

idiographic Pertaining only to an individual person, as contrasted with *nomothetic*.

I-E Scale (Rotter) A paper-and-pencil measure of the degree to which one has an *internal* or *external locus of control* (as a *generalized expectancy*).

imitation Making one's own behavior similar in some way to that of a model.

implicit pole (Kelly) Pole of a construct used to indirectly interpret an event by acting as a contrast (cf. *explicit pole*).

independent variable In an *experiment*, the variable that is systematically varied by the experimenter and is expected to influence the *dependent variable*.

indirect counterimitation Avoiding the general type or class of behavior which one has seen a model perform.

indirect imitation Performing the general type or class of behavior that one has seen a model perform.

individual traits (Allport) Those important characteristics of the individual that do not lend themselves to comparison across persons.

inferiority complex (Adler)   Exaggerated, neurotic reaction to one's weaknesses.

insight (psychoanalysis)   Emotional experiencing and accepting of parts of one's *unconscious*; necessary for cure in *psychoanalysis* (therapy).

instinctoid needs (Maslow)   Biologically-based human needs.

internal frame of reference   A person's subjective view of the world.

internal locus of control (Rotter)   The belief that the reinforcements we get in life are due to our own effort and ability.

interpretation (psychoanalysis)   Psychoanalyst's pointing out *unconscious* meanings to a patient.

intrapsychic conflict (psychoanalysis)   Discord within the personality occurring when the aims of *id, ego,* and *superego* are at odds.

intrapsychic events   Processes occurring in the mind (usually in the *unconscious*), such as thoughts, images, and wishes.

latency   In Freud's developmental sequence, the period between the *phallic* and *genital stages.*

latent content   Underlying meaning of a dream (cf. *manifest content*).

L-data (Cattell)   Information that can be gathered from the life records of the individual.

libido (Freud)   *Psychic energy* of the sexual drive.

locus of control (Rotter)   The generalized way that the person perceives the source of his or her outcomes (see *external* and *internal locus of control*).

manifest content   What a person remembers and reports of a dream (cf. *latent content*).

methodological behaviorism   The approach to personality which emphasizes objectivity, direct observation of phenomena, precise definitions, and controlled experimentation.

midlife crisis (Jung)   The crisis people in their late 30s through the middle 40s experience when they come to realize that many of their goals have been set by others.

moral anxiety (Freud)   Experience of guilt or shame resulting from an id-superego conflict (cf. *neurotic anxiety, objective anxiety*).

need (Murray)   A tendency to seek or produce particular effects or temporary end states.

negative reinforcement   Removal of an aversive stimulus contingent on the performance of a desired response, which results in an increase in the response (cf. *positive reinforcement*).

neuroses   A generic term for mental disorders that generally affect people in a limited sphere of their lives; symptoms include anxiety, depression, and physical complaints.

neurotic anxiety (Freud)   Unrealistic fear or vague apprehension resulting from an id-ego conflict (cf. *moral anxiety, objective anxiety*).

nomothetic   Pertaining to people in general (cf. *idiographic*).

NREM (nonrapid eye movement) period Period of Stage 1 sleep not associated with dreaming (cf. *REM period*).

objective anxiety (Freud) Fear from a realistic, external threat (cf. *moral anxiety, neurotic anxiety*).

object relations Psychoanalytic term for interpersonal relations.

observational learning The process by which the behavior of one person is changed through observing the behavior of another (rather than through direct experience, as in *classical* and *operant conditioning*).

Oedipus complex (Freud) The conflict in the *phallic stage* involving the child's unconscious wish to have sexual relations with the opposite-sexed parent and at the same time to do away with the same-sexed parent.

operant conditioning Learning process in which a behavior is strengthened or weakened because of its consequences.

oral eroticism Pleasure from sucking and taking things in through the mouth during the early part of the *oral stage*.

oral sadism Pleasure from biting and chewing in the later part of the *oral stage*; begins with the eruption of teeth.

oral stage Freud's first *psychosexual stage* of development (first year of life) in which *libido* is centered in the mouth area.

organismic valuing process (Rogers) Process by which the *self-actualizing tendency* evaluates experiences as maintaining or enhancing the person.

overt behavior Behavior that can be observed directly by others (cf. *covert behavior*).

paradoxical sleep Phase of Stage 1 sleep in which the person is both alert and relaxed; associated with dreaming; same as *REM period*.

participant modeling The combination of a therapist's live modeling and *prompting,* with closely supervised practice by the client.

peak experience (Maslow) Intensely fulfilling and meaningful experience.

penis envy (Freud) Woman's desiring to be like a man; part of the *Electra complex*.

perceptual defense Unconscious mechanism that keeps a person from experiencing threatening ideas.

perceptual distortion (Rogers) Changing how one perceives an experience to make it consistent with one's *self-concept*.

permeability (Kelly) Degree to which a construct is able to interpret new experiences.

personal unconscious (Jung) Part of the mind containing images that we are not immediately aware of, but that we can become aware of easily; parallel concept to Freud's *preconscious*.

personality coefficient (Mischel) Term coined to describe the small correlation (between .20 and .30) which is the most that is usually found when any personality dimension inferred from a questionnaire is related to another type of response.

person-centered approach (Rogers)   Extension of the principles of *client-centered therapy* to other endeavors, such as education and international relations.

person variables (Mischel)   The relatively enduring cognitive and behavioral attributes of an individual.

phallic stage   Freud's third *psychosexual stage* of development (ages 4 to 5) where *libido* is centered in the genital area; *Oedipus complex* occurs in this stage.

phenomenological knowledge (Rogers)   Understanding another person from that person's perspective.

phobia   Strong, irrational fear of a particular situation or object.

pleasure principle (Freud)   Immediate discharge of intrapsychic tension; the principle by which the *id* operates (cf. *reality principle*).

positive regard (Rogers)   Esteem from others in the form of acceptance, respect, sympathy, warmth, or love.

positive reinforcement   Presentation of a stimulus contingent on the performance of a desired response, which results in an increase in the response (cf. *negative reinforcement*).

positive self-regard (Rogers)   *Positive regard* that has been internalized and thus comes directly from the person and not from others.

post-Freudian   Psychoanalytic theories and practices that are somewhat based on Freud's but deviate from them in varying degrees (cf. *Freudian*).

preconscious (Freud)   Part of the mind that contains information we are not immediately aware of but that we can become aware of easily.

predictive efficiency (Kelly)   How well a *construct* anticipates events; the measure of the validity of a *construct*.

press (Murray)   An environmental circumstance that influences behavior.

primary anxiety (Freud)   Intense, negative experience in infants resulting from a need not being immediately satisfied.

primary needs (Murray)   Needs of biological origin, representing the physiological requirements of the organism.

primary process (Freud)   *Id* process that reduces intrapsychic tension by producing a mental image of an object that will satisfy the need (cf. *secondary process*).

projection   *Defense mechanism* in which a person attributes threatening impulses to another person (e.g., "I don't want to kill you; you want to kill me").

projective hypothesis   Assumption that when people are forced to impose meaning on an ambiguous stimulus, the response will reflect significant parts of their personality; basis for *projective techniques*.

projective techniques Indirect personality assessment procedures that present subjects with ambiguous stimuli (e.g., an inkblot) on which they must impose meaning.

prompting Reminding or instructing a person to perform a behavior so that it can be reinforced.

psychic energy (Freud) Unitary energy source for all psychological functions.

psychoanalysis Three common meanings: theory of personality, approach to research, and procedures for changing personality. All three were originally developed by Freud and subsequently extended and modified by other psychoanalysts.

psychosexual stages (Freud) Periods in one's life representing the development of the *libido* (sexual drive); specifically, the *oral, anal, phallic,* and *genital stage.*

psychosocial stages Periods proposed by *post-Freudians* (e.g., Erikson, Sullivan) that represent the development of social behaviors (cf. *psychosexual stages*).

punishment A consequence that reduces the likelihood of future occurrence of the behavior which preceded it; usually an aversive consequence.

Q-data (Cattell) Information about a person gathered from questionnaires and interviews.

radical behaviorism The position that psychology should be concerned only with objective environmental events (stimuli) and overt behavior (responses).

range of convenience (Kelly) Events that a *construct* is able to predict.

rational-emotive therapy (RET) Ellis's version of *cognitive restructuring* therapy.

rationalization *Defense mechanism* in which a person finds a sensible reason or "excuse" for performing or thinking about an unacceptable behavior.

reaction formation *Defense mechanism* involving overemphasis on acting or thinking in ways opposite to a threatening impulse.

reality principle (Freud) Process of postponing tension reduction until an appropriate situation or object in the external world is found; the principle by which *ego* operates (cf. *pleasure principle*).

reciprocal determinism (Bandura) The theoretical assumption that personality develops through a continuing interaction among personal, behavioral, and environmental factors.

regression *Defense mechanism* in which the person repeats a behavior that led to satisfaction in an early stage of development.

reinforcement value (Rotter) A person's subjective preference for a given reinforcer relative to other possible reinforcers in a given situation.

reliability Measure of the "repeatability" or stability of a test or measure; prerequisite for *validity*.

REM (rapid eye movement) period Phase of Stage 1 sleep associated with dreaming. Also called *paradoxical sleep*.

repression The most basic *defense mechanism* which involves completely putting out of consciousness a threatening experience.

resistance Any behavior that interferes with the progress of psychotherapy.

response acquiescence The tendency to agree with personality test items, regardless of their content.

response cost Removal of a valued item or privilege, contingent on the performance of an unwanted behavior.

response deviation The tendency to answer personality test items in an uncommon direction.

response sets Characteristic and consistent ways of responding to personality test items, regardless of what the items say.

restatement of content (Rogers) *Client-centered therapy* technique in which the therapist rephrases what the client says (cf. *clarification of feelings*).

retest reliability Degree to which the same (or equivalent forms of) test administered more than once yields the same basic results.

Role Construct Repertory Test (Rep Test) Assessment device developed by Kelly for finding the constructs a person uses to construe other people.

Rorschach inkblots The most popular *projective technique*; subjects describe what they see in ambiguous, nearly symmetrical figures.

scatter diagram A graphic representation of the correlation between two variables; the stronger the relationship, the more the points look like a straight line.

schedule of reinforcement The rate or time interval at which desired responses are reinforced.

secondary disposition (Allport) A trait that manifests itself in only a few areas of personality.

secondary process (Freud) *Ego* process that reduces intrapsychic tension by problem solving and dealing directly with external reality (cf. *primary process*).

self-actualization tendency (Maslow, Rogers) Unique, inborn inclination to behave in ways that result in maintaining and enhancing the person; leads people to become all that they can be.

self-concept (Rogers) How we view ourselves, including how we actually view ourselves (real self) and our *ideal self;* also called "self."

self-efficacy (Bandura) People's convictions that they can successfully execute the behavior required to produce a desired outcome in a particular situation.

self-instructional training (Meichenbaum)   A cognitive-behavioral therapy procedure that teaches clients *cognitive restructuring* through modeling and cognitive behavior rehearsal.

shaping   Reinforcing progressively closer approximations to the desired behavior.

signal anxiety (Freud)   Discomfort that warns the *ego* to institute *defense mechanisms* to prevent the intense experience of *primary anxiety.*

social desirability   The tendency to answer personality test items in the most socially accepted direction, irrespective of whether such answers are correct for the respondent.

source trait (Cattell)   The underlying *dispositions* that determine behavior. They are often identified by *factor analysis.*

statistical significance   An estimate of the likelihood that a particular research finding (e.g., a difference between two groups or a correlation between two variables) occurred by chance; by convention, a result must have a chance likelihood of less than 5 in 100 to be called statistically significant.

statistical test   Mathematical test used to determine *statistical significance.*

stimulus control   Behavior that occurs only when certain environmental circumstances (*discriminative stimuli*) are present.

stress inoculation training (Meichenbaum)   A cognitive-behavioral therapy which prepares clients to deal with stress-inducing events by teaching them self-control coping skills and then having them rehearse these skills while gradually being exposed to stressors.

sublimination   *Defense mechanism* in which unacceptable desires are channeled into socially acceptable outlets.

superego (Freud)   Aspect of the personality incorporating ideals and the moral standards of one's parents and culture (cf. *ego, id*).

suppression   Conscious forgetting of threatening thoughts; not a Freudian *defense mechanism* because it operates consciously.

surface traits (Cattell)   Clusters of overt behavior that seem to go together, but do not necessarily have a common cause (cf. *source traits*).

symptom substitution   Concept that treating only the symptom and not the underlying cause of an abnormal behavior will lead to the development of another (substitute) symptom; psychoanalytic argument against *behavioral therapies.*

systematic desensitization (Wolpe)   A *behavioral therapy* technique based on counterconditioning; the client is gradually exposed to increasingly more anxiety-evoking stimuli while making a response that is essentially incompatible with anxiety (e.g., relaxation).

target behaviors   In *behavioral therapy,* the specific behaviors which the client and therapist are trying to encourage, eliminate, or modify.

T-data (Cattell) Information gained from putting subjects in objective test situations without telling them which aspects of their behavior are being observed or evaluated.

temporal consistency Behavior that remains consistent and stable over time in the same or similar situations.

Thematic Apperception Test (TAT) A projective test consisting of pictures about which the respondent must make up a story.

theoretical constructs The basic terms and building blocks of a theory; they do not actually exist but are invented to describe or explain phenomena.

therapeutic alliance In *post-Freudian psychoanalysis,* a cooperative relationship between patient and analyst.

time out (from positive reinforcement) Withdrawing a client's access to positive reinforcers for a brief, preset time period immediately after an unwanted behavior occurs.

token economy A systematically controlled environment in which clients earn tokens for performing various behaviors; the tokens can later be exchanged for tangible reinforcers and privileges.

transference Feelings a patient has for a psychoanalyst that are inappropriate *displacements* from the patient's past. Working through transference is critical in *Freudian* psychoanalytic psychotherapy.

Type A behavior A pattern of responding characterized by a high competitive drive coupled with a continuous rush to meet deadlines ("hurry sickness"); it is predictive of later heart attacks.

unconditional positive regard (Rogers) Esteem (*positive regard*) from others that does not depend on the person's behaviors and is thus nonevaluative.

unconditional positive self-regard (Rogers) *Unconditional positive regard* that has been internalized and thus comes directly from the person and not from others.

unconditioned response (UCR) In *classical conditioning,* the response elicited by an *unconditioned stimulus* (cf. *conditioned response*).

unconditioned stimulus (UCS) In *classical conditioning,* a stimulus that naturally or automatically elicits a particular response.

unconscious Part of the mind containing information of which we have no knowledge. For Freud, most personality is unconscious.

undoing *Defense mechanism* involving restitution for an unacceptable act.

validity The extent to which a test or measure indicates what it is intended to measure.

variable-interval schedule A *reinforcement schedule* in which the individual is reinforced for the first response made after a period of time that varies randomly around a specified time value.

variable-ratio schedule A *reinforcement schedule* in which the number of responses required for reinforcement varies randomly around a particular number.

vicarious consequences Rewards and punishments administered to a model which influence the observer's subsequent likelihood of performing the modeled behavior.

wish fulfillment (Freud) Satisfying a desire through a mental image rather than in reality; part of *primary process*.

REFERENCES

Abraham, K. (1927). The influence of oral eroticism on character formation. In K. Abraham (Ed.), *Selected papers on psychoanalysis*. London: Hogarth.

Adams-Webber, J. R. (1979). *Personal construct theory: Concepts and applications*. Chichester, England: Wiley.

Adler, A. (1964). *Social interest: A challenge to mankind*. New York: Putnam (Capricorn Books).

Adler, A. (1973). *Superiority and social interest: A collection of later writings*. (H. L. Ansbacher & R. R. Ansbacher, Eds.). New York: Viking Press.

Ainsworth, M. D. (1974). Infant-mother attachment and social development: Socialization as a product of reciprocal responsiveness to signals. In M. P. Richards (Ed.), *The integration of the child into a social world*. Cambridge: Cambridge University Press.

Ainsworth, M. D. (1984). Attachment. In N. S. Endler & J. McV. Hunt (Eds.), *Personality and the behavior disorders* (rev. ed.). New York: Wiley.

Ainsworth, M. D., Bell, S. M., & Stayton, D. C. (1971). Individual differences in a strange-situation behavior in one-year-olds. In H. R. Schaffer (Ed.), *The origins of human social relations*. New York: Academic Press.

Allport, G. W. (1960). *Personality and social encounter: Selected essays*. Boston: Beacon Press.

Allport, G. W. (1961). *Pattern and growth in personality*. New York: Holt, Rinehart & Winston.

Allport, G. W. (1966). Traits revisited. *American Psychologist, 21*, 1–10.

Allport, G. W., & Allport, F. H. (1928). *The A-S reaction study*. Boston: Houghton Mifflin.

Anastasi, A. (1968). *Psychological testing* (3rd ed.). New York: Macmillan.

Anastasi, A. (1976). *Psychological testing* (4th ed.). New York: Macmillan.

Ansbacher, H. L., & Ansbacher, R. R. (1956). *The individual psychology of Alfred Adler: A systematic presentation in selections from his writings*. New York: Harper & Row.

Aronson, E. (1972). *The social animal*. San Francisco: Freeman.

Aserinsky, E., & Kleitman, N. (1953). Regularly occurring periods of eye motility, and concomitant phenomena, during sleep. *Science, 118*, 273–274.

Aspy, D. (1972). *Toward a technology for humanizing education*. Champaign, IL: Research Press.

Aspy, D., & Roebuck, F. (1974). From humane ideas to humane technology and back again, many times. *Education, 95*, 163–171.

Atkinson, J. W. (Ed.). (1958). *Motives in fantasy, action, and society*. Princeton, NJ: Van Nostrand.

Atkinson, J. W., & Litwin, G. H. (1960). Achievement motive and test anxiety

REFERENCES

conceived as motive to approach success and motive to avoid failure. *Journal of Abnormal and Social Psychology, 60,* 52–63.

Atkinson, J. W., & McClelland, D. C. (1948). The projective expression of needs, II. The effect of different intensities of the hunger drive on thematic apperception. *Journal of Experimental Psychology, 38,* 643–658.

Azrin, N. H., & Thienes, R. M. (1978). Rapid elimination of enuresis by intensive learning without a conditioning apparatus. *Behavior Therapy, 9,* 342–354.

Bandura, A. (1965). Influence of models' reinforcement contingencies on the acquisition of imitative responses. *Journal of Personality and Social Psychology, 1,* 589–595.

Bandura, A. (1969). Social learning theory of identificatory processes. In D. A. Goslin (Ed.), *Handbook of socialization theory and research.* Chicago: Rand McNally.

Bandura, A. (1977a). Self-efficacy: Toward a unifying theory of behavioral change. *Psychological Review, 84,* 191–215.

Bandura, A. (1977b). *Social learning theory.* Englewood Cliffs, NJ: Prentice-Hall.

Bandura, A. (1978). Reflections on self-efficacy. In S. Rachman (Ed.), *Advances in behaviour research and therapy* (Vol. 1). Oxford: Pergamon Press.

Bandura, A. (1982). Self-efficacy mechanism in human agency. *American Psychologist, 37,* 122–147.

Bandura, A. (1983a). Self-efficacy determinants of anticipated fears and calamities. *Journal of Personality and Social Psychology, 45,* 464–469.

Bandura, A. (1983b). Temporary dynamics and decomposition of reciprocal determinism: A reply to Phillips and Orton. *Psychological Review, 90,* 166–170.

Bandura, A. (1984). Recycling misconceptions of perceived self-efficacy. *Cognitive Therapy and Research, 8,* 231–255.

Bandura, A. (1986a, in press). From thought to action: Mechanisms of personal agency. *New Zealand Journal of Psychology.*

Bandura, A. (1986b). *Social foundations of thought and action: A social cognitive theory.* Englewood Cliffs, NJ: Prentice-Hall.

Bandura, A., & Adams, N. E. (1977). Analysis of self-efficacy theory of behavioral change. *Cognitive Therapy and Research, 1,* 287–308.

Bandura, A., Adams, N. E., & Beyer, J. (1977). Cognitive processes mediating behavioral change. *Journal of Personality and Social Psychology, 35,* 125–139.

Bandura, A., Adams, N. E., Hardy, A. B., & Howells, G. N. (1980). Tests of the generality of self-efficacy theory. *Cognitive Therapy and Research, 4,* 39–66.

Bandura, A., & Cervone, D. (1983). Self-evaluative and self-efficacy mechanisms governing the motivational effects of goal systems. *Journal of Personality and Social Psychology, 45,* 1017–1028.

Bandura, A., & Mischel, W. (1965). Modification of self-imposed delay of reward through exposure to live and symbolic models. *Journal of Personality and Social Psychology, 2,* 698–705.

Bandura, A., Reese, L., & Adams, N. E. (1982). Microanalysis of action and fear arousal as a function of differential levels of perceived self-efficacy. *Journal of Personality and Social Psychology, 43,* 5–21.

Bandura, A., & Schunk, D. H. (1981). Cultivating competence, self-efficacy, and intrinsic interest through proximal self-motivation. *Journal of Personality and Social Psychology, 41*, 586–598.

Bandura, A., & Walters, R. H. (1963). *Social learning and personality development.* New York: Holt, Rinehart & Winston.

Bannister, D. (Ed.). (1985). *Issues and approaches in personal construct theory.* Orlando, FL: Academic Press.

Barnard, D. (1984). The personal meaning of illness: Client-centered dimensions of medicine and health care. In R. F. Levant & J. M. Shlien (Eds.), *Client-centered therapy and the person-centered approach: New directions in theory, research, and practice.* New York: Praeger.

Barrett-Lennard, G. T. (1962). Dimensions of therapist response as causal factors in therapeutic change. *Psychological Monographs, 76* (43, Whole No. 562).

Barrios, F. X. (1985). A comparison of global and specific estimates of self-control. *Cognitive Therapy and Research, 9*, 455–469.

Beck, A. T. (1976). *Cognitive therapy and the emotional disorders.* New York: International Universities Press.

Beck, A. T. (1984). Cognitive approaches to stress. In R. Woolfold & P. Lehrer (Eds.), *Principles and practice of stress management.* New York: Guilford Press.

Beck, J. G. (1985). Sexual dysfunction. In M. Hersen & C. G. Last (Eds.), *Behavior therapy casebook.* New York: Springer.

Berger, R. J., & Oswald, I. (1962). Eye movements during active and passive dreams. *Science, 137*, 601.

Bergin, A. E., & Jasper, L. G. (1969). Correlates of empathy in psychotherapy: A replication. *Journal of Abnormal Psychology, 74*, 477–481.

Bergin, A. E., & Solomon, S. (1970). Personality and performance correlates of empathic understanding in psychotherapy. In J. T. Hart & T. M. Tomlinson (Eds.), *New directions in client-centered therapy.* Boston: Houghton Mifflin.

Bergin, A. E., & Strupp, H. H. (1972). *Changing frontiers in the science of psychotherapy.* Chicago: Aldine-Atherton.

Bergman, A., & Ellman, S. (1985). Margaret S. Mahler: Symbiosis and separation-individuation. In J. Reppen (Ed.), *Beyond Freud: A study of modern psychoanalytic theorists.* Hillsdale, NJ: Analytic Press.

Bertrand, S., & Masling, J. M. (1969). Oral imagery and alcoholism. *Journal of Abnormal Psychology, 74*, 50–53.

Bettelheim, B. (1976). *The uses of enchantment.* New York: Knopf.

Birney, R. C. (1968). Research on the achievement motive. In E. F. Borgatta & W. W. Lambert (Eds.), *Handbook of personality theory and research.* Chicago: Rand McNally.

Birns, B. (1965). Individual differences in human neonates' responses to stimulation. *Child Development, 36*, 249–256.

Blanck, G., & Blanck, R. (1974). *Ego psychology: Theory and practice.* New York: Columbia University Press.

Block, J. (1965). *The challenge of response sets.* New York: Appleton-Century-Crofts.

REFERENCES

Block, J. (1977). Advancing the psychology of personality: Paradigmatic shift or improving the quality of research? In D. Magnusson & N. S. Endler (Eds.), *Personality at the crossroads*. Hillsdale, NJ: Erlbaum.

Boffey, P. M. (1986, May 14). Psychotherapy is as good as drug in curing depression, study finds. *The New York Times*, pp. A1, B11.

Bonarius, H., Holland, R., & Rosenberg, S. (Eds.). (1981). *Personal construct psychology: Recent advances in theory and practice*. New York: St. Martin's Press.

Bootzin, R. R. (1985). Insomnia. In M. Hersen & C. G. Last (Eds.), *Behavior therapy casebook*. New York: Springer.

Bootzin, R. R., & Nicassio, P. M. (1978). Behavioral treatments for insomnia. In M. Hersen, R. M. Eisler, & P. M. Miller (Eds.), *Progress in behavior modification* (Vol. 6). New York: Academic Press.

Bornstein, R. F., & Masling, J. (1985). Orality and latency of volunteering to serve as experimental subjects: A replication. *Journal of Personality Assessment, 49,* 306–310.

Bottome, P. (1957). *Alfred Adler: A portrait from life*. New York: Vanguard.

Boudin, H. M. (1972). Contingency contracting as a therapeutic tool in decelerating amphetamine use. *Behavior Therapy, 3,* 602–608.

Bozarth, J. D. (1984). Beyond reflection: Emergent modes of empathy. In R. F. Levant & J. M. Shlien (Eds.), *Client-centered therapy and the person-centered approach: New directions in theory, research, and practice*. New York: Praeger.

Breger, L., & McGaugh, J. L. (1966). Learning theory and behavior therapy: A reply to Rachman and Eysenck. *Psychological Bulletin, 65,* 170–173.

Breuer, J., & Freud, S. (1955). Studies in hysteria. In J. Strachey (Ed.), *The standard edition of the complete psychological works of Sigmund Freud* (Vol. 2). London: Hogarth. (Originally published, 1893–1895.)

Brown, N. O. (1959). *Life against death*. New York: Random House.

Brown, R. (1965). *Social psychology*. New York: Free Press.

Bruch, H. (1973). *Eating disorders: Obesity, anorexia nervosa and the person within*. New York: Basic Books.

Bruch, H. (1978). *The golden cage: The enigma of anorexia nervosa*. Cambridge, MA: Harvard University Press.

Bruner, J. S. (1956). A cognitive theory of personality. *Contemporary Psychology, 1,* 355–356.

Brunson, B. I., & Matthews, K. A. (1981). The Type A coronary-prone behavior pattern and reactions to uncontrollable stress: An analysis of performance strategies, affect, and attributions during failure. *Journal of Personality and Social Psychology, 40,* 906–918.

Burnham, J. C. (1968). Historical background for the study of personality. In E. F. Borgatta & W. W. Lambert (Eds.), *Handbook of personality theory and research*. Chicago: Rand McNally.

Buros, O. K. (Ed.). (1965). *The sixth mental measurements yearbook*. Highland Park, NJ: Gryphon Press.

Buros, O. K. (Ed.). (1972). *The seventh mental measurements yearbook*. Highland Park, NJ: Gryphon Press.

Buss, A. H., & Plomin, R. (1984). *Temperament: Early developing personality traits.* Hillsdale, NJ: Erlbaum.

Buss, A. H., Plomin, R., & Willerman, L. (1973). The inheritance of temperaments. *Journal of Personality, 41,* 513–524.

Buss, D. M., & Craik, K. H. (1985). Why *not* measure that trait? Alternative criteria for identifying important dispositions. *Journal of Personality and Social Psychology, 48,* 934–946.

Butcher, J. N. (1979). Use of the MMPI in personnel selection. In J. N. Butcher (Ed.), *New developments in the use of the MMPI.* Minneapolis: University of Minnesota Press.

Camp, B. W., & Bash, M. A. S. (1981). *Think aloud: Increasing social and cognitive skills—A problem-solving program for children (primary level).* Champaign, IL: Research Press.

Campbell, D. T. (1960). Recommendations for APA test standards regarding construct, trait, or discriminant validity. *American Psychologist, 15,* 546–553.

Campbell, D. T., & Fiske, D. W. (1959). Convergent and discriminant validation by the multitrait-multimethod matrix. *Psychological Bulletin, 56,* 81–105.

Cantwell, D. P. (1972). Psychiatric illness in the families of hyperactive children. *Archives of General Psychiatry, 27,* 414–417.

Cartwright, R. D., & Ratzel, R. (1972). Effects of dream loss on waking behaviors. *Archives of General Psychiatry, 27,* 277–280.

Carver, C. S., & Glass, D. C. (1978). Coronary-prone behavior pattern and interpersonal aggression. *Journal of Personality and Social Psychology, 36,* 361–366.

Cattell, R. B. (1957). *Personality and motivation structure and measurement.* Yonkers, NY: New World Book.

Cattell, R. B. (1965). *The scientific analysis of personality.* Baltimore: Penguin.

Cattell, R. B. (1979). *Personality and learning theory* (Vol. 1). New York: Springer.

Cattell, R. B., & Kline, P. (1977). *The scientific analysis of personality and motivation.* New York: Academic Press.

Cattell, R. B., & Warburton, F. W. (1967). *Objective personality and motivation tests: A theoretical introduction and practical compendium.* Urbana: University of Illinois Press.

Cavell, T. A., Frentz, C. E., & Kelley, M. L. (1986). Consumer acceptability of the single case withdrawal design: Penalty for early withdrawal? *Behavior Therapy, 17,* 82–87.

Cervone, D., & Peake, P. K. (1986). Anchoring, efficacy, and action: The influence of judgmental heuristics on self-efficacy judgments and behavior. *Journal of Personality and Social Psychology, 50,* 492–501.

Chambliss, C. A., & Murray, E. J. (1979a). Cognitive procedures for smoking reduction: Symptom attribution versus efficacy attribution. *Cognitive Therapy and Research, 3,* 91–96.

Chambliss, C. A., & Murray, E. J. (1979b). Efficacy attribution, locus of control, and weight loss. *Cognitive Therapy and Research, 3,* 349–354.

Cheyne, J. A. (1971). Effects of imitation of different reinforcement combinations to a model. *Journal of Experimental Child Psychology, 12,* 258–269.

REFERENCES

Chiang, H., & Maslow, A. H. (Eds.). (1977). *The healthy personality: Readings* (2nd ed.). New York: Van Nostrand.

Chodorkoff, B. (1954). Self-perception, perceptual defense, and adjustment. *Journal of Abnormal and Social Psychology, 49,* 508–512.

Colarusso, C. A., & Nemiroff, R. A. (1979). Some observations and hypotheses about the psychoanalytic theory of adult development. *International Journal of Psycho-Analysis, 60,* 59–71.

Colletti, G., Supnick, J. A., & Payne, A. A. (1985). The smoking self-efficacy questionnaire (SSEQ): Preliminary scale development and validation. *Behavioral Assessment, 7,* 249–260.

Comrey, A. L. (1973). *A first course in factor analysis.* New York: Academic Press.

Conley, J. J. (1984). Longitudinal consistency of adult personality: Self-reported psychological characteristics across 45 years. *Journal of Personality and Social Psychology, 47,* 1325–1333.

Cooperman, M., & Child, I. L. (1971). Differential effects of positive and negative reinforcement on two psychoanalytic character types. *Journal of Consulting and Clinical Psychology, 37,* 57–59.

Crabtree, A. (1985). *Multiple man: Explorations in possession and multiple personality.* New York: Praeger.

Crain, W. C. (1980). *Theories of development.* Englewood Cliffs, NJ: Prentice-Hall.

Crandall, V. J. (1967). Achievement behavior in young children. In *The young child: Reviews of research.* Washington, DC: National Association for the Education of Young Children.

Crandall, V. J., Dewey, R., Katkovsky, W., & Preston, A. (1964). Parents' attitudes and behaviors and grade-school children's academic achievement. *Journal of Genetic Psychology, 104,* 53–66.

Crandall, V. J., Katkovsky, W., & Preston, A. (1962). Motivational and ability determinants of young children's intellectual achievement behaviors. *Child Development, 33,* 643–661.

Crockett, W. H. (1982). The organization of construct systems: The organization corollary. In J. C. Mancuso & J. R. Adams-Webber (Eds.), *The construing person.* New York: Praeger.

Cronbach, L. J. (1949). Statistical methods applied to Rorschach scores: A review. *Psychological Bulletin, 46,* 393–429.

Cronbach, L. J. (1959). Review of the California Psychological Inventory. In O. K. Buros (Ed.), *Fifth mental measurements yearbook.* Highland Park, NJ: Gryphon Press.

Cutter, H. S. G., Boyatzis, R. E., & Clancy, D. D. (1977). The effectiveness of power motivation training in rehabilitating alcoholics. *Journal of Studies on Alcohol, 38,* 131–141.

Dahlstrom, W. G. (1980). Screening for emotional fitness: The Jersey City case. In W. G. Dahlstrom & L. Dahlstrom (Eds.), *Basic readings on the MMPI: A new selection on personality measurement.* Minneapolis: University of Minnesota Press.

Damon, A. (1955). Physique and success in military flying. *American Journal of Physical Anthropology, 13,* 217–252.

Daniels, D., & Plomin, R. (1984). Origins of individual differences in infant shyness. *Developmental Psychology, 21,* 118–121.

Davis, R. W., & Hajicek, J. O. (1985). Effects of self-instructional training on a mathematics task with severely behaviorally disordered students. *Behavioral Disorders, 10,* 211–218.

Davison, G. C., & Neale, J. M. (1974). *Abnormal psychology: An experimental-clinical approach.* New York: Wiley.

DeCharms, R. (1976). *Enhancing motivation in the classroom.* New York: Irvington, Halsted-Wiley.

Decker, P. J., & Nathan, B. R. (1985). *Behavior modeling training: Principles and applications.* New York: Praeger.

Dement, W. C. (1964). Experimental dream studies. In J. H. Masserman (Ed.), *Science and psychoanalysis. Scientific proceedings of the academy of psychoanalysis* New York: Grune and Stratton.

Dement, W. C. (1965). An essay on dreams: The role of physiology in understanding their nature. In *New directions in psychology* (Vol. 2). New York: Holt, Rinehart & Winston.

Dement, W. C., & Kleitman, N. (1957). The relation of the eye movements during sleep to dream activity: An objective method for the study of dreaming. *Journal of Experimental Psychology, 53,* 339–346.

Dement, W. C., & Wolpert, E. (1958). The relation of eye movements, body motility, and external stimuli to dream content. *Journal of Experimental Psychology, 55,* 543–553.

Diamond, C. T. P. (1985). Becoming a teacher: An altering eye. In D. Bannister (Ed.), *Issues and approaches in personal construct theory.* Orlando, FL: Academic Press.

DiClemente, C. C. (1981). Self-efficacy and smoking cessation maintenance. *Cognitive Therapy and Research, 5,* 175–187.

DiClemente, C. C., Prochaska, J. O., & Gilbertini, M. (1985). Self-efficacy and the stages of self-change of smoking. *Cognitive Therapy and Research, 9,* 181–200.

Diener, E., & Larsen, R. J. (1984). Temporal stability and cross-situational consistency of affective, behavioral, and cognitive responses. *Journal of Personality and Social Psychology, 47,* 871–883.

Doherty, W. (1983). Impact of divorce on locus of control orientation in adult women: A longitudinal study. *Journal of Personality and Social Psychology, 44,* 834–840.

Dollard, J., & Miller, N. E. (1950). *Personality and psychotherapy.* New York: McGraw-Hill.

DuPreez, P. D. (1977). *Kelly's "matrix of decision" and the politics of identity.* Paper presented at the Second International Conference on Personal Construct Psychology, Oxford University. Cited in Adams-Webber, J. R. (1979). *Personal construct theory: Concepts and applications.* Chichester, England: Wiley.

D'Zurilla, T. (1965). Recall efficiency and mediating cognitive events in "experimental repression." *Journal of Personality and Social Psychology, 37,* 253–256.

REFERENCES

D'Zurilla, T., & Goldfried, M. (1971). Problem solving and behavior modification. *Journal of Abnormal Psychology, 78*, 107–126.

D'Zurilla, T., & Nezu, A. (1982). Social problem-solving in adults. In D. Kendall (Ed.), *Advances in cognitive-behavioral research and therapy* (Vol. 1). New York: Academic Press.

Eagle, M. N. (1984). *Recent developments in psychoanalysis: A critical evaluation.* New York: McGraw-Hill.

Eastman, C., & Marzillier, J. S. (1984). Theoretical and methodological difficulties in Bandura's self-efficacy theory. *Cognitive Therapy and Research, 8*, 213–229.

Edwards, A. L. (1953). *Manual for Edwards Personal Preference Schedule.* New York: Psychological Corporation.

Edwards, A. L. (1957). *The social desirability variable in personality research.* New York: Dryden.

Edwards, A. L. (1970). *The measurement of personality traits by scales and inventories.* New York: Holt, Rinehart & Winston.

Edwards, A. L., & Abbott, R. D. (1973). Measurement of personality traits: Theory and technique. In P. Mussen & M. Rosenzweig (Eds.), *Annual Review of Psychology,* (Vol. 24). Palo Alto, CA: Annual Reviews.

Ellenberger, H. F. (1970). *The discovery of the unconscious: The history and evolution of dynamic psychiatry.* New York: Basic Books.

Ellis, A. (1962). *Reason and emotion in psychotherapy.* New York: Lyle Stuart.

Ellis, A. (1970). *The essence of rational psychotherapy: A comprehensive approach in treatment.* New York: Institute for Rational Living.

Epstein, S. (1966). Some theoretical considerations on the nature of ambiguity and the use of stimulus dimensions in projective techniques. *Journal of Consulting Psychology, 30*, 183–192.

Erdelyi, M. H. (1974). A new look at the new look: Perceptual defense and vigilance. *Psychological Review, 81*, 1–25.

Erdelyi, M. H. (1985). *Psychoanalysis: Freud's cognitive psychology.* New York: Freeman.

Erikson, E. H. (1954). The dream specimen of psychoanalysis. *Journal of the American Psychoanalytic Association, 2*, 5–56.

Erikson, E. H. (1963). *Childhood and society.* New York: Norton.

Erikson, E. H. (1968). *Identity, youth, and crisis.* New York: Norton.

Eysenck, H. J. (1952). *The scientific study of personality.* London: Routledge & Kegan Paul.

Eysenck, H. J. (1961). The effects of psychotherapy. In H. J. Eysenck (Ed.), *Handbook of abnormal psychology.* New York: Basic Books.

Eysenck, H. J. (1964). *Crime and personality.* Boston: Houghton Mifflin.

Eysenck, H. J. (1975). *The inequality of man.* San Diego: Edits Publishers.

Eysenck, H. J. (1977). *Crime and personality.* London: Routledge & Kegan Paul.

Eysenck, H. J. (1982). *Personality genetics and behavior.* New York: Praeger.

Eysenck, H. J. (1985). Incubation theory of fear/anxiety. In S. Reiss & R. R. Bootzin (Eds.), *Theoretical issues in behavior therapy.* Orlando, FL: Academic Press.

Fairbairn, W. R. D. (1952). *Psychoanalytic studies of the personality*. London: Tavistock Publications and Routledge & Kegan Paul.

Felton, B., & Kahana, E. (1974). Adjustment and situationally bound locus of control among institutionalized aged. *Journal of Gerontology, 29*, 295–301.

Fenichel, O. (1945). *The psychoanalytic theory of neurosis*. New York: Norton.

Fernandez, J. (1983). The token economy and beyond. *Irish Journal of Psychotherapy, 2*, 21–41.

Fiedler, F. E. (1950). A comparison of therapeutic relationships in psychoanalytic, non-directive, and Adlerian therapy. *Journal of Consulting Psychology, 14*, 436–445.

Findley, M. J., & Cooper, H. M. (1983). Locus of control and academic achievement: A literature review. *Journal of Personality and Social Psychology, 44*, 419–427.

Fischer, M. (1973). Genetic and environmental factors in schizophrenia. *Acta Psychiatrica Scandinavica.* (Suppl. 238).

Fisher, S. (1973). *The female orgasm*. New York: Basic Books.

Fisher, S., & Greenberg, R. P. (1977). *The scientific credibility of Freud's theories and therapy*. New York: Basic Books.

Fiske, D. W. (1971). *Measuring the concepts of personality*. Chicago: Aldine.

Fiske, D. W., & Pearson, P. H. (1970). Theory and techniques of personality measurement. In *Annual Review of Psychology* (Vol. 21). Palo Alto, CA: Annual Reviews.

Floderus-Myrhed, B., Pedersen, N., & Rasmuson, S. (1980). Assessment of heritability for personality based on a short form of the Eysenck Personality Inventory. *Behavior Genetics, 10*, 153–162.

Fodor, E. M. (1984). The power motive and reactivity to power stresses. *Journal of Personality and Social Psychology, 47*, 853–859.

Fordyce, W. E. (1976). *Behavioral methods for chronic pain and illness*. St. Louis: Mosby.

Franks, C. M. (1984). Behavior therapy: An overview. In C. M. Franks, G. T. Wilson, P. C. Kendall, & K. D. Brownell (Eds.), *Annual review of behavior therapy: Theory and practice* (Vol. 10). New York: Guilford.

Fransella, F., & Bannister, D. (1977). *A manual for repertory grid technique*. London: Academic Press.

French, E. G., & Lesser, G. S. (1964). Some characteristics of the achievement motive in women. *Journal of Abnormal and Social Psychology, 68*, 119–128.

French, T., & Fromm, E. (1964). *Dream interpretation*. New York: Basic Books.

Freud, A. (1958). Adolescence. *Psychoanalytic Study of the Child, 13*, 255–278.

Freud, A. (1966). *The ego and the mechanisms of defense* (rev. ed). New York: International Universities Press.

Freud, S. (1953). The interpretation of dreams. In J. Strachey (Ed. and Trans.), *The standard edition of the complete psychological works of Sigmund Freud* (Vols. 4 and 5). London: Hogarth. (Originally published, 1900.)

Freud, S. (1957). On the history of the psycho-analytic movement. In J. Strachey (Ed. and Trans.), *The standard edition of the complete psychological works of Sigmund Freud* (Vol. 14). London: Hogarth. (Originally published, 1914.)

REFERENCES

Freud, S. (1959). Character and anal eroticism. In J. Strachey (Ed. and Trans.), *The standard edition of the complete psychological works of Sigmund Freud* (Vol. 9). London: Hogarth. (Originally published, 1908.)

Freud, S. (1961a). *The interpretation of dreams* (J. Strachey, Ed. and Trans.). New York: Science Editions. (Originally published, 1900.)

Freud, S. (1961b). Two encyclopedia articles. In J. Strachey (Ed. and Trans.), *The standard edition of the complete psychological works of Sigmund Freud* (Vol. 18). London: Hogarth. (Originally published, 1923.)

Freud, S. (1963). Introductory lectures on psycho-analysis. In J. Strachey (Ed. and Trans.), *The standard edition of the complete psychological works of Sigmund Freud* (Vol. 16). London: Hogarth Press. (Originally published, 1916–1917.)

Freud, S. (1964a). An outline of psychoanalysis. In J. Strachey (Ed. and Trans.), *The standard edition of the complete psychological works of Sigmund Freud* (Vol. 23). London: Hogarth. (Originally published, 1940.)

Freud, S. (1964b). Femininity. In J. Strachey (Ed. and Trans.), *The standard edition of the complete psychological works of Sigmund Freud* (Vol. 22). London: Hogarth. (Originally published, 1933.)

Freud, S. (1964c). New introductory lectures on psychoanalysis. In J. Strachey (Ed. and Trans.), *The standard edition of the complete psychological works of Sigmund Freud* (Vol. 22). London: Hogarth. (Originally published, 1933.)

Freud, S. (1965). *New introductory lectures on psychoanalysis.* New York: Norton. (Originally published, 1933.)

Freud, S., & Jung, C. G. (1974). *The Freud/Jung letters* (W. McGuire, Ed.). Princeton: Princeton University Press.

Friedman, H. S., Hall, H. S., & Harris, M. J. (1985). Type A behavior, nonverbal expressive style, and health. *Journal of Personality and Social Psychology, 48,* 1299–1315.

Friedman, M., & Rosenman, R. H. (1974). *Type A behavior and your heart.* London: Wildwood House.

Fromm, E. (1947). *Man for himself: An inquiry into the psychology of ethics.* New York: Holt, Rinehart & Winston.

Fromm, E. (1963). *The art of loving.* New York: Bantam.

Fromm, E. (1973). *The anatomy of human destructiveness.* New York: Holt, Rinehart & Winston.

Gallagher, J. J. (1953). The problem of escaping clients in non-directive counseling. In W. U. Snyder (Ed.), *Group report of a program of research in psychotherapy.* Psychotherapy Research Group, Pennsylvania State University.

Galton, F. (1884). Measurement of character. *Fortnightly Review, 42,* 179–185.

Garfield, S. L., & Bergin, A. E. (Eds.). (1985). *Handbook of psychotherapy and behavior change* (3rd ed.). New York: Wiley.

Garn, S. M., & Gertler, M. M. (1950). An association between type of work and physique in an industrial group. *American Journal of Physical Anthropology, 8,* 387–397.

Gauthier, J., & Ladouceur, R. (1981). The influence of self-efficacy reports on performance. *Behavior Therapy, 12,* 436–439.

Gedo, J. E. (1979). *Beyond interpretation*. New York: International Universities Press.

Geer, J. H. (1968). A test of the classical conditioning model of emotion: The use of nonpainful aversive stimuli as unconditioned stimuli in a conditioning procedure. *Journal of Personality and Social Psychology, 10,* 148–156.

Geer, J. H., Davison, G. C., & Gatchel, R. I. (1970). Reduction of stress in humans through nonveridical perceived control of aversive stimulation. *Journal of Personality and Social Psychology, 16,* 731–738.

Gilligan, C. (1982). *In a different voice: Psychological theory and women's development*. Cambridge, MA: Harvard University Press.

Glass, D. C. (1977a). *Behavior patterns, stress, and coronary disease*. Hillsdale, NJ: Erlbaum.

Glass, D. C. (1977b). Stress, behavior patterns and coronary disease. *American Scientist, 65,* 177–187.

Glueck, S., & Glueck, E. (1950). *Unraveling juvenile delinquency*. New York: Commonwealth Fund.

Glueck, S., & Glueck, E. (1956). *Physique and delinquency*. New York: Harper & Row.

Goffman, E. (1959). *The presentation of self in everyday life*. Garden City, NY: Doubleday.

Goldfried, M. R., & Wachtel, P. L. (Speakers). (1985). *Dialogue on psychotherapy integration* (Cassette Recording No. 1). Falls Church, VA: C.A.S.E.T. Associates.

Goldstein, A. P., & Michaels, G. Y. (1985). *Empathy: Development training and consequences*. Hillsdale, NJ: Erlbaum.

Goleman, D. (1985, December 10). Esalen wrestles with a staid present. *The New York Times,* pp. C1, C6.

Goleman, D. (1985, December 31). Scientists find city is a series of varying perceptions. *The New York Times,* pp. C1, C6.

Gough, H. G. (1956). *California Psychological Inventory*. Palo Alto, CA: Consulting Psychologists Press.

Gough, H. G. (1960). Theory and measurement of socialization. *Journal of Consulting Psychology, 24,* 123–130.

Gould, D., & Weiss, M. (1981). Effect of model similarity and model self-talk on self-efficacy in muscular endurance. *Journal of Sport Psychology, 3,* 17–29.

Graham, W., & Balloun, J. (1973). An empirical test of Maslow's need hierarchy theory. *Journal of Humanistic Psychology, 13,* 97–108.

Grasha, A. F. (1978). *Practical applications of psychology*. Cambridge, MA: Winthrop.

Greene, J. (1982, September). The gambling trap. *Psychology Today,* pp. 50–55.

Greenson, R. R. (1965). The working alliance and the transference neurosis. *Psychoanalytic Quarterly, 34,* 155–181.

Greenson, R. R. (1967). *The technique and practice of psychoanalysis*. New York: International Universities Press.

Grieser, C., Greenberg, R., & Harrison, R. H. (1972). The adaptive function of sleep: The differential effects of sleep and dreaming on recall. *Journal of Abnormal Psychology, 80,* 280–286.

REFERENCES

Guntrip, H. (1969). *Schizoid phenomena, object relations and the self*. New York: International Universities Press.

Haaga, D. A., & Davison, G. C. (1986). Cognitive change methods. In F. H. Kanfer & A. P. Goldstein (Eds.), *Helping people change: A textbook of methods* (3rd ed.). Elmsford, NY: Pergamon.

Hall, C. S. (1955). *A primer of Freudian psychology*. New York: New American Library.

Hall, C. S., & Van de Castle, R. L. (1963). An empirical investigation of the castration complex in dreams. *Journal of Personality, 33,* 20–29.

Hall, M. H. (1968, July). A conversation with Abraham Maslow. *Psychology Today,* 35–37, 54–57.

Hall, R. V., Lund, D., & Jackson, D. (1968). Effects of teacher attention on study behavior. *Journal of Applied Behavior Analysis, 1,* 1–12.

Halpern, J. (1977). Projection: A test of the psychoanalytic hypothesis. *Journal of Abnormal Psychology, 86,* 536–542.

Hanley, C. (1956). Social desirability and responses to items from three MMPI scales: D, Sc, and K. *Journal of Applied Psychology, 40,* 324–328.

Hansen, D. J., St. Lawrence, J. S., & Christoff, K. A. (1985). Effects of interpersonal problem-solving training with chronic aftercare patients on problem-solving component skills and effectiveness of solutions. *Journal of Consulting and Clinical Psychology, 53,* 167–174.

Harlow, H. F., & Harlow, M. K. (1972). The language of love. In T. Alloway, L. Krames, & P. Pliner (Eds.), *Communication and affect: A comparative approach.* New York: Academic Press.

Harrell, T. W. (1972). High earning MBAs. *Personnel Psychology, 25,* 523–530.

Harri-Augstein, S. (1985). Learning-to-learn languages: New perspectives for the personal observer. In D. Bannister (Ed.), *Issues and approaches in personal construct theory.* Orlando, FL: Academic Press.

Harris, B. (1979). Whatever happened to little Albert? *American Psychologist, 34,* 151–160.

Harris, J. G., Jr. (1980). Nomovalidation and idiovalidation: A quest for the true personality profile. *American Psychologist, 35,* 729–744.

Hartley, D. E., & Strupp, H. H. (1983). The therapeutic alliance: Its relationship to outcome in brief psychotherapy. In J. Masling (Ed.), *Empirical studies of psychoanalytical theories* (Vol. 1). Hillsdale, NJ: Analytic Press.

Hartmann, H. (1951). Ego psychology and the problem of adaptation. In D. Rapaport (Ed. and Trans.), *Organization and pathology of thought: Selected sources.* New York: Columbia University Press.

Hartmann, H. (1958). *Ego psychology and the problem of adaptation*. New York: International Universities Press.

Hartmann, H. (1964). *Essays in ego psychology*. New York: International Universities Press.

Hathaway, S. R., & Monachesi, E. D. (1952). The Minnesota Multiphasic Personality Inventory in the study of juvenile delinquents. *American Sociological Review, 17,* 704–710.

Hayden, B. C. (1982). Experience—a case for possible change: The modulation corollary. In J. C. Mancuso & J. R. Adams-Webber (Eds.), *The construing person.* New York: Praeger.

Heelan, P. A. (1983). *Space-perception and the philosophy of science.* Berkeley: University of California Press.

Heppner, P. P., & Anderson, W. P. (1985). The relationship between problem-solving self-appraisal and psychological adjustment. *Cognitive Therapy and Research, 9,* 415–427.

Heppner, P., Neal, G., & Larsen, L. (1984). Problem-solving training as prevention with college students. *Personnel and Guidance Journal, 62,* 514–519.

Hjelle, L. A., & Ziegler, D. J. (1981). *Personality theories: Basic assumptions, research, and applications* (2nd ed.). New York: McGraw-Hill.

Hobson, J. A., & McCarley, R. W. (1977). The brain as a dream state generator: An activation-synthesis hypothesis of the dream process. *American Journal of Psychiatry, 134,* 1335–1438.

Hoffer, A., & Pollin, W. (1970). Schizophrenia in the NAS–NPC panel of 15,909 veteran twin pairs. *Archives of General Psychiatry, 23,* 469–477.

Hogan, W. A., & Johnson, D. P. (1985). Elimination of response cost in a token economy program and improvement in behavior of emotionally disturbed youth. *Behavior Therapy, 16,* 87–98.

Hollander, E. P. (1964). *Leaders, groups, and influence.* New York: Oxford University Press.

Holmes, D. S. (1972). Repression or interference? A further investigation. *Journal of Personality and Social Psychology, 22,* 163–170.

Holmes, D. S. (1978). Projection as a defense mechanism. *Psychological Bulletin, 85,* 677–688.

Holmes, D. S., McGilley, B. M., & Houston, B. K. (1984). Task-related arousal of Type A and Type B persons: Level of challenge and response specificity. *Journal of Personality and Social Psychology, 46,* 1322–1327.

Holmes, D. S., & Tyler, J. D. (1968). Direct versus projective measurement of achievement motivation. *Journal of Consulting and Clinical Psychology, 32,* 712–717.

Holtzman, W. H., Thorpe, J. S., Swartz, J. D., & Herron, E. W. (1961). *Inkblot perception and personality: Holtzman Inkblot Technique.* Austin: University of Texas Press.

Honikman, B. (1976). Construct theory as an approach to architectural and environmental design. In P. Slater (Ed.), *Explorations of intrapersonal space* (Vol. 1). London: Wiley.

Hopper, R. B., & Kirschenbaum, D. S. (1985). Social problem solving and social competence in preadolescents: Is inconsistency the hobgoblin of little minds? *Cognitive Therapy and Research, 9,* 685–701.

Horner, M. S. (1973). A psychological barrier to achievement in women: The motive to avoid success. In D. C. McClelland & R. S. Steele (Eds.), *Human motivation: A book of readings.* Morristown, NJ: General Learning Press.

Horney, K. (1939). *New ways in psychoanalysis.* New York: Norton.

REFERENCES

Houston, B. K. (1983). Psychophysiological responsivity and the Type A behavior pattern. *Journal of Research in Personality, 17,* 22–39.

Houts, A. C. (1981). *Initial clinical judgement in psychotherapy: The role of theoretical orientation.* Unpublished doctoral dissertation, State University of New York at Stony Brook.

Huber, C. H. (1985). Pure versus pragmatic RET. *Journal of Counseling and Development, 63,* 321–322.

Hudson, R. (1974). Images of the retailing environment: An example of the use of the repertory grid methodology. *Environment and Behavior, 6,* 470–495.

Hyman, R. (1964). *The nature of psychological inquiry.* Englewood Cliffs, NJ: Prentice-Hall.

Inkeles, A., & Levinson, D. J. (1969). National character: The study of modal personality and sociocultural systems. In G. Lindzey & E. Aronson (Eds.), *The handbook of social psychology* (Vol. 4, 2nd ed.). Reading, MA: Addison-Wesley.

Isaacs, W., Thomas, J., & Goldiamond, I. (1960). Application of operant conditioning to reinstate verbal behavior in psychotics. *Journal of Speech and Hearing Disorders, 25,* 8–12.

Jackson, D. D. (1960). (Ed.). *The etiology of schizophrenia.* New York: Basic Books.

Jackson, D. N., & Messick, S. (1958). Content and style in personality assessment. *Psychological Bulletin, 55,* 243–252.

Jackson, S. R., & Bannister, D. (1985). Growing into self. In D. Bannister (Ed.), *Issues and approaches in personal construct theory.* Orlando, FL: Academic Press.

Jaffe, P. G., & Carlson, P. M. (1976). Relative efficacy of modeling and instructions in eliciting social behavior from chronic psychiatric patients. *Journal of Consulting and Clinical Psychology, 44,* 200–207.

James, W. (1890). *Principles of psychology* (Vols. 1 and 2). New York: H. Holt.

Jenkins, C. D., Rosenman, R. H., & Friedman, M. (1967). Development of objective psychological tests for the determination of the coronary-prone behavior pattern in employed men. *Journal of Chronic Diseases, 20,* 371–379.

Jenkins, C. D., Rosenman, R. H., & Zyanski, S. J. (1974). Prediction of clinical coronary heart disease by a test for the coronary-prone behavior pattern. *New England Journal of Medicine, 290,* 1271–1275.

Johnson, G. B. (1966). Penis envy or pencil needing? *Psychological Reports, 19,* 758.

Jones, E. (1927). The early development of female sexuality. *International Journal of Psycho-Analysis, 8,* 459–472.

Jones, E. (1953). *The life and works of Sigmund Freud* (Vol. 1). New York: Basic Books.

Jourard, S. M. (1974). *Healthy personality: An approach from the viewpoint of humanistic psychology.* New York: Macmillan.

Jung, C. G. (1933). *Modern man in search of a soul* (W. S. Dell & C. F. Baynes, Trans.). New York: Harcourt Brace.

Jung, C. G. (1969). General aspects of dream psychology. In *The collected works of C. G. Jung* (Vol. 8). Princeton: Princeton University Press.

Kagan, J., & Moss, H. A. (1960). *Birth to maturity*. New York: Wiley.

Kanfer, F. H., & Hagerman, S. M. (1985). Behavior therapy and the information-processing paradigm. In S. Reiss & R. R. Bootzin (Eds.), *Theoretical issues in behavior therapy*. Orlando, FL: Academic Press.

Kaplan, R. M., Atkins, C. J., & Reinsch, S. (1984). Specific efficacy expectations mediate exercise compliance in patients with CAPD. *Health Psychology, 3*, 223–242.

Katz, H. A., & Rotter, J. B. (1969). Interpersonal trust scores of college students and their parents. *Child Development, 40*, 657–661.

Kaufman, I. C. (1974). Mother-infant relations in monkeys and humans: A reply to Prof. Hinde. In N. F. White (Ed.), *Ethology and psychiatry*. Toronto: University of Toronto Press.

Kelly, D., & Taylor, H. (1981). Take and escape: A personal construct study of car "theft." In H. Bonarius, R. Holland, & S. Rosenberg (Eds.). *Personal construct psychology: Recent advances in theory and practice*. New York: St. Martin's Press.

Kelly, G. A. (1955). *The psychology of personal constructs* (Vols. 1 and 2). New York: Norton.

Kelly, G. A. (1961). Suicide: The personal construct point of view. In N. L. Farberow & E. S. Schneidman (Eds.), *The cry for help*. New York: McGraw-Hill.

Kelly, G. A. (1969). The autobiography of a theory. In B. Maher (Ed.), *Clinical psychology and personality: Selected papers of George Kelly*. New York: Wiley.

Kelly, G. A. (1970). A brief introduction to personal construct theory. In D. Bannister (Ed.), *Perspectives in personal construct theory*. New York: Academic Press.

Kelly, G. A. (1980). A psychology of the optimal man. In A. W. Landfield & L. M. Leitner (Eds.), *Personal construct psychology: Psychotherapy and personality*. New York: Wiley.

Kendall, P. C. (1984). Cognitive processes and procedures in behavior therapy. In C. M. Franks, G. T. Wilson, P. C. Kendall, & K. D. Brownell, *Annual review of behavior therapy: Theory and practice* (Vol. 10.) New York: Guilford Press.

Kern, S. (1973). Freud and the discovery of child sexuality. *History of Childhood Quarterly, 1*, 117–141.

Kernberg, O. (1975). *Borderline conditions and pathological narcissim*. New York: Jason Aronson.

Kernberg, O. (1976). *Object-relations theory and clinical psychoanalysis*. New York: Jason Aronson.

Keyes, D. (1981). *The minds of Billy Milligan*. New York: Random House.

Kipnis, D. (1971). *Character structure and impulsiveness*. New York: Academic Press.

Klein, G. S. (1976). *Psychoanalytic theory: An exploration of essentials*. New York: International Universities Press.

Klein, M. (1981). On Mahler's autistic and symbiotic phases: An exposition and evaluation. *Psychoanalysis and Contemporary Thought, 4*, 69–105.

Kleinmuntz, B. (1967). *Personality measurement: An introduction*. Chicago: Dorsey Press.

Kline, P. (1972). *Fact and fantasy in Freudian theory*. London: Methuen.

REFERENCES

Klinger, E. (1966). Fantasy need achievement as a motivational construct. *Psychological Bulletin, 66,* 291–308.

Klopfer, B., & Davidson, H. H. (1962). *The Rorschach technique: An introductory manual.* New York: Harcourt, Brace & World.

Kluckhohn, F., & Strodtbeck, F. (1961). *Variations in value orientation.* Evanston, IL: Row, Peterson.

Knapp, P. H., Levin, S., McCarter, R. H., Wermer, H., & Zetzel, E. (1960). Suitability for psychoanalysis: A review of 100 supervised analytic cases. *Psychoanalytic Quarterly, 29,* 459–477.

Knapp, R. R. (1976). *Handbook for the Personal Orientation Inventory.* San Diego: Edits Publishers.

Kohut, H. (1971). *The analysis of self.* New York: International Universities Press.

Kohut, H. (1977). *The restoration of self.* New York: International Universities Press.

Kosinski, J. N. (1970). *Being there.* New York: Harcourt Brace Jovanovich.

Krasner, L., & Ullmann, L. P. (1973). *Behavior influence and personality: The social matrix of human action.* New York: Holt, Rinehart & Winston.

Kretschmer, E. (1926). *Physique and character: An investigation of the nature of constitution and of the theory of temperament* (W. J. H. Sprott, Trans.). New York: Harcourt.

Kris, E. (1950). On preconscious mental processes. *Psychoanalytic Quarterly, 19,* 540–560.

Kuhn, T. S. (1962). *The structure of scientific revolutions.* Chicago: University of Chicago Press.

Kuhn, T. S. (1970). *The structure of scientific revolutions* (2nd ed.). Chicago: University of Chicago Press.

Kurtz, R. R., & Grummon, D. L. (1972). Different approaches to the measurement of therapist empathy and their relationship to therapy outcomes. *Journal of Consulting and Clinical Psychology, 39,* 106–115.

Labouvie-Vief, G., & Gonda, J. (1976). Cognitive strategy training and intellectual performance in the elderly. *Journal of Gerontology, 31,* 327–332.

Landfield, A. W., & Leitner, L. M. (Eds.). (1980). *Personal construct psychology: Psychotherapy and personality.* New York: Wiley.

Langer, E. J., & Abelson, R. P. (1974). A patient by any other name . . . "Clinician group difference in labeling bias." *Journal of Consulting and Clinical Psychology, 42,* 4–9.

LaPiere, R. T. (1934). Attitudes vs. actions. *Social Forces, 13,* 230–237.

Last, C. G. (1985). School phobia. In M. Hersen & C. G. Last (Eds.), *Behavior therapy casebook.* New York: Springer.

Lavin, N. I., Thorpe, J. G., Barker, J. C., Blakemore, C. B., & Conway, C. G. (1961). Behavior therapy in a case of transvestism. *Journal of Nervous and Mental Disease, 33,* 346–353.

Lazarus, A. A. (1981). *The practice of multimodal behavior therapy.* New York: McGraw-Hill.

Lazarus, R. S. (1961). *Adjustment and personality.* New York: McGraw-Hill.

Lefcourt, H. M. (1973). The function of the illusions of control and freedom. *American Psychologist, 28,* 417–425.

Lefcourt, H. M. (Ed.). (1981). *Research with the locus of control construct: Assessment methods.* (Vol. 1.). New York: Academic Press.

Lefcourt, H. M. (1982). *Locus of control: Current theory and research* (2nd ed.). Hillsdale, NJ: Erlbaum.

Lesser, G. S. (1973). Achievement motivation in woman. In D. C. McClelland & R. S. Steele (Eds.), *Human motivation: A book of readings.* Morristown, NJ: General Learning Press.

Lesser, G. S., Krawitz, R., & Packard, R. (1963). Experimental arousal of achievement motivation in adolescent girls. *Journal of Abnormal and Social Psychology, 66,* 59–66.

Lessler, K. (1964). Cultural and Freudian dimensions of sexual symbols. *Journal of Consulting Psychology, 28,* 46–53.

Levant, R. F., & Shlien, J. M. (Eds.). (1984). *Client-centered therapy and the person-centered approach: New directions in theory, research, and practice.* New York: Praeger.

Levin, R. B., & Gross, A. M. (1985). The role of relaxation in systematic desensitization. *Behaviour Research and Therapy, 23,* 187–196.

Levine, F. J., & Slap, J. W. (1985). George S. Klein: Psychoanalytic empiricist. In J. Reppen (Ed.), *Beyond Freud: A study of modern psychoanalytic theorists.* Hillsdale, NJ: Analytic Press.

Levinson, D. (1977). The mid-life transition. *Psychiatry, 40,* 99–112.

Levinson, D. J., Darrow, C. N., Klein, E. B., Levinson, M. H., & McKee, B. (1978). *The seasons of a man's life.* New York: Knopf.

Levis, D. J. (1985). Implosive theory: A comprehensive extension of conditioning theory of fear/anxiety to psychopathology. In S. Reiss & R. R. Bootzin (Eds.), *Theoretical issues in behavior therapy.* Orlando, FL: Academic Press.

Levy, L. H. (1970). *Conceptions of personality: Theories and research.* New York: Random House.

Lewinsohn, P. M., Mischel, W., Chaplin, W., & Barton, R. (1980). Social competence and depression: The role of illusory self-perceptions. *Journal of Abnormal Psychology, 89,* 203–212.

Lewis, M. (1967). The meaning of a response, or why researchers in infant behavior should be Oriental metaphysicians. *Merrill-Palmer Quarterly, 13,* 7–18.

Lewis, O. (1961). *The children of Sanchez: Autobiography of a Mexican family.* New York: Random House.

Liebert, R. M. (1973). Observational learning: Some social applications. In P. J. Elich (Ed.), *The Fourth Western Symposium on Learning.* Bellingham: Western Washington State College.

Liebert, R. M., & Baron, R. A. (1972). Some immediate effects of televised violence on children's behavior. *Developmental Psychology, 6,* 469–475.

Liebert, R. M., & Fernandez, L. E. (1969). Vicarious reward and task complexity as determinants of imitative learning. *Psychological Reports, 25,* 531–534.

Liebert, R. M., & Fernandez, L. E. (1970). Effects of vicarious consequences on imitative performance. *Child Development, 41,* 847–852.

REFERENCES

Liebert, R. M., & Fischel, J. (1986). *The elimination disorders.* Unpublished manuscript, State University of New York at Stony Brook.

Liebert, R. M., Sobol, M. P., & Copemann, C. D. (1972). Effects of vicarious consequences and race of model upon imitative performance. *Developmental Psychology, 6,* 453–456.

Liebert, R. M., & Spiegler, M. D. (1970). *Personality: An introduction to theory and research.* Chicago: Dorsey Press.

Liebert, R. M., Sprafkin, J. N., & Davidson, E. S. (1982). *The early window: Effects of television on children and youth* (2nd ed.). Elmsford, NY: Pergamon.

Lietaer, G. (1981). The client-centered approach in the seventies. Part I: A structured review of the literature. *Tijdschrift voor Psychotherapie, 7,* 81–102.

Lietaer, G. (1984). Unconditional positive regard: A controversial basic attitude in client-centered therapy. In R. F. Levant & J. M. Shlien (Eds.), *Client-centered therapy and the person-centered approach: New directions in theory, research, and practice.* New York: Praeger.

Lindzey, G., & Herman, P. S. (1955). Thematic Apperception Test: A note on reliability and situational validity. *Journal of Projective Techniques, 19,* 36–42.

Lloyd, C., & Chang, A. F. (1979). The usefulness of distinguishing between a defensive and a nondefensive external locus of control. *Journal of Research in Personality, 13,* 316–325.

Loehlin, J. C., & Nichols, R. C. (1976). *Heredity, environment, and personality.* Austin: University of Texas Press.

Loewenstein, R., Newmann, L. M., Schur, M., & Solnit, A. J. (Eds.). (1966). *Psychoanalysis—a general psychology: Essays in honor of Heinz Hartmann.* New York: International Universities Press.

Long, B. C. (1985). Stress-management interventions: A 15-month follow-up of aerobic conditioning and stress inoculation training. *Cognitive Therapy and Research, 9,* 471–478.

Lorand, S. (1946). *Technique of psychoanalytic therapy.* New York: International Universities Press.

Lubin, B., Wallis, R. R., & Paine, C. (1971). Patterns of psychological test usage in the United States: 1935–1969. *Professional Psychology, 2,* 70–74.

Lundin, R. W. (1961). *Personality.* New York: Macmillan.

Lykken, D. T. (1957). A study of anxiety in the sociopathic personality. *Journal of Abnormal and Social Psychology, 55,* 6–10.

MacKinnon, D. W., & Dukes, W. F. (1962). Repression. In L. Postman (Ed.), *Psychology in the making.* New York: Knopf.

Maddi, S. R. (1976). *Personality theories: A comparative analysis* (3rd ed.). Chicago: Dorsey Press.

Mahler, M. (1968). *On human symbiosis and the vicissitudes of individuation: Infantile psychosis* (Vol. 1). New York: International Universities Press.

Mahler, M., Bergman, A., & Pine, F. (1975). *The psychological birth of the infant: Symbiosis and individuation.* New York: Basic Books.

Mahoney, M. J. (1974). *Cognition and behavior modification.* Cambridge, MA: Ballinger.

Maletzky, B. M. (in press). *The treatment of the sexual offender.* New York: Wiley.

Malinowski, B. (1927). *Sex and repression in savage society.* London: Routledge & Kegan Paul.

Manicas, P. T., & Secord, P. F. (1983). Implications for psychology of the new philosophy of science. *American Psychologist, 38,* 399–413.

Manning, M. M., & Wright, T. L. (1983). Self-efficacy expectancies, outcome expectancies, and the persistence of pain control in childbirth. *Journal of Personality and Social Psychology, 45,* 421–431.

Marks, I. (1981). *Cure and care of neuroses: Theory and practice of behavioral psychotherapy.* New York: Wiley.

Marks, P. A., & Seeman, W. (1963). *An atlas for use with the MMPI: Actuarial description of abnormal personality.* Baltimore: Williams & Wilkins.

Masling, J. M. (1960). The influence of situational and interpersonal variables in projective testing. *Psychological Bulletin, 56,* 65–85.

Masling, J. (Ed.). (1983). *Empirical studies of psychoanalytic theories* (Vol. 1). Hillsdale, NJ: Analytic Press.

Masling, J. (Ed.). (1985a). *Empirical studies of psychoanalytic theories* (Vol. 2). Hillsdale, NJ: Analytic Press.

Masling, J. (1985b). Orality, pathology, and interpersonal behavior. In J. Masling (Ed.), *Empirical studies of psychoanalytic theories* (Vol. 2). Hillsdale, NJ: Analytic Press.

Masling, J. M., Johnson, C., & Saturansky, C. (1974). Oral imagery, accuracy of perceiving others, and performance in Peace Corps training. *Journal of Personality and Social Psychology, 30,* 414–419.

Masling, J., O'Neill, R., & Katkin, E. S. (1981). Orality and latency of volunteering to serve as experimental subjects. *Journal of Personality Assessment, 45,* 20–22.

Masling, J. M., Rabie, L., & Blondheim, S. H. (1967). Obesity, level of aspiration, and Rorschach and TAT measures of oral dependence. *Journal of Consulting Psychology, 31,* 233–239.

Masling, J. M., Weiss, L., & Rothschild, B. (1968). Relationships of oral imagery to yielding behavior and birth order. *Journal of Consulting and Clinical Psychology, 32,* 89–91.

Maslow, A. H. (1955). Deficiency motivation and growth motivation. In M. R. Jones (Ed.), *Nebraska symposium on motivation, 1955* (Vol. 3). Lincoln: University of Nebraska Press.

Maslow, A. H. (1962). *Toward a psychology of being.* Princeton, NJ: Van Nostrand.

Maslow, A. H. (1963). Self-actualizing people. In G. B. Levitas (Ed.), *The world of psychology* (Vol. 2). New York: Braziller.

Maslow, A. H. (1967). A theory of metamotivation: The biological rooting of the value-life. *Journal of Humanistic Psychology, 7,* 93–127.

Maslow, A. H. (1968). *Toward a psychology of being* (2nd ed.). Princeton, NJ: Van Nostrand.

Maslow, A. H. (1970). *Motivation and personality* (rev. ed.). New York: Harper & Row.

Maslow, A. H. (1971). *The farther reaches of human nature.* New York: Viking Press.

REFERENCES

Matson, J. L., & DiLorenzo, T. M. (1984). *Punishment and its alternatives: A new perspective for behavior modification.* New York: Springer.

Matthews, K. A. (1982). Psychological perspectives on the Type A behavior pattern. *Psychological Bulletin, 91,* 293–323.

Matthews, K. A., & Carra, J. (1982). Suppression of menstrual distress symptoms: A study of Type A behavior. *Personality and Social Psychology Bulletin, 8,* 146–151.

Matthews, K. A., Helmreich, R. L., Beane, W. E., & Lucker, G. W. (1980). Pattern A, achievement striving, and scientific merit: Does Pattern A help or hinder? *Journal of Personality and Social Psychology, 39,* 962–967.

May, R. (1967). Existential psychology. In T. Millon (Ed.), *Theories of psychopathology.* Philadelphia: Saunders.

Mayo, L. L., & Norton, G. R. (1980). The use of problem solving to reduce examination and interpersonal anxiety. *Journal of Behavior Therapy and Experimental Psychiatry, 11,* 287–289.

McArthur, L. Z., & Eisen, S. V. (1976). Achievements of male and female storybook characters as determinants of achievement behavior by boys and girls. *Journal of Personality and Social Psychology, 33,* 467–473.

McCarley, R. W., & Hobson, J. A. (1977). The neurobiological origins of psychoanalytic dream theory. *American Journal of Psychiatry, 134,* 1211–1221.

McClelland, D. C. (1961). *The achieving society.* Princeton, NJ: Van Nostrand.

McClelland, D. C. (1965). Toward a theory of motive acquisition. *American Psychologist, 20,* 321–333.

McClelland, D. C. (1967). *The achieving society.* New York: Free Press.

McClelland, D. C. (1977). The impact of power motivation training on alcoholics. *Journal of Studies on Alcohol, 38,* 142–144.

McClelland, D. C. (1978). Managing motivation to expand human freedom. *American Psychologist, 33,* 201–210.

McClelland, D. C. (1979). Inhibited power motivation and high blood pressure in men. *Journal of Abnormal Psychology, 88,* 182–190.

McClelland, D. C. (1982). The need for power, sympathetic activation, and illness. *Motivation and Emotion, 6,* 31–61.

McClelland, D. C., Atkinson, J. W., Clark, R. A., & Lowell, E. I. (1953). *The achievement motive.* New York: Appleton-Century-Crofts. (Reprinted 1976 by Irvington Publishers.)

McClelland, D. C., & Burnham, D. H. (1976). Power is the great motivator. *Harvard Business Review, 54,* 100–110.

McClelland, D. C., Davis, W. N., Kalin, R., & Wanner, E. (1972). *The drinking man.* New York: Free Press.

McClelland, D. C., & Winter, D. G. (1969). *Motivating economic achievement.* New York: Free Press.

McConachie, H. (1983). Fathers, mothers, siblings: How do they see themselves? In P. Mittler & H. McConachie (Eds.), *Parents, professionals and mentally handicapped people.* London: Croom Helm.

McConachie, H. (1985). How parents of young mentally handicapped children construe their role. In D. Bannister (Ed.), *Issues and approaches in personal construct theory*. Orlando, FL: Academic Press.

McCoy, M. M. (1980). Culture-shocked marriages. In A. W. Landfield & L. M. Leitner (Eds.), *Personal construct psychology: Psychotherapy and personality*. New York: Wiley.

McCoy, M. M. (1981). Positive and negative emotion: A personal construct theory interpretation. In H. Bonarius, R. Holland, & S. Rosenberg (Eds.), *Personal construct psychology: Recent advances in theory and practice*. New York: St. Martin's Press.

McCrae, R. R., & Costa, P. T. (1984). Personality is transcontextual: A reply to Veroff. *Personality and Social Psychology Bulletin, 10,* 175–179.

McFarland, R. A. (1953). *Human factors in air transportation*. New York: McGraw-Hill.

McGaw, W. H., Rice, C. P., & Rogers, C. R. (1973). *The steel shutter*. La Jolla, CA: Film Center for Studies of the Person.

McIntyre, J. J., & Teevan, J. J., Jr. (1972). Television violence and deviant behavior. In G. A. Comstock & E. A. Rubinstein (Eds.), *Television and social behavior* (Vol. 3). *Television and adolescent aggressiveness*. Washington, DC: U.S. Government Printing Office.

McKeachie, W. J. (1961). Motivation, teaching methods, and college learning. In M. R. Jones (Ed.), *Nebraska symposium on motivation, 1961* (Vol. 9). Lincoln: University of Nebraska Press.

McKenna v. Fargo, (1978). 451 F. Supp. 1355.

Mead, M. (1949). *Male and female*. New York: William Morrow.

Mearns, D., & McLeod, J. (1984). A person-centered approach to research. In R. F. Levant & J. M. Shlien (Eds.), *Client-centered therapy and the person-centered approach: New directions in theory, research, and practice*. New York: Praeger.

Meichenbaum, D. (1975). Enhancing creativity by modifying what subjects say to themselves. *American Educational Research Journal, 12,* 129–145.

Meichenbaum, D. (1985). *Stress inoculation training*. Elmsford, NY: Pergamon.

Meichenbaum, D. (1986). Cognitive-behavior modification. In F. H. Kanfer & A. P. Goldstein (Eds.), *Helping people change: A textbook of methods* (3rd ed.). Elmsford, NY: Pergamon.

Meichenbaum, D., Gilmore, B., & Fedoravicius, A. (1971). Group insight vs. group desensitization in treating speech anxiety. *Journal of Consulting and Clinical Psychology, 36,* 410–421.

Meichenbaum, D., & Goodman, J. (1971). Training impulsive children to talk to themselves: A means of developing self-control. *Journal of Abnormal Psychology, 77,* 115–126.

Merrill, R. M., & Heathers, L. B. (1956). The relation of the MMPI to the Edwards Personal Preference Schedule on a college counseling center sample. *Journal of Consulting Psychology, 20,* 310–314.

Messer, S. B. (Speaker). (1985). *Points of contact: Psychoanalytic therapy and behavior therapy* (Cassette Recording No. 5). Falls Church, VA: C.A.S.E.T. Associates.

REFERENCES

Mettlin, C. (1976). Occupational careers and the prevention of coronary-prone behavior. *Social Science and Medicine, 10*, 367–372.

Meyers, A., Mercatoris, M., & Sirota, A. (1976). Use of covert self-instruction for the elimination of psychotic speech. *Journal of Consulting and Clinical Psychology, 44*, 480–483.

Miller, K., & Treacher, A. (1981). Delinquency: A personal construct theory approach. In H. Bonarius, R. Holland, & S. Rosenberg (Eds.), *Personal construct psychology: Recent advances in theory and practice.* New York: St. Martin's Press.

Miller, N. E., & Dollard, J. (1941). *Social learning and imitation.* New Haven: Yale University Press.

Miller, S. M., Lack, E. R., & Asroff, S. (1985). Preference for control and the coronary-prone behavior pattern: "I'd rather do it myself." *Journal of Personality and Social Psychology, 49*, 492–499.

Miller, W. R. (Ed.). (1980). *The addictive behaviors: Treatment of alcoholism, drug abuse, smoking, and obesity.* New York: Pergamon.

Millon, T. (Ed.). (1967). *Theories of psychopathology.* Philadelphia: Saunders.

Mischel, W. (1966). Theory and research on the antecedents of self-imposed delay of reward. In B. A. Maher (Ed.), *Progress in experimental personality research* (Vol. 3). New York: Academic Press.

Mischel, W. (1968). *Personality and assessment.* New York: Wiley.

Mischel, W. (1973). Toward a cognitive social learning reconceptualization of personality. *Psychological Review, 80*, 252–283.

Mischel, W. (1976). *Introduction to personality* (2nd ed.). New York: Holt, Rinehart & Winston.

Mischel, W. (1979). On the interface of cognition and personality: Beyond the person-situation debate. *American Psychologist, 34*, 740–754.

Mischel, W. (1982). A cognitive-social learning approach to assessment. In T. V. Merluzzi, C. R. Glass, & M. Genest (Eds.), *Cognitive assessment.* New York: Guilford.

Mischel, W. (1984). Convergences and challenges in the search for consistency. *American Psychologist, 39*, 351–364.

Mischel, W. (1986). *Introduction to personality: A new look* (4th ed.). New York: Holt, Rinehart & Winston.

Mischel, W., & Baker, N. (1975). Cognitive appraisals and transformations in delay behavior. *Journal of Personality and Social Psychology, 31*, 254–361.

Mischel, W., & Ebbesen, E. (1970). Attention in delay of gratification. *Journal of Personality and Social Psychology, 16*, 329–337.

Mischel, W., Ebbesen, E., & Raskoff, A. (1971). Cognitive and attentional mechanisms in delay of gratification. Unpublished manuscript, Stanford University.

Mischel, W., & Moore, B. (1973). Effects of attention to symbolically presented rewards upon self-control. *Journal of Personality and Social Psychology, 28*, 172–179.

Mischel, W., & Moore, B. (1980). The role of ideation in voluntary delay for symbolically presented rewards. *Cognitive Therapy and Research, 4*, 211–221.

Mischel, W., & Peake, P. K. (1982). Beyond *deja vu* in the search for cross-situational consistency. *Psychological Review, 89,* 730–755.

Mischel, W., & Peake, P. K. (1983). Analyzing the construction of consistency in personality. In M. M. Page (Ed.), *Nebraska symposium on motivation, 1982.* Lincoln: University of Nebraska Press.

Mitchell, J. (1974a). On Freud and the distinction between the sexes. In J. Strouse (Ed.), *Women & analysis: Dialogues on psychoanalytic views of femininity.* New York: Grossman.

Mitchell, J. (1974b). *Psychoanalysis and feminism.* New York: Pantheon.

Modell, A. (1975). The ego and the id: 50 years later. *International Journal of Psycho-analysis, 56,* 57–68.

Moll, A. (1912). *The sexual life of the child.* New York: Macmillan. (German edition, 1909.)

Montague, E. K. (1953). The role of anxiety in serial rote learning. *Journal of Experimental Psychology, 45,* 91–96.

Moore, B., Mischel, W., & Zeiss, A. (1976). Comparative effects of the reward stimulus and its cognitive representation in voluntary delay. *Journal of Personality and Social Psychology, 34,* 419–424.

Morris, B. S. (1949). Officer selection in the British Army, 1942–1945. *Occupational Psychology, 23,* 219–234.

Morrison, J. K., & Cometa, M. C. (1982). Variations in developing construct systems: The experience corollary. In J. C. Mancuso & J. R. Adams-Webber (Eds.), *The construing person.* New York: Praeger.

Morrison, J. R., & Stewart, A. M. (1971). A family study of the hyperactive child syndrome. *Biological Psychiatry, 3,* 189–195.

Motley, M. T., & Baars, B. J. (1978). Laboratory verification of "Freudian" slips of the tongue as evidence of prearticulatory semantic editing. In B. Ruken (Ed.), *Communication yearbook 2.* New Brunswick, NJ: Transaction.

Mowrer, O. H., & Mowrer, W. M. (1938). Enuresis—A method for its study and treatment. *American Journal of Orthopsychiatry, 8,* 436–459.

Mullahy, P. (1948). *Oedipus: Myth and complex.* New York: Grove Press.

Mullen, J., & Abeles, N. (1972). Relationship of liking, empathy, and therapist's experience to outcome of therapy. In *Psychotherapy, 1971. An Aldine annual.* Chicago: Aldine-Atherton.

Murray, H. A. (1951). Uses of the Thematic Apperception Test. *American Journal of Psychiatry, 107,* 577–581.

Murray, H. A. (1962). *Explorations in personality.* New York: Science Editions.

Musante, L., MacDougall, J. M., & Dembroski, T. M. (1984). The Type A behavior pattern and attributions for success and failure. *Personality and Social Psychology Bulletin, 10,* 544–553.

Neale, J. M., & Liebert, R. M. (1986). *Science and behavior: An introduction to methods of research* (3rd ed.). Englewood Cliffs, NJ: Prentice-Hall.

Neale, J. M., & Weintraub, S. (1977). Personal communication.

Neimeyer, G. J., & Hudson, J. E. (1985). Couples' constructs: Personal systems in marital satisfaction. In D. Bannister (Ed.), *Issues and approaches in personal construct theory.* Orlando, FL: Academic Press.

REFERENCES

Neisser, U. (1967). *Cognitive psychology*. New York: Appleton-Century-Crofts.

Neisser, U. (1976). *Cognition and reality*. San Francisco: Freeman.

Nicol, S. E., & Gottesman, I. I. (1983). Clues to the genetics and neurobiology of schizophrenia. *American Scientist, 71*, 398–404.

Nisbett, R. E., & Wilson, T. (1977). Telling more than we can know: Verbal reports on mental processes. *Psychological Review, 84*, 231–259.

Nisenson, S., & DeWitt, W. A. (1949). *Illustrated minute biographies*. New York: Grosset & Dunlap.

Noll, V. H. (1951). Simulation by college students of a prescribed pattern on a personality scale. *Educational and Psychological Measurement, 11*, 478–488.

Norman, W. T. (1961). Development of self-report tests to measure personality factors identified from peer nominations. *USAF ASK Technical Note*. No. 61–44.

Norman, W. T. (1963). Toward an adequate taxonomy of personality attributes: Replicated factor structure in peer nomination personality ratings. *Journal of Abnormal and Social Psychology, 66*, 574–583.

Nystedt, L., & Magnusson, D. (1982). Construction of experience: The construction corollary. In J. C. Mancuso & J. R. Adams-Webber (Eds.), *The construing person*. New York: Praeger.

O'Hare, D. P. A., & Gordon, I. E. (1976). An application of repertory grid technique to aesthetic measurement. *Perceptual and Motor Skills, 42*, 1183–1192.

O'Leary, A. (1985). Self-efficacy and health. *Behaviour Research and Therapy, 23*, 437–451.

Orgler, H. (1963). *Alfred Adler: The man and his work*. New York: Putnam (Capricorn Books).

Ortega, D. M., & Pipal, J. E. (1984). Challenge seeking and the Type A coronary-prone behavior pattern. *Journal of Personality and Social Psychology, 46*, 1328–1334.

OSS Assessment Staff. (1948). *Assessment of men*. New York: Holt, Rinehart & Winston.

Öst, L.-G., & Hugdahl, K. (1985). Acquisition of blood and dental phobia and anxiety response patterns in clinical patients. *Behaviour Research and Therapy, 23*, 27–34.

Overall, J. E. (1964). Note on the scientific status of factors. *Psychological Bulletin, 61*, 270–276.

Parnell, R. W. (1953). Physique and choice of faculty. *British Medical Journal, 2*, 472–475.

Passini, F. T., & Norman, W. T. (1966). A universal conception of personality structure? *Journal of Personality and Social Psychology, 4*, 44–49.

Pavlov, I. P. (1927). *Conditioned reflexes*. New York: Liveright.

Pekarik, E. G., Prinz, R. J., Liebert, D. E., Weintraub, S., & Neale, J. M. (1976). The Pupil Evaluation Inventory: A sociometric technique for assessing children's social behavior. *Journal of Abnormal Child Psychology, 4*, 83–97.

Pellegrini, D. S., & Urbain, E. S. (1985). An evaluation of interpersonal cognitive problem solving training with children. *Journal of Child Psychology and Psychiatry and Allied Disciplines, 26,* 17–41.

Perry, M. A., & Furukawa, M. J. (1986). Modeling methods. In F. H. Kanfer & A. P. Goldstein (Eds.), *Helping people change: A textbook of methods.* Elmsford, NY: Pergamon.

Pfiffner, L. J., Rosén, L. A., & O'Leary, S. G. (1985). The efficacy of an all-positive approach to classroom management. *Journal of Applied Behavior Analysis, 18,* 257–261.

Phares, E. J. (1976). *Locus of control in personality.* Morristown, NJ: General Learning Press.

Phares, E. J. (1978). Locus of control. In H. London & J. E. Exner (Eds.), *Dimensions of personality.* New York: Wiley-Interscience.

Phares, E. J. (1979). Defensiveness and perceived control. In L. C. Perlmuter & R. A. Monty (Eds.), *Choice and perceived control.* Hillsdale, NJ: Erlbaum.

Phares, E. J. (1984). *Introduction to personality.* Columbus, OH: Charles E. Merrill.

Piacentini, J. C., Schaughency, E. A., & Lahey, B. B. (1985). Tantrums. In M. Hersen & C. G. Last (Eds.), *Behavior therapy casebook.* New York: Springer.

Pierce, J. V. (1961b). *Sex differences in achievement motivation.* Quincy, IL: Quincy Youth Development Project.

Piotrowski, C., Sherry, D., & Keller, J. W. (1985). Psychodiagnostic test usage: A survey of the society for personality assessment. *Journal of Personality Assessment, 49,* 115–119.

Plomin, R. (1986). Behavioral genetic methods. *Journal of Personality, 54,* 226–261.

Plomin, R., & Foch, T. T. (1980). A twin study of objectively assessed personality in childhood. *Journal of Personality and Social Psychology, 39,* 680–688.

Popper, K. (1963). *Conjectures and refutations: The growth of scientific knowledge.* New York: Harper.

Posner, M. (1973). Coordination of internal codes. In W. Chase (Ed.), *Visual information processing.* New York: Academic Press.

Prociuk, T. J., & Breen, L. J. (1977). Internal-external control and information-seeking in a college academic situation. *Journal of Social Psychology, 101,* 309–310.

Quarti, C., & Renaud, J. (1964). A new treatment of constipation by conditioning: A preliminary report. In C. M. Franks (Ed.), *Conditioning techniques in clinical practice and research.* New York: Springer.

Rachlin, H. (1977). [Review of *Cognition and behavior modification* by M. J. Mahoney.] *Journal of Applied Behavior Analysis, 10,* 369–374.

Ramond, C. K. (1953). Anxiety and task as determiners of verbal performance. *Journal of Experimental Psychology, 46,* 120–124.

Rank, O. (1929). *The trauma of birth.* New York: Harcourt, Brace.

Rank, O. (1959). *The myth of the birth of the hero.* New York: Vintage.

Raskin, N. (1974). Studies on psychotherapeutic orientation: Ideology in practice. *AAP Psychotherapy Research Monographs.* Orlando, FL: American Academy of Psychotherapists.

REFERENCES

Rathod, P. (1981). Methods for the analysis of rep grid data. In H. Bonarius, R. Holland, & S. Rosenberg (Eds.), *Personal construct psychology: Recent advances in theory and practice*. New York: St. Martin's Press.

Read, P. P. (1974). *Alive: The story of the Andes survivors*. Philadelphia: Lippincott.

Rees, L. (1961). Constitutional factors and abnormal behavior. In H. J. Eysenck (Ed.), *Handbook of abnormal psychology*. New York: Basic Books.

Reisman, D., Glazer, N., & Denney, R. (1950). *The lonely crowd*. New York: Doubleday.

Reuman, D. A., Alwin, D. F., & Veroff, J. (1984). Assessing the validity of the achievement motive in the presence of random measurement error. *Journal of Personality and Social Psychology, 47*, 1347–1362.

Rhodewalt, F. (1984). Self-involvement, self-attribution, and the Type A coronary-prone behavior pattern. *Journal of Personality and Social Psychology, 47*, 662–670.

Roazen, P. (1975). *Freud and his followers*. New York: Knopf.

Robin, A. L., & Foster, S. L. (in press). *Parent-adolescent problem solving and communication*. New York: Guilford.

Robins, L. N. (1966). *Deviant children grown up: A sociological and psychiatric study of sociopathic personality*. Baltimore, MD: Williams & Wilkins.

Rock, I. (1983). *The logic of perception*. Cambridge, MA: MIT Press.

Rogers, C. R. (1942). *Counseling and psychotherapy*. Boston: Houghton Mifflin.

Rogers, C. R. (1959). A theory of therapy, personality, and interpersonal relationships, as developed in the client-centered framework. In S. Koch (Ed.), *Psychology: A study of a science* (Vol. 3). New York: McGraw-Hill.

Rogers, C. R. (1961). *On becoming a person*. Boston: Houghton Mifflin.

Rogers, C. R. (1963). The concept of the fully functioning person. *Psychotherapy: Theory, Research, and Practice, 1*, 17–26.

Rogers, C. R. (1964). Toward a science of the person. In T. W. Wann (Ed.), *Behaviorism and phenomenology*. Chicago: University of Chicago Press.

Rogers, C. R. (1965). *Client-centered therapy*. Boston: Houghton Mifflin.

Rogers, C. R. (1973). Some new challenges. *American Psychologist, 28*, 379–387.

Rogers, C. R. (1974). In retrospect: Forty-six years. *American Psychologist, 29*, 115–123.

Rogers, C. R. (1975). Empathic: An unappreciated way of being. *The Counseling Psychologist, 5*, 2–10.

Rogers, C. R. (1979). The foundations of the person-centered approach. *Education, 100*, 98–107.

Rogers, C. R. (1980). *A way of being*. Boston: Houghton Mifflin.

Rogers, C. R. (1983). *Freedom to learn for the 80s*. Columbus, OH: Charles E. Merrill.

Rogers, C. R., & Dymond, R. F. (Eds.). (1954). *Psychotherapy and personality change*. Chicago: University of Chicago Press.

Rogers, C. R., & Ryback, D. (1984). One alternative to nuclear planetary suicide. In R. F. Levant & J. M. Shlien (Eds.), *Client-centered therapy and the person-centered approach: New directions in theory, research, and practice*. New York: Praeger.

Rogers, C. R., & Truax, C. B. (1967). The therapeutic conditions antecedent to change: A theoretical view. In C. R. Rogers, D. J. Kiesler, & C. B. Truax (Eds.), *The therapeutic relationship and its impact: A study of psychotherapy with schizophrenics.* Madison: University of Wisconsin Press.

Rogers, W. R. (1984). Person-centered administration in higher education. In R. F. Levant & J. M. Shlien (Eds.), *Client-centered therapy and the person-centered approach: New directions in theory, research, and practice.* New York: Praeger.

Rokeach, M., & Kliejunas, P. (1972). Behavior as a function of attitude-toward-object and attitude-toward-situation. *Journal of Personality and Social Psychology, 22,* 194–201.

Rosen, B. C., & D'Andrade, R. G. (1959). The psychosocial origins of achievement motivation. *Sociometry, 22,* 185–218.

Rosén, L. A., O'Leary, S. G., Joyce, S. A., Conway, G., & Pfiffner, L. J. (1984). The importance of prudent negative consequences for maintaining the appropriate behavior of hyperactive students. *Journal of Abnormal Child Psychology, 12,* 581–604.

Rosenbaum, M., & Hadari, D. (1985). Personal efficacy, external locus of control, and perceived contingency of parental reinforcement among depressed, paranoid, and normal subjects. *Journal of Personality and Social Psychology, 49,* 539–547.

Rosenberg, S. (1977). New approaches to the analysis of personal constructs in person perception. In J. K. Cole & A. W. Landfield (Eds.), *Nebraska symposium on motivation, 1976* (Vol. 24). Lincoln: University of Nebraska Press.

Rosenman, R. H. (1978). Introduction. In T. M. Dembroski, S. M. Weiss, J. L. Shields, S. G. Haynes, & M. Feinleib (Eds.), *Coronary-prone behavior.* New York: Springer-Verlag.

Rosenman, R. H., Brand, R. J., Jenkins, C. D., Friedman, M., Straus, R., & Wurm, M. (1975). Coronary heart disease in the Western Collaborative Group Study: Final follow-up experience of 8½ years. *Journal of the American Medical Association, 233,* 872–877.

Rosenman, R. H., Friedman, M., Straus, R., Wurm, M., Kositchek, R., Haan, W., & Werthessen, N. T. (1964). A predictive study of coronary heart disease: The Western Collaborative Group Study. *Journal of the American Medical Association, 189,* 15–22.

Rosenman, R. H., Friedman, M., Straus, R., Wurm, M., Kositchek, R., Haan, W., & Werthessen, N. T. (1970). Coronary heart disease in the Western Collaborative Group Study: A follow-up experience of 4½ years. *Journal of Chronic Disease, 23,* 173–190.

Rosenwald, G. C. (1972). Effectiveness of defenses against anal impulse arousal. *Journal of Consulting and Clinical Psychology, 39,* 292–298.

Ross, A. O. (1963). Deviant case analysis: A neglected approach to behavior research. *Perceptual and Motor Skills, 16,* 337–340.

Rotter, J. B. (1954). *Social learning and clinical psychology.* Englewood Cliffs, NJ: Prentice-Hall.

Rotter, J. B. (1966). Generalized expectancies for internal versus external control of reinforcement. *Psychological Monographs, 80,* 1–28.

REFERENCES

Rotter, J. B. (1967). A new scale for the measurement of interpersonal trust. *Journal of Personality, 35,* 651–665.

Rotter, J. B. (1971). Generalized expectancies for interpersonal trust. *American Psychologist, 26,* 443–452.

Rotter, J. B. (1980). Interpersonal trust, trustworthiness, and gullibility. *American Psychologist, 35,* 1–7.

Rotter, J. B. (1981). The psychological situation in social learning theory. In D. Magnusson (Ed.), *Toward a psychology of situations: An interactional perspective.* Hillsdale, NJ: Erlbaum.

Rotter, J. B. (1982). *The development and application of social learning theory.* New York: Praeger.

Royce, J. R., & Powell, A. (1983). *Theory of personality and individual differences: Factors, systems, and processes.* Englewood Cliffs, NJ: Prentice-Hall.

Rush, A. J., Beck, A. T., Kovacs, M., & Hollon, S. (1977). Comparative efficacy of cognitive therapy and pharmacotherapy in the treatment of depressed outpatients. *Cognitive Therapy and Research, 1,* 17–37.

Rushton, J. P., Russell, R. J. H., & Wells, P. A. (1985). Personality and genetic similarity theory. *Journal of Social and Biological Structures, 8,* 63–86.

Rychlak, J. (1973). The psychology of personal constructs: George A. Kelley. In J. Rychlak (Ed.), *Introduction to personality and psychotherapy.* Boston: Houghton Mifflin.

Sarbin, T. R., Taft, R., & Bailey, D. E. (1960). *Clinical inference and cognitive theory.* New York: Holt, Rinehart & Winston.

Sarnoff, I., & Corwin, S. M. (1959). Castration anxiety and the fear of death. *Journal of Personality, 27,* 374–385.

Scarr, S. (1969). Social introversion-extroversion as a heritable response. *Child Development, 40,* 823–832.

Schachter, S., & Latané, B. (1964). Crime, cognition, and the autonomic nervous system. In D. Levine (Ed.), *Nebraska symposium on motivation, 1964* (Vol. 12). Lincoln: University of Nebraska Press.

Schaefer, W. S., & Bayley, N. (1963). Maternal behavior, child behavior, and their intercorrelations from infancy through adolescence. *Monographs of the Society for Research in Child Development, 28,* 1–27.

Schafer, R. (1950). [Review of *Introduction to the Szondi Test: Theory and practice* by S. Deri.] *Journal of Abnormal and Social Psychology, 45,* 184–188.

Schaffer, H. R., & Emerson, P. E. (1964). Patterns of response to physical contact in early human development. *Journal of Child Psychology and Psychiatry, 5,* 1–13.

Schramm, W., Lyle, J., & Parker, E. (1961). *Television in the lives of our children.* Stanford, CA: Stanford University Press.

Schreiber, F. R. (1974). *Sybil.* New York: Warner.

Sears, F. S. (1962). *Correlates of need achievement and need affiliation and classroom management, self-concept, achievement, and creativity.* Unpublished manuscript, Stanford University.

Sears, R. R. (1943). *Survey of objective studies of psychoanalytic concepts*. New York: Social Science Research Council, Bulletin 51.

Sechrest, L. (1963). The psychology of personal constructs: George Kelly. In J. M. Wepman & R. W. Heine (Eds.), *Concepts of personality*. Chicago: Aldine.

Sechrest, L. (1977). Personal construct theory. In R. J. Corsini (Ed.), *Current personality theories*. Itasca, IL: Peacock.

Seeman, J. (1984). The fully functioning person: Theory and research. In R. F. Levant & J. M. Shlien (Eds.), *Client-centered therapy and the person-centered approach: New directions in theory, research, and practice*. New York: Praeger.

Seligman, M. E. P. (1971). Phobias and preparedness. *Behavior Therapy, 2*, 307–320.

Shane, M. (1977). A rationale for teaching analytic technique based on a developmental orientation and approach. *International Journal of Psycho-Analysis, 58*, 95–108.

Shaw, B. F. (1977). Comparison of cognitive therapy and behavior therapy in the treatment of depression. *Journal of Consulting and Clinical Psychology, 45*, 543–551.

Sheehy, G. (1976). *Passages: Predictable crises of adult life*. New York: Dutton.

Sheehy, G. (1981). *Pathfinders*. New York: William Morrow.

Sheldon, W. H. (1942). *The varieties of temperament: A psychology of constitutional differences*. New York: Harper & Row.

Sherwood, G. G. (1979). Classical and attributive projection: Some new evidence. *Journal of Abnormal Psychology, 88*, 635–640.

Sherwood, M. (1969). *The logic of explanation in psychoanalysis*. New York: Academic Press.

Shlien, J. M. (1984). Secrets and the psychology of secrecy. In R. F. Levant & J. M. Shlien (Eds.), *Client-centered therapy and the person-centered approach: New directions in theory, research, and practice*. New York: Praeger.

Shostrom, E. L. (1963). *Personal Orientation Inventory*. San Diego: EDITS/Educational & Industrial Testing Service.

Shostrom, E. L. (1964). An inventory for the measurement of self-actualization. *Educational and Psychological Measurement, 24*, 207–218.

Shostrom, E. L. (1974). *Manual for the Personal Orientation Inventory*. San Diego: EDITS/Educational & Industrial Testing Service.

Shostrom, E. L., Knapp, L. F., & Knapp, R. R. (1976). *Actualizing therapy: Foundations for a scientific ethic*. San Diego: EDITS/Educational & Industrial Testing Service.

Silverman, L. H. (1976). Psychoanalytic theory: "The reports of my death are greatly exaggerated." *American Psychologist, 31*, 621–637.

Skinner, B. F. (1938). *The behavior of organisms*. New York: Appleton-Century-Crofts.

Skinner, B. F. (1948). *Walden two*. New York: Macmillan.

Skinner, B. F. (1953). *Science and human behavior*. New York: Macmillan.

Skinner, B. F. (1956). A case history in scientific method. *American Psychologist, 11*, 221–233.

REFERENCES

Skinner, B. F. (1964). Behaviorism at fifty. In T. W. Wann (Ed.), *Behaviorism and phenomenology*. Chicago: University of Chicago Press.

Skinner, B. F. (1971). *Beyond freedom and dignity*. New York: Knopf.

Skinner, B. F. (1974). *About behaviorism*. New York: Knopf.

Snyder, C. R. (1974a). Acceptance of personality interpretations as a function of assessment procedures. *Journal of Consulting and Clinical Psychology, 42*, 150.

Snyder, C. R. (1974b). Why horoscopes are true: The effects of specificity on acceptance of astrological interpretations. *Journal of Clinical Psychology, 30*, 577–580.

Snyder, C. R., & Larson, G. R. (1972). A further look at student acceptance of general personality interpretations. *Journal of Consulting and Clinical Psychology, 38*, 384–388.

Snyder, F. (1965). The organismic state associated with dreaming. In N. W. Greenfield (Ed.), *Psychoanalysis and current biological thought*. Madison: University of Wisconsin Press.

Snyder, W. U. (1947). *Casebook of non-directive counseling*. Boston: Houghton Mifflin.

Sokolov, A. N. (1972). *Inner speech and thought*. New York: Plenum.

Sperry, R. W. (1976). Changing concepts of consciousness and free will. *Perspectives in Biology and Medicine, 20*, 9–19.

Spiegler, M. D. (1980, November). Behavioral primary prevention: Introduction and overview. In M. D. Spiegler (Chair), *Behavioral primary prevention: A challenge for the 1980s*. Symposium presented at the meeting of the Association for Advancement of Behavior Therapy, New York.

Spiegler, M. D. (1981, November). *The nature and treatment of avoidance behavior in obese persons*. Paper presented at the International Conference on the Treatment of Addictive Behaviors, Grand Canyon, Arizona.

Spiegler, M. D. (1983). *Contemporary behavioral therapy*. Palo Alto, CA: Mayfield.

Spiegler, M. D. (1985, August). *Treating guilt within the framework of personal construct theory*. Paper presented at the International Congress on Personal Construct Theory, Cambridge, England.

Spiegler, M. D. (1986). Abnormal psychology. In T. Pettijohn, C. P. Bankart, H. Fitzgerald, S. Misovich, M. D. Spiegler, & Triplet (Eds.), *The encyclopedic dictionary of psychology* (3rd ed.). Guilford, CT: Dushkin.

Spiegler, M. D. (1987). *Individual behavior change projects: Teaching behavior modification actively*. Unpublished manuscript, Providence College.

Spiegler, M. D., & Agigian, H. (1977). *The Community Training Center: An educational-behavioral-social systems model for rehabilitating psychiatric patients*. New York: Brunner/Mazel.

Spiegler, M. D., & Liebert, R. M. (1970). Some correlates of self-reported fear. *Psychological Reports, 26*, 691–695.

Spiegler, M. D., & Weiland, A. (1976). The effects of written vicarious consequences on observers' willingness to imitate and ability to recall modeling cues. *Journal of Personality, 44*, 260–273.

Spielberger, C. D. (1966). Theory and research on anxiety. In C. D. Spielberger (Ed.), *Anxiety and behavior*. New York: Academic Press.

Spielberger, C. D., & Gorsuch, R. L. (1966). *Mediating processes in verbal conditioning: Report of United States Public Health Service Grants MH-7229, MH-7446, and HD-947.* Unpublished manuscript, Vanderbilt University.

Stagner, R. (1976). Traits are relevant: Theoretical analysis and empirical evidence. In N. S. Endler & D. Magnusson (Eds.), *Interactional psychology and personality.* Washington, DC: Hemisphere.

Staw, B. M., & Ross, J. (1985). Stability in the midst of change: A dispositional approach to job attitudes. *Journal of Applied Psychology, 70,* 469–480.

Steele, R. S. (1979). Psychoanalysis and hermeneutics. *The International Review of Psycho-Analysis, 6,* 389–411.

Steele, R. S. (1982). *Freud and Jung: Conflicts of interpretation.* London: Routledge & Kegan Paul.

Steele, R. S. (1985). Paradigm lost: Psychoanalysis after Freud. In Buxton (Ed.), *Points of view in the modern history of psychology.* New York: Academic Press.

Steele, R. S. (1986). Deconstructing histories: Toward a systematic criticism of psychological narratives. In T. Sarbin (Ed.), *Psychology and narrative.* New York: Praeger.

Stephan, C., & Linder, H. B. (1985). Suicide, an experience of chaos or fatalism: Perspectives from personal construct theory. In D. Bannister (Ed.), *Issues and approaches in personal construct theory.* Orlando, FL: Academic Press.

Stern, D. N. (1983). The early development of schemas of self, of other, and of various experiences of "self with other." In J. D. Lichtenberg & S. Kaplan (Eds.), *Reflections on self-psychology.* New York: International Universities Press.

Strean, H. S. (1985). *Resolving resistances in psychotherapy.* New York: Wiley.

Strickland, B. R. (1977). Internal-external control of reinforcement. In T. Bass (Ed.), *Personality variables in social behavior.* Hillsdale, NJ: Erlbaum.

Strickland, B. R. (1978). Internal-external expectancies of health-related behaviors. *Journal of Consulting and Clinical Psychology, 46,* 1192–1211.

Strickland, B. R. (1979). Internal-external expectancies and cardiovascular functioning. In L. C. Perlmuter & R. A. Monty (Eds.), *Choice and perceived control.* Hillsdale, NJ: Erlbaum.

Strube, M. J., Berry, J. M., Goza, B. K., & Fennimore, D. (1985). Type A behavior, age, and psychological well-being. *Journal of Personality and Social Psychology, 48,* 203–218.

Strube, M. J., Turner, C. W., Cerro, D., Stevens, J., & Hinchey, F. (1984). Interpersonal aggression and the Type A coronary-prone behavior pattern: A theoretical distinction and practical implications. *Journal of Personality and Social Psychology, 47,* 839–847.

Strube, M. J., & Werner, C. (1985). Relinquishment of control and the Type A behavior pattern. *Journal of Personality and Social Psychology, 48,* 688–701.

Strupp, H. H. (1967). *An introduction to Freud and modern psychoanalysis.* Woodbury, NY: Barron's.

Stumphauzer, J. S. (1972). Increased delay of gratification in young prison inmates through imitation of high-delay peer-models. *Journal of Personality and Social Psychology, 21,* 10–17.

REFERENCES

Sullivan, H. S. (1953). *The interpersonal theory of psychiatry.* New York: Norton.

Sulloway, F. J. (1979). *Freud, biologist of the mind.* New York: Basic Books.

Supnick, J. A., & Colletti, G. (1984). Relapse coping and problem solving training following treatment for smoking. *Addictive Behaviors, 9,* 401–404.

Swan, G. E., & MacDonald, M. L. (1978). Behavior therapy in practice: A national survey of behavioral therapists. *Behavior Therapy, 9,* 799–807.

Swanson, H. L. (1985). Effects of cognitive-behavioral training on emotionally disturbed children's academic performance. *Cognitive Therapy and Research, 9,* 201–216.

Szasz, T. S. (1960). The myth of mental illness. *American Psychologist, 15,* 113–118.

Tanner, J. M. (1955). *Growth at adolescence.* Springfield, IL: Charles C Thomas.

Tausch, R. (1980). Personal communication, 1973. Cited in C. R. Rogers, *A way of being.* Boston: Houghton Mifflin.

Taylor, J. A. (1953). A personality scale of manifest anxiety. *Journal of Abnormal and Social Psychology, 48,* 285–290.

Taylor, J. A., & Spence, K. W. (1952). The relationship of anxiety level to performance in serial learning. *Journal of Experimental Psychology, 44,* 61–64.

Thigpen, C. H., & Cleckley, H. (1954). A case of multiple personality. *Journal of Abnormal and Social Psychology, 49,* 135–151.

Thomas, A., & Chess, S. (1977). *Temperament and development.* New York: Brunner/Mazel.

Thomas, A., Chess, S., & Birch, H. G. (1970). The origin of personality. *Scientific American, 223,* 102–109.

Thompson, C. M. (1941). The role of women in this culture. *Psychiatry, 4,* 1–8.

Thompson, C. M. (1942). Cultural pressures in the psychology of women. *Psychiatry, 5,* 331–339.

Thompson, C. M. (1943). Penis envy in women. *Psychiatry, 6,* 123–125.

Thompson, C. M. (1950). Cultural pressures in the psychology of women. In P. Mullahy (Ed.), *A study of interpersonal relations.* New York: Hermitage Press.

Thompson, C. M. (1957). *Psychoanalysis: Evolution and development.* New York: Grove.

Torgersen, A. M. (1985). Temperamental differences in infants and 6-year-old children: A follow-up study of twins. In J. Strelau, F. Farley, & A. Gale (Eds.), *The biological bases of personality and behavior* (Vol. 1). New York: Hemisphere.

Tryon, W. W. (1979). The test-trait fallacy. *American Psychologist, 34,* 402–406.

Turk, D., Meichenbaum, D., & Genest, M. (1983). *Pain and behavioral medicine.* New York: Guilford.

Turner, J. H. (1974). *The structure of sociological theory.* Chicago: Dorsey Press.

Tversky, A. (1977). Features of similarity. *Psychological Review, 84,* 327–352.

Ullmann, L. P., & Krasner, L. (1975). *A psychological approach to abnormal behavior.* (2nd ed.). Englewood Cliffs, NJ: Prentice-Hall.

Ulrich, R. E., Stachnik, T. J., & Stainton, N. R. (1963). Student acceptance of generalized personality interpretations. *Psychological Reports, 13,* 831–834.

Vaillant, G. E. (1977). *Adaptation to life*. Boston: Little, Brown.

Van de Castle, R. L. (1971). *The psychology of dreaming*. Morristown, NJ: General Learning Press.

Vander Goot, M. (1981). Styles of elaboration in women "becoming liberated." In H. Bonarius, R. Holland, & S. Rosenberg (Eds.), *Personal construct psychology: Recent advances in theory and practice*. New York: St. Martin's Press.

van der Veen, F. (1970). Client perception of therapist conditions as a factor in psychotherapy. In J. T. Hart & T. M. Tomlinson (Eds.), *New directions in client-centered therapy*. Boston: Houghton Mifflin.

Veroff, J. (1955). *Development and validation of a projective measure of power motivation*. Unpublished doctoral dissertation, University of Michigan.

Veroff, J. (1957). Development and validation of a projective measure of power motivation. *Journal of Abnormal and Social Psychology, 54*, 1–8.

Veroff, J., Atkinson, J. W., Feld, S. C., & Gurin, G. (1960). The use of thematic apperception to assess motivation in a nationwide interview study. *Psychological Monographs, 74* (12, Whole No. 499).

Verplanck, W. S. (1956). The operant conditioning of human motor behavior. *Psychological Bulletin, 53*, 70–83.

Viederman, M. (1974). Adaptive and maladaptive regression in hemodialysis. *Psychiatry, 37*, 68–77.

von Euen, E. (1975). [The psychology of diet behavior: Examinations of patients with kidney failure.] *Zeitschrift fur Psychotherapie und medizinische Psychologie, 1974, 24*, 31–35. (Abstracted in *Psychological Abstracts, 53*, No. 10307.)

Waldron, I. (1978). The coronary-prone behavior pattern, blood pressure, employment and socioeconomic status in women. *Journal of Psychosomatic Research, 22*, 79–87.

Waldron, I., Hickey, A., McPherson, C., Butensky, A., Gruss, L., Overall, K., Schmader, A., & Wolmuth, D. (1980). Type A behavior pattern: Relationships to variation in blood pressure, parental characteristics, and academic and social activities of students. *Journal of Human Stress, 6*, 16–26.

Warren, W. G., & Parry, G. (1981). Personal constructs and death: Some clinical refinements. In H. Bonarius, R. Holland, & S. Rosenberg (Eds.), *Personal construct psychology: Recent advances in theory and practice*. New York: St. Martin's Press.

Wasik, B. (1984). *Teaching parents effective problem-solving: A handbook for professionals*. Unpublished manuscript, University of North Carolina, Chapel Hill.

Watson, J. B. (1914). *Behavior: An introduction to comparative psychology*. New York: H. Holt.

Watson, J. B. (1919). *Psychology from the standpoint of a behaviorist*. Philadelphia: Lippincott.

Watson, J. B., & Rayner, R. (1920). Conditioned emotional reactions. *Journal of Experimental Psychology, 3*, 1–14.

Watson, N. (1984). The empirical status of Rogers's hypotheses of the necessary and sufficient conditions for effective psychotherapy. In R. F. Levant & J. M. Shlien (Eds.), *Client-centered therapy and the person-centered approach: New directions in theory, research, and practice*. New York: Praeger.

REFERENCES

Webb, W. B. (1975). *Sleep: The gentle tyrant.* Englewood Cliffs, NJ: Prentice-Hall.

Webster-Stratton, C. (1984). Randomized trial of two parent-training programs for families with conduct-disordered children. *Journal of Consulting and Clinical Psychology, 52,* 666–678.

Weidner, G., & Matthews, K. A. (1978). Reported physical symptoms elicited by unpredictable events and the Type A coronary-prone behavior pattern. *Journal of Personality and Social Psychology, 36,* 1213–1220.

Weinberg, R. S., Hughes, H. H., Critelli, J. W., England, R., & Jackson, A. (1984). Effects of preexisting and manipulated self-efficacy on weight loss in a self-control group. *Journal of Personality Research, 18,* 352–358.

Weinberg, R. S., Yukelson, D., & Jackson, A. (1980). Effect of public and private efficacy expectations on competitive performance. *Journal of Sport Psychology, 2,* 940–949.

Weisberg, P., & Waldrop, P. B. (1972). Fixed-interval work habits of Congress. *Journal of Applied Behavior Analysis, 5,* 93–97.

Weiss, S. L. (1972). Perceived effectiveness of psychotherapy: A function of suggestion? *Journal of Consulting and Clinical Psychology, 39,* 56–59.

Weitzman, B. (1967). Behavior therapy and psychotherapy. *Psychological Review, 74,* 300–317.

Weitzmann, E. (1961). A note on the EEG and eye movements during behavioral sleep in monkeys. *EEG Clinical Neurophysiology, 13,* 790–794.

Wesman, A. G. (1952). Faking personality test scores in a simulated employment situation. *Journal of Applied Psychology, 36,* 112–113.

West, D., Horan, J., & Games, P. (1984). Component analysis of occupational stress inoculation applied to registered nurses in an acute care hospital setting. *Journal of Counseling Psychology, 31,* 209–218.

White, R. W. (1959). Motivation reconsidered: The concept of competence. *Psychological Review, 66,* 297–333.

White, R. W. (1960). Competence and the psychosexual stages of development. In M. R. Jones (Ed.), *Nebraska symposium on motivation, 1960* (Vol. 8). Lincoln: University of Nebraska Press.

White, R. W. (1963). *Ego and reality in psychoanalytic theory: Psychological issues* (Monograph No. 11). New York: International Universities Press.

White, R. W. (1976). *The enterprise of living: A view of personal growth* (2nd ed.). New York: Holt, Rinehart & Winston.

Whyte, L. (1960). *The unconscious before Freud.* New York: Basic Books.

Wicker, A. W. (1971). An examination of the "other variables" explanation of attitude-behavior inconsistency. *Journal of Personality and Social Psychology, 19,* 18–30.

Willerman, L. (1973). Activity level and hyperactivity in twins. *Child Development, 44,* 288–293.

Willerman, L. (1975). *Individual and group differences.* New York: Harper's College Press.

Willerman, L., & Plomin, R. (1973). Activity level in children and their parents. *Child Development, 44,* 854–858.

Williams, R. B., Jr., Friedman, M., Glass, D. C., Herd, J. A., & Schneiderman, N. (1978). Mechanisms linking behavioral and pathophysiological processes. In T. M. Dembroski, S. M. Weiss, J. L. Shields, S. G. Haynes, & M. Feinleib (Eds.), *Coronary-prone behavior*. New York: Springer-Verlag.

Wilson, G. (1986). The behaviour therapy of W. S. Gilbert. *the Behavior Therapist, 2*, 32–34.

Wilson, G. T. (1982). Clinical issues and strategies in the practice of behavior therapy. In C. M. Franks, G. T. Wilson, P. C. Kendall, & K. D. Brownell (Eds.), *Annual review of behavior therapy: Theory and practice* (Vol. 8). New York: Guilford.

Wilson, G. T. (1984). Fear reduction methods and the treatment of anxiety disorders. In C. M. Franks, G. T. Wilson, P. C. Kendall, & K. D. Brownell (Eds.), *Annual review of behavior therapy: Theory and practice* (Vol. 10). New York: Guilford.

Wilson, W. R., & Rajecki, D. W. (1974). Effects of the presence of familiar objects on the tendency of chicks to peck in a novel situation. *Revue du Comportement Animal, 8*, 95–102.

Winnicott, D. W. (1958). *Collected papers: Through pediatrics to psychoanalysis*. New York: Basic Books.

Winnicott, D. W. (1965). *The maturational processes and the facilitating environment*. New York: International Universities Press.

Winter, D. G. (1967). *Power motivation in thought and action*. Unpublished doctoral dissertation, Harvard University.

Winter, D. G. (1968). Need for power in thought and action. In *Proceedings of the 76th Annual Convention of the American Psychological Association, 3*, 429–430.

Winter, D. G. (1972). The need for power in college men: Action correlates and relationship to drinking. In D. C. McClelland, W. N. Davis, R. Kalin, & E. Wanner (Eds.), *The drinking man*. New York: Free Press.

Winter, D. G. (1973). *The power motive*. New York: Free Press.

Wolk, S., & Kurtz, J. (1975). Positive adjustment and involvement during aging and expectancy for internal control. *Journal of Consulting and Clinical Psychology, 43*, 173–178.

Wolpe, J. (1958). *Psychotherapy by reciprocal inhibition*. Stanford, CA: Stanford University Press.

Wolpe, J. (1978a). Cognition and causation in human behavior and its therapy. *American Psychologist, 33*, 437–446.

Wolpe, J. (1978b). Self-efficacy theory and psychotherapeutic change: A square peg in a round hole. In S. Rachman (Ed.), *Advances in behaviour research and therapy* (Vol. 1). Oxford: Pergamon.

Wolpe, J., & Lazarus, A. A. (1966). *Behavior therapy techniques: A guide to the treatment of neurosis*. New York: Pergamon.

Woodruffe, C. (1985). Consensual validation of personality traits: Additional evidence and individual differences. *Journal of Personality and Social Psychology, 48*, 1240–1252.

Woodworth, R. S. (1920). *Personal data sheet*. Chicago: Stoelting.

REFERENCES

Worchel, P. (1955). Anxiety and repression. *Journal of Abnormal and Social Psychology, 51*, 201–205.

Wright, J., & Mischel, W. (1982). Influence of affect on cognitive social learning variables. *Journal of Personality and Social Psychology, 43*, 901–914.

Wright, J., & Mischel, W. (1986). *Predicting cross-situational consistency: The role of person variables and situation requirements.* Unpublished manuscript, Columbia University.

Wrightsman, L. S. (1969). Wallace supporters and adherence to "law and order." *Journal of Personality and Social Psychology, 13*, 17–22.

Wylie, R. C. (1968). The present status of self theory. In E. F. Borgatta & W. W. Lambert (Eds.), *Handbook of personality theory and research.* Chicago: Rand McNally.

Yalom, I. D., & Lieberman, M. A. (1971). A study of encounter group casualties. *Archives of General Psychiatry, 25*, 16–30.

Yates, A. J. (1971). *Behavior therapy.* New York: Wiley.

Yates, B. T., & Mischel, W. (1979). Young children's preferred attentional strategies for delaying gratification. *Journal of Personality and Social Psychology, 37*, 286–300.

Zeller, A. (1950). An experimental analogue of repression, II. The effect of individual failure and success on memory measured by relearning. *Journal of Experimental Psychology, 40*, 411–422.

Zeller, A. (1951). An experimental analogue of repression, III. The effect of induced failure and success on memory measured by recall. *Journal of Experimental Psychology, 42*, 32–38.

Zetzel, E. (1956). Current concepts of transference. *International Journal of Psycho-Analysis, 37*, 369–376.

Zucker, R. A., Manosevitz, M., & Lanyon, R. I. (1968). Birth order, anxiety, and affiliation during a crisis. *Journal of Personality and Social Psychology, 8*, 354–359.

Zuckerman, M. (1983). The distinction between trait and state scales is *not* arbitrary: Comment on Allen and Potkay's "On the arbitrary distinction between traits and states." *Journal of Personality and Social Psychology, 44*, 1083–1086.

Name index

i

SUBJECT INDEX